Contents in Brief

Table of Contents

3 Patterns of Colonial Social Structure — 57

4 Colonial Administration and Politics

5 Revolution and Independence, 1763–1783

6 Establishing the Republic, 1781–1800

7 The Emergence of a National Culture

8 The Jeffersonian Era, 1800–1824

9 The Growth of Democratic Government, 1824–1844

10 American Culture Comes of Age

11 Westward Expansion, 1824–1854

List of Maps & Charts

About the Authors

Dr. Brian R. Farmer received his PhD from Texas Tech University in 1996 and has been teaching on the college level since 1991. He is the author of numerous books and articles including *The Question of Dependency and Economic Development* (Lexington Books, 1999), *American Political Ideologies* (McFarland Press, 2005), *American Conservatism: History Theory and Practice* (Cambridge Scholars Press, 2006), *Understanding Radical Islam* (Peter Lang Publishing, 2007), and *Radical Islam in the West* (McFarland Press, 2011). Dr. Farmer is currently a professor of social sciences at Amarillo College.

Carl N. Degler was born in Orange, New Jersey, in 1921 and educated in the public schools of New Jersey. He earned his BA in history at Upsala College in 1942, served in the U.S. Army Air Forces from 1942–1945, received his MA in 1947, and his PhD in 1952 from Columbia University. Moving from an instructor to a professor at Vassar College (1952–1968), he joined the faculty of Stanford University in 1968 and was named the Margaret Byrne Professor of American History in 1972. He became an emeritus in 1990. Degler also served as a visiting professor at the Columbia University graduate school (1963–1964) and as Harmsworth Professor of American History, Oxford University, 1973–1974.

His principal publications include the following: *Out of Our Past: The Forces that Shaped Modern America* (New York, 1959; 2nd revised ed., 1984); *The Age of the Economic Revolution* (Chicago, 1967, rev. ed., 1977); *Affluence and Anxiety* (Chicago, 1968, rev. ed., 1975); *Neither Black Nor White: Slavery and Race Relations in Brazil and the United States* (New York, 1971); *The Other South: Southern Dissenters in the Nineteenth Century* (New York 1974, Gainesville, FL, 2000); *Place Over Time the Continuity of Southern Distinctiveness* (Baton Rouge, LA 1977); *At Odds: Women and the Family from the Revolution to the Present* (New York, 1980); *In Search of Human Nature: the Fall and Revival of Darwinism in American Social Thought* (New York, 1991). Degler has also edited *Pivotal Interpretations in American History* (2 vols., 1966) and *The New Deal* (Chicago, 1970). He wrote an introduction to Charlotte Perkins Gilman's *Women and Economics* [orig. 1898] (New York, 1966). Since 1954, he has published seventy-five articles and more than one hundred book reviews.

Neither Black Nor White won the Pulitzer Prize in History, 1972, the Bancroft Prize of Columbia University, and the Beveridge Prize of the American Historical Association. *In Search of Human Nature* was awarded the Ralph Waldo Emerson Prize by Phi Beta Kappa in 1991. Degler received the Dean's Award for Teaching in 1979 and honorary degrees from Oxford University, Colgate University, Ripon College, and Upsala College.

Carl Degler has served as president of the Pacific Coast branch of the American Historical Association (1974–1975), president of the Organization of American Historians (1978–1979), president of the Southern Historical Association, and president of the American Historical Association (1985–1986).

He was a fellow of the American Council of Learned Societies (1964–1965), the John Simon Guggenheim Foundation (1972–1973), the National Endowment of the Humanities (1976–1977 and 1983–1984), and the Center for Advanced Studies in the Behavioral Sciences (1979–1980). Degler is an elected member of the American Academy of Arts and Sciences, the American Philosophical Society, the American Antiquarian Society, and the Society of American Historians.

About the Authors

Vincent P. De Santis, late professor emeritus of history at the University of Notre Dame, earned a doctoral degree from Johns Hopkins University and became a specialist in American political history and the Gilded Age/Progressive Era. De Santis joined the Notre Dame faculty in 1949 and spent his entire academic career there. De Santis authored such influential books as *Republicans Face the Southern Question* and *The Shaping of Modern America: 1877–1916,* and was a contributor to the textbook, *The Democratic Experience.* Officially retiring in 1982, he continued to write and teach a course on "American Presidents from FDR to Clinton" until his passing in 2011.

Foreword

~The opportunity to take a fresh look at the nation's history is always an exciting one. This text represents a solid interpretation of traditional economic and political history, while also including many original insights into social and cultural changes that have influenced and been influenced by economic and political events. Special attention has also been paid to the role of technology. In fact what emerges is a vivid picture of the interrelationship of a nation's technology with its culture and its political and economic life. It is hoped that students will gain insights into the ideas and events that inspired this nation's founding and continue to influence its development.

The book that results is an engrossing story of a young nation engaged in what Thomas Paine described as a "bold and sublime experiment" in government. We hope you enjoy the story of the continuing effort to realize the high ideals of this nation's founding.

Special Acknowledgements

In the earlier iteration of *Introduction to American History,* the textbook had been a collaboration among Carl N. Degler, Thomas C. Cochran, Vincent P. De Santis, Holman Hamilton, William H. Harbaugh, James M. McPherson, Russel B. Nye, and Clarence L. Ver Steeg. These prestigious authors had brought to it many strengths which resulted in a well received and respected textbook for nearly two decades.

We must also extend our appreciation to the many other historians and scholars whose work is reflected in this edition, including Dr. Brian R. Farmer, who provided extensive editing, writing, and updating. Special gratitude goes to those teachers and historians who read the manuscript for the previous editions and gave their comments: Frank W. Abbott, University of Houston, Downtown College; Thomas J. Archdeacon, University of Wisconsin at Madison; Morris H. Holman, Eastfield College; Arthur McClure, Central Missouri State University; and Thomas R. Tefft, Citrus College.

Finally, we want to acknowledge the contributions of Dee Andrews of California State University, East Bay, who consulted on early American history, and John Snetsinger of California State Polytechnic University, San Luis Obispo, who consulted about twentieth-century diplomatic history.

The Publisher

Dedication

IN MEMORY OF GLEN

Preface

New to This Edition

This two-volume *Introduction to American History* text has undergone significant revisions for 2015 in an effort to create a more comprehensive and readable text for students. A number of chapters have been rearranged so that discussions of culture follow discussions of major events rather than vice versa and some redundancy has been eliminated. Key terms are now in bold in the body text so that they are easier to find, and definitions of the key terms appear on the outside margins of the pages. Selected bibliographies have been included so that readers know where the material is coming from and where to go for further reading. New material has been added throughout the text, including new material on the French colonial experience; expanded discussions of slavery and the slave trade; the "New South"; the nineteenth century West; the Triangle Shirtwaist Factory fire; the Spanish Flu Pandemic of 1918, crime in the Prohibition era—including Hoover's FBI and Public Enemy #1 John Dillinger—the Baby Boom; and more recent history of the Obama administration. The brief biography of Abraham Lincoln, his reelection, and assassination are now covered in the chapter on the Civil War so that courses that end with the Civil War (rather than Reconstruction) will have the needed material. Volume II now begins with Reconstruction as "Chapter 15," so as to preserve continuity from Volume I. The discussions of culture in the Gilded Age, Jazz Age, and cold war eras now follow the discussion of major events and international politics in these epochs. Similarly, the culture shift that occurred between 1963 and 1980 now follows the discussion of politics and events for the time period. The final result is a more readable and understandable text that better meets the needs of students in the twenty-first century.

Pedagogical Features

The text contains a number of pedagogical features that are intended to stimulate student interest and enhance learning.

Chapter Openers

Each chapter begins with a chapter opener that is intended not only to pique the reader's attention but also preview the topics to be discussed in the chapter and provide insight into the chapter's themes.

Chapter Summaries

At the end of each chapter is a chapter summary that provides a concise summary of the major events and themes covered in that chapter.

Timelines

Accompanying the chapter summaries are timelines that provide a chronology of the key events covered in each chapter designed to help students place the events in their proper context.

Key Terms

Each chapter is also followed by a list of key terms—each with a concise definition provided to help students understand the important people, places, and events, as well as why they are considered important. The key terms are presented in bold in the body text and their definitions appear in the outside margins of the pages.

Pop Quizzes

A pop quiz is included at the end of each chapter to help students review the material and cognitively assemble the material in a manageable way.

Bibliographies

Selected bibliographies are included at the end of each chapter to help students know where the material comes from and to assist them if they desire to pursue further reading.

Supplements & Resources

Instructors Supplements

A complete teaching package is available for instructors who adopt this book. This package includes an online lab, instructor's manual, test bank, course management software, and PowerPoint™ slides.

BVT*Lab*	An online lab is available for this textbook at www.BVTLab.com, as described in the BVT*Lab* section below.
Instructor's Manual	The instructor's manual helps first-time instructors develop the course, while offering seasoned instructors a new perspective on the material. Each section of the instructor's manual coincides with a chapter in the textbook. The user-friendly format begins by providing learning objectives and detailed outlines for each chapter. Then, the manual presents lecture discussions, class activities and/or sample answers to the end-of-chapter review questions, along with citations that provide the rationale for the answers. Lastly, additional resources—books, articles, web-sites—are listed to help instructors review the materials covered in each chapter.
Test Bank	An extensive test bank is available to instructors in both hard copy and electronic form. Each chapter has one hundred multiple choice questions ranked by difficulty and style, as well as twenty written-answer questions. Each question is referenced to the appropriate section of the text to make test creation quick and easy.
Course Management Software	BVT's course management software, Respondus, allows for the creation of tests and quizzes that can be downloaded directly into a wide variety of course management environments such as Blackboard, WebCT, Desire2Learn, ANGEL, E-Learning, eCollege, Canvas, Moodle, and others.
PowerPoint Slides	A set of PowerPoint slides includes about forty slides per chapter, comprising a chapter overview, learning objectives, slides covering all key topics, key figures and charts, as well as summary and conclusion slides.

Student Resources

Student resources are available for this textbook at www.BVTLab.com. These resources are geared toward students needing additional assistance, as well as those seeking complete mastery of the content. The following resources are available:

Study Guide	For each chapter, the study guide includes a chapter summary, learning objectives, key terms, and a generous set of review questions (essay, multiple choice, true or false, and fill in the blank) referenced to the subsections of the chapter.
Practice Questions	Students can work through hundreds of practice questions online. Questions are multiple choice or true/false in format and are graded instantly for immediate feedback.
Flashcards	BVT*Lab* includes sets of flashcards that reinforce the key terms and concepts from each chapter.
Chapter Summaries	A convenient and concise chapter summary is available as a study aid.
PowerPoint Slides	All instructor PowerPoints are available for convenient lecture preparation and for students to view online for a study recap.

BVT*Lab*

BVT*Lab* is an affordable online lab for instructors and their students. It includes an online classroom with a grade book and chat room, a homework grading system, extensive test banks for quizzes and exams, and a host of student study resources. Even if a class is not taught in the lab, students can still utilize the resources described below.

Course Setup	BVT*Lab* has an easy-to-use, intuitive interface that allows instructors to quickly set up their courses and grade books, and to replicate them from section to section and semester to semester.
Grade Book	Using an assigned passcode, students register for the grade book, which automatically grades and records all homework, quizzes, and tests.
Chat Room	Instructors can post discussion threads to a class forum and then monitor and moderate student replies.
Student Resources	All student resources for this textbook are available in BVT*Lab* in digital form.
eBook	Students who have purchased a product that includes an eBook can download the eBook from a link in the lab. A web-based eBook is also available within the lab for easy reference during online classes, homework, and study sessions.

Customization

BVT's Custom Publishing Division can help you modify this book's content to satisfy your specific instructional needs. The following are examples of customization:

- Rearrangement of chapters to follow the order of your syllabus

- Deletion of chapters not covered in your course

- Addition of paragraphs, sections, or chapters you or your colleagues have written for this course

- Editing of the existing content, down to the word level

- Customization of the accompanying student resources and online lab

- Addition of handouts, lecture notes, syllabus, etc.

- Incorporation of student worksheets into the textbook

All of these customizations will be professionally typeset to produce a seamless textbook of the highest quality, with an updated table of contents and index to reflect the customized content.

Chapter 1

(Getty Images, Wikimedia Commons)

The Clash of Civilizations

CHAPTER OUTLINE

1.1 Those Who Came First

Before the voyage of Christopher Columbus in 1492 initiated European colonization of the New World, there were approximately four million indigenous people in what would become the United States, organized into a multiplicity of tribes and speaking hundreds of discrete languages. Clearly, humans had inhabited the Western Hemisphere for thousands of years before Columbus arrived. The exact date of the arrival of the first Americans is in dispute, but historians generally believe that they arrived somewhere between 15,000 and 20,000 years ago. Prior to the twentieth century, historians believed that the earliest humans had only arrived in North America 3,000–4,000 years ago. Then a discovery was made near Folsom, New Mexico, in 1908 that proved that humans had in fact arrived in North America thousands of years earlier. Nineteen flint spear points were found amid the bones of a giant bison—a species that has been extinct for 10,000 years. One of the spear points was still stuck between the ribs of an extinct giant bison, thus proving that the spear points had not merely been dropped on the site at a later date. These **"Folsom Points"** proved that the first Americans had migrated to the Western Hemisphere at least 10,000 years ago.

Folsom Points

Nineteen flint spear points, discovered near Folsom, NM, that prove that the first Americans had migrated to the Western Hemisphere at least ten thousand years ago

1.1a The Land Bridge to Alaska

It is believed that these earliest Americans emigrated from Asia during the earth's last ice age when massive continental glaciers covered much of North America. With more water trapped on land in the form of ice (and therefore not in the ocean), the ocean level was low enough to expose a **land bridge to Alaska** across the Bering Strait from Asia. Thousands of migrants then moved south over the millennia and spread themselves across a vast region. Using the tools of archaeology, genetics, climatology, and dendrochronology (using tree rings to date events in the past), scholars have been able to learn a fair amount about these people.

During the earth's last ice age, when massive continental glaciers covered much of North America, it is believed that thousands of migrants moved south over the millennia and spread themselves across a vast region. (iStockphoto)

Land bridge to Alaska
Exposed ground during the last ice age that was part of the Bering Strait between Asia and Alaska, used by the first Americans to migrate to America from Asia

Agricultural revolution
The transition from hunting and gathering to the domestication of plants and animals, which allowed vast changes in lifestyle and technology to take place

1.1b The Earliest Americans

The earliest Americans were nomadic hunters who had developed weapon and tool making techniques. These first Americans apparently specialized in hunting mammoths—long-extinct, elephant-like creatures that they killed and processed for food, clothing, and building materials. Most likely, these earliest Americans first migrated to America while following their prey.

In situations where the data are not entirely conclusive, scholars have attempted to make educated guesses. It appears that about 11,000 years ago the early Americans were confronted with a major crisis when a period of global warming evidently caused the mammoths and other big game animals they hunted (mastodons, camels, and ancient species of horses) to become extinct. Thus, as the early Americans spread out over the Western Hemisphere, they were forced to adapt to a changing environment. They developed new food sources, including smaller animals, fish, nuts, berries, and insects. Then, about five thousand years ago, they began to cultivate corn, squash, and beans. This shift from hunting and gathering to cultivating basic crops is normally referred to as the **agricultural revolution**.

1.1c The Agricultural Revolution

The agricultural revolution brought great changes to Native American cultures in addition to changes in dietary patterns. Agriculture allows a food surplus, since many crops—especially grain crops—can be stored and preserved for long periods of time. The same could not be said for meat in the era prior to refrigeration. The development of agriculture and a food surplus allowed Native Americans to settle in one place, and therefore also allowed the development of technology and culture, and the accumulation of goods. As long as people hunted and gathered to sustain themselves, they were forced to limit their possessions. Following animal herds made it necessary for people to travel with as few possessions as possible; hence, there was little room for sculptures or painted pottery or other items that did not directly contribute to survival. As a consequence, the development of technology and numerous art forms was greatly hindered. Similarly, population growth was hindered in nomadic societies, as women could not have more children than they could carry or nurse at one time. After the development of agriculture, however, people were able to have more children because the children would not have to be carried or keep up with the rest of the group while the tribe followed the herds. In short, technological advancement and advancement in the arts accompanied the development of agriculture, both because agricultural people had more leisure time and because they no longer had to keep their possessions at a minimum.

Gradually, the Native Americans developed substantial civilizations, though the civilizations—including their living standards—varied greatly. For example, the Karankawa tribes of the Gulf Coast of Texas had a formidable reputation for cannibalism and bestiality. In the words of one Spanish traveler in the sixteenth century, "They are cruel, inhuman, and ferocious. When one nation makes war with another, the one that conquers puts all the old men and old women to the knife and carries off the little children for food to eat on the way." In contrast to the Karankawas were the Coahuitecans, who lived near the mouth of the Rio Grande and subsisted primarily by digging and grubbing. The Coahuiltecan diet consisted of spiders, ant eggs, lizards, rattlesnakes, worms, insects, agave bulbs, stool, lechuguilla, maguey, rotting wood, and deer dung. The Coahuiltecans roasted mesquite beans and ate them with sides of dirt. They also ate products from what was known as the "second harvest"—seeds and similar items picked from human feces. In addition, they ate prickly pear cactus and chewed another cactus, called peyote, that produces a hallucinogenic effect. When the Coahuiltecans caught fish, they roasted them whole, set them in the sun for several days to collect flies and maggots, and then ate the bug-enriched food. Because food was obviously scarce for the Coahuiltecans, they also frequently practiced infanticide because they did not have enough food to go around.

1.1b The Advanced Societies

In contrast to the Coahuiltecans, other Native Americans built technologically advanced and elaborate societies. For example, in Peru, the **Incas** assembled an empire of approximately six million people with irrigated farmland, paved roads, and a complex political system. In southern Mexico and the Yucatan, the **Mayas** assembled a civilization that had a written language, an advanced system of mathematics, an accurate calendar, an advanced agricultural system, and impressive pyramids—many of which stand to this day. Similarly, the **Aztecs** of central Mexico constructed an elaborate political system complete with educational and medical systems that rivaled those of Europe in the sixteenth century. The Aztec capitol, **Tenochtitlan**, had a population of over 250,000 with impressive temples equal in size to the Great Pyramid of Egypt. In comparison, Seville, Spain—the port from which the Spanish sailed—had a population of approximately 50,000 at that time. The Aztec religion, however, required human sacrifice on a massive scale, as evidenced by the one hundred thousand skulls the Spanish found at one location in 1519. The Aztecs also shocked the Spanish by bringing them a meal soaked in human blood when they mistook the Spanish for bloodthirsty "gods" according to their own religious folklore, which foretold of the coming of white men.

In the territory that was to become the United States, there were no Native American societies as advanced and elaborate as the Mayas, Aztecs, or Incas; however, there were numerous Native American societies prior to Columbus that are worthy of note. We can look more closely at a few of these groups about whom the most is known.

1.1c The Anasazi

After arriving in the Southwest in the fifteenth century, the Navajos called the people who had inhabited the region earlier the **Anasazi**, meaning "ancient ones" in Navajo. This name is still commonly employed to refer to this society, whose members built so well that some of their structures have survived for a thousand years—all while wringing a living from a harsh environment. Ancestors of the modern Pueblo Indians, the Anasazi lived in what is now called the Four Corners region, where the states of Arizona, New Mexico, Utah, and Colorado come together. They learned how to grow corn, beans, and squash in this arid region in such a way as to take advantage of virtually every precious drop of rainfall. They even built irrigation devices to improve their chances of watering the crops adequately. Moreover, archeologists have discovered parrot feathers among their remains, which could only have originated some 1,500 miles to the south in Mesoamerica. We know, therefore, that the Anasazi traded with those who were a long way away. Further, there is compelling evidence that the Anasazi knew

Incas
Advanced Native American civilization of the Andes

Mayas
Advanced Native American civilization of the Yucatan Peninsula

Aztecs
Advanced Native American civilization of the south Central Mexican Plateau

Tenochtitlan
The capital city of the Aztecs

Anasazi
The cliff dwelling Native American society in the American Southwest

The Aztec religion required human sacrifice on a massive scale as evidenced by the hundred thousand skulls the Spanish found. (Wikimedia Commons)

Mound-builders
The Mississippian Native
American culture that built
earthen burial mounds

Cahokia
The largest settlement of the
Mississippian culture

how to keep track of key dates, such as the solstices, because various ruins contain spirals which are pierced by a dagger of sunlight at noon—only on the day in question. And finally, the four hundred some miles of roads in one of the most important Anasazi regions, Chaco Canyon in New Mexico, attest to a complex web of interconnectedness within the region itself. The Anasazi road system connected Chaco Canyon by road to more than seventy outlying villages. Several of the Anasazi roads were almost one hundred miles long.

It is their buildings, however, that have captivated succeeding generations since the first Euro-Americans discovered the structures in the mid-nineteenth century. Some were built into hillsides—hence the term *cliff-dweller* that has been used to characterize the Anasazi. Others were free-standing and built on a scale that suggests a people with a sophisticated social structure. The largest complex is called Pueblo Bonito, and it is located in Chaco Culture National Historical Park. With at least 650 rooms, and stretching up to four stories, Pueblo Bonito poses many mysteries: Was it an apartment complex, a ceremonial center, a storehouse for supplies? What is certain is that the people who built it included master architects and skilled masons.

Beginning around 300 BC, the Anasazi culture flourished for more than a millennium. Then, for reasons which are still not known with certainty, around AD 1150 the Anasazi abandoned their carefully constructed dwellings and moved on. Generations of archeologists have wrestled with many explanations, including environmental stress, conflict, and soil exhaustion, but no definitive answer has been found.

The Cliff Palace is the largest cliff dwelling in North America. The structure was built by the Ancient Pueblo Peoples in Colorado, in the Southwestern United States. (Wikimedia Commons, © 2006 Sascha Brück)

1.1f The Mound-Builders

In contrast to the Anasazi, the people who lived in the Mississippi watershed enjoyed a lush environment with abundant water and a temperate climate. What the two groups had in common, however, was their ambitious building projects, developed around the same time: AD 900–1100. At the largest settlement of **mound-builders—Cahokia**, located in Illinois just across the Mississippi from St. Louis—there were more than one hundred earthen mounds, used for ceremonial purposes. The principal one, Monks Mound, is the largest prehistoric earthen construction in the Western Hemisphere, rising one hundred feet with a base spreading over fourteen acres. It is believed that these Native Americans were sun worshipers and that the purpose of the mounds was to elevate elites nearer to the divine power of the sun. Sun calendars have been unearthed at this site, too, as well as other evidence of a complex social organization ruled by powerful chiefs. In one mound, a man—presumably a chief—was buried with the bodies of more than sixty people who were evidently executed at the time of the chief's burial. Several bodies, thought to be either servants or enemies, were buried with their hands cut off. Also in the mound were found the bodies of fifty young women, presumably wives, who evidently had been strangled. The entire Cahokia site encompasses almost twenty acres, and it is estimated that it was once home to twenty thousand people, easily the largest settlement in North America prior to Columbus.

Also known as the "Mississippians," these people had a well-developed agricultural system, once again based on corn, beans, and squash. They were able to supplement this diet with animal protein, thanks to abundant hunting and fishing, and consequently had a good enough food supply to support the construction of actual cities, with houses built around plazas. They, too, engaged in extensive trade; and they, too, abandoned their sites—circa AD 1500—for reasons which are not fully known. The contributing factors may have been some combination of war, disease, and depletion of natural resources.

1.1g The Five Nation Iroquois

When we discuss the Iroquois, we are talking about a group who came into intense contact with Europeans, and who were subsequently entered into the historical record. Member tribes of the Iroquois included the Seneca, Cayuga, Oneida, Onondaga, and Mohawk people. They lived in large villages in the woodlands of modern day New York and Ontario, Canada. Their success in the cultivation of corn and other crops allowed them to build permanent settlements comprised of bark-covered longhouses, some up to one hundred feet in length, which housed as many as ten families each. Women were the primary agriculturalists whereas male jobs centered on hunting and warfare, which was frequent. Iroquoian societies were matrilineal, with property of all sorts—including land, children and inheritance—belonging to women. Women were considered the heads of households and family clans, and they selected the male chiefs that governed the tribes. Jesuit priests who lived among them in New France were much struck by their culture, including the close attention they paid to dreams, and by their child-rearing practices, which seemed overly permissive to the Europeans.

It was their breakthrough in political organization, however, for which they are best-known. One hundred or so years before the Europeans arrived—that is, in the fifteenth century—there was apparently a substantial enough population increase among the Iroquois that they began to put pressure on the hunting grounds of neighboring tribes, such as the Algonquian. Not surprisingly, this led to even more frequent warfare. Scholars believe that it was this increase in conflict that led the Five Nations to form a confederacy for mutual defense. In the early sixteenth century, a prophet by the name of Deganawida appeared among them. He and his chief disciple, Hiawatha, preached the benefits of unity and peace; this persuaded the Five Nations to form a Great League of Peace and Power that remained powerful well into the eighteenth century, the eve of the American Revolution.

Pictured are deer-like creatures which were totem symbols of the Iroquois, a confederacy of Five Nations. (iStockphoto, MPI/Getty Images)

1.1ƒ Commonalities

Although they varied greatly, certain elements were held in common among the different native peoples. First, one can say with certainty that none had gender roles at all like those held among the Europeans—who were profoundly patriarchal. In some tribes, such as the Iroquois, the sexual division of labor favored relatively greater equality between men and women than anything known to the Old World.

Another commonality lay in their religious beliefs. Despite all of the differences among the tribes, they had in common a way of looking at the world and its origins that is called *animistic*. For the native peoples, the distinction made by Europeans between "natural" and "supernatural" was nonexistent. The native world was filled with spirits. Rivers, the sun, the moon, forests, the ocean, great rocks, and so on—all had spirits that one must take care not to disturb. Moreover, unlike the Judeo-Christian tradition, in which creation was an all-male undertaking, most tribes had cosmologies in which there were Great Mother figures, as well as Great Fathers. The natives also had their own creation myths and their own "fall of man" myths. For instance, the Cherokees believed that the land was created by a busy water bug who built the continent one grain of sand at a time by diving to the bottom of the ocean and bringing earth to the surface. After trillions of trips, the continents were built. As for the mountains and valleys, a giant bird swooped down and scraped the earth with its wings, carving out valleys and depositing the earth into hills and mountains in the process. The Cherokees also explained their fall from grace as being the result of a Cherokee who distracted God. According to the Cherokees, God kept all the animals in a cave and allowed the Cherokees to eat them as needed until a Cherokee boy distracted God's attention from his guard duty, allowing all the animals to escape. The Cherokee, therefore, had been forced to chase the escaped game ever since.

Tragically, another commonality lay in their vulnerability to European pathogens. There were no hogs and cattle in the Western Hemisphere prior to the arrival of the Europeans, and it is from these animals that smallpox and influenza are believed to have originated. The Europeans had resistances to these diseases from centuries of contact with hogs and cattle, whereas the indigenous peoples of the Western Hemisphere had none. The conquerors brought these animals and the accompanying diseases, to which American Indians had never before been exposed—and the native peoples succumbed in ghastly numbers. Demographers estimate that, typically, only about one-tenth of the original native population of a given area was left after a generation or so of contact with Europeans. Warfare played a role in this decimation, but its role was secondary to that of disease.

1.2 Background to Colonization

1.2a The Beginnings of European Expansion

America had been discovered as early as AD 1000, when the Vikings dominated northern Europe and the northern Atlantic. Erik the Red led a group of Norsemen from Iceland to Greenland, geographically a North American island, in AD 982. There, Erik came into contact with indigenous people of North America and established a permanent settlement. In AD 1001, Erik's son, **Leif Erikson**, made a voyage from Greenland to North America and landed perhaps at Labrador or Newfoundland. Leif made three more voyages, the last in 1014 when he began a colony he named "Viinland" on the north coast of Newfoundland at a place now called L'Anse aux Meadows. The indigenous peoples of Newfoundland resisted the Norse incursion vigorously. In one engagement, just as the Norse were about to be wiped out in battle, Freydis—the illegitimate daughter of Erik the Red and the first white woman known to North American history—saved the Norse by bearing her breasts, slapping them with a sword, and screaming ferociously. At these sights and sounds, the indigenous attackers turned and fled.

Unfortunately, once established, the Norse colonists quarreled among themselves and ended up destroying their own colony. The Norse abandoned Viinland after their brief settlement in 1014, but continued to visit North America for another hundred years. A twelfth century Norse coin recovered from a Native American site in Maine proves that the Norse had continuing contact with North America at least until the early twelfth century.

In spite of this relatively long period of contact between the Norse and North America, their adventures did not stimulate European expansion into the New World. Obviously, a significant change had taken place in western Europe by the time of Columbus' voyage in 1492, not only making overseas expansion possible but also instilling an adventurous spirit among Europeans; thus they were even more eager to explore new lands and new opportunities.

Essentially, it was a change from medieval agrarianism and the feudal mindset to the economic developments characteristic of early modern Europe and a more inquiring mind. In the Middle Ages, western Europe had been dominated by the feudal and manorial system in which each family's place in society—ranging from the peasantry to the nobility—was determined by the relationship of the male head of the household to the land. The commodities produced were consumed by the inhabitants of the manor. The rise of early modern capitalism brought with it a revival of trade, the rise of the city, the emergence of a merchant class, the idea of production for an outside market, and the growth of banking. As a result, people were no longer dependent exclusively upon their relationship to the land. Business transactions brought an accumulation of money, and money could be employed to finance new enterprises.

The mind of Europe was awakened. The Crusades, beginning in the eleventh century, introduced western Europe to the ways of the Near East and to such exotic commodities as spices and silk. Italian merchants—most notably, Marco Polo—journeyed all the way to China and Japan to trade. Fear of the unknown and of new experiences that had gripped many people in the Middle Ages began to disappear with the Renaissance of the fifteenth century, giving way to the spirit of innovators, whose minds were stimulated by a curiosity about the unknown and a wish to exploit the riches of the East. The Renaissance fostered a more expansive outlook and encouraged more creative thinking. This time period also witnessed greater centralization of political authority under a group of leaders whom historians call the New Monarchs. The New Monarchs gained power over the local nobles, who had dominated in the feudal system, and extracted taxation on a national scale, which could be used to fund expansion. As a result, the nation-state system emerged in Europe.

Portugal was the first nation bordering the Atlantic to engage in wide-scale exploration, especially along the western coast of Africa. This primacy was not accidental. Portugal was the first of the Atlantic nations to be unified, giving its leaders an opportunity to look outward, no longer preoccupied with internal disorder. During the fifteenth century, a time in which most of Europe was beset by war and internal upheaval, Portugal enjoyed internal peace and reasonably efficient government. Portugal's location, at the intersection of the Mediterranean and Atlantic, also encouraged the Portuguese to look outward and consider the maritime possibilities. The Portuguese were aware that Arab caravans crossed the Sahara to bring back gold, slaves, and ivory from sub-Saharan Africa. Arab traders also spoke of how the Mandingo king, Musa of Mali, controlled more gold than anyone in Europe. The Portuguese believed that an Atlantic voyage to the West African coast south of the Sahara could tap into Africa's riches and undercut the Arab traders.

Prince Henry the Navigator
The Portuguese prince who provided the impetus for the great era of European navigation

Among the most forward-looking of the Portuguese leaders was **Prince Henry the Navigator** (1394–1460), who established a center for the study of cartography and astronomy, and for the improvement of ships and seamanship. The Portuguese studied the Arab ships, borrowed from their design, and then improved upon them. The Portuguese increased the ratio of length to width from a standard 2:1 ratio to 3:1, borrowed the lateen (triangular) sail from the Arabs, and created a new kind of ship called the Caravel—an example of which was the *Niña*, used on Columbus' first voyage. The Portuguese also learned how to mount heavy cannons on their ships, made full use of the compass, and borrowed from the Arabs the astrolabe—a device that permitted the calculation of latitude simply from looking at the stars. Prince Henry sponsored some fifteen voyages along the African coast and launched Portugal's era of expansion. The Portuguese began colonization efforts by taking possession of the uninhabited Madeira Islands off the northwest coast of Africa in 1418, followed by the Azores due west of Portugal in 1427, and then the Cape Verde Islands off of Africa's west coast in 1450.

Trade between the Europeans and West Africans was not new; it had been going on indirectly for hundreds of years. West Africans had been producing iron for centuries and had been supplying Europe with most of its gold for centuries as well through trade caravans across the Sahara. Beginning in the 1440s, the trade relationship changed as the Portuguese colonists began using African slave labor on sugar plantations and in vineyards throughout their new colonies. The Portuguese would purchase their slaves from African traders, who often sold enemies captured through tribal warfare. The Portuguese were thus able to build a profitable slave trade by exploiting rivalries between the tribes on the West African coast. Slavery, and the agricultural products that were profitably produced through the use of slave labor, became a major impetus to overseas exploration. For the first three hundred years after Columbus, the majority of people brought to the Western Hemisphere were not European settlers but rather African slaves brought to the Americas to provide the labor for sugar, rice, indigo, tobacco, and later cotton plantations.

Because of the profits made possible by slavery and African gold, Portuguese exploration was able to continue, as was their expansion throughout the fifteenth century. By the 1480s, Portugal sought a water route to Asia that would take them around the tip of Africa. Portugal was eventually rewarded when Bartholomew Diaz rounded Africa's southernmost Cape of Good Hope in 1488, followed by Vasco da Gama, who reached India by way of the Cape of Good Hope in 1498. Da Gama's voyage lasted over two years, but resulted in large profits from the spices that Da Gama eventually brought back to Portugal from India. Subsequent Portuguese sailors would eventually come to trade in both Japan and Indonesia. Settlement of the lands where the Portuguese traded, however, was not a major Portuguese goal. Only when Pedro Alvares Cabral accidentally discovered Brazil in 1500 (he was blown off course while trying to round the Cape of Good Hope) did the Portuguese attempt to settle a faraway land where their mariners traded.

Successful overseas expansion required the support of a stable government and a unified nation-state. The significance of national unity was underscored when Columbus' voyage in 1492 coincided with the expulsion of the Islamic Moors from Spain, when Granada was captured by Spanish soldiers. For the first time in centuries, the entire Iberian Peninsula was united under Christian rule. Columbus' voyage, sailing west to reach the fabulous riches of the East, marked the great historical divide which eventually made the Atlantic, rather than the Mediterranean, the principal artery of trade and communication.

Treaty of Tordesillas

Negotiated by Pope Alexander VI, this treaty divided the new territory by a line of longitude located 270 leagues west of the Azores. Any land west of the line belonged to Spain, and those lands east of the line belonged to Portugal.

1.26 Christopher Columbus

Christopher Columbus was born and raised in Genoa, Italy, in 1451 to a master weaver. Columbus began his life on the sea at age 14; in 1476, he journeyed to Lisbon where he would do most of his sailing as a young man in the service of Portugal. Through his seafaring experience, Columbus became intrigued by the possibility of reaching Asia by sailing west. Like most fifteenth century mariners, Columbus was aware that the Greek scholar Ptolemy had postulated that the earth was round six centuries before Christ. However, Columbus thought that the world was much smaller than it actually is and expected to find Asia approximately 2,500 miles west of the Canary Islands. His calculations were only off by about 8,000 miles. When Columbus was unable to find anyone in Portugal who would finance his expedition, he turned to Spain, where Queen Isabella agreed to finance his voyage. Isabella outfitted Columbus with his three small ships—the *Niña*, the *Pinta*, and the *Santa Maria*—and ninety men, including the Pinzon brothers, who would navigate. Columbus was a religious man and believed his voyage to be part of a divine mission. In the words of Columbus, "God made me the messenger of the new heaven and the new earth, and he showed me the spot where to find it."

Unable to find anyone in Portugal who would finance his expedition, Columbus turned to Spain, where Queen Isabella agreed to finance his voyage. Columbus believed himself to be a messenger appointed by God to seek out the new heaven and the new earth. (Wikimedia Commons)

On October 12, 1492—only thirty-three days after leaving the Canary Islands—Columbus landed in the Bahamas after a smooth voyage across calm seas. He named the island San Salvador. Columbus found neither the gold nor the black pepper he had hoped to bring back; instead, he brought seven Native Americans, whom he misnamed "Indians," back to Spain with him. In Columbus' diary he described the natives as friendly, but "naked as their mothers bore them." Columbus also reported that the natives had no knowledge of metals because when he showed them swords "they took them by the edge and through ignorance cut themselves." The natives called themselves "Tainos," which meant "good" or "noble" in their language; and they engaged in agriculture, growing cassava, sweet potatoes, corn, cotton, and tobacco. The natives also fished and traveled from island to island in canoes. Columbus did notice, however, small pieces of gold in the noses of some of the natives, and he sought to find the source of the gold so that he could bring it back to Spain.

Upon Columbus' return, the Spanish awarded him the title "Admiral of the Ocean Sea," and the seven Tainos were all baptized as Christians. In 1493, Columbus returned to the Caribbean with seventeen ships and a thousand men and began a colony on the Island of Hispaniola. Upon his return, Columbus found that the thirty-nine men he had left on the island had all been killed by the Tainos. Columbus' men had kidnapped Taino women and forced them into personal harems. The Tainos retaliated by killing all of the Spaniards, showing that the Native Americans were not completely passive.

Finding neither gold nor spices, Columbus forced the natives to bring him either cotton or gold to ship to Spain to make his voyage profitable. Columbus imposed a quota for natives of twenty-five pounds of cotton or a hawk's bell full of gold. Those that did not comply were severely punished by having a hand, nose, or ear cut off. When those efforts also failed to produce the desired profits, Columbus began selling the natives into slavery.

In 1494, Spain and Portugal almost went to war over who would control the riches of the newly found territories. Spain insisted on complete control over the lands discovered by Columbus, while Portugal wanted their share of the new discoveries. More importantly, Portugal wanted to exclude Spain from the coast of Africa, which had been explored extensively by Portugal. Pope Alexander VI negotiated a settlement of the dispute that became the **Treaty of Tordesillas**. The Treaty divided the new territory (which all parties still believed to be Asia) by a line of longitude located 270 leagues west of the Azores. Any land west of the line belonged to Spain, and those lands east of the line belonged to Portugal. Unknown to all parties at the time, much of undiscovered Brazil lay east of the line.

With the bulk of the new land secured for Spain by the pope, Columbus made a third voyage in 1498 where he reached the coast of South America, which he still believed was part of Asia. He died in 1506, never realizing that he had, in fact, discovered an entirely different continent. In 1500, Italian explorer **Amerigo Vespucci** published an account of his voyages across the Atlantic that was sufficient to convince European mapmakers that Columbus had indeed discovered a previously unknown continent, rather than simply a new passage to Asia. It is from Amerigo Vespucci that America got its name. From 1519 to 1522, **Ferdinand Magellan**—a Portuguese mariner in the service of Spain—led a voyage around the globe (though Magellan himself was killed in a skirmish with natives in the Philippines), thus putting to rest forever the questions of whether or not the earth is round and whether Asia could be reached from Europe by sailing west.

The efforts of Portugal and Spain to find new routes to the East were prompted, in large part, by their desire to challenge the commercial monopoly of the Italians. Italian cities, because of their geographical position, dominated trade with the East by way of the Mediterranean. By sailing around the world—and showing a substantial profit despite the loss of all but one ship, the commander, and most of the men—the expedition of Ferdinand Magellan proved that the Mediterranean could be bypassed, and the Italian monopoly broken.

Spain followed the voyage of Columbus by establishing an American empire, thereby setting an example that the other nations of western Europe would attempt to imitate. The Spaniards constructed a tightly knit, closely supervised colonial system with the object of making its American colonies a source of wealth for the mother country, while preventing any encroachment by other nations. All of the Spanish conquests, including those of Columbus, were cloaked under the guise of spreading Christianity. Wherever Columbus went, he planted a cross and made (as he said) the "declarations that are required" to claim the land for Spain and Christianity. Spanish explorers that came after Columbus would be required to read to natives a document known as the ***Requerimiento*** (requirement) that informed the natives of the "truth" of Christianity, and the necessity to swear immediate allegiance to the pope and the Spanish crown. The natives were informed that they would be the slaves of the Spanish, and those who rejected these blessings of Christianity deserved to die. The actual text of the document read thusly:

> I certify to you that, with the help of God, we shall powerfully enter into your country and shall make war against you in all ways and manners that we can, and shall subject you to the yoke and obedience of the Church of Their Highnesses. We shall take you and your wives and your children, and shall make slaves of them, and as such shall sell and dispose of them as Their Highnesses may command. And we shall take your goods, and shall do you all the mischief and damage that we can, as to vassals who do not obey and refuse to receive their Lord and resist and contradict him.

Generally, the *Requerimiento* was read to the bewildered natives in Spanish (which most natives could not understand)—after the natives had already been put in chains.

1.2c Columbus' Tainted Image

Although Columbus has been enshrined as an American hero (though he never actually set foot in the area that is now the United States) and Columbus Day is a national holiday in the U.S., the true history of Columbus is more mixed; his savagery was such that he has been denounced in many places in Latin America in a manner similar to the Soviet denunciation of Stalin in the 1950s. The denunciation of Columbus is not without warrant. Long before the *Requerimiento*, Columbus had begun kidnapping and enslaving the Native Americans—even on his very first voyage. On one occasion during Columbus' first voyage, he sent a raiding party ashore to capture some women to keep the males he had already captured company because, as he wrote in his journal, his past experience in African slave trading taught him that "the Indian men would behave better in Spain with women of their own country than without them."

On Columbus' second voyage, he embarked on a much larger slave roundup and gathered 1,600 natives on the Island of Hispaniola, 550 of whom he took back to Spain. The involuntary nature of the roundup was described by Italian nobleman Michele da Cuneo, who wrote, "Among them were many women who had infants at the breast.

BVT Lab

Visit www.BVTLab.com to explore the student resources available for this chapter.

Christopher Columbus, explorer from Genoa (present day Italy), headed four voyages across the Atlantic Ocean. Columbus began the movement of further exploration and later colonization by European countries of the American continents. (Wikimedia Commons)

They, in order the better to escape us … left their infants anywhere on the ground and started to flee like desperate people." Of the 550 slaves Columbus took back to Spain, 200 died en route; and many of the others died shortly after reaching Spain. Of the event, Columbus wrote, "in the name of the Holy Trinity, we can send from here all the slaves and brazil-wood which could be sold." Columbus even viewed the native death rate optimistically, writing that "although they die now, they will not always die. The Negroes and Canary Islanders died at first." And die they did.

Spanish historian Peter Martyr described the situation in 1516 thusly, "Packed in below deck, with hatchways closed to prevent their escape, so many slaves died on the trip that a ship without compass, chart, or guide, but only following the trail of dead Indians who had been thrown from the ships could find his way from the Bahamas to Hispaniola." This, unfortunately, was only the beginning of a campaign of rape, murder, and genocide, perpetrated by Columbus and the Spanish on Hispaniola.

Upon Columbus' arrival in Hispaniola in 1493, he demanded quotas of food, gold, cotton, and sex from the natives. To ensure cooperation, Columbus ordered that an ear or nose should be cut off of anyone who did not comply. Concerning the sex demands, Columbus was most explicit. Columbus friend, Michele da Cuneo, reported that he was personally given a beautiful Caribe woman by Columbus during Columbus' second voyage. Da Cuneo stated:

"I conceived desire to take pleasure. I wanted to put my desire into execution but she did not want it and treated me with her finger nails in such a manner that I wished I had never begun. But seeing that, I took a rope and thrashed her well, for which she raised such unheard of screams that you would not have believed your ears. Finally, we came to an agreement."

In 1500, Columbus wrote to a friend and gleefully proclaimed, "A hundred castellanoes are as easily obtained for a woman as for a farm, and it is very general and there are plenty of dealers who go about looking for girls; those from nine to ten are now in demand."

In 1495, the natives attempted a rebellion, which Columbus brutally put down. According to a witness to the slaughter, "The soldiers mowed down dozens with point blank volleys, loosed the dogs to rip open limbs and bellies, chased fleeing Indians into the bush to skewer them on sword and pike, and with God's aid soon gained a complete victory." The Spanish reports of their own deliberate cruelty are legion. In the words of one observer, "For a lark they tore babes from their mother's breast by their feet and dashed their heads against the rocks. The bodies of other infants they spitted … together." After losing in battle, many natives chose suicide rather than a life of slavery for the Spanish. As Pedro de Cordoba wrote in 1517:

"Occasionally a hundred have committed mass suicide. The women, exhausted by labor, have shunned conception and childbirth … Many, when pregnant, have taken something to abort and aborted. Others after delivery have killed their children with their own hands, so as not to leave them in such oppressive slavery."

The Spanish annihilation of the natives on Hispaniola was thorough and complete. At one point, the Spanish even hunted the natives for sport and then fed them to the dogs. Historians estimate the population of Hispaniola to have been as high as eight million upon Columbus' arrival. By 1496, Columbus' brother Bartholomew estimated the population of adults at 1.1 million. By 1516, the native population was only 12,000; and by 1555, there were no Native Americans remaining. Elsewhere in the Caribbean, what natives still survived had all been enslaved by the Spanish by 1525. Although the vast majority in this great holocaust surely died from European diseases such as influenza, the brutal Spanish policies of slavery and subordination clearly share the blame. What's more, this pattern of genocide perpetrated by the Spanish was carried out on other Caribbean

Islands as well, including the Bahamas, where Columbus first landed. By 1516, Spanish historian Peter Martyr reported that the Bahamas were "deserted." Similar proceedings were repeated in Puerto Rico and Cuba.

1.2b The Conquistadores

Very early in the sixteenth century, the Spanish ceased to view the New World as an obstacle to reaching Asia's wealth and began to look at the New World as a place that could provide riches for Spain, in and of itself. Thus began the era of the **Conquistadores**. In 1519, the Spanish, under **Hernán Cortés**, began an exploration of Mexico with the purpose of finding and conquering a great kingdom that they had heard of during their conquest of the Caribbean. Aided by a native woman named Malinali, whom Cortés received from a native chief in the Yucatan, Cortés eventually found the capital of the Aztec empire at Tenochtitlan (present-day Mexico City). The name Aztec was given to them by the Spanish; the people referred to themselves as Mexicans. The Aztec leader, **Montezuma**, mistook the Spaniards for the coming of the Aztec god Quetzalcoatl, whose arrival had been prophesied in the Aztec religion. Malinali had previously informed Cortés about the legend of Quetzalcoatl, encouraging Cortés to don some native ceremonial regalia indicating to the Aztecs that he was indeed the prophesied god. Hoping to please the god, Montezuma sent Cortés not only a large quantity of food soaked in human blood but also a large golden disk the size of a cartwheel—proof of the Aztec's wealth. Montezuma welcomed the Spanish into Tenochtitlan and presented Cortés and his men with gifts, but Cortés quickly took Montezuma hostage and held him under house arrest. Cortés then ruled from the background, attempting to use Montezuma as a puppet until the Aztecs revolted on June 30, 1520. Cortés and his men were forced to flee from Tenochtitlan to Tlaxcala, approximately one hundred miles away, where they made an alliance with an Aztec enemy, the Tlaxcalans. Cortés and his men had also left behind the deadly smallpox virus, producing an epidemic so horrible in Tenochtitlan that the Aztecs lacked the manpower to bury all the bodies.

Monument marking the encounter between Montezuma Xocoyotzin and conquistador Hernán Cortés in 1519 (Fabioj at the English language Wikipedia)

In the spring of 1521, Cortés, his men, and tens of thousands of Tlaxcalan allies laid siege to the city. Cortés destroyed the Aztec's food and water supplies and burned the magnificent Aztec public buildings, marketplaces, parks, gardens, and aviaries containing thousands of wondrous birds. The city that the Spanish had, just months earlier, described as the most beautiful city on earth quickly became a place of rubble, dust, flame, and death. Because the city was built on canals, burning was not always the most efficient means of destruction, so the Spanish crushed houses and other buildings and piled the debris into the canals. Cortés wrote that his intention was to kill everyone in Tenochtitlan, and that there were so many bodies in the streets that the Spanish were forced to walk upon them. Lastly, the Spanish burned the books of Aztec religion and learning, and fed Aztec priests to Spanish dogs.

The Spanish conquerors fanned out from Tenochtitlan, searching for more gold and plunder. As a result, 95 percent of the indigenous populations of Mexico and South America would perish. It is estimated that the Native American population in the Western Hemisphere just before the arrival of Columbus was approximately eighty million—equal to that of Europe. It is also estimated that only approximately 5 percent of these Native Americans lived in what is now the United States and Canada.

In addition to the slaughter initiated by Columbus, it is estimated that Spanish troops under Pedro de Alvarado alone were responsible for as many as five million deaths in southern Mexico and Central America between 1525 and 1540. In South America, the Spanish under **Francisco Pizarro** in 1532 repeated the pattern established by Columbus, Cortés, and Alvarado when they conquered the Incan empire of six million people, using only two hundred men. Pizarro and his men captured the Incan Emperor Atahualpa and held him for ransom. The Incas responded with a pile of gold and silver equal to fifty years' worth of precious metal production in Europe in the sixteenth century. After receiving the ransom, the Spanish then executed Atahualpa anyway. Over the next one hundred years, 95 percent of the Incan population would perish.

To replace the Native American population, the Spanish immigrated to the New World in large numbers. In 1574, long before the English had established a successful colony in the New World, the Spanish population in Mexico City alone exceeded 15,000; throughout the New World, it exceeded 160,000. By 1650, over 450,000 Spaniards had immigrated to the New World, more than two hundred Spanish cities and towns had been founded, and Mexico City boasted a university. Most of the immigrants were single males seeking economic opportunity. The principal agency used by Spain to transplant the culture of the Old World to the New was the Catholic Church—the only church in existence in the Western world at the time that the Spanish colonial system was founded. The Church established missions throughout the New World, many of which are located in Florida and the southwestern United States.

The Spanish colonial policy—unlike that which was later introduced by the English—considered native people subjects of the sovereign and American resources as wealth to be plundered. The result was a fusion of cultures still characteristic of Latin America today, as well as the shipment of 200 tons of gold and 16,000 tons of silver back to Spain between 1500 and 1650. The influx of metals into Spain, however, had the negative effect of producing inflation since gold and silver were at that time used as currency; therefore the money supply expanded faster than the growth of tangible goods.

The Spanish colonial system also extended into territory that has since become part of the United States. As early as 1512, Ponce de Leon had begun launching expeditions from the West Indies to explore the coast of Florida, returning on a second voyage some seven years later. In 1528 Panfilo de Narvaez led a disastrous expedition of about six hundred men—equipped with horses, livestock, and other supplies—which landed on the Gulf Coast of Florida. After exploring the region extending westward to Alabama and encountering illness, starvation, and hostile natives, the survivors of the expedition were forced to kill their horses and build barges of horse hide in an attempt to follow the coastline to Mexico. The barges foundered, and the Spanish were forced ashore on the Texas coast. The Spanish then attempted to trek overland to Spanish settlements in Mexico. Only four members of the group, led by Cabeza de Vaca, reached Mexico City some eight years later, after suffering almost unbelievable hardship—including enslavement by native tribes in Texas. In 1539, **Hernando de Soto** and six hundred men landed in Florida, and de Soto and his men explored the southeastern United States all the way to Texas. In 1542 De Soto himself died and was buried in the Mississippi River before his men turned back without ever finding another city of gold like Tenochtitlan.

1.2e The _Encomiendas_

The Spanish empire in the New World was primarily the effort of private entrepreneurs, with little direct support from the Spanish government. For individuals who desired to launch expeditions into the New World, it was required that they first get licenses from the Spanish government. Those who obtained licenses (**_encomiendas_**) were essentially rewarded with possession of conquered native villages. _Encomenderos_ (those with _encomiendas_) were given the authority to demand labor from the natives, in return for legal protection and religious guidance.

1.2f Spanish Colonization in the United States

In 1565 **Pedro Menéndez de Avilés** founded St. Augustine, the earliest continuous settlement within the present limits of the United States. Spanish expansion into what is today Texas, the American Southwest, and California was sufficiently influential to leave an enduring imprint. Spanish soldiers and Franciscan priests established a chain of garrisons and mission stations throughout the territory. Santa Fe, New Mexico, was founded in 1610 and San Antonio, Texas, in 1718. In the eighteenth century more than twenty missions were organized in California, including San Diego, San Francisco, and Santa Barbara.

By the end of the sixteenth century, the Spanish empire was the largest in the history of the world, encompassing most of South America, Central America, Mexico, the Caribbean, Florida, and the southwestern United States, in addition to Spain itself.

The Spanish, however, had imposed upon the colonies a small ruling class, which existed to serve the Spanish crown, and had not established anything resembling European society in the New World. The fact that the Spanish colonists were largely single men (men outnumbered women ten to one) meant that the Spanish men in America typically took Native American wives, and thus fused bloodlines and cultures. Eventually, what emerged in Latin America became known as the "fifth great race" (the Latin Americans). The majority of people in Latin America by the eighteenth century were *mestizos* or persons of mixed Spanish and Native American ethnicity. However, men from the Spanish ruling class were more likely than commoners to bring their European wives with them; consequently, Latin America became dominated, in general, by an ethnically European elite class ruling over the mestizo masses. The Europeans also brought approximately eleven million African slaves to Latin America, further diversifying the ethnic mix. Brazil and the Caribbean were the destination for most of the African slaves, and the population of Haiti is still over 90 percent of African origin in the twenty-first century. In contrast, in some of the more remote regions of Latin America, such as in the Amazon Basin and some areas high in the Andes, the Spanish mixed very little with the indigenous populations; thus, the Native American populations in those areas remained much larger than those in North America, and have remained so through the present.

The Spanish imported new crops to the Western Hemisphere, including sugar and bananas, and new livestock, including cattle, pigs, sheep, goats, cats, chickens, and, perhaps most importantly, horses. With no natural enemies, the new animals grew rapidly in population in the new land. The Native Americans quickly learned to cultivate the new crops and domesticate the new animals—thus furthering the spread of the flora and fauna, but also changing forever the Native American cultures. By the mid-nineteenth century, for instance, the Great Plains Indians of North America were known for their expertise in horsemanship. The exchange was not all one way, however. The Spanish also brought New World crops, like corn and tobacco, back with them to Europe along with Native American slaves—and an epidemic of syphilis. This transatlantic exchange of people and goods became known as the **Columbian exchange**.

The sixteenth century belonged to the Spanish, who had not only discovered the New World but also exploited it for their own enrichment. As the sixteenth century came to a close, however, the Spanish empire was beginning its decline; the Spanish were facing new challenges from the French, Dutch, and English in Europe, on the open seas, and in the New World. The Spanish had subdued the people of the New World and instituted the Columbian exchange, thus providing a model for those who would come later. The lesson that the Spanish example taught the rest of Europe was that there were riches in the New World for the taking. As other European powers rose to challenge Spanish dominance, they would launch their own expeditions purposed to do just that. The Treaty of Tordesillas benefited Portugal by, in effect, granting it a vast expanse east of the Andes in South America that, though not discovered until later, eventually became a flourishing Portuguese colony in what is now known as Brazil. With South America carved up between the Spanish and Portuguese, France, England, and the Netherlands looked to North America as a place to find their fortunes.

1.2g France in the New World

The earliest explorer to the New World sailing under the flag of France was Italian-born **Giovanni da Verrazzano**, who came to North America in 1524 in search of the **Northwest Passage**, believed to lead to Asia. Verrazzano sailed the East Coast of North American, from Nova Scotia to the Carolinas, but could find no such passage. A decade later, **Jacques Cartier** made the first of his three voyages (1534–1543) to North America in search of the Northwest Passage and a legendary wealthy kingdom known as Saguenay. Cartier sailed up the St. Lawrence River to the Great Lakes, but found neither Saguenay nor the Northwest Passage. The severity of the Canadian winters caused Cartier and the French to cease exploration of the northern latitudes of the New World until the seventeenth century when **Samuel de Champlain** revived French colonization efforts.

Mestizos

Persons of mixed Spanish and Native American heritage

Columbian exchange

The exchange of food, clothing, language, plants, animals, and disease between Europe and the Americas

Giovanni da Verrazzano

Earliest explorer to the New World sailing under the flag of France, in 1524

Northwest Passage

A nonexistent water passage sought by the Europeans, believed to cut through North America to Asia

Jacques Cartier

French explorer who explored from the St. Lawrence River to the Great Lakes (1534–1543) in search of the Northwest Passage and a legendary, wealthy kingdom known as Saguenay, but found neither

Samuel de Champlain

Champlain made eleven voyages between 1600 and 1635 to the area that is now Canada, planting permanent settlements in Quebec (in 1608) and Acadia (now Nova Scotia).

Statue of Giovanni da Verrazzano, an Italian-born explorer who sailed under the flag of France to seek out a Northwest passage to Asia, and the first of many to seek out such a route unsuccessfully (Wikimedia Commons, louis-garden)

Quebec
An area of French Canada
along the St. Lawrence River
at Montreal and Quebec City

Acadia
An area of French Canada
along the Atlantic, in what is
now Nova Scotia

Huguenots
French Protestants

Jesuits
A well-educated, but
religiously uncompromising,
Catholic order that
established missions in New
France

Jean Baptiste Colbert
French minister to the king
who fostered population
growth in New France

**Father Jacques
Marquette**
Jesuit priest who explored
the Mississippi River in 1673

Robert de La Salle
Explored the Mississippi for
France in 1682

Champlain made eleven voyages, between 1600 and 1635, to the area that is now Canada, planting permanent settlements in **Quebec** in 1608 and **Acadia** (now Nova Scotia). New France, as the collection of French settlements in North America was called, was slow to grow, being virtually all male. Trading in furs was the most lucrative enterprise, and it flourished in a wilderness setting. Settlers from farms and villages intruded upon the wilderness and its inhabitants.

Champlain sought friendly relations with the Native Americans, and the French colonists married and cohabited with Native American women. Champlain desired to convert the Native Americans to Christianity, and he attempted to ensure that there would be religious freedom for both Catholics and French Protestants (known as **Huguenots**) in the New World. Champlain's efforts at ecumenism were thwarted in 1625, however, when France declared that only the Catholic religion could be practiced in New France.

By the 1630s, the Society of Jesus, also called the **Jesuits**—a well-educated but religiously uncompromising Catholic order—had begun establishing missions in New France. Though the Jesuits had little tolerance for Protestants, they allowed Native American converts to retain all aspects of their native cultures that did not conflict with Catholicism. By 1670, the Jesuits had converted ten thousand Native Americans to Christianity. Their efforts were hindered, however, by the fact that they often performed baptisms for Native Americans who were dying of small pox. Other Native Americans perceived a correlation between death and baptism, and therefore resisted conversion. This resistance to conversion helped French fur traders eventually become more influential with the Native Americans than the Jesuits. Instead of the focal point being the Jesuit Missions, approximately 25 percent of the population of New France became concentrated in three fur-trading cities on the St. Lawrence River: Montreal, Three Rivers, and Quebec.

Beginning in 1663, King Louis XIV and his minister, **Jean Baptiste Colbert**, began exercising tighter control over New France. Government was comprised of a governor and an intendant (judge), as well as soldiers sent to New France to protect the king's possession. In an effort to boost population growth, Colbert sent 774 women to New France and offered bonuses to couples who produced large families. Families were provided with land, livestock, seeds, and tools. Colbert also threatened to impose fines on fathers whose children failed to marry before the end of their teens. In five years the population in New France doubled. By 1700, the population of New France had grown to an estimated fourteen thousand. The French developed wheat agriculture on the fertile land along the St. Lawrence River, and New France was self-sufficient in food production by 1700. The success of agriculture combined with the fur trade to make New France economically prosperous, but the harsh Canadian winters caused most French immigrants to the New World to begin to look elsewhere.

The French encouraged exploration further inland, sending Jesuit priests along with specially selected explorers. In 1673, **Father Jacques Marquette**, whose personal goal was to establish missions among the Illinois natives, was ordered by his superior in Quebec to accompany Louis Joliet (picked by the governor of New France) to explore the "Great River," the Mississippi. Accompanied by five trappers, Marquette and Joliet followed the Wisconsin River down to the Mississippi River, which awed them with its grandeur. No less a surprise, downstream they found the roaring Missouri River, emptying into the Mississippi.

Marquette kept a lively journal describing the buffalo, the Native Americans they met, the heat—it was mid-July—and their experiences and encounters along the route. After feasting on dog meat and other delicacies with the Indians along the Arkansas River, the explorers decided to return to Canada—in part because of their fear of capture by the Spanish, should they proceed to the mouth of the Mississippi.

Robert de La Salle launched a less successful expedition in 1682, although he did reach the mouth of the Mississippi. These expeditions not only gave New France a strong claim to the interior of the territory of mid-America but also encouraged the French to fortify the Mississippi and Ohio rivers, laying the groundwork for an inevitable clash of interests between the British and French in North America. The French also developed colonies in the West Indies at St. Dominique (Haiti), Guadeloupe, and Martinique, based on sugar plantation agriculture and African slave labor.

1.2ʰ English Expansion

John Cabot

First English explorer to North America in 1497

Sir Walter Raleigh

Responsible for planting the English colony at Roanoke

Roanoke

The first English attempt at colonization in North America in 1585, which ended in failure in 1588

Although **John Cabot**, representing the English crown, explored the eastern coast of North America within a decade of Columbus' voyage (1497), successful English settlement was delayed for a century. Cabot himself landed on the North American coast, perhaps at Newfoundland or Labrador, but did not journey further than the range of a crossbow from the shore line. The English would not attempt to establish a settlement in North America until 1583, when Henry Gilbert led an expedition to Newfoundland. Though Gilbert was successful in at least landing on the coast of Newfoundland, he was proceeding along the coast of the island in search of a good place for a military outpost when he became caught in a storm and was lost at sea, thus leaving England without a North American colony.

1.2ⁱ The Lost Colony of Roanoke

Undeterred by Gilbert's failure, in 1585 **Sir Walter Raleigh** dispatched a group under the command of Richard Grenville to an island called **Roanoke**, off the coast of North Carolina. The English experienced problems with the natives almost immediately when the English accused the natives of theft in the case of a missing silver cup. In retaliation, the English destroyed a native village, leading to enmity with them. When Sir Francis Drake arrived on the island in the spring of 1586, the colonists boarded his ship and abandoned the colony. The next year (1587), Raleigh dispatched another expedition of ninety-one men, seventeen women, and nine children, who he hoped would begin a successful plantation. Shortly after arrival, one of the women gave birth to a daughter, Virginia Dare, who was the first person born in North America to English parents. Dare's grandfather, John White, returned to England a few weeks after her birth to recruit more settlers and bring more supplies. When he returned to Roanoke in 1590, he found the island deserted with no clues to the fate of the settlers, other than the inscription "Croatoan" carved on a post.

Sir Walter Raleigh dispatched two groups to the island of Roanoke. The first expedition experienced irreconcilable difficulties with the natives, and the second disappeared mysteriously. (Wikimedia Commons)

Theories abound as to what happened to the settlers. Some argue that they were all killed in a war with the American Indians; others argue that they were adopted by the natives and then taken off the island. Perhaps segments of both theories are correct, but no conclusive evidence has ever been found to prove either. In any case, it would be twenty years before another English group would attempt to establish a colony in North America.

In spite of the failure at Roanoke, other factors would lead to further English colonization attempts in North America. The economic, religious, and political factors that led to the establishment of the English colonies were entirely different from those that had influenced the Spanish colonies. Two outstanding economic changes took place in trade and agriculture. Whereas no trading companies flourished in 1500, over two hundred English trading companies were operating aggressively by 1600, including the Muscovy Company (1553), the Levant Company (1592), and the famous East India Company (1600). In 1500, German and Italian merchants dominated English trade. By 1600, this domination had been eliminated, and a strong group of English merchants had emerged. In 1500, most of

A tobacco brand was named for Virginia Dare, the first person born in North America to English parents. (Wikimedia Commons)

Map 1.1 Voyages of Exploration

Line of the Treaty of Tordesillas 1494

To Spain

To Portugal

GREENLAND

ICELAND

Norsemen c. 1000

Hudson 1609
To Novaya Zemlya

Cabot

Hudson Bay

Hudson

NORTH
AMERICA

NEW
FRANCE

Norsemen

Corte-Real

St. Lawrence R.

Hudson 1610

Cabot 1498

ENGLAND

UNITED
NETHERLANDS

Cabot 1497

Cartier 1534-35

EUROPE

FRANCE

NEW ENGLAND

Cartier

NEW NETHERLANDS

Verrazano

Hudson 1609

Corte-Real 1501

PORTUGAL

SPAIN

VIRGINIA

Columbus 1st 1493

AZORES

Verrazano 1524

MADEIRA IS.

Columbus 1st voyage 1492

CANARY
IS.

SAN
SALVADOR

Columbus 2nd voyage 1493

Gulf of Mexico

HISPANIOLA

Vespucci

Columbus 4th voyage 1502

CAPE
VERDE
IS.

AFRICA

NEW SPAIN

2nd

4th
Caribbean
Sea

3rd

Columbus 3rd voyage 1498

Vespucci 1499

NEW
GRANADA

Cabral 1500

ATLANTIC OCEAN

SOUTH
AMERICA

BRAZIL

PACIFIC OCEAN

PERU

Explorers' routes	Colonial Powers c. 1650	
←		English
◄ - - -		French
◄ - -		Dutch
←		Spanish
◄ ·····		Portuguese

the raw wool raised in England was shipped to Flanders to be made into cloth. By 1600, the textile industry in England absorbed much of the wool produced there.

These economic changes had a direct effect upon the development of the English colonies. The first three successful English colonies in America—Plymouth, Virginia, and Massachusetts Bay—were planted by cooperatively owned, joint-stock companies, precursors of modern corporations, in which a number of investors pooled their capital. Many of those engaged in the American enterprises had gained their experience in trading elsewhere, and they continued to participate in trading enterprises throughout the world. As Charles M. Andrews, a prominent historian of the colonial period, has written: "English America would hardly have been settled at this time had not the period of occupation coincided with the era of capitalism in the first flush of its power."

This experience in trade influenced mercantilist thought in England. Mercantilism embodied a set of economic ideas held throughout western Europe from 1500 to 1800, though the details differed from country to country. The mercantilist advocated that the economic affairs of the nation should be regulated to encourage the development of a strong state. A number of propositions were customarily included in this policy: A nation could become stronger by exporting more than it imported, resulting in a "favorable balance of trade." National self-sufficiency could be encouraged by subsidy of domestic manufacturers. A nation's wealth was to be measured by the amount of precious metals it could obtain (thus the emphasis on the accumulation of bullion). Labor should be regulated for the well-being and benefit of the state. And colonies should be established to provide the nation with those raw materials that it was unable to produce at home.

Although this does not exhaust the list of propositions supported by mercantilist thinkers, it does show that trade was considered one of the most important measures of a nation's wealth, and that colonies were valued because they contributed to that wealth. In England, the mercantile emphasis between 1500 and 1600 was upon internal regulation. After 1600, the emphasis was on external regulation—particularly the commercial relationship between England and its colonies. The phenomenal increase in English mercantile activity not only provided an agency— the joint-stock company—to create colonies but also provided a national purpose for doing so.

A second significant economic change took place in agriculture. Between 1500 and 1600, an enclosure movement gained strength in Britain. Essentially, "enclosure" meant that smaller landholdings in certain areas of England were incorporated into larger holdings, forcing some people off of the land. The result was a dislocation of population that caused many political thinkers to conclude that England was overpopulated, and that almost anyone should be permitted to go to the New World to reduce this burden. Spain, by contrast, had restricted immigration to selected individuals favored by the crown.

In the sixteenth century, the Protestant Reformation swept through Europe and profoundly affected the religious and political development of England, which in turn placed an enduring stamp upon its colonies in America. In 1500, England (and the Continent) was still within the fold of the Catholic Church. By 1600, not only had England broken away and established the national Anglican Church, but the religious rupture had also encouraged the rise of religious splinter groups.

The story of this religious rupture in England is too involved for extended treatment in this text; however, of particular importance is the fact that, in the process of waging his contest with the Roman Catholic Church, **King Henry VIII** enlisted the aid of Parliament. Parliament passed a series of enactments creating a national church, culminating in the **Act of Supremacy (1534)**, which made Henry—instead of the pope—the ecclesiastical sovereign of England. Eventually, by means of further parliamentary acts, lands in England belonging to the Roman Catholic Church were taken over by the king, greatly enhancing his wealth.

King Henry VIII
King of England (1509–1547) who broke England away from the Catholic Church— and began the Anglican Church—when the Catholic Church refused to grant him a divorce

Act of Supremacy (1534)
Declared that Henry VIII, instead of the pope, was the ecclesiastical sovereign of England

With Parliament's help, King Henry VIII of England broke with the Roman Catholic Church and established the Anglican Church, which made him the ecclesiastical sovereign of England. (Wikimedia Commons)

Although the ramifications of these actions invaded almost every sphere of English life, two consequences had a particularly strong effect on the colonies: (1) The king, by utilizing the support of Parliament, demonstrated that in practice, the authority of the crown was limited—a concept carried to the English colonies in America, and in direct opposition to Spanish doctrine (which held that the power of the sovereign was to be without restriction). (2) The break with the Catholic Church opened the way for a wider diversity of religious groups.

Some people, believing that separation from the Catholic Church should never have taken place, remained Roman Catholics. Others felt that Henry VIII (and later, Elizabeth I) had not gone far enough. The **Puritans**, an impassioned and vocal minority, believed that the Reformation in England had stopped short of its goal—that ritual should be further simplified and that the authority of crown-appointed bishops should be lessened. However, they resolved to stay within the Anglican Church and attempt to achieve their goals—that is, to "purify" the church—without further division. The Separatists, a small minority, believed that each congregation should become its own judge of religious orthodoxy. They were no more willing to give allegiance to the crown than they had been to give it to the pope. This religious factionalism was transferred to the American colonies. Of the first four settlements, Virginia was Anglican, Plymouth was Separatist, Massachusetts Bay was Puritan, and Maryland was Catholic.

Early in the seventeenth century, a number of English "dissenters"—men and women who were dissatisfied with the political, economic, and/or religious conditions in England—were ready to migrate to the New World; and English trading companies provided an agency for this kind of settlement.

Timeline

20,000–12,000 BC	Asian peoples migrate to North America across the Bering Strait.
9,000 BC	Global warming leads to the extinction of mammoths and other large game animals.
1,500 BC	Agriculture develops in North America.
300 BC	Beginning of Anasazi culture
900–1100 CE*	Mississippian culture
982 CE	Erik the Red reaches North America.
1001 CE	Leif Erikson establishes a Norse settlement in North America.
1095 CE	Crusades begin.
1150 CE	Anasazi culture vanishes.
1418	Portugal takes the Madeira Islands and begins colonization.
1477	Marco Polo's *Travels* is published in Europe.
1492	Columbus lands in the New World.
1497	John Cabot is the first English explorer to North America.
1498	Vasco Da Gama reaches India via the Cape of Good Hope.
1493–1555	Spanish savagery and European diseases decimate native populations in the Caribbean and Central America.
1512–1565	Spain explores the southern portion of North America.
1519–1521	Cortés conquers the Aztecs.
1519–1522	Magellan's expedition sails around the world.
1532–1535	Pizarro conquers the Incas.
1565	Spain founds a colony at St. Augustine, Florida.
1585–1588	The first English colonization attempt fails at Roanoke.
1608	Champlain plants French colonies at Quebec and Acadia.

* *Common Era*

The first Americans migrated over a land bridge from Asia to the Western Hemisphere during the last ice age, some 15,000 years ago. Eventually, the descendants of these hunting and gathering societies would develop agriculture, including irrigated agriculture, 3,000 years before the arrival of Columbus. Advanced societies were developed in the Andes, Yucatan, and Central Valley of Mexico by the Incas, Mayas, and Aztecs, who built pyramids, produced advanced mathematics, and created accurate calendars.

The journeys of Marco Polo overland to Asia prompted Europeans to seek an easier route to Asia, via the sea, to exploit Asian wealth in gold and spices. Norse explorers, under Leif Erikson, began a colony in North America in 1001, but abandoned it the next year; and the Western Hemisphere remained unknown to Europeans. Portugal pioneered navigation and exploration under Prince Henry the Navigator in the fifteenth century, culminating in Vasco da Gama's successful voyage to Asia around the Horn of Africa in 1498. Meanwhile, Columbus, seeking a western water route to Asia on behalf of Spain, landed in the New World in 1492, touching off an age of European exploration and colonization. The Spanish conquered Native American societies with horses, swords, guns, and European diseases. Meanwhile, the English and French, who arrived later to the colonization game, would plant colonies in North America. The first permanent Spanish settlement in the U.S. was at St. Augustine, Florida, established in 1565, while the French planted colonies in 1608 in what are now Quebec and Nova Scotia. The first English attempt at colonization in North America, at Roanoke in 1585, ended in failure in 1588.

KEY TERMS

BIBLIOGRAPHY

A

Andrews, Pat. *Voices of Diversity.* Guilford, CT: Dushkin, 1993.

Axtell, James. *The Invasion Within: The Contest of Cultures in Colonial North America.* New York: Oxford University Press, 1986.

———. *Natives and Newcomers: The Cultural Origins of North America.* New York: Oxford University Press, 2000.

B

Boxer, Charles R. *The Portuguese Seaborne Empire: 1415–1825.* New York: Knopf, 1969.

Brinkley, Alan. *American History: A Survey.* 11th ed. Boston, MA: McGraw-Hill, 2003.

C

Clendinnen, Inga. *Aztecs: An Interpretation.* New York: Cambridge University Press, 1995

Coe, Michael D. *The Maya,* 8th ed. London: Thames and Hudson, 2011.

D

Davis, David Brion. *Slavery and Human Progress.* New York: Oxford University Press, 1986.

Davis, Ralph. *The Rise of the Atlantic Economies.* Ithaca, NY: Cornell University Press, 1973.

Dipolla, Carlo M. *Guns, Sails, and Empire: Technological Innovation and the Early Phases of European Expansion 1400–1700.* London: Sunflower University Press, 1965.

E

Ellerbe, Helen. *The Dark Side of Christian History.* Orlando, FL: Morningstar and Lark, 1995.

F

Fagan, Brian. *The Great Journey: The Peopling of Ancient America.* Gainesville, FL: The University Press of Florida, 1987.

G

Garraty, John A. *The American Nation: A History of the United States to 1865.* 7th ed. New York: HarperCollins, 1991.

Gibson, Charles. *Spain in America.* New York: Harper Torchbooks, 1966.

Greenblatt, Stephen. *Marvelous Possessions: The Wonder of the New World.* Chicago, IL: University of Chicago Press, 1991.

H

Hemming, John. *The Conquest of the Incas.* New York: Houghton Mifflin, 1970.

J

Johnstone, Ronald L. *Religion in Society: A Sociology of Religion.* 4th ed. Englewood Cliffs, NJ: Prentice Hall, 1992.

Joseph, Alfred M., ed. *America in 1492: The World of the Indian Peoples before the Arrival of Columbus.* New York: Alfred A. Knopf, 1991.

L

Lockhart, James, and Stuart B. Schwartz. *Early Latin America: A History of Colonial Spanish America and Brazil.* New York: Cambridge University Press, 1983.

Lowen, James. *Lies My Teacher Told Me: Everything Your American History Textbook Got Wrong.* New York: Touchstone, 2007.

M

MacGowan, Kenneth, and Joseph A. Hester. *Early Man in the New World.* New York: Anchor Books, 1962

Morison, Samuel Eliot. *The European Discovery of America: The Northern Voyages, A.D. 500–1600.* New York: Oxford University Press, 1971.

———. *The European Discovery of America: Volume 2: The Southern Voyages, 1492–1616.* New York: Oxford University Press, 1974

Muccigrosso, Robert. *Basic History of Conservatism.* Melbourne, FL: Krieger, 2001.

Muller, Jerry Z. *The Other God that Failed: Hans Freyer and the Deradicalization of German Conservatism.* Princeton, NJ: Princeton University Press, 1987.

Muller, Jerry Z. *Conservatism: An Anthology of Social and Political Thought from David Hume to the Present.* Princeton, NJ: Princeton University Press, 1997.

Murrin, John R., Paul E. Johnson, James M. McPherson, Gary Gerstle, Emily S. Rosenberg and Norman L. Rosenberg. *Liberty, Equality, Power.* Fort Worth, TX: Harcourt Brace, 1996.

N

Nash, Gary B., Julie Roy Jeffrey, John R. Howe, Peter J. Frederick, Allen F. Davis, and Allan M. Winkler. *The American People: Creating a Nation and a Society.* 4th ed. New York: Longman, 1998.

O'Sullivan, John, and Edward F. Keuchel. *American Economic History: From Abundance to Constraint.* New York: Markus Wiener, 1989.

Padgen, Anthony. *European Encounters with the New World: From Renaissance to Romanticism.* New Haven, CT: Yale University Press, 1994.

Quinn, David B. *England and the Discovery of America, 1481–1620.* New York: Alfred A. Knopf, 1974.

Sahlins, Marshall. *Stone Age Economics.* New York: Routledge. 1972.

Sale, Kirkpatrick. *The Conquest of Paradise: Christopher Columbus and the Columbian Legacy.* New York: Plume, 1990.

Schwartz, Stuart B. *Victors and Vanquished: Spanish and Nahua Views of the Conquest of Mexico.* Boston: Bedford/St. Martin's, 1999.

Shaffer, Lynda Norene. *Native Americans before 1492: The Moundbuilding Centers of the Eastern Woodlands.* Armonk, NY: M. E. Sharpe, 1992.

Stannard, David E. *American Holocaust: Columbus and the Conquest of the New World.* New York: Oxford University Press, 1993.

Wolf, Eric. *Europe and the People without History.* Berkeley, CA: University of California Press, 2010.

POP QUIZ

1. The discovery of the Folsom Points suggests that the earliest immigrants to America arrived _____.
   a. 10,000 years ago
   b. 6,000 years ago in the Garden of Eden
   c. In 1492
   d. 1,000,000 BC

2. A Native American tribe with a reputation for cannibalism and bestiality was the _____ tribe.
   a. Anasazi
   b. Coahuiltecan
   c. Karankawa
   d. Maya

3. Which of the following best characterizes the Aztecs?
   a. an elaborate political system
   b. temples that rival the pyramids of Egypt
   c. a capital (Tenochtitlan) with over 250,000 in population
   d. all of the above

4. Which of the following is true of the Iroquois?
   a. They were matrilineal.
   b. They built bark covered longhouses of up to a hundred feet in length.
   c. They formed a confederacy for mutual defense.
   d. All of the above

5. In 1014, why did the Norseman abandon Viinland?
   a. Because natives tortured Freydis by slicing her breasts
   b. The colony was wiped out by Indian attacks.
   c. Because they were quarreling amongst themselves
   d. They didn't; they froze to death in the harsh Canadian winter.

6. The new Portuguese ship that provided a boost to exploration was the _____.
   a. caramel
   b. caravel
   c. catamaran
   d. capri

7. On October 12, 1492, Columbus landed on _____.
   a. Long Island
   b. the site that would become Jamestown, Virginia
   c. Plymouth Rock
   d. an island in the Bahamas that he named "San Salvador"

8. The explorer who headed the first expedition to voyage around the world was _____.
   a. Christopher Columbus
   b. Ferdinand Magellan
   c. Vasco de Gama
   d. Amerigo Vespucci

9. What was the primary effect of the influx of gold and silver from the New World?
   a. It made Spain the wealthiest nation in Europe for centuries to come.
   b. It caused monetary inflation in Europe.
   c. Spain abandoned the monetization of gold and silver.
   d. All of the above

10. The Spanish who explored what is now the United States had which of the following in common?
    a. They all found "cities of gold."
    b. None of them found "cities of gold" on the scale of Tenochtitlan.
    c. They all rejected Catholic Christianity.
    d. They all established permanent settlements in what is now the U.S.

11. Mestizos are _____.
    a. persons of Spanish ancestry
    b. persons of Native American ancestry
    c. persons of mixed Spanish and Native American ancestry
    d. persons who do not know their ancestry

12. The French explorer that planted settlements in Acadia and Quebec was _____.
    a. Giovanni da Verrazzano
    b. Steven Colbert
    c. Samuel de Champlain
    d. Rene Quebec

13. The first successful English colony in what is now the United States was planted by _____.
    a. a Christian mission
    b. land grants from the King to an English proprietor
    c. a joint-stock company
    d. none of the above

14. Ferdinand Magellan was killed in the _____.

15. The Protestant Reformation split the _____ _____.

ANSWER KEY: 1.a 2.c 3.d 4.d 5.c 6.b 7.d 8.b 9.b 10.b 11.c 12.c 13.c 14. Philippines 15. Catholic Church

Chapter 2

(Wikimedia Commons)

Founding the Colonies of North America

2.1 The English Settlements

As of 115 years after Columbus' discovery of America, the English had not established a single permanent foothold in the Western Hemisphere. As late as 1600, even though they had made several voyages and two attempts at settlement, they had not one colony to show for their efforts. By 1700, however, some twenty colonies—with some 350,000 inhabitants—stretched all the way from Newfoundland on the North Atlantic to the island of Barbados in the southern Caribbean. Heavy losses originally deterred growth, but promoters and settlers learned to adjust to the new environment. Thus, by the end of the 1600s, their settlements had taken root, attained prosperity, and entered into a stage of steady growth. The English dream of expansion overseas had become a reality, and Britain looked with pride upon its American empire.

2.1a Founding Virginia

The first permanent English colony in America was Virginia, begun at **Jamestown** in 1607. In the year 1606, King James I granted a group of London merchants the privilege of establishing colonies in "the part of America commonly called Virginia." Securing a charter, this Virginia Company of London raised sufficient funds through the sale of shares to outfit three ships—the *Godspeed, Discovery,* and *Susan Constant*—with 144 men and send them to Virginia. On May 14, 1607, the 104 men and boys who survived the voyage established a settlement, Jamestown, on a peninsula extending from the banks of the James River. The site was initially chosen because it appeared to be a good location for a defensible fort and the colonists wanted to avoid the native attacks that were believed to have destroyed the ill-fated colony at Roanoke. Unfortunately, the colonists did not choose their site wisely. The peninsula was low and swampy, in addition to being hot and humid in the summer, with the result that mosquitoes were abundant. Consequently, the colonists were quickly stricken with malaria outbreaks.

The early Jamestown settlers had no experience in colonization. Many of them had come for adventure rather than from any desire to become permanent residents in the wilderness. They knew nothing of subsistence farming and displayed little ingenuity. Approximately a third of the original colonists were "gentlemen" that were, in the words of **Captain John Smith**, "averse to work." Another third of the colonists were criminals who had been given a second chance in the New World. According to Smith, they were also averse to work. Although the James River teemed with fish, early colonists nearly perished for want of food. Instead of fishing and engaging in agricultural pursuits, the colonists spent their time on fruitless hunts for gold. Of the 104 that landed in Jamestown in May, only 38 survived until a ship full of supplies arrived in January—and even that many might not have survived if it were not for the natives offering to barter food for English goods throughout the fall of 1607. This pattern of failure and death would continue over the next several years as new colonists arrived. Of the first five thousand people who migrated to Virginia, fewer than one thousand survived. The winter of 1609–1610 was particularly harsh and became known as the "starving time." John Smith had alienated the natives by raiding their food supplies, so the natives retaliated by killing off livestock in the woods and keeping the colonists barricaded within their settlement. The English lived by eating dogs, cats, rats, snakes, toadstools and horsehides—and even cannibalizing the bodies of the dead. One man reportedly sat and watched his wife die and then quickly chopped up her body and salted down the pieces. The man was executed for eating what Smith referred to as "powdered wife." The English imposed draconian laws for stealing food, including the death penalty for stealing a bunch of grapes. One man was nailed to a tree by his tongue for stealing three pints of oatmeal.

2.1b Reorganization

Tobacco was a profitable crop in the New World and was in high demand in Europe. By 1700, thirty-five million pounds of tobacco had been exported from Chesapeake Bay. (iStockphoto)

Upon the colonists' arrival in Jamestown, leadership of the colony had been divided between several members of an ineffective ruling council. In the fall of 1608, however, John Smith became the council president and imposed his will on the community. Smith traded with the natives for food when he could, but organized raids to steal their food at other times. He also kidnapped natives and forced them to explain to the English how to plant corn. In 1609, Smith returned to England after suffering a severe powder burn. Smith's successors, Sir Thomas Dale and Sir Thomas Gates, imposed harsh discipline, organizing settlers into work gangs and sentencing offenders to flogging, hanging, or being broken on the wheel. The Virginia Company raised money by selling stock and recruited new immigrants by providing free passage to the New World for people who would serve the Company for seven years. Eventually, Dale decided that colonists would work harder if he permitted private ownership of land. Still, life in Virginia was harsh, and mortality rates remained high. Over nine thousand people immigrated between 1610 and 1622, but the population was only two thousand in 1622.

Gradually, the Jamestown colonists devised ways of making a livelihood. **John Rolfe** developed the skill of growing tobacco profitably and planted the first tobacco crop in

1612. Rolfe's contribution ensured Virginia's prosperity, for tobacco became a commodity much in demand in Europe very soon after its introduction from the New World. The first commercial shipment of tobacco reached England in 1617. In 1620, the colony—with fewer than a thousand residents—sent sixty thousand pounds of tobacco across the waters. By 1700, there were approximately one hundred thousand colonists in Chesapeake Bay, and they exported thirty-five million pounds of tobacco. The Virginia colony was finally an economic success, but one built on smoke. Even King James' denunciation of tobacco as "loathsome to the eye, hateful to the nose, harmful to the brain, and dangerous to the lungs" failed to slow the expansion of tobacco exports.

2.1c Indentured Servitude

Tobacco is a labor intensive crop, and successful cultivation required Virginia planters to find a reliable supply of low-cost labor. To fill this need, Virginia tobacco growers turned to **indentured servants**—those who willingly sold themselves into a form of temporary slavery for a set number of years (normally four) in exchange for passage to the New World. Of the seventeenth century immigrants to the Chesapeake colonies, 80 percent came as indentured servants. Approximately 75 percent were single males under age 25.

Life was harsh for indentured servants in the seventeenth century Chesapeake colonies. Approximately half of the indentured servants died before fulfilling their indenture contract and securing their freedom. Harsh working conditions on the tobacco plantations, along with tropical diseases, decimated the indentured workforce. Masters often cared only if their servants survived the years of their contracts and thus worked them from "can" (can see, or sunrise) to "can't" (can't see, or sundown). Indentured servants could also be sold for the remainder of their contract and therefore had no control over whom they might work for. Masters were even known to gamble away indentured servants in card games. Women could also be sold into indenture and often endured sexual abuse from masters. To make matters worse, women had time added to their indenture contracts (two years) for pregnancy and childbirth. Time was also added for both men and women for attempting to run away or committing crimes, such as stealing food or livestock. Women could be released from indenture through marriage if prospective grooms had the resources with which to purchase their indenture contracts; hence, many indentured women actively sought husbands. Both women and men received compensation at the end of their indenture contracts in the form of one suit of clothing and one barrel of corn. The more important benefit, of course, was the freedom to seek one's own economic prosperity in the New World.

2.1d Pocahontas

Pocahontas was the daughter of the native chief **Powhatan** and described by Smith as a "well-featured, but wanton young girl," probably 11 years old. She became famous both for saving the life of John Smith and for marrying the English tobacco planter, John Rolfe, and thus securing a temporary peace between the English and the natives. Shortly after arriving in Jamestown in December 1607, John Smith wrote that he was "feasted by the Indians according to their best, barbarous manner" and then taken and held down upon a rock where a native with a large rock threatened to "beat out his braines." Right before the native was to crush his skull, Pocahontas placed her own head on the rock next to Smith's so as to save him from certain death. Smith wrote that Pocahontas "hazarded the beating out of her own braines" to save his. Instead of a story of romance, however, historians generally interpret it as being part of a staged ceremony that signified Powhatan's power over the life and death of Smith; it was most likely a staged ceremony of subordination.

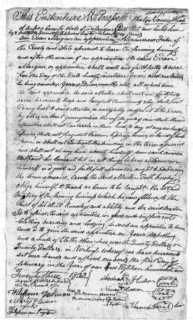

In the seventeenth century, 80 percent of immigrants came to the New World as indentured servants. Servants willingly sold themselves into slavery (by signing a contract, such as the above example) in exchange for passage to the New World. (Wikipedia, The Cooper Collection of U.S. Historical Documents, photographs and digital restoration by Centpacrr)

Pocahontas was eventually captured by the English in a raid on Powhatan's camp in 1613. When Powhatan refused English ransom demands, Pocahontas remained with the English, converted to Christianity, and married the English tobacco planter, John Rolfe. After giving birth to a son, Thomas Rolfe, Pocahontas accompanied Rolfe back to England in 1616 and became known as a gracious woman in English society. Unfortunately, her life in England was short-lived as Pocahontas died of European diseases in 1617, probably at the age of 21.

Instead of a love story, historians generally interpret the story of Pocahontas and John Smith as part of a staged ceremony that signified Powhatan's power over the life and death of Smith—a ceremony of subordination. (Wikimedia Commons)

Quakers

A fundamentalist and pacifist sect that preached equality of the sexes and suffered persecution at the hands of the Puritans in both England and in America

Royal colony

A colony ruled by a governor who was appointed by the monarch

George Calvert

Founder of the colony of Maryland

2.1e Religion in Jamestown

Virginia's Charter declared that the Anglican Church would be the official state religion of the colony and that bringing Christianity to the natives was the true purpose of the colony. John Smith, however, debunked this façade by stating that "it was absurd to cloak under the guise of religion the true intentions of profit." Smith added that what quickened the heart of most Chesapeake folk was "a close horse race, a bloody cock fight, or a fine tobacco crop." The religion of Jamestown was officially Anglican; but the passion of the people was most certainly tobacco, which was not only the primary source of income but also smoked constantly by virtually all inhabitants. Still, most of the colonists of Jamestown were nominally Anglican; and attendance at Sunday services and conformity to Anglican doctrines were required of all Virginia colonists. The Anglicans did not officially allow religious dissent; Baptists, Presbyterians, Catholics, **Quakers**, and other "heretics" were persecuted, whipped, fined, imprisoned, and forced to financially support the Anglican Church through a church tax. Anglican Church courts punished fornicators, blasphemers, and served notice on those who spent Sundays "goeing a fishing." Fines were imposed for fornication; and in 1662, a law was passed making the fine double if one were caught "fornicating with a negro."

2.1f Governing Virginia

In governing the colony, the Virginia Company at first adopted a policy of having severe laws administered by a strong-armed governor. After this failed, it made the momentous decision to let the settlers share in their own government. When Governor George Yeardley arrived in Virginia in 1619, he carried instructions to annually call an assembly to consist of two members, or burgesses, from each of the various local units in the colony. These burgesses were to be elected by residents on a basis of almost complete male suffrage. This assembly, which met in the church at Jamestown in the summer of 1619, was the first representative law-making body in English America and as such was the forerunner of representative government in the United States. Even when the Virginia Company at last succumbed to bankruptcy in 1624 and lost its charter, with the result that Virginia became a **royal colony**, the company's greatest contribution was preserved intact: The Virginia House of Burgesses continued to meet. It was ironic that this transfer took place under King James I, for it meant that the very monarch who spoke in terms of absolute power of the monarchy and the divine right of kings was also, unwittingly, the one who permitted representative government in America to become a regular part of the system of colonial government under the crown.

In 1649 Lord Baltimore sponsored the Maryland Toleration Act to guarantee freedom of worship to Christians. The act marked an advance in the direction of full religious freedom in the New World. (Wikipedia Commons)

2.1g Catholic Maryland

While Virginia was gradually gaining vitality, a neighboring colony was developing to the north. In 1632, Sir **George Calvert**, First Lord Baltimore, received from King Charles I a charter for the tract of land extending from the fortieth degree of north latitude to the south bank of the Potomac River. Calvert, a Roman Catholic, intended to make Maryland a refuge for oppressed Catholics. He died before he could settle his grant, but his son **Cecilius** became lord proprietor and sent his brother Leonard to take possession of Maryland. The first group of Catholic settlers landed on March 25, 1634.

A **proprietary colony**, such as the one the Calverts obtained, was a return to a feudal and baronial system, which in the seventeenth century was becoming outmoded. The manorial system of land tenure—which made the inhabitants of Maryland tenants of the Calverts instead of landowners—was the source of much unrest and would never have lasted at all had the Calverts not made tenancy similar to ownership. Calvert planned an aristocratic society ruled from the top, but those who immigrated to Maryland created their own democratic structures and often ignored rule from above.

In order to attract settlers and make the colony profitable, the Calverts encouraged Protestants as well as Catholics to come to Maryland from the outset. Though most of the manorial families were Catholic, Catholics never constituted a majority of the general population. Calvert attracted settlers with low cost land, with the result that the vast majority of immigrants came to Maryland for economic opportunity rather than freedom from religious persecution. Nevertheless, unlike in Virginia, Catholics and Anglicans in Maryland held separate worship; and Lord Baltimore would not allow the Jesuits in the colony to place any restrictions upon Protestants. In 1649, he sponsored the famous **Maryland Toleration Act**, which guaranteed freedom of worship to all Christians. This was not yet full liberty of conscience because there was a death penalty for non-Christians; however, the act marked an advance in the direction of full religious freedom.

With an economy based on tobacco agriculture, Maryland economically resembled Virginia in the seventeenth century; but Maryland became more open both religiously and politically. Maryland granted citizenship rights to women and Native Americans; and a black man, named **Matthias de Souza,** became the first African American to vote in North America in 1647. **Margaret Brent** became the first woman to exercise the franchise in the same election.

Religious tolerance would end in 1689, however, when the Anglicans in Maryland accused the Calverts of refusing to bow to the new Protestant king in England, **William of Orange**. In reality, the Calverts had simply not yet received word of the new king. Anglicans deposed the Calverts; they also declared the end of Catholic worship and closed, and later destroyed, the Catholic churches. Catholics would not be able to worship in public again in Maryland until the American Revolution. The Anglicans were also harsh to the **Puritans**, whom they viewed as traitors for failing to aid in the revolt against the Calverts. As a result, Puritans were arrested and jailed for treason. The Anglicans then made the Anglican Church the official state church of the colony. Interestingly, while Maryland was ending religious toleration, England was culminating its Glorious Revolution by passing it.

By the early seventeenth century, Virginia, Maryland, Plymouth, and Massachusetts Bay were established as colonies; the risk of founding new colonies was reduced; and territories in Pennsylvania, the Carolinas, New Jersey, and New York were soon claimed by the crown or other European groups. (Wikimedia Commons)

2.1f) Proprietary Colonies

Except for Maryland, the original colonies were established by joint-stock companies; but after 1660, almost all of the newly founded colonies were proprietaries. Joint-stock companies as a whole did not make a profit, and business enterprisers became less interested in investing in colonial establishments. After 1660, King Charles II began to grant large segments of American land to those who had supported the Stuart claim to the throne during the period of the English Civil War that had led to temporary abolition of the

Cecilius Calvert
Son of George Calvert, proprietor of Maryland who ensured religious freedom in Maryland

Proprietary colony
A colony where one or more individuals are granted the powers of the state and all others are tenants of the proprietors, rather than owning the land themselves

Maryland Toleration Act
1649 law declaring freedom of worship for all Christians in Maryland

Matthias de Souza
African American who voted in Maryland in 1647

Margaret Brent
Woman who voted in Maryland in 1647

William of Orange
England's Protestant king in 1689

Puritans
Protestant fundamentalist faction that sought to "purify" the Anglican Church, but was persecuted in England by King Charles I and immigrated to Massachusetts Bay in 1630

monarchy. Proprietors had been unsuccessful in the late sixteenth century because they could neither command sufficient capital nor sustain a colonizing effort over an extended period of time. But with the successful founding of Virginia, Maryland, Plymouth, and Massachusetts Bay in the early seventeenth century, the risk of founding proprietary colonies appeared greatly reduced. As a result, the territory of the Carolinas was given to a number of proprietors in 1663, and Pennsylvania was founded as a proprietary colony in 1682. New Jersey began as a proprietorship but eventually was made a crown (or royal) colony, in which affairs were directed by crown officials. New York also began as a proprietary colony, under the Duke of York, after its capture from the Dutch. It became a crown colony when York ascended the throne as James II.

2.1i The English and the Native Americans

The relationship between the English in North America and the Native Americans was different from that between the indigenous peoples and any other European group. For example, a small number of Spanish conquistadors under Hernán Cortéz were able to dominate Mexico by conquering the Aztecs, who held lesser tribes in subordination. But the English in North America faced a different situation that produced a decidedly different result. Powerful tribes blocked the westward expansion of the English settlers. In the triangular area between Lakes Ontario, Erie, and Huron, there were the Hurons. They faced the Iroquois in New York and Pennsylvania, the Susquehannas in Pennsylvania and Virginia, and the Cherokees in the Carolinas—all along the spine of the Appalachians. And in the Mississippi Valley below the Ohio River, there were the Chickasaws and, further south, the Choctaws. In addition, there were many other tribes interspersed throughout. However, no single nation had achieved ascendancy. The defeat of one tribe did not mean the defeat of all.

The relationship between the English and the Native Americans differed from that between the indigenous peoples and other European groups. In the Southern Mississippi Valley, Choctaws—such as those depicted in this painting—clashed with English settlers. (Wikimedia Commons)

Since the most powerful groups of Native Americans did not dwell along the Atlantic seacoast at that time, white settlers from England first encountered friendly tribes or warlike tribes that were easily defeated. If the American Indians had joined forces to drive the English from North America at any time during the first half century of colonization, they could have succeeded. Lack of desire, and perhaps lack of unity of purpose, explains their failure to do so—not an absence of power.

From the beginning, the English treated Native Americans as members of separate nations or separate tribes, never as subjects of the crown. Warfare and negotiation involved two nations: England and the particular tribe or nation in question. In contrast to the fusion of cultures that took place under the Spanish colonial system, white and Native American cultures remained separate in English America.

2.2 The Coming of Africans

The first Africans came to Virginia in 1619, as part of what would become a vast and very profitable Atlantic trade in human flesh—a trade that had begun about a hundred years earlier with the slaves sent to the West Indies. Records do not reveal whether the Africans brought to Virginia in 1619 came as servants or slaves, but it is known that by 1650 Virginia had both black freemen and black slaves. African immigration grew slowly during the seventeenth century. In 1680, Africans (mostly slaves) comprised only 4 percent of the total population, widely scattered throughout the eastern seaboard.

Late in the seventeenth century, the pace of importation of African slaves quickened. Most were brought to the Southern Colonies: Maryland, Virginia, North Carolina, South Carolina, and eventually Georgia. By the beginning of the American Revolution, blacks comprised 20 percent of the population and the number of blacks (four hundred thousand) was equal to the total population of New England. Given the size of this single ethnic group, it is hardly surprising that the unwilling immigrants from Africa had an enduring impact on life in what was to become the United States of America.

BVT *Lab*

Flashcards are available
for this chapter at
www.BVTLab.com.

2.2a The Rise of Slavery

Blacks from Africa and the West Indies were by far the largest group of immigrants to come to the English colonies in North America during the eighteenth century. It was a forced migration. The first blacks were brought to Virginia in 1619; and evidence indicates that, until the middle of the seventeenth century, they were both slaves and servants. The numbers involved were relatively insignificant. Less than 4 percent of the population of Virginia in 1670 was composed of slaves, with similar percentages in New York and Rhode Island. Then, in the 1690s, slavery suddenly boomed. The proportion of slaves in the population of Virginia rose to 25 percent in 1720 and to 41 percent in 1750. Slavery became the labor base upon which the large-scale plantation systems in Virginia, Maryland, and North and South Carolina were founded.

Two considerations in particular account for the abrupt change. First, neither intellectual nor moral restraint existed. Blacks were considered property rather than people. Liberty, as understood in the seventeenth and eighteenth centuries, protected property, and as a consequence protected slavery. No important social institution within Virginia, or indeed in the Western world, condemned slavery in 1700. Whites justified slavery with multiple verses from the Bible. Apostle Paul's command to slaves to obey their masters (Ephesians 6:5) was perhaps most important.

Slavery did not develop as much in the Northern Colonies because of the colder climate, shorter growing season, and prevalence of agriculture based on grain crops (corn and wheat) that are less labor intensive. Northern farms also tended to be smaller so that family labor was sufficient in most circumstances. Given that slaves require sustenance year-round and that there was not work in agriculture in the North for most of the year, slavery did not make economic sense in the higher latitudes. George Washington, for instance—who owned almost three hundred slaves in northern Virginia—eventually concluded that his plantation would have been more profitable if he had used wage labor due to his responsibility to take care of older slaves that could no longer work, but who required healthcare.

Washington, like other slave owners, required his slaves to work from dawn to dusk and "be diligent all the while." In short, slave life was harsh. Washington and other slave owners also instituted whipping so as to impose discipline on the slaves and ensure that they did not slack in their work. Washington's calculations aside, the slave system did work and was generally profitable for slave owners—otherwise they would have shifted to wage labor long before slavery was abolished at the end of the Civil War.

A second contributing factor in the rise of slavery was the fact that Virginia, Maryland, and South Carolina were desperately in need of workers. In the seventeenth century, indentured servants had been the primary labor force in Virginia and Maryland; and indentures in modest numbers were introduced into New England as well, even though family labor predominated. But beginning in the late seventeenth century, and accelerating in the eighteenth century, indentured servants were increasingly attracted to the Middle Colonies. As a result, the Southern Colonies were correspondingly desperate for labor, especially as large landholdings became more numerous.

The chief motivation behind the increase in black slave importation in the Southern Colonies, then, was economic. Although twice as expensive as an indentured servant at the outset, a slave provided permanent service; and in every colony the offspring of female slaves were by law also slaves, in perpetuity. Soon, slaves outstripped land as an investment. A broadside written by Thomas Nairne of South Carolina in 1704 informed prospective colonists of the relative costs of establishing a plantation. For a modest plantation of two hundred acres, the cost of two slaves constituted one half of all costs—including tools, land, a house, livestock, and a year's provisions. The land cost only £6 compared with £80 for the two slaves.

In America, slavery's development was also partially a response to landowners' desire for a more pliable labor force. Wage laborers could always choose other options in the vast expanse that was America. If wage laborers were unhappy with their working conditions or wages, they could always walk off the job and head west to the endless frontier where they could subsist through hunting and gathering.

As England rose as a naval force in the seventeenth century, the slave trade increased thanks to British seafaring power. Eventually, half of all British merchant ships would be

Middle Passage

The slave journey aboard sailing ships from Africa to the New World

Seasoned slaves

Slaves who had survived one year in the New World, giving them a greater market value

slave ships, and approximately five hundred thousand people would come to America in bondage from Africa. Eleven million more African slaves would be transported to Latin America and the Caribbean, with Brazil as the number one destination.

The human cargo arrived in colonial America from Africa under particularly cruel conditions. The first part of the slaves' passage was from their local village, where they were captured, to the African coast, where they were sold to African middlemen. These middlemen kept the slaves in holding areas known as "factories" for up to a year before they were sold to European traders. The slaves would be branded while waiting and then sold to a European slave-ship captain. Once the transaction was complete, the traders would load the slaves onto ships for the infamous **Middle Passage** between the African coast and their landing point in the Western Hemisphere. One in seven people would not survive the four to six week voyage from Africa. If the ship became stuck in calm water with insufficient wind, food, and water, then the slaves would simply be tossed overboard. Others died of disease. Two competing goals were in play for the traders. On the one hand, it was in their economic interest to deliver their goods alive and in good enough health to be capable of work. On the other hand, they wanted to cram as many people into the hold as possible, once again to maximize profits. Typically, the captives made the long voyage to America below deck and in shackles.

Arrival in the New World, however, did not end the slaves' risk of death. The slaves would be purchased at auction when they landed in the New World, then transported to the plantations of their new owners. Before transportation to their final destination, slaves would be branded again. To make matters worse, an estimated one-third of the new immigrants from Africa would die during their first year in the New World due to European diseases. Those who survived the first year were much more likely to survive thereafter; they were known as **seasoned slaves** and had a higher market value.

Once slaves reached their final destinations, the captives found they were the property of people who spoke an unfamiliar language and had unfamiliar customs and laws. Given such unfavorable circumstances, scholars debate the extent to which slaves were able to reconstitute their own culture, religious traditions, and family life—which was centered more on extended kin networks than was the European model. What is clear is that much of American culture—jazz being the prime example—has been profoundly influenced by the African legacy. Hence, we know that despite all of the suffering, the Africans were not entirely stripped of their culture, as had been formerly thought.

Jazz music is a significant piece of culture that has been greatly influenced by the legacy of the African Americans who came to this country as slaves. (Shutterstock)

By 1775, 20 percent of the population of the English colonies in North America was composed of blacks, most of them slaves. More than four hundred thousand lived in the colonies of Maryland, Virginia, North Carolina, South Carolina, and Georgia—a number almost equal to the total population of New England.

Although it has often been asserted that the British Royal African Company brought most of the slaves to America, in reality free traders were the principal conveyors of blacks. New Englanders, infrequently the Dutch, and later Southern merchants or planters—all imported slaves from the Caribbean as well as from Africa. Most of the colonies tried to end, by law, the increasing importation of slaves; each act adopted by the individual colonial legislatures, however, was rejected by the British Board of Trade. Because of the profitability of the slave trade, Britain considered it to be the basis for its entire trading structure. Indeed, a charge excised from the Declaration of Independence, which condemned the crown for imposing slaves upon the colonies, had a basis in fact.

Several myths were spread to feed a racial bias, including that the slaves came to the English colonies with no skills and that the culture of Africa was vastly inferior to that of the Western world. In truth, most slaves came with skills equal to those of an ordinary laboring Englishman. For example, the original source of the rice that became a successful crop in South Carolina was Madagascar, where Africans had been cultivating it for centuries. When Eliza Pinckney of South Carolina was unsuccessful in making the commercial indigo dye with a white overseer, she imported a black slave whose knowledge—together with her own perseverance—culminated in an important marketable staple.

The agricultural tools of the African farmer and the English leaseholder did not vary greatly. In time, the transplanted African became the skilled worker in the Southern Colonies—the cook, cooper, cobbler, and blacksmith. It was not unusual for a planter to put in a request for a slave from a special region of Africa because of the particular skills of its inhabitants.

The cultivation of a number of popular crops—including rice, tobacco, and cotton—was very labor intensive; in the case of rice, it required working in mosquito-infested swamps. African slaves, with their greater resistance to tropical diseases, provided a low-cost solution for farmers and plantation owners. (Wikimedia Commons, Kimberly Vardeman)

2.2b Slave Life

Depending on which colony they lived in and what type of work they were in engaged in, life for slaves varied across the American colonies. Approximately 75 percent of slaves were involved in agriculture, and most of the rest were involved in domestic servitude; consequently, slavery was primarily a way of organizing agricultural work so as to produce the greatest profits for land owners. The cultivation of a number of agricultural crops, including rice, tobacco, and cotton, was very labor intensive. In the case of rice, it required working in mosquito-infested swamps—something that few laborers for hire were inclined to do. African slaves, with their greater resistance to tropical diseases, provided the solution.

Most of the African slaves in the colonies, an estimated 80 percent, lived and worked on large plantations with two hundred slaves or more; and most slaves, by far, lived in the Southern Colonies, with South Carolina having the most slaves in the seventeenth century. Most Southerners, however, did not own slaves. Only one in five Southerners owned slaves, and 80 percent of slave owners owned fewer than five slaves.

Once on the plantation in America, slaves lived as family units in rustic, small, crowded slave cottages. Marriage between slaves, while illegal, was often informally encouraged and practiced as slave owners understood that slave men with wives and children were less likely to rebel. Slave owners could then threaten to sell family members as a way to ensure discipline, hard work, and other preferred behaviors. It was not always a mere threat, however. Most slaves would experience the loss of family members through sale, as slave reproduction often exceeded plantation labor demands. The sale of excess laborers, therefore, was often economically expedient for the masters.

Slave breeding was also common, as slave owners desired to increase their slaveholdings through reproduction. Women who resisted the forced breeding would be subjected to the whip. Some women were also forced to satisfy the sexual desires of the master or other male members of the master's family. These relations often produced children, causing difficulties in the slave cottages as slave patriarchs raised the master's illegitimate children.

Not all slave/master sexual relations were forced, however. Some slave women sought sexual relations with the master as a way to improve their lives and the lives of their children. Slave mistresses were more likely to have jobs in the house rather than the field, often had nicer clothing, and often took more frequent baths. Furthermore, the children of the master and the slave woman often received special treatment and preferred jobs on the plantation.

2.2c Slave Resistance and Rebellion

The devastating social consequences of slavery pervaded every aspect of colonial life. Conflict between blacks and whites led to the enactment of elaborate codes for the conduct of slaves. Runaway slaves were normally caught, and the consequences for runaways were dire. That being the case, the most common forms of slave revolt were covert kinds of resistance—such as faking illness, slacking work, breaking tools, and moving as slowly as masters would allow while staying ahead of the whip.

Mose

A settlement begun by the Spanish in Florida in 1738 for slaves who escaped from the British

Stono Rebellion

The largest slave revolt in American history where over twenty whites and sixty slaves were killed

New York Conspiracy Trials

In the arson conspiracy trials that lasted the summer of 1741, four whites and eighteen slaves were hanged, thirteen slaves were burned alive, and seventy were banished to the West Indies. One man, John Uty, who was a clergyman and Latin teacher who had just arrived in New York, was hanged as a likely Spanish priest.

Salem Village

Site of the famous Salem witch trials of 1692

2.2b Mose

Beginning in the 1680s, Spain offered freedom to slaves from the English colonies who could make their way to Florida and who accepted Catholicism. In 1738, the Spanish governor in Florida established a town north of St. Augustine for escaped slaves from the British colonies. The town, Gracia Real de Santa Teresa de Mose (**Mose** for short), was administered by an African American Catholic convert named Francisco Menendez, a name he took at his Catholic baptism. Menendez was an escaped slave from Carolina who learned not only to speak but also to read and write Spanish. Menendez was given charge of Mose in 1738, and Mose became the first community of free blacks in what is now the United States.

2.2c Stono Rebellion

In 1739, the Spanish governor of Florida also offered freedom to any slaves who could make their way to Florida from Carolina (there were no slaves in Georgia at the time). This announcement, along with word about a free settlement for blacks in Mose, ignited the **Stono Rebellion** in South Carolina—the largest slave revolt in American history. On a Sunday morning before dawn, a group of some twenty slaves attacked a country store and killed the store's two shopkeepers while confiscating the store's guns and ammunition. The slave rebels placed the severed heads of their victims on the store's front steps and then headed toward Spanish Florida, attacking Southern plantations along the way and enticing other slaves to join their rebellion. The slave rebels burned and plundered over half a dozen plantations and killed over twenty white men, women, and children. A force of whites was quickly assembled to put down the revolt; and over sixty rebels were killed—their heads placed atop mileposts along the road as reminders to other slaves of the consequences of rebellion.

The fate of these rebels illustrated the fact that, at the time, slaves had no chance of overturning slavery; rebellion would only lead to death for the rebels. The Stono Rebellion stunned the white population, however; and fear of future revolts prompted defensive measures. Laws were passed to restrict the importation of slaves and to encourage the importation of white indentured servants. White settlements were promoted on the frontier as protection for older, slave-centered communities.

The next year, Georgia's governor, James Oglethorpe, retaliated against the Spanish for inciting the Stono Rebellion and led both an invasion of Florida and an attack on Mose; he managed to disperse the free blacks living there before being forced to retreat by the Spanish. Oglethorpe reported that Spanish priests were living in disguise among the free blacks at Mose and that the Spanish were instigating slave revolts in the British colonies.

Punishment for slave rebellion could be extremely harsh. The whip was commonly used to keep slaves working throughout the day or in retaliation for resistance. (Wikimedia Commons)

Oglethorpe's report spread panic and fear of slave revolt throughout the British colonies. New York City, in particular, was gripped by panic because, with over two thousand slaves, it had the largest concentration of slaves in North America at that time. A slave revolt there in 1712 had led to the execution of twenty-one slaves. In the summer of 1741, a series of fires in the city were blamed on a white tavern owner and a number of slaves. The conspiracy trials that followed lasted through the summer of 1741. Sixteen-year-old witness Mary Burton was granted immunity for her testimony. She had worked at the tavern in question and caused a sensation when she testified that it had been the center of a plot by the pope to murder the city's white population and install the tavern's white owner, John Hughson, as king of the Africans. By the time the courts were finished, four whites and eighteen slaves were hanged, thirteen slaves were burned alive, and seventy were banished to the West Indies. One man, John Uty—a clergyman and Latin teacher who had just arrived in New York—was hanged as a likely Spanish priest. The **New York Conspiracy Trials** of 1741 have often been compared to the Salem witch trials in terms of their irrationality and panic, but more people were executed in New York in 1741 (thirty-five) than in **Salem Village** (twenty).

2.3 The Pilgrims in Plymouth

Colonists arriving on the *Mayflower* at **Plymouth Rock** off Cape Cod on November 11, 1620, made the first permanent settlement in New England. They had been granted permission to settle farther south, but their ship had been blown off course. A small, devoted band of Separatists—part of a larger number of religious dissenters who had left England for Holland in 1608—were at the core of the group of about a hundred settlers. The Separatists viewed the Anglican Church as corrupt and beyond correction; thus, proper service to God required that they separate themselves from the Anglican Church and establish their own separate society. The Separatists first moved to rural England, but finding it impossible to escape Anglican decadence in England, moved to the Netherlands in 1608. The Separatists

Protestant pilgrims, like those who sailed to the New World on the Mayflower, *are led in prayer prior to their departure from England for their new home. Women and children are shown, perhaps to emphasize the importance of family in the community; and a rainbow is depicted symbolizing hope and divine protection. (Wikimedia Commons)*

would find constructing a pure society of uncorrupted Christians in the Netherlands to be futile as well. In the words of Separatist leader **William Bradford**, "many of their children, by the great licentiousness of youth in Holland, and the manifold temptations of the place, were drawn away by evil examples." Unsuccessful in the Netherlands, the Separatists obtained permission to settle in the New World, in the lands granted to the Virginia Company. In August 1620, 102 **Pilgrims** boarded the *Mayflower* to immigrate to the New World. The expedition, which put out from Plymouth, England, was financed by a joint-stock company in which the Separatists, their fellow passengers, and outside investors participated.

During their eleven week voyage, the Pilgrims were blown off course and ended up far north of the Virginia Company's lands. Realizing that they had no legal authority to settle at Plymouth, the Pilgrims drew up the Mayflower Compact the day they arrived; the document would provide security, order, and a claim to legitimacy. In the document, the Pilgrims agreed to "covenant and combine ourselves together into a civil Body Politick, for our better Ordering and Preservation." The signatories also agreed to enact and obey just laws. William Bradford was quickly elected governor.

Unfortunately, the Pilgrims got off to a difficult start in the New World. William Bradford's wife jumped overboard and committed suicide by drowning in Plymouth Harbor before ever setting foot in North America. For the rest of the Separatists arriving that November, the weather was harsh and food was scarce. As a result, half of the Pilgrims died the first winter and they were only able to build seven houses. More might have died of starvation had the Pilgrims not stolen corn from the natives while the natives were away from their houses toiling in the fields. Bradford credited God with sending the Native Americans away so that the Pilgrims could steal the natives' food. The Pilgrims at first attempted a communal lifestyle with no private property, but Bradford disappointedly explains that this early attempt at communism was abandoned in 1623 because it apparently sapped the work ethic.

Squanto, the legendary helpful Native American, arrived at the Pilgrim's camp in March 1621 with the simple greeting, "Welcome Englishmen." Obviously, this meant that Squanto had previous experience with Englishmen—but Bradford viewed Squanto as a "special instrument sent from God for the Pilgrims' good." Historians believe that Squanto had been sold into slavery in Virginia in 1614 and had been transported to Spain, France, and then England where he

The legendary Squanto, historically described as a great helper to the settlers, may actually have been a slave, traded several times throughout France and Europe and then returned to North America. Squanto may have helped the settlers, but his primary motive was likely personal gain through trade. (Wikimedia Commons)

convinced the Newfoundland Company that he could be a useful guide and trade broker. It appears that, consequently, the English Newfoundland Company returned Squanto to North America.

Plymouth Rock

The landing site of the Pilgrims in North America in November 1620

Mayflower

The ship that carried the Pilgrims to America

William Bradford

The leader of the Pilgrims and author who wrote *Of Plymouth Plantation*, which chronicles their efforts in the new world

Pilgrims

A Separatist group in England that viewed the Anglican Church as corrupt beyond repair, migrated to the Netherlands, and then went on to America in 1620

Squanto

Native American trade broker who befriended and aided the Pilgrims

John Winthrop

Puritan leader and
author from whom
we have a historical
record of the Puritans in
Massachusetts Bay

Bradford writes that Squanto taught the Pilgrims the "Indian way" of planting corn, directing that the Pilgrims place four fish in each corn mound and that the corn mounds be one and a half feet apart. In reality, historians doubt that either the Pilgrims or the Native Americans could have followed such a method, since it would have meant using 27,844 fish per acre—or 2,784,400 fish per one hundred acres. Furthermore, there is no evidence that any other Native Americans in North America were using fish for fertilizer in the manner and quantity purportedly prescribed by Squanto. Instead, there is evidence that fish waste was used for fertilizer in coastal Spain and France in the seventeenth century. It has therefore been suggested that, in actuality, Squanto gained the fish-for-fertilizer idea during his time as a slave in Europe. Evidence also suggests that Squanto often kept portions of goods traded between the English and natives for his own personal profit. Historians believe that he coerced Native Americans into trading with the English by telling them that the plague was kept in the ground by the English and that they would release it on the Native Americans if they refused to trade. Instead of an instrument from God, it appears that Squanto was primarily a salesman and an opportunist.

2.3a The Great Migration

Although the character and heroism of the Pilgrims of Plymouth bequeathed a poetic heritage to the American people, the larger colony of Massachusetts Bay contributed more to New England's civilization. The main body of Puritan settlers, under the leadership of **John Winthrop**, arrived in the summer of 1630 on the *Arbella*. This was one of four ships that carried the first wave of the Great Migration; between 1630 and 1640, the Great Migration brought some twenty thousand people into Massachusetts. The Pilgrims of Plymouth would essentially be overwhelmed and absorbed by the larger Puritan society. The Puritans, like the Pilgrims before them, were a splinter group from the Anglican Church who viewed the Anglican Church as corrupt. In contrast to the Pilgrims, who viewed the Anglican Church as beyond reform, the Puritans sought to reform or "purify" the Anglican Church from within.

The Winthrop group had managed to obtain a royal charter for the Massachusetts Bay Company. Unlike other colonial enterprises, this company vested control not in a board of governors in England but rather in the members of the company who themselves were emigrating. They came bringing their charter with them and were self-governing, subject only to the English crown. Voting privileges were granted to those who were members of the Congregational Puritan Church of the colony; and during the early years of settlement, a close relationship between church and state was the key to authority and lifestyle. In all cases, however, the civil magistrates—not the clergy—held preeminence.

Similar to other seventeenth century colonies, the Puritans of Massachusetts Bay suffered hardships upon their arrival in the New World. Over two hundred Puritans died the first year, including Winthrop's son and eleven of his servants. A group of over one hundred decided that immigration to the New World had been a mistake and boarded boats back to England. In spite of these problems, Puritans would continue to emigrate from England due to the persecution of Puritans at the time by the Anglican King Charles I, who charged Anglican Bishop William Land with "harrying them [the Puritans] out of the land." During the ten years after the landing of the *Arbella*, Massachusetts Bay became the most populous English colony in the New World. From towns established at Boston, Cambridge, Dorchester, Salem, and elsewhere, groups would break away, from time to time, and move into fresh territory. In the summer of 1636, for example, the Reverend Thomas Hooker, with about one hundred of his followers, set out on foot from Cambridge and settled a new township at Hartford, in what became Connecticut. Other towns proliferated in similar fashion.

2.3b Puritan Society

Puritan society was democratic in form from the very beginning—at least, for Puritan men—and stressed religion, work, family, and education. Leaders in the Puritan community were university trained ministers, and Harvard University was begun in 1636 as a theological seminary for Puritans. In 1647, all towns with at least fifty families were ordered to establish elementary schools; and towns of a hundred families were required to establish secondary schools, making the Puritan colonies of New England the most educated of the American colonies.

New England Puritans often expressed themselves in prose and poetry. Sometimes their tone was harsh, but it was always unmistakably clear. Sermons were cultivated as a literary form and were published by the press founded in Massachusetts Bay in 1639—the first printing press in the New World. This press became the voice of Puritanism in America. Its productivity was fabulous, exceeding the output of the presses of Cambridge and Oxford in England.

Pictured is Massachusetts Hall, Harvard's oldest building (1720). University trained ministers were leaders in the Puritan community, and Harvard University was begun in 1636 as a theological seminary for Puritans. (Wikimedia Commons, Daderot)

The Puritans began democratic self-government almost immediately. Male church members elected a governor and colonial legislature, as well as local selectmen who handled most political matters. Once annually, all townspeople would meet to decide local political matters (a practice that continues in small New England towns through the present). Puritans had a multiplicity of municipal offices including surveyors of deer, town criers, measurers, and purchasers of grain; of all adult males, 10 percent held some sort of municipal office.

Each Puritan town was founded by a grant from the Massachusetts Colony General Court in Boston. Settlement grants were given only to groups of Puritans that signed a compact signifying the unity of their purpose. After receiving a charter from Boston, Puritan communities enjoyed much local autonomy.

The New England Puritans turned to congregationalism as a form of church government, but they attempted informally to establish close ties among the individual congregations by means of synods—or assemblies of delegates—to discuss and make decisions on ecclesiastical affairs. Theoretically, each congregation could select its own course of action; but in practice, a consensus of the Puritan leaders usually determined the course.

It would be a mistake, however, to think that the Puritan clergy were all-powerful; indeed, conformity to Puritan beliefs was enforced by civil authority. Lay leaders like John Winthrop, not the leading ministers, were primarily responsible for the banishment of colonials who protested against Puritan doctrines.

The premises of New England Puritanism affected every sphere of life—political, economic, cultural, social, and intellectual. For example, land was distributed to church congregations so that a social-religious community could be created and sustained. Settlements by towns enabled the Puritans to build their lives and activities around the church, and made it so that designated practice could easily be enforced. With the Puritans in political control, and thus able to determine those groups who were to receive land grants, the goal of creating a Bible Commonwealth could be realized.

2.3c Puritan Success

Puritans had astounding success in terms of survival, when compared to the Chesapeake colonies. Ordinary settlers came as family units with men and women almost equal in numbers. Very few were indentured servants. The Puritans' economy was a mix of agriculture, fishing, timber, and fur trade. Puritans farmed in open fields shared by all and grazed livestock in open meadows. Firewood was cut from communal woodlands. Life expectancy had reached 60 years by 1700—exceeding life expectancy in England—and 90 percent of Puritan colonists survived childhood to marry (only 50 percent of Americans survived childhood in 1900). The Puritan population doubled every twenty-seven years to reach one hundred thousand in population by 1700. Furthermore, most of the population increase is accounted for by natural increase, since only 25,000 people immigrated to New England in the seventeenth century. Large scale Puritan immigration ended after 1642, due to the English Civil War that ended their persecution.

In contrast to the Puritans' success, an influx of 75,000 immigrants to Chesapeake in the seventeenth century only yielded a total population of seventy thousand by 1700.

Roger Williams

Puritan who was banished
from Massachusetts Bay for
heresy and credited with
founding the colony of
Rhode Island

Anne Hutchinson

Puritan woman banished
from Massachusetts Bay for
heresy and who joined with
Roger Williams in Rhode
Island

John Calvin

Protestant leader in
Reformation Europe whose
ideas spawned the Puritan
movement in England

**Doctrine of
predestination**

The Calvinist and Puritan
idea stating that before the
creation of the world, God
predestined his "elect" for
heaven

By 1680, the average Massachusetts household had a kitchen, parlor, and sleeping loft, in contrast to the single room dwellings that were still found in Chesapeake at that time; and Puritan living standards were already equal to those in England.

2.3d The Spreading Colonies of New England

Either because they had offended the ruling authorities, or because they were discontented with a thoroughgoing Puritan commonwealth that punished nonconformists severely and tried to impose its religious tenets upon all, colonists occasionally left Massachusetts Bay. Freedom of conscience or religion was not a virtue of Massachusetts Bay. **Roger Williams**, pastor of the church at Salem, complained publicly that the clergy's interference in politics threatened the freedom of individual congregations; because of this, and because he questioned the right of the settlers to take land from the American Indians, he was banished from the colony in 1635. Williams fled in the dead of winter to the Narragansett Indians and arranged, in January 1636, to purchase land from the American Indians in order to build a small settlement that he called Providence. It wasn't long before other fugitives from the persecution of Massachusetts Bay's Puritan clergy found their way to Williams' colony—including a group led by the religious rebel, **Anne Hutchinson**.

The Providence settlers made a compact which provided for the separation of church and state. Other groups came to the area and settled at Portsmouth, Newport, and Warwick; and in 1644, Parliament granted Williams a charter that united the various groups, located in what is now Rhode Island, into one civil government. A royal charter in 1663 reiterated the liberties that had been established earlier. This charter remained the basis of Rhode Island's laws until 1842. Rhode Island was far ahead of its time in its legal provisions. As early as 1647, for example, it outlawed trials for witchcraft and imprisonment for debt. The Rhode Island Constitution did not, however, provide for complete religious freedom. In particular, the Rhode Island Constitution of 1644 denounced Catholics and Quakers for "Belching out fire from Hell."

A group of Massachusetts Bay emigrants settled a colony at New Haven, still under conservative Puritan leadership. As in Massachusetts, only church members were permitted to vote—a policy that, in effect, gave the church political control over the affairs of the colony. Since the scriptures made no mention of jury trials, New Haven—in contrast to other New England colonies—forbade such trials and left the dispensation of justice in the hands of the magistrates.

In 1662, Connecticut received a royal charter that confirmed the rights of self-government and provided for the Fundamental Orders, a platform of government extending the franchise to non-church members. New Haven, to its distress, was subsequently absorbed into Connecticut, and its citizens thereby gained the guarantees of Connecticut's charter.

Other Massachusetts Bay residents moved into New Hampshire and Maine, where settlers had already established themselves in small fishing villages. Massachusetts laid claim to both regions; but after many disputes, New Hampshire gained a royal charter and freed itself from the domination of Massachusetts in 1679. Maine did not become separate until 1820.

2.3e Puritanism

As a movement, Puritanism sought to religiously and politically return society to a "better, vanished time"—in this case, the time of the Christian Church in the days of the Acts of the Apostles. The Puritans viewed the first century as an uncorrupted golden age of Christianity, which had become corrupted over the centuries—complete with the addition of defiling and unnecessary traditions, rules, and decorations—first by the Catholic Church and then the Anglican Church. Human history, in the Puritan view, was a history of religious (and therefore human) decline and increasing human depravity.

The Puritans were heavily influenced by **John Calvin** and believed Calvin's **doctrine of predestination**, which holds that before the creation of the world, God exercised his divine grace and chose a few human beings to receive eternal life. Only God, however, could know who the elect are, and nothing could change God's choices. If one were among the elect, however, one would be expected to act like it so that the saintly behavior would be visible to all.

An obvious problem with the Puritan predestination doctrine is that if one is predestined to eternal bliss, and nothing can change God's mind, why worry about sin? In another apparent contradiction, the Puritans stressed the conversion of "those who could not find God's truth in their hearts." If the decision was predestined by God before the beginning of the world, and has nothing to do with humans, why evangelize?

Puritan "logic" was not a method of discovery or of learning the truths of science and nature. Instead, Puritan logic was a rhetorical means of communicating the knowledge passed from God to others. Since the Puritans already knew the truth, there was little need for inductive reasoning.

Nevertheless, the Puritans viewed the salvation of themselves, as well as the salvation of others within the congregation, as the concern of everyone in the Puritan community; and each Puritan was responsible for helping others to achieve their spiritual goals. To further this purpose, the Puritans engaged in **Holy Watching**, or moral surveillance of each other to ensure that they did not sin. Puritan houses were built in close proximity so that Puritans could hear their neighbors and know what they were doing. Curtains on the windows were forbidden so that one could see inside of the house of one's neighbor and ensure that no one inside was engaging in sin. The physical layout of the towns was such that houses faced inward toward their neighbors so as to allow Puritans to keep better watch on one another and guard against ungodly behavior.

Holy Watching
The Puritan responsibility to keep a watch on others in the community as a measure against sin

2.3f Puritans and Human Nature

Puritans espoused a negative view of human nature, believing that humans are naturally bad and untrustworthy. Consequently, single men and women were prevented from living alone because, left to their own devices, it was expected that they would sin. In the words of Thomas Hooker, "Every natural man and woman is born as full of sin as a toad is of poison." In order to compensate for the depravity of human nature, Puritans believed that coercion was necessary to ensure proper behavior; and civil and religious transgressions were therefore severely punished. Puritans also believed that people were naturally slothful, but that work was Godly; and therefore work was stressed as the primary method of serving God. To ensure that Puritans served God faithfully through work, the Puritans meted out punishment for laziness.

Puritans purged themselves of all luxuries to focus on God's work. Physical beauty and aesthetics were disparaged. In 1634, the General Court forbade garments with any lace, silver or gold thread, all cutworks, embroidered or needlework caps, all gold and silver girdles, hatbands, belts, ruffs, beaver hats, and all clothing whereby the nakedness of the arm may be discovered. The Court also forbade long hair, and neither Christmas nor Easter was celebrated. Religious wedding ceremonies were also outlawed; couples were married by a magistrate in a civil ceremony, instead.

Laws were also passed ensuring that no one engaged in any form of entertainment, which was considered sinful. Prohibited entertainment included sledding, swimming, music, and dancing. According to Puritan leader Increase Mather, "Mixt or Promiscuous Dancing of Men and Women could not be tolerated since the unchaste Touches and Gesticulations used by Dancers have a palpable tendency to that which is evil." Also prohibited were cards, dice, shuffleboard, and other games of chance. To make sure that Puritans did not waste time entertaining themselves, the Court specifically forbade enjoyment when one might be better employed—as well as on the Sabbath, Sunday walks, and visits to the harbor. In 1670, John Lewis and Sarah Chapman were convicted of "engaging in things tending much to the dishonor of God, the reproach of religion, and the prophanation of the holy Sabbath." Lewis and Chapman were, more specifically, "sitting together on the Lord's Day, under an apple tree in Goodman Chapman's orchard." Perhaps the most notorious case of all, however, was the case of Thomas Granger, who was executed in 1642 for having sex with a mare, two cows, five calves, two goats, five sheep, and a turkey. All of the animals were also put to death—according to the instructions of Leviticus 20:15—and their carcasses were thrown in a pit; all were ordered to make no use of them.

BVT Lab

Visit www.BVTLab.com to explore the student resources available for this chapter.

2.3g Puritan View of the Bible

The Puritans viewed the Bible as a complete guide to societal organization and believed that "God's laws," as outlined in their Holy book, should also be the basis of civil law. In the Puritan mindset, everything that occurred in the world was somehow analogous to some event in the Bible and therefore a reproduction of divine will. The fact that the Bible was "complete" meant that anything that could not be justified by a passage found somewhere in the Bible was forbidden. In the minds of the Puritans, they spoke when the Bible spoke and were silent when the Bible was silent. The Puritans were extremely legalistic in their approach to the Bible and paid great attention to Biblical details, so much so that they could be criticized for paying more attention to the Biblical "trees" than to the forest. The Puritans conceived of themselves as a covenanted people. In essence, the "covenant theology" held that God had made a contract with humans setting down the terms of salvation. God had pledged himself to abide by these terms. This covenant in no way changed the doctrine that God elected the saints, but it explained why certain people were elected and others were not. Individuals knew that they were numbered among the elect by experiencing God's grace and exhibiting this *regeneration*—spiritual rebirth—before their peers. The Puritans firmly opposed all religious enthusiasms and any evidence of self-revelation (the doctrine that God revealed himself directly to an individual).

The Puritans conceived of themselves as a covenanted people. In essence, the "covenant theology" held that God had made a contract with humans setting down the terms of salvation. (iStockphoto)

2.3h Puritans and Free Thought

Like the seventeenth century Anglicans and the Catholics whom they disparaged, the Puritans refused, absolutely, to tolerate those who thought differently from themselves on religious matters; such heretics were vigorously persecuted. The Puritans believed that they possessed the correct interpretation of the Bible to the exclusion of all groups with whom they disagreed. As a consequence, if anyone offered a persuasive argument that shook the Puritans' certainty, or if someone developed a clever line of reasoning that could confuse the Puritan or cause him to question his beliefs, the Puritans suspected that Satan must somehow be involved. In order to prevent such confusion, settlement grants in the Puritan colony were granted only to groups of Puritans who signed a compact signifying the unity of their purpose. The compact stated, "We shall live by all means, labor to keep off from us such as are contrary minded, and receive only such unto us as may be probably of one heart with us."

2.3i Hutchinson Heresy

In 1636, the Puritan Community of Boston became divided between the male clergy and the theological teachings of Anne Hutchinson. Hutchinson considered herself a devout Puritan, but she challenged the Puritan view of women as subservient. In I Timothy 2:10–11, the writer states that women should be submissive to men, silent in Church, and not teach men. Hutchinson essentially violated all three—by teaching her own version of the gospel—and built up a major following who would meet at her home after church services. Hutchinson had no official church training or standing, but gained the wide respect of converts within the community, thanks to her teachings. Hutchinson preached that salvation was through grace, which she viewed as more important than works, thus violating the premium placed on works in orthodox Puritan theology. Hutchinson also stated that the "Holy Spirit was absent in the Preaching of some Ministers," thus challenging the spirituality, and legitimacy, of Puritan leadership.

Hutchinson was therefore placed on trial by male clergy and judges in 1637, convicted of sedition and contempt, and banished as a "woman not fit for our society, cast out and delivered to Satan to become a heathen and a leper." Hutchinson was also convicted of the heresy of prophecy, the "erroneous" claim that God revealed his will directly to a believer instead of exclusively through the Bible. On the stand at her trial, Hutchinson claimed that "the Lord hath let me see which was the clear ministry and which was wrong by the Voice of God's own Spirit into my Soul." In claiming that God had spoken to her directly, Hutchinson committed heresy before the Puritans' very eyes. In all, Hutchinson was convicted of preaching eighty-two heresies and banished from the Massachusetts colony, only to help found the colony of dissenters in Rhode Island.

2.3j Puritans and Quaker Persecution

In furtherance of their goal of unity, the Puritans persecuted Quakers for blasphemy when members of the competing sect began arriving in Massachusetts in the 1650s. The General Court ordered that any Quaker literature found in the colony should be publicly burned, and the first Quakers that arrived in Boston (a pair of housewives) were arrested before they had even disembarked from their ship.

The Puritan interpretation of "contrary minded" was essentially broadened to include not just those who thought differently but also anyone who acted differently or looked different. For instance, Puritans identified the Quakers as "persons who wore hats in the presence of magistrates" (a violation of Puritan customs) and disliked the Quakers' use of outdated terms such as "thee" and "thou" in conversation.

A statue of Puritan religious dissident Anne Hutchinson is seen outside the Statehouse in Boston. (Wikimedia Commons)

In fact, the first two Quakers arrested in Massachusetts Bay were identified, arrested, and committed to jail because one of them was heard using the word "thee" in conversation.

In that instance, the two Quaker women were jailed, stripped naked, and body-searched for marks of the devil—the Puritan belief being that the Devil's children (witches) had marks on their bodies where the Devil had physically touched them when he made them his own. The windows of the jail were boarded so that the women could not infect the rest of the community with their heresies, after which the women were deported to Barbados, in spite of the fact that there was no law, per se, against Quakerism at the time. The Quaker books that were in the possession of the women were then burned in a ceremony in the public marketplace.

In October 1656, the Puritans passed a law against "that cursed sect of heretics lately risen up in the world," charging fines of ship captains who brought Quakers to Massachusetts and larger fines of Puritans who sheltered Quakers. Finally, it was decreed, "What person or persons soever shall revile the office or persons of magistrates or ministers, as is usual with the Quakers, such persons shall be severely whipped or pay the sum of five pounds."

The Quakers reacted to the persecution by choosing martyrdom, and Quaker efforts to infiltrate the Puritan community actually increased, rather than decreased, as a result. The Puritans retaliated the next year by passing the following harsher law—which included the extremes of corporal punishment and amputation—against Quakerism.

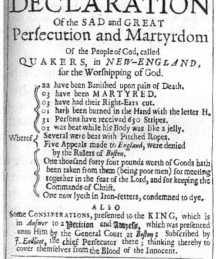

In 1656, the Puritans passed a number of laws resulting in the persecution of Quakers. Puritans arrested and jailed Quakers for their beliefs and lifestyle. (Wikimedia Commons)

And it is further ordered, that if any Quaker or Quakers shall presume, after they have once suffered what the law requireth, to come into this jurisdiction, every such male Quaker shall for the first offense have one of his ears cut off, and be kept at work in the house of correction till he can be sent away at his own charge, and for the second offense shall have his other ear cut off, and kept in the house of correction, as aforesaid; and every woman Quaker that hath suffered the law here and shall presume to come into this jurisdiction shall be severely whipped, and kept at the house of correction at work till she be sent away at their own charge, and so for her coming again she shall be alike used

Mary Dyer

Quaker woman executed
by the Puritans in 1660 for
heresy

as aforesaid; and for every Quaker, he or she, that shall a third time herein again offend, they shall have their tongues bored through with a hot iron, and kept at the house of correction, close to work, till they be sent away at their own charge.

Three people lost ears for violating this law; and there were numerous beatings, imprisonments, and other tortures. One man was beaten with 117 blows from a corded whip and left for dead. A witness to the event stated, "His flesh was beaten black and as into jelly, and under his arms the bruised flesh and blood hung down, clotted as it were into bags; and it was so beaten into one mass, that the signs of one particular blow could not be seen."

In October 1658, the General Court passed another new law that required that anyone guilty of Quaker disorders would be banished from the territory "upon pain of death." The law was quickly implemented, with the result that in May 1659, the General Court banished six persons from Salem, Massachusetts, for Quakerism; and two young Quaker children were promptly sold into slavery in order to satisfy claims against their parents.

Puritans considered Quakers heretics, and Mary Dyer was martyred for her Quaker beliefs. In this painting by an unknown nineteenth-century artist, Dyer is being led to the gallows to be hung at Boston Common on June 1, 1660. (Wikimedia Commons)

More banishments of Quakers followed in the summer of 1659, with the result that several Quakers, prepared to die as martyrs, defied the law by returning to Boston in protest during a meeting of the General Court. A group of Puritans from Salem who sympathized with the Quakers came to the court with them, one person bringing linen "wherein to wrap the dead bodies of those who were to suffer." The General Court proceeded to arrest all of the protesters, over twenty people in total, and incarcerate them in the Boston jail. The court then selected three persons from those incarcerated—William Robinson, Marmaduke Stevenson, and **Mary Dyer** (who formerly had been a follower of Anne Hutchinson)—and sentenced them to death. The two men were hanged, but Mary Dyer was given a reprieve and taken down from the scaffold at the execution due to unrest among the Puritan audience. Dyer would continue to defy the Puritan Courts, however, and was hanged for her defiance the next year.

Two Quaker women performed the outrageous act of parading naked in public as a protest against their unjust treatment by the Puritans. The parading women were quickly caught and punished. The sentence passed on one of the women by the Essex County Court was as follows:

The wife of Robert Wilson, for her barbarous and inhuman going naked through the town, is sentenced to be tied at a cart's tail with her body naked downward to her waist, and whipped from Mr. Gidney's gate till she come to her own house, not exceeding thirty stripes.

Similarly, Quaker woman Lydia Wardell was ordered by the court to be, "severely whipped and to pay costs to the Marshall of Hampton upon her presentment for going naked into Newbury meeting house."

Each of the Puritans' escalating stern actions, however, only caused the Quakers to be even more defiant, with the result that the number of Quakers awaiting execution overflowed the jails; and the waiting list for Quaker trials grew to an unmanageable length that overwhelmed the Puritan courts. It soon became clear that either the Puritans would have to develop new tactics in order to deter the Quakers or they would have to engage in a bloodbath of unprecedented proportions. In late 1661, the Massachusetts General Court received a letter from King Charles II prohibiting the use of either corporal or capital punishment in cases involving Quakers, thus laying the issue to rest.

2.3k Puritans and Witches

Malleus Maleficarum

Catholic Church manual from 1484 on witches and witch trials

Concerning witches, the Puritan rationale had its origin in Exodus 22:18, which states, "Thou shalt not suffer a witch to live." The Bible itself, however, does not contain a complete and concise discussion of how to identify and apprehend witches, so the Puritans were forced to rely on traditions that had developed over the prior centuries. Many of the Puritans' ideas concerning witches had been shaped by the Catholic Church in Medieval Europe prior to the Protestant Reformation. The Puritans were merely the beneficiaries of these ideas, which had been developed and handed down over the centuries. The official, pre-Enlightenment Catholic Church position on witches was spelled out in detail in the *Malleus Maleficarum* of 1484, written by Heinrich Kramer and James Sprenger. The ideas contained therein remained prevalent in society among Protestants and Catholics alike throughout the seventeenth century English colonies.

Kramer and Sprenger explained for the Catholic Church the concept of witches, their power, and how they should be dealt with by the authorities. The *Malleus Maleficarum* was approved by the Catholic Church as valid in 1487, and its prescriptions and procedures served as the official policies of the Inquisition from the late fifteenth through the sixteenth century. In this truly incredible work, Kramer and Sprenger argue that "devils" can "truly and actually remove men's members" as well as "work some prestidigitatory illusion so that the male organ appears to be entirely removed and separate from the body." Furthermore, Kramer and Sprenger explain that witches are able to "collect male organs in great numbers, as many as twenty or thirty members together, and put them in a bird's nest, or shut them up in a box, where they move themselves like living members, and eat oats and corn, as has been seen by many and is a matter of common report." Kramer and Sprenger also provide the story of a "certain man," who explained:

> [W]hen he had lost his member, he approached a known witch to ask her to restore it to him. She told the afflicted man to climb a certain tree, and that he might take which he liked out of a nest in which there were several members. And when he tried to take a big one, the witch said: You must not take that one; adding, because it belonged to a parish priest.

Kramer and Sprenger go on to explain how men can be turned into "werewolves," both voluntarily and involuntarily, and how one such werewolf was condemned by the court of Dole, Lyons, in 1573 to be burned alive. Other fictional creatures described by Kramer and Sprenger include fauns, trolls, and incubus (with penises of ice) and succubus devils, both of which are purported to have sex with humans.

In cases of witches, the Puritan court accepted without question the idea that Satan could take the "shape" of persons and use that shape to terrorize innocent Christians (as had been argued by Kramer and Sprenger two centuries before). The Puritans also contended that the Devil could not assume the shape of an innocent person. Thus, if someone testified that they were visited by a "specter" in the shape of a particular person, it was a foregone conclusion that said person was guilty of "signing the Devil's book," allowing him to use that person's shape.

During an early hearing in the Salem witch proceedings, a young girl had been named as one whose shape had terrorized the other young girls in Salem Village. When the Puritan authorities inquired of the girl "How comes your appearance to hurt these (girls)?" the girl replied, "How do I know, he that appeared in the shape of Samuel, a glorified saint, may appear in anyone's shape." The girl was referencing I Samuel 28: 7–17, where the Witch at Endor conjures the shape of the prophet Samuel at the behest of Israel's King Saul. Through the Bible itself, she had just proven that because the Devil had taken the shape of Samuel—a prophet and an "innocent" man of God—that if he [Devil] could take the shape of humans, he must be able to take the shape of innocent humans. The Puritans, however, were not persuaded by the testimony and continued to condemn persons to death based on "spectral evidence."

The Puritans also altered the rules of evidence in witch trials. Puritans normally followed the rule that two eye-witnesses were necessary for conviction in capital cases. In witch trials, however, they abandoned this standard; instead, they ruled that any two witnesses—even if they were not eye-witnesses, or if they were testifying about other events at other times—would be sufficient for conviction at a witch trial. The Puritans' efforts to squelch heresy and witchcraft would inevitably end in failure due to the massive immigration and accompanying religious diversity that would eventually render the narrow Puritan experience untenable.

2.3l Witches of Salem Village

In Salem Village, the famous witch trials were preceded by a series of sermons by Samuel Parris in 1692 on demons, the devil, and witchcraft. Following Parris' sermons, nine-year-old Betty Parris and her 11-year-old cousin, Abigail Williams, baked "witch-cakes" with the aid of Tituba, the Jamaican slave of Betty's father, Samuel. The cakes were made with cornmeal and human urine and were eaten by the two young girls. Afterward, the two girls were reported to have been seized with fits and to have made wild gestures and noises. The strange behavior then spread to other young girls in the village. The village elders interrogated the young girls, who confessed that they had been bewitched by Tituba and two other old women. Tituba admitted to having practiced witchcraft in the Caribbean prior to coming to Salem. With the confession to witchcraft, fear gripped the town and other persons came forward with similar tales of bewitching.

Foremost among the accusers was the family of Thomas Putnam, who had recently been left out of his father's will and whose family was suffering from economic hardship. Thomas Putnam himself accused twelve persons of witchcraft, while his daughter, Ann, accused twenty-one; his brother, Edward, thirteen; and another Putnam cousin, sixteen. Any personal misfortunes, bad harvests, illnesses, or even bad dreams in Salem Village were blamed on witches. One woman was accused of witchcraft for stroking a cat and causing a nearby batch of milk to turn sour. The trials lasted through the summer of 1693 and nineteen witches were eventually hanged on Witches Hill. One man convicted of witchcraft, eighty-one-year-old Giles Corey, was crushed under heavy rocks. The panic finally ended when officials from Harvard declared that, henceforth, no one could be convicted upon spectral evidence. That being the case, the remaining suspects were released and the ordeal was over—but more people had already been executed for witchcraft in Salem, that summer, than in any other witch-related incident in American history.

Pictured is a dramatic courtroom scene from the Salem Witch Trials. Fourteen women and five men were accused of witchcraft or association with witchcraft and executed by hanging. One man, Giles Corey, was crushed to death under heavy stones. At least five more of the accused died in prison. (Wikimedia Commons)

2.3m Puritans and the Natives

The natives in Massachusetts Bay were estimated to number around 125,000 in population in 1600; but when English fishermen brought smallpox to the area, an epidemic wiped out over half of the population by 1610—twenty years prior to the arrival of the Puritans. In 1633, three years after the Puritans' arrival, a second smallpox epidemic hit the natives and again wiped out over half the population. The Puritans believed that the epidemic was proof that God had granted them the Native American's land. After the plagues, the remaining Native Americans welcomed the Puritans because they now had surplus land, but lacked the manpower to tend and clear it all. The natives also benefited from trade with the Puritans, who had many things that the natives could use—including steel blades, axes, guns, and steel kettles for boiling water and cooking food. The remaining Massachusetts Bay natives also recognized the value of English protection from tribal enemies to the north and thus hoped that the Puritans could strengthen their own security.

Puritans sought to Christianize the Native Americans and succeeded in converting over a thousand natives by 1640. The Puritan Charter claimed that the Puritans' "Principal end is to convert the Natives to Christianity." Some natives resisted Christianization leading to a war in 1637, which was won by the Puritans. William Bradford credited God with giving the Puritans the victory over the Native Americans in the Pequot War. He recounted how the Puritans massacred four hundred natives in a raid on the Native American village, with most of the them dying in a fire set by the Puritans to burn them out of their homes. In the words of Bradford:

> It was a fearful sight to see them thus frying in the fire and the streams of blood quenching the same, and horrible was the stink and scent thereof; but the victory seemed a sweet sacrifice, and they gave the praise thereof to God, who had wrought so wonderfully for them, thus to enclose their enemies in their hands and give them so speedy a victory over so proud and insulting an enemy.

By the close of the war, all of the Native Americans in eastern Massachusetts were essentially under Puritan control; however, in order to aid in the conversion of the natives, and to avoid a future security threat, it was decreed that all Puritan men were to be trained in the use of firearms.

2.4 The Capture of New York

In 1609 **Henry Hudson**, an Englishman in the employ of the Dutch East India Company, sailed the Hudson River as far as the present town of Albany while in search of a "Northwest Passage" to Asia. In 1623, after the monopoly of a private Dutch company in the area had run out, the Dutch West India Company was formed to develop trade in the region along the river that Hudson had discovered. In 1626, Dutch West India Company director Peter Minuit purchased Manhattan Island from the natives for trade goods equal to a dozen beaver pelts. A settlement was begun in Manhattan known as "New Amsterdam," which became the trading center for the new Dutch colony named **New Netherland**.

Despite incompetent governors, quarreling inhabitants, and frequent wars with the natives, the colony made progress; and New Amsterdam (New York City) became an important shipping point for furs and farm products. By the 1660s, with a population of 2,500, it was second only to Boston as a trading port. The colony, as a whole, had about 8,000 settlers, many of whom were not Dutch.

Since the citizens of Holland were largely content, the new company had trouble finding colonists; thus, the early settlers included French Protestant refugees and non-Dutch emigrants from Holland. From the very beginning, New Netherland was a polyglot region. The Dutch tried to attract settlers by granting patroonships—allotments of eighteen miles of land along the Hudson River—to wealthy stockholders who would bring fifty families to the colony. Only one patroonship succeeded; and the settlers that were attracted were diverse peoples from Sweden, Holland, France, and Germany. The Dutch sent a minister of the Dutch Reformed Church to oversee religion in the new colony, and the minister wrote back and complained that the colonists were unreceptive. In his words, "Several groups of Jews have recently arrived, adding to the religious mixture of Papists, Mennonites, and Lutherans among the Dutch, and many Puritans and many other atheists who conceal themselves under the name of Christians." In response to this diversity, the Dutch West India Company ensured religious freedom for the colony of New Netherland in 1664, declaring that "the consciences of men should be free and unshackled."

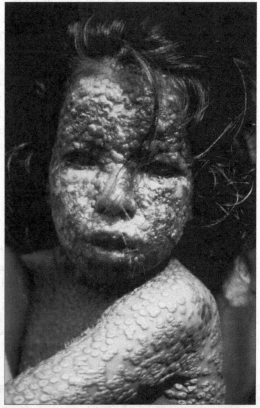

Pictured here is a young child with smallpox, which was brought to the New World by English fishermen. A smallpox epidemic killed off approximately half of the American Indian population. Puritans took this as a sign that God had given them the American Indians' land. (Wikimedia Commons)

Henry Hudson
Explored the Hudson River in 1609 in search of the Northwest Passage

New Netherland
Dutch colony in what is now New York

William Penn

The founder of the
Pennsylvania Colony

"Great Treaty"

Perhaps mythical, but
probably a series of treaties
between Penn and the
natives purchasing land from
the natives and ensuring
peace

The English had never admitted the right of the Dutch to the territory they were occupying. In 1664, Charles II named his brother, James, Duke of York, proprietor over lands occupied by the Dutch in the New World. When York sent out an expedition to take over New Netherland, the English claimed that it was not an act of war but merely an action to regain rightfully English territory from the Dutch West India Company. With an English fleet in the harbor of New Amsterdam, the Dutch governor, Peter Stuyvesant, surrendered on September 9, 1664. The town and territory were both rechristened New York in honor of the royal proprietor. The English then lost the colony back to the Dutch in a second war in 1673, before recapturing the colony permanently in 1675. The Duke of York continued to support the religious freedom that had begun under the Dutch; New York never had a state-church blend in leadership, such as in Massachusetts and Virginia. New York City grew quickly due to its harbor location and access to the interior via the Hudson and Oneida rivers.

The Dutch occupation of the Hudson Valley, however, had benefited the English far more than the new rulers cared to admit. Had the Dutch not been in possession of the land during the first half of the seventeenth century, the thin line of English colonies along the coast might have been taken by France since English settlements on the Atlantic seaboard were too sparse and weak, at the time, to prevent the French from moving down the Hudson from Canada.

2.4a The Jerseys

Soon after the Duke of York took over New Netherland in 1664, he granted the land between the Hudson and the Delaware to John Lord Berkeley and Sir George Carteret, Royalists who had defended the island of Jersey against the Parliamentarians during the English Civil War. Berkeley sold his proprietary right to two Quakers, and in 1676 the province was divided into East Jersey (belonging to Carteret) and West Jersey (which became a Quaker colony). The later division of the two portions of New Jersey among the many heirs of the proprietors created a land problem so complex that it vexes holders of real estate in that state to the present day.

In 1681 King Charles II granted to William Penn (a Quaker) land that stretched between New Jersey and Maryland, naming him and his heirs forever owners of the soil of Pennsylvania, as the domain was called. Penn established Pennsylvania as a colony that would offer refuge to persecuted Christians from all lands. (Wikimedia Commons)

2.5 Penn's Experiment

In 1681, King Charles II granted to **William Penn**, a Quaker, a charter to the land between New Jersey and Maryland, naming him and his heirs forever owners of the soil of Pennsylvania, as the domain was called. Penn set about establishing a colony that would serve as a refuge for persecuted Christians, especially Quakers, from all lands. He drew up his celebrated first Frame of Government and made various concessions and laws to govern the colony, which already had a conglomerate group of English, Dutch, Swedish, and Finnish settlers scattered here and there. After his own arrival in Pennsylvania, he provided for the calling of a popular assembly on December 4, 1682, which passed the "Great Law," guaranteeing, among other things, the rights of all Christians to liberty of conscience. Penn's colony is generally considered to have been the most democratic and free anywhere in the New World, to that point. Legislative power was vested in a directly elected assembly and suffrage was granted to all free males, not just Church members. Trial by jury was guaranteed to all citizens.

Penn was determined to keep peace with the American Indians and careful to purchase the land that his settlers occupied. The tradition of a single **"Great Treaty"** signed under an ancient elm at Kensington is probably a myth, but Penn held many powwows with the American Indians and negotiated treaties of peace and amity after purchasing needed land. To the credit of Penn and the Quakers, these agreements with the American Indians were, for the most part, conscientiously kept. Penn's colony became the only colony where land from the American Indians was purchased, rather than taken. In the words of Voltaire, "This was the only league between the Indians and Christians that was never sworn to and never broken."

Penn's colony, assembled by way of treaty with the American Indians, became the only colony where land was purchased from the natives, rather than taken. (Wikimedia Commons)

2.5a Quakers

Like Puritans and Pilgrims, Quakers were a fundamentalist Protestant sect that regarded the Anglican Church as corrupt and renounced its formalities and rituals. Based on their reading of Hebrews Chapters 4–8, Quakers rejected all church officials and institutions, instead claiming that every individual could claim salvation on an individual basis. Quakers were persecuted in England after the 1650s because they challenged the legitimacy of the existing church (and therefore the political hierarchy, since Anglican clergymen sat in the upper house of Parliament).

Quakers were despised by English nobles for their failure to observe customary deference (for instance, the tipping of one's hat to noblemen). The Quakers refused such deference because they believed that all men were equal before God; consequently, no one should be tipping one's hat in deference to anyone else based on birthright. Quakers also refused to pay church taxes that went to the Anglican Church; refused to sign witness oaths on the Bible (Jesus said "swear not"); and refused to participate in violence, including military service, taking Jesus' admonition to "turn the other cheek" literally. All of these beliefs and practices set them at odds with the Anglican Church and the political authority in England.

2.5b Quaker Laws

Though persecuted by others both in England and in the New World, the Quakers, like both the Anglicans and Puritans, used civil government to enforce religious morality. One of Pennsylvania's first laws provided severe punishment for "all offenses against God, such as, lying, profane talking, drunkenness, drinking of healths, obscene words, all prizes, stage plays, cards, dice, May games, gamesters, masques, revels, bull-baitings, cock-fightings, bear baitings, and the like, which excite the people to rudeness, cruelty, looseness, and irreligion."

2.5c Pennsylvania's Economy and Growth

Pennsylvania's growth from the first was phenomenal. Penn's success was largely due to his own skill as a promoter, for he wrote enticing tracts and went on preaching journeys to describe the opportunities offered by his colony. Mennonites from Switzerland and Germany—especially Pietists from the Rhineland, which had so often been overrun by invading armies—were soon coming to Pennsylvania in large numbers. Dutch sectarians, French Huguenots, Presbyterian Scots from Ulster, Baptists from Wales, and distressed English Quakers also came. Somewhat after the Mennonites, Lutheran emigrants from Germany swarmed into Pennsylvania's back country, where they cleared the forests and developed fertile farms. From the beginning, Pennsylvania was prosperous. Pennsylvania avoided the starvation periods that beset the other colonies due to fertile ground and a longer growing season than in the northeast; they also lacked the tropical diseases that plagued the South. Philadelphia became a major international port due to its excellent harbor on the Delaware River, and the city had become larger than New York City by 1700.

From the beginning, Pennsylvania was prosperous. The city of Philadelphia, which was larger than New York City by 1700, became a major international port because of its excellent harbor on the Delaware River. (Wikimedia Commons, author Nicholas A. Tonelli, uploaded to Commons by Franz Liszt)

John Colleton

Planter from Barbados who was named one of the eight lords proprietor of Carolina, for his support of the restoration of the English monarchy, by King Charles II

2.6 **Settlement of the Carolinas**

Among the later colonies to be settled was Carolina, which also began as a proprietorship. In 1660, the monarchy was restored in England and King Charles II rewarded those who helped him regain the throne—including a Barbadian planter named **John Colleton** and seven other men—with a charter to establish a colony south of Chesapeake and north of Spanish Florida. The proprietors drew up an instrument of government called the Fundamental Constitutions (probably the handiwork of the English political philosopher John Locke). This document provided for a hierarchy of colonial nobility and set up a platform of government with a curious mixture of feudal and liberal elements. Eventually it had to be abandoned in favor of a more workable plan of government; but for the short term, Colleton and the small group of nobles officially monopolized political power in the new colony. However, they also followed the Chesapeake example of settlement by enticing immigration through the promise of 150 acres of free land and freedom of religion. In 1670, the first settlement was founded just across from present day Charleston.

Most of the early settlers were Englishmen from the English Caribbean colony of Barbados. Carolina was the only seventeenth century English colony to be settled principally by colonists from other colonies, rather than from England. The colonists were a diverse mix of Swiss, Scottish, Irish, French, and English settlers, and African slaves (who made up a quarter of the first settlers). Religious diversity prevented any group from creating a church/state relationship. The new settlers, however, generally ignored the political rule of the nobles and opted instead for local self-rule.

2.6a **Carolina Economy**

The leaders of Carolina sought to exploit the Native Americans for deerskin trade. In the words of Colleton, "All of Carolina is one continuous deer park." Settlers, however, found greater profit in selling natives as slaves in New England or the West Indies. Local planters would arm and reward one tribe for helping them bring in enemy tribes—and then they would capture the tribe that had helped them and sell them into slavery, as well. By 1700, the native population of Carolina was essentially wiped out. The shortage of natives caused the British to begin the importation of African slaves to South Carolina since white Europeans refused to work in the swamps of the Carolina rice and indigo plantations. In 1680, South Carolina was 80 percent white. By 1720, South Carolina was 70 percent black. Like Virginia and Maryland, the climate of South Carolina was conducive to malaria and high mortality rates—and African slaves proved more resistant to malaria. John Colleton described it thusly, "Carolina is in the Spring Paradise, the Summer Hell, and in the Autumn, a Hospital."

2.6b **The Division of Carolina**

The division of Carolina into two distinct colonies came about gradually. English settlers were already occupying land around Albemarle Sound when the proprietors received their charter, and Albemarle continued to attract a smattering of settlers. It was geographically remote from the other settlement on the Ashley and Cooper rivers to the south. As the two separate sections gained population, they set up separate legislative assemblies, approved by the proprietors. In 1710, the proprietors appointed a governor of North Carolina, "independent of the governor of Carolina," thus recognizing the separation of North Carolina from South Carolina. In 1721, South Carolina was declared a royal province and eight years later North Carolina also became a crown colony. North and South Carolina also had different economies and different demographics. North Carolina's economy was a mix of livestock, tobacco, and naval stores. Naval stores included lumber,

Map 2.1 Georgia and the Carolinas

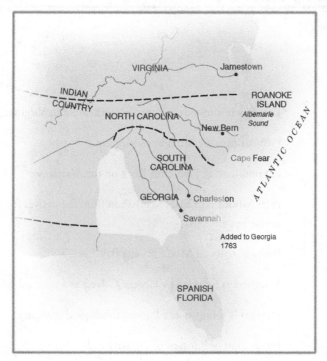

rope, and pine tar for sailing ships. Those who worked in the pine tar industry gained the name "tar heels." In terms of population, while South Carolina's population was 70 percent African slaves by 1720, North Carolina had remained 80 percent white.

2.6c Georgia

Georgia, founded in 1732, was administered by twenty trustees in England for two decades. Georgia was established to serve many purposes: as an extension of the southern provincial frontier; as a buffer or a first line of defense between the Spanish colony of Florida and the English settlements; as a planned Utopia where the trustees hoped to establish a model society; as a refuge for persecuted Protestants from Europe; as a new opportunity for men who had been released from debtor's prisons in England; as an Enlightenment project to make productive use of England's "deserving poor"; and as a model "colony" that would produce commodities that England wanted, notably silk and citrus fruits.

In its inception, Georgia was governed strictly by its Board of Noble Trustees and had no popularly elected assembly. The trustees brought in silkworms from China and grapes from France for their planned economy of silk and wine. Alcohol was prohibited in Georgia so as to dissuade the laziness of poor people and "second chance" criminals. Slavery was prohibited for the same reasons.

The "model colony" envisioned by the Board of Trustees never materialized, however, due to multiple problems. The wine business failed in Georgia due to grape-eating bugs and birds. The silk business also failed because it turned out that silkworms needed the trees from China and Georgia birds feasted on the imported silkworms. As a consequence, the population of Georgia was only

Silkworms were imported from China and grapes from France for Georgia's planned economy of silk and wine. However, the silk business failed because the insects needed the trees in China to feed on. The birds ate the rest of the population. (Wikimedia Commons, Dennis Jarvis)

2,800 in 1750; hence, Parliament passed the legalization of slavery and alcohol in Georgia. Georgia then developed into a rice and indigo plantation economy based on slave labor, like South Carolina.

Timeline

1607	Jamestown is founded as the first settlement in Virginia.
1619	First Africans are brought to Virginia.
1620	Pilgrims land at Plymouth Rock on the *Mayflower*.
1626	Peter Minuit purchases Manhattan from the natives for goods equal to twelve beaver pelts.
1630	Puritans arrive in Massachusetts Bay.
1632	Maryland is founded by George Calvert as a planned refuge for Catholics.
1636	Harvard is founded as a Puritan theological seminary.
1642	Persecution of Puritans in England ends.
1649	Maryland Toleration Act
1660	Execution of Mary Dyer
1663	Carolina is founded as a proprietary colony.
1670	Settlement is started near present-day Charleston, South Carolina.
1675	England defeats the Netherlands in a war and gains permanent control of the colony on the Hudson, renamed New York.
1681	King Charles II grants a charter for a colony to William Penn.
1688–1691	Glorious Revolution in England installs Protestant William of Orange to the throne, and England passes religious toleration while Maryland deposes the Calverts and ends religious toleration.
1692	Witch Trials in Salem Village
1732	Georgia is founded as a colony for the deserving poor.
1738	Mose is founded by the Spanish in Florida as a community of runaway slaves.
1739	Stono Rebellion
1741	New York Conspiracy Trials

CHAPTER SUMMARY

$\mathcal{B}$eginning with the colonization of Jamestown by the Virginia Company in 1607 and proceeding through the establishment of Georgia as a colony for the "deserving poor" in 1732, the English successfully colonized the east coast of what is now the United States, with thirteen colonies from Georgia to New Hampshire. The colonies were diverse, though most were proprietary colonies where profit and the lure of economic advancement were the primary motives for immigration. With the exception of New England, most seventeenth century emigrants from Europe arrived as indentured servants seeking economic opportunity, the majority of them single men. In New England, immigrants arrived as family units fleeing persecution—with the greatest influx taking place between 1630 and 1642. African slaves were brought to North America as early as 1619 (in Virginia) and comprised 80 percent of the population of South Carolina by the early eighteenth century.

Although all were English colonies, they were diverse both economically and culturally. Puritans dominated New England, and others—nominally Anglican, but with religious diversity—were prevalent elsewhere. Pennsylvania was unique as a planned refuge for Quakers with a goal of peace with Native American tribes, emphasized by the practice of purchasing land, rather than seizing it. Maryland was unique as a "planned refuge for Catholics" that never actually attained a Catholic majority, but which nevertheless enjoyed religious tolerance until 1789, when an Anglican revolt removed the Calverts as Catholic proprietors.

Religious tolerance prevailed in New York and other areas where religious diversity precluded dominance by any one group, but Puritanism dominated in New England where charters called for the rejection of all that were "contrary-minded." The Calvinist-influenced Puritans arrived in America to practice their religion freely, but denied religious freedom to others in their midst—persecuting, banishing, and even executing heretics or those who thought differently. Quakers, in particular, bore the brunt of the Puritan persecution. Consequently, Rhode Island was founded by persons banished from the Puritan community; and Willian Penn set about establishing a colony that would serve as a refuge for persecuted Christians, especially Quakers, from all lands.

Native Americans were generally viewed as obstacles to colonial progress—in spite of sometimes profitable trade and cases where European colonists were saved from starvation by Native Americans, such as at Plymouth in 1620. Land was purchased from the natives rather than taken in Pennsylvania, but armed struggles between whites and natives began almost the moment the English arrived at Jamestown and continued intermittently throughout the seventeenth century.

The first African slaves were brought to Virginia in 1619 and increased greatly in number after that, especially in the Southern Colonies. Slaves increased in the Southern Colonies with the decline of indenture and the rise of England as a naval power. Southern Colonies, such as South Carolina, grew into rice, indigo, and tobacco-based export economies built on African slave labor by the end of the seventeenth century.

The thirteen English colonies were founded over the course of 126 years, beginning in 1607, in what is now the United States. Although they were diverse in terms of culture and economics, they shared an English heritage and English colonial experience that would bind them together to eventually form one nation before the eighteenth century came to a close.

KEY TERMS

BIBLIOGRAPHY

A

Andrews, Pat. *Voices of Diversity*. Guilford, CT: Dushkin, 1993.

B

Bailyn, Bernard. *The Peopling of British North America: An Introduction*. New York: Vintage, 1988.

Battis, Emery. *Saints and Sectaries: Anne Hutchinson and the Antinomian Controversy in the Massachusetts Bay Colony*. Chapel Hill, NC: University of North Carolina Press, 2011.

Bishop, George. *New England Judged by the Spirit of the Lord*. Whitefish, MT: Kessinger Publishing, 2003.

Boxer, Charles R. *The Dutch Seaborne Empire*. New York: Penguin, 1995.

Bradford, William. *Of Plymouth Plantation 1620–1647*. New York: Random House, 1981.

Brinkley, Alan. *American History: A Survey*. 11th ed. Boston, MA: McGraw-Hill, 2003.

C

Chinard, Gilbert, Ed. *A Huguenot Exile in Virginia: Or Voyages of a Frenchman Exiled for His Religion with a Description of Virginia and Maryland*. New York: The Press of the Pioneers, 1934.

Colden, Cadwallader. *The Letters and Papers of Cadwallader Colden*. New York: AMS Press, 1973.

Cremin, Lawrence A. *American Education: The Colonial Experience 1607–1783*. New York: HarperCollins, 1970.

Cross, Barbara M., Ed. *The Autobiography of Lyman Beecher*. Cambridge, MA: Harvard University Press, 1961.

D

Dandelion, Pink. *The Quakers: A Very Short Introduction*. New York: Oxford University Press, 2008.

E

Eccles, W. J. *France in America*. East Lansing, MI: Michigan State University Press, 1990.

Ellerbe, Helen. *The Dark Side of Christian History*. Orlando, FL: Morningstar and Lark, 1995.

Erikson, Kai. *Wayward Puritans: A Study in the Sociology of Deviance*. Boston, MA: Allyn and Bacon, 1966.

G

Greene, Jack P. *Pursuits of Happiness: The Social Development of Early Modern British Colonies and the Formation of American Culture*. Chapel Hill, NC: University of North Carolina Press, 1988.

H

Hall, David D. *Worlds of Wonder, Days of Judgment: Popular Religious Belief in Early New England*. Cambridge, MA: Harvard University Press, 1990.

Highman, John. *Strangers in the Land*. New Brunswick, NJ: Rutgers University Press, 1955.

J

Jordan, Winthrop. *White over Black: American Attitudes toward the Negro 1550–1812*. Chapel Hill, NC: University of North Carolina Press, 1968.

K

Kenny, Kevin. *Peaceable Kingdom Lost: The Paxton Boys and the Destruction of William Penn's Holy Experiment*. New York: Oxford University Press, 2011.

Kupperman, Karen, Ed. *Captain John Smith: A Selected Edition of His Writings*. Chapel Hill, NC: University of North Carolina Press, 1988.

Kupperman, Karen O. *Providence Island, 1630–1641: The Other Puritan Colony*. Cambridge, UK: Cambridge University Press, 1995.

L

Labaree, Leonard Woods. *Conservatism in Early American History*. Ithaca, NY: Great Seal Books, 1948.

———. *Royal Instructions to British Colonial Governors, 1670–1776*. New York: D. Appleton-Century, 1935.

Land, Aubrey C., Ed. *Law, Society, and Politics in Early Maryland: Proceedings on the First Conference of Maryland History, June 14–15, 1974*. New York: Johns Hopkins University Press, 1977.

M

Mather, Cotton. *Wonders of the Invisible World*. Temecula, CA: Reprint Services, 1999.

Miller, Perry. *The New England Mind: The Seventeenth Century*. Cambridge, MA: Belknap, 1983

Miller, Perry, and Thomas H. Johnson Eds. *The Puritans: A Sourcebook of Their Writings*. New York: Harper, 1968.

Mitchell, Robert. *Calvin's and the Puritans' View of the Protestant Ethic*. Lanham, MD: University Press of America, 1979.

Morgan, Edmund S. *American Slavery, American Freedom: The Ordeal of Colonial Virginia*. New York: W. W. Norton & Company, 2003.

———. *Visible Saints: The History of a Puritan Idea*. Ithaca, NY: Cornell University Press, 1965.

———. *Roger Williams: The Church and the State*. New York: W. W. Norton & Company, 2007.

Murphy, Francis. "Introduction." In Bradford, William, *Of Plymouth Plantation 1620–1647*. New York: Random House, 1981.

BIBLIOGRAPHY

Murrin, John M. "Religion and Politics in America from the First Settlements to the Civil War." In Mark A. Noll, ed., *Religion and American Politics: From the Colonial Period to the 1980s*. New York: Oxford University Press, 1990.

Murrin, John R., Paul E. Johnson, James M. McPherson, Gary Gerstle, Emily S. Rosenberg, and Norman L. Rosenberg. *Liberty, Equality, Power: A History of the American People*. Fort Worth, TX: Harcourt Brace, 1996.

N

Nash, Gary B., Julie Roy Jeffrey, John R. Howe, Peter J. Frederick, Allen F. Davis, and Allan M. Winkler. *The American People: Creating a Nation and a Society*. 4th ed. New York: Longman, 1998.

O

O'Sullivan, John, and Edward F. Keuchel. *American Economic History: From Abundance to Constraint*. New York: Markus Wiener, 1989.

P

Patterson, Orlando. *Slavery and Social Death. A Comparative Study*. Cambridge, MA: Harvard University Press, 1985.

Q

Quinn, David B. *England and the Discovery of America 1481–1620*. New York: Alfred A. Knopf, 1974.

R

Russell, David Lee. *Oglethorpe and Colonial Georgia: A History 1733–1783*. Jefferson, NC: McFarland Press, 2006.

Rink, Oliver. *Holland on the Hudson. An Economic and Social History of Dutch New York*. Ithaca, NY: Cornell University Press, 1989.

S

Saunders, William L., Ed. *The Colonial Records of North Carolina*. Temecula, CA: Reprint Services Corporation, 1999.

Stanard, William G. and Mary N. Stanard. *The Colonial Virginia Register*. Albany, NY: Joel Munsell's Sons, 1902.

W

Weber, David J. *The Spanish Frontier in North America*. New Haven, CT: Yale University Press, 1994.

Weir, Robert. *Colonial South Carolina: A History*. Columbia, SC: University of South Carolina Press, 1997.

Wright, Louis B. *The First Gentlemen of Virginia: Intellectual Qualities of the Early Colonial Ruling Class*. Charlottesville, VA: University of Virginia Press, 1970.

Y

Yazawa, Melvin, Ed. *Diary and Life of Samuel Sewall*. New York: St. Martin's Press, 1998. Pop Quiz

1. The product that King James I denounced as "loathsome to the eye, hateful to the nose, harmful to the brain, and dangerous to the lungs" was

   _____.

   a. alcohol

   b. tobacco

   c. marijuana

   d. peyote

2. Which of the following is true of Pocahontas?

   a. She was killed by the English in a raid on Powhatan's camp.

   b. She committed suicide by jumping overboard on the Thames River upon her arrival in England.

   c. She died of European diseases after moving to England.

   d. She died while being forced to read Shakespeare after moving to England.

3. Which of the following is true of Maryland in the early seventeenth century?

   a. It allowed religious freedom.

   b. It allowed citizenship rights for blacks.

   c. It allowed citizenship rights for women.

   d. All of the above

4. What was most important reason for the importation of African slaves in the eighteenth century?

   a. humanitarian, as Africans willingly sold themselves into slavery so as to enjoy the privilege of living in America

   b. economic, due to the need to remedy the labor shortage in the colonies

   c. luxury, as most Americans had become wealthy enough to own slaves to relieve themselves of domestic chores

   d. religious, as black Christians believed that God was sending them on an exodus from Africa like the ancient Israelites

5. Which of the following is true of the Stono Rebellion?

   a. It was the largest slave rebellion in North America in the eighteenth century.

   b. It led to the death of at least twenty whites and sixty slaves.

   c. It led to widespread panic in the British colonies.

   d. All of the above

6. Which of the following is true of the Pilgrims who arrived on the *Mayflower*?

   a. They were Puritans who wanted to reform the Anglican Church.

   b. They were Separatists who viewed the Anglican Church as so corrupt that they must separate themselves from it.

   c. They had great success in founding a colony of uncorrupted Christians in the Netherlands.

   d. They believed in an economy of pure, unrestrained capitalism.

7. In contrast to the Pilgrims, what did the Puritans want to do?

   a. They wanted to separate themselves from the Anglican Church.

   b. They wanted to "purify" the Anglican Church.

   c. They wanted to establish the Catholic Church in North America.

   d. They wanted to ensure freedom of religious thought to everyone.

8. Who established the colony of Providence?

   a. Roger Williams

   b. Thomas Hooker

   c. John Winthrop

   d. William Penn

9. Which of the following is true of Thomas Granger?

   a. He was the founder of the first animal rights group in America.

   b. He claimed that he could talk to animals.

   c. He preached better living through celibacy.

   d. He was executed in 1642 for bestiality.

10. Puritan punishment of Quakers included

    _____.

    a. whippings

    b. amputations of the ears

    c. executions

    d. all of the above

11. Puritans in the late seventeenth century believed which of the following?

    a. that the Devil could terrorize people by taking the "shape" of humans

    b. that the Devil was prevented by God from taking the shape of humans

    c. that the Devil was prevented by God from harming humans

    d. Both b and c

12. What happened after the Puritans massacred four hundred Indians by burning their village?

    a. The Puritans gave praise to God.

    b. The Puritans wept for the Indian dead.

    c. The Puritans passed a law against killing innocent women and children in warfare.

    d. The Puritans invited the remaining Indians to Thanksgiving dinner.

13. Which of the following is true of the Quakers?

    a. They rejected all Anglican Church officials and rituals.

    b. They believed that everyone must tip their hats to Quakers.

    c. They believed that women must be subordinate and silent in the Church.

    d. They required that everyone pay church taxes and swear oaths on the Bible.

14. Which of the following is true of South Carolina in the seventeenth century?

    a. Cotton was the most important crop.

    b. The population suffered from malaria and other tropical diseases.

    c. There was a complete absence of deer due to mosquitoes.

    d. Tobacco was the most important crop.

15. In Puritan society only _____ _____ _____ could vote.

Chapter 3

MONTCALM TRYING TO STOP THE MASS.

(Wikimedia Commons)

Patterns of Colonial Social Structure

CHAPTER OUTLINE

3.1 Colonial Social Structure

3.1a Influences on Cultural Development

In intellectual and social life, as in political and economic life, the first English settlers in America shared attitudes, ambitions, and habits of thought with their peers in the home country. During the colonial period, however, these characteristics were modified. In part, this was because of changing intellectual life in England, which affected the colonies in a variety of ways. In addition, it was because men and women born and educated in America knew only the ways of their colonial neighbors, first-hand, and experienced English culture and intellectual currents second-hand.

Furthermore, the immigration of non-English peoples brought added diversity and dimension to the social and intellectual scene. An evaluation of the degree of distinctiveness of American culture depends upon the relative weight placed upon these influences—English, American, and non-English. Because individual historians have placed different emphases upon these factors, their judgments have differed; all agree, however, that conditions in the New World influenced social and intellectual development.

3.1b Influence of English Society

In Elizabethan England, the social rank of a family was determined strictly by the status of the male head of the household. The top level of this patriarchal and paternalistic society consisted of noble families, whose position depended upon extensive landholdings and the favors that accrued to a privileged segment of society. The nobility was not quite a closed circle. Younger sons who did not inherit a substantial estate or title generally sought their fortunes through the life of the **gentry**, through commercial connections, or through such professions as the army and the church. Although it was possible for a highly successful entrepreneur to penetrate the nobility, full-fledged acceptance was often delayed for general generations.

Below the nobility ranked the gentry, the country gentlemen. The life of the gentry centered on the land. The country gentleman knew his tenants and their problems; and he experienced first-hand the uncertainties, as well as the blessings, of farming. The gentry served as the backbone of governing authority, in part because the sovereign encouraged their participation as a shield against ambitious nobles. The gentry formed the largest group in Parliament, and they held those local offices which were mainly responsible for enforcing the statutes of the state. Marriage alliances between gentry and families engaged in trade were fairly frequent; and families in the gentry class often contributed younger sons to trade, to adventure, to the military, to the church, and sometimes to the universities.

In England, the people of the highest social rank were the nobility. Below the nobility came the gentry, and below the gentry, the yeoman. (Wikimedia Commons)

Below the gentry ranked the yeomen, who could be leaseholders or owners of small estates. In Elizabethan days the dirt farmer was the **yeoman**, a man attached to the soil who lived a simple life and farmed with frugality. The laborers and servant classes of Elizabethan England ranked below the yeomen. A laborer might have been an apprentice who, in time, would enter a trade and make a good living; alternatively, he might have been a man who worked for daily wages and whose chances of rising to a better social and economic position were remote. In the same fashion, to be a servant could mean to serve a family in the gentry with the expectation that, by means of a good marriage or hard work, an elevation of status could be secured; alternatively, it could involve the meanest kind of position, from which no increase in status seemed possible.

The English social structure was not transplanted, intact, to America. Established members of the English aristocracy did not emigrate, as they were relatively content and well off at home; a primitive New World wilderness simply held no incentive for them. Occasionally, younger sons of noble families came to America to try their fortune, but even this was rare.

For the other end of the social structure—day laborers and servants—immigration to the New World was restricted by transportation costs; servants were transported by the gentry class. Sometimes, laborers immigrated by taking advantage of the system of *indentured servitude,* in which they bound themselves to a master for service in the colonies for a specified length of time, usually three to five years, in exchange for their passage. This system became widespread after the mid-seventeenth century.

The first settlers, then, were drawn principally from the yeomanry and the gentry, the latter bringing servants with them. At the outset, these class divisions, and their patriarchal framework, were scrupulously maintained. In early Massachusetts, to cite an illustration, a laborer's wife who appeared in church wearing a frock or hat of a quality—which, in the eyes of the elders, exceeded her station—was severely admonished.

3.1c Influence of the American Environment

Modifications to this structure took place during the colonial period and gave rise to a social structure indigenous to English America. The gradual growth of a system of indentured servitude enabled people without money to immigrate to America, where they eventually became yeoman farmers or free laborers. Men who arrived as hired servants or as yeomen sometimes acquired substantial estates through industry or good fortune. Ships' captains who brought immigrants to certain colonies claimed **headrights**, an allotment of fifty acres of land for each person transported; these grants formed the nucleus around which some landed estates were formed. Labor was so scarce that a skilled workman could not only make a good living but could also become an employer. Men of modest means who engaged in trade built up strong mercantile firms, and wealth brought an elevation of social status and often political power.

One of the most important determinants of social position in America was the possession of land; and its abundance—as the Native Americans lost ground—helped encourage a more mobile society. Nowhere was this more clearly demonstrated than in the Chesapeake colonies. In the first century of settlement, the vast majority of the settlers in Virginia and Maryland were yeomen or indentured servants, who were able to rise to the status of yeomen after completing their term of servitude. During various crises of the seventeenth century—especially the Puritan ascendancy of the 1640s and 1650s in England and immediately after the restoration of the Stuart monarchy in 1660—members of the gentry class or, more rarely, younger sons of nobles immigrated to Virginia. However, they acted as no more than leaven to the loaf. The Virginia gentry class that gradually emerged was made up primarily of those who had risen to this status in America—it was not a gentry group transplanted to America.

Headrights

An allotment of fifty acres of land, granted by some colonies to a planter or ship captain for each person transported

Anne Bradstreet

Recognized by many as the most sensitive colonial poet

3.1b Women in Colonial America

The practice of bringing families to the New World set the English colonies apart from those of other nations. Women were in great demand, not only to serve as companions or to satisfy sexual appetites, but also as partners in the enterprise of settlement. John Winthrop of Massachusetts, who preceded his wife to New England, wrote her most lovingly of the life and excitement they would share in America. Some women became influential. The religious views of Anne Hutchinson of Massachusetts led to her being ousted from the colony but attracted a following that found refuge with her near Providence—though she and her family were eventually killed by American Indians. **Anne Bradstreet** is now often recognized as the most sensitive poet of colonial America. Most women, like most men, worked day in and day out in the fields and the household, making a living, raising a family, and looking forward to better times. Whether laboring as slaves, indentured servants, or housewives, they made an essential contribution to the success of the colonial economy.

A yeoman (or laborer) could become an apprentice and enter, in time, a trade on his own and make a decent living.
(Wikimedia Commons)

Women in colonial America did not have the vote and could not, in most cases, hold property. Their opportunities were severely restricted. None became lawyers or ministers. Some practiced a trade, such as blacksmithing or printing, but almost none made a name in business. Yet their influence was keenly felt, and without them there could have been no society to win its freedom and found a nation. Some scholars have suggested that extreme Protestant devotion to the Bible may have offered women a strong incentive for becoming literate; and this may, in turn, have laid the groundwork for the reformation of women's roles, white and black, in the new nation.

3.1c The Structure of Colonial Society

The structure that evolved in colonial society differed from that of English society in three important respects. First, the top level of English society—the nobility—was left behind during emigration. Second, an immigrant's class in America did not exactly correlate with the class to which he or she had belonged in England. Third, the levels of society were present in somewhat different proportions.

In America, there were more slaves who were condemned to perpetual servitude and who had little if any mobility, but there were fewer servants because the opportunities to acquire land and other forms of wealth were so abundant. American society ranged, therefore, from the colonial elite—the important merchants in Massachusetts

Francis Daniel Pastorious

Founder of Germantown in Pennsylvania

James Logan

Emerged as the "first citizen" of Pennsylvania through his success in the fur trade

and Rhode Island, the planters along the Chesapeake and in the Carolinas, and the large landholders in New York and Pennsylvania—to the small farmers and skilled workers, to the unskilled workers and servants, and finally, at the base, to the slaves.

The special contours of American society also reflected a modification of male professional opportunities. An upper-class Englishman could advance professionally through the church, the military, or the law. Although the church in New England offered an avenue for advancement for a time, by the eighteenth century in America, a man looking for advancement generally sought out land and commerce—not the church. Moreover, American men, accustomed to their special militia forces, could not advance professionally through naval or military service. Instead, a man who had already achieved status as a merchant or landholder was placed in command of a colonial militia.

Not until the 1730s and 1740s did the practice of law gain sufficient status to become an avenue for advancement. In earlier periods, merchants and landholders frequently served as their own lawyers. Only as colonial society became more sophisticated did the practice of law become a profession. A number of colonials, some of whom already held substantial social position—James Otis and John Adams in New England, John Dickinson in the Middle Colonies, and Patrick Henry and Charles Pinckney in the Southern Colonies—improved their status by becoming experts in the practice of law. The seed of American society was English, but the American environment dramatically affected social growth. The country's evolution, as a result, was distinctive—not a replica.

3.2 Minorities in the Colonies

In the eighteenth century, the population of the colonies included large groups of non-English: Irish, Germans, Scots, and French. These minorities gave a flavor to American society that endures to the present day.

Two groups of Americans—the Native Americans and the Africans—were excluded, however, from the colonial social structure. True, black Americans were very much a part of the economic structure, and trade with the Native Americans had great economic significance for the colonists. But in both cases the relationship between the races was marked by a cultural clash rather than cultural fusion; and in both cases white culture had enough power to establish its dominance.

3.2a European Minorities

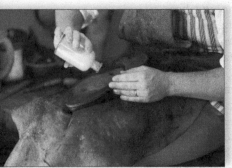

At the lower end of the colonial social hierarchy were small farmers and skilled workers (such as this leather craftsman); unskilled workers and servants; and finally, at the base, the slaves. (iStockphoto)

The reasons for the inflow of non-English Europeans were numerous, but a change of policy in England was a critical factor. By the eighteenth century, England was less enthusiastic about exporting its population to America. As its agriculture became increasingly commercial, as trade expanded a hundredfold, and as manufacturing began to take root, its people were needed at home. As the supply of labor from the mother country was reduced, the Middle and Southern Colonies, especially, brought indentured servants from northern and western Europe.

Francis Daniel Pastorious, a man of exceptional intellect, led the first German settlers into Pennsylvania in 1683, founding Germantown north of Philadelphia. But the principal immigration of Germans did not begin until after 1710. From then until 1770, a wave of 225,000 German immigrants came to the New World— almost half of whom migrated to Pennsylvania. Statistically, about 80 percent settled in the Middle Colonies of Pennsylvania, New York, and New Jersey, and about 20 percent settled in the Southern Colonies from Maryland to Georgia. Less than 1 percent settled in New England.

The settlement of newcomers from France, Scotland, and Ireland tended to conform to the pattern of the German immigration. In fact, the migration of Scotch-Irish from northern Ireland to Pennsylvania became so heavy that **James Logan** of Pennsylvania observed: "It looks as if Ireland is to send all its inhabitants hither … The common fact is that if they thus continue to come they will make themselves proprietors of the Province."

Map 3.1 Early Settlements in the Middle Colonies

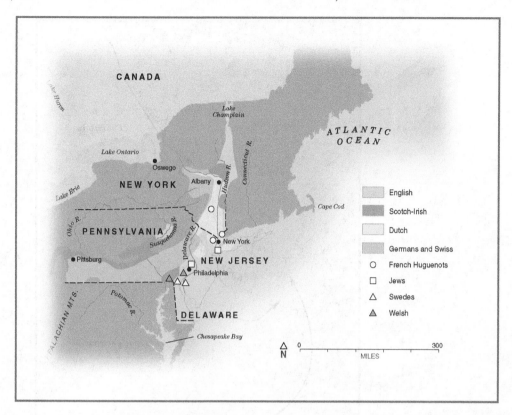

The consequences of non-English immigration were numerous. The population of provincial America grew; demographic patterns changed; and new cultural patterns and influences, such as German Pietism, were introduced. In those colonies where immigration was greatest—such as Pennsylvania, where Quakers constituted the elite and the Germans and the Scotch-Irish were regarded as the lower classes—the social structure was affected. New sources of labor became available at a time when colonial economic expansion demanded them. The colonies became more cosmopolitan, with a broader interaction of cultures.

The non-English influence was primarily cultural, not political. English political customs and institutions, modified by American colonial conditions, continued to be practiced without challenge because most of the newcomers had never before experienced self-government. Non-English cultural life in the broadest sense—the classical music of the Moravians, the new languages, Scottish Presbyterianism, and the special methods of breeding high-grade cattle brought by the Scottish Highlanders—enriched provincial America.

The population growth provided by the new immigrants occurred mainly in the country rather than in the cities. In fact, this was one of the few periods in American history in which the urban proportion of the population declined rather than increased. Yet the five major colonial cities—Boston, Newport, New York, Philadelphia, and Charleston—tripled their populations between 1690 and 1742. More significantly, a great number of smaller urban communities developed—port towns in Massachusetts and inland towns such as Albany.

In each case the importance of the urban areas exceeded a strict population count because, as centers for distribution of goods and commodities, they became more influential economically, politically, socially, and culturally. By 1776 Philadelphia, ranking second among the cities within the British Empire, had become an important cultural center with its scientific societies, its university, its public library, its newspaper, and its first citizen, **Benjamin Franklin**—amateur scientist, inventor, and noted publisher of ***Poor Richard's Almanack***.

Benjamin Franklin

America's most prominent representative of Enlightenment thinking

Poor Richard's Almanack

Eighteenth century publication, edited by Ben Franklin, which became the best selling publication in America other than the Bible

Map 3.2 Routes to the Interior

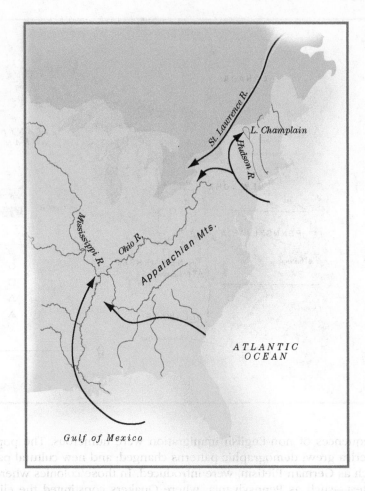

3.26 Native Americans in the Colonies

In need of labor, English settlers sometimes tried to make slaves of Native Americans captured in skirmishes, but it did not work. The captives could too easily slip off and return to their own people. Around 1700, in some colonies—South Carolina, for instance—captured Native Americans were shipped off to the West Indies as slaves.

Efforts were also made to convert Native Americans to English ways. Schools were established for them in several colonies, but the Native Americans resumed their traditional ways and customs once they returned to their own people.

On occasion, the practice of treating a Native American people as a foreign power had gratifying results for the English. When Iroquois and Cherokee leaders were brought to London to sign treaties of friendship, the crown made these occasions festive and special. Both Native American nations remained invaluable allies of England for a century.

Also during the colonial period, powerful nations of Native Americans blocked English access to the interior of the continent. These Native Americans controlled interior trade, thanks to their defensive position along the Appalachian range; and they were strengthened by their ability to play European rivals, France and England, against each other. They held the balance of power in America for a century (1660–1760). Not until the French had been eliminated as a major participant in colonization were the English finally able to penetrate the Appalachian barrier in any great numbers.

Ironically, by forcing the American provincials to stay principally in the coastal areas, the Native Americans may have contributed to their own destruction. Prevented from moving westward, the colonists established a mature, vigorous, developed society from which to launch an assault to conquer the inland wilderness. If the English had been able to penetrate deeply into the interior of America soon after settlement, the strength provided by cohesive, highly developed colonies would not have been achieved.

BVT Lab

Flashcards are available for this chapter at www.BVTLab.com.

Also, if deep penetration had been possible, the tie with England would unquestionably have been much less influential. The political experience of the settlements would have been less sophisticated, and therefore less valuable—for only relatively stable communities could provide such experience. By facilitating the creation of a vigorous, structured, provincial society, the formidable Native American barrier thus contributed to the development of political, economic, and intellectual institutions. These institutions, in turn, became so deep-rooted that the sweeping westward movement of the nineteenth century failed to alter them in any fundamental way.

Trade represented one of the most important contacts between the settlers and the Native Americans and accounted for the founding of many of the first modest, provincial fortunes. In South Carolina, for example, the early road to riches was gained not by raising rice but by trading in deerskins, one of the most valuable exports from the Carolinas until well into the eighteenth century. In Pennsylvania, James Logan's emergence as the first citizen of that colony was made possible through what he called the "stinking" fur trade. In New York, the trade brought a fortune and a title to Sir William Johnson.

During the eighteenth century, the locus of the fur trade shifted. By 1730 New England's share was limited, if not negligible. The Middle Colonies, the area of greatest expansion, had become the center of the trade, with New York and Pennsylvania well in the lead. In the South, Virginia had controlled the principal trade with the Cherokees and the Chickasaws in the late seventeenth century, but early in the eighteenth century South Carolina developed into a serious rival. Then Georgia moved into contention. By the mid-eighteenth century, New York and Georgia were perhaps the two colonies most deeply engaged in trade with the natives.

Recently, scholars have begun to also focus on a more informal trade: that which took place between English and Native American women. Historian Laurel Thatcher Ulrich has written about "exchange relations" in needlework and basketry between members of the two groups—for example, using a Native American basket in the collections of the Rhode Island Historical Society as the point of departure for exploring the nature and meaning of such relations in the colonial period.

Informal trade, or "exchange relations," between English and Native American women established a beneficial relationship between two very different groups of people. Needlework and basketry were commonly swapped. Pictured is a transitional blanket, woven circa 1880–1885. The thick handspun yarns and synthetic dyes are typical of pieces made during the transition from blanket weaving to rug weaving, when more weavings were sold to outsiders. (Wikimedia Commons)

3.2c Non-English Settlers in the Borderlands

While the English settlers were being held in check, Spanish and French colonists were settling in territory that would eventually become part of the United States. From the sixteenth century to the early nineteenth, the Spanish advanced into Florida, Texas, the American Southwest, and along the Pacific coastline of California. Outside of the territory that would become the United States, the French established their first settlement in Quebec, Canada, in 1608; and in the seventeenth and eighteenth centuries, they posted settlements of explorers and soldiers from New Orleans to the western Great Lakes and from the headwaters of the Ohio River, near present-day Pittsburgh, to its outlet into the Mississippi.

The Spanish and French coupled exploration and conquest with missionary stations. Many of the Spanish missions in the American Southwest and California—originally housing a garrison of soldiers, a parcel of priests, and a community of American Indians—remain to be visited today. Those established by France proved somewhat less durable.

The objective of the Spanish defense of its borderlands was to extend the empire and "to Christianize, civilize, and purify" the "Indians" at the same time. To achieve these goals, the Spanish established a chain of **presidios**, or army outposts, from Florida to California. These were linked to and often coupled with mission stations. A presidio consisted of some sixty or more soldiers, often living in a modest hut surrounded by a mud palisade. They were accompanied by their families, American Indian servants and warriors, and other hangers-on (various types of frontier adventurers).

The missions, somewhat in contrast, tried to organize American Indian society. On the whole, the priests (largely Franciscans) did not find many settled American Indian

The Spanish and French coupled exploration and conquest with missionary stations. Many of the Spanish missions were built and established in the American Southwest and California, and many of the structures still stand today. (iStockphoto)

communities and so set out to establish them. They gathered the American Indians into mission stations typically made up of a *plaza*, or square, dominated by the church and surrounded by official buildings, granaries, blacksmith shops, tanneries, stables, and living quarters for both the American Indians and the missionaries.

The object was to impose Spanish "civilization" upon these created American Indian communities. American Indians learned to speak the Spanish language, to cultivate crops, to raise livestock, and to raise and ride horses. They also learned carpentry, European style, became wine-makers and candlemakers, and were held, of course, to daily sessions of work and prayer.

A traveler to the missions in California described how everyone, American Indians and missionaries alike, awakened at first light. They attended prayers and mass, after which *atole*, a type of barley ground up and boiled, was served for breakfast. Then everyone was sent out to work. Men tilled the soil, and women cared for the household and the children. A bell summoned the workers for the noonday meal of a stew made of wheat, corn, peas, and beans. The inhabitants of the mission station worked for several hours in the afternoon, after which everyone, once again, attended religious services.

Hunting and fishing were allowed, and the American Indians raised livestock. At the same time, they retained some of their traditional lifestyle. Their shelters, clothing, and games remained the same. Intermarriage between the Spanish and American Indians was encouraged, and, in some mission stations, polygamy was permitted.

Out of this came the mixed Spanish-Indian customs: the rodeo; cattle roundup; and the stylized concept of the cowboy with chaps, lasso, and lariat, riding a bronco. Out of this also came the fierce Apache warrior on horseback, defending the tribe against further colonial encroachment. Much more subtle, as an outgrowth of the Spanish colonization of the border-lands, was the hybridization of people and customs in the region, which has endured. Among some of the peoples in the Southwest, such as the Navajos, the Hopis, and the Pueblos, there has been extraordinary cultural survival over the centuries, with tribal groups in some instances holding on to their religious beliefs in tandem with their Catholic practices.

The French did not impose themselves in the same way through their mission-garrison stations. Instead, trading played a larger role. The French did not attempt to keep whole American Indian populations under their control, but they wooed and won the friendship of many tribes who stood against English encroachment. They also fortified the Mississippi and Ohio river basins, as well as the region surrounding the Great Lakes.

3.2b End of the Barrier to Expansion

In the wars that erupted during the eighteenth century between England and France, Native Americans played a key role. Each side tried to win allies among them, and for almost a century there was a standoff. But in the Great War for Empire (1754–1763), the English defeated the French and caused them to abandon North America. In the process, the Native Americans—who had previously been able to take advantage of the rivalry between England and France to suit their own interests—abruptly lost their strategic position. For 150 years the English settlements had failed to penetrate more than two hundred miles into the interior of North America; it was not by chance that they were suddenly able to surge thousands of miles to finally reach the Pacific Ocean in the first few decades of the nineteenth century.

3.3 The Seventeenth Century: An Age of Faith

In America's intellectual and religious life, as in its social structure, English ideas and practices were taken and modified by the American environment. The late sixteenth and early seventeenth centuries in Europe were an Age of Faith, and the characteristics of this age were indelibly stamped upon the English colonies in America. The Protestant

Reformation in Europe had unleashed a flood of ideas concerning the role of the church, qualifications for church membership, and the individual's relationship with God—particularly a person's degree of free will. Were individuals elected by God and thus saved from eternal damnation? Or could each person win salvation through individual faith and the exercise of free will? The English of the early seventeenth century were endlessly concerned with points of doctrine like these.

3.3a Changes in the New World

During the seventeenth century, Puritanism in America was gradually modified by New World conditions. These modifications affected theology, church practice, and everyday life. The changes were many, but for the purposes of this text a single example—the adoption of the **Half-Way Covenant** in 1662—will suffice.

The Puritan church was presumed to be made up exclusively of God's elect, the covenanted people. Children of the elect, however, sometimes failed to evidence "conversion" and thereby to demonstrate the election which would qualify them for full membership within the church. As the body of church members became smaller in proportion to the total population, the clergy feared that the influence of the church in the community at large would be seriously undermined. By the terms of the Half-Way Covenant, therefore, the children of the elect who had not entered full membership in the church were nevertheless permitted to have their children baptized. Baptism enabled their children to participate in some, though not all, of the sacraments

MONTCALM TRYING TO STOP THE MASSACRE.

In the Great War for Empire (1754–1763) the English defeated the French, leading to the French abandonment of North America. This also caused the Native Americans to lose their strategic position in fending off the English from assuming more land in the West. (Wikimedia Commons)

of the church. This opening wedge made an association with the church possible without proof of "election." It was gradually widened until a number of prominent ministers advocated opening the church to those who tried to live according to the precepts of the church—even if they could not demonstrate election.

The New World environment affected other areas of Puritan intellectual life as well. The intellectual vigor of Harvard College declined. Its intellectual direction became, at least to old-line Puritans, "radical," which meant that it diverged from early Puritan precepts and intellectual rigor. The enforcement of the school acts (that required Puritan towns to build schools) lagged, and few intellectuals of late seventeenth-century New England could match the intellectual creativity of the first-line Puritans.

Making the terms of church membership easier was important outside intellectual and spiritual life as well. During most of the seventeenth century, only male church members could vote in the colony-wide elections of Massachusetts Bay. As a result, a substantial majority of the population failed to qualify for the franchise. Thus, broadening church membership had direct political effects. Then a new charter made property ownership the basis for suffrage in 1691, and the Puritans lost outright control of Massachusetts. Even so, the Congregational Church, as a social-religious institution, was a powerful influence in New England well into the nineteenth century.

Half-Way Covenant
Children of the Puritan "elect" who had not entered full membership in the church were permitted to have their children baptized, which enabled their children to participate in some, though not all, of the sacraments of the church

3.3b The Transplanted Anglicans

In the Age of Faith, the Anglican Church was transplanted to Virginia. From there, it expanded into the Carolinas and Maryland, and in the eighteenth century, to the Middle Colonies and New England. In contrast to Puritanism in America, Anglicanism did not center on formal theological inquiries and dogmas. The theological structure of Anglicanism was exclusively the product and concern of the clerical hierarchy within England, and a highly learned Anglican ministry did not immigrate to America along with other members of the faith.

As a result, the influence of the New World environment on the Anglican faith is measured in terms of the modification of church practices and ceremonies—not the modification of doctrine. For example, while the Anglican Church in England was highly centralized and carefully supervised by its hierarchy, in America it became a decentralized

Old field schools

Schools on plantations in Virginia, where children of the gentry were taught by a minister, the wife of a planter, or an indentured servant

The Enlightenment

An era of explosion of scientific thinking and scientific inquiry predicated on the idea that human society can progress through reason and scientific analysis

Sir Isaac Newton

Published *Mathematical Principles of Natural Philosophy* (1697), which set forth, by precise demonstration, the laws of motion and gravitation

Deism

The belief in a Supreme Being or Creator that created the universe and all that is in it, but that would not intervene in human affairs or interfere with the laws of nature

church ruled by lay members. In fact, the clergy who immigrated to America were almost impotent before the lay leaders.

The Anglican parishes in seventeenth-century America were much too large, and this affected church practices. A minister could not readily serve a congregation when its membership was widely scattered. Lay leaders, therefore, began to read the services on the Sabbath, and they soon exercised a role in religious functions that violated the canons of the church.

Because people found it difficult to travel ten or twelve miles to church on horseback or by boat, attendance at services suffered. Moreover, because of the distances, weddings took place on the plantation rather than in church; and the dead were buried in unconsecrated family plots rather than on church ground—another violation of church ordinances.

The absence of a guiding intellectual premise in the Chesapeake colonies dramatically affected education. The scattered nature of the settlements made community schools impractical. By the time the children arrived at the schoolhouse by horseback or boat, it would be time for them to return home. Consequently, responsibility for education was placed upon the family, not upon the community; and the finances and intellectual values of an individual family determined what, and how much, children learned.

Obviously, in a plantation system that made public schools well-nigh impossible, the Virginia gentry had a decided educational advantage over lesser folk. Occasionally, when enough plantations were close to each other, **old field schools** were founded in which the children were taught by a minister or by the wife of a planter. More often, a family or a group of families hired an indentured servant to teach the children. With no way of obtaining an advanced education in the colonies, those planters who wished their children to receive a college education sent them to England.

3.4 The Eighteenth-Century Mind

3.4a The Enlightenment

During the seventeenth century, English intellectual life underwent a transformation triggered by the momentous advance of science and the application of the theoretical framework of science to all phases of human experience. The writings of the father of scientific reasoning, Francis Bacon, marked the beginning of a movement called **the Enlightenment**. This movement was consummated by the great scientific discoveries of **Sir Isaac Newton**, whose *Mathematical Principles of Natural Philosophy* (1697) set forth, by precise demonstration, the laws of motion and gravitation. Newton was to the eighteenth century what Einstein was to the twentieth.

Sir Isaac Newton, 1642–1727 (Wikimedia Commons)

The Enlightenment also affected religious thinking. Newton had used reasoning to discover laws in the physical universe. Many reasoned that laws must also govern the relationship between the human race and the spiritual universe. In this view, God was seen as the Prime Mover who had created the universe with a perfectly operating, harmonious system of unchangeable laws—the laws of nature. Once the universe had been created, so the reasoning went, God no longer took an active part in ruling it; and the natural laws set the requirements for human behavior.

Fortunately, these laws could be discovered; and once they were known, people had only to adjust their lives and their political and educational systems accordingly—in conformity with the requirements set by natural law. The closer we came to alignment between human activity and the laws of nature, the closer human institutions would be to perfection.

In this view, people were perfectible and progress was inevitable. These ideas about God and the universe were called **Deism**, and they contrasted sharply with many of the basic tenets of Puritanism. The Deists believed that there was a God, or Supreme Being, who created the Universe—but they viewed him essentially as a "great watchmaker," who set all of the laws of nature in motion, but who no longer intervenes in human affairs. The Deists did not accept Jesus of Nazareth as the son of God, instead viewing him as a "cynic sage," endowed with great wisdom. As for the meaning of human existence, the Deists believed that life is what humans make of it and little if anything is left to fate or some Divine plan. Prominent Deists included Ben Franklin, who described himself as a "thorough Deist" in his autobiography; Thomas Paine; Ethan Allen; and perhaps Thomas Jefferson, though he himself stated, "I never told anyone my own religion."

In spite of the influence of Deism on some prominent Americans, it should be emphasized that the ideas of the Enlightenment affected only a small minority of the English and far fewer colonials. Most people went about their daily lives unaware of intellectual trends. Enlightenment ideas did not gain strong advocates in America until the mid-eighteenth century, and even then their influence was sharply restricted. Whereas in Europe Enlightenment ideas permeated literature as well as politics, in America these ideas found expression chiefly in political thought. The Declaration of Independence appeals to the "laws of nature and nature's God."

The Enlightenment constituted only one current in the mainstream of intellectual life in eighteenth-century America. Whereas the English Age of Faith had dominated seventeenth-century colonial America, the widespread immigration of non-English groups brought a diversity of cultures. By the eighteenth century, the colonies reflected what was to become a characteristic of the American mind—a wide diversity of intellectual streams.

3.46 The Growth of Toleration

The Toleration Act adopted by Parliament in 1689 gave sufferance to all Protestant sects in England. In America, the background for toleration had been laid as early as 1636, when Roger Williams founded Rhode Island.

In a sense, Williams backed into the principle of religious toleration. He had found the Puritans of Massachusetts Bay to be imperfect in their religious fervor, and he consequently vowed to pray only with those he knew to be regenerate, or spiritually reborn. Because he was unsure of almost all others, he was finally forced to pray only with his wife. From this restricted, impractical position, Williams took the long step to religious toleration on the premise that since he could not determine precisely which persons were regenerate, he had no alternative but to extend toleration to everyone with religious convictions. Williams' ultimate attitude of toleration was well in advance of the mainstream, both in England and in America.

The Maryland Toleration Act of 1649 lent impetus to the growth of toleration, though it arose not from broad humanitarian principles but from immediate circumstances. Maryland, established originally as a Catholic refuge, was being heavily populated by Protestants. The Catholics had not only become a minority, but they were also seriously threatened by persecution because of the Puritan domination in Europe. The Toleration Act, advocated by Lord Baltimore, was intended to protect the Catholic minority and to forestall action against Baltimore's proprietorship.

Toleration flourished in the eighteenth century, in part because of seventeenth-century precedents, but more importantly because the realities of the eighteenth century made intolerance an anachronism. The migration of dissenter sects from Germany; the emergence of an intercolonial Presbyterian church, increasingly fortified by newly arrived Scots and Scotch-Irish; the spread of Anglicanism throughout the colonies; the migrations south, from Pennsylvania to Georgia; the settlements of Jews in Rhode Island, Georgia, and other colonies; the application of the English Toleration Act in America—all of these developments made toleration a necessity. The sheer diversity of religious faiths made any other course highly impractical.

Toleration for provincial America did not mean disruption of church-state establishments, however. Householders of all faiths were taxed to maintain the Anglican Church in Virginia and the Congregational Church in Massachusetts—although in each colony people could practice other faiths without other undue molestation. The separation of church and state did not become a question of principle until during and after the American Revolution, when it was apparent that no single church was sufficiently strong to be elevated to the status of a national church.

BVT Lab

Visit www.BVTLab.com to explore the student resources available for this chapter.

Secularism

A concern with human and worldly affairs, rather than with religious matters

Great Awakening

Religious revival of the mid-eighteenth century

3.4c The Rise of Secularism

Greater toleration, in turn, provided a climate in which **secularism**—a concern with worldly rather than religious matters—could grow. The people who immigrated to America in the eighteenth century were primarily seeking opportunity, not religious toleration. If toleration had been their principal desire, the German Pietists could easily have migrated to Rhode Island—and at an earlier date. But choice Pennsylvania land, in combination with religious toleration, proved to be a superior attraction. Moreover, the new generations of native-born Americans turned with avidity to enrichment and advancement. They were less concerned than their seventeenth-century forebears with the saving of souls.

Perhaps the best index of the rise of secularism is the production of the provincial press. In the eighteenth century, newspapers flourished. The first was published in Boston in 1704; and by the 1750s almost every colony had one newspaper, and a number had several. In contrast to Michael Wigglesworth's "Day of Doom" of the seventeenth century (a religious poem that warns Puritans of the impending Judgment Day where God sentences sinners to hell), almanacs (annual publications that gave information to farmers for the best time to plant, along with weather forecasts, tide tables, and other tabular information) became the best-sellers of the eighteenth century. *Poor Richard's Almanack,* which Benjamin Franklin edited in Philadelphia from 1732 to 1758, sold ten thousand copies a year and became the most popular reading matter in the colonies—except for the Bible.

The emergence of secularism can also be detected in the appearance of touring companies of English actors. Williamsburg had a theater in 1716. In the 1770s, several satirical, patriotic plays by Mercy Otis Warren were published, as were the verses of Phillis Wheatley, who had been brought from Africa as a slave.

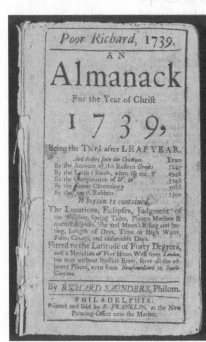

From the rise of secularism came the production of the provincial press. This led to the printing of newspapers and almanacs, such as Benjamin Franklin's best-selling Poor Richard's Almanack. *(Wikimedia Commons)*

3.4d The Great Awakening

The growth of toleration and the emergence of secularism should not obscure a third significant and persistent theme of eighteenth-century intellectual and social life. This was, of course, the **Great Awakening**—an evangelical religious movement, involving a series of revivals preached by stirring evangelists—which swept through colonial America and caused great excitement.

There are numerous reasons why the colonies experienced a religious "awakening" in the eighteenth century, but one of the most prominent is certainly the changing demographics of the time. The sex imbalance between men and women in the Southern Colonies, which had been so severe in the beginning of the seventeenth century, had largely disappeared by the mid-seventeenth century. Thus the Southern Colonies, like those in the north, became societies based on the family unit rather than the young, single, male laborer and adventurer. The family-based society introduced numerous different social dynamics, among them an increase in religiosity. In addition, rural America at the time was an extremely "unchurched" society, due to a shortage of trained clergymen from England and the difficulty of attending church from rural areas in the horse-drawn era. Most historians estimate church membership in the colonies to have been approximately 10 percent in the mid-seventeenth century. In Virginia in 1761, for instance, there were only sixty clergymen for a colony with a population of 350,000. Furthermore, churches were small, averaging only about seventy members. That being the case, it appears that less than 2 percent of Virginians in 1761 were attending church with any regularity. Thus, the colony was primed for a religious revival.

To compound matters further, many of the clergymen who immigrated to America were—simply put—the worst England had to offer. Drunkenness, brawling, and womanizing were, unfortunately, all too common among colonial clergymen. The clergymen were also trained in theological seminaries in England, often making it difficult for them to connect with the common, uneducated people of the American colonies.

The Great Awakening began in the Middle Colonies, and there were three main reasons for this. First, German immigration—much of which fed into to the Middle Colonies—carried with it the Pietist movement from Europe, adding even greater diversity to the mix. Second, the rapid expansion that was characteristic of the Middle Colonies tended to overtax traditional religious institutions and thus to encourage the creation of new organizations and new forms for religious expression. Third, a church-state relationship did not exist to thwart an evangelical movement.

In the 1730s, the Great Awakening extended into New England, where its fire-and-brimstone preachers drew large revivalist crowds in cities and towns alike. In the 1740s and 1750s, the movement reached into the Southern Colonies—carried along, in part, by the southward migration of the Scotch-Irish and Germans along the eastern edge of the Appalachians.

Among the noted preachers associated with the Great Awakening was **Jonathan Edwards** of the Northampton Church in Massachusetts. Often called the greatest theologian America has produced, he used Enlightenment reasoning to construct a theological response to Enlightenment ideas. Beginning in the 1720s, many New England ministers had begun to preach a theology that based salvation on both human moral effort and divine grace. Edwards opposed this tendency and reasserted the absolute justice of God's power to elect or to condemn as he chose, defending with exceptional skill the basic Calvinistic position that God was omnipotent and that, before God, humans were impotent.

Another gifted evangelist who lit the fires of religious revival in America was **George Whitefield**, an Anglican who arrived and toured the American seaboard in 1739. Whitefield customarily addressed huge crowds, including a farewell sermon to 2,500 in Boston in 1740. Whitefield also successfully connected his religious message with the politics of his age, attacking wealthy merchants, who were hated by the common people, as "gripping and merciless usurers who heaped up vast estates" at the expense of the common people.

Two years later, evangelist **James Davenport** would take the political thesis even further. Upon his arrival in Boston, Davenport found that every church was closed to him; consequently, Davenport took his message to the street—and probably reached more people with his message than he might have reached in the churches themselves.

Simultaneously, **William Robinson** began preaching at tent revivals in the rural South. Robinson and other preachers (including Davenport) so stirred up the rural masses that the Virginia governor banned all traveling preachers in 1750. This only spurred the circuit riders to greater resolve, and the "persecution" helped them prove to the masses that they were genuinely men of God sent to do the Lord's work.

Successful preachers stressed the conversion experience and often eschewed theological arguments in favor of playing to emotions. New Light tent revivals were replete with speaking in tongues, barking, jerking, uncontrollable dancing, falling, and slithering on the ground like snakes. In some instances, people crawled on the ground on all fours and dragged their tongues on the ground in displays of humility. Tent revivals could last for a weekend or an entire week and became immense social gatherings in rural areas. Some revivals also involved drunkenness, and it has been claimed that as many souls were conceived as were saved among those in attendance. Successful preachers also tended to be uneducated ministers who were able to speak to the common people in their own language. Given that preaching was not reserved only for those with theological training but was open to anyone who felt the spirit, the number of preachers quickly and exponentially multiplied.

3.4e Lasting Impact, Division, and Dissent

The Great Awakening caused divisions within existing church organizations. Church members attracted to the evangelical group were called **New Lights**, and they attempted to wrest control of the church from the conservative members who held power, the Old Lights. The Awakening fervor was also responsible for the founding of four colleges by separate religious denominations: Dartmouth (Congregationalist), Princeton (Presbyterian), Brown (Baptist), and Rutgers (Dutch Reformed). The premise in each

Jonathan Edwards
Theologian who skillfully challenged the ideas of the Enlightenment

George Whitefield
A dynamic clergyman who toured the colonies from 1739 to 1740 and provided a spark for the Great Awakening

James Davenport
A dynamic clergyman who came to America in 1742 and preached in the streets because the churches closed their doors to him

William Robinson
Great Awakening preacher who held tent revivals in the rural South

New Lights
A new breed of clergymen, churches, and church members (typically focused on emotion and the conversion experience) spawned by the Great Awakening

case was that the existing institutions of higher learning—Yale, for instance, which had been founded in 1701—were unsuitable for training acceptable New Light ministers. The Awakening also altered the face of American religion so that the Methodists, who made up only 3 percent of Americans in the mid-eighteenth century, were the largest denomination in America by the mid-nineteenth century. Baptists and Presbyterians also experienced exponential growth.

The Awakening, because it was an intercolonial movement, strengthened intercolonial ties as well; and many historians have advanced the idea that, by emphasizing the individual and his or her relationship with God, it aroused a democratic spirit that influenced the revolutionary generation. This generalization cannot be proven or disproven, but it seems fair to suggest that by scrutinizing traditional institutions—in this case, ecclesiastical institutions—the Awakening encouraged a climate of freedom. It also offered women the power of choice—to stay with an Old Light congregation or to affiliate with the New Lights. This was no mean thing in a period when married women were unable to control property, except under unusual circumstances, and women in general lacked a political voice.

As immigration increased in the early eighteenth century, and with it religious diversity, the more established Puritans and Anglicans voiced their opposition, labeling sectarianism and diversity as heresy, a violation of God's will, and contrary to Apostle Paul's admonition, "Let all things be done decently and in order" (I Corinthians 14:40). Puritans and Anglicans viewed the new sects not only as erroneous and heretical but also as exceedingly unruly and therefore unpleasing to God. Issac Stiles, a Puritan clergyman, described members of other religious sects as:

> subversive of peace, discipline, and government, lay open the sluices, and make a gap to let in a flood of confusion and disorder, and very awfully portend the ruin of these churches. If sectarianism increased, Connecticut would soon be an habitation of dragons and a court for owls.

Anglicans, like the Puritans, tended to believe that their church was the only one (among English-speaking Protestant churches) founded on the principle of apostolic succession. Therefore, the Anglican Church was the only one that was valid. To the Anglicans, ministers in other sects were not truly ordained; and other sects were a perversion of sound church doctrine, organization, and discipline that undermined civil society. For example, Lieutenant Governor Colden of New York essentially blamed land riots in the 1760s on trouble caused by "religious dissenters from the diverse sects."

Similarly, Anglican minister Jonathan Boucher described the sectarians as those referenced by Apostle Paul as "persons having itching ears and unstable in all their ways," who are "easily tossed about with every wind of doctrine." Boucher declared that "those who are not for the [Anglican] Church are against it." He viewed the dissenting sects as representative of revolts not only against the church but also against the state and society. Boucher argued for rigid enforcement of regulations and laws against dissenting sects and warned of the ultimate destruction of society if the sects went unpunished.

Anglicans and Puritans, however, were also disdainful of each other. Anglicans were particularly appalled by the democratic leanings within the Puritan community, which they viewed as an affront to the hierarchical structure of the Anglican Church. In the words of Samuel Johnson, Anglican rector of Stratford in 1760:

> All the disadvantages it [Puritan Connecticut] labors under are owing to its wretched constitution, being little more than a mere democracy, and most of them upon a level, and each man thinking himself an able divine and politician; hence the prevalence of rigid enthusiasms and conceited notions and practices in religion, and republican and mobbish principles and practices, next door to anarchy, in polity.

Johnson's sentiments were most certainly the dominant views of the Anglican Church hierarchy throughout the early colonial period; however, by the time of the American Revolution and the subsequent writing of the American Constitution, the Anglicans had come to recognize that suppression of dissent, no matter how distasteful, was no longer possible. Nevertheless, during the reign of King James II, the governors of all royal provinces had the following instructions: "to permit a liberty of conscience to all persons except Papists, so they be contented with a quiet and peaceable enjoyment of the same, not giving offense or scandal to the government."

Virginia Statute for Religious Freedom
Written by Thomas Jefferson, the statute separated church and state in Virginia.

Eventually, the diversity of the population—produced by massive immigration—would mean that laws punishing heretics and dissenters would be overturned and eliminated on a state by state basis, starting at the end of the Seven Years War and continuing to the Jacksonian era. Thomas Jefferson's famous **Virginia Statute for Religious Freedom** of 1786, declaring that "no one shall be compelled to contribute to any opinion with which he disagrees," became a model for other states to follow and its ideas gradually supplanted official intolerance as the norm.

The Anglican Church, in particular, had a proclivity to oppose the movement toward freedom of conscience in the colonial period, given that it was the established church not only in a number of the colonies but in the mother country as well. Thus, for specifically political reasons, the Anglican Church was motivated to retain its preferred positions both in England and in the colonies; coupled with theological and ideological motivations, the Anglicans could be expected to resist religious tolerance. This resistance was futile in the long run, however, as the Awakening proved that religious diversity was unavoidable and that complete unity of religious thought was impossible. Furthermore, the Awakening enlarged the idea that ordinary persons could challenge both religious and political authorities, thus helping to lay the groundwork for the American Revolution, which would arise on the tail of the Awakening.

3.4f The Enlightenment in America

The greatest influence of the Enlightenment in America was the encouragement it gave to scientific inquiry. Cotton Mather, the most prominent New England clergyman of the late seventeenth and early eighteenth centuries, was attracted to scientific investigation. He was an advocate of smallpox inoculations when others greeted this medical advance with uncertainty or fear. William Byrd II of Virginia, along with other colonials, belonged to England's Royal Society and frequently sent observations of New World phenomena to his friends in England.

The contribution of most colonials was to that aspect of science called "natural history." Almost every botanical specimen collected in America constituted a contribution to knowledge because it added to the storehouse of scientific information. John Bartram, who collected specimens throughout the provinces and cultivated rare species in his garden in Philadelphia, was called the finest contemporary "natural botanist" by Carolus Linnaeus of Sweden, the foremost botanist in Europe. A celebrated work was Mark Catesby's extraordinary *Natural History of Carolina*.

In America, the Enlightenment encouraged scientific inquiry. Cotton Mather was a prominent New England clergyman and Puritan. Mather drew great attention to scientific investigation regarding issues, such as smallpox inoculations, which were controversial. (Wikimedia Commons)

Of the colonists, Benjamin Franklin was foremost in his contribution to theoretical science although many of his provincial contemporaries pursued related investigations with vigor and persistence. Fortunately for Franklin, he entered a field of physics (electricity) in which relatively little work had been done up to that point; thus he was not handicapped by his lack of background—particularly his limited knowledge of mathematics. Both his identification of lightning as electricity (though it was his son William, not Ben, who dangerously flew the kite in the lightning storm), and his observations concerning the flow of electricity and the equalization that took place between highly charged particles and those less highly charged, were contributions that won him a reputation throughout Europe.

Endowed with an active and inventive mind, as well as quick wit, Franklin is also famous for having invented bifocals, the lightning rod (which greatly reduced the incidence of barn fires in America), and the Franklin Stove—a much more efficient way to burn wood than a brick fireplace.

Franklin also demonstrates the fact that science (although it has become increasingly important in colleges) was first pursued most fervently by those outside of institutions of learning. As proper eighteenth-century generalists, these men were interested in politics, science, writing, and other broad-gauged, stimulating activities. The impact of science in colonial America makes it clear that the Enlightenment, unlike Puritanism, was peculiarly the possession of the educated and socially elite.

This does not mean, however, that the effects of the Enlightenment were not felt by all. For one thing, provincial America—because it was a new, actively forming society—appeared, in the eyes of some European and American observers, to be an ideal laboratory for the Enlightenment. Free from the incrustations of the centuries, American society could presumably adjust to the unchangeable laws of nature more readily than could European societies. Indeed, American intellectuals were confident that a perfect society was already being created.

In political thought and practice, too, provincial Americans—regardless of status or location—embraced many Enlightenment ideas. That citizens have a right to challenge the government when it stands athwart the laws of nature, and a subsequent right to replace such a government with one that conforms to nature's laws, were two assumptions of the Enlightenment that deeply penetrated the American mind.

3.4g Colonial Roots of American Culture

Colonial America made no great progress in the arts, nor could such manifestations of cultural life be expected of a people whose principal energies were devoted to creating a new civilization. Yet Philadelphia stood as a cosmopolitan city, second in population only to London within the British Empire. The American cities in the aggregate, as well as the American countryside, provided a stimulating atmosphere that nourished people of intelligence, indeed of genius, whose contributions would endure beyond those of most of their cultivated counterparts in England.

The standard criteria for evaluating the level of intellectual life, therefore, did not apply to provincial America. More important than artistic expression were a zest for learning, the exploration of new modes of society, an emphasis on mobility, and the ability of these new societies to prosper and to set examples that, in time, would be imitated. The "American Mind," fashioned from the experiences of the seventeenth and eighteenth centuries, formed the foundation upon which American nationhood and an American culture were later built.

Here, Benjamin Franklin—born in New England but who enjoyed his prime in Philadelphia—can be seen as the best example of colonial American culture. A man of the Enlightenment, interested in all of the new ideas, he also devoted himself to bettering his adopted city. He played a role in founding the first public library there, as well as the first volunteer firefighting company, and two colleges—the University of Pennsylvania, and Franklin and Marshall College. An early advocate of colonial unity, he would play a role second only to that of George Washington in the success of the American Revolution.

Timeline

1608	French establish their first settlement in North America at Quebec, Canada.
1636	Roger Williams founds Rhode Island.
1649	Maryland Toleration Act
1660	Restoration of the Stuart Monarchy
1662	Adoption of the Half-Way Covenant in Massachusetts
1683	Francis Daniel Pastorious leads the first German settlers into Pennsylvania.
1690–1742	Boston, Newport, New York, Philadelphia, and Charleston triple their populations.
1691	Property ownership is established as the basis for the franchise in Massachusetts.
1697	Isaac Newton's *Mathematical Principles of Natural Philosophy* demonstrates the laws of motion and gravitation.
1704	First newspaper in the colonies published in Boston.
1710–1770	Wave of 225,000 German settlers immigrate to North America.
1730–1760	The Great Awakening spreads across America.
1732–1758	Ben Franklin is editor of *Poor Richard's Almanack.*
1739	George Whitefield arrives in Boston.
1754–1763	Great War for Empire
1776	Philadelphia is the second largest city in the British Empire.
1786	Thomas Jefferson's Virginia Statute for Religious Freedom

Colonial culture in the eighteenth century very much reflected English heritage—from language, to social and intellectual life, to politics. This was true despite the colonies developing diversity due to the ethnic mix of immigrants arriving from Europe and the unique features of colonial frontier life that contrasted with life in England.

Because African slaves had provided a solution to the immense labor demands of the colonies, and hostile Native American tribes to the west forced most colonists to remain near the eastern seaboard, the colonists formed thriving, urban centers—such as Philadelphia—along the East Coast. Not all Native Americans were hostile, however; and the colonists developed a thriving fur trade with them, as well as trade with Europe. Meanwhile, France was developing a trading empire on the Mississippi River and St. Lawrence River that hindered English expansion in the North, while the Spanish established a series of missions and presidios in the South from Florida along the coastal bend and through Texas and the Southwest, all the way to California. The French barrier to English expansion would finally be eliminated in the Great War for the Empire (1754–1763).

The eighteenth century, in colonial America, was an age of both faith and reason. Led by the writings of Isaac Newton, the European Enlightenment spread to the American colonies, with American icon Benjamin Franklin the most noteworthy American contributor. Enlightenment thinkers believed that humans could progress through reason and scientific inquiry. Coterminous with the Enlightenment was the rise of Deism, the adherents of which held that there was a Supreme Being or Creator that did not interfere in human affairs or the laws of nature.

While the Enlightenment spread, the colonies simultaneously experienced a Great Awakening, or religious revival. The shift from a society dominated by single men to one dominated by families, the arrival of gifted evangelists, a focus on emotion and the conversion experience, and the idea that anyone with "inspiration" could preach the Gospel—all contributed to the Awakening. The older, established churches divided into New Light and Old Light factions, sometimes within individual congregations. The Awakening also had lasting effects on education, as reflected by the emergence of Universities affiliated with New Light religious organizations. The emotional focus, and the idea that any inspired individual can preach, have remained prevalent in American religious culture ever since.

Finally, the religious diversity that accompanied the Awakening eventually forced a movement to separate Church and State. The idea that one could challenge authority (which arose during the Awakening) would surface again in the 1770s—but this time, the authority challenged would be political rather than religious.

KEY TERMS

BIBLIOGRAPHY

A

Andrews, Pat. *Voices of Diversity.* Guilford, CT: Dushkin, 1993.

B

Bailyn, Bernard. *The Peopling of British North America: An Introduction.* New York: Vintage, 1988.

———. *Voyagers to the West: A Passage in the Peopling of North America on the Eve of the Revolution.* New York: Vintage, 1988.

Bishop, George. *New England Judged by the Spirit of the Lord.* Whitefish, MT: Kessinger Publishing, 2003.

Brewer, John. *The Sinews of Power: War, Money, and the English State 1688–1783.* Cambridge, MA: Harvard University Press, 1990.

Brinkley, Alan. *American History: A Survey.* 11th ed. Boston, MA: McGraw-Hill, 2003.

Bushman, Richard L. *The Refinement of America: Persons, Houses, Cities.* New York: Vintage, 1993.

C

Coalter, Milton J. *Gilbert Tennent, Son of Thunder: A Case Study of Continental Pietism's Impact on the First Great Awakening in the Middle Colonies.* Westport, CT: Praeger, 1986.

Chinard, Gilbert, Ed. *A Huguenot Exile in Virginia: Or Voyages of a Frenchman Exiled for His Religion with a Description of Virginia and Maryland.* New York: The Press of the Pioneers, 1934.

Colden, Cadwallader. *The Letters and Papers of Cadwallader Colden.* New York: AMS Press, 1973.

Cremin, Lawrence A. *American Education: The Colonial Experience 1607–1783.* New York: HarperCollins, 1970.

Cross, Barbara M., Ed. *The Autobiography of Lyman Beecher.* Cambridge, MA: Harvard University Press, 1961.

D

Dandelion, Pink. *The Quakers: A Very Short Introduction.* New York: Oxford University Press, 2008.

E

Eccles, W. J. *France in America.* East Lansing, MI: Michigan State University Press, 1990.

Ellerbe, Helen. *The Dark Side of Christian History.* Orlando, FL: Morningstar and Lark, 1995.

Erikson, Kai. *Wayward Puritans: A Study in the Sociology of Deviance.* Boston, MA: Allyn and Bacon, 1966.

F

Ferguson, Robert A. *The American Enlightenment.* Cambridge, MA: Harvard University Press, 1997.

G

Greene, Jack P. *Pursuits of Happiness: The Social Development of Early Modern British Colonies and the Formation of American Culture.* Chapel Hill, NC: University of North Carolina Press, 1988.

H

Hall, David D. *Worlds of Wonder, Days of Judgment: Popular Religious Belief in Early New England.* Cambridge, MA: Harvard University Press, 1990.

Hatch, Nathan O. *The Sacred Cause of Liberty. Republican Thought and the Millennium in Revolutionary New England.* New Haven, CT: Yale University Press, 1977.

Highman, John. *Strangers in the Land.* New Brunswick, NJ: Rutgers University Press, 1955.

Hirschman, Albert O. *The Passions and the Interests: Political Arguments for Capitalism before Its Triumph.* Princeton, NJ: Princeton University Press, 1997.

J

Jernegan, Marcus Wilson. *Laboring and Dependent Classes in Colonial America 1607–1783.* Westport, CT: Greenwood Press, 1980.

Jordan, Winthrop. *White over Black: American Attitudes toward the Negro 1550–1812.* Chapel Hill, NC: University of North Carolina Press, 1968.

K

Kidd, Thomas S. *The Great Awakening: The Roots of Evangelical Christianity in Colonial America.* New Haven, CT: Yale University Press, 2009.

Kenny, Kevin. *Peaceable Kingdom Lost: The Paxton Boys and the Destruction of William Penn's Holy Experiment.* New York: Oxford University Press, 2011.

L

Labaree, Leonard Woods. *Conservatism in Early American History.* Ithaca, NY: Great Seal Books, 1948.

———. *Royal Instructions to British Colonial Governors, 1670–1776.* New York: D. Appleton-Century, 1935.

Levy, Barry. *Quakers and the American Family: British Settlement in the Delaware Valley.* New York: Oxford University Press, 1992.

BIBLIOGRAPHY

M

May, Henry F. *The Enlightenment in America*. New York: Oxford University Press, 1978.

McCusker, John J. and Russell R. Menard. *The Economy of British America 1607–1789*. Chapel Hill, NC: University of North Carolina Press, 1991.

Miller, Brandon Marie. *Good Women of a Well-Blessed Land: Women's Lives in Colonial America*. New York: Lerner, 2003.

Miller, Perry. *The New England Mind: The Seventeenth Century*. Cambridge, MA: Belknap, 1983.

Miller, Perry, and Thomas H. Johnson Eds. *The Puritans: A Sourcebook of Their Writings*. New York: Harper, 1968.

Mitchell, Robert. *Calvin's and the Puritans' View of the Protestant Ethic*. Lanham, MD: University Press of America, 1979.

Morgan, Edmund S. *American Slavery, American Freedom: The Ordeal of Colonial Virginia*. New York: W. W. Norton & Company, 2003.

———. *Inventing the People: The Rise of Popular Sovereignty in England and America*. New York: W. W. Norton & Company, 1989.

———. *Visible Saints: The History of a Puritan Idea*. Ithaca, NY: Cornell University Press, 1965.

Murrin, John M. "Religion and Politics in America from the First Settlements to the Civil War." In Mark A. Noll, Ed., *Religion and American Politics: From the Colonial Period to the 1980s*. New York: Oxford University Press, 1990.

Murrin, John R., Paul E. Johnson, James M. McPherson, Gary Gerstle, Emily S. Rosenberg, and Norman L. Rosenberg. *Liberty, Equality, Power: A History of the American People*. Fort Worth, TX: Harcourt Brace, 1996.

N

Nash, Gary B., Julie Roy Jeffrey, John R. Howe, Peter J. Frederick, Allen F. Davis, and Allan M. Winkler. *The American People: Creating a Nation and a Society*. 4th ed. New York: Longman, 1998.

Noll, Mark O. *Princeton and the Republic 1768–1822: The Search for a Christian Enlightenment in the Era of Samuel Stanhope Smith*. Vancouver, BC: Regent College Publishing, 2004.

O

O'Sullivan, John, and Edward F. Keuchel. *American Economic History: From Abundance to Constraint*. New York: Markus Wiener, 1989.

P

Patterson, Orlando. *Slavery and Social Death. A Comparative Study*. Cambridge, MA: Harvard University Press, 1985.

Plumb, J. H. *The Growth of Political Stability in England 1675–1725*. New York: MacMillan, 2001.

R

Russell, David Lee. *Oglethorpe and Colonial Georgia: A History 1733–1783*. Jefferson, NC: McFarland Press, 2006.

Rink, Oliver. *Holland on the Hudson. An Economic and Social History of Dutch New York*. Ithaca, NY: Cornell University Press, 1989.

S

Saunders, William L., Ed. *The Colonial Records of North Carolina*. Temecula, CA: Reprint Services Corporation, 1999.

Stanard, William G. and Mary N. Stanard. *The Colonial Virginia Register*. Albany, NY: Joel Munsell's Sons, 1902.

U

Ulrich, Laurel Thatcher. *Good Wives: Image and Reality in the Lives of Women in Northern New England 1650–1750*. New York: Vintage, 1991.

W

Ward, W. Reginold. *The Protestant Evangelical Awakening*. Cambridge, UK: Cambridge University Press, 2002.

Webb, Stephen S. *The Governors General: The English Army and the Definition of Empire, 1569–1681*. Chapel Hill, NC: University of North Carolina Press, 1987.

Weir, Robert. *Colonial South Carolina: A History*. Columbia, SC: University of South Carolina Press, 1997.

Wright, Louis B. *The First Gentlemen of Virginia: Intellectual Qualities of the Early Colonial Ruling Class*. Charlottesville, VA: University of Virginia Press, 1970.

Y

Yazawa, Melvin, Ed. *Diary and Life of Samuel Sewall*. New York: St. Martin's Press, 1998.

POP QUIZ

1. A majority of German immigrants to the English colonies lived in _____.
   a. the South
   b. the Middle Colonies
   c. New England
   d. the Chesapeake colonies

2. In the English social structure, below the yeomen were the _____.
   a. nobles
   b. merchants
   c. laborers and servants
   d. large landowners

3. For what were ships' captains given fifty acres of land?
   a. For each slave brought into the colonies
   b. For each indentured servant brought into the colonies
   c. For each immigrant brought into the colonies
   d. For each family brought into the colonies

4. How did the structure of colonial society differ from that of England?
   a. In the colonies, the top level of English society, the nobility, was shorn off.
   b. In the colonies, women did not work.
   c. In the colonies, there were no wealthy people.
   d. In the colonies, there were far fewer slaves.

5. The largest percentage of German, Scotch, and Irish immigrants settled in _____.
   a. Canada
   b. New England
   c. the Southern Colonies
   d. Pennsylvania and the Middle Colonies

6. Spanish efforts to convert the American Indians to Christianity focused on the _____.
   a. presidios
   b. missions
   c. baptistries
   d. rodeos

7. Which of the following was true of the Anglican Church in the American colonies?
   a. Due to the difficulty of travel, attendance suffered.
   b. All weddings were held at the church.
   c. All burials were on church grounds.
   d. Anglican community schools dominated education in the Chesapeake colonies.

8. Why did religious tolerance flourish in the eighteenth century colonies?
   a. Because the colonists were so naturally tolerant, having suffered persecution in England
   b. Because even though there were multiple religious denominations, they were all Christian.
   c. Because the sheer diversity of religious faiths made any other course highly impractical
   d. Because all of the colonists were carrying guns, which made them more tolerant and polite

9. The people who migrated to America in the eighteenth century were primarily seeking _____.
   a. economic opportunity
   b. religious freedom
   c. the chance to own slaves
   d. to live in a free, democratic society

10. Successful preachers and movements during the Great Awakening stressed _____.
    a. Bible education
    b. theological argument and debate
    c. the conversion experience and emotion
    d. the eurcharist

11. Ben Franklin invented which of the following?
    a. the electric light bulb
    b. the lightning rod
    c. contact lenses
    d. the kite

12. The religion of the Enlightenment was _____.

13. According to Jonathan Edwards, humans were _____ in the eyes of God.

14. The second best selling book in the colonies, after the Bible, was _____.

15. A concern with worldly things rather than religious values is a major element of _____.

(Wikimedia Commons)

Chapter 4

Colonial Administration and Politics

CHAPTER OUTLINE

4.1 English Administration of the Colonies

In London, administrative agencies to govern the colonies were slow in evolving. Originally, a committee of the **King's Privy Council** (the Lord Commissioners for Plantations) directly supervised the colonies. Variations of this committee operated until 1675, when the **Lords of Trade** were created— an agency whose vigorous actions set a new standard in colonial policy. It opposed the crown's disposition toward proprietary grants and advocated revoking them, thereby bringing such colonies under direct royal control.

The most important effort of the Lords of Trade was made in 1686, when it established the **Dominion of New England**. The charter of Massachusetts Bay had been annulled in 1684, and the Dominion represented an attempt to centralize the authority of the crown by creating a super-colony, including

The seal of the Dominion of New England
(Wikipedia Commons)

King's Privy Council
An executive body that advised the king on affairs of state and issued orders on the behalf of the monarch

Lords of Trade
An administrative body created by King Charles II in 1675 to create stronger ties between the colonial governments and the crown

Dominion of New England
A failed attempt at administrative union of the New England Colonies, New York, and New Jersey, 1686–1689

Massachusetts, New Hampshire, Connecticut, Rhode Island, Plymouth, New York, and New Jersey. It was expected that eventually Pennsylvania would also be incorporated within the framework of the Dominion. The crown, acting upon the recommendation of the Lords of Trade, appointed Edmond Andros as governor, stipulating that Andros was to reside in Boston while his deputy resided in New York. No provision was made for an assembly, although there was to be a council of advisers. Andros, unfortunately, was of limited mind and petty spirit. He was scarcely the man to carry out such a dramatic, far-reaching colonial experiment. Resentment was intense among the colonies included within the Dominion, not only because their original charters had been arbitrarily set aside and the equally arbitrary Andros appointed, but also because they lacked a representative assembly.

England's Glorious Revolution of 1688 deposed the despotic James II and firmly championed Parliament—and thus representative government—in England. This twist of fate provided an opportunity for the colonials to overthrow the Dominion. Acting on the premise that Governor Andros now represented a discarded royal regime, the colonials imprisoned him as a signal of their allegiance to the new government in England set up under William and Mary. Each colony that had been included within the Dominion hastily returned to its previous path of colonial self-government except for Plymouth, which was absorbed by Massachusetts. Thus the Glorious Revolution marked the end of an experiment to consolidate the colonies within a larger framework and to administer them more directly.

In many respects, the experiment of the Dominion of New England was a turning point in colonial political affairs. At the time, the colonials were not yet strong enough to defeat the royal will. If the experiment had been a success, individual self-government within the colonies would have been eliminated and the entire course of American history might have been changed. With the fall of the Dominion, the individual colonies received a new lease on life—and they used it to gain strength both politically and economically.

In 1696 the Lords of Trade were replaced by the Board of Trade, an administrative agency that survived into the period of the American Revolution. During the eighteenth century, Parliament was overwhelmed with its own problems—namely, the internal political transition to parliamentary supremacy in England and the turmoil of foreign policy—and could not spare the time to formulate new policies for the empire. As a result, the general policies that had been formulated very early in the century continued to be followed throughout the period—despite changing circumstances. The instructions issued to a governor in 1750 were little changed from instructions given in 1700. The American provinces were changing, England was changing, and the world was changing—but British imperial policy remained, for the most part, the same.

4.1a Political Structures in the Colonies

The English colonies in America experienced a vigorous political life, in contrast to the colonies of other western European countries. The concept of self-government was transferred to the English colonies almost from the outset in most settlements, but the political structure generally took more definitive shape early in the eighteenth century.

The political structures that evolved in royal, proprietary, and **charter colonies** were remarkably similar. Each colony had a **governor** who executed colonial laws, served as commander in chief of the militia, presided over the colony's highest court of appeals, and enforced relevant British enactments. In a proprietary colony like Pennsylvania, the governor looked after the interests of the proprietor, most notably in the disposition of land; he was also expected to enforce the imperial policies laid down by the English authorities. Usually the crown appointed the governor, although in proprietary colonies the proprietor held this prerogative. In the charter colonies of Rhode Island and Connecticut, the governor was elected by the legislature. The colonies of Rhode Island, Connecticut, and Massachusetts Bay were charter colonies. In a charter colony, the king granted a charter to the colonial government that established the rules under which the colony was to be governed. The charters of Rhode Island and Connecticut granted the colonists significantly more political liberty than other colonies. Rhode Island and Connecticut continued to use their colonial charters as their state constitutions after the American Revolution.

Most colonies had a **council** whose members served as advisers to the governor. This council comprised the upper house of the legislature and sat as the highest court of appeal in the colony. Generally, the crown appointed council members upon the recommendation of the governor, but exceptions were made. Members of the council were customarily the more affluent colonials, many of whom had powerful friends in England. In a number of colonies, the council, although acting in self-interest, was the spokesman for the people against the prerogative of the governor; the council wished to control office patronage, the distribution of lands, and the like.

The freemen elected a colonial **assembly**, which served as the lower house of the legislature. By the eighteenth century, every colony had instituted property requirements as a requisite for freemanship (full citizenship in the colony), but recent research has demonstrated that these requirements did not seriously restrict the number of eligible voters. Property requirements for officeholding, however, were frequently much higher than the requirements for suffrage; thus a member of the assembly had to be a person of some means. "Professional politicians," who had no other means of livelihood, were rare in the provinces.

During the eighteenth century the assemblies of every colony gained power. Among the specific powers obtained by most assemblies were the rights to initiate legislation, to judge the qualifications of their own members, and to elect their speakers. The assemblies were somewhat less successful in determining when elections should be held and in extending their membership.

Whereas the basic constitutional position of the English authorities was that the power of the assemblies and the grant of self-government itself were merely an extension of "the royal grace and favor"—to be offered, modified, or even eliminated as the crown determined—the constitutional position held by the assemblies was that their power and authority derived from the consent of the governed. The assemblies conceived of themselves as replicas of the British House of Commons; and they attempted to imitate it in waging their contest for power against the prerogative of the governor, who represented the crown or the proprietor.

Conflicts were inevitable between constitutional positions that differed so markedly. The principal expression of this conflict arose between the assemblies and the governor. The assemblies attempted to restrict the scope of the governor's operations by controlling the disbursement of funds appropriated by the legislature, by failing to appropriate monies for projects asked for by the governor, and occasionally by refusing to pay the governor's salary until he accepted the legislation passed by the assembly.

4.1b Local Government

At the time the colonies were founded, the structures of English local government was transplanted, for the most part, to the New World. Among the more important officials were the county sheriffs and the justices of the peace. Other positions that were important in England, such as lord lieutenant, did not flourish in the New World. Local government in the United States today descends directly from the colonial period.

Local disputes over land titles and other matters were settled by the county courts. The justices of the peace in cooperation with the sheriff enforced colonial legislation, and the sheriff collected taxes. In practice, therefore, local government served as a major link between the people and the colonial government.

4.1c Colonial Politics

In every colony, at some time or another, domestic disputes developed, which were fought out in the political arena. The issues of land, currency, proportionate representation, defense, and trade with Native Americans were among those that arose most frequently. In a colony such as Virginia, where tobacco was the principal staple, tobacco inspection acts aroused lively political disputes. Seldom did political parties develop. Generally, a coalition—drawn, in most cases, from various parts of a province—formed to support or defeat a particular measure. Once the issue was decided, the coalition disintegrated.

A political split between the eastern and western parts of the province was characteristic of Pennsylvania, which was growing at a swifter pace than most of its sister colonies. By contrast, the major political division in New York was between influential families whose wealth was based on land and influential families whose wealth was based on commerce. These political divisions and the conflicts they aroused were evidence not of internal disorder but of political maturity—of vigorous, healthy self-government in action.

Assembly

Lower house of the colonial legislatures elected by propertied freemen

BVT Lab

Flashcards are available for this chapter at www.BVTLab.com.

4.2 Colonial Economy

4.2a New England

The rise of capitalism throughout western Europe, which coincided with the founding of the English colonies, determined that the American provincial economy would be capitalistic in orientation, with an emphasis on trade, production for market, and eventually regional specialization. Each colony's economy, at the outset, was rather primitive—merely an appendage of the economy of the mother country. Shortly after the mid-eighteenth century, however, an indigenous, well-developed, capitalist economy emerged.

The economic development of New England was strongly influenced by the systems of land distribution and of trade. In the seventeenth century, land was granted by the legislature to groups—usually church congregations—which in turn distributed the land among their members. The result was the encouragement of the famous New England township system, whose principal aim was to maintain an effective social-religious community. After provisions for the church, a village green, and sometimes a school were made, each family was customarily granted a town lot. Plots of land outside the town were then distributed among members of the group, with common land retained for grazing purposes and a specified number of acres reserved for latecomers.

Distributing the land in this fashion meant that all members of the group would be in close proximity to the church, the heart of the Puritan community. It also meant that sending youngsters to school would raise no serious problems and that towns would become the basis for representative government, with town meetings providing the political structure to resolve local issues.

In the eighteenth century, the New England land system changed. Because it was no longer so important to plant a concentrated social-religious community, church groups were seldom in charge of settlement along western frontier lands. Instead, people of influence and means began to buy large blocks of land for speculative purposes, selling off smaller parcels to individual farmers or prospective farmers.

Even in the older towns, conditions changed. Original settlers or descendants of original settlers moved out, often selling their land to newcomers. Absentee ownership of town lots and township lands was common. Whereas in the seventeenth century town proprietors were nearly always residents of the town, this was less often the case in eighteenth-century communities.

Although farming was the predominant occupation in New England until 1640, trade gained increasing importance thereafter. From 1640 to 1660, the English were preoccupied with civil war and political upheaval at home, and colonials began to replace the English merchants as the trading enterprisers. It was at this time that the developing resources of New England fisheries helped to open up trade between the Puritans of New England and Puritans who had settled in the West Indies.

New England merchants gradually gained a position of economic and political primacy. By the end of the seventeenth century, they had already begun to replace the Puritan magistrates as the source of economic and political power. By the 1760s they constituted the single strongest voice in New England.

It is important to remember that merchants were not alone in their dependence on trade for prosperity. The artisans who repaired canvas and built vessels, and the farmers who exported meat products—in fact, the entire population in one way or another—were partly dependent upon prosperous commercial relations. Meat, fish, and lumber (the principal articles of export) found their major market in the West Indies. New England was also dependent on its role as a carrier of exports from other provinces and of imports from England.

For labor, New Englanders depended largely on members of their own families, though they sometimes hired local servants and imported indentured servants. New England, in contrast to some of the other regions, was attractive to skilled workers because they could find a ready market for their talent in an area dominated by a town system. Each town needed a carpenter and a blacksmith, for example. Slavery, though never as important to the economy as it was further south, was fully legal in each of the **New England Colonies**.

4.2b The Southern Colonies

Three significant factors affected the economic development of the **Southern Colonies**: the distribution of land, the evolution of the plantation system, and the tremendous production of staples for market. In the seventeenth-century, the Chesapeake colonies of Virginia and Maryland distributed land directly to individuals—in contrast to the practice in early New England. Moreover, the settlers were scattered up and down the rivers of the Chesapeake area instead of settling in groups. Each planter aimed to have his own landing, where an ocean-going vessel could readily load the tobacco he produced and unload the goods he had ordered from England. This method of settlement made the county the basis of local government, discouraged the establishment of a school system because of the distances involved, and markedly influenced the transplantation of the Anglican Church.

In the seventeenth century, the average landholding was relatively small since labor to cultivate extensive landholdings was lacking. The headright system, whereby a planter or ship captain could obtain fifty acres of land for each dependent or servant brought to the colonies, allowed the first accumulations of land to occur. Even so, it was not until the eighteenth century, when American colonists obtained control of the machinery to distribute land, that large grants became fairly common.

Although slaves were imported into the Chesapeake colonies and into South Carolina in the seventeenth century, the principal labor force was composed of indentured servants, including convicts and paupers who were sentenced to labor in America. Over 1,500 indentures were imported annually into Virginia, alone, in the 1670s and the 1680s.

In the following years, the plantation system became larger; and the black slave became a relatively less expensive source of labor as the **Middle Colonies**—New York, New Jersey, Pennsylvania, and Delaware—expanded to compete for indentured servants. At the same time, the supply of English indentures decreased because the demand for labor in England was also on the rise. As a result, the institution of slavery became fastened upon the eighteenth-century Southern Colonies. A society that had been made up largely of yeomen now became dominated by the plantation elite, whose power rested on the ownership of black slaves.

Tobacco continued to be the main staple in the Chesapeake colonies. Rice became prominent in South Carolina, however; and indigo—introduced by Elizabeth Pinckney—became yet another important crop. In addition, naval stores became a major export of North Carolina, and deerskins were the most important good obtained through trade with the American Indians.

In the seventeenth century, no merchant group developed in the southern colonies because planters sold directly to English merchants. In the eighteenth century, an important merchant group developed in strategically located Charleston, South Carolina—trade center for a vast hinterland. No major tensions developed between merchants and planters in the South, however, because the prosperity of one was directly related to the well-being of the other. In fact, the same individual might belong to both groups since many merchants bought land and planters sometimes became merchants.

4.2c The Middle Colonies

During the eighteenth century, English migration decreased because demand for laborers and opportunities for advancement greatly increased at home, as Britain expanded its trade and manufacturing. However, a tremendous influx of non-English peoples—Germans, Scotch-Irish, Irish, Swiss, and French Huguenots—into the Middle Colonies resulted in the expansion of that region at a rate exceeding that of New England or the Southern Colonies.

The reasons for the migration of non-English peoples were fundamentally economic, although religious intolerance and fear of destructive wars at home sometimes played a part. Opportunities for the Scotch-Irish in Ireland were limited, whereas opportunities in the New World appeared much more attractive. German Pietists came to Pennsylvania in large numbers because that colony offered an attractive land policy as well as religious toleration.

Southern Colonies

The colonies south of Pennsylvania

Middle Colonies

New York, New Jersey, Delaware, and Pennsylvania

Tobacco was a staple product in the development of the Southern Colonies. (iStockphoto)

Regulatory acts

Imperial regulations imposed in the seventeenth century to prevent foreign commercial competition and the competition of colonial manufactures with those of the mother country

Land policies in Pennsylvania, New Jersey, and New York varied greatly. In New York, land was granted to royal favorites, who established extensive manors. An ordinary settler was often forced to accept a leasehold and become a renter instead of obtaining a clear title to the land. The distribution of lands in Pennsylvania was much more favorable. Small grants could be obtained by outright purchase. In fact, Scotch-Irish settlers on the frontier of Pennsylvania frequently assumed title to the land by right of settlement and refused to pay the proprietors.

New York and Philadelphia developed into major ports in the eighteenth century, with Philadelphia becoming the second largest city within the British Empire. Both cities developed a strong mercantile class and attracted skilled artisans (cabinetmakers, silversmiths, gunsmiths, and the like) and exported grain—the principal commodity of the Middle Colonies, which became the "breadbasket" of colonial America.

Pennsylvania's rapid growth and early economic maturity reflected the astonishing general growth of the colonies. The original "handful" of English settlers had become 250,000 strong by 1700. By 1760, the colonies provided a good livelihood for a population of approximately two million—almost half the population of England. No wonder, then, that trade quadrupled, that banking and currency became important issues, that tradesmen and merchants carried on sophisticated economic practices, that a stable society was formed, and that the American economic system was, finally, sufficiently developed to sustain the shock of political separation from the mother country and to finance a war for independence. All the ingredients of a well-developed, commercial, capitalist economy were present.

4.20 English Regulatory Acts

As the economy of the American provinces matured, a series of **regulatory acts** were passed to prevent foreign commercial competition and the competition of colonial manufactures with those of the mother country. Although restrictions were placed on the tobacco trade as early as the 1620s, a series of enactments passed from 1651 to 1700 laid the actual framework for the English imperial system.

The Navigation Act of 1651 was designed primarily to reduce competition from foreign shipping. It provided that non-European goods brought to England or its possessions could be transported only in English (including colonial) ships, and that goods from the Continent could be brought into England or its possessions only in vessels belonging to the country that had produced the goods. A second Navigation Act (often called the Enumeration Act), passed in 1660, closed the loophole that had permitted colonials to import directly from Europe. It provided that all goods, regardless of origin, could only be imported into or exported from an English colony in English ships. "Enumerated" goods—including sugar, cotton, indigo, dye goods, and tobacco—of colonial origin were to be shipped only to England or its other colonies; they could not be exported directly to other European nations.

The Enumeration Act was particularly hard on Virginia and Maryland, for it meant that colonial tobacco—which the English market could not absorb—had to be shipped to England and then reexported to Continental markets. Re-exportation costs—including handling charges, storage charges, and the costs of frequent loss of tobacco stored in English warehouses—were extremely high. Historians have suggested that the enumeration of tobacco produced an economic depression in Virginia and Maryland in the late seventeenth century and was responsible for the later concentration of land ownership, since only the large-scale producer could handle the disadvantages of the market.

In 1663 a third Navigation Act—the Staple Act—required that most commodities (excluding salt, servants, and wine) imported into the colonies from Europe had to be shipped from England in English-built ships. But the colonists found a loophole. Often ships stopped at several colonial ports before returning to Europe. Colonial merchants would load enumerated goods at one port supposedly designated for a later colonial port; actually the goods would remain on the ship and go directly to Europe.

To close this loophole, a fourth Navigation Act was passed in 1673. It provided that whenever a vessel carried enumerated commodities, a plantation duty—that is, a bond—had to be paid before the ship could clear a colonial port. A final enactment in 1696 provided for the creation of vice-admiralty courts in America, placing the enforcement of the navigation laws in the hands of men appointed directly by the crown. Research indicates that the burden of the Navigation Acts was greater at the end of the seventeenth century than at any other time during the colonial period and that the acts were seldom evaded. Evasion was to come later with the Molasses Act of 1733.

Whereas in the seventeenth century the English regulations were directed principally at commerce, in the eighteenth century, with the maturing of the American economy, the regulations were directed principally at manufactures. The Woolen Act of 1699, which forbade colonial export of wool products, had little impact upon the American colonies because their exportation of textiles was limited anyway. But the Hat Act of 1732—which prohibited exportation of hats from one colony to another and severely restricted the colonial hat industry—adversely affected New York and New England, who had been usurping a vital European market. The act eliminated this colonial enterprise, greatly benefiting London hatters, who had exerted pressure in Parliament to pass the bill.

The Molasses Act of 1733 placed a heavy duty upon sugar, rum, molasses, and other commodities imported into the colonies from the non-British West Indies. This enactment seriously hampered the trade of the American colonies. They had been importing these commodities—molasses in particular—in quantity from Spanish and French colonies at a price cheaper than could be obtained in the British West Indies. Because the act seriously encroached upon this customary channel of trade, the Molasses Act was evaded by extensive smuggling.

The Iron Act of 1750 encouraged the colonial production of pig iron and bar iron for use by the English iron and steel industry, but prohibited the building of slitting mills, forges, and other iron-finishing equipment in the colonies. Certain colonies, notably Pennsylvania, defied the prohibition; and when war broke out between France and England in 1754, the home authorities were unable to enforce the act with vigor. After 1763, of course, the continual crises between the mother country and the colonies prevented effective enforcement of all of the above-mentioned acts.

4.2c Conflict with the Native Americans

Throughout the seventeenth century, there was conflict with the Native Americans, who saw themselves being dispossessed of their land and their way of life. In 1622, for example, the Powhatans, under **Opechancanough**, nearly succeeded in wiping out the new settlement of Jamestown in Virginia. After the English murdered a Powhatan war captain and religious leader, Nemattanew, Chief Opechancanough and the Powhatans waged a war on the white population of Virginia that led to the death of approximately 25 percent of the English population. By the time the armed whites were finally able to subdue the Native Americans, Virginia was bankrupt.

After Opechancanough's revolt, the English adopted a policy of **perpetual enmity** toward the Natives in Virginia and only viewed them as obstacles to English progress that must be eradicated. John Smith was given orders from Captain William Tucker to "root out the Indians from being any longer a people." From England, John Smith wrote that many believed that the orders would be good for the plantations because "now we have just cause to destroy them by all means possible." In 1623, the English invited the Native Americans to a feast in celebration of peace and then served them poisoned wine, thus leading to the death of approximately two hundred natives.

The following decade, 1636–1637, the Puritans fought a bitter war of annihilation against the Pequot Indians. In the **Pequot War**, William Bradford writes that the Puritans burned a native village full of unarmed women and children. Bradford notes that it was "frightful to see the Indians frying in the fire and their blood quenching the same." Then he notes the stench from burning flesh, but credits God with the victory.

From 1636–1637, the Puritans fought a bitter war of annihilation against the Pequot people. The English, trying to eradicate those who had lived on this land first, burned villages full of unarmed women and children. (Wikimedia Commons)

Map 4.1 King Philip's War (1675–1676)

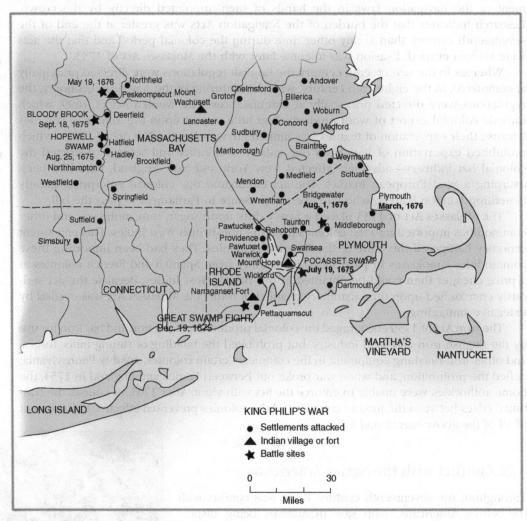

KING PHILIP'S WAR
- ● Settlements attacked
- ▲ Indian village or fort
- ★ Battle sites

0 ——— 30
Miles

King Philip's War

War waged against the Puritans by Chief Metacomet in 1675 that devastated New England before Metacomet was killed and the revolt subdued

Metacomet

Native American leader—also known as "King Philip"—who led the bloody revolt known as King Philip's War against the Puritans in 1675

The next big war between whites and Native Americans in New England occurred in 1675–1676. Known as **King Philip's War**, it entailed fierce fighting along the frontier. By 1671, the Plymouth colonists had forced Native American leader **Metacomet** (referred to as King Philip by the colonists) to surrender the natives' stock of guns and accept a treaty of submission acknowledging English rule. In 1675, a Native American informant was murdered by other Native Americans; the Puritans retaliated by executing three natives who were accused of the murder. The executions sparked a war of retaliation led by Metacomet; the Native American tribes banded together and launched an offensive against their white oppressors, who now had superior numbers and greater technology.

At first, the Native Americans scored resounding victories. Under King Philip, the Native Americans attacked fifty-two of the ninety Puritan towns in the area, completely destroying thirteen of them. In reaction, Massachusetts passed the first military draft law in American history in 1676. With the help of the new draftees, the colonists managed to thwart the Native American offense and had nearly exterminated the Narragansetts, Wampanoags, and Nipmucks by the spring of 1676. King Philip was killed in battle, and his head was on public display in Plymouth for twenty-five years. The conflict left so strong a legacy that one scholar, Mary Beth Norton, has argued that it was a contributing factor in the hysteria about witches that erupted in Salem in 1692. The estimated cost of the war was greater than all the personal property held in New England. Fear of evoking another war with the Native Americans prevented the New England colonists from extending their boundaries any further into native territory for the next forty years.

4.2f Bacon's Rebellion

A serious rebellion in Virginia, **Bacon's Rebellion** was fought among white men. It was precipitated by a belief held by a faction of settlers that they were not receiving enough protection against the natives. Led by a twenty-five-year-old wealthy planter named **Nathaniel Bacon**, five hundred former indentured servants took up arms against the constituted authorities in 1676.

Violence had erupted periodically, in the 1660s and early 1670s, between whites and natives, and then overflowed in the summer of 1675 when a group of frontiersmen attacked and killed a small group of Susquehannocks. In retaliation, the local tribes attacked and killed thirty-six Virginians during the winter of 1675. In turn, the frontiersmen retaliated, under the leadership of Bacon, with a series of attacks on the Native Americans.

Bacon stated that his goals were "not only to ruine and extirpate all Indians in General, but all manner of trade and commerce with them." Bacon also targeted the elite planters, or "**grandees**," who nominally controlled the government for their private gain. In the words of Bacon, "See what spounges have suckt up the Publique Treasure."

Bacon was a cousin of **Governor Berkeley** and demanded that Berkeley appoint him to lead the army. Berkeley refused, pronounced Bacon a rebel, and threatened to punish him for treason. Berkeley then called for new elections of the Virginia House of Burgesses, hoping to purge Bacon's supporters from the legislature. To Berkeley's surprise, however, Bacon's supporters swept the election; Bacon himself was elected to the House of Burgesses.

In June 1676, the Virginia House of Burgesses passed a series of laws known as **Bacon's Laws**. The laws gave landowners a voice in setting tax levies, forbade office-holders from demanding bribes for carrying out their duties, placed limits on the holding of multiple offices, and required officials to have been residents of Virginia for at least three years. The House also declared that all free men could vote (effectively abolishing property requirements).

Bacon followed his legislative success by marching into Jamestown with five hundred armed men and demanding a commission to fight the natives. Faced with overwhelming firepower, Berkeley pardoned Bacon for any wrongdoing, and authorized his military campaign. Thus, Bacon and his army departed to go fight their Native American enemies—but the elite planters complained to Governor Berkeley that Bacon was more dangerous than his targets, and urged the governor to reconsider. Berkeley complied by again charging Bacon with treason and sending three hundred militiamen into the Virginia wilderness to apprehend Bacon. When Bacon learned that he had again been branded a traitor, he declared war against Berkeley and the other grandees and headed into the wilderness to recruit more soldiers. Bacon then waged war against both the natives and Berkeley's forces for three months. Berkeley's militia retaliated by plundering the homes of Bacon's supporters. Both Berkeley and Bacon recruited slaves and indentured servants by promising freedom to them if they joined their cause. Hence, most of Bacon's rebels were discontented indentured servants who desired freedom and land held by Native Americans.

In September 1676, Bacon marched on Jamestown, defeated Berkeley's militia, burned the Statehouse, and forced the governor to flee. Berkeley then sent word of the crisis to England; and the king responded by sending over a thousand troops—though it took three months to get a message to England and to receive the troops back from the king as a reply. In October 1676, before the troops arrived, Bacon died—of either swamp fever or dysentery—and most of his followers disbanded. Berkeley then rounded up twenty-three known Bacon followers and hanged them without a

Pictured is "Bacon's Castle," where Nathaniel Bacon and his fellow rebels stayed during the uprising against the Native Americans and Berkeley's militia. (Wikimedia Commons)

trial. The king launched an investigation into the entire affair, which resulted in the removal of Governor Berkeley. The new governor, installed by the king, subsequently nullified

Bacon's Rebellion

Revolt in 1675 by landless Virginians led by Nathaniel Bacon aimed at taking Native American land and reducing the power of the large land owners, or grandees

Nathaniel Bacon

Leader of Bacon's Rebellion in 1675, who accomplished the goals of gaining Native American land and reducing grandee power, but who died of swamp fever

Grandees

Large land owners in Virginia with political power who supported Governor Berkeley and opposed Bacon's Rebellion

Governor Berkeley

Virginia governor in 1675 who supported the grandees and opposed Bacon's Rebellion

Bacon's Laws

1676 laws passed in the midst of Bacon's Rebellion that gave landowners a voice in setting tax levies, forbade officeholders from demanding bribes for carrying out their duties, placed limits on the holding of multiple offices, and required officials to have been residents of Virginia for at least three years (The House also declared that all free men could vote.)

Pueblo Revolt

A revolt in 1680 of Pueblo Indians against Spanish rule in the area that is now New Mexico, where the Pueblos successfully drove the Spanish out of the territory, only to have them return twelve years later

Bacon's Laws and imposed an export tax on tobacco to pay for all the damages caused by Bacon's Rebellion.

In the end, Bacon's Rebellion secured Native American land for the white settlers, and through the expansion into that land, quelled the divisive land tension between white colonists. A slowdown in immigration to Chesapeake during the 1680s and 1690s, due largely to an improving economy in England, also reduced land pressures and tension.

4.2g The Pueblo Revolt

Finally, although we have been focusing on the English colonies, it should be mentioned that the Spanish Empire was in decline in the seventeenth century, thus diminishing Spain's ability to control its vast holdings. Much of the wealth Spain gained in the New World had been in the form of gold, but this wealth—shipped from the Western Hemisphere to Europe—had the long-term effect of diminishing the value of gold in Europe, due to oversupply. From 1560 to 1648, the Spanish were dealing with revolts against their rule in both the Netherlands and Belgium, which eventually ended with Dutch independence at the close of the Thirty Years War (1648). During that same time, most of western Europe was embroiled in a bloody war between the Protestants and Catholics. The resistance against Spain spread to the periphery; in North America in 1680, the Pueblo Indians (descendants of the Anasazi) staged an uprising called the **Pueblo Revolt** (also known as the Popé's Rebellion) that succeeded in driving the Spanish out of colonial New Mexico for the next thirteen years. Led by the Shaman Popé, villagers from some two dozen pueblos repudiated Christianity and even massacred several hundred Spaniards, driving the remaining two thousand men south along the Rio Grande. The Pueblos were reconquered in the 1690s.

BVT Lab

Visit www.BVTLab.com to explore the student resources available for this chapter.

4.3 Britain Wins Supremacy in North America

4.3a Early Border Conflicts

The shifting balance of power in eighteenth-century Europe—brought about, in part, by the emergence of France and Britain as the major nations of the Western world—produced a ceaseless contest for position in both the Old World and the New. To the English colonials, the strength of New France was a particular danger. French fur traders in the wilderness were capable of stirring up the American Indians to hostility against English traders and settlers—who were beginning to penetrate the transmontane region—and French control over the interior threatened to curb the westward expansion of the English colonies in America. The French, however, also had a problem in that the French population in North America in 1690 was only twelve thousand, as compared to two hundred thousand English—and the French were scattered from Quebec to the Gulf of Mexico.

The growth of both French and English ambitions in the New World led to protracted wars between the two in that same territory. The French and British were at war for nineteen of the twenty-four years spanning 1689 to 1713—King William's War (1689–1697) and Queen Anne's War (1702–1713). The War of the Spanish Succession—or Queen Anne's War, as it is known in America—saw conflict between the British colonists and both Spanish and French forces.

The British colonists had also been heavily involved in the English war effort in Massachusetts during King William's War—in which the French attacked New England, proving to the colonists that British military protection was necessary for their security. Of the able-bodied men in Massachusetts, 20 percent participated in the war; the death rate for colonial soldiers was 25 percent. The war debts incurred by the colony of Massachusetts (£50,000) exceeded the colony's GDP. The war left numerous widows and orphans in its wake, and left Massachusetts with a war ravaged economy. As a consequence, the New England economy would not rebound for a generation. Nevertheless, the war ended with a British victory; the Peace of Utrecht officially ended Queen Anne's War in 1713, and the British gained Newfoundland and Nova Scotia, along with the

Hudson Bay Territory (Ontario), from the French. The British takeover of these areas eventually caused an outmigration of French inhabitants who did not desire to be ruled by the British. In 1754, after two generations of trying unhappily to live under British rule, flotillas of refugees left French Acadia (Nova Scotia) for New Orleans (which was still possessed by France). The locals misunderstood the Acadians when they arrived in New Orleans, due to differences in dialect, and the "Acadians" became known as **Cajuns**.

4.3b King George's War

In 1739, Great Britain attacked Spain in a conflict that soon merged with the War of the Austrian Succession, or **King George's War** (1744–1748). Believing that the time was ripe to neutralize French power in Canada, the governor of Massachusetts organized a force of militia. In one of the most audacious—and lucky—episodes in the colonial wars, the Americans captured a fort on Cape Breton Island known as Louisbourg on June 17, 1745. In 1748, however, the British returned the fortress to the French in exchange for Madras, India.

4.3c Start of the Great War for Empire

The French now showed a greater determination than ever to hold Canada and the Ohio and Mississippi valleys. In furtherance of their goals, they erected blockhouses to fortify the Ohio and Allegheny river valleys against the British.

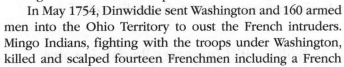

In the meantime, planters from Virginia and Maryland had organized the Ohio Company to exploit virgin lands as far west as the present site of Louisville, Kentucky. In 1753, to prevent these western lands from falling into the possession of the French, the governor of Virginia sent George Washington—a young surveyor—into the Ohio Valley to remonstrate with the French commander. George Washington delivered a letter from the Royal Governor of Virginia, **Robert Dinwiddie**, to a French outpost near Lake Erie, warning the French that they were intruding on Virginia land. Washington returned with a scornful reply from the French, as well as military intelligence about France's positions.

Royal Governor of Virginia, Robert Dinwiddie (Wikimedia Commons)

In May 1754, Dinwiddie sent Washington and 160 armed men into the Ohio Territory to oust the French intruders. Mingo Indians, fighting with the troops under Washington, killed and scalped fourteen Frenchmen including a French commander—a massacre unintended by Washington. Washington knew there would be a French retaliation and quickly assembled a fort called **Fort Necessity**, built in just one week, in an indefensible position. Washington received two hundred reinforcements, but his Native American allies abandoned the colonists and instead helped the French, who attacked the Fort in July 1754. A third of Washington's men were killed or wounded in the battle and Washington was forced to surrender. The French then sent Washington back to the Virginia governor with the message that the French would not depart from the disputed territory. Thus began the conflict that was to develop into the **French and Indian War**, a war that would explode in Europe as the

On June 17, 1745, the Americans—in one of the most daring episodes of the colonial wars—captured Louisbourg, a fort on Cape Breton Island. (Wikimedia Commons, Tango7174)

Seven Years War (1756–1763), allying England and Prussia against France, Austria, and Spain. In 1754, England and France each dispatched three thousand troops into the New World and charged them with securing their colonial territory.

Cajuns
French Acadians from Nova Scotia who immigrated to the province of New Orleans in 1754 in order to escape British rule (The word "Acadian" was misunderstood by the locals in New Orleans as "Cajun.")

King George's War
A War for Empire between the British and French (1744–1748) in which the British tried unsuccessfully to oust the French from North America

Robert Dinwiddie
Virginia governor who sent young George Washington to order the French to withdraw from Virginia at the outset of the French and Indian War

Fort Necessity
A fort hastily built by George Washington and his men and subsequently surrendered to the French at the outset of the Seven Years War

French and Indian War
The final War for Empire between Britain and France (1754–1763) that resulted in the end of French influence in North America

4.3d Albany Congress

With the danger of an Indian war threatening the whole frontier, the colonies were particularly concerned with counterbalancing the Native Americans allied with the French. To conciliate the powerful Iroquois, who had given invaluable support to the English in the past, the British government called a conference in Albany, New York, comprised of commissioners from seven different colonies. This **Albany Congress** was more important for its political proposals than for its few accomplishments in dealing with the disaffected Iroquois.

Because the delegates realized that a closer union of the colonies was needed to provide better collective defense and control of Native American affairs, they listened attentively to the **Plan of Union** put forward by one of Pennsylvania's leading citizens, Benjamin Franklin. Franklin's proposals would have brought all of the colonies under "one general government" with an executive and legislature, but with each colony retaining its separate existence and government. Ben Franklin's plan for a union of the colonies could not be agreed upon by the seven colonies. Although all agreed a union for defense was needed, none could agree on the actual form. Thus, no colony gave the plan serious consideration, and the British government disregarded it altogether. The Iroquois left the conference with thirty wagonloads of gifts, but never committed to help the English.

4.3e Fort Duquesne, 1755

Because they engaged in more trade with the French, the Iroquois initially helped them rather than the English. To protect the colonies, the British government sent two regiments of regulars and a British fleet, but the French and American Indians routed the British army under General Edward Braddock. In an attempt to dislodge the French from **Fort Duquesne**—a strategic position that controlled the upper Ohio Valley—a detachment of regulars and colonial militia under British General Edward Braddock marched toward the fort; but they were ambushed and routed by French and American Indian forces. Almost half of the two thousand British were killed, including Braddock. Washington narrowly escaped, having two horses shot out from underneath him, but the young soldier survived. With the loss of Braddock, young Washington was given the responsibility of protecting more than three hundred miles of the Virginia frontier against incursions by Native American and French marauders. The year 1755 was a period of almost unrelieved misfortune for the British; and for the next two or three years the war raged intermittently and disastrously along the whole frontier, with the French under Marquis de Montcalm winning a succession of victories in the north.

4.3f William Pitt Increases British Resolve

By 1757, the British had not accomplished their objectives. French Canada, with only seventy thousand inhabitants, was winning the war against the British colonies even though they were endowed with a population nearly twenty times larger. In 1757, **William Pitt**, who was determined to break the French resistance in the New World, became the British prime minister. Pitt realized that part of the trouble in America lay in the incompetence of Britain's officers. To remedy this, he ordered to America fresh troops under a new command. He also won more wholehearted cooperation from the American provincials by promising that Britain would reimburse the individual colonies for their war expenditures.

Pitt dispatched 23,000 new British army troops to North America in 1757 and 1758, along with a naval force of 14,000. Pitt also altered British strategy to focus on cutting off French trade with the natives. Pitt correctly surmised that if Iroquois' trade were disrupted, the Iroquois would likely change sides. The overwhelming force of the British army was successful in defeating the French in several major battles in 1758, resulting in British control of the St. Lawrence River. With British control of the St. Lawrence, the Iroquois were effectively cut off from French trade goods, thus convincing them to change sides and aid the English. With the Iroquois on their side, the British took Fort Duquesne from the French in 1758. In 1759, the Iroquois helped the English defeat the French at Forts Niagara and Ticonderoga.

4.3g The Capture of Quebec

The victory that finally decided the issue in Canada came on September 13, 1759, when British General James Wolfe led a successful attack on **Quebec**—which had been under siege since late June. General Wolfe's five thousand men scaled a rocky cliff and surprised the French, defeating them on the Plains of Abraham after taunting them out of their impenetrable fort. The capture of Quebec sealed the fate of France in North America. The British took Montreal in 1760; and the war continued in the Caribbean until 1763, when it was finally settled with the Peace of Paris.

Elsewhere—in Europe and India—British arms were also victorious; France could do nothing but capitulate. In 1762 France ceded Louisiana to Spain in recompense for aid in the war and a year later, by the Treaty of Paris, ceded to Great Britain all of Canada except the tiny Islands of St. Pierre and Miquelon. Paradoxically, the very magnitude of the British victory paved the way for the disintegration of the British Empire in America.

4.3h Proclamation of 1763

In order to have good relations with the American Indian tribes, the English issued the Proclamation of 1763, in which England reserved all land west of the Appalachians to the American Indians, and all whites living west of the Appalachians were ordered to withdraw. The Proclamation of 1763 failed miserably. Neither England nor the colonies had the resources necessary for its enforcement, and whites west of the Appalachians refused to pull up and move east.

With help from the Iroquois, the English defeated the French at Forts Niagara and Ticonderoga. (Wikimedia Commons, Mwanner)

> **Quebec**
>
> The French colony in North America that was taken by the British in the Seven Years War

4.3i Ramifications of the Seven Years War

The ramifications of the Seven Years War were immense. Although the French would later temporarily gain the land between the Mississippi River and the Rocky Mountains from Spain, they would quickly sell the territory to the United States in 1803, after which the French were never again to be a colonial force in North America.

The long and costly war also had major economic ramifications. The war left England and the colonies with massive debt; and the booming, wartime colonial economy was followed by an economic recession. There were huge human casualties in the colonies (especially in New England), resulting in a sex imbalance in New England (women outnumbered men) and an overabundance of widows and orphans.

The war also had major political ramifications, as the colonial legislatures gained power at the expense of colonial governors. During the war, governors were forced to make numerous concessions to the legislatures in efforts to gain legislative support for the British war effort. The war also left the colonies replete with a generation of seasoned military veterans who would be less averse to taking up arms later when they believed their livelihood was threatened. Additionally, the colonies gained a sense of national identity through working together in the war against the French. Finally, France was no longer a security threat to the colonies, and therefore the colonists no longer viewed English military protection in the colonies as necessary. When the British Crown would insist that the colonists do their part to support the British military, the colonists would therefore resist.

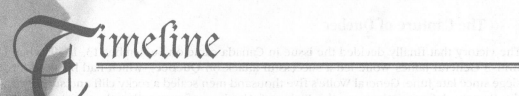

Timeline

1622	—	Opechancanough's revolt
1636–1637	—	Pequot War in New England
1640–1660	—	Political unrest and civil war in England
1651	—	Navigation Act
1660	—	Second Navigation Act (Enumeration Act)
1663	—	Third Navigation Act (Staple Act)
1673	—	Fourth Navigation Act
1675	—	Lords of Trade is created.
1675–1676	—	Bacon's Rebellion in Virginia
	—	King Philip's War in New England
1680	—	Pueblo Revolt
1686	—	Lords of Trade creates the Dominion of New England.
1688	—	Glorious Revolution elevates the power of Parliament in England.
1689–1697	—	King William's War
1696	—	Lords of Trade is replaced by the Board of Trade.
	—	Creation of vice-admiralty courts in America to place enforcement of navigation laws in the hands of men appointed directly by the crown
1699	—	The Woolen Act forbade colonial export of wool products.
1702–1713	—	Queen Anne's War
1713	—	Peace of Utrecht
1732	—	Hat Act prohibited exportation of hats from one colony to another.
1733	—	Molasses Act placed a heavy duty upon sugar, rum, molasses, and other commodities imported into the colonies from the non-British West Indies.
1740–1744	—	King George's War
1750	—	The Iron Act encouraged the colonial production of pig and bar iron for use by the English iron and steel industry.
1754	—	Acadians leave Nova Scotia for New Orleans.
	—	George Washington is defeated by the French at Fort Necessity.
1754–1763	—	French and Indian War
1755	—	George Washington and General Edward Braddock are defeated near Fort Duquesne by the French.
1756	—	William Pitt becomes prime minister.
1758–1759	—	British take Forts Duquesne, Niagara, and Ticonderoga.
1759	—	British capture Quebec
1760	—	British capture Montreal
1763	—	Peace of Paris: France cedes French possessions in North America to England.
	—	Proclamation of 1763 orders white settlers to return east of the Appalachians.

CHAPTER SUMMARY

English administration of its colonies in North America was slow to develop, beginning with the King's Privy Council, progressing through the Lords of Trade in 1675 to Board of Trade in 1696, and culminating with rule by Parliament after the Glorious Revolution of 1688. The colonies in North America also had their own governing structures that included royal governors, who were representatives of the king; colonial councils, which served as the upper houses of the legislatures as well as the high courts; and colonial assemblies, which were elected by freemen—though there were normally property requirements for voting. The members of the colonial councils were members of the elite class and often appointed by the King, whereas members of the assemblies represented the common people in the colonies.

The American provincial economy emerged from its agricultural base with a new emphasis on trade, production for market, and eventually, regional specialization. In New England, shipping merchants gradually gained a position of economic and political primacy; artisans who repaired canvas and built vessels, and farmers who exported meat products, were also important. For labor, New Englanders depended largely on members of their own families, though they sometimes hired local servants or imported indentured ones. In the Southern Colonies, plantation agriculture developed using primarily African slave labor and indentured servants. In the Middle Colonies, grain agriculture developed along with artisanship and international shipping. Philadelphia became the second largest city in the British Empire. A series of English Regulatory Acts, or Navigation Acts, between 1651 and 1700 were designed to prevent foreign commercial competition and the competition of colonial manufactures with those of the mother country.

Throughout the seventeenth century, there was bloody conflict between the colonists and the Native Americans. In Virginia, Opechancanough's revolt in 1622 resulted in perpetual enmity between the English and the Native Americans, while five decades later in 1675, land pressures in Virginia led to Bacon's Rebellion—and another Native American defeat. Meanwhile, in New England, Puritans burned entire Native American villages in the Pequot War of 1637 and put down the bloody Native American revolt led by Metacomet in King Philip's War (1675–1676). The English, however, were not the only Europeans to find themselves in disputes with the Native Americans, as the Spanish suffered heavy losses and found themselves expelled from territory they claimed in the Southwest during the Pueblo Revolt of 1680.

In the eighteenth century, the British found themselves involved in wars for empire with France, including Queen Anne's War, King George's War, and the Seven Years War. Finally, in 1763, the French were expelled from North America by the British and would never again be a colonial force in North America. The British were left in debt, despite their victory; and the colonists would not be inclined to help pay—especially with France no longer a threat in North America.

KEY TERMS

BIBLIOGRAPHY

A

Anderson, Fred. *Crucible of War: The Seven Years War and the Fate of the British Empire in North America 1754–1766*. New York: Vintage, 2001.

Andrews, Pat. *Voices of Diversity*. Guilford, CT: Dushkin, 1993.

B

Bailyn, Bernard. *The Origins of American Politics*. New York: Vintage, 1970.

Brewer, John. *The Sinews of Power: War, Money, and the English State 1688–1783*. Cambridge, MA: Harvard University Press, 1990.

Brinkley, Alan. *American History: A Survey*. 11th ed. Boston, MA: McGraw-Hill, 2003.

Bushman, Richard L. *The Refinement of America: Persons, Houses, Cities*. New York: Vintage, 1993.

C

Calhoun, Robert. *Revolutionary America: An Interpretive Overview*. New York: Harcourt Brace, 1976.

Colden, Cadwallader. *The Letters and Papers of Cadwallader Colden*. New York: AMS Press, 1973.

Countryman, Edward. *The American Revolution: Revised Edition*. New York: Hill and Wang, 2003.

Cremin, Lawrence A. *American Education: The Colonial Experience 1607–1783*. New York: HarperCollins, 1970.

Cross, Barbara M., Ed. *The Autobiography of Lyman Beecher*. Cambridge, MA: Harvard University Press, 1961.

D

Dickerson, Oliver Morton. *American Colonial Government 1696–1795*. Charleston, SC: Nabu Press, 2011.

Drake, Samuel Adams. *The Border Wars of New England, Commonly Called King William's and Queen Anne's Wars*. Charleston, SC: BiblioLife, 2009.

E

Eccles, W. J. *France in America*. East Lansing, MI: Michigan State University Press, 1990.

Ellis, George W., and John E. Morriss. *King Philip's War*. Scituate, MA: Digital Scanning, 2001.

H

Hirschman, Albert O. *The Passions and the Interests: Political Arguments for Capitalism before its Triumph*. Princeton, NJ: Princeton University Press, 1997.

Hoeveler, David J. *Creating the American Mind: Intellect and Politics in the Colonial Colleges*. Lanham, MD: Rowman and Littlefield, 2007.

J

Jennings, Francis. *Empire of Fortune: Crowns, Colonies, and Tribes in the Seven Years' War in America*. New York: W. W. Norton & Company, 1990.

Jernegan, Marcus Wilson. *Laboring and Dependent Classes in Colonial America 1607–1783*. Westport, CT: Greenwood Press, 1980.

Jordan, Winthrop. *White over Black: American Attitudes toward the Negro 1550–1812*. Chapel Hill, NC: University of North Carolina Press, 1968.

K

Kopperman, Paul E. *Braddock at the Monogahela*. Pittsburgh, PA: University of Pittsburgh Press, 2003.

L

Labaree, Leonard Woods. *Conservatism in Early American History*. Ithaca, NY: Great Seal Books, 1948.

———. *Royal Instructions to British Colonial Governors, 1670–1776*. New York: D. Appleton-Century, 1935.

M

Marston, Daniel. *The Seven Years War*. New York: Osprey, 2001.

McCusker, John J. and Russell R. Menard. *The Economy of British America 1607–1789*. Chapel Hill, NC: University of North Carolina Press, 1991.

Morgan, Edmund S. *American Slavery, American Freedom: The Ordeal of Colonial Virginia*. New York: W. W. Norton & Company, 2003.

———. *Inventing the People: The Rise of Popular Sovereignty in England and America*. New York: W. W. Norton & Company, 1989.

Murrin, John R., Paul E. Johnson, James M. McPherson, Gary Gerstle, Emily S. Rosenberg, and Norman L. Rosenberg. *Liberty, Equality, Power: A History of the American People*. Fort Worth, TX: Harcourt Brace, 1996.

N

Nash, Gary B., Julie Roy Jeffrey, John R. Howe, Peter J. Frederick, Allen F. Davis, and Allan M. Winkler. *The American People: Creating a Nation and a Society*. 4th ed. New York: Longman, 1998.

Newbold, Robert C. *The Albany Congress and Plan of Union 1754*. New York: Vantage Press, 1954.

O

O'Sullivan, John, and Edward F. Keuchel. *American Economic History: From Abundance to Constraint*. New York: Markus Wiener, 1989.

BIBLIOGRAPHY

P

Patterson, Orlando. *Slavery and Social Death. A Comparative Study*. Cambridge, MA: Harvard University Press, 1985.

Peckham, Howard H. *The Colonial Wars*. Chicago, IL: University of Chicago Press, 1965.

———. *Pontiac and the Indian Uprising*. Detroit, MI: Wayne State University Press, 1994.

Phillips, Leon. *The Fantastic Breed: Americans in King George's War*. New York: Doubleday, 1968.

Pocock, Tom. *The Very First World War 1756–1763*. London: Michael O'Mara, 1999.

R

Reid, Stuart. *King George's Army 1740–1793*. New York: Osprey Publishing, 1995.

Russell, David Lee. *Oglethorpe and Colonial Georgia: A History 1733–1783*. Jefferson, NC: McFarland Press, 2006.

Rink, Oliver. *Holland on the Hudson. An Economic and Social History of Dutch New York*. Ithaca, NY: Cornell University Press, 1989.

Roberts, David. *The Pueblo Revolt: The Secret Rebellion that Drove the Spaniards Out of the Southwest*. New York: Simon and Schuster, 2005.

S

Saunders, William L., Ed. *The Colonial Records of North Carolina*. Temecula, CA: Reprint Services Corporation, 1999.

Stanard, Mary Mann Page. *The Story of Bacon's Rebellion*. Toronto: University of Toronto Libraries, 2011.

Stanard, William G. and Mary N. Stanard. *The Colonial Virginia Register*. Albany, NY: Joel Munsell's Sons, 1902.

U

Ubbelodhe, Carl. *American Colonies and the British Empire, 1607–1783*. Arlington Heights, IL: Harlan Davidson, 1975.

Ulrich, Laurel Thatcher. *Good Wives: Image and Reality in the Lives of Women in Northern New England 1650–1750*. New York: Vintage, 1991.

W

Ward, W. Reginold. *The Protestant Evangelical Awakening*. Cambridge, UK. Cambridge University Press, 2002.

Webb, Stephen S. *The Governors General: The English Army and the Definition of Empire, 1569–1681*. Chapel Hill, NC: University of North Carolina Press, 1987.

Weir, Robert. *Colonial South Carolina: A History*. Columbia, SC: University of South Carolina Press, 1997.

Wright, Louis B. *The First Gentlemen of Virginia: Intellectual Qualities of the Early Colonial Ruling Class*. Charlottesville, VA: University of Virginia Press, 1970.

Y

Yazawa, Melvin, Ed. *Diary and Life of Samuel Sewall*. New York: St. Martin's Press, 1998.

POP QUIZ

1. The Lords of Trade established the Dominion of New England with the goal of _____.
   a. granting greater local autonomy to the colonists
   b. centralizing the authority of the Crown
   c. ridding New England of witches
   d. abolishing slavery in New England

2. Which of the following was typically a duty of the colonial assemblies?
   a. initiating legislation
   b. executing the laws
   c. acting as the highest court of appeal
   d. all of the above

3. Duties of the sheriff included which of the following?
   a. clearing the forests of men who robbed from the rich and gave to the poor
   b. enforcing the law
   c. collecting taxes
   d. both b and c

4. In eighteenth century New England, how did the land system change?
   a. Only church groups were granted land.
   b. Only secular groups were granted land.
   c. People of means began to buy large blocks of land for speculative purposes, selling off smaller parcels to individuals.
   d. Land was given to individual yeoman farmers who would work the land.

5. Which of the following was true under the headright system?
   a. A planter could obtain fifty acres of land for each dependent or servant brought to the colonies.
   b. A planter could obtain fifty acres of land from those who did not have their "headright" (i.e., suffered from mental illness).
   c. A planter could obtain any land he wanted, simply by firing a gun and heading right for it.
   d. A planter could obtain fifty acres of land if he had his head right and supported the Anglican church.

6. In the seventeenth century, why couldn't a merchant group develop in the Southern Colonies?
   a. The Southerners were ignorant of the navigational skills necessary for sea voyages to England.
   b. The Southerners sold directly to English merchants.
   c. Southerners sought self-sufficiency and opposed trade with England.
   d. All of the above

7. Under the Hat Act of 1732, which of the following was true?
   a. Hats could be exported only to England.
   b. Hats could be purchased only from England.
   c. Hats could not be exported from one colony to another.
   d. Hats could no longer be worn in the colonies.

8. Which of the following is true of King Philip's War?
   a. The war was an easy victory for the colonists.
   b. King Philip of Britain lost his head on the battlefield.
   c. The Indians were hindered in the war by their inability to make fire.
   d. The war was so costly for the colonists that they did not expand to take any more Indian land in New England for forty years.

9. Which of the following were included in Bacon's Laws?
   a. Laws that gave landholders a voice in tax levies
   b. Laws that limited voting rights to property owners
   c. Laws that allowed the governor to hold multiple offices
   d. Laws that made it legal for public officials to accept bribes to perform their duties

10. In King George's War in 1745, the American colonists captured _____.
    a. Cape Breton Island
    b. Greenland
    c. Quebec
    d. Jacques Le Bleu

11. What occurred near Fort Duquesne in 1755?
    a. The French scored a resounding victory against British troops led by General Edward Braddock and George Washington.
    b. The French defeated the British with the result that George Washington was given command of all British troops.
    c. British troops led by General Edward Braddock and George Washington scored a resounding victory against the French.
    d. British and French troops fought to a stalemate before both armies withdrew.

12. Colonial merchants could trade freely with nations other than England. T   F

13. The French were the biggest winners in the French and Indian War. T   F

14. The Glorious Revolution of 1688 drove _____ from the throne.

15. Another name for the French and Indian War was the _____ _____ _____.

Chapter 5

(Wikimedia Commons)

Revolution and Independence, 1763–1783

CHAPTER OUTLINE

5.1 Background of the Revolution

5.1a The Character of the Revolution

The American Revolution was the first of its kind in modern times. Even more remarkably, it was founded on the principles of self-government and the protection of individual liberty. Because of this, it became a beacon—lighting the way for people the world over.

Although it is often thought of in terms of "the Americans versus the British," the American Revolution was, in fact, many-sided. It was the War for Independence in which the colonies fought for separation from the strongest nation in the world—Great Britain—but it was also a civil war, one in which Englishmen fought Englishmen and colonials fought colonials. It was part of a world war fought in two hemispheres and involved not only the United States and England but also France and Spain. It involved a struggle for power within each colony, pitting Patriots against Loyalists and elites against commoners. Additionally, it was a nationalist movement that inspired the colonies (after separating from Britain) to form a lasting union—a monumental event that Americans today take for granted, though it was not necessarily predestined. Although the purpose of the Revolution was not to establish a democracy—any more than it was to establish a union—one of the results of the struggle was a greater political voice for the average white, male American.

Finally, it should be remembered that this first modern revolt—the American colonies against Britain—occurred under the most enlightened and least burdensome imperial system in Europe at that time. The whites who lived in English colonies then enjoyed far more privileges in every sphere of life than did their counterparts in French and Spanish colonies.

Why were the least restricted colonials the first to revolt? The American colonials had enjoyed certain liberties for a century or more; and they had no intention of seeing these liberties restricted—even if, comparatively, they were better off than colonials elsewhere. They also did not want to pay taxes to a government located so far away, especially not one in which they believed they were inadequately represented. Although the Revolution was not inevitable, any action to limit existing privileges naturally produced friction. How much friction would build depended upon the course of events to follow and the responses made by American colonials and British authorities.

BVT *Lab*

Flashcards are available for this chapter at www.BVTLab.com.

5.1b Early Provocations and Crises

The crises within the empire from 1763 to 1776 were provoked by a series of specific enactments, but to review the prelude to revolution in such narrow terms is to misconstrue the essential issues that were in dispute. An adjustment in the relationship between Britain and its colonies was made inevitable by several sweeping changes that had occurred throughout the eighteenth century.

The colonial and commercial systems of Britain had been established in the seventeenth century and were based on the mercantilist theory—already several centuries old—which viewed a colony's importance primarily in terms of the wealth that could be extracted from it. During the course of the eighteenth century, colonies gained importance for the role they played in British commerce. Moreover, when the system was inaugurated, England possessed few colonies. After the Peace of 1763, Britain had more than thirty colonies scattered throughout the world, each with its own individual characteristics. Did the policies initiated in the 1660s suit conditions in the colonies in the 1760s? Could the same system be applied to such diverse locations as India and Massachusetts?

Even before the specific crises that occurred between 1763 and 1776, British-colonial relationships were in need of adjustment to meet new and changing realities. Three major changes were clearly evident. First, the American colonies had matured, from the early days of Jamestown, to become bustling commercial and agricultural successes. Second, the political transition in England, by which **Parliament** had steadily gained power at the expense of the crown, required a redefinition of relationships within the empire. Third, the colonies in the New World had become a critical factor in the European balance of power.

By 1760 the British colonies in America were no longer infants, dependent solely upon the protection of the mother country. From limited self-government to mature self-government; from inexperience to experience with authority; from a primitive to a complex, well-developed indigenous economy—this had been the course of the American colonies. Any imperial system that failed to recognize these realities was doomed.

As it existed, the imperial system had become, in many ways, an anachronism. The American provinces had transformed into an insatiable market for British goods, but the British system failed to adjust to this fact. The American colonies required a more

Map 5.1 North America After the Treaty of Paris (1763)

enlightened money and banking policy, but the British continued to use outdated theories. The American colonies produced statesmen, and even geniuses, but most American talent went unacknowledged.

The political transition in England required a rethinking of the constitutional structure of the empire. The colonies had been established under the auspices of royal charters. They had been administered through the king, the executive authority. As Parliament assumed greater authority, fundamental questions arose. Did Parliament have unlimited legislative supremacy over the colonies? Did Parliament gain the executive power previously exercised by the crown? The home authorities said yes, but American colonials said no. Moreover, the Industrial Revolution of the eighteenth century in England introduced new problems with regard to mercantile theories—notably the importance of colonies as a market—that were never resolved.

During the eighteenth century, the Spanish, French, and British colonies in the New World had become increasingly critical factors in the European balance of power. Beginning particularly with the Peace of Utrecht in 1713, the European powers attempted to establish equilibrium in that balance. The scales were clearly tipped in England's favor by the Peace of Paris in 1763, however, when Britain acquired New France in North America as well as French possessions elsewhere in the world.

These British acquisitions created uneasiness and uncertainty throughout western Europe, and France began to explore avenues to redress the balance of power. Soon after 1763, the French saw an opportunity to even the score—not by recapturing lost colonies or by capturing British colonies, but by encouraging a separation between Britain and its colonies in America. This is what inspired French intervention in 1778, on behalf of the Americans.

Any one of these major changes in the eighteenth century—the maturation of the colonies, the political and economic transformation in Britain, the changes in the balance of power in North America—would have inevitably produced problems in the relationship between England and the colonies. Together, these changes were powerful enough to inspire a revolution.

Map 5.2 Territorial Growth 1775

Boundary between Mississippi River and
49th parallel uncertain due to misconception that
source of Mississippi River lay further north

5.1c The Constitutional Issue

As mentioned previously, the British and the American colonials had differing ideas about the constitutional structure of the empire. The British assumed that the self-government practiced by the separate colonies was a privilege granted by the mother country—which could at any time be enlarged, curtailed, or even eliminated. The ultimate authority rested in Britain. Under this view, the colonies possessed no power except that granted by English authorities.

The colonials, on the other hand, held that self-government rested upon the consent of the governed (the colonial electorate)—not upon royal grace and favor. The Americans believed that they possessed rights (at first called the Rights of Englishmen, later called American Rights) that Britain could in no way curtail. Each colonial assembly viewed itself as struggling against a royal governor (and thus against the king), much like the House of Commons in its struggle to gain power at the king's expense.

During the Seven Years War, the colonial assemblies gained power—in relation to the colonial governors—as a result of their roles in extracting taxation from the colonists. Governors were unable to collect the necessary taxes without assistance from the colonial assemblies. The assemblies would only agree to provide assistance, however, if the governors conceded some of their power.

The rising power of Parliament, along with the rising power of the colonial assemblies, posed an additional question: What were the limits to the legislative power of Parliament over the colonies? Conflict on this point was inevitable, and it became a critical issue in the revolutionary crisis that developed.

5.1b Constitutional Confrontations

During the French and Indian War, several British policies annoyed the American provincials. In 1759 the Privy Council instructed the governor of Virginia to refuse to sign any bill that failed to include a "suspending clause"—that is, a clause preventing the act from becoming effective until it had been approved by English authorities. In 1761, general **writs of assistance** empowered officers of the British customs service to break into and search homes and stores for smuggled goods (goods that had been brought to the colonies by colonial merchants who failed to pay British customs duties). This provoked strong opposition from the provincials, who claimed that the writs were contrary to law and to the natural rights of men. In that same year, the Privy Council prohibited the issuance in New York and New Jersey of judicial commissions with unlimited tenure, specifying that such commissions must always be subject to revocation by the king—even though, in England, judges no longer held their posts at the king's pleasure. In 1764, the **Currency Act** extended, to all colonies, the restrictions on the issuance of paper money that previously had applied only to Massachusetts. All colonists would now have to pay British merchants in gold or silver, thus severely diminishing colonial buying power in an economy that was already in recession following the Seven Years War.

5.1c Problems of Defense and Western Lands

The Peace of Paris of 1763 eliminated the French threat to English expansion on the North American continent, and made available to English colonials opportunities in the West (west of the Appalachians, primarily the Ohio Valley) that had been denied them for a quarter century. However, the Peace of Paris raised problems with regard to the administration and distribution of this newly available land. It also raised the issue of how to raise the necessary revenue to pay the cost of administering the ever-growing empire. Most important, the Peace of Paris, by eliminating the French threat, made the American provincials bolder in stating their views since they no longer felt that they needed English protection against the French. Once they had adopted a position, the colonists became more resolute in holding it.

One of the principal problems faced by the British was the settlement of the territory west of the Alleghenies. The issue was complicated by a revolt—**Pontiac's Rebellion, 1763**—of western Native Americans under the leadership of Pontiac, chief of the Ottawa tribe. Farms and villages along the whole of the colonial frontier, from Canada to Virginia, were laid to waste. The uprising was put down largely by British troops, but the problem of future defense assumed great importance. The incident was compounded by a previous policy of appointing a commander in chief for America, the fact that the British now controlled a French Canadian population that did not desire British rule, and the fact that the British viewed the American colonies as unruly (an image fostered by incidents like the Boston Impressment Riot of 1747). Taken together, these factors produced a major decision on the part of the British: to quarter ten thousand British regulars on the American mainland and in the West Indies.

However well-intentioned, this action met with stern provincial resistance. Americans who had faced the French threat at close quarters for a century could not understand why British troops were needed now, after the French menace had been eliminated. Ill will between the British Redcoats and the colonials increased the tension, especially in New York (after 1765) and in Boston (after 1768), where the troops were stationed. Moreover, the colonials were not accustomed to the accepted British practice of expecting the people who were being "defended" to quarter the troops. **The Quartering Act of 1765**, which required New York colonials to house the soldiers and to make supplies available, was bitterly resented. It should be noted that the British never actually intended for the colonists to quarter the British army in private homes, except as a last resort. Instead, the British expected the colonists to fund and build barracks for the troops. The threat of quartering soldiers in private homes was intended as motivation for the colonists to build more appropriate accommodations. Instead, the Quartering Act provided colonial revolutionaries with a clear symbol of British oppression.

Writs of assistance
Empowered officers of the British customs service to break into and search homes and stores for smuggled goods

Currency Act, 1764
Required that the colonists discontinue issuance of paper currency and that all British merchants must be paid in specie

Pontiac's Rebellion, 1763
A bloody, Native American revolt in the West in 1763, put down by the British

The Quartering Act of 1765
Required that the colonists provide housing and supplies for British troops

In 1763, the Native Americans in the West revolted under the leadership of Pontiac. This caused problems for the British, who wished to settle the territory west of the Alleghenies. (Images.com)

Map 5.3 Proclamation of 1763

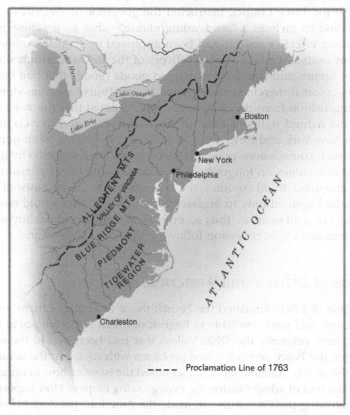

---- Proclamation Line of 1763

The solution to the problem of western lands beyond the Appalachians was equally irritating. If the westernmost colonies (like Pennsylvania, New York, Virginia, and the Carolinas) were permitted to extend their boundaries further, colonies without a hinterland (like Connecticut, Rhode Island, New Jersey, and Maryland) would be placed at a disadvantage. Should new colonies, therefore, be formed in the territory beyond the Appalachians?

The answer formulated by the British government was the **Royal Proclamation Line of 1763**, which established a line along the crest of the Appalachians, west of which colonials could not take up land. This policy of delay seemed sensible in London, but the colonials were impatient to take advantage of the new territory. Virginians had specifically fought in the French and Indian War to open this area for settlement. Not only were frontiersmen eager to exploit these opportunities, but land companies in Pennsylvania, Virginia, and New England—whose membership included both affluent colonials and Englishmen—wished to act. For these men, the Proclamation Line was a disappointment and an unexpected barrier to enterprise and opportunity.

The Proclamation Line, intended originally as a temporary measure to gain time for a permanent policy, was not revoked before the Revolution. Meanwhile, the Quebec Act of 1774 further annoyed the provincials by annexing the western lands north of the Ohio River to the Province of Quebec. The former French colony, viewed by the colonials as the enemy, was to be rewarded, while the faithful colonists—who had fought to free that territory from French control—were denied the fruits of their labor.

The problems of distributing western lands and defending a growing empire did not directly bring about a revolution, but these issues did cause a lingering resentment. When added to the other irritations of British rule, they decreased the probability of a compromise and increased feelings of hostility.

5.1f Aftermath of the Seven Years War

The Seven Years War not only effectively redrew the map of North America and eliminated France as a major colonial power in that region, it also had an immense and lasting political and economic impact on the British colonies in the New World. The war had produced an economic boom in the colonies as American merchants were awarded contracts to outfit the British military with ships, arms, uniforms, shoes, and food. When some thirty thousand British troops departed from North America, however, an economic recession and accompanying unemployment followed as the war orders ceased.

During the war, colonial governments licensed American privateers (legally commissioned pirates) to attack and seize French shipping, often at great profits to the privateers. For example, John MacPherson seized eighteen French ships through privateering in 1758, and profited enough that he purchased an estate near Philadelphia for £14,000. With the close of the war, this lucrative but dangerous business would cease. All colonists who served in the war had not been so fortunate, however. To illustrate the point, the 1764 census of Boston counted 3,612 adult females but only 2,941 adult males. This sex imbalance was created by war deaths, and it resulted in increased poverty in New England, due to a severe widow and orphan problem.

Finally, the Seven Years War left England with massive financial obligations. The forward placement of troops in the colonies was costly, and England was saddled with £145 million in debt from the war. In order to service the debt and finance the forward placement of troops, British Prime Minister George Grenville would propose new taxation both in England and the colonies. Without the threat of the French, the colonists would view the forward placement of troops, as well as the new taxation, as unnecessary—and colonial contentment with being British subjects, which appears to have been widespread as late as 1762, would come to an abrupt end.

5.1g The Stamp Act

British Prime Minister George Grenville, while perhaps neither imaginative nor clever, was remarkably determined. He came into office just at the close of the French and Indian War. Alongside most of his countrymen, he believed that it was the American colonists who would benefit most from the vast territory bordering the Ohio and Mississippi rivers, recently won from the French. Therefore, he was determined that the colonists should pay at least part of the cost of defending and pacifying this territory. At the time, no revenue was coming from the colonists to aid in imperial defense. Duties imposed by the Molasses Act of 1733 were being evaded by smugglers. In fact, the American customs service was costing more to operate than it was collecting in fees.

Thus, in 1764 Grenville led Parliament to adopt the Revenue Act, or Sugar Act, intended to produce revenue—a purpose clearly stated in its preface—by enforcing the payment of customs duties on sugar, wine, coffee, silk, and other goods. The act declared that a number of colonial commodities could only be imported from England and required tighter control over ships' cargo. American shippers would have to post bonds guaranteeing observance of the Revenue Act before loading their cargoes. The act also strengthened the admiralty courts, where the violators of British customs laws were prosecuted. Although the act reduced the duty on molasses bought from non-British sources from six pence to four pence per gallon—on the surface, an attractive reduction—provincials had previously been smuggling in molasses for no more than a pence and a half per gallon in the form of a bribe to customs officials. Now Grenville intended to enforce the trade laws with stricter administrative procedures. The crux of the issue, however, was the British intention to tax the colonists for purposes of revenue. Before this, duties had been imposed merely as a means of regulating the trade of the empire. The New York legislature protested that any tax by Parliament solely for the purpose of raising revenue, rather than controlling trade, violated the rights of overseas English subjects who were taxed without representation in Parliament.

The issue of taxation, raised by the Sugar Act, was brought to a crisis by the **Stamp Act of 1765**, which provoked opposition throughout the colonies. Grenville announced his intention to extend to America the stamp duties that he had already imposed on England. Grenville gave the colonies almost one year to propose an alternative way to raise the same amount of revenue before the act would go into effect. Instead of coming up with a plan, the colonists spent the next year denouncing the idea of the Stamp Act;

and the year elapsed with the colonists offering no revenue-raising plan of their own. As a consequence, in November 1765 the Stamp Act went into effect, placing a stamp fee on all legal documents, deeds and diplomas, custom papers, newspapers, liquor licenses, playing cards, and dice. It directly affected every articulate element in the community, including lawyers, merchants, preachers, and printers. Moreover, the act raised not only the question of who had the right to tax but also the more significant questions: Who had power and over what? Could Parliament legislate for the colonials in all matters? Was Parliament's authority without limit? Or were there bounds beyond which it could not reach—bounds based upon certain rights inherent to all Englishmen?

5.1ƒ Reaction to the Stamp Act

The massive American reaction to the Stamp Act shocked the British government. The ensuing conflict was contested on two levels: that of action and that of constitutional debate. In almost every colony, British Stamp Act collectors were forced to resign—sometimes under the threat of force. Newspapers defied the act by printing skulls and crossbones in the space where the stamps belonged. **Sons of Liberty** were organized in key colonies to enforce a colonially self-imposed prohibition on the use of stamps.

Occasionally, mob spirit carried opposition to extremes, as it did in Massachusetts when a band of provincials rioted in Boston in what is known as the Stamp Act Riot. On August 14, 1765, Bostonians hanged an effigy of Boston Stamp Distributor Andrew Oliver from a tree on the south end of town. That evening, a crowd of several thousand people paraded the effigy through town and held a mock trial before beheading and burning the effigy. The crowd then destroyed the new stamp distribution office at the wharf. Oliver resigned as stamp distributor the next day out of fear for his life; and twelve days later another angry mob ransacked the home of the lieutenant governor, Thomas Hutchinson, whom the Bostonians mistakenly believed to be in support of the Stamp Act. A reward of £300 was offered for the arrest and conviction of the riot organizers, but not a single person came forward with a lead. The courts and the ports, which could not operate legally without using the stamps, continued—after a momentary lull—to carry out their regular functions in defiance of the act.

In the Virginia House of Burgesses, Patrick Henry introduced resolutions declaring that only the general assembly of a colony has the right to tax the residents of the colony. (Wikimedia Commons)

Boston's riots sparked similar actions by other Sons of Liberty in almost fifty colonial towns, and stamp distributors resigned throughout the colonies. Each colonial legislature met to decide on a course of action, the most famous incident occurring in the Virginia House of Burgesses, where Patrick Henry introduced resolutions declaring that the "General Assembly of this Colony have the only and *sole exclusive* Right and Power to lay Taxes and Impositions upon the Inhabitants of This Colony." Any other course, said Henry, would tend "to destroy British as well as American Freedom." One of Henry's resolutions—which did not pass because the Virginia House of Burgesses feared it might be treasonous—declared it "illegal, unconstitutional, and unjust" for anyone outside of Virginia to tax Virginians. Henry also resolved that Virginians did not have to obey any externally imposed tax and labeled anyone who denied Virginia's exclusive right to tax as "an enemy of the colony." Though Henry's radical resolutions failed to pass, they were widely circulated throughout the colonies creating a furor. Massachusetts governor Francis Bernard termed the Virginia resolves as "an alarm bell for the disaffected."

At the invitation of Massachusetts, nine colonies sent delegates to New York in October 1765 to form the Stamp Act Congress, in which a set of resolutions was adopted denying the authority of Parliament to tax the colonials. A boycott of British goods by the colonists—an example of the use of economic coercion to achieve political ends—was introduced on the theory that the colonial market was so necessary to Britain that it would abandon the act to regain the market. It should be noted that scholars of women's history have argued that the use of the boycott following the Stamp Act began to bring women into the political process, since consumer choices about what to buy were traditionally a woman's domain.

Moreover, in many instances women were required to produce the goods no longer being purchased from England.

On the second level, that of defining constitutional theory, the respective arguments of the colonials and the authorities in England developed differently. Colonials argued that they could not be free without being secure in their property and that they could not be secure in their property if, without their consent, others could take it away through taxation. This argument revealed the close tie between property and liberty in the minds of the eighteenth-century Anglo-Americans.

The British responded by saying that the Americans were not being taxed without their consent because they were "virtually," if not directly, represented in Parliament. They argued that many areas in Britain—notably Manchester and other substantial communities—were not directly represented in Parliament (the British did not require members of Parliament to live in their districts), but that no one denied that an act of Parliament had authority over those communities. The same concept of **virtual representation**, asserted the British leaders, applied to the colonies. Just as a member of Parliament who represented Manchester might live in London, a member of Parliament who represented Virginia might live in London.

The colonies vigorously opposed this interpretation of representation. Most of the colonial legislatures echoed Maryland's argument "that it cannot, with any Truth or Propriety, be said, that the Freemen of this Province of Maryland are Represented in the British Parliament." Daniel Dulany, a Maryland attorney, in his *Considerations on the Propriety of Imposing Taxes in the British Colonies,* argued that even those people in Britain who did not have the right to vote were allied in interest with their contemporaries. "But who," he asked, "are the Representatives of the Colonies?" Who could speak for them?

> The Right of Exemption from all Taxes without their consent, the Colonies claim as *British* Subjects. They derive this Right from the Common Law, which their Charters have declared and confirmed … A Right to impose an internal Tax on the Colonies, without their Consent *for the single Purpose of Revenue,* is denied; a Right to regulate their Trade without their Consent is admitted.

In brief, the colonists argued, Parliament had power, but not unlimited power. It could *legislate,* and thus impose external duties to regulate trade; but it could not *levy a tax for revenue.* In time, as the revolutionary crisis intensified, the colonial position was modified to deny Parliament's authority to legislate or tax the colonists for any purpose, whatsoever.

A view much closer to the eventual stand taken by the colonists was expressed by **George Mason** of Virginia, who implicitly denied the indefinite subordination of the colonies:

> We rarely see anything from your [the English] side of the water free from the authoritative style of a master to a school boy: 'We have with infinite difficulty and fatigue got you excused this one time; pray be a good boy for the future, do what your papa and mama bid you.'

He warned the British that "such another experiment as the stamp-act would produce a general revolt in America."

Parliament backed down—not on the principle at issue, but on the act itself. The Stamp Act was repealed in 1766. At the same time, however, the **Declaratory Act** was passed, stating that Parliament possessed the authority to make laws binding the American colonists "in all cases whatsoever." The Americans mistakenly believed not only that their arguments were persuasive but also that the economic pressure brought on by the boycott of English goods had been effective. The boycott, in fact, only delayed British reaction—but the Americans, unaware of the failure, would come to employ the boycott as a standard weapon against the British in each following crisis.

Virtual representation
The British idea that members of Parliament living in England represented the colonists in Parliament

George Mason
Warned the British that another action like the Stamp Act would lead to revolt in America

Declaratory Act
Asserted the right of Parliament, in 1766, to enact legislation "in all cases whatsoever"

5.1i The Townshend Duties

The next major crisis arose in 1767. The British Parliament enacted the **Townshend Duties** on glass, lead, paper, paints, and tea in 1767. They had been misinformed by Benjamin Franklin, who in February 1766 had told the House of Commons that the provincials object only to internal taxes—not taxes on trade. These import, or *external,* taxes were designed to exploit the distinction between internal taxes and external duties that Parliament mistakenly supposed the Americans were making. At the same time, Parliament reorganized the customs service by appointing a Board of Customs Commissioners to be located in Boston. The Townshend Duties also designated that customs officials were to be paid directly from the duties collected (an incentive for customs officials to be diligent collectors).

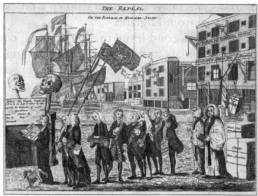

Pictured is a 1776 illustration representing the repeal of the Stamp Act. George Grenville is depicted carrying the tiny coffin, followed by British dukes and two bishops. (Wikimedia Commons)

The Massachusetts House of Representatives responded to the Townshend Duties by sending a circular letter written by **Samuel Adams**, denouncing the Townshend Duties, to all the other colonies. Adams declared that the payment of customs officials from duties collected was unconstitutional. Parliament quickly demanded that Massachusetts rescind the circular; and when they refused, Parliament declared the Massachusetts legislature to be dissolved.

5.1j The *Liberty* Incident

Tension mounted in Boston in the summer of 1768 when customs officials seized the *Liberty,* a ship owned by John Hancock, for evading customs duties. An angry mob of Bostonians reacted by attacking the customs officials, who fled to the safety of a British warship in Boston Harbor. In response, the British sent two regiments of troops to Boston, at least in part because of the urging of Customs Commissioners. By the time all the British troops were in place, there were 4,000 British soldiers in Boston—which, at the time, only had a total population of 16,000. Such numbers were, perhaps, a formula for disaster, especially without any other accompanying political stimulants, as the British troops competed with Boston men for part-time employment and the attention of Boston women.

John Hancock (Wikimedia Commons)

Although the Townshend Duties failed to awaken the same heated reaction as the Stamp Act, they again brought to light the differences in colonial versus British theories of the empire, and posed once more the question: What were the limits to the power of Parliament? Again the American colonists resorted to a boycott, although no intercolonial congress was called. **John Dickinson**, in his *Letters from a Farmer in Pennsylvania,* reaffirmed the position of the colonials that duties, even external duties, could not be levied primarily to obtain revenue, though measures enacted to regulate trade were admitted as a proper prerogative of Parliament. Dickinson's essays were not revolutionary in tone or in spirit. Neither, however, did they back away from the fundamental position taken by the colonists—that they alone could levy a tax upon themselves.

As for the British, the Board of Customs Commissioners—charged with enforcing the Navigation Acts, the Sugar Act of 1764, and the Townshend Duties—carried out its responsibilities in such a perfidious way that the commissioners were properly accused of customs racketeering. But the real significance of the Board was the breadth of opposition it aroused. Those colonists most vulnerable to its activity—particularly New England merchants—were not the only ones disposed to stand against the British. A consensus of opposition pervaded all the colonies, many of which experienced no serious problems with customs officials. This consensus was made possible because of the more profound issue at hand: Where did the regulatory power of Parliament end and that of the colonials begin?

The Townshend Duties disappointed their advocates, for the duties did not produce the revenue expected due to colonial boycotts that caused imports of British goods to decline as much as 40 percent. In 1770, therefore, the British repealed the Townshend Duties (except the duty on tea, which was retained as a symbol of Parliament's right to tax). The Americans relaxed their opposition and reopened their ports to British goods, although they condemned tea drinking as unpatriotic.

5.1k Boston Massacre

Finally, violence erupted in February 1770, as colonists surrounded the house of Ebenezer Richardson, a low-level British customs official. As colonists smeared a batch of "Hillsboro Paint" (a mixture of feces and urine) on the building, Richardson fired his gun into the crowd in an attempt to get them to disperse and accidentally killed a seventeen-year-old boy. Although the boy's death was an accident, some view it as the first death of the American Revolution.

Violence would be even greater in the following months. On March 5, 1770, what would be called the **Boston Massacre** occurred; by coincidence, the Townshend Duties were repealed that same day. A small group of townspeople, described by the Boston lawyer John Adams as a "motley rabble of saucy boys, negroes, and mulattoes, Irish teagues and outlandish Jack Tars," shouted cat-calls and insults and hurled snowballs and rocks at British troops on duty. The crowd referred to the British soldiers as "lobsterbacks," due to their red coats, and referred to a British soldier as a "damned rascally scoundrel lobster son of a bitch." A scuffle erupted, and the Redcoats opened fire, killing five persons and wounding six more. One of the slain was Crispus Attucks—an escaped slave who, according to one witness, had led the charge against the redcoats.

Acting governor Thomas Hutchinson ordered the removal of the British regiments in Boston to an island in the harbor to prevent further bloodshed. Hutchinson then jailed the eight British soldiers until they could stand trial. The British soldiers were then defended in the colonial court by John Adams and Josiah Quincy. Adams did so in order to show the British that even unpopular suspects in America could receive a fair trial. All but two of the British soldiers were acquitted. The remaining two were convicted of manslaughter, but given the "benefit of clergy" and thus were merely branded on their thumbs in punishment.

Following the trial, a form of informal truce developed between the colonists and the British. Imports of British goods again increased; and the American boycotts essentially collapsed—though the colonists continued to boycott tea since the British had symbolically retained the small Townshend Duty on it. At the end of 1771, it appeared that revolt might be averted after all.

Boston Massacre

Incident, in 1770, in which Bostonians heckled British troops and pelted them with rocks until the troops fired into the crowd, killing five

The bloody Boston Massacre occurred on March 5, 1770, when a mob of angry townspeople began taunting British soldiers on duty, throwing rocks and snowballs. The soldiers opened fire, killing five people and injuring six more. (Wikimedia Commons)

5.2 'Tis Time to Part

5.2a The Boston Tea Party and the Coercive Acts

Beginning in 1772, the informal truce collapsed and new unrest erupted. In June 1772, a British patrol boat, the *Gaspee*, ran aground in Narragansett Bay, south of Providence. The *Gaspee's* commander, Lieutenant Dudingston, was detested by the colonists for what they viewed as overzealous prosecution of smugglers and illegally seizing ships' cargo. Colonists seized the opportunity for revenge and burned the *Gaspee* to the water level as it sat helpless in Narragansett Bay. To make matters worse, the colonists arrested Lieutenant Dudingston and convicted him of illegally seizing what he contended was smuggled rum and sugar. The British attempted to try the colonial culprits for the arson, but no witnesses to the events could be found. Shortly thereafter, Governor Thomas Hutchinson announced that the governor and colonial judges would now be paid by the British

Crown rather than the local legislature. The colonists viewed the action as an attempt by the British to bias the courts and government against them. In reaction, a **Committee of Correspondence** was established in Massachusetts at the urging of Samuel Adams, John Adams' radical cousin. By the end of 1772, eighty Massachusetts towns had such committees. Furthermore, all but three of the other colonies had followed the Massachusetts pattern and formed such committees by the end of 1773, in order to keep one another informed of possible British action.

5.26 Tea Act Crisis

In 1773 and 1774, with the **Boston Tea Party** and the passage of the **Coercive Acts** (denounced as "Intolerable Acts" by the colonists), the conflict between Great Britain and its colonies entered a new and conclusive phase. Throughout the early 1770s, colonists had been drinking moderate amounts of English tea (from India) and paying moderate duties on the tea without major objections—but they were also smuggling in large quantities of Dutch tea, thus cutting into the tea sales of Britain's East India Company and British government revenues gained from taxes on tea. The Tea Act of May 1773 permitted the British East India Company—which was near bankruptcy but had an excess stock of around seventeen million pounds of tea in English warehouses—to market ("dump" would perhaps be a better term) tea in America. The East India Company's overstock had been caused partially by colonial boycotts and partially by competition from Dutch tea smuggled into the colonies. Normally, the East India Company sold its tea to British wholesalers, who in turn sold to American wholesalers, who then distributed the tea to local colonial merchants for sale to the public. By eliminating English middlemen and British import taxes, the Tea Act would allow the colonists to purchase less expensive tea while enabling the East India Company to undersell even smuggled Dutch tea. The British government would get modest revenue from the small Townshend Duty that remained on tea, and the East India Company would be saved from bankruptcy. The company was also authorized to employ its own agents in this transaction, rather than go through public auction to the independent wholesalers, and thus cut out the middlemen. In effect, the East India Company was given the means to seize monopolistic control of the American market.

With this act, the British reawakened the latent hostility of the American colonists. Some Americans objected to what they viewed as a British attempt to control American trade. Colonial merchants denounced the "monopoly" given to the East India Company and predicted that other monopolies would follow and colonial middlemen of all types would be eliminated. Others viewed the Tea Act as a British plot to induce Americans into buying more duties tea. Many colonists believed that the real goal of the act was to increase British revenue, which in turn would be used to pay royal governors and judges. The Tea Act was, therefore, viewed by many as an insidious example of Parliament's claim to the power to tax and legislate for the colonies "in all cases whatsoever," a principle that many colonists

Map 5.4 Boston and Vicinity (1775)

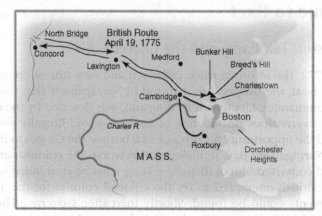

rejected. When Americans drank the tea, they would also be "swallowing" the British right to tax Americans and control their trade.

Before any of the East India Company's tea arrived in Boston, the Sons of Liberty had already pressured British tea agents to resign and vowed that the "obnoxious" tea would be stopped at the water's edge. When the ships carrying the tea arrived, they were met with unbroken opposition. In some ports, the ships were forced to return to England without unloading; in other cases, the tea was placed in a warehouse to prevent its distribution. In Boston, five thousand people gathered at the Old South Church on December 16, 1773. The colonists resolved that the governor, Thomas Hutchinson, must clear the ships for a return to England; the Governor refused. At nightfall, a band of 100 to 150 colonists, haphazardly disguised as American Indians, dumped 342 chests of tea—valued at £11,000 (approximately $1 million in 2010)—into the harbor.

In protest to Tea Act, the Sons of Liberty had vowed that the East India Company's tea would be refused at the water's edge. At nightfall, a band of more than one hundred colonists (haphazardly disguised as Indians) dumped 342 chests of tea—valued at £11,000 (approximately $1 million in 2010)—into the harbor. (Wikimedia Commons)

Declaration of Independence
Printed July 4, 1776, declaring American independence from Britain

The reaction in England was prompt and decisive; the prevailing mood in Parliament was that punitive legislation must be passed to teach those property-destroying Massachusetts provincials a lesson. This position was endorsed even by members of Parliament previously well-disposed toward the Americans. In quick succession, three Coercive Acts were passed: the Boston Port Act (March 31, 1774), which closed that port to commerce until the colonists paid for all of the destroyed tea; the Massachusetts Government Act (May 30, 1774), which altered the manner of choosing the Governor's Council from election by the lower house to appointment by the governor, authorized the governor to prohibit all but annual town meetings, installed General Thomas Gage as governor of Massachusetts, and indicated to the Americans, more significantly, that parliamentary power knew no limits; and finally, the Administration of Justice Act (May 30, 1774), which removed certain cases involving crown officials from the jurisdiction of Massachusetts courts. British officials were declared immune from local court trials for acts committed while suppressing civil disturbances in the colonies.

The other colonies immediately rallied to the support of Massachusetts in opposing these "Intolerable Acts"—much to the surprise of the British authorities, who had expected the support rather than the condemnation of the remaining colonies. After all, had not British property been wrongfully destroyed?

No action on the part of the Americans revealed the basic issue so clearly. The debate, at its heart, was not over customs racketeering, the presence of Redcoats, the problem of western lands, or even the issue of taxes. The conflict at hand was simple: Who had power and over what?

The Coercive Acts set in motion a series of actions and counteractions that led directly to separation. If there was any one point at which the Revolution became inevitable, it was in 1774, with the passage of the Coercive Acts and the colonial response to those acts. The colonists asked themselves: What would Parliament do next? Change the administration of justice in Virginia? Eliminate self-government in New York? Close the port of Philadelphia? Once the supremacy of Parliament in all areas was conceded, self-government would live merely on sufferance.

The colonials, at this stage, were not calling for independence. Such a step was too frightening. The Americans had lived within the British Empire for more than a century. They had been content with being British until as late as 1763. The British government, with all of its flaws, was still the most enlightened government of its time—where rule of law was a fact, and "liberty" was a word that meant something. The idea of separating from Britain in the 1770s was like changing, today, the form of government under which we have lived since 1789. It was not a step to be taken—as the revolutionary fathers later declared in the **Declaration of Independence**—for light or transient causes.

First Continental Congress

Meeting in Philadelphia in 1774, the Congress claimed that the colonists were not represented in Parliament and claimed that each colonial government had the exclusive right to legislate and tax its own people.

Minutemen

Colonial militiamen that fought against the British

Lexington and Concord

The first shots of the Revolution took place at Lexington, and the first significant engagement the same day at Concord.

Second Continental Congress

In 1775, this body appointed George Washington commander in chief of the provincial forces surrounding Boston, authorized the outfitting of a navy, and authorized a paper currency issue of $2 million.

George Washington

Commander of the Continental army

5.2c The Provincials Act

Events proceeded once again on two levels—that of action and that of theory. The **First Continental Congress** was called to meet in Philadelphia in September 1774. A number of important decisions made early in the deliberations set the tone of the meeting. Carpenters' Hall, instead of the legislative chambers of Pennsylvania (which many viewed as a den of loyalist activism), was selected as the meeting hall—a victory for Samuel Adams of Massachusetts and others who wished to take firm action against Britain. A more important show of strength came when resolutions proposing a union of colonies were offered, resolutions regarded as conciliatory. They were tabled by a close vote; and the Suffolk Resolves were adopted, asserting that the colonies should make no concessions until Britain first repealed the Coercive Acts. The burden of conciliation was thus placed upon British authorities.

In addition, the First Continental Congress adopted a series of resolutions embodying its position and sent them off to the king. The colonists claimed that they were not represented in Parliament and that each colonial government had the exclusive right to legislate and tax its own people. The colonists acquiesced to British trade regulations—so long as the regulations were not covert forms of raising revenue. At the same time, a Continental Association was established to cut off trade with the British. Although the Continental Congress avowed its "allegiance to his majesty" and its "affection for our fellow subjects" in Great Britain, the stand it took placed Britain on notice.

5.2d Lexington and Concord

When the First Continental Congress adjourned, its members agreed to meet again in the spring of 1775 if no action was forthcoming from Britain. Conditions failed to improve; in fact, they became worse. In Massachusetts, **minutemen** were training to guard against possible actions by British Redcoats stationed in Boston. Guns, powder, and other military stores were being collected at Concord.

On April 18, 1775, the British military governor sent out from Boston about seven hundred British regulars to destroy the colonists' military stores at Concord. As the British marched from Boston toward Concord, Paul Revere and William Dawes mounted their horses and rode out to warn the minutemen of the British advance. When the British reached Lexington, between Boston and Concord, they were met by about seventy-five colonial minutemen. The British demanded that the colonists lay down their weapons and disperse. Someone—no one knows who—fired a shot; and for the next few minutes both sides opened fire. By the time the firing stopped, the Americans were dispersing; eight had been killed, and ten were wounded. The first shots of the Revolution, termed by the Americans as the "shots heard round the world," had been fired. The British then continued their march toward Concord, some fifteen miles west of Lexington, while the colonists gathered in defense. When the British arrived, they were unable to find the bulk of the Americans' ammunition, which had been quickly removed; the British burned what little they did find.

The British were then engaged by the minutemen at Concord's Old North Bridge, where two Americans and three British soldiers were killed. The British retreated to Boston, but the colonists—hiding in the trees—attacked them along the way. Before their day was spent, they had suffered nearly three hundred casualties and had escaped total destruction only because reinforcements came from Boston. Dogging the regulars all the way, the minutemen encamped on the land approaches to Boston and began a siege. The colonial effort had not come without a cost, however, as ninety-five Americans were killed by the time the British reached Boston. With the confrontations at **Lexington and Concord**, the American Revolution had begun.

5.2e Second Continental Congress and Revolt

When the **Second Continental Congress** met in May 1775, the thin line between peace and war was vanishing. Congress appointed a Virginian, **George Washington**, as commander in chief of the provincial forces surrounding Boston. His nomination by John Adams, a

Massachusetts man, revealed the determined effort of the Americans to present a united front. Congress also authorized the outfitting of a navy under the command of Commodore Esek Hopkins of Rhode Island. In order to finance the war effort, Congress authorized a paper currency issue of $2 million. Congress also tried to win Canada to its cause, but failed. Meanwhile, on May 10, New England forces led by Benedict Arnold and Ethan Allen captured Fort Ticonderoga on Lake Champlain. Subsequently, they moved northward to seize points along the Canadian border.

5.2f Bunker Hill

In June, colonists seized Breed's Hill and Bunker Hill in Boston with the intention of shelling the British positions on the peninsula of Boston. The colonists set up defenses on Breed's Hill, and General William Howe and 2,500 British troops assaulted the hill on June 17, 1775, in an effort to drive them off. In what the colonists referred to as the battle of Bunker Hill (though it was actually fought on Breed's Hill), the colonists twice turned the British back before the British were able to take the hill—after the colonists ran out of ammunition. It was due to the ammunition shortage that the famous order, "don't fire until you see the whites of their eyes," was issued, as the colonists needed to make sure that every shot counted. The battle lasted only two hours, but the British suffered a thousand casualties; the Americans, four hundred. Though the British accomplished their objective, the battle proved to the colonists that they were capable of competing with the British army. In the words of British General Henry Clinton, "It was a dear bought victory; another such would have ruined us."

The heavy casualties on both sides also reduced any chance for a negotiated settlement, and the spilling of so much blood only caused each side to become more determined to force the other to submit militarily. General Howe perhaps erred at Bunker Hill in failing to pursue the Americans as they fled the battlefield. If Howe had pushed westward after the battle, many military historians suggest that he might have decisively defeated the Continental army. Instead, Howe held his army in Boston and abandoned the town without a fight nine months later.

5.2g Declaration of Causes and the Olive Branch Petition

In July 1775, Congress adopted the "Declaration of the Causes and Necessity of Taking up Arms"—in essence, a declaration of war—in an attempt to assure fellow Britons that dissolution of the union was not intended, but that neither would Americans back away from their convictions. "Our cause is just. Our union is perfect. Our internal resources are great, and, if necessary, foreign assistance is undoubtedly attainable." The Declaration stated that the British government had left the American people with only two alternatives: "unconditional submission to the tyranny of irritated ministers or resistance by force." Congress simultaneously pursued war and peace, however, as they also drafted and sent to the king an "Olive Branch Petition" that humbly begged the king to remove obstacles to reconciliation. Congress also moved to secure the neutrality of the Native American tribes, established a postal system, and approved plans for a military hospital.

In August 1775, the king declared that his subjects were in rebellion, effectively rejecting the Olive Branch Petition, and began to recruit foreign mercenaries and prepare the British regulars. Twenty thousand British troops were sent to the colonies to quell the rebellion. Parliament also passed the "Prohibitory Act," which closed the colonies to all overseas trade and made no concessions to American demands. The British enforced the Prohibitory Act with a naval blockade of colonial ports.

During the remainder of 1775, the Americans, under Benedict Arnold and Richard Montgomery, attempted the conquest of Canada—chiefly in order to deprive Britain of a base of attack before British reinforcements could arrive. After capturing Montreal, Montgomery pushed northeastward and Arnold pushed north, toward Quebec, from the territory of Maine. Arnold's contingent was decimated by smallpox and freezing rain, and more colonists died in the campaign from disease than from battle with the British. Nevertheless, Arnold and the colonists heroically reached Quebec and jointly attacked the British with Montgomery; even so, the American attack was repulsed and the Americans were forced to withdraw.

BVT *Lab*

Visit www.BVTLab.com to explore the student resources available for this chapter.

5.2ℏ Momentum Toward the Declaration

Beginning in January 1776, the movement for independence gained ground. On January 1, 1776, the British gave the Americans a military shove by shelling Norfolk, Virginia—an act that was viewed as barbaric by the colonists. The same month, **Thomas Paine** published his *Common Sense*, asserting "'tis time to part." To this point, few Americans had questioned the legitimacy of the king; but in this pamphlet, Paine condemned the monarchy as a form of government in bold language, stating that "nature disapproves it; otherwise she would not so frequently turn it to ridicule by giving mankind an ass for a lion." Paine not only denounced the monarchy, in general, but also King George in particular, referring to him as a "Royal Brute" and the "hardened sullen-tempered Pharaoh of England." To replace the monarchy, Paine advocated republican government based on the consent of the people. Appreciatively read by thousands upon thousands, *Common Sense* helped to crystallize opinion. The denunciation of the king as an "ass" helped to break down the traditional British deference that most Americans still had for the monarchy. The British also gave the independence movement a boost when news that the British were using Hessian mercenaries reached the colonies. The use of mercenaries, who had a reputation for raping and pillaging, was considered ungentlemanly and an improper thing for the British to do in a dispute with their American brothers. By late spring a number of colonies instructed their delegates to the Continental Congress to advocate independence.

On June 7, 1776, Richard Henry Lee of Virginia, once again reflecting the unity of the colonials regardless of region, introduced a resolution calling for independence. Thomas Jefferson was appointed chair of a committee to draft the document that was presented to Congress on June 28. Congress debated the document on July 1. Though many delegates were apprehensive, it was adopted on July 2 by a unanimous vote, with twelve colonies voting for independence and New York abstaining so that the vote could be unanimous.

The Declaration of Independence (iStockphoto)

5.2ℹ The Declaration of Independence

Action and theory were, by this point, moving together. In 1774 James Wilson, later a Supreme Court justice, had published *Considerations on the Authority of Parliament*, which posed a series of questions:

> And have those, whom we have hitherto been accustomed to consider as our fellow-subjects, an absolute and unlimited power over us? Have they a natural right to make laws, by which we may be deprived of our properties, of our liberties, of our lives? By what title do they claim to be our masters? ... Do those, who embark freemen in Great Britain, disembark slaves in America?

Wilson answered by affirming, without qualification, that Parliament had no authority over the colonies. Their dependence upon Britain was exclusively through the crown. The colonies were "different members of the British Empire ... independent of each other, but connected together under the same sovereign."

Wilson's assumption underlay the philosophy of the Declaration of Independence. The colonists directed the entire document against the king. Nowhere is Parliament mentioned.

The Continental Congress could have separated from Britain by means of a simple declarative resolution. An elaborate document to explain the reason for revolution was unnecessary. That such a document was written is, in itself, an insight into the nature of the Revolution—for it did not feature tattered flags, starved and desperate people, or lawlessness. Its leadership included some of the most substantial and prominent individuals in America. Because of their influential position and their regard for law, they and their associates felt a deep need to explain to a "candid world" why they took such a drastic step.

Although five delegates of the Continental Congress, among them John Adams and Benjamin Franklin, were assigned the task of writing the Declaration, the draft was composed primarily by Thomas Jefferson of Virginia. The members of the committee made modest changes, and the document was then debated in Congress, where more changes were made.

The Declaration was based on the philosophy that underlay John Locke's treatises on the occasion of England's Glorious Revolution of 1688. The similarity in ideas and even in phraseology is striking. The Declaration appealed to the highest authority within the intellectual structure of the eighteenth century, "the Laws of Nature and Nature's God." It asserts that all men are created equal, that each person is endowed with certain rights that cannot be set aside, and that included among these rights are "life, liberty, and the pursuit of happiness."

What this felicitous phrase meant was to be defined more carefully later, in state and national constitutions. The Declaration reaffirmed what Americans in their experience had long practiced: Governments, based upon the consent of the governed, are established to secure these rights; and if governments become destructive to these rights, they should be abolished. The king, the symbol of the British government, had failed to honor his obligation to protect these rights, and instead had become destructive to them; thus, the king's government should be abolished.

The Declaration includes a list of specific charges that add up to a devastating indictment, too often treated by historians as an excuse or a rationalization for an act already taken. The list of grievances was meant to show that the Declaration was not based on transient causes but rather upon a long pattern of abuse. With the acceptance of the Declaration by the Continental Congress, the British view that the rights of the colonies depended on the sufferance of the royal grace and favor was forever demolished. Ben Franklin added some gallows humor that reflected the grave nature of the situation when he stated to John Hancock, "we must all hang together, or surely we will all hang separately" when signing the Declaration of Independence.

With the Declaration, the character of the conflict changed, also. Whereas the colonials had been secretly soliciting aid from France since 1775, the Continental Congress, representing an independent people, now established ministries throughout Europe to obtain recognition and help for the independent colonies, soon to become the United States. Washington, who had been leading a militia force to obtain recognition of the rights of colonials, now headed an army fighting for American independence. Thirteen colonies became thirteen states with the problem of working out appropriate constitutions.

Facing the experience of union, the Americans also had to work out an acceptable constitutional structure for the national government. With the Declaration, the Continental Congress was no longer an extralegal body of rebels but rather the symbol of a sovereign nation.

5.2j The Internal Revolution

Emphasis has been placed on the principal issue: What were the limits of Parliament's power? But historians have investigated a second question: Within each colony, who was to possess authority? Points of view have varied widely regarding the answer. Some have insisted that the issue of who was going to rule at home was preeminent, that the break with Britain was brought about by radical dissenters within each colony who were so anxious to overthrow the power structure in their colony that they worked for revolution to accomplish this goal. Other historians contend that those who held power in the late colonial period were willing to fight to maintain it. This argument is fueled by the undoubted fact that in many colonies, the number of people living in poverty was on the increase in the years before the Revolution.

The present consensus among historians is perhaps best expressed as follows: Conflicts within individual colonies contributed to the coming of the Revolution because some people hoped to correct grievances under a new regime. However, this internal struggle for control was not the decisive or preeminent force behind the Revolution. The principal issue was the conflict over the constitutional framework of the empire. Even without an internal struggle, the Revolution would have occurred. The internal grievances were related, however, to later developments in the revolutionary and post-revolutionary periods as Americans set about to resolve their own problems. Between the explosive potential for human freedom contained in the words of the Declaration and the heady release of democratic fervor in the early days of the new nation, those developments would be transformative.

5.2k The Loyalists

The Declaration of Independence was a divisive rather than a unifying document; and it had an impact upon every colony, county, and town, and almost every family. With its adoption, people had a decision to make: Would they remain loyal to Britain and its government? Or would they join those who advocated independence and be called rebels?

Regardless of their political views or associations, the present generation of Americans claims the American Revolution as their rightful heritage and regards, consequently, this decision as a foregone conclusion. But the literal "patriots" of 1776 were those who upheld the existing British government: The word *patriotism* derives from *patrios*, meaning "established by forefathers."

In discussing the division between those who supported separation from Britain and those who opposed it, historians have customarily used rather gross figures, holding that one third of the revolutionary generation remained loyal to Britain, one third remained uncommitted, and one third supported independence. Closer examination reveals that the percentage varied substantially among colonies as well as among localities within colonies. Furthermore, the percentage of **Loyalists** versus Revolutionaries was fluid and changed over time.

The best recent figures indicate that 20 percent, about five hundred thousand, of the white population became Loyalists. During and after the Revolution, as many as a hundred thousand people left the American colonies for Canada, England, the West Indies, and other places of refuge. Historian Robert R. Palmer has calculated that twenty-four persons per thousand of the population left the colonies compared with five persons per thousand of the population in France during the French Revolution—a startling fact that raises the issue of Loyalists to a new level of importance.

These divisions were reflected among families and friends. Gouverneur Morris of New York took up the cause of independence. His mother and many other members of his family remained loyal to Britain. Benjamin Franklin's son William, who was governor of New Jersey, became a Loyalist, causing Franklin to write that his son caused him more personal grief by this act than he had experienced in a lifetime. Close friends and trading associates Thomas Willing and Robert Morris of Philadelphia took opposite sides: Willing remained a supporter of the crown, while Morris became a principal leader of the Revolution.

Some of the most distinguished and honored leaders in these and other provinces left. Daniel Dulany of Maryland, who wrote so convincingly about the evils of the Stamp Act, could not bring himself to accept independence. Neither could Joseph Galloway, Speaker of the House in Pennsylvania. Chief Justice William Smith of New York finally decided to migrate to Canada after refusing to take a loyalty oath to the revolutionary government in New York.

To list these names tends to imply that only the upper social strata became Loyalists, but the total of five hundred thousand—a full 20 percent of the white population—demonstrates that people from every social class became Loyalists. Slaves left plantations to follow the British in the hope of gaining freedom; servants and artisans also sought the protection of the British government and army.

During the course of the War for Independence, it is estimated that as many as thirty thousand Loyalists served in the British army. In 1780 alone, as many as eight thousand Loyalists served in the British forces. Washington's forces at that time numbered no more than nine thousand.

What is more difficult to ascertain is the number of Loyalists who remained in the colonies, trying not to offend the supporters of the Revolution but assisting the British troops when they came. The colonies of Georgia, New York, and South Carolina were the staunchest Loyalist strongholds, followed by New Jersey and Massachusetts. Indeed, the

British planned military campaigns in these provinces with the expectation that Loyalists would flock to their standard. The decision to concentrate on New York in 1776 and again in 1777 was based, at least in part, on this assumption. The decision in 1779–1780 to redirect the military effort to Georgia and South Carolina was also prompted by the expectation of winning support throughout the countryside.

Loyalists who did not wish to speak out had good reason to retain a low profile. To leave was to abandon their homes and land, and few Loyalists were able to convert their possessions into cash. Revolutionary governments confiscated Loyalists' property to be resold to the highest bidders. For this and many other reasons, few Loyalists, with the critical exception of those who immigrated to Canada, left an imprint upon their adopted homelands.

Those who left for England were probably the ones who became most disenchanted. The nation and the government they had held in such high esteem seemed unrecognizable at close range. The rampant corruption, the flagrant bidding for position and favor, even the lifestyle of eighteenth-century England—all seemed alien to provincial leaders. Persons accustomed to leadership in the colonies became, for the most part, inconsequential in England. One dedicated Loyalist, Henry Van Schaack, longed to return to America and eventually did so. On the whole, the Loyalists became lost among their contemporaries, and in many respects to history, because they chose the losing side.

5.3 Prosecuting the War

5.3a The Continental Congress

To make independence a reality, the war had to be won. Although the Continental Congress had neither a specific grant of authority nor a fixed constitutional basis until 1781, it resolved financial, military, diplomatic, and constitutional questions during this critical period. Occasionally, action lagged and arguments centered upon trivialities, but the Continental Congress should be remembered for its major achievements rather than for its minor failures. It unified the American war effort and fashioned an instrument of national government without violating individual liberty and without producing dissension so divisive as to splinter the Revolution. Most of America's greatest leaders of the Revolutionary generation served at one time or another in the Congress, gaining their first political experience at the national rather than at the colony-state level.

5.3b Revolutionary Finance

One of the early problems facing Congress was how to finance the war. Four major methods were used: Loan Office Certificates, the equivalent of present-day government bonds; requisitions, that is, requests for money and later supplies from individual states; foreign loans, which were insignificant until 1781; and paper currency.

Pictured is a fifty-five dollar bill of Continental currency from 1779. This is an example of some of our country's first paper money, developed for use by Benjamin Franklin.
(Wikimedia Commons, Beyond My Ken)

The first issues of paper money were made by Congress before the Declaration of Independence. This avenue of revenue was one that had been used by many colonies during that period. At first the paper money circulated at its face value; but as more money was issued, its value declined (although intermittently the value of the currency increased when successful military operations revived hopes for a quick victory). By the spring of 1781, the value had declined so precipitously that paper currency cost more to print than it was worth once it was printed. Up to that point, however, paper money had paid for no less than 75 percent of the cost of the war.

After 1781 foreign loans became especially important because these loans provided capital for the establishment of a national bank, the Bank of North America. From it the government borrowed money in excess of the bank's capitalization. After 1781,

Morris Notes—a form of paper currency backed by the word of Robert Morris, the superintendent of finance—helped to restore the public credit. At the conclusion of the war, the national government, as well as the various states, had incurred a substantial debt that was to figure into the movement to write the Federal Constitution of 1787.

5.3c Military Strategy

The British did not take advantage of perhaps their most promising military strategy: blockading all the American ports. An intensive blockade, if it had been coordinated with swift, devastating land campaigns to lay waste the resources of the Americans, might have brought success—for the British, in order to win, had to demand unconditional surrender. The Americans, to be successful, needed an army in the field as a symbol of resistance. Any negotiations automatically recognized the United States as an independent nation because a sovereign power does not negotiate with rebels.

After leaving Boston in the spring of 1776, the British were concentrated in the middle states, with an eye to dividing the United States physically between north and south—crippling its unity and exploiting the possibility of support from American Loyalists, which was much stronger in New York than in Massachusetts. Control of New York, with its excellent harbor and river connections to the interior, was also viewed as crucial to the strangulation of American trade. The British also believed that control of the Hudson River system would allow them to isolate New England, which they viewed as the center of the rebellion. British forces could then descend on New England from Canada while simultaneously pushing northward from New York and strangling New England trade with the blockade. The British believed that once New England was subdued, Loyalists in the Middle Colonies would force New York, Pennsylvania, and New Jersey to fall in line. When the New York strategy failed to sufficiently divide the colonists and end the war, the British emphasis shifted to the Southern theater of operations beginning in 1780 with the intention of exploiting Loyalist sentiments in the South so as to subdue troublesome rebels in Virginia.

5.3d Slavery and the Revolution

General George Washington
(Wikimedia Commons)

Policy on enlisting blacks in the Continental forces changed throughout the course of the war. At the beginning of the fighting, the Continental army and most state militias accepted black enlistments, both slaves and freemen. Prince Estabrook, a black man, fought at Lexington, for example; and Peter Salem fought at Lexington, Concord, and Bunker Hill. One Rhode Island regiment included 125 blacks, of whom 30 were freemen.

Early attitudes changed. A Council of War convened by General Washington in Massachusetts in October 1775 decided not to accept further enlistment of blacks because other troops, especially those from the South, refused to accept them as equals. Free blacks protested to Washington, and in December 1775 he ordered the reopening of enlistments to free blacks. Meanwhile, he requested that the Continental Congress review the issue. In January 1776 Congress ruled that free blacks who had already served could reenlist; other blacks, whether slave or free, were excluded. State militias followed the pattern set by the Continental army.

The British attitude fluctuated as much as that of the American provincials. The British recognized that recruiting slaves would cripple the planter colonies, so they promised freedom in exchange for service. They offered indentured servants the same promise. When planters found their slaves leaving to answer the British call, they became alarmed and angry. In Virginia, slave patrols were doubled to catch runaways. At the very least, each planter in the Southern colonies tended to keep a sharper eye on the men and women in bondage due to the British action.

Toward the end of 1776 and early in 1777, manpower shortages caused Continental policy to change once again—and blacks were recruited for the Continental and state navies. The state of Maryland enlisted blacks in its militia, and even the Virginia militia was willing to accept blacks. By 1779 the Continental Congress recommended that

South Carolina and Georgia raise a military force of five thousand black soldiers. Owners of slaves who enlisted were to be compensated, and the slaves in return would receive freedom and $50 in cash. The two states rejected the recommendation, but enlistment of blacks did grow in the North. In 1781 Baron Von Closen found that one fourth of the encampment of soldiers at White Plains was composed of blacks.

Although slavery would continue after the Revolution, a few faltering steps were taken toward emancipation during the war years. In 1780, Pennsylvania provided for the gradual abolition of slavery. In 1784, Connecticut and Rhode Island followed Pennsylvania's lead; soon thereafter New York and New Jersey followed suit. In 1783 the Supreme Court of Massachusetts ruled that the phrase "men are created free and equal" meant what it said, thereby freeing slaves in that state. Massachusetts was the only state where slaves were freed by the state against the will of their masters. In contrast, a proposal in the Maryland legislature to free slaves lost by a vote of 32 to 22. Significantly, no grand plan of emancipation was adopted anywhere in the new nation.

The reason for the continuation of slavery was largely the attitude of whites toward blacks. Jefferson, in a public statement called *The Summary View,* acknowledged that slaves should be freed, but he also declared that blacks were inferior human beings. He could never bring himself to free his own slaves, and Washington eventually did so only upon his death. The fear of living with blacks as equals, the loss of property, and the social consequences paralyzed the movement to free the slaves. Consequently, the possibility that slavery could be ended during the Revolution faded, only to be taken up again by a later generation that resolved the issue on the battlefield.

5.3e The War in the North

In March 1776 Washington forced the British under **General Sir William Howe** to abandon Boston by capturing Dorchester Heights—from which they could shell British positions from the high ground. Howe then loaded his troops on transports and sailed to Nova Scotia to prepare for an attack on New York. Howe took with him more than a thousand Loyalists who preferred residence in Canada to independence from Great Britain, thus demonstrating the division among the American colonists even in the revolutionary hotbed of Boston.

In an effort to prevent Howe's taking New York, Washington moved south and occupied Brooklyn Heights on Long Island. There, on August 27, 1776, Howe—with an army of 33,000—attacked and defeated Washington, who withdrew to Manhattan Island under the cover of night and fog after suffering some 1,500 casualties. Washington then attempted to hold his ground against the British by occupying forts Washington and Lee on either side of the Hudson River. In November, Howe attacked the forts, forcing Washington to retreat across New Jersey into Pennsylvania. Howe pursued Washington across New Jersey and at one point was only one hour behind the fleeing Continental army, but Howe decided to rest his men for a day and allowed Washington to escape. The Continental Congress, meeting in Philadelphia, fled to Baltimore as the British army approached.

Military historians tend to argue that Howe failed to press his advantage while he had Washington on the run and contend that had Howe attacked Washington's army at Philadelphia, he would have taken the city and crushed the Continental army. Instead, Howe decided to winter his Hessian troops in quarters along the Delaware River and delay his advance until spring, confident that the colonists would be unable to mount an attack. As fate would have it, on December 25, 1776, in a freezing rainstorm, Washington moved his army across the Delaware in the dead of night and attacked the unsuspecting Hessians early in the morning, taking nine hundred prisoners. Washington read to the troops these famous words from a Thomas Paine

Washington moved his army across the Delaware River during the night to spring an attack on the unsuspecting Hessians the following morning. (Wikimedia Commons)

Map 5.5 Central Campaigns (1776–1778)

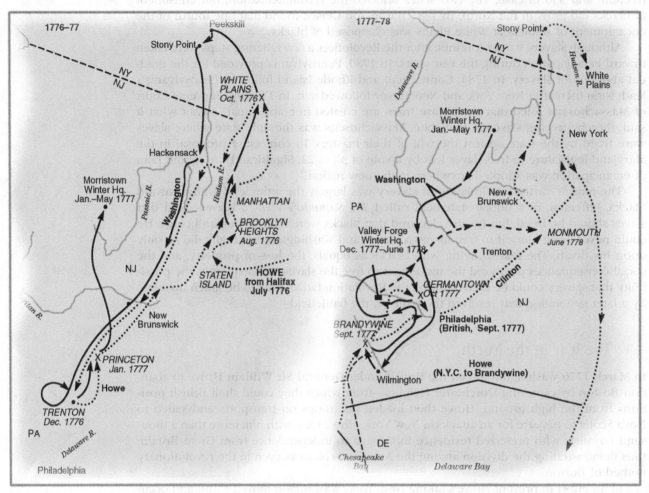

1776–77

Peekskill
Stony Point
WHITE PLAINS Oct. 1776 X
Hackensack
NY NJ
Morristown Winter Hq. Jan.–May 1777
Passaic R.
Washington
Hudson R.
MANHATTAN
BROOKLYN HEIGHTS Aug. 1776
NJ
STATEN ISLAND
HOWE from Halifax July 1776
New Brunswick
X PRINCETON Jan. 1777
Howe
TRENTON Dec. 1776
PA
Delaware R.
Philadelphia

1777–78

Stony Point
NY NJ
Hudson R.
White Plains
Morristown Winter Hq. Jan.–May 1777
New York
Washington
Delaware R.
PA
New Brunswick
Valley Forge Winter Hq. Dec. 1777–June 1778
Trenton
GERMANTOWN X Oct 1777
MONMOUTH June 1778
Clinton
NJ
Philadelphia (British, Sept. 1777)
BRANDYWINE Sept. 1777 X
Wilmington
Howe (N.Y.C. to Brandywine)
DE
Chesapeake Bay
Delaware Bay

pamphlet entitled "American Crisis": "These are the times that try men's souls … The summer soldier and the sunshine patriot will, in this crisis shrink from the service of their country, but he that stands it now deserves … love and thanks."

Pictured are General Washington and his army at Valley Forge. The freezing weather, poor-quality food, shortages of blankets and shoes, and plights of disease took 2,500 soldiers' lives here. (Wikimedia Commons)

A week later on January 3, Washington continued his surprise attacks with an assault on Princeton before moving his army to winter quarters at Morristown. The colonial victories in New Jersey were important less for their strategic significance than for their boost to morale. The victories convinced many Americans that they should continue the fight. The strategic prize, New York City, would be occupied by British troops for the duration of the Revolution, however.

In 1777, Howe bestirred himself sufficiently to send an army by sea against Philadelphia. Washington proceeded overland south of Philadelphia and met units of Howe's army at Brandywine Creek on September 11, 1777. He was badly outmaneuvered and suffered defeat. Howe entered Philadelphia with ease, but British units were severely tested when Washington launched an unexpected counterattack at Germantown on October 4. Just when it appeared that the American army would prevail, Washington's troops suddenly retreated in confusion.

Though the American army was defeated, its offensive spirit aided the cause of independence at home and in France. Washington then withdrew his army to **Valley Forge**, Pennsylvania, where a combination of freezing weather, bad food, a shortage of blankets and shoes, and disease cost 2,500 American lives. Washington complained to Congress that nearly three thousand of his men were "unfit for duty because they are bare foot and otherwise naked."

Map 5.6 Northern Campaigns (1777)

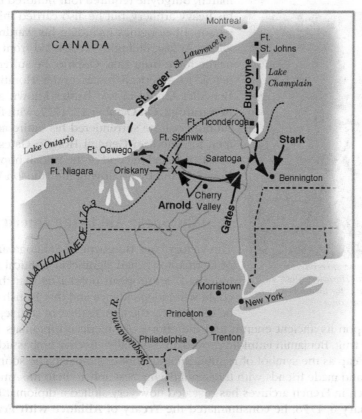

Food and clothing were available in different states, but states were reluctant to send their own supplies of blankets, shoes, and food for use outside of their own territory. To make matters worse, the American supply lines were fraught with corruption. Teamsters who hauled barrels of salt pork drained out the brine to lighten their load, thus allowing the meat to rot in transit. Blankets were delivered to Washington's army that proved to be only a fourth of the normal size, and gunpowder purchased by the Continental army often turned out to be defective.

5.3f Saratoga

In the meantime, the British had planned a three-pronged attack to capture the Hudson Valley and thus isolate New England from the colonies to the south. From Canada, **General Sir John Burgoyne** was to push southward down Lake Champlain and the upper Hudson, with the expectation of joining General Howe moving up the Hudson from New York City. General Burgoyne would then join Howe in an attack on Philadelphia and the occupation of other rebel territory to the south. But Howe had received conflicting orders and decided that the immediate capture of Philadelphia was more urgent than cooperating with Burgoyne, thus delaying his scheduled rendezvous with Burgoyne's army descending from the north.

Burgoyne had also expected to converge with a third British force under General Barry St. Leger (mostly Loyalists and Native Americans) moving eastward from Lake Ontario along the Mohawk Valley, but this force was beaten back by American troops (many of whom were German in ethnicity) and other Native Americans at the Battle of Oriskany. The Americans suffered heavy losses—five hundred of the eight hundred Americans were killed—but the British forces were forced to retreat and would not rendezvous at Albany with Burgoyne. Nevertheless, throughout the summer of 1777, Burgoyne pressed southward toward Albany. Burgoyne captured Fort Ticonderoga in July after three thousand American defenders—low on food and supplies—fled when they saw the coming British army. However,

Valley Forge
Site near Philadelphia, Pennsylvania, where Washington wintered his troops in 1777–1778 in freezing conditions with inadequate supplies

General Sir John Burgoyne
British general defeated at Saratoga

Burgoyne's troops were accompanied by some one thousand laundresses, cooks, and musicians, as well as four hundred Native American warriors and scouts, thus slowing their march. Burgoyne required four hundred horses to pull his heavy artillery, but he also carried thirty trunks of personal belongings including his wardrobe and fine wines. At last, failing to receive aid from either Howe or the force from Lake Ontario, he suffered complete defeat to American forces under Horatio Gates and Benedict Arnold in two battles known as the **Battle of Saratoga**. On October 17, 1777, with food supplies running out, he surrendered his entire army of 5,800 men to American General Horatio Gates. Burgoyne's defeat signaled the end of the British hope of isolating New England by occupying the Hudson Valley.

On October 17, 1777, General Sir John Burgoyne surrendered his entire army of 5,800 men to American General Horatio Gates. The British could no longer isolate New England for themselves by occupying the Hudson Valley. (Wikimedia Commons)

Battle of Saratoga

Major colonial victory that led to French assistance and the Treaty of Alliance with France

Treaty of Alliance with France

France agreed to a permanent alliance with the U.S., and the U.S. agreed not to stop short of full independence; both agreed not to sign a separate peace with England.

5.3g European Aid to the Americans

The victory over Burgoyne at Saratoga and the Battle of Germantown had significant political results. They indicated to European politicians that the Americans could win independence and that British power could be crippled by the loss. France, of course, was anxious for revenge upon its ancient enemy, and the efforts of American diplomats in Paris now began to bear fruit. Benjamin Franklin proved an especially effective ambassador to France. Wearing a fur cap as the symbol of republican and frontier simplicity, he soon became the toast of Paris and made friends with those politicians best able to help the American cause. Recent research in French archives has revealed how very skilled a diplomat he was.

On February 6, 1778, he consummated the **Treaty of Alliance with France**. France recognized American independence, thus granting America status as an independent nation under international law. France promised to the United States full military support until U.S. independence was recognized by England, and both France and the United States agreed that neither would sign a separate peace with England. Finally, the United States was to be militarily allied with France indefinitely. France immediately supplied limited funds to aid the American cause and in 1780 dispatched troops and ships. French ports were now opened to such war vessels as the Americans had, and privateers could attack British vessels and stand a better chance of getting away to a safe haven. The French navy provided sea power that the colonies had previously lacked.

Eager to gain the access to American markets that Great Britain had long prevented, Holland also provided aid—largely in the form of loans underwritten by the French. Thus European aid, prompted by self-interest, contributed to the American victory. Since Spain was at the time closely allied to France, America expected aid from Spain also—but Spanish actions never fulfilled American expectations.

5.3h New Campaigns in the North

General William Howe, notorious for his dilatoriness, was relieved in 1778 by Sir Henry Clinton, who evacuated Philadelphia and returned to New York for a new campaign in the North. Washington, without the power to inflict defeat, could only hang on the flanks of the British army. He established a base at White Plains, New York, and saw to it that West Point on the Hudson was fortified. The arrival off the coast of New York of a French naval force under Count d'Estaing did little to help the American cause, for D'Estaing showed little audacity and soon sailed away to the West Indies. Only from the western frontier was the news encouraging. American George Rogers Clark, leading a group of colonial frontiersmen, helped to hold the West against the British.

5.3i The War in the South

Thousands of slaves in the South could be freed by a British victory, and in 1778 the British adopted a new strategy designed to take advantage of this destabilizing factor and existing Loyalist sentiments in the South. The British hoped to reestablish British rule in the Southern Colonies one by one—beginning with lightly-defended Georgia and then moving north up the southern colonial coast. The British captured Savannah in December 1778 and subsequently installed a Loyalist government. Then an oath was signed by 1,400 Georgia militiamen, swearing allegiance to the king and that they would fight for the British against American rebels. In April and May 1780, the British laid siege to Charleston, where 3,300 Americans were forced to surrender after five weeks of fighting. As in Georgia, pardons were offered to Carolinians who swore loyalty oaths to the king and then proved their loyalty by taking up arms for the British. When the Continental army under Horatio Gates attempted a counterattack at Camden, South Carolina, in August, American militiamen dropped their weapons and ran when they saw the approaching British cavalry. By the second day of the battle, when the Americans tried to regroup, only seven hundred of the three thousand American troops showed up—the rest had been either killed or captured, or had deserted.

The British victories in the South were aided by information the British gained from America's most famous traitor, Benedict Arnold. Arnold had been a hero at Saratoga; but he had been denied the command of the Southern army that was given to Horatio Gates, whom Arnold (and many military historians) viewed as Arnold's inferior on the battlefield. Instead, Arnold was given command of a fort at West Point—a post he did not want. This, combined with his relationship with a pro-British lover, evidently pushed Arnold to espionage. Arnold's treason was discovered when a man was caught carrying plans of West Point's defense from Benedict Arnold to British general, Henry Clinton.

Map 5.7 Southern Campaigns (1780–1781)

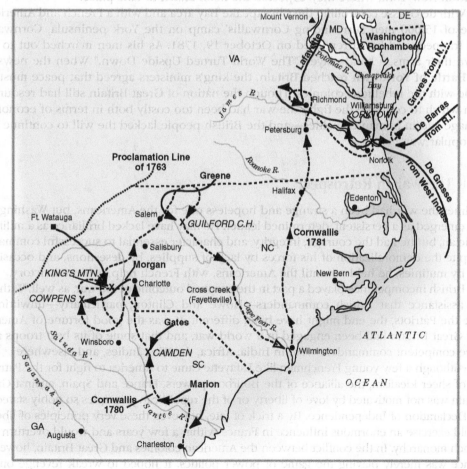

In South Carolina, Washington appointed General Nathanael Greene to replace Horatio Gates after the defeat at Camden; Greene divided his army into small guerrilla bands and launched a series of hit and run attacks on the British. Some six thousand men engaged in twenty-six battles with the British and Loyalists, and the guerrilla war spread into Georgia and North Carolina. Both Patriots and Loyalists committed murders and atrocities and ravaged their opponents' property, and the Southern backcountry slipped into near anarchy. In the worst of these fratricidal skirmishes, on October 7, 1780, Patriots massacred 1,400 Loyalists at King's Mountain in western South Carolina. In January 1781, the Patriots followed with a brilliant victory involving Daniel Morgan and his farmer-cavalrymen at the Battle of Cowpens, South Carolina, where local militia units (backed by the Continental army) defeated the British army. These successes turned the tide in the Carolinas. By autumn, those British who had not moved north to Virginia with Cornwallis were pocketed in a small area around Charleston, South Carolina.

5.3j Battle of Yorktown

Meanwhile in 1780, the French dispatched an army of 5,500 men under an able soldier, the Count de Rochambeau, to aid Washington. These troops encamped at Newport, while Rochambeau and Washington waited to see what success collaborative effort would bring. The Count de Grasse, a brilliant French naval commander with a well-equipped squadron, had arrived in the West Indies.

After an exchange of correspondence, de Grasse decided that his squadron could attack more successfully in the Chesapeake than in the harbor of New York. A decision was made for a coordinated land and sea attack in Virginia, where Cornwallis' army—supplemented by troops under the turncoat Benedict Arnold—was being engaged by forces led by French general Lafayette. Washington and Rochambeau began to move their armies southward—a maneuver that the British believed was a feint to catch them off guard in New York, where they expected the main attack to take place.

With de Grasse controlling the Chesapeake Bay area and with a French and American force of 15,000 men surrounding Cornwallis' camp on the York peninsula, Cornwallis was trapped; and he surrendered on October 19, 1781. As his men marched out to lay down their arms, a band played "The World Turned Upside Down." When the news of the **Battle of Yorktown** reached Britain, the king's ministers agreed that peace must be made with the rebellious colonies. Though the nation of Great Britain still had resources with which to continue the fight, the war had been too costly both in terms of economic damage and in human casualties—and the British people lacked the will to continue the unpopular war.

5.3k The War in Retrospect

At times the war had been a strange and hopeless one for the Americans, but Washington had emerged as a persistent, determined leader. He may have lacked brilliance as a military tactician, but he had the courage, integrity, and character essential to successful command. Despite the demoralization of his forces by lack of supplies, by desertions, and occasionally by mutinies, he held on until the Americans, with French help, achieved victory.

British incompetence played a part in the eventual outcome of the war, as well. Without the assistance that British commanders—Howe and Clinton, particularly—unwittingly gave the Patriots, the end might have been different. It was the good fortune of America that Great Britain had been engaged in a world war, and that some of its best troops and more competent commanders were in India, Africa, the West Indies, and elsewhere.

Although a few young Frenchmen like Lafayette came to America to fight for the Patriots out of sheer idealism, the alliance of the Bourbon powers, France and Spain, against Great Britain was not motivated by love of liberty or of the republican principles so nobly stated in the Declaration of Independence. By a trick of fate, however, these very principles of liberty would exercise an enormous influence in France within a few years and would overturn the French monarchy. In the conflict between the American colonies and Great Britain, however, France was merely playing the game of power politics. It hoped to wreak revenge on an ancient enemy and perhaps to regain some of the American territory it had lost.

Spain also had an interest in territory west of the British possessions in North America. To weaken Great Britain's strength in the New World would provide possible opportunities for later aggrandizement there for both France and Spain. A weak and struggling republic without money and friends would be easy to dominate and perhaps to devour.

France had promised its neighbor, Spain, that it would help wrest Gibraltar from the British, but had attacked Gibraltar in vain. Now France proposed to appease Spain with territory west of the Appalachians. In the peace negotiations, which had begun even before Yorktown, the disposition of western territories was a critical consideration.

Treaty of Paris

1783 peace treaty concluding the American Revolution and guaranteeing American independence

5.3 The Peace of Paris, 1783

To negotiate a peace with England, Congress appointed five commissioners: Benjamin Franklin, envoy in France; John Jay, American agent in Spain; John Adams, envoy in Holland; Henry Laurens; and Thomas Jefferson. Only the first three, assembled in Paris, took an active part in the discussions. At the outset, Jay was suspicious of the motives of the Count de Vergennes, the French foreign minister, and of the British agent, Richard Oswald. Oswald had come with instructions to treat the commissioners as if they represented rebellious colonies. Jay insisted that Oswald go back and obtain new instructions on how to treat the representatives of the "Thirteen United States," which would be tantamount to recognizing, at the outset, the independence of the new republic. This Oswald did.

Although the commissioners had received from Congress full power to negotiate the best treaty possible, Congress had specifically instructed them to take no steps that France would not approve. Since Jay was convinced that France was determined to sacrifice American interests to satisfy Spain, he persuaded Adams and Franklin to deal secretly with England and to make a preliminary treaty that promised favorable terms.

The news leaked out, and Vergennes was incensed. Franklin, a great favorite of the French, managed to placate him by admitting that their action was merely an "indiscretion." Nevertheless, the preliminary treaty had established the pattern for the final treaty, which was signed on September 3, 1783.

Great Britain, partly to sow dissension between the Bourbon allies and partly to win the friendship of the late colonies and keep them from becoming satellites of France, offered such favorable terms that Vergennes in anger declared that the English were ready to "buy peace rather than make it." Instead of letting Spain have the trans-Appalachian region, Great Britain agreed that the Mississippi should be the western boundary of the United States. Although Franklin had tried to obtain all of Canada "to insure peace," it was agreed that the Great Lakes should determine the northern border. In the end, Great Britain gave the Floridas back to Spain, and the treaty set the southern border of the United States at 31° north latitude. The provisions of the treaty seemed clear, but in some areas the boundary lines were not stated precisely. In Maine (at that time still part of Massachusetts), the border remained in dispute for years.

The treaty also provided that American citizens were to enjoy the same fishing rights in Canadian waters as British subjects. The two countries agreed that the Mississippi River would be forever open to navigation by both American and British shipping. The British demanded restitution of Loyalist property confiscated during the war, but all Congress could do was to recommend that this be done. The treaty also stipulated that the United States would not impede the payment of debts to the British, but Congress had no means by which to force any American debtors to pay their British creditors. Since Congress also had no authority over the states, it was agreed that suits might be brought by British subjects in the state courts for the recovery of debts. Congress finally ratified the **Treaty of Paris** on January 14 of the next year, 1784.

5.4 Effects of the War

Wars traditionally result in social and financial upheavals, and the American Revolution was no exception. Within the twenty years of controversy and war, old and settled traditions were altered; and the patterns of a new society emerged. Obviously, one of the most

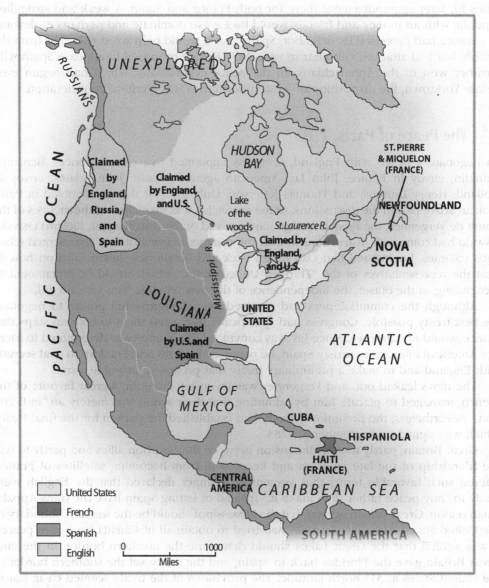

Map 5.8 North America in 1783

UNEXPLORED

RUSSIANS

PACIFIC OCEAN

Claimed by England, Russia, and Spain

Claimed by England and U.S.

HUDSON BAY

Lake of the woods

St. Laurence R.

Claimed by England and U.S.

ST. PIERRE & MIQUELON (FRANCE)

NEWFOUNDLAND

NOVA SCOTIA

LOUISIANA

Mississippi R.

UNITED STATES

Claimed by U.S. and Spain

ATLANTIC OCEAN

GULF OF MEXICO

CUBA

HISPANIOLA

HAITI (FRANCE)

CENTRAL AMERICA

CARIBBEAN SEA

SOUTH AMERICA

United States
French
Spanish
English

0   1000
Miles

important changes was the fact that the colonists were no longer English. Consequently, as soon the Revolutionary War ended, the new government faced a number of problems, not the least of which was what to do about those who had remained loyal to George III.

5.4a The King's Friends

The Treaty of Paris of 1783 contained two clauses concerning the American Loyalists. One recommended that they be restored their "estates, rights, and properties"; the other, that refugees be allowed to return for a year, without persecution or prosecution, to settle their affairs. The states, however, did not always follow these recommendations. The bitter war that "set Nabor against Nabor" had created fierce antagonism. Loyalists who had served with the British—there were twenty-one Loyalist regiments in the British army—faced being beaten, tarred and feathered, and possibly hanged. As a consequence, most Loyalists who fled did not return.

There were two waves of Loyalist migration, one in the early years of the war, the other near and after its close. Refugees in the first wave went chiefly north to Canada. Of those in the second wave, the "late Loyalists" of 1781–1784, some were probably motivated as much by the promise of cheap land as by loyalty to the King. Estimates are hard to substantiate, but about sixty thousand Loyalists, in all, left the United States. Of these, forty thousand went to Canada, ten thousand to England, and most of the rest (including over a thousand free blacks and slaves) to the West Indies and Africa.

5.4b "Our Old Home"

The Loyalists who went to England, chiefly to London and Bristol, were first lionized and then neglected. Governor Hutchinson of Massachusetts, who on arrival was offered a baronetcy (which he could not afford) and an honorary Oxford degree, wrote two years later, "We Americans are plenty here, and cheap. Few if any of us are much consulted or inquired after."

Some liked London, of course, but others found that they did not like the British and that the British, with their prejudice against colonials, did not particularly like them. Britain's tightly woven, hierarchical society had few openings for them in the usual vocations—church, military, law, politics—and not many had the capital or connections needed for business.

Then, too, the Loyalists were not British but rather British-American, and England was not home. "I would rather die in a little country farmhouse in New England," said Hutchinson, "than in the best nobleman's seat in Old England." Nevertheless, a parliamentary commission, appointed in 1783 to deal with Loyalist war claims, eventually paid out three million pounds distributed among about two thirds of the claimants.

5.4c "Go to Hell or Halifax"

Loyalists who went to Canada did much better. The British promised half-pay to ex-officers as well as land, lumber, seeds, stock, tools, and clothing, and kept most of their promises. The larger number went to Nova Scotia—to the great port city of Halifax or to the fertile St. John valley. Others went to the St. Lawrence area. Since the Maritime Provinces of Canada were a geographical and economic extension of New England, and central Upper Canada (north of the St. Lawrence River) was a similar extension of New York State, the Loyalists easily fit into Canadian society. In fact, the British in 1784 created the province of New Brunswick to separate them from the more conservative society of Nova Scotia.

The British promised better opportunities to Loyalists who went to Canada. They promised they would grant half-pay to ex-officers, as well as land, lumber, seeds, stock, tools, and clothing—and they kept most of their promises. The majority went to Nova Scotia, to the great port city of Halifax. (iStockphoto)

The arrival of the Loyalists had a significant impact on subsequent Canadian history. It placed thriving English-speaking settlements where none had been before, thus reinforcing Canada's "Britishness" at a crucial point in its development. Without the arrival of the Loyalists, Upper Canada might have gravitated toward New York State, the Maritimes toward New England, and present-day Canada might not exist. Refugees from one North American nation, in a sense, became the founders of another. "By Heaven," wrote Loyalist Edward Winslow from New Brunswick, "we will be the envy of the American States. I am in the midst of as cheerful a society as any in the world." But one Loyalist wife wrote, as she saw the last ships depart for Massachusetts, "Such a feeling of loneliness came over me that though I had not shed a tear through the entire war, I took my baby in my lap and sat down on the moss and wept."

5.4d Unrestricted Trade

No longer were the American colonies a source of raw materials supplied exclusively to Great Britain. Dutch, French, Spanish, and Portuguese ships could slip into American ports and load up tobacco, wheat, corn, meat, rice, and other products needed in Europe. Despite the war—perhaps even as a result of it—some American merchants made more money than ever before; and some European commodities, received in exchange for produce, were more abundant during the war than they had been previously.

War profiteers made a few fortunes; more important, however, a network of colonial merchants experienced the challenges and problems of unrestricted trade on an international scale. Patriotism did not keep some dealers from making 200 or 300 percent profit on clothing and supplies needed by the Continental soldiers. New industries, particularly war industries, developed. Iron foundries multiplied. Gunsmiths flourished, and factories for the manufacture of muskets, gunpowder, and cannons were built—particularly in New England and Pennsylvania. Since the usual trade in English woolens and other fabrics was cut off, cloth making was encouraged.

5.4e The Westward Movement

With the elimination of the Proclamation of 1763's prohibition against movement into the trans-Appalachian region, fresh migrations began. Frontiersmen were soon filtering into valleys and clearings beyond the mountains. In 1776, Virginia had organized into a county a portion of what later became the state of Kentucky. Before the Revolution, frontiersmen from Virginia had settled on the Watauga River in what became Tennessee. After the Revolution, uprooted citizens and restless souls all along the frontier began a trek west that would continue until, one day, the American continent as far west as the Pacific would be occupied. Land companies were organized, and within a few years speculation in western lands became an obsession. Thus, in many ways, one could see the native peoples as losers in the Revolution, alongside the British. In the course of twenty years of imperial struggle—and then the war for independence itself—Native Americans first lost their French allies and then the British as a restraint on American expansionism.

5.4f Modifications to American Society

The Revolution also brought social changes. The most immediate result was the elimination of royal governors, other British officials, and the cliques of socially elite who had gathered around them. Even in colonies that had not had royal officials, those who were loyal to the mother country were swept out and new leaders took their places.

Yet, as important as these changes were, the United States nowhere experienced the kind of social revolution that swept France a few years later. The structure of American society was modified rather than completely abolished and built anew. In Virginia, for example, the influence of the tidewater aristocrats diminished somewhat and back-country politicians of the type represented by Patrick Henry gained power. But the families that had produced leaders before the Revolution still continued to supply many of the leaders in the new nation.

One reason the new republic moved with relative ease from the status of a colony to that of a self-governing nation was the tradition of local responsibility established in all of the colonies early in the development of the British settlements. This inheritance from the British tradition of local self-government ensured a reservoir of leadership from which individuals could be drawn for any level of responsibility required.

Though lacking a French-style social revolution, it must still be said, in summation, that within a generation or so after the Treaty of Paris, American society had undergone extraordinarily rapid change. As the noted historian Joyce Appleby has argued in a recent book, all sorts of Americans reinvented themselves in the first decades of the new nation—started small businesses, created new products, established organizations, and found themselves ready to take chances, in general.

5.4g American Nationalism

There were a number of conditions after the American Revolution that favored the growth of American nationalism. For one thing, many idealistic democratic and humanitarian tendencies were accentuated or set in motion. Slavery, imprisonment for debt, and humiliating punishments were regarded with growing disfavor. The idea of universal education at state expense was voiced. Small businesses and manufacturing were stimulated, first by American war demands and the severing of trade with England, and later by the patriotic impulse to purchase American-made goods. Conversely, American patriotism and nationalism also proved to have a dark and dangerous side. During the Revolution and the early national period, large Loyalist estates were confiscated and divided; and church establishments were attacked—especially the Anglican Church, due to its ties with England and prevalent Loyalism during the Revolution.

Americans were far from being of one mind about these matters. They did believe, however, that they could, through honest effort and the fortunate circumstances of their society, forge ahead in ways that the nations of the Old World could not. The Americans were a "new" people, as Crèvecoeur put it. They were ready to teach the rest of the world and were no longer content to be taught. Indeed, Americans considered the United States to be superior to England and Europe in every way. It was, they hoped, the model of a new kind of New World.

"Americans are fanatically proud of their own wild country," remarked an English traveler during the period, "and love to disparage the rest of the world." It was America's mission to lead other nations to revolution against the forces of ignorance and oppression or just as Joel Barlow wrote, "to excite emulation throughout the kingdoms of the earth, and meliorate the conditions of the human race." It was America's responsibility to extend the concepts of liberty, equality, and justice over all the earth. This responsibility, James Wilson would say at the Constitutional Convention, was "the great design of Providence in regard to this globe."

In order to accomplish this mission, Americans felt compelled to cultivate their "Americanness," emphasize their differences with Europe, and develop their own culture in terms of their own national purpose. "Every engine should be employed to render the people of the country national," wrote Noah Webster, "to call their attachment home to their own country." If the United States was to succeed as an experiment in self-government, the people who governed themselves must have deep faith in it. The patriotic impulse was considered essential to the creation of a national character.

As a consequence, there was a trend in fashion toward American-made **homespun clothing** even if the American threads were inferior to their British counterparts. American churches—including, but not limited to the Anglicans and the Catholics—broke with their British hierarchies. The Anglican Church even underwent a name change to become the American Episcopal Church. Education was altered to include American history, complete with the American heroes of the Revolution, including General Washington, Jefferson and his Declaration, and the words and exploits of Patrick Henry, Thomas Paine, John Adams, Samuel Adams and the Sons of Liberty, along with many more. American language education was also altered with the introduction of *Noah Webster's Speller*, including American spellings and pronunciations of words that, by 1783, had become different from those in England. The forging of a truly American identity separate from England, and separate from the identities of the thirteen individual colonies, had begun.

5.4f The Articles of Confederation

Soon after the Declaration of Independence, a committee was appointed to draw up **Articles of Confederation** to bind the thirteen states together into a union. It took more than a year to draft the Articles, and they then had to be submitted to the states for ratification. This took until the spring of 1781. In the meantime—during almost the entire war—the rebel colonies operated under the authority of the extralegal Continental Congress.

Among the most important contributions of the Articles were their preservation of the union and their definition of powers to be granted to the central government as opposed to the state governments. The delay in ratifying the Articles of Confederation was due chiefly to a conflict of economic interests. Massachusetts, Connecticut, New York, Virginia, Georgia, and the Carolinas—under the terms of colonial charters, royal grants, American Indian treaties, or proprietary claims—all asserted ownership of tremendous grants of land in the West. To be able to retain these western lands would be a great economic boon, since the sale of the back regions would provide the state governments with a steady income and make it unnecessary for them to tax their citizens at all.

Naturally, the advantage that would come to states with western land claims was resented by the states with fixed boundaries. For example, Rhode Island could claim no

Homespun clothing
Inferior, American-made clothing worn by the newly independent Americans as an expression of their national identity

Articles of Confederation
America's first constitution that created a weak confederal form of government with most of the power residing in the states

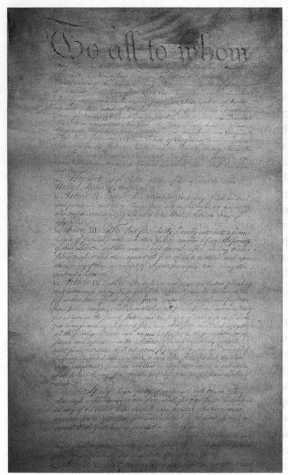

The Articles of Confederation, ratified by all thirteen colonies in 1781, were the basis for the United States government until the Constitution was drafted. (Wikimedia Commons)

land west of Rhode Island due to the existence of Connecticut. Conversely, Virginia claimed as much land west along its latitude as it could. The "landless" states such as Rhode Island protested that the War for Independence was being fought for the benefit of all and that every state should share in the rewards to be found in western territory. Thus, these landless states were reluctant to sign the Articles of Confederation until the westward limits of the existing states were set and until Congress, the central government, was given authority to grant lands and to create new states beyond these limits.

The debate was not motivated entirely by the question of the equality of the states, however. Land speculators had formed companies in Maryland and Pennsylvania, for example, and had made purchases from the American Indians in the Ohio Valley. Now they wished for governmental validation of their titles. How could they secure clear title to land claimed by Virginia and New York when such states were inclined not to recognize American Indian purchases made by out-of-state residents?

Eventually, after considerable political maneuvering and propagandizing, both sides gave in. Between 1777 and 1781, the land companies vacated their claims to western territory purchased from the American Indians; and upon the recommendation of a congressional committee in 1780, the landed states—led by Virginia, New York, and Connecticut—gave up claim to most of the trans-Appalachian country, thus making the western lands the territory of the nation. In February 1781 the last of the landless states, Maryland, ratified the Articles; and on March 1, the Confederation was formally proclaimed. The problem of western lands was now placed squarely before the new central government.

When the war was over, many thoughtful citizens throughout the country feared that the loose provisions of the Articles of Confederation would not permit the evolution of a nation strong enough to survive. For example, in foreign policy much would depend upon the power of a centralized authority. Furthermore, a central authority was required to establish the financial stability of the nation and to deal with problems of credit, the issuance of money, and the maintenance of national defense. These problems and their solutions would form an important chapter in constitution-making.

A final word should be said about the American Revolution, not only as a symbol in the history of the United States, but also as a guiding light for generations of people the world over. As the first anti-imperialist, anti-monarchial revolution of modern times, the American Revolution inspired imitators in Europe and Latin America in the nineteenth century and in Africa and Asia in the twentieth. The principles of the Revolution—government by consent of the governed, and the existence of inviolate rights that no government can invade—spoke to the hearts and minds of people in other nations. While the fact was, and is, that the American Revolution is not exportable—other people and other nations are the products of their own particular circumstances and experiences—the language, idealism, and ideas of the American Revolution have taken on a life of their own, one that transcends national boundaries.

Timeline

1759	The Privy Council instructs the governor of Virginia to refuse to sign any bill that fails to include a "suspending clause."
1761	General writs of assistance empowers officers of the British customs service to break into and search homes and stores for smuggled goods.
1763	Pontiac's Rebellion
	Peace of Paris concludes Seven Years War.
1764	Currency Act restrictions on the issuance of paper money force colonists to pay British merchants in gold or silver.
	Revenue Act or Sugar Act declares that a number of commodities could be imported only from England.
1765	Quartering Act requires colonists to provide housing for British troops.
	Stamp Act Riots
1766	Declaratory Act declares that Parliament can legislate in all matters "whatsoever," but Stamp Act is repealed.
1767	Townshend Act imposes new duties on a number of commodities.
1768	*Liberty* Incident
1770	Repeal of Townshend Duties except for a symbolic duty on tea
	Boston Massacre, March 5
1772	*Gaspee* Incident: colonists burn a British ship in Providence harbor.
1773	Tea Act and Boston Tea Party
1774	Quebec Act annexes lands in the northwest to Quebec.
	Coercive Acts or "Intolerable Acts"
	First Continental Congress meets at Carpenter's Hall in Philadelphia.
1775	First shots of the Revolution are fired at Lexington on April 18.
	Second Continental Congress appoints George Washington as commander of troops around Boston.
	Battle of Bunker Hill on June 17 reduces chances for negotiations.
	Olive Branch Petition is rejected by England.

1776

News arrives in January that England is using Hessian mercenaries.

Thomas Paine publishes *Common Sense*.

British withdraw from Boston in March.

George Washington is defeated at Long Island in August.

Richard Henry Lee proposes a Declaration of Independence in June.

Declaration of Independence goes to the printer on July 4.

Washington is defeated at Manhattan in November.

Washington crosses the Delaware River on December 25 and defeats Hessian mercenaries at Trenton on December 26.

1777

Washington suffers defeat at Brandywine Creek on September 11.

Washington is defeated at Germantown on October 4.

Washington withdraws to winter his army at Valley Forge, Pennsylvania.

Saratoga: 5,800 British surrender to Horatio Gates on October 17.

1778

Treaty of Alliance with France on February 6

British capture Savannah in December.

1780

Pennsylvania provides for gradual abolition of slavery.

British capture Charleston in May.

Patriots massacre 1,400 Loyalists at King's Mountain on October 7.

1781

British are defeated at Cowpens, South Carolina, in January.

Yorktown: British General Cornwallis surrenders on October 19, trapped between American and French troops.

1783

Massachusetts Supreme Court abolishes slavery.

Treaty of Paris officially concludes Revolutionary War, September 3.

CHAPTER SUMMARY

At the close of the Seven Years War in 1763, Americans were generally content to continue being British; however, a number of changes brought about by the war itself would lead to an American revolt against England in less than a generation. The Seven Years War left England deeply in debt and also with new, unruly territory to control with the acquisition of French Canada. The British viewed the American colonies as unruly as well, as evidenced by incidents such as the Boston Impressment riot a generation earlier. Consequently, the British determined that forward placement of troops in the American colonies—as well as in the newly acquired, former French colonies—was necessary to ensure order.

Forward placement of troops, however, was expensive; and that, coupled with the debt incurred from the Seven Years War, induced the British to impose taxes on the colonists to extract from them what the British viewed as their share of the burden. In the British view, the British troops had not only provided security for the colonists in the Seven Years War, they were also continuing to provide security from which the colonists benefited.

In the view of the colonists, however, forward placement of troops in the American colonies was unnecessary because the French had effectively been removed from North America as a threat. Consequently, the colonists rejected both the new British taxes and the new British restrictions on trade, engaging in boycotts of British goods, rioting, and eventually dumping a large shipment of tea in Boston Harbor.

When the British had finally had enough and sent troops to "quell the rebellion," most Americans favored resistance—though whether or not it would result in American independence remained unclear. British use of Hessian mercenaries, combined with Thomas Paine's *Common Sense,* produced enough sentiment to inspire the Declaration of Independence in July 1776; and the war became a war for independence. Though Americans lost most of the battles, the superior British army was never able to completely squelch the rebellion. The shocking American victory at Saratoga resulted in French assistance and a Treaty of Alliance with France. The British moved the war south in an attempt to exploit stronger Loyalist sentiments in the South and scored major victories at Savannah and Charleston; but when the French arrived at Yorktown to trap General Cornwallis and 7,500 British troops between the Americans and the French, the British decided that it was time to negotiate an end to the costly war.

The Revolution brought a number of changes to American society in addition to self-rule. The former colonists now had a new American identity, language, and culture as they attempted to forge a new Republic and deal with the social and economic problems left over from the war. Slavery had been abolished in Massachusetts and was in the process of being abolished in other northern states. Questions remained over the weakness of the Confederation, however, as contentious issues over western lands had delayed ratification of the Articles of Confederation until 1781. Nevertheless, the principles of the American Revolution—freedom and self-rule—would be a guiding beacon to the world for centuries to come.

KEY TERMS

BIBLIOGRAPHY

A

Alexander, Edward. *A Revolutionary Conservative, James Duane of New York*. New York: Columbia University Press, 1938.

Ammerman, David. *In the Common Cause: American Response to the Coercive Acts of 1774*. Charlottesville, VA: University of Virginia Press, 1974.

B

Bailyn, Bernard. *The Ideological Origins of the American Revolution*. Cambridge, MA: Belknap Press, 1992.

Bassett, John, Ed. *The Writings of Colonel William Byrd, of Westover in Virginia, Esq*. New York: Doubleday, 1989.

Boucher, Jonathan. *Reminiscences of an American Loyalist, 1738–1789*. Port Washington, NY: Kennikat Press, 1967.

Brewer, John. *Party Ideology and Popular Politics at the Accession of George III*. Cambridge, UK: Cambridge University Press, 1981.

Brinkley, Alan. *American History: A Survey* 11th ed. Boston, MA: McGraw-Hill, 2003.

C

Calhoon, Robert M. *The Loyalists in Revolutionary America 1760–1781*. New York: Harcourt Brace, 1973.

———. *Revolutionary America: An Interpretive Overview*. New York: Harcourt Brace, 1976.

Chernow, Ron. *Alexander Hamilton*. New York: Penguin, 2005.

Colden, Cadwallader. *The Letters and Papers of Cadwallader Colden*. New York: AMS Press, 1973.

Countryman, Edward. *The American Revolution: Revised Edition*. New York: Hill and Wang, 2003.

D

Dowd, Gregory E. *A Spirited Resistance: The North American Indian Struggle for Unity, 1745–1815*. Baltimore, MD: Johns Hopkins University Press, 1993.

Dull, Jonathan R. *A Diplomatic History of the American Revolution*. New Haven, CT: Yale University Press, 1987.

F

Faragher, John Mack. *Daniel Boone: The Life and Legend of an American Pioneer*. New York: Henry Holt, 1992.

Farquhar, Michael. *Great American Scandals*. New York: Penguin, 2003.

Ferguson, James E. *The Power of the Purse: A History of American Public Finance*. Chapel Hill, NC: University of North Carolina Press, 1961.

Fischer, David Hackett. *Paul Revere's Ride*. New York: Oxford University Press, 1995.

Fleming, Thomas. *1776: Year of Illusions*. New York: W. W. Norton & Company, 1975.

———. *Beat the Last Drum: The Siege of Yorktown, 1781*. Boston, MA: St. Martin's Press, 1966.

Fliegelman, Jay. *Declaring Independence: Jefferson, National Language, and the Culture of Performance*. Palo Alto, CA: Stanford University Press, 1993.

Flower, Milton. *John Dickinson: Conservative Revolutionary*. Charlottesville, VA: University of Virginia Press, 1983.

Foner, Eric. *Tom Paine and Revolutionary America*. New York: Oxford University Press, 2004.

G

Gruber, Ira D. *The Howe Brothers and the American Revolution*. Chapel Hill, NC: University of North Carolina Press, 2011.

J

Jameson, J. Franklin *The American Revolution Considered as a Social Movement*. Boston, MA: Beacon Press, 1965.

Jensen, Merrill. *The New Nation: A History of the United States During the Articles of Confederation*. Boston, MA: Northeastern University Press, 1981.

K

Klein, Rachel N. *Unification of a Slave State: The Rise of the Planter Class in the South Carolina Backcountry, 1760–1808*. Chapel Hill, NC: University of North Carolina Press, 1992.

L

Labaree, Benjamin W. *The Boston Tea Party*. Boston, MA: Northeastern, 1979.

Labaree, Leonard Woods. *Conservatism in Early American History*. Ithaca, NY: Great Seal Books, 1948.

Lincoln, Charles Henry. *The Revolutionary Movement in Pennsylvania, 1770–1776*. Philadelphia, PA: University of Pennsylvania Press, 1968.

BIBLIOGRAPHY

Mackesy, Piers, and John W. Shy. *The War for America 1775–1783*. Lincoln, NE: Bison Books, 1993.

Miller, Perry, and Thomas H. Johnson, Eds. *The Puritans: A Sourcebook of their Writings Volume II*. New York: Harper, 1968.

McCullough, David. *1776*. New York: Simon and Schuster, 2006.

———. *John Adams*. New York: Simon and Schuster, 2008.

Morgan, Edmund S., and Helen S. Morgan. *The Stamp Act Crisis: Prologue to Revolution*. Chapel Hill, NC: University of North Carolina Press, 1995.

Nagle, Robert. *American Conservatism: An Illustrated History*. New York: Allied Books, 1988.

Norton, Mary Beth. *The British Americans: Loyalist Exiles in England, 1774–1789*. Edinburgh, UK: Constable, 1974.

———. *Liberty's Daughters: The Revolutionary Experience of American Women 1750–1800*. Ithaca, NY: Cornell University Press, 1996.

Palmer, Robert R. *The Age of the Democratic Revolution: Vol. I, The Challenge*. Princeton, NJ: Princeton University Press, 1969.

Quarles, Benjamin. *The Negro in the American Revolution*. Chapel Hill, NC: University of North Carolina Press, 1996.

Roark, James L., Michael P. Johnson, Patricia Cline Cohen, Sarah Stage, Alan Lawson, and Susan M. Hartmann. *The American Promise: A History of the United States Volume II*. 3rd ed. New York: Bedford/St. Martin's, 2005.

Royster, Charles. *A Revolutionary People at War: The Continental Army and the American Character, 1775–1783*. Chapel Hill, NC: University of North Carolina Press, 1996.

Schlesinger, Arthur M. Sr. *The Colonial Merchants and the American Revolution, 1763–1776*. Temecula, CA: Reprint Services Corporation, 1993.

Schneider, Carol, and Herbert C. Schneider Ed. *Samuel Johnson: His Career and Writings, 1929 Edition*. Bristol, UK: Thoemmes Press, 2002.

Shy, John. *Toward Lexington: The Role of the British Army in the Coming of the American Revolution*. Princeton, NJ: Princeton University Press, 1965.

Watts, John. *Letter Book of John Watts: Merchant and Councilor of New York*. New York: New York Historical Society, 1928.

Weigley, Russell F. *The Partisan War: The South Carolina Campaign of 1780–1782*. Columbia, SC: University of South Carolina Press, 1975.

Wills, Garry. *Inventing America: Jefferson's Declaration of Independence*. Boston, MA: Mariner, 2002.

Wood, Gordon S. *The Creation of the American Republic 1776–1787*. Chapel Hill, NC: University of North Carolina Press, 1998.

Wright, Louis B. *The First Gentlemen of Virginia: Intellectual Qualities of the Early Colonial Ruling Class*. Charlottesville, VA: University of Virginia Press, 1970.

Zobel, Hiller B. *The Boston Massacre*. New York: W. W. Norton & Company, 1996.

POP QUIZ

1. Which of the following is an important factor in understanding the American Revolution?
   a. the fact that the American colonies had matured in terms of self-government and experience with authority
   b. the fact that the British had not allowed any self-government in the colonies whatsoever
   c. the fact that the British imposed taxes on the colonies, but not on citizens in England
   d. the fact that the colonists felt that they had no connection with British culture

2. Which of the following was required by the Currency Act of 1764?
   a. that the colonies issue paper money, causing inflation
   b. that debts to British merchants could only be paid in gold or silver
   c. that "In God We Trust" be removed from colonial currency
   d. that all colonial currency be backed by land holdings

3. The Quebec Act of 1774 angered Americans by _____.
   a. annexing the land north of the Ohio River to Quebec
   b. granting land north of the Ohio River to Indians
   c. declaring that French was an official language in Quebec
   d. requiring that Americans who had moved to Quebec withdraw east of the Appalachians

4. Colonial newspapers protested the Stamp Act by _____.
   a. calling for revolution
   b. failing to print any newspapers so long as the stamp was required
   c. printing a skull and crossbones in the space where the stamp was required
   d. printing their own counterfeit stamps

5. The colonists argued which of the following about British power?
   a. that the British could legislate to regulate trade
   b. that the British could impose taxes, but only for the purpose of raising revenue
   c. that Parliament had the power to enact legislation in all cases whatsoever
   d. that the government of England had no power to make laws in the colonies

6. Which of these occurred in what is known as the Gaspee Incident?
   a. A British lieutenant, who referred to himself as "The Great Gaspee," declared himself ruler of the colonies.
   b. The colonists burned a British ship in Providence Harbor.
   c. The captain of the British ship, *Gaspee,* bombarded Providence.
   d. Colonists in Providence destroyed the home of Rhode Island Governor Gaspee.

7. At the First Continental Congress in Philadelphia in 1774, what did the delegates resolve?
   a. that the colonists should make no concessions until Parliament repealed the Coercive Acts
   b. that the colonists would accept no British trade regulations
   c. that the colonists must declare independence
   d. all of the above

8. The Declaration of the Causes and Necessity of taking up Arms asserted that the colonists were left with only two choices _____.
   a. unconditional submission to tyranny or resistance by force
   b. outright rebellion or a negotiated peace
   c. fight or flight
   d. liberty or death

9. *Common Sense* contained which of the following?
   a. a call for calm negotiation and peace
   b. a denunciation of the monarchy and King George personally in bold language
   c. a denunciation of the leaders of the Revolution
   d. a call for a return to laws based on the Bible

10. All of the following were used to finance the revolution *except* _____.
    a. foreign loans
    b. an income tax
    c. selling bonds
    d. issuing paper money

11. For what is Nathanael Greene famous?
    a. for dividing his army into small guerrilla bands
    b. for marching his army to songs played by army bands
    c. for banning army bands as too noisy
    d. for naming blood poisoning after his dying brother, Gan Greene

POP QUIZ

12. The British did not allow black men to serve in their army. T   F

13. Thomas Jefferson believed that black people were equal to whites. T   F

14. The Treaty of Alliance with France took place after the Battle of _____ in 1777.

15. Under the _____, western land became national territory in 1781.

ANSWER KEY: 1 a   2 b   3 a   4 c   5 a   6 b   7 a   8 a   9 b   10 b   11 a   12 F   13 F   14 Saratoga   15 Articles of Confederation

Chapter 6

(Wikimedia Commons)

Establishing the Republic, 1781–1800

CHAPTER OUTLINE

6.1 The Search for Stability

6.1a Balancing Federal with Local Authority

The first two decades of American life after the Revolution were the years in which the work of independence was completed, the Republic shaped, the national character determined, the federal system established, and a foreign policy developed. Fortunately for the nation born during this period, it was blessed with an extraordinary generation of leaders. These men met the challenges forthrightly and left a legacy of dedicated and creative work that still fascinates their countrymen and women.

Federalism

A way of organizing government where there is division of powers between the central government (the U.S. government) and the political subunit governments (the states)

Articles of Confederation

America's first constitution, proposed in 1776 and ratified in 1781, that created a confederal form of government with all of the power in the states and a weak national government

Of prime importance in the political life of the United States throughout its history has been the problem of **federalism**—the division of power between the states and the federal government—or more simply, the issue of local control or states' rights versus national power or central authority. The origins of this problem are to be found in the British imperial system of the mid-eighteenth century. At the center of this system had stood Great Britain, whose government had directed foreign affairs and intercolonial relations with the view of keeping the machinery and policies of the empire working in harmony. At the extremities of this system had been the colonies themselves, each of which had attained the right to govern its internal affairs.

In practice, however, the dividing line between imperial and local affairs was variously interpreted; out of the conflict rose the American Revolution. With the Declaration of Independence, the American colonies rejected the government in London altogether and united, sufficiently, under the pressures of war to set up a central authority of their own making—the Confederation.

When Richard Henry Lee, on June 7, 1776, offered a resolution to the Continental Congress to declare American independence, he also proposed that "a plan of confederation be prepared and transmitted to the respective colonies for their consideration and approbation." A little over a month later, on July 12, a committee headed by John Dickinson of Pennsylvania presented such a plan to the Continental Congress. On November 15, 1777, after more than a year of debate, the **Articles of Confederation** were approved and sent to the states for ratification, a process that took four years—the Articles of Confederation would not be ratified until 1781. During almost the entire Revolutionary War, therefore, the country operated under the authority of the Continental Congress without a formal central government.

Because the loyalty of individual Americans was strongly attached to their states, it was readily agreed that the states should hold the sovereign powers of government. The Articles were designed to create an assembly of equal states, each of which retained its "sovereignty, freedom, and independence, and every Power, Jurisdiction, and right." The Articles of Confederation, therefore, created a loose confederation of states with a new Congress almost exactly like the wartime Continental Congress then in existence, in which each state—regardless of size, population, or wealth—had an equal vote. The Articles delegated to Congress the power to declare war, make peace, conclude treaties, raise and maintain armies, maintain a navy, establish a postal system, regulate American Indian affairs, borrow money, issue bills of credit, and regulate the value of the coinage of the United States and the several states. However, nine of the thirteen states had to give their consent before any legislation of importance could be enacted, and enforcement of the decisions of Congress depended upon the cooperation of all the states. Ultimately, all power therefore rested in the states rather than in the national government. For example, Congress could make treaties but could not force the states to live up to their stipulations. It could authorize an army but could not fill its ranks without the cooperation of each state. It could borrow money but had to depend on requisitions from the states to repay its debts. Nor did the Articles provide standing agencies of enforcement. Congress could pass laws, but there was no formal executive or judicial branch to execute and adjudicate them. The day-to-day operations of government were handled rather precariously by officials or committees appointed by Congress.

Richard Henry Lee
(Wikimedia Commons)

Pictured is John Trumbull's famous depiction of the drafting committee presenting its work to the Continental Congress on July 12, 1776 (though the Articles of Confederation were not ratified until 1781). (Wikimedia Commons)

Because of their recent quarrels with Parliament over questions of taxation and commercial regulation, the states also withheld two key powers from their new central government: the power to levy taxes (Congress could merely request contributions from the state legislatures) and the power to regulate commerce. This proved to be problematic during the Revolution, as states actually fulfilled only ten percent of Congressional requisitions. Without the power to tax and regulate commerce, the Confederation could not depend upon a regular and adequate supply of revenue to sustain its own functions, nor could it attempt to foster a national economy, a factor essential to the political unity of America.

The central government, therefore, was what the Articles called it—nothing more than "a firm league of friendship." Sharing a common cause and facing common danger, such as an invading British army on American soil, its members could work together with some measure of effectiveness. Any suspicion that Congress would infringe upon their own right of independent action, however, would throw the states on their guard—and once imminent danger passed, the states tended to work independently rather than together.

Pictured is Richard Henry Lee reading the Declaration of Independence in Philadelphia. (AP Wide World Photos)

6.16 The State Governments

The Declaration of Independence in 1776 had made necessary the creation of two kinds of government: central and local. While only tentative motions were made toward centralization, the people were quick to make the transition from colonial government to state government. Actually the process was one of revision and adaptation, since each of the former colonies already possessed a government with its own methods of operation. Indeed, two states (Connecticut and Rhode Island) continued to operate under their colonial charters by simply deleting all references to the British crown. Ten other states completed new constitutions within a year after the Declaration of Independence, and the last (Massachusetts) had made the transition by 1780. The state constitutions, though varying in detail, reflected both the colonial experience and the current revolutionary controversy.

The framers of these constitutions placed the center of political authority in the legislative branch, where it would be especially responsive to popular and local control. As a Massachusetts town meeting bluntly resolved in 1778, "The oftener power Returns to the hands of the people, the Better ... Where can the power be lodged so Safe as in the Hands of the people?" Members of the legislature, if they wished to be reelected, had to keep in mind the feelings of their people "back home." Legislators were held constantly accountable by being restricted to brief terms: in ten states the lower house, which originated tax legislation, was newly elected every year; in Connecticut and Rhode Island it was every six months; in South Carolina, every two years.

Framers of the constitutions, remembering their recent troubles with royal governors and magistrates, restricted the powers of governors and justices almost to the vanishing point. The average governor, jokesters claimed, had just about enough authority to collect his salary. Opposition to a single, strong executive was so intense that in Pennsylvania the position of the governor was abolished and replaced with a council of twelve.

The imbalance of power among the branches of government often severely hampered the states' abilities to meet and solve the political and economic problems that faced them during and after the war. Yet whatever their shortcomings, these constitutions were the first attempts to translate the generalities of the Declaration into usable instruments of government. They were constructed on the premise, novel to the eighteenth century, that a government should be formed under a *written* document—thus recognizing for the first time in modern political life the difference between fundamental law and statute law and between rule of law and rule of men. The introduction of such precisely formed instruments of governmental law, on such a grand scale, was a major contribution to the science of government.

Northwest Ordinance of 1787

After the lands to the northwest had been surveyed and divided into townships in 1785, it provided an orderly process for governing and the eventual transition to statehood.

The state constitutions reaffirmed the powerful colonial tradition of individual freedom in their bills of rights, which guaranteed each citizen freedom of religion, speech, and assembly, trial by jury, the right of habeas corpus, and other natural and civil rights. In general, they extended the voting franchise to the majority of white, male citizens. In all states, a man had to own some property to vote. In many, he had to own a more substantial amount to hold office. Since property formed the basis for voting qualifications, and since the states quickly enlarged opportunities to own land, most white males could probably meet the requirements. New Jersey even gave the vote to women, only to withdraw it later in 1807. Over the years, gradual abolition of property qualifications further widened the suffrage; all property requirements had been eliminated, on a state-by-state basis, by 1852.

The popular fear of governmental power tended to render the state governments politically and financially impotent. Afraid to antagonize the voters, who could quickly run them out of office, legislators had difficulty, for example, in passing effective measures of taxation. Even when they did so, revenue men were hard put in forcing collections from the people.

6.2 The Confederation Period

Such was the political framework within which the new nation entered the "critical period," 1783–1789, from the close of the Revolutionary War to the inauguration of the federal government under the Constitution. The term *critical period* was first introduced by historian John Fiske in 1889, and still possesses some utility. On the one hand, historians have come to believe that the years of the Confederation were more creative and constructive than once was supposed. During these years, a peace was won on terms highly favorable to the United States; an orderly policy for western territorial expansion was established; a postwar recession was overcome and replaced by economic prosperity; and the population increased. Finally, at the end of the critical period, the Constitution was born. In general, the achievements of the period were due to the efforts of particular individuals and groups, and to some of the more foresighted state governments. The central government was much too dependent on the conflicting whims of the several states to be consistently effective.

6.2a Establishing a Western Policy

The solution to the western land problem (See Chapter 5)—which had kept the last state, Maryland, from ratifying the Articles until 1781—was of paramount importance to the new government. It represented a first step toward nationalization and made certain that the nation, as it moved west, would gradually evolve as a unit rather than as thirteen colonies with a set of permanently dependent territories. It also meant that, since Congress now controlled all the western lands, it could determine a central policy for the development of this vast unpopulated territory.

During and after the Revolution, a stream of settlers poured west, creating an urgent need for a systematic plan of land sale and territorial government. A land ordinance passed by Congress in 1785 provided for a government survey to divide the land of the Northwest Territory (north of the Ohio River, west of Pennsylvania, and east of the Mississippi River) into townships of thirty-six square miles. Each township was to be split into thirty-six sections of one square mile (640 acres) each, and each section into quarter sections. Four sections in every township were reserved as bounties for soldiers of the Continental army, and another section was set aside for the use of public schools. The remainder of the land was to be sold at public auction for at least one dollar an acre, in minimum lots of 640 acres.

The Ordinance of 1785 proved advantageous to wealthy land speculators, who bought up whole townships and resold them at handsome profits. Sensing even greater returns, a group of speculators (including some congressmen and government officials) pressed for further legislation to provide a form of government for the Northwest. The result was the **Northwest Ordinance of 1787**, based largely on a similar ordinance drafted by Jefferson in 1784 but never put into effect.

Map 6.1 Western Lands Ceded by the States (1782–1802)

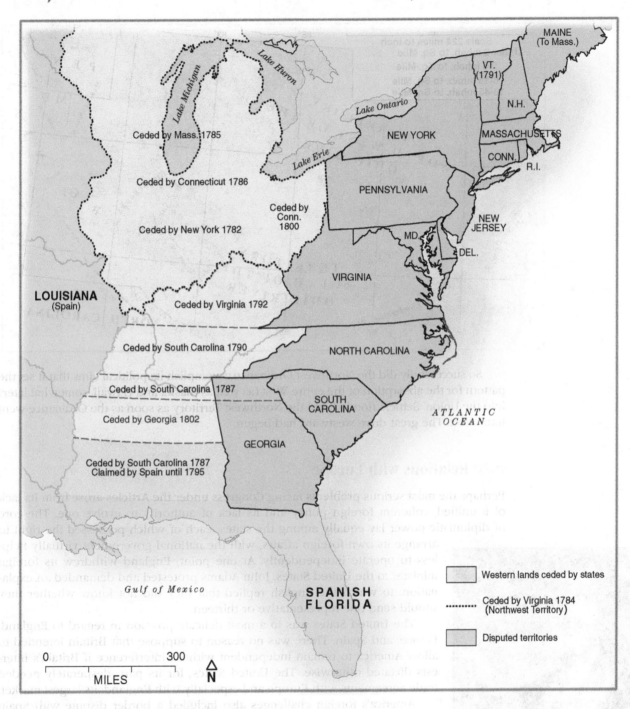

MAINE
(To Mass.)

VT.
(1791)

N.H.

Lake Michigan

Lake Huron

Lake Ontario

Ceded by Mass. 1785

NEW YORK

MASSACHUSETTS

Lake Erie

CONN.

R.I.

Ceded by Connecticut 1786

PENNSYLVANIA

Ceded by Conn. 1800

Ceded by New York 1782

NEW JERSEY

MD.

DEL.

VIRGINIA

LOUISIANA
(Spain)

Ceded by Virginia 1792

Ceded by South Carolina 1790

NORTH CAROLINA

Ceded by South Carolina 1787

SOUTH CAROLINA

ATLANTIC OCEAN

Ceded by Georgia 1802

GEORGIA

Ceded by South Carolina 1787
Claimed by Spain until 1795

Gulf of Mexico

SPANISH FLORIDA

Western lands ceded by states

Ceded by Virginia 1784
(Northwest Territory)

Disputed territories

0   300

MILES

N

Though it favored the wealthy land speculator over the indigent farmer, the Northwest Ordinance did provide an orderly process for translating the unsettled Northwest from frontier to statehood. It provided that Congress should appoint from among the landholders of the region a governor, a secretary, and three judges. When the territory reached a population of five thousand free, adult males, a bicameral legislature was to be established. When there were sixty thousand free inhabitants (the population of the smallest state at the time), the voters might adopt a constitution, elect their own officers, and enter the Union on equal terms with the original thirteen states. The Ordinance provided that no less than three and no more than five states were to be formed from the Northwest Territory. Slavery was forbidden in the area, and freedom of worship and trial by jury were guaranteed.

Map 6.2 Trans-Allegheny Settlements (1790)

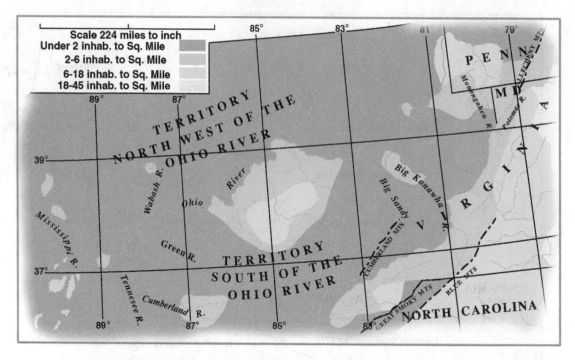

So successfully did the Northwest Ordinance accomplish its political aims that it set the pattern for the absorption of the entire West (as well as Alaska and Hawaii, somewhat later) into the Union. Settlers flooded into the Northwest Territory as soon as the Ordinance went into effect. The great drive westward had begun.

6.26 Relations with Europe

Perhaps the most serious problems facing Congress under the Articles arose from its lack of a unified, coherent foreign policy and its lack of authority to evolve one. The core of diplomatic power lay equally among the states, each of which possessed the right to arrange its own foreign affairs, with the national government virtually helpless to operate independently. At one point, England withdrew its foreign minister to the United States. John Adams protested and demanded an explanation, to which the English replied that they did not know whether they should send one representative or thirteen.

The United States was in a most delicate position in regard to England, France, and Spain. There was no reason to suppose that Britain intended to allow America to remain independent without interference if Britain's interests dictated otherwise. The United States, for its part, desperately needed trade agreements with Europe and especially with England, its largest market.

America's foreign challenges also included a border dispute with Spain over Florida. When the Spanish, who controlled the lower Mississippi and New Orleans, closed these territories to American trade in 1784, the nation was in trouble. The closing of the Mississippi effectively shut down vital trade to the American interior, and the livelihood of the nation was in peril. If Congress could not open the Mississippi to trade, a number of Western leaders favored either taking New Orleans by force or joining a British protectorate that might help them to do so. Washington felt that the West, in 1784, was so near to secession that "the touch of a feather" might divide it from the country.

Secretary of Foreign Affairs John Jay (Wikimedia Commons)

The Spanish, who needed American trade, seemed willing to negotiate; and in 1785 the Spanish minister Diego de Gardoqui discussed terms with Secretary of Foreign Affairs John Jay. Both diplomats were bound by specific instructions that led to a stalemate, but eventually Jay agreed to a commercial treaty in 1786. This treaty would have

Map 6.3 Territorial Growth 1790

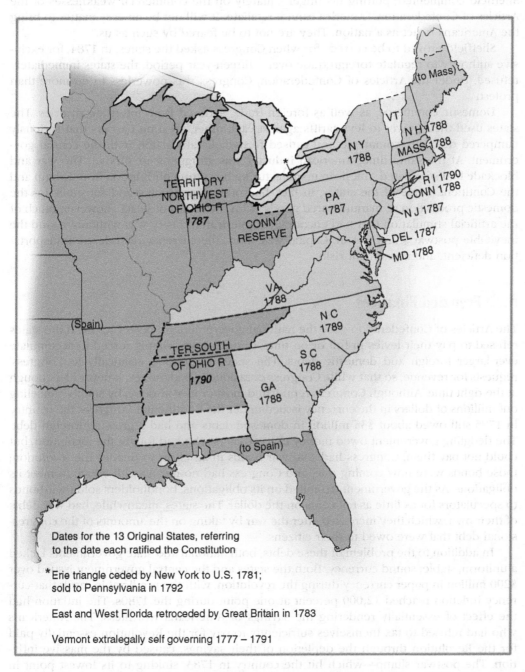

VT

N H 1788

N Y 1788

MASS 1788

R I 1790

CONN 1788

PA 1787

N J 1787

DEL 1787

MD 1788

(to Mass)

TERRITORY NORTHWEST OF OHIO R *1787*

CONN RESERVE

VA 1788

N C 1789

(Spain)

TER. SOUTH OF OHIO R *1790*

S C 1788

GA 1788

(to Spain)

Dates for the 13 Original States, referring to the date each ratified the Constitution

*Erie triangle ceded by New York to U.S. 1781; sold to Pennsylvania in 1792

East and West Florida retroceded by Great Britain in 1783

Vermont extralegally self governing 1777 – 1791

allowed the United States to trade with Spain but not with its colonies—if the Americans would "forbear" navigation of the Mississippi River though not the *right* to use it.

Such a roar of protest went up from the West that Jay let the negotiations lapse. The Spanish helped matters in 1788 by opening the river under restrictions with which the West could live, though not happily, until the issue was settled by the Pinckney Treaty of 1795. These negotiations with Spain not only pointed to the impotence of the Articles in foreign affairs but also left those in the western United States with a lingering suspicion of those in the eastern portion.

6.2c The Difficulties of Trade

When the colonies left the imperial system, thus giving up their favored economic position, American merchants and shippers found themselves in cutthroat competition

Chapter 6 Establishing the Republic, 1781–1800   145

with the British, Dutch, and French for world markets. John Adams tried, unsuccessfully, for three years to make some kind of trade agreement with England—but as Lord Sheffield commented, putting his finger squarely on the commercial weaknesses of the Articles of Confederation, "America cannot retaliate. It will not be an easy matter to bring the Americans to act as a nation. They are not to be feared by such as us."

Sheffield proved to be correct, for when Congress asked the states, in 1784, for exclusive authority to regulate foreign trade over a fifteen-year period, the states immediately refused. Under the Articles of Confederation, Congress was powerless to do more than protest.

Domestic commerce, as well as foreign trade, suffered from interstate rivalries. The states used their power to levy tariffs against each other, creating barriers that seriously hampered domestic commerce and caused further dissatisfaction with the central government. At the same time, American industry was struggling to survive. The war and blockade had stimulated American manufacturing by cutting off imports from Britain and the Continent. Some of the states, in fact, had offered premiums and subsidies for the domestic production of manufactured goods. With the return of peace, however, much of the artificial stimulation that had encouraged American industry was withdrawn; and the inevitable postwar slump set in. Capital was short, the currency disordered, transportation deficient, and investment risky.

6.2b **Frenzied Finances**

The Articles of Confederation gave the national government no power to tax. If the states refused to pay their levies in full or on time, Congress was simply forced to accumulate ever-larger foreign and domestic debts. The states responded erratically to Congress' requests for revenue, so that while Congress occasionally had money, it never had enough at the right time. Although Congress repudiated most of its war debts by simply canceling out millions of dollars in the currency issued under the Continental Congress, the country in 1785 still owed about $35 million in domestic debts and had a growing foreign debt. The fledgling government owed money to its soldiers who had fought the revolution, but could not pay them. Congress had sold war bonds in an effort to finance the revolution; those bonds were now coming due, and Congress had no means with which to meet its obligations. As the government defaulted on its obligations, bondholders sold their bonds to speculators for as little as ten cents on the dollar. The states, meanwhile, had war debts of their own, which they increased after the war by taking on the amounts of the congressional debt that were owed to their citizens.

In addition to the problem of these debts, both national and state governments lacked a uniform, stable, sound currency. Both the states and the central government issued over $200 million in paper currency during the revolution, with the predictable result that currency inflation reached 12,000 percent at one point during the 1780s. The inflation had the effect of essentially rendering the savings of Americans worthless. The Americans who had refused to tax themselves sufficiently to pay for the Revolution essentially paid for the Revolution through the depletion of their savings, caused by the massive inflation. The postwar slump—which hit the country in 1783, sinking to its lowest point in mid-1786—affected the farmers and the small debtors most of all. In states where farmers and other small debtors controlled the legislatures, the solution seemed easy: Seven state legislatures simply approved the issue of paper money in larger quantities. In addition, to help distressed farmers, these states passed "stay laws" to prevent creditors from foreclosing on mortgages.

6.2c **Crisis and Rebellion**

At the depth of the depression in 1786, there was a severe hard money shortage. Farmers, especially, were experiencing difficulty. The problems were most acute in Massachusetts, where the debt situation led to a decree by the state government that all debt must be repaid at face value, and new taxes were levied by the state to pay the state's debts. The citizens of Massachusetts, however, lacked the resources with which to pay the new taxes.

Twenty-nine Massachusetts towns declared their inability to meet their obligations. Tax collector Peter Wood of Marlborough, Massachusetts, reported that "there was not … the money in possession or at command among the people" to meet their obligations. Protest meetings in several states won some concessions from the legislatures; in Massachusetts, however, a Hampshire County convention of fifty towns met and passed resolutions condemning the state legislature, lawyers, court fees, and of course the taxation. The Massachusetts county courts became the targets of the citizens' wrath when they issued writs of foreclosure on farmers that had been demanded by creditors and the state taxing authorities. When mobs of unruly men forced the closure of the courts at Northampton, Worcester, and Springfield—thus preventing farm foreclosures and prosecutions for debt—Governor James Bowdoin sent in the state militia to scatter them.

In reply to Bowdoin, **Daniel Shays**, a veteran of the Revolution and Bunker Hill, began organized resistance to the Massachusetts government. Shays issued a set of demands, including a demand for new paper money issues, tax relief, a moratorium on debts, and the abolition of imprisonment for debt. Shays organized a band of some 1,200 farmers in the winter of 1786 for an attack on the Springfield Arsenal, from which he hoped to get arms. The governor sent a militia force of some three thousand men (paid for by contributions from Boston businessmen) to protect the arsenal, and Shays' poorly mounted attack by outnumbered farmers, in February, 1787, failed miserably. Four of Shays' men were shot and killed by the Massachusetts militia and twenty were wounded, sending Shays' rebels into retreat. Shays fled toward Canada; but he was caught, arrested, and imprisoned by Massachusetts authorities. Over a thousand of his followers were also arrested and jailed. Samuel Adams, who only a decade earlier had led a revolt against the taxation policies of the British government, denounced Shays and the rebels for treason. Two of the rebels were executed; and sixteen more were sentenced to death, but later were granted reprieves. Four thousand more gained leniency by confessing their misconduct and swearing a loyalty oath to the state. The Massachusetts legislature passed a Disqualification Act that prohibited the rebels from voting, holding public office, serving on juries, working as schoolmasters, or operating taverns for a period of up to three years.

Daniel Shays

Led a rebellion of Massachusetts farmers against taxation and foreclosures on farms in 1786 (Shays' Rebellion convinced many that a stronger national government was needed.)

A monument stands at the place of the final battle of Shays' Rebellion, in Sheffield, Massachusetts. (Wikimedia Commons)

Shays' Rebellion had swift effects in Massachusetts. Governor Bowdoin was defeated in the next election by John Hancock, and the legislature prudently decided to grant the farmers some measure of relief. Debtor laws in Massachusetts were reformed, and Shays and his followers were released. The effect on the country at large was equally swift, and much greater, as the rebellion shook the confidence of elites in the ability of the Confederation to maintain order. Abigail Adams exemplified the attitudes of the elites in a letter to Thomas Jefferson, where she wrote, when "ignorant, restless desperadoes, without conscience or principles" could persuade "a deluded multitude to follow their standards …" who could be safe anywhere in the land? Similarly, George Washington wrote, "There are combustibles in every state which a spark might set fire to."

6.3 Framing a New Constitution

6.3a The Drift Toward a New Government

Even the most earnest states' rights advocates were willing to admit the existence of imperfections in the Articles of Confederation, and proposals for conventions to discuss amending them had already appeared in the New York legislature in 1782 and in Massachusetts in 1785. In 1786, under the cloud of Shays' Rebellion, Congress agreed that the Articles needed revision. As James Monroe told Jefferson, "Some gentlemen have

Anti-Federalists

The faction that opposed
the Constitution, largely
because they believed that
the national government
and the president would
be too powerful under the
Constitution

inveterate prejudices against all attempts to increase the powers of Congress, others see the necessity but fear the consequences."

James Madison called for a meeting of delegates at Annapolis, Maryland, in 1786, to discuss needed changes in the Articles of Confederation and hopefully reach agreement on a uniform tariff. The lack of a uniform tariff had seriously hindered American trade and rendered the Confederation impotent in its efforts to retaliate against high British tariffs on American goods. New York, with its busy harbor, opposed high tariffs, preferring more open trade policies in an attempt to boost trade in the port of New York. No agreement was reached in the convention of 1786, and only five states even participated; it provided, however, the opportunity for Alexander Hamilton of New York to seize the initiative. At Annapolis, Hamilton called upon the states to appoint delegates to a meeting to be held in May 1787 at Philadelphia, to discuss ways "to render the Constitution of the Federal Government adequate to the exigencies of the Union." Since at almost the same time Daniel Shays' men, pursued by Boston militia, were providing an example of the kind of "exigency" Hamilton referred to, his call found receptive audiences in the states. Congress adopted his suggestion and authorized a convention "for the sole and express purpose of revising the Articles of Confederation and reporting to Congress and the several legislatures such alterations and provisions therein."

While there were those who believed that the Articles could be amended and reworked into an effective and efficient government, a number of determined political leaders—among them Alexander Hamilton, James Madison, John Jay, and Henry Knox—were convinced that the country's interests demanded a much stronger central government. They believed in executive and judicial control, rather than legislative, and did not fully trust the decentralized, mass-dominated state governments. There was a general belief among the mercantile and financial classes that, as Madison wrote, the United States needed the kind of government that would "support a due supremacy of the national authority, and leave in force the local authorities so far as they can be subordinately useful."

Samuel Adams, among others, became known as an Anti-Federalist because he opposed a federal form of government, which would empower the national government at the expense of the states. (Wikimedia Commons)

6.36 The Question of Federalism

The meetings in Philadelphia began on May 25, 1787, but conspicuously absent were many of the popular leaders of the pre-revolutionary era. These men, like Samuel Adams and Patrick Henry, became known as **Anti-Federalists** due to their opposition with a federal form of government that would place more power in the national government at the expense of the states. These men had involved themselves in the Revolution when it still comprised a scattering of colonial protests and then state revolts, rather loosely guided by the Continental Congress. Deeply devoted to winning independence for their own states, most of them continued to believe that the states should be governed without the interference of a strong central government. Some Anti-Federalists, like George Clinton of New York, had a vital stake in local state politics, which the enlargement of the powers of a continental government might endanger. Others saw the need to strengthen the Confederation but insisted that the supremacy of the states should not be basically altered. Others feared a strong executive, due to what they viewed as abuses of executive power under the English monarch. All of the Anti-Federalists were passionately convinced that a republican system could survive only on the local level, under their watchful eyes. A republic on a continental scale was beyond their imagination.

The fifty-five delegates who made their appearance in the Philadelphia State House held generally broader views. George Washington (chosen presiding officer of the convention) and Benjamin Franklin were distinguished representatives of an older generation, long experienced in guiding the military and diplomatic affairs of the colonies as a whole.

Though Washington, in particular, contributed little to the proceedings at the convention, his presence gave the convention legitimacy in the eyes of the public. Most of the delegates, however, were in their thirties or forties. Their careers had only begun when the Revolution broke out, and their public reputations had been achieved as a result of their identification with the continental war effort. With the coming of peace, these "nationalists" had been disquieted by the ease with which the states slid back into their old provincial ways. In vainly advocating revenue and commercial powers for the Confederation Congress, Robert Morris, James Wilson, Gouverneur Morris, James Madison, Alexander Hamilton, Charles Pinckney, and others began to see the futility of trying to govern a large country with thirteen states following diverse policies. These men who favored placing more power in the national government became known as **Federalists**.

The Federalists distrusted unchecked power in government as much as their opponents did and favored retaining state autonomy as much as possible. They believed, however, that under the current system power *was* being exercised in one quarter without effective restraints. Jefferson branded it the "legislative tyranny" of the states. There was no way to appeal the decisions of the state legislators. The state executive and judicial branches, and even the central Confederation, were powerless to overrule the legislative branches in the thirteen states. In addition, nations abroad were beginning to look with contempt upon the disunited states, and there were even dangerous signs of territorial encroachments—by Britain in the northwest and by Spain in the south and southwest. The English had not withdrawn all of their troops from American soil in the Ohio Valley, as Americans had expected after the Peace of Paris. The British remained in an effort to exploit trade with Native American tribes in the Ohio Valley, and also to induce the Americans to pay their British debts. Spain controlled the mouth of the Mississippi River and therefore could cut off trade to the American interior by closing the Mississippi to American trade at their discretion. The U.S. had no standing army and was too weak militarily to do anything about either the Spanish or the British situation. National survival, commerce, and prestige, the Federalists insisted, demanded that a stronger central government be created.

Federalists

The faction—led by Alexander Hamilton, James Madison, and John Jay—that favored a stronger national government with a stronger executive and ratification of the Constitution, forged in Philadelphia in 1787

6.3c The Philosophy of the Constitution

The feeling of urgency that permeated the minds of the delegates goes far toward explaining their eagerness to reach compromises on matters in dispute. Whenever the debates became deadlocked, speakers would arise and warn of the consequences should the convention fail. Said Elbridge Gerry at mid-session, "Something must be done or we shall disappoint not only America, but the whole world ... We must make concessions on both sides." And Caleb Strong warned, "It is agreed, on all hands, that Congress is nearly at an end. If no accommodation takes place, the Union itself must soon be dissolved."

Such warnings climaxed a series of heated arguments during the meetings. There were 569 votes taken at the convention, sixty just to decide on one executive in the form of the president. Of the fifty-five people who attended the convention, only thirty-nine signed the document and four voted against it. Of the three New York delegates who attended, only Alexander Hamilton remained until the end; the other two left in disgust. In the end, the document that emerged is best viewed as a political compromise, since the founders were not in agreement on many details.

The delegates generally believed that the central government must be empowered to act without the mediation of the states and to exercise its will directly upon individual citizens. It must have its own administrative agencies, with the ability to enforce its own laws and treaties, to collect its own revenues, and to regulate commerce and other matters of welfare affecting the states generally.

In addition, they believed that power in government, though imperative, must somehow be held in check. Like most enlightened people of the eighteenth century, they recognized that human nature was not perfect. "Men are ambitious, vindictive, and rapacious," said Alexander Hamilton; and while his language was strong, his appraisal of human nature was generally shared by his colleagues. They agreed with the French political philosopher Montesquieu that "men entrusted with power tend to abuse it." The system advocated by Montesquieu to prevent this evil was to distribute the functions of government among three coequal branches of government, each of which would hold a veto or check on the power of the others. This doctrine of **separation of powers** had earlier been outlined by John Adams:

> A legislative, an executive, and a judicial power comprehend the whole of what is meant and understood by government. It is by balancing each of these powers against the other two that the efforts in human nature toward tyranny can alone be checked and restrained, and any degree of freedom preserved in the constitution.

That a three-branch system had failed in the state governments did not shake the delegates' faith in the *principle* of separation of powers. For the most part, the states had only gone through the motions of creating three branches. In actuality, they had not given the executive and judicial branches sufficient checks on the legislatures, which in some states were running riot with government power.

Finally, most of the delegates were committed to some form of Federalism—the political system that would unite the states under an independently operating central government while permitting them to retain some portion of their former power and identity. Few agreed with George Read of Delaware that the states "must be done away." Even Alexander Hamilton, who formally introduced such a scheme, acknowledged that the Convention might "shock the public opinion by proposing such a measure." It was generally agreed that the states must remain. The argument arose over how, in operating terms, power could be properly distributed between the states and the national government.

6.3ᵭ The Convention at Work

The Virginia Plan proposed a national executive; a national judiciary; and a national legislature consisting of two houses, both representing the states proportionally. After much debate and amendment, this plan became the United States Constitution—the oldest written constitution still in use by any nation in the world. (iStockphoto)

Four days after the Convention opened, Edmund Randolph of Virginia proposed fifteen resolutions, drafted by his colleague James Madison. The general intent was clear at once: to proceed beyond mere revision of the Articles of Confederation in favor of forming a new national government. The founders held essentially conflicting goals since they desired to both increase national government power and retain state sovereignty. In order to solve this dilemma, Randolph's plan called for a national government sufficient for security, powerful enough to prevent dissension among the states, and strong enough to provide for national development. This **Virginia Plan** proposed a national executive, a national judiciary, and a national legislature consisting of two houses, both representing the states proportionally according to either population or tax contributions, with the lower house popularly elected and the upper house chosen by members of the lower one. Although William Paterson proposed a rival **New Jersey Plan**, which in substance would merely have enlarged the taxation and commerce powers of the Confederation Congress, it was never seriously considered. The Virginia Plan, after four months of debate, amendment, and considerable enlargement, became the United States Constitution.

Although the delegates agreed upon the main features of the new government, discord over the details almost broke up the convention. That a breakup was avoided is attributable in part to the delegates' recognition of the undeniable need for a new form of government, thus forcing the delegates into compromise and concession. They were pressed to balance special interest against special interest, the large states against the small, section against section, in order to work out a constitution that the majority could accept. No state would be perfectly satisfied with the result, but each could feel that the half loaf it garnered for its interest was far better than none.

Major opposition to the original Virginia Plan came from the small states. In the existing Congress, each of their votes was equal to that of any large state—but under the proposed system of proportional representation in the national legislature they would be consistently outvoted by the larger, more populous states. Delegates from the large states retorted that government should represent people, not geography. "Is [a government] for men," asked James Wilson, "or for the imaginary beings called States?" The issue came down to the question of how federal the federal government should be. In acknowledging the permanence of the states, were the delegates obligated to go further and introduce the concept of the states into the very structure and representation of the new central government?

The final answer to this question was yes; and in the end, the large states gave in. After the New Jersey Plan was rejected and the principle of a bicameral (two-house) legislature established, the small states—while hesitating to object to proportional representation in the lower house—persisted in claiming the right of equal representation for states in the Senate, or upper house. By threatening to walk out of the convention, they won. In essence, this **Great Compromise**, as it came to be called, was hardly a compromise at all. The major issue concerned representation in the Senate; and when the large states conceded on this point, they received no concession in return. The major crisis of the convention, however, had been resolved.

In the process of accepting this two-house legislature, the delegates acknowledged not only a balance between large and small states but also a balance between the common people and the propertied interests. Many delegates had argued against giving the people a direct voice in government; "The people," said Roger Sherman, "should have as little to do as may be about the government. They want information, and are constantly liable to be misled." Elbridge Gerry pointed to the "evils" that "flow from the excess of democracy." Other delegates agreed, however, with James Madison, who stated, "that the great fabric to be raised would be more stable and durable, if it should rest on the solid foundation of the people themselves." Thus, the basis of representation in the lower house was set at one representative for every forty thousand persons—each representative to be elected by voters eligible to elect "the most numerous branch of [their] State legislature." On the other hand, the senators of the upper house—two from each state—were to be chosen by the state legislatures, putting them at a second remove from popular control. As a result, the Senate was expected to represent the more conservative interests, "to consist," as John Dickinson noted, "of the most distinguished characters, distinguished for their rank in life and their weight of property." In sum, the two houses of Congress were to balance the rights of the lower and higher ranks of society, but with the edge given to the higher.

Another issue arose over the manner of choosing the president, the head of the executive branch of the new government. To have the national legislature appoint him, as the original Virginia Plan proposed, might mean, it was argued, that a candidate to that high office would be "a mere creature of the legislature." A second plan, championed by James Wilson, called for popular election of the president, but the delegates had too great a distrust of unchecked democracy to find this plan fully acceptable. Other proposals sought to bring the states into the elective process by having either the state legislatures or the governors combine to elect the nation's chief executive.

The final compromise embodied elements from all these plans. Each state legislature was to appoint a number of presidential "electors" equal to the total number of senators and representatives to which the state was entitled in Congress. The electors would meet in their own states and vote for two presidential candidates, and the candidate receiving the majority of votes from all the states would become president. It should be noted that the method of choosing the electors was left to the decision of the state legislatures. Thus, the legislatures might decide to keep the power of appointment in their own hands, as most of them did—or they could submit the appointment to popular vote, a method that became widespread only much later. In either case, the electoral system was intended to minimize popular influence in the choice of the president.

In effect, this presidential compromise echoed the earlier issue of proportional representation. In the first phase of the election, the popular vote, votes would be drawn on the basis of population. In the second phase, the **Electoral College**, voting would be on the basis of statehood—as each state would give all its votes to the President of the Senate to be counted. Few of the delegates, however, believed that the election would end in the Electoral College. It was believed that each state would try to advance a native son, and thus no candidate would receive a majority of the electoral vote. In that event, the election would be referred to the House of Representatives, where votes would be taken by state delegations, each state having one vote.

Great Compromise
The compromise over apportionment that created a bicameral Congress with a lower house apportioned by population and an upper house apportioned equally among the states at two senators per state

Electoral College
The constitutional system of electing the president in which each state chooses electors based on its representation in Congress to cast the actual vote for the presidency

Three-Fifths Compromise

The compromise between North and South over apportionment in the House of Representatives where five slaves would equal three free men for purposes of representation and taxation

The conflict between North and South was not so serious in the convention as it was later to become, but the differing sectional economies did arouse specific issues regarding governmental structure and powers. Because the South was an agricultural region dependent on a world market for its staple exports like tobacco and rice, it wanted to have commercial regulation—tariffs and export duties—eliminated or minimized. Southerners were also committed to slavery—not necessarily with moral conviction as to its justice, but because of their inescapably large investment in slave labor. Finally, the Southern states (six in number and comparatively less populous than the Northern states) were aware that in Congress they would be outnumbered by the North. They thus felt compelled to secure constitutional guarantees for their sectional interests before launching a new government in which they would be consistently outvoted.

In the North, on the other hand, agricultural products like grain and livestock had, for the most part, a ready domestic market. Many Northerners were more interested in having the government promote shipping and foster manufacturing by means of protective tariffs. Many also roundly condemned slavery and demanded an end to the "nefarious" slave trade. Their stance, however, was not entirely without self-interest. The convention had already agreed that direct taxes were to be assessed on the basis of population. The North was quite willing to have slaves counted as part of the population in apportioning such taxes, thus upping the South's assessments. Conversely, Northerners objected to counting slaves in apportioning representation in the House of Representatives—a plan that would enlarge the Southern delegations.

The convention resolved these differences by negotiating compromises. In regard to commerce, the South won a ban on export taxes and a provision requiring a two-thirds vote in the Senate for ratification of treaties. In return, the North secured a provision that a simple congressional majority was sufficient to pass all other acts of commercial regulation. The slave trade was not to be prohibited before the year 1808, but a tax of $10 could have been imposed on each slave imported. The so-called **Three-Fifths Compromise** specified that five slaves would equal three free men for purposes of both taxation and representation.

The influence of the states in the framework of the new constitution was greater than some nationalists would have liked. One of the most important factors shaping the delegates' decisions was their practical recognition that they had to offer a constitution that the people would approve, and popular loyalty to the respective states was too strong to be ignored.

New powers granted to the national government under the Constitution were designed to remedy the primary concerns of the time. The Constitution empowered congress to construct a standing army and navy to provide for the security of the United States. Congress was granted the power to impose tariffs, both to raise revenue for the American government and to aid American commerce in competition with overseas competitors. Congress was empowered not only to raise revenue but also to pay the debts of the United States. Congress was empowered to establish uniform laws of bankruptcy in an effort to help resolve some of the contentious debt problems present in the states. Congress also was given the power to regulate interstate commerce, a power that has grown immensely since its inception, and the power to coin money and regulate its value. Congress was also given exclusive authority over foreign policy. Two vague clauses—the power to "provide for the common defense and the general welfare," and the power to make all laws "necessary and proper" for the carrying out of its powers—provided the potential for great expansion of national governmental powers, if the clauses were interpreted broadly.

6.3e Referral to the States

By the close of the summer, the Constitution was slowly taking shape, and on September 17, 1787, twelve state delegations voted approval of the final draft. Edmund Randolph and George Mason of Virginia, along with Elbridge Gerry of Massachusetts, refused to sign it, feeling that it went too far toward consolidation and concerned because it lacked a bill of rights (Randolph later decided to support it, anyway). The remaining thirty-nine delegates affixed their signatures and sent the document to Congress with two recommendations from Article VII: that it be submitted to state ratifying conventions specifically called for that purpose, rather than directly to the voters; and that it be declared officially operative when nine (not thirteen) states had accepted it, since there was real doubt that any document so evolved could ever get unanimous approval. Some of the delegates feared that they had far exceeded their instructions to *revise* the Articles, for the document they sent to Congress certainly represented much more than revision.

6.3f Federalists and Anti-Federalists

The new Constitution met with great favor and equally great opposition in the states. Its strongest supporters, the Federalists, were drawn from the ranks of bankers, lawyers, businessmen, merchants, planters, and men of property in the urban areas. Hamilton and Jay favored it in New York. Madison, Randolph, and John Marshall argued for it in Virginia. And the fact that Washington and Franklin, the two most honored Americans, supported it was much in its favor.

The Federalist Papers

A series of essays by Alexander Hamilton, James Madison, and John Jay explaining the Constitution and how they expected the new government under the Constitution to work (The *Federalist Papers* were influential in the ratification debates over the Constitution.)

Opposition to its ratification came from the small farmers, laborers, and the debtor, agrarian classes. It is misleading, however, to arrange the argument over ratification on lines of economic interest alone. Obviously there were businessmen and merchants who voted for the document because they felt it would mean expanded markets, better regulation of commerce, greater credit stability, and less control of trade by the states. Just as obviously, there were farmers and debtors who voted against it for equally self-interested economic reasons. The lines of demarcation between rich and poor, or mercantile and agrarian interests, were by no means so clear in the voting as one might expect. Claiming that the nation could obtain progress and prosperity under the Articles if they were revised, the Anti-Federalists accused the convention of creating a government that eventually, as George Mason of Virginia thought, might "produce either a monarchy or a corrupt aristocracy." There was "apprehension," Rufus King of New York told Madison, "that the liberties of the people are in danger." In Massachusetts, the pioneering woman historian Mercy Otis Warren, who belonged to an elite family, opposed the Constitution on these grounds.

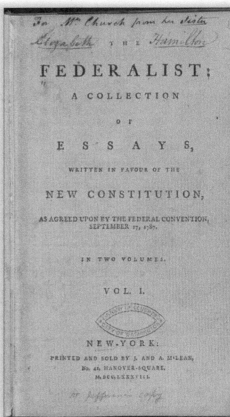

Happily for the fate of the Constitution, the Federalists, who might more accurately have been called "Nationalists," possessed a group of leaders of great drive and organizational skill. It was not easy to out-argue or outmaneuver men such as Hamilton, Jay, Madison, James Wilson, or Henry Knox. Furthermore, they had the initiative and kept it, giving their opposition little time to temporize or organize. The Federalists immediately began an energetic campaign for ratification in their own states. In New York, where opposition was strong, the Constitution was brilliantly defended in a series of eighty-five newspaper articles written by Hamilton, Madison, and Jay. The essays later were collected in a single volume called *The Federalist: A Collection of Essays, Written in the Favour of the New Constitution* (also known as **The Federalist Papers** or *The New Constitution*)

Pictured is the first printing of The Federalist Papers *(1788)—a collection of eighty-five essays, written by Alexander Hamilton, James Madison, and John Jay, defending the Constitution. (Wikimedia Commons)*

The Anti-Federalists had only a few such talented leaders. George Clinton, Patrick Henry, Elbridge Gerry, Luther Martin, and James Warren were able men, but none of them were capable of producing the brilliant *Federalist* papers or of handling the New York campaign as Hamilton did. The Anti-Federalists tried to fight the battle piecemeal, without a positive program, and showed a curious reluctance to match the aggressive, shrewd campaigning of the Federalists.

It has sometimes been fashionable among historians, particularly in the early twenty-first century, to consider the struggle over ratification as a contest between "conservatives" and "liberals." If the Declaration of Independence represented "radical" or revolutionary thought, the Constitution, it was assumed, represented a conservative counterrevolution that undid some of the Revolution's work. On reexamination, however, it becomes less clear which side deserves which label. It was the Federalists, after all, who had proposed the bold, decisive change to carry to completion the powerful nationalism engendered by the revolutionary effort. This was a daring step—to create from a bundle of disparate states a single, unified nation bound together by common consent and national pride. The Anti-Federalists, fearful of any power not under their direct restraint, preferred the status quo. To them, apparently, the great experiment in federalism suggested by the Constitution seemed too new and too dangerous. They could not conceive of a nationalized government that did not threaten republican principles.

6.3g Ratification of the Constitution

The ratification of the document proceeded smoothly in most of the smaller states, which were generally satisfied with the compromises set up to protect them. By January 1788 five states (Delaware, New Jersey, Georgia, Connecticut, and Pennsylvania) had accepted it, with strong opposition recorded only in Pennsylvania. The Massachusetts state convention ratified the Constitution by a vote of 187 to 168 after a long dispute, and then only after attaching a strong recommendation for a bill of rights. Maryland and South Carolina ratified, while New Hampshire, the ninth state, took two conventions (the second by a margin of nine votes) to accept it in June 1788. Legally, the Constitution could now go into effect—yet most people understood that without New York and Virginia, it could not function successfully.

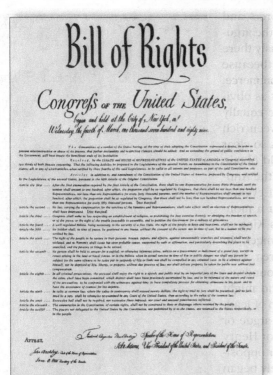

The Bill of Rights comprises the first ten amendments, proposed by a committee chaired by James Madison, to the United States Constitution. These constitutional amendments came into effect on December 15, 1791. (iStockphoto)

In Virginia, the Federalists won a narrow victory, 89 to 79, on June 25. Like Massachusetts, Virginia attached proposals for twenty changes and a recommendation for a specific bill of rights. In New York, Hamilton and the Federalists pulled the document through on July 26—by the breathtakingly small margin of 30 to 27. North Carolina refused to ratify the Constitution until a bill of rights was actually attached to it and finally approved it in late 1789. Rhode Island held out until 1790.

The debates over the ratification indicated that the chief issue was the Constitution's lack of a bill of rights, so in 1789 the First Congress proposed twelve amendments (ten of which were ratified in 1791) to guarantee popular government and individual freedom. Of the ten, the First prohibited Congress from interfering with freedom of speech, press, religion, and assembly. The Fifth placed the citizen under "due process" of law, and the Sixth and Seventh guaranteed trial by jury. The Tenth reserved to the people and to the states all powers not delegated to the federal government, thereby providing a guarantee of decentralized political power. Thus the **Bill of Rights** wrote into law those "self-evident truths" and "natural rights" on which the Declaration had based its case for independence.

The ideas expressed in the Constitution were themselves implicit in the Articles of Confederation, the Declaration of Independence, and the revolutionary arguments. The Constitution merely gave those ideas explicit, final form. The idea that government should protect life, liberty, and property was already accepted. The idea that government should be powerful enough to perform its functions was already recognized, even in the Articles—though there were sharp differences of opinion over how powerful that need be.

No one at the convention, and very few people in the states, argued for retention of the Articles without change. The question was, did the Constitution change the direction of government too much? The difference between the Articles and the Constitution lay almost wholly in the amount and quality of the authority granted to that "more perfect union."

6.4 Launching the Government

6.4a Washington and Federalist Rule

After the balloting for president and for Congress in January 1789, under the terms of the new Constitution, the presidential electors met in February to choose George Washington

Map 6.4 Vote on Ratification of the Constitution

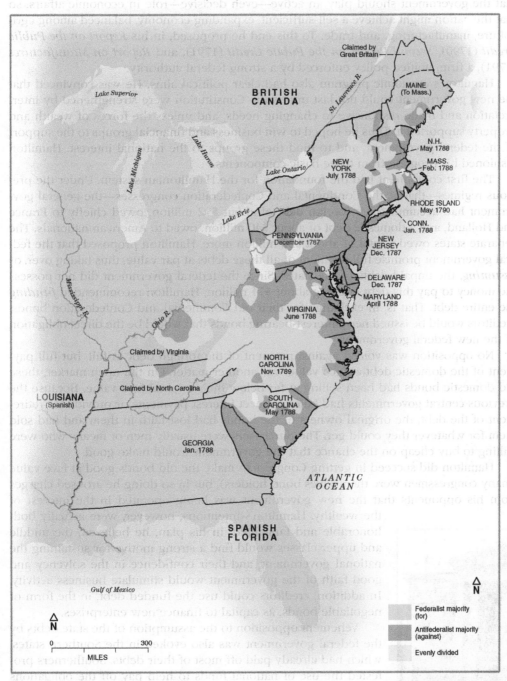

Claimed by Great Britain

BRITISH CANADA

MAINE (To Mass.)

N.H. May 1788

MASS. Feb. 1788

RHODE ISLAND May 1790

NEW YORK July 1788

CONN. Jan. 1788

NEW JERSEY Dec. 1787

PENNSYLVANIA December 1787

DELAWARE Dec. 1787

MD.

MARYLAND April 1788

VIRGINIA June 1788

Claimed by Virginia

NORTH CAROLINA Nov. 1789

Claimed by North Carolina

SOUTH CAROLINA May 1788

LOUISIANA (Spanish)

GEORGIA Jan. 1788

ATLANTIC OCEAN

SPANISH FLORIDA

Gulf of Mexico

Lake Superior

Lake Michigan

Lake Huron

Lake Ontario

Lake Erie

St. Lawrence R.

Mississippi R.

Ohio R.

0   300
MILES

Federalist majority (for)

Antifederalist majority (against)

Evenly divided

as the first President of the United States. John Adams—who had received the smaller number of electoral ballots—was installed as vice president in mid-April; and on April 30, Washington, standing on the balcony of the Federal Building at Broad and Wall Streets in New York, was inaugurated as president.

For the first few months of the new administration, Congress and the president moved carefully. Congress quickly created the three executive departments of State, Treasury, and War; and Washington chose Thomas Jefferson, Alexander Hamilton, and Henry Knox to serve as their Secretaries. Congress then passed a tariff on imports and a tonnage duty on foreign vessels, both intended to raise revenue and to protect American trade. The Judiciary Act of 1789 created the office of Attorney General, a Supreme Court, three circuit courts, and thirteen district courts, filling in the outlines of the federal legal system.

Hamilton's assumption plan

The U.S. government would assume, at face value, all government debts incurred under the Articles of Confederation.

Washington left the most critical problem of his first term to Alexander Hamilton, his confident young Secretary of the Treasury. Hamilton believed, as most Federalists did, that the government should play an active—even decisive—role in economic affairs, so that the nation might achieve a self-sufficient, expanding economy, balanced among agriculture, manufacturing, and trade. To this end he proposed, in his *Report on the Public Credit* (1790), *Second Report on the Public Credit* (1791), and *Report on Manufactures* (1791), a firm, unified policy enforced by a strong federal authority.

Hamilton's economic program also had clear political aims. He was convinced that the new government could not last unless the Constitution were strengthened by interpretation and made responsive to changing needs, and unless the forces of wealth and property supported it. Thus he hoped to win business and financial groups to the support of the federal government, and to bind these groups to the national interest. Hamilton fashioned his program from three basic components.

The first component laid the foundation for the Hamiltonian system. Under the previous regimes—that is, the Continental and Confederation congresses—the general government had accumulated a foreign debt of about $12 million, owed chiefly to France and Holland, and a domestic debt of about $40 million, owed to American nationals. The separate states owed a total of about $22 million more. Hamilton proposed that the federal government promise full payment of all these debts at par value, thus taking over, or *assuming*, the unpaid debts of the states. Since the federal government did not possess the money to pay this debt, totaling about $74 million, Hamilton recommended *funding* the entire debt. That is, in exchange for their old Continental and Confederation bonds, creditors would be issued new, interest-bearing bonds that would be the direct obligation of the new federal government.

No opposition was voiced against payment of the foreign debt in full, but full payment of the domestic debt at face value was another matter. On the open market, these old domestic bonds had been selling at far below their original face value. Because the previous central governments had failed to meet interest payments or provide for retirement of the debt, the original owners of the bonds had lost faith in them and had sold them for whatever they could get. The purchasers were usually men of means who were willing to buy cheap on the chance that the government would make good.

Hamilton did succeed in getting Congress to make the old bonds good at face value (many congressmen were themselves bond holders), but in so doing he aroused charges from his opponents that the new government was being operated in the interest of the wealthy. Hamilton's intentions, however, were actually both honorable and farsighted. In his plan, he believed, the middle and upper classes would find a strong motive for sustaining the national government, and their confidence in the solvency and good faith of the government would stimulate business activity. In addition, creditors could use the funded debt, in the form of negotiable bonds, as capital to finance new enterprises.

Vehement opposition to the assumption of the state debts by the federal government was also evoked in the Southern states, which had already paid off most of their debts. Southerners protested the use of national funds to help pay off the obligations of states with large outstanding debts, such as the New England states. **Hamilton's assumption plan** was defeated on its first vote in the House, but he finally won in a bargain with Jefferson. In exchange for an agreement to locate the new national capital in the South (on the Potomac across from Virginia), Jefferson's congressional forces agreed to assume the debts of the states.

The second part of Hamilton's plan called for the creation of a central bank, somewhat like the Bank of England, which would serve as a depository for federal funds, issue paper money (which the Treasury by law could not do), provide commercial interests with a steady and dependable credit institution, and serve the government with short-term loans.

Part of Hamilton's assumption plan called for the creation of a central bank, which would act as a depository for federal funds, issue paper currency, provide commercial interests with a dependable credit institution, and also issue the government short-term loans. The First Bank of the United States was chartered by Congress on February 25, 1791, and still stands in Philadelphia, Pennsylvania. (Wikimedia Commons)

BVT Lab

Improve your test scores. Practice quizzes are available at www.BVTLab.com.

Some leaders in and out of Congress objected to this proposal on the grounds that four-fifths of the bank's funds were to come from private sources, which might then control the bank's (and the nation's) fiscal policies. And, more important, opponents of the bank argued that it was unconstitutional. Jefferson and Madison, among others, argued that since the federal government was not specifically authorized by the Constitution to create a national bank, it would be unconstitutional for Congress to do so.

Hamilton, aware that the bank bill might set an important precedent, argued that Congress was authorized by the Constitution to do what was "necessary and proper" for the national good. If the proposed bank fell within this definition, as he believed it did, the Constitution gave Congress "implied powers" to act in ways not precisely defined in the document. He took the position "that every power vested in a government is in its nature sovereign and includes, by force of the term, a right to employ all the means requisite and fairly applicable to the attainment of the ends of such power …"

Jefferson, to the contrary, argued that the federal government possessed only those powers explicitly granted to it in the Constitution, and that all others, as the Tenth Amendment said, were reserved to the states. Jefferson argued that the language of the Constitution must be strictly construed. "To take a single step beyond the boundaries thus especially drawn around the powers of Congress," he wrote, "is to take possession of a boundless field of power, no longer susceptible of any definition." Neither the "general welfare" nor the "necessary and proper" clause of the Constitution, he maintained, could be so broadly interpreted. Washington and Congress, however, accepted Hamilton's argument, and in 1791 created the Bank of the United States with a charter for twenty years.

6.4c The Whiskey Rebellion

In order to help finance the new national government's obligations, Hamilton proposed to levy an excise tax on a number of commodities to supply money to the federal Treasury for, he wrote, "… the creation of debt should always be accompanied by the means of its extinguishment." One of the items included in the bill, passed in 1791, was a 25 percent excise tax on whiskey to be paid by farmers when they brought their grain to the distillery. The cost would then be passed on to consumers in the form of higher prices for whiskey. In western Pennsylvania and North Carolina, conversion into whiskey was an efficient way of getting grain to market and avoiding the high transportation costs of shipping their excess bulk grain over the mountains to the market in the east. Hamilton's excise tax was, therefore, a tax on the farmers' most valuable cash crop. Farmers viewed the tax as especially oppressive since they already paid half the value of their crop to the distillery to distill their grain, and after the tax was taken out of the farmers' remaining half, less than a third remained. Hamilton exacerbated the farmers' anger by his flippant comment that "farmers drink too much anyway."

Farmers in western Pennsylvania gathered in meetings the summer of 1792, and a farmers' convention in Pittsburgh denounced the tax and declared that the people would prevent its collection. Collections fell off in this area of Pennsylvania in 1792, and irritated farmers manhandled a few tax collectors in 1793. In fact, some were even tarred and feathered. One tax collector in particular, John Neville, had his house burned to the ground in July 1794 by an angry agrarian crowd estimated at five hundred. Neville escaped, but one man in the crowd that attacked Neville's house was killed and several were wounded, as a dozen soldiers inside Neville's house fired into the crowd. This violent incident appeared to be the beginning of a larger revolt, as the next year a sizable force of as many as seven thousand angry whiskey makers vowed to march on Pittsburgh to challenge federal authority at its nearest point.

Memories of Daniel Shays were still fresh in Congress, and President Washington acted quickly. He issued a proclamation ordering the Pennsylvanians to return to their homes and declared western Pennsylvania in a state of rebellion. President Washington then mounted his horse and led Alexander Hamilton and Henry Lee with a force of 15,000 militiamen—more troops than the average strength of the continental army during the American Revolution—to Pennsylvania. Upon the arrival of federal troops, the farmers promptly scattered; Hamilton, determined to teach the unruly frontiersmen a lesson in federal authority, saw to it that a score of the ringleaders were arrested and tried, and two were sentenced to death. Washington wisely pardoned the rebels, but neither Hamilton nor Federalism was ever again popular in that region of Pennsylvania.

Hamilton viewed the government's action in the **Whiskey Rebellion** as a smashing success, the prevention of another Shays' Rebellion, but others—including Thomas Jefferson and ardent Federalist Fisher Ames—opposed the use of federal troops on American citizens, viewing it as an abuse of power and proof that the national government had been granted too much power under the Constitution.

6.5 Developing an American Indian Policy

At the close of the Revolution, the conflict between American Indians and white Americans remained as insoluble as ever. Of the losers in the Revolution, the American Indians—most of whom had fought with the British—lost most. The Peace Treaty simply left them out. Britain ceded the lands west to the Mississippi to the Americans without mentioning the American Indians who lived there, while the Americans considered them a conquered people whose lands were subject to confiscation.

"With respect to the Indians," wrote one of the negotiators, "we claim the right of pre-emption; with respect to all other nations, we claim the sovereignty over the territory." Though tribal leaders protested to the British negotiators that they had no right to give away American Indian lands, and to the Americans that they had no right to abrogate previous treaties, neither side listened.

6.5a "Noble Red Man" or "Barbaric Savage"?

Federal and state policy toward the American Indians was greatly influenced by white Americans perceptions of them. Whites found American Indians to be difficult to negotiate with—for few Americans fully understood American Indian psychology, politics, or culture. Both American Indians and whites were heirs of two hundred years of constant and vicious warfare. White explorers and settlers, almost from their first contacts with the American Indians, had developed contrasting images of the "noble red man" on the one hand, and the "barbaric savage" on the other.

Some Americans, particularly the educated minority, viewed the various American Indian cultures with respect and sympathized with the natives' plight. These Americans hoped the tribes could be assimilated into American society. Both President Washington and his secretary of war, Henry Knox (who had charge of American Indian affairs), believed in assimilation. Knox reaffirmed American Indian land claims in a series of reports in early 1789. "Instead of exterminating part of the human race," he wrote, Americans should instead take pride in having "imparted knowledge of cultivation and the arts to the aboriginals of the country."

Others tended to see the American Indians as irredeemably—though tragically—savage, incapable ever of learning the ways of civilization. Meanwhile, the possibility of an alliance between the western tribes and the British army, still in Canada, posed a threat to the Ohio-Indiana frontier.

In fact, although the British had promised in the Peace of Paris to give up their posts in the Northwest, they apparently intended to hold them as long as possible. Orders from the Colonial office to the governor-general of Canada, one day before the proclamation of the Treaty in 1784, instructed British commanders to do exactly that. For these reasons, many Americans were convinced that the only sound policy toward the American Indians was removal.

6.5b Assimilation or Removal

Relations with the American Indians developed over two phases in the years before 1812. From the end of the war until the election of Washington in 1789, Congress assumed that all American Indian lands belonged to the United States and that all tribes were under government control. Congress appointed commissioners to handle Indian affairs, but most direct dealings with the tribes were carried out by the states.

Land was generally the largest issue. Both federal and state policies were to move American Indians off of land that settlers wanted—but this required more military power and money than either federal or state governments possessed. The removal policy also raised questions among those who saw this as a moral problem, as well as a military and political one.

Little Turtle
Native American chief in the Ohio Valley who rebelled against white encroachment from 1790 to 1794

By 1786, both state and federal governments realized that establishing an effective, acceptable American Indian policy involved a large set of complex issues. The central problem was how to establish white settlements in American Indian country and still treat them with humanity and justice. The lure of open, fertile land, a growing nationalism, and the need for strategic defenses against France, Spain, and British Canada—all had to be balanced against the new nation's desire to act in accordance with the principles of its revolution and a Christian conscience.

American leaders, therefore, reactivated the British colonial policy of recognizing native land rights and acquiring the necessary acres by treaties and purchases—establishing, meanwhile, strict boundaries to control the advance of white settlers. The Northwest Ordinance of 1787, which had officially opened the West to settlement, stated that natives should be dealt with in "utmost good faith," their "property, rights and liberty" protected, their lands "never to be taken from them without their consent."

Pictured are Delaware American Indians hunting buffalo across the plains. As land and game disappeared, tribes were pushed ever farther west by treaties and expansion. If this had continued unchecked, the race in its entirety might have disappeared. (WikiPaintings)

This new policy did not fully satisfy the national conscience, however. At best, it was a temporary solution. Plenty of Americans, particularly on the frontier, simply did not care; conversely, many others did not want their country—which they believed to be a new and better experiment in enlightened government—held responsible for the destruction of an entire people.

In the view of the Enlightenment, natives were as much part of the human race as were white men. Such differences as existed between the two were seen as the results of education and environment. The solution, then, was to "civilize" American Indians by giving them education, religious training, and the means of making a living, thus bringing them into the mainstream of American society. "In leading them to agriculture, to manufacture, and civilization," said Jefferson, "I trust and believe we are acting for their greatest good."

Westward expansion was thus given a moral basis by being seen as an extension of the advantages of a "higher" social order to a "lower" group. It was a common principle in European thought and would continue to be for some time—whether the subjected people were Gauls or Aztecs or Maoris.

6.5c Clashes on the Frontier

Treaties negotiated with the tribes of the Northwest brought only temporary peace, while in the South the Spanish encouraged the Creeks' harassment of frontier settlements. The Mohawks, led by chief Joseph Brant; the Miami, led by Chief **Little Turtle**; and the Shawnee, led by chief Blue Jacket—all led raids against white settlements in Indiana, Ohio, and western Pennsylvania, spreading panic and challenging white control of the Ohio Valley. Meanwhile, the doubling of the American white population to almost four million between the French and Indian War and 1790 created land pressure in the West, as thousands of white settlers moved into the Ohio Valley. In such a situation, the Native American resistance was predictable. In response to this resistance, the white Americans took military action.

In 1790, General Josiah Harmar and 1,400 men, under orders from Secretary of War Henry Knox, marched into western Ohio burning native villages as they went. This expedition against the American Indians in the Ohio country was ambushed and scattered by the Miami and Shawnee under Little Turtle and Blue Jacket. Two hundred of Harmar's men were killed, and Harmar was court-martialed for his inept leadership in the humiliating defeat. In 1791, the U.S. government sent General Arthur St. Clair to Ohio with a larger force of some two thousand men—but the results were no better. St. Clair and his men were reduced to about 1,400 through desertion due to the cold Ohio weather that autumn, and Little Turtle and a thousand Miami Indians ambushed the remaining troops in northwestern Ohio on November 4. Over half of St. Clair's men were killed or wounded, and all but three of the two hundred female "camp followers" that accompanied St. Clair's men were also killed. The natives scalped and dismembered the dead and dying and pursued the fleeing survivors out of Ohio. With over nine hundred dead, St. Clair's defeat was the most costly defeat for the U.S. in the history of the American Indian wars. President Washington denounced St. Clair as "worse than a murderer" and demanded his resignation. In 1793–1794, however, the tide began to turn as the Tennessee militia temporarily stabilized the southwestern frontier in a series of small, intense engagements.

General Arthur St. Clair's defeat was the most costly defeat for the U.S. in the history of the American Indian wars. President Washington denounced St. Clair as "worse than a murderer" and demanded his resignation. (Wikimedia Commons)

Washington then gave command to General "Mad Anthony" Wayne, who took four thousand men into northwestern Ohio, where the British had authorized the construction of a fort inside American boundaries. After the signing of the Jay Treaty, the British did an about face and cut off arms sales to the Native Americans. Without British weapons, the American Indians (armed with only tomahawks) would be no match for the American forces. Wayne established two military camps, Fort Greenville and Fort Recovery, in western Ohio. Fort Recovery was built on the site of St. Clair's defeat in 1791, and Wayne's men literally had to pick through skeletal remains in order to construct the fort. Wayne defeated the remaining American Indian forces at the **Battle of Fallen Timbers**, so called because a recent tornado had felled so many trees, in the late summer of 1794. The next year, the twelve strongest tribes ceded most of the Ohio country to the United States in return for $25,000 worth of shirts, axes, knives, blankets, kettles, mirrors, ribbons, thimbles, and liquor, by the Treaty of Greenville. In subsequent years, the American government continued to supply an annual shipment of liquor to the American Indians in an attempt to keep them pacified. The unfortunate result was rampant alcoholism among the Ohio tribes. In 1800, Little Turtle proclaimed that "more or us have died since the Treaty of Greenville than we lost by the years of war before, and it is all owing to the introduction of liquor among us ... This liquor that they introduce into our country is more to be feared than the gun and the tomahawk."

6.6 **The Perils of Neutrality**

6.6a **The French Revolution**

The outbreak of the French Revolution forced the Washington administration into the first real test of its foreign policy. A good many Americans in 1789 welcomed the news of the French uprisings as the logical outcome of their own revolution. "In no part of the world," wrote John Marshall later, "was the French Revolution hailed with more joy than in America." The overthrow of the French monarchy and its replacement with what the new French government called a "republic" based on the ideals of "liberty, equality, and fraternity" seemed in concert with American Revolutionary ideals. The execution of King Louis XVI and the Reign of Terror that followed—during which France devolved into fratricidal chaos—led many to sober second thoughts, however, while the French declaration of war against England, Holland, and Spain in February 1793 introduced the difficult question of neutrality directly into American foreign policy.

One segment of opinion, holding that Britain was still the United States' major enemy, favored the French cause. Furthermore, technically the United States was still obligated under the Treaty of Alliance (signed in 1778 during the American Revolution) to defend France when it was attacked. France had aided the U.S. against Britain during America's time of need; therefore, some argued that the U.S. must aid France during theirs. Others felt that British trade was so essential to American prosperity that the United States, whatever its sympathies with revolution, could not afford to offend the world's greatest naval and economic power. Still others, observing the chaos of Jacobin Paris, saw France as a threat to the security and order of society everywhere—even to Christianity itself. Up to a third of the population of western France died in the chaos of the French Revolution, and some twenty thousand were guillotined as "enemies of the Republic." Regardless of the slogans of "Liberty, Equality, and Fraternity," many Americans viewed this carnage as nothing worthy of support.

When Washington received news of the outbreak of war between France and Britain in April 1793, he declared a "fair and impartial policy." Although avoiding the word "neutrality"—because Washington believed that since Congress declared war, Congress must also declare neutrality—Washington's proclamation guaranteed the belligerents the "friendly and impartial conduct" of the United States. America, he believed, needed peace—the opportunity to build up its strength—more than anything else. "If this country is preserved in tranquility twenty years longer," he wrote, "it may bid defiance in a just cause to any power whatever." His proclamation, which was to influence American foreign policy for the next half-century, derived from his firm conviction that the United States should avoid, at all reasonable costs, the "brawlings of Europe." The following year, Congress passed a Neutrality Act that made Washington's position the official American policy.

Edmond Charles Genet

French diplomat who came to America seeking American aid to France in its war with England and Holland, but forced to seek political asylum in the U.S. when the political situation changed in France

6.66 Genet Affair

Official neutrality aside, many Americans continued to support France both in spirit and in deed. The supporters of the French Republic noted that the American Republic had been born in blood as well, and concluded that the shedding of blood was therefore sometimes necessary for the establishment of liberty. In the words of John Bradford of the *Kentucky Gazette:*

President Washington's decision to grant political asylum to French diplomat Edmond Charles Genet, who was charged with treason, began a powerful American policy still used today. (Wikimedia Commons)

> Instead of reviling the French republicans as monsters, the friends of royalty in this country should rather admire their patience in so long deferring the fate of their perjured monarch, whose blood is … atonement for the safety of many guilty thousands that are still suffered to remain in the bosom of France.

Citizens' associations in support of the French Revolution, known as Democratic-Republican societies, formed throughout the American states. In 1793, these associations received a boost with the arrival of **Edmond Charles Genet**, an envoy dispatched from France to the United States for the purpose of garnering support for the French Republic in its war with England. Instead of meeting with the president or other members of Washington's administration, however, Genet landed in Charleston, South Carolina, where pro-French sentiments were much stronger. Upon his arrival in the U.S., Genet began commissioning American privateers to seize British ships and cargo—a clear violation of American neutrality. Genet even publicly urged Congress to reject Washington's "friendly and impartial policy" and support Republican

Jay's Treaty

Treaty of London with England, in 1794, that preserved peace with England and resumed normal trade, but was unpopular in the U.S.

Pinckney's Treaty

In 1795, set the border with Spain at 31° north latitude and opened the Mississippi River to American trade

France. Washington reacted by demanding that Genet be recalled to France under the premise that his conduct could lead to "war abroad and anarchy at home." Before Genet could return to France, the political situation changed in the tumultuous political atmosphere of revolutionary France; and Genet was charged with treason, for which the penalty was death. President Washington granted Genet political asylum under the condition that he withdraw from public life. In doing so, Washington began the American tradition of political asylum that has continued through the present.

6.6c Strained Relations with Britain

The British navy was large, the French navy small, and the British blockade of France very effective. When the French, desperate for trade, opened up their ports in the West Indies to American ships, the British immediately declared that any trade with France was a military act and that ships caught at it were subject to seizure. Not only did British men-of-war confiscate American cargoes, but they also forcibly "impressed" a number of American seamen into British naval service, claiming that some American sailors were really deserters. Still, although American ships were in danger wherever they went in Atlantic waters, wartime trade was so lucrative that many American merchants felt that the profit was worth the risk; and incidents multiplied.

6.6d Jay's Treaty

Hoping to reduce tensions, Congress passed an embargo act in 1794 that forbade British ships to call at American ports and forbade American ships to sail in areas where they might be subject to British seizure. Since this hurt American trade more than it hindered the British navy, the embargo lasted less than two months. American protests, however, induced the British to relax some of their rules; and in 1794 Washington requested that Chief Justice John Jay sail for London to discuss a treaty to settle outstanding differences.

Jay's arguments were no doubt good ones, but perhaps more important, French military successes persuaded the British that it was unwise to antagonize the United States unduly. Under the terms of **Jay's Treaty** (the Treaty of London, signed in 1794), the British agreed to evacuate the frontier posts by 1796, to open the British West Indies to American trade under certain condition, to admit American ships to East Indian ports on a nondiscriminatory basis, and to refer to a joint commission the payment of pre-Revolutionary War debts and settlement of the northwest boundary dispute.

The British simply refused to discuss other important points at issue, however, including impressments and the Indian question; and they made far fewer concessions than Jay had been instructed to get. Washington reluctantly submitted the treaty to the Senate, which narrowly ratified the Treaty. Not only was the Washington administration severely criticized for the settlement, but also Jay himself was burned in effigy in various cities. Alexander Hamilton suffered bombardment of eggs and tomatoes when he attempted to speak in support of Jay's Treaty. Americans opposed to the Treaty began a campaign of graffiti where they painted on fences the slogan, "Damn John Jay, and Damn everyone who won't Damn John Jay."

Not all the news was bad, however. Jay's Treaty allowed the U.S. to avoid what could have been a disastrous war with England and resume normal trade, thus boosting American well-being both in terms of security and economic well-being. Spain, badly mauled by France in the land war, had signed a separate peace in 1795 and, fearing British retaliation for its defection, needed American friendship. In **Pinckney's Treaty** (the Treaty of San Lorenzo), signed on October 27, 1795, Spain recognized the line of 31° latitude as the United States' southern boundary (Spain had claimed land in the American Southeast north to the Ohio River) and granted the United States free navigation of the Mississippi with a three-year right of deposit at New Orleans.

Map 6.5 Pinckney's Treaty (1795)

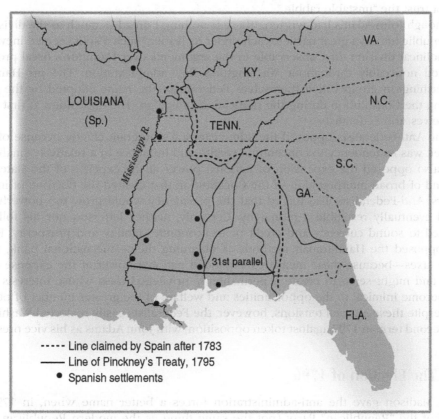

- ----- Line claimed by Spain after 1783
- —— Line of Pinckney's Treaty, 1795
- ● Spanish settlements

6.7 Early Political Parties

6.7a The Emergence of Party Politics

The dispute over Jay's Treaty revealed a deep division in Washington's administration, as well as growing public opposition to a number of Federalist policies. The French Revolution, the Franco-British War, and the subsequent problems in foreign relations created further political differences in Congress. By 1792 opposing factions had begun to coalesce around the two strong men of Washington's cabinet, Hamilton and Jefferson.

Hamilton and Jefferson represented contrasting views of what the American government should be. Both views were implicit in the Declaration and the Constitution, and both still lie beneath the stream of partisan politics. These contrasting views have come to be known as Hamiltonian and Jeffersonian democracy.

Hamilton had no confidence in "the people in the mass." "I have long since learned," he wrote Washington, "to hold public opinion of little value." Most people, he believed, were unreliable and easily swayed by passions, self-interest, and false rhetoric. Since political, social, and economic systems were intertwined, an effective government should be an active force ("a strong government, ably administered," as John Jay of New York put it) in promoting the good of the total society. Its control should be vested in those few who had skill and talent—"the rich and wellborn," Hamilton once called them—who would use it best to ensure the forward thrust of the nation.

Jefferson believed deeply in the ability of the majority of people to govern themselves if properly prepared and allowed to do so. In his view, the individual—in whom he found "substantial and genuine virtue"—was much more important than the state; and the individual's right to pursue liberty and happiness was paramount. People were capable of ruling themselves; thus they needed no strong central government to do it for them. "That government is best," he said, "which governs least." A central government was needed, of course, for foreign policy, defense, commerce, and like matters; too much control, however, of the individual "begets subservience and venality" and corrupts him.

Democratic-Republican
The first democratic political opposition party that coalesced around Thomas Jefferson

It was ironic that it was Jefferson, the Virginia planter-aristocrat, who did not trust the "rich and wellborn" few, and Hamilton, the illegitimate child of a Scottish merchant, who did not trust the "unstable rabble."

Though John Adams had written, "there is nothing I dread as much as the division of the Republic into two great parties, each under its leader," such a split seemed inevitable. This political division, first observable in the arguments over Hamilton's fiscal program, widened noticeably throughout Washington's first administration. The pro-Hamilton, pro-Washington group called themselves Federalists—the name adopted by the forces favoring the Constitution during the ratification campaign. The opposition at first called themselves Anti-Federalists.

The Anti-Federalists opposed the administration's program chiefly because of what they felt was its tendency to concentrate wealth and influence in a relatively small class. They also opposed the expansion of national power at the expense of the states, and the kind of broad interpretation of the Constitution that created the doctrine of implied powers. Anti-Federalists also feared that the presidency would grow too powerful and would eventually resemble a monarchy. Certainly, neither Jefferson nor his followers objected to sound currency and credit or to economic stability and prosperity. Rather, they opposed the Hamiltonian methods of obtaining them—the national bank, tariffs, excise taxes—because these measures expanded national power at the expense of the states and might serve to create a permanently privileged class whose interests could well become inimical to the opportunities and welfare of the greater number of people.

Despite these internal tensions, however, the Federalists easily reelected Washington for a second term in 1792 against token opposition, with John Adams as his vice president.

6.76 The Election of 1796

James Madison gave the anti-administration forces a better name when, in 1792, he spoke of the "Republican" Party (not the same thing as the modern Republican Party, but rather the ancestor of the modern Democratic Party). This designation (sometimes **Democratic-Republican**) shortly displaced Anti-Federalist." Into this loosely organized opposition group, formed about the commanding figure of Thomas Jefferson, came such men as James Monroe and James Madison of Virginia, George Clinton and Aaron Burr of New York, Albert Gallatin and Alexander Dallas from Pennsylvania, Willie Jones, the North Carolina back-country leader, and others from the middle and Southern states. Among the Federalists were Hamilton, Philip Schuyler, and John Jay of New York, Timothy Pickering and John Adams of Massachusetts, Thomas Pinckney of South Carolina, and John Marshall of Virginia.

When Jefferson—convinced that he could no longer work with Hamilton and the administration, dominated by members of what would become the Federalist Party—resigned as secretary of state in 1793, Republican partisan politics began in earnest. Hamilton resigned from the Treasury in 1795, partly because he could not afford to neglect his law and business interests. He still remained the most powerful Federalist leader since Washington decided not to run again in 1796.

Washington's achievements as president have been overshadowed by his image as "The Father of His Country" and by the dramatic contest during his second term between Hamilton and Jefferson. Washington was not the scholar or thinker that Jefferson, Hamilton, Adams, and Madison were; nor is he remembered for his talents as an orator. On a personal level, Washington was notoriously aloof and addicted to appearances—writing more letters as president concerning his plantation at Mount Vernon than concerning the policies of the nation. Moreover, when Washington solicited advice from his advisors, he was more likely to ask how he should appear in any given situation than what policies should be pursued. Generally, his greatest accomplishments as president are often listed as stepping down after two terms and reducing the fear that the presidency would grow into a monarchy by his unassertiveness in his official capacities. Washington's unassertiveness, in turn, stemmed from his goal of being a "disinterested gentleman." Washington believed that becoming involved in political bickering was not becoming of a gentleman and believed that he himself should appear to be above the fray. Presidents typically do

Map 6.6 Presidential Elections of 1796 and 1800

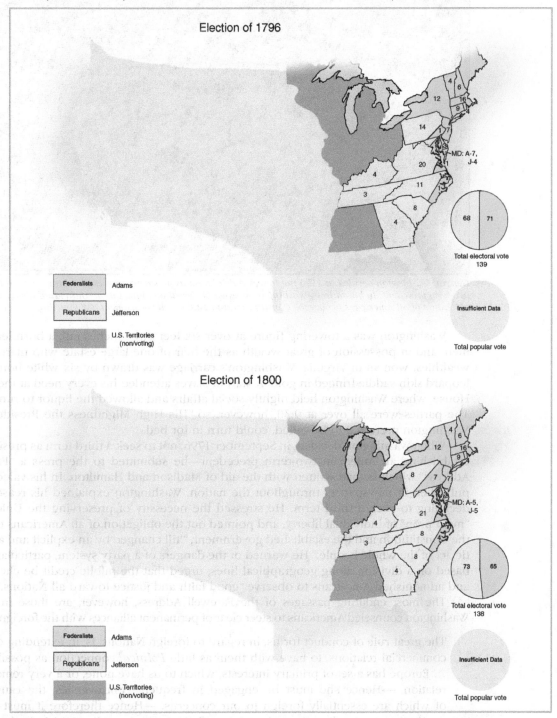

Election of 1796

MD: A-7, J-4

68 | 71

Total electoral vote
139

Insufficient Data

Total popular vote

Federalists — Adams

Republicans — Jefferson

U.S. Territories (non/voting)

Election of 1800

MD: A-5, J-5

73 | 65

Total electoral vote
138

Insufficient Data

Total popular vote

Federalists — Adams

Republicans — Jefferson

U.S. Territories (non/voting)

not go down in history as great leaders if they avoid assuming policy leadership or publicly taking a stand on issues of substance.

More recently, however, historians have pointed out Washington's real skill as an administrator, as his guiding hand held the fledgling nation together, and the importance of his contributions to the efficiency of the newly created government. Since almost every act of his first term set a precedent, Washington did more than anyone else to establish the tone of the presidential office and to establish the whole set of delicate relationships among the executive, the cabinet, the Congress, and the judiciary. Moreover, he imbued the fledgling nation with his immense dignity.

General Washington decided in 1796 not to seek a third term as president, thus establishing the presidential two-term precedent. In his address, Washington stressed preservation of the Union, individual liberty, and the obligation of all Americans to obey the Constitution and established government. (Wikimedia)

Washington was a towering figure at over six feet three inches tall, a born leader of men, and in possession of great wealth as the heir of one large estate who married the wealthiest woman in Virginia. Washington's carriage was drawn by six white horses, his leopard skin saddle fringed in gold. A staff of slaves attended his every need at the White House, where Washington held nightly social affairs and allowed the liquor to run freely. The parties were all over at 9:30, however, so "His High Mightiness the President," as Washington preferred to be called, could turn in for bed.

When Washington decided, in September 1796, not to seek a third term as president—establishing an American two-term precedent—he submitted to the press a "Farewell Address" which he had written with the aid of Madison and Hamilton. In his valedictory, published in newspapers throughout the nation, Washington explained his reasons for declining to seek a third term. He stressed the necessity of preserving the Union, the "main prop" of individual liberty, and pointed out the obligation of all Americans to obey the Constitution and the established government, "'till changed by an explicit and authentic act of the whole People." He warned of the dangers of a party system, particularly one based on a division along geographical lines; urged that the public credit be cherished; and admonished Americans to observe "good faith and justice toward all Nations."

The most enduring passages of the Farewell Address, however, are those in which Washington counseled Americans to steer clear of permanent alliances with the foreign world:

> The great rule of conduct for us, in regard to foreign Nations, is, in extending our commercial relations, to have with them as little *Political* connection as possible … Europe has a set of primary interests, which to us have none, or a very remote relation. —Hence she must be engaged in frequent controversies, the causes of which are essentially foreign to our concerns. —Hence therefore it must be unwise in us to implicate ourselves, by artificial ties in the ordinary vicissitudes of her politics … Taking care always to keep ourselves … on a respectably defensive posture, we may safely trust to temporary alliances for extraordinary emergencies.

After eight years in office, Washington left behind a government that possessed a reasonably good civil service, a workable committee system, an economic program, a foreign policy, and the seeds of a body of constitutional theory. He also left behind a party beginning to divide. The election of 1796 gave clear indication of the mounting strength of the Republican opposition. Thomas Jefferson and Aaron Burr campaigned for the Republicans, John Adams and Thomas Pinckney for the Federalists. The margin of Federalist victory was slim: Adams had 71 electoral votes, Jefferson 68. Since Jefferson had more votes than Pinckney, he became vice president.

6.7c Federalists and Republicans

It is too broad a generalization to say that the Federalists represented the conservative, commercial, nationalistic interests of the northeastern and middle Atlantic states, and the Republicans the more radical, agrarian, debtor, states' rights interests of the South and West—though there is more than a germ of truth in the generalization. In reality, the two parties drew support from all kinds of people in different parts of the country.

The differences in the parties reflected many factors—personalities, religious and educational backgrounds, ideologies, economic interests, political necessities, and the like. It would be more accurate to say that these parties were loose combinations of certain economic, social, and intellectual groupings, held together by a set of common attitudes and interests.

Fundamentally, they reflected two different opinions about the qualities of human nature. Hamiltonians were acutely aware of the "imperfections, weaknesses, and evils of human nature." They believed that if people were fit to govern themselves at all, it must only be under rigid controls imposed upon them by society and government. Jeffersonians, on the other hand, believed that people were, by inclination, rational and good. If freed from the bonds of ignorance, error, and repression, they might achieve real progress toward an ideal society. Others, of course, took positions between these two extremes.

These contrasting concepts of human fallibility were reflected in contemporary political opinions about the structure and aim of government. The Federalists emphasized the need for political machinery to restrain the majority. They believed in a strong central government and a strong executive, with the active participation of that government in manufacturing, commerce, and finance. They believed that leadership in society belonged to a trained, responsible, and (very likely) wealthy class that could be trusted to protect property as well as human rights.

The Jeffersonian Republicans distrusted centralized authority and a powerful executive, preferring instead a less autonomous, more decentralized government modeled more on confederation than on federalism. They believed in the leadership of what Jefferson called "a natural aristocracy," founded on talent and intelligence rather than on birth, wealth, or station. Most Republicans believed that human nature in the aggregate was naturally trustworthy and that it could be improved through freedom and education—and therefore that wise self-government, under proper conditions, would be possible.

6.8 The Trials of John Adams

6.8a The XYZ Affair

John Adams took office at a difficult time, for the Federalist Party that had elected him was showing strain at the seams. Hamilton still dictated a large share of party policy from private life. He did not like Adams and had maneuvered before the election in an attempt to defeat him. Adams himself was a stubbornly honest man, a keen student of government and law—but also blunt, a trifle haughty, and sometimes tactless.

Adams' administration promptly found itself in trouble. Within his party there was a violently anti-French group, including Adams' secretary of state, Thomas Pickering, who virtually demanded a declaration of war against France. The French minister to the United States, Pierre Adet, had openly tried to influence the 1796 election in favor of Jefferson and the Democratic-Republican Party. The French, angry at Jay's Treaty and at an American neutrality that appeared to favor Britain, began seizure of American ships at sea carrying British goods. By March 1797, three hundred American ships had been seized by French privateers. France also refused to receive Adams' new minister to France, Charles Cotesworth Pinckney. Adams, who did not want war, sent John Marshall, C. C. Pinckney, and Elbridge Gerry to Paris in 1797 to try to find some way out.

The French foreign minister, Talleyrand, dealing with the American commission through three intermediaries called (for purposes of anonymity) X, Y, and Z, demanded not only a loan of $12 million to the French government but also a bribe of $240,000, and an apology for negative comments that John Adams had made about France—a

XYZ Affair

Incident in which three French diplomats demanded bribes from American diplomats prior to negotiations

Quasi-War with France

Period of agitation between France and the U.S., 1797–1800, where both France and the U.S. seized merchant ships at sea

Alien and Sedition Acts

Acts of Congress under the Adams administration that allowed the president to imprison or deport aliens he considered dangerous and made it a federal crime to utter malicious statements against the Adams administration

request which the Americans indignantly refused with Pinckney's retort of "no, not a sixpense." When the news of the **XYZ Affair** leaked out, the ringing slogan "Millions for defense, but not one cent for tribute!" (based on Pinckney's reply) became a rallying point for the anti-French faction in Congress. Adams asked Congress to prepare for war, and the French accelerated the seizure of American ships at sea. The U.S. Navy was sent to the Caribbean to repel the French navy, and with powder and shot provided by the British, captured over a hundred French privateers in what historians refer to as the **Quasi-War with France**—since plenty of shots were fired on the open sea, but war was never officially declared.

6.8b The Convention of 1800

Capitalizing on the war fever, Congress created a Department of the Navy, built a number of new ships, armed American merchantmen, and authorized an army of ten thousand men. Though his own party leaders (Hamilton among them) argued that war with France was inevitable, Adams refused to listen—and as it turned out, the French did not want war either. Adams received scathing reviews from Republican newspapers and even endured abuse from members of his own party. After nearly a year of undeclared naval war, where each nation seized the other nation's merchant ships at sea, the French government suggested that if an American mission were to be sent to Paris it would be respectfully received.

In the year 1800, control of France was in the hands of Napoleon Bonaparte. (Wikimedia Commons)

By the time the American commissioners arrived in France in March 1800, the country was in the hands of Napoleon Bonaparte, who quietly agreed to a settlement of differences. The Convention of 1800 avoided a war and also dissolved the French-American alliance forged during the Revolution. "The end of war is peace," said Adams, "and peace was offered me." John Adams got his peace—but probably at the expense of victory, in the coming elections, for himself and his party.

6.8c The Alien and Sedition Acts

The popular outcry against France, and the Quasi-War with France that carried from 1797 through 1800, gave the Federalists a good chance, they believed, to cripple their Republican political opponents under the cover of protecting internal security. The country was honeycombed, so the Federalist press claimed, with French agents and propagandists who were secretly at work undermining the national will and subverting public opinion. Since most immigrants were inclined to vote Republican, the Federalist Congress passed a series of anti-Republican acts in 1798—the **Alien and Sedition Acts**. The Alien Acts, which lengthened the naturalization period from five to fourteen years, empowered the president to deport undesirable aliens and authorized him to imprison such aliens as he chose in times of war. Though he signed the bill, Adams did not like the acts and never seriously tried to enforce them.

As the second step in its anti-Republican campaign, Congress passed the Sedition Act. Under this act, a citizen could be fined or imprisoned or both for "writing, printing, uttering, or publishing" false statements or any statements which might bring the president or Congress "into contempt or disrepute." Since this last clause covered almost anything Republicans might say about Federalists, its purpose was quite plainly to muzzle the opposition and its primary targets were newspaper editors that opposed the Adams administration. Under the Sedition Act, twenty-five editors and printers were prosecuted and twelve were convicted for criticizing the Adams Administration—though they were later pardoned and their fines returned by the Jeffersonians.

Republicans opposed the Acts on the grounds that they were in violation of the free speech and free press protections of the Bill of Rights. The judiciary branch, however, was dominated by Federalist judges who would not rule against the Federalist Congress or the Adams administration. Public opinion sided with the Republicans. The legislatures of Kentucky and Virginia (home to Republican leaders Jefferson and Madison) passed resolutions in 1798 and 1799 (Jefferson drafted Kentucky's; Madison, Virginia's) condemning the laws and asking the states to join in nullifying them as violations of civil rights. Actually none did, but the **Kentucky and Virginia Resolutions** furnished the Jeffersonians with excellent ammunition for the approaching presidential campaign. The Kentucky and Virginia resolutions also put forth the idea that states could nullify federal laws that they found to be unconstitutional. Finally, although the United States as yet had no strong tradition of civil liberties, the Alien and Sedition laws helped to create one by pointing out how easily those rights of free speech and free press, guaranteed by the Bill of Rights, could be violated.

Kentucky and Virginia Resolutions
Nullification resolutions passed by Virginia and Kentucky condemning the Alien and Sedition Acts

6.8ᵔ The Election of 1800

Washington's death in December 1799 (from a throat and upper respiratory infection along with the detrimental medical treatment of bloodletting) symbolized the passing of the Federalist dynasty. The party that had emerged around him was in dire distress, divided into wrangling factions.

The Federalists had been unable to maintain a balance between the nationalist business interests, which formed the core of their support, and the rapidly growing influence of the middle and lower urban and agrarian classes that came from the South, the West, and the Mid-Atlantic. After Washington, who had held the party together by the force of his persona, no Federalist leader found a way to absorb and control the elements of society that, after 1796, began to look to Jefferson for leadership. The clash of personalities within the Federalist camp, of course, damaged the party further.

John Adams, who through his entire term had to face the internal opposition of the Hamiltonians as well as the Republicans from without, deserves more credit than he is often given. Except for Adams' stubborn desire to keep the peace, the United States might well have entered into a disastrous war with France, and without him the Federalist Party—under Hamilton's control—would probably have killed itself ten years sooner than it did. Adams' decision to stay out of war, made against the bitter opposition of his own party, was not only an act of courage but very likely his greatest service to the nation.

Although Hamilton circulated a pamphlet violently attacking the president, the party had no other satisfactory candidate for the election of 1800 and decided to nominate Adams again, choosing Charles Cotesworth Pinckney to run with him. The Republicans picked Jefferson and Burr once more, hoping thus to unite the powerful Virginia and New York wings of the party. The campaign was one of the bitterest in American history. In the end, the Republicans—who won the Mid-Atlantic States and the South—emerged with a small edge in total electoral votes.

Under the Constitution, the candidate with the most votes were president and vice president, respectively. When the Republican electors all voted for Jefferson and Burr, they created a tie between the two for president. This threw the election into the House of Representatives, still controlled by lame-duck Federalists. The Federalists' hatred of Jefferson was so intense that many of them preferred Burr. At the same time, Burr's own party wanted Jefferson, but Burr refused to step aside. Hamilton, much as he disagreed with Jefferson's principles, considered Burr a political adventurer and deeply distrusted him—as well he should have, given that Burr killed him in a duel a few years later. Hamilton therefore threw his influence in Congress behind Jefferson, who was declared president by the House of Representatives on February 17, 1801. Subsequent historians have seen this election as particularly significant because it was the first one in American history in which the party in power lost and then turned that power over to its victorious opponents peacefully, and in legal, democratic fashion.

Timeline

1776	Richard Henry Lee proposes a Declaration of Independence and "Confederation" on June 12.
1777	Articles of Confederation are approved by the Continental Congress on November 15 and sent to states for ratification.
1781	Articles of Confederation are ratified by the states.
1784	Spain closes the Mississippi River to American trade.
	Congress asks the states for the exclusive power to regulate trade, but states refuse.
1785	A Land Ordinance passed by Congress provides for a government survey to divide the land of the Northwest Territory into townships
1786	Annapolis Convention fails to settle on a uniform tariff.
1787	Shays' Rebellion against taxation and farm foreclosures in February
	Northwest Ordinance provides an orderly process for translating the unsettled Northwest from frontier to statehood.
	Constitutional Convention is held in Philadelphia.
1788	Spain opens restricted Mississippi River trade to the U.S.
	Constitution is ratified by the required nine states.
1789	Bill of Rights is sent to the states for ratification.
	Constitution goes into effect.
	New Congress is elected in January and George Washington is elected president by the Electoral College.
	Judiciary Act of 1789 creates the office of Attorney General, a Supreme Court, three circuit courts, and thirteen district courts.
	Outbreak of the French Revolution in July
1790	Rhode Island ratifies the Constitution, the last state to do so.
1791	Congress creates the Bank of the United States.

Timeline

1793 — Revolutionary France declares war against England, Holland, and Spain.

Washington's proclamation of effective neutrality

Genet Affair

1790–1794 — War with Native Americans in the Ohio Valley results in a white victory in the Battle of the Fallen Timbers in 1794.

1794 — Whiskey Rebellion in Pennsylvania is put down by federal troops under the command of President George Washington.

Jay Treaty preserves peace with England in spite of unpopularity in America.

1795 — Pinckney Treaty sets border with Spain and opens the Mississippi to U.S. trade.

1796 — John Adams is elected president.

1797 — XYZ Affair

1797–1800 — Quasi-war with France

1798 — Alien and Sedition Acts

1798–1799 — Kentucky and Virginia Resolutions

1800 — Treaty of 1800 secures peace with France and ends Alliance of 1778.

Thomas Jefferson is elected president in the House of Representatives after his running mate, Aaron Burr, attempts to steal the election.

CHAPTER SUMMARY

When the colonists declared their independence in July 1776, they were left with the difficult task of forming a government and governing the nation while at war with England. The thirteen states were united for their defense against England, but very diverse in their interests otherwise, and spread from Georgia to New Hampshire along the Eastern seaboard. When Richard Henry Lee of Virginia proposed a Declaration of Independence in June 1776, the Continental Congress also began work on forging the Articles of Confederation, America's first constitution. Divisions among the states, however—especially a dispute over land in the West—delayed the ratification of the Articles of Confederation until 1781. Furthermore, the governmental structure created under the Articles of Confederation quickly proved to be insufficient.

With no standing army, America suffered from a lack of security: British troops remained on American soil after the Revolution, there were problems with Native Americans on the frontier, and Spain closed the Mississippi River to American shipping. The national government was in debt, but did not have the power to tax; and states would not send the money requisitioned by Congress to pay the debts. Both the national government and the states issued paper money, with the result that inflation reached 12,000 percent. Foreign trade remained confused since the states could not agree on a uniform tariff. Finally, when farmers in Massachusetts under Daniel Shays rebelled against taxation and farm foreclosures, many felt that the Articles of Confederation had to be revised.

The Constitutional Convention was held in the summer of 1787 and attended by fifty-five delegates from throughout the U.S. Though the authors of the Constitution disagreed on numerous issues, they eventually settled on a federal form of government with one executive and a bicameral legislature with one house apportioned by population and the other apportioned equally among the states, having two senators per state. The authors of the Constitution created a government with separation of powers in an attempt to prevent concentration of power and to ensure liberty.

Two-thirds of the states had to ratify the Constitution. Those opposed to its ratification, known as Anti-Federalists, argued that the national government and the president would grow too powerful under the Constitution. Federalists, led by Alexander Hamilton, James Madison, and John Jay, argued that Federalism, separation of powers, and checks and balances would prevent the national government from growing too powerful and destroying state sovereignty. The Constitution was ratified in 1788, and a Bill of Rights was added to the Constitution in 1791 to help guard against arbitrary government power.

In 1794, when a group of Pennsylvania farmers rebelled against a federal excise tax on whiskey, both Federalists and Anti-Federalists felt vindicated. George Washington led the federalized troops to Pennsylvania to quell the rebellion, an action that proved to Anti-Federalists that the national government was too powerful under the Constitution. Conversely, Federalists were satisfied that the government had been able to restore order.

By 1796, opposition to the policies of the Federalists began to coalesce around Thomas Jefferson; and the first democratic opposition political party, the Democratic-Republican Party, was born. The Democratic-Republican Party became the first opposition party to win an election in 1800, when Thomas Jefferson defeated the incumbent, John Adams, in spite of the underhanded machinations of Jefferson's running mate, Aaron Burr, who attempted to hijack the election from Jefferson in the House of Representatives.

During the same time period, the young Republic was faced with major challenges from abroad as the French Revolution of 1789 quickly led to war between the great monarchical powers of Europe and Revolutionary France. President George Washington proclaimed "a fair and impartial policy," essentially meaning American neutrality in 1793—but neutrality would prove difficult as France seized American merchant ships at sea. In what is known as the Quasi-War with France, Americans retaliated by seizing French merchant ships.

The Quasi-War with France produced a domestic backlash as Congress passed the Alien and Sedition Acts, authorizing the president to deport or imprison aliens deemed to be dangerous and prohibiting criticism of the Adams administration. Antagonisms with France would finally come to an end with the convention of 1800 that normalized relations, but not quickly enough to save the unpopular Adams administration. With the election of Jefferson, America would move into a new era as the eighteenth century came to a close.

KEY TERMS

BIBLIOGRAPHY

B

Brodie, Fawn M. *Thomas Jefferson: An Intimate History*. New York: W. W. Norton & Company 2010.

Brookshier, Richard. *Rules of Civility: 110 Precepts that Guided Our First President in War and Peace*. Charlottesville, VA: University of Virginia Press, 2003.

C

Chernow, Ron. *Alexander Hamilton*. New York: Penguin-Putnam, 2004.

Combs, Jerald A. *The Jay Treaty: Political Battleground of the Founding Fathers*. Berkeley, CA: University of California Press, 1970.

Cross, Barbara M. Ed. *The Autobiography of Lyman Beecher*. Cambridge, MA: Harvard University Press, 1961.

D

Dahl, Robert. *How Democratic Is the American Constitution?* New Haven, CT: Yale University Press, 2003.

DeConde, Alexander. *The Quasi War: Politics and Diplomacy of the Undeclared War with France, 1797–1801*. New York: Charles Scribner, 1966.

E

Elkins, Stanley, and Eric McKitrick. *The Age of Federalism: The Early American Republic, 1788–1800*. New York: Oxford University Press, 1995.

Ellis, Joseph J. *His Excellency: George Washington*. New York: Random House, 2004.

Ellis, Richard E. *The Jeffersonian Crisis: Courts and Politics in the Young Republic*. New York: Oxford University Press, 1971.

F

Ferguson, James E. *Power of the Purse: A History of American Public Finance*. Chapel Hill, NC: University of North Carolina Press, 1961.

Freeman, Douglas S. *Washington*. New York: Simon and Schuster, 1996.

H

Hofstadter, Richard. *The Rise of Legitimate Opposition in the United States 1780–1840*. Berkeley, CA: University of California Press, 1970.

Horsman, Reginald. *The Diplomacy of the New Republic, 1776–1815*. New York: Harlan Davidson, 1985.

J

Jacoby, Susan. *Freethinkers: A History of American Secularism*. New York: Henry Holt, 2004.

K

Ketcham, Ralph. *Presidents Above Party: The First American Presidency, 1789–1829*. Chapel Hill, NC: University of North Carolina Press, 1987.

Kerber, Linda. *Federalists in Dissent: Imagery and Ideology in Jeffersonian America*. Ithaca, NY: Cornell University Press, 1980.

Kohn, Richard H. *Eagle and the Sword: The Federalists and the Creation of the Military Establishment in America, 1783–1802*. New York: Free Press, 1985.

M

McCollough, David. *John Adams*. New York: Simon and Schuster, 2001.

McCoy, Drew R. *The Elusive Republic: Political Economy in Jeffersonian America*. Chapel Hill, NC: University of North Carolina Press, 1996.

Miller, John C. *The Federalist Era, 1789–1801*. Charleston, SC: Nabu Press, 2011.

Miner, Brad. *The Concise Conservative Encyclopedia*. New York: Simon and Schuster, 1996.

Muccigrosso, Robert. *Basic History of Conservatism*. Melbourne, FL: Krieger, 2003.

N

Newmyer, R. Kent. *The Supreme Court Under Marshall and Taney*. New York: Harlan Davidson, 2006.

R

Rutland, Robert Allen. *The Ordeal of the Constitution: The Anti-Federalists and the Ratification Struggle*. Boston, MA: Northeastern University Press, 1983.

———. *The Birth of the Bill of Rights, 1776–1791*. Boston, MA: Northeastern University Press, 1991.

BIBLIOGRAPHY

Schlessinger, Arthur Jr. *The Age of Jackson.* New York: Little, Brown, 1945.

Sharp, James R. *American Politics in the Early Republic: The New Nation in Crisis.* New Haven, CT: Yale University Press, 1993.

Slaughter, Thomas P. *The Whiskey Rebellion: Frontier Epilogue to the American Revolution.* New York: Oxford University Press, 1988.

Smelser, Marshall. *The Democratic Republic, 1801–1815.* Long Grove, IL: Waveland Press, 1992.

Smith, James M. *Freedom's Fetters: The Alien and Sedition Laws and American Civil Liberties.* Ithaca, NY: Cornell University Press, 1966.

Starkey, Marion L. *A Little Rebellion.* New York: Alfred A Knopf, 1955.

Stinchcombe, William. *The XYZ Affair.* Santa Barbara, CA: Greenwood Press, 1980.

Sword, Wiley. *President Washington's Indian War: The Struggle for the Old Northwest 1790–1795.* Norman, OK: University of Oklahoma Press, 1993.

Wienceck, Henry. *An Imperfect God: Washington, His Slaves, and the Creation of America.* New York: Houghton Mifflin, 2003.

White, Leonard B. *The Jeffersonians: A Study in Administrative History, 1801–1829.* New York: Macmillan, 1961.

POP QUIZ

1. How many votes did each state have in the Confederation Congress?

   a. one

   b. two

   c. it depended on the state's population

   d. four

2. A square mile section contained how many acres?

   a. 36

   b. 640

   c. 12

   d. 460

3. What was a major impediment to making foreign trade agreements in the years between the Revolution and the Constitution?

   a. Most Americans did not want foreign trade.

   b. America lacked enough merchant ships for effective foreign trade.

   c. Congress blocked all trade agreements.

   d. Foreign trade suffered from interstate rivalries.

4. Which of the following did Alexander Hamilton, James Madison, and Henry Knox believe?

   a. that states needed more power

   b. that the nation needed a stronger central government

   c. that power should be centered in the legislative branch

   d. that power should be decentralized into mass-dominated state governments

5. The New Jersey Plan favored _____.

   a. slave states

   b. small states

   c. large states

   d. the North

6. A power that allowed for great potential expansion of congressional power was _____.

   a. the power to make "all laws necessary and proper"

   b. the power to grant titles of nobility

   c. the power to pass ex post facto laws

   d. the power to impose bills of attainder

7. Which of the following is true about the Whiskey Rebellion?

   a. Farmers opposed a federal excise tax on whiskey.

   b. Alexander Hamilton and George Washington led the U.S. Army to put down a rebellion by Pennsylvania farmers.

   c. Pennsylvania farmers abused federal tax collectors, even burning down the house of tax collector John Neville.

   d. All of the above

8. Which of the following is true of Jay's Treaty?

   a. The British agreed to evacuate their posts in the American West.

   b. The treaty was very popular in the South.

   c. The treaty ended the British policy of impressment.

   d. Alexander Hamilton had great success on a speaking tour in support of the treaty.

9. In George Washington's farewell address, he admonished the nation to steer clear of _____.

   a. presidents who speak poorly and use bad grammar

   b. socialism

   c. permanent alliances

   d. politicians under six feet tall

10. In the Pinckney Treaty of 1795, _____.

    a. the French Revolution was declared to be at an end

    b. Spain ceded west Florida to the U.S.

    c. the Spanish boundary with the U.S. was set at 31 degrees north latitude

    d. the "Quasi-War" with France and the Alliance of 1778 were ended

11. Taxes on imports were banned by the Constitution. T F

12. Anti-Federalists opposed the Constitution. T F

13. Hamilton argued that a central bank was constitutional because it was allowed by the _____ _____ doctrine, which allowed Congress to act for the _____ _____ of citizens.

14. In negotiating the Treaty of London (Jay's Treaty), the British refused to discuss _____.

15. In the election of 1796, _____ _____ faced _____ _____.

(Wikimedia Commons)

Chapter 7

The Emergence of a National Culture

CHAPTER OUTLINE

7.1 The Framework of the American Mind

Two great intellectual movements—the Age of Reason and the Age of Romanticism—provided the structure of ideas within which Americans achieved their independence. The United States itself, almost purely a creation of the eighteenth century, emerged at a time when the Western world was shifting from one system of thought to another, the two involving quite different views of human nature, the world, and the deity.

7.1a The Professionalization of Science

The intellectual impact of the Enlightenment (or Age of Reason) manifested itself most clearly in the advancement of American science in the late eighteenth century. The colonies had been settled in the scientific age of Galileo and Newton. American intellectuals were never far from the center of the great scientific revolution that marked the European Enlightenment, and lived, like other educated people of their time, by contemporary scientific attitudes. They believed that all problems would respond to scientific investigation. Deriving their view from Newtonian science, they saw the universe as mechanistic, governed by constant natural laws that were discoverable through human reason. They believed that all knowledge was fundamentally scientific and that the inductive method of thinking was, quite possibly, the only trustworthy method of arriving at truth. From science, the leaders of American thought believed they might find solutions to the problems of human society.

The Revolution suspended practically all scientific activity. Immediately after it, as Dr. Amos Eaton (himself a scientist) wrote, "A thirst for natural science seemed to pervade the United States like the progress of an epidemic." The nation was especially fortunate in receiving a number of brilliant immigrants and refugees during and after the war. Thomas Cooper, geologist and economist, came from England, as did Joseph Priestley, one of the world's greatest chemists; Pierre du Pont de Nemours, a noted chemist, arrived from France. Meanwhile, the United States possessed a number of highly competent scientists among its native-born. President Jefferson was a scientist of repute himself, and the Lewis and Clark expedition that he sent westward in 1804 (to be discussed later) was one of the most significant scientific projects in American history.

Though long neglected by the colleges and universities, the study of science began to appear in the curriculum, usually as astronomy, chemistry, or physics. Indeed, science was becoming a profession rather than a hobby for interested amateurs. The tremendous growth in the amount of scientific knowledge, and the equally great impact of that knowledge on contemporary life, meant that there was no longer a place for the "natural philosopher" who took all scientific knowledge as his province. The day of the academic jack-of-all-trades like Dr. Samuel Latham Mitchill of Columbia, who ranged through chemistry, medicine, mathematics, botany, zoology, and poetry, was nearly over.

American scientists readily admitted that they had made no major contributions to scientific theory and that Europe and England still dominated the various fields. Yet American achievements were not negligible, especially in identifying and classifying the flora and fauna of their continent and in exploring the extent of its resources. Americans were confident that their own great scientific contributions would inevitably come.

In Kansas City, Missouri, stands a statue of Meriwether Lewis and William Clark, who (accompanied by Sacajawea) led the first United States expedition to the Pacific Coast. The expedition, commissioned by President Thomas Jefferson, was one of the most significant scientific projects in American history. (Plantspedia)

7.16 "The Best Mechanics in the World"

While America had produced few scientists of worldwide repute (always excepting Franklin), Americans were quick to apply scientific knowledge to practical ends. Born in the midst of the Industrial Revolution, the United States knew no other than a technological environment. The steam engine, the iron industry, the chemical revolution, and the discovery of electricity, for example—all preceded Yorktown. Americans embraced technology with great enthusiasm. Machinery, Salmon P. Chase would write, "is an almost infinite power. It is in modern times by far the most efficient cause of human improvement, producing almost unmingled benefit, to an amount and extent of which we have as yet but a very faint conception."

Technology was particularly important to a new nation that needed to catch up with the rest of the industrialized world. One of Congress' first acts in 1790, after the Constitution had been ratified and gone into effect, would be to pass a patent law; and the first patent went to a process for making potassium carbonate, essential to the glass-making industry. By 1830 the United States Patent Office was issuing, annually, four times as many patents as were being issued in England. Foreign visitors often commented on "Yankee ingenuity." Americans, a French observer wrote, "are the best mechanics in the world ... engineers from birth." The country had ample power, unparalleled natural resources, and a chronic shortage of labor. A stream of new processes and new machines supplied the missing element needed for an efficient, productive society.

When the country needed something done, somebody quickly invented or adapted a machine, tool, or technique to do it. Examples are too numerous to list, but included the iron I-beam, the copying lathe, the breech-loading rifle, the iron plow, the electromagnet, the milling machine, the miner's lamp, the compound steam engine, Portland cement, the screw propeller, the stone-crusher, the high-speed steam printing press, insulated wire, wire nails, the spinning mule, the ice refrigerator, canned food, the railroad T-rail—to name a few— were all in use before 1830. These, and many other technologies like them, had immediate economic value and powerful influence on the way Americans lived and worked.

The New England textile industry is a case in point. The area had plenty of water power and good transportation, but a labor shortage. Before 1800, cloth was made almost wholly by hand—but after 1820, it was made almost entirely by machinery. Cheap, factory-made cloth of good quality had effects in the home, in society, in the domestic market, and in world trade.

Concurrently, the increasing use of the **cotton gin** (invented in by **Eli Whitney** in 1793 for separating the cotton fiber from the seed) combined with stepped-up demands for cotton to influence Southerners' way of life. Prior to Whitney's cotton gin, farmers tediously plucked cotton fibers from each cotton seed by hand. Because of the gin, the southern climate, the nature of the land, and the presence of cheap slave labor, the South was in an economic position to supply what expanding American and international markets needed. If there had been no cotton gin, slavery might have been far less profitable. Thus, it is clear that the gin was a potent factor in affecting both the status of slavery and the proslavery thinking of many Southerners. By the time of the Civil War, a full 20 percent of the British workforce was employed in the textile industry, most of which was driven by cotton from the American south. In the words of British historian Lord Macaulay, "What Peter the Great did to make Russia dominant, Eli Whitney's invention of the cotton gin has more than equaled in relation to the power and progress of the United States."

The invention of the cotton gin, recreated here, greatly influenced Southerners' pro-slavery thinking. Slaves were cheap, and labor was needed to feed the growing demand for cotton and textile products in America and Britain. (Wikimedia Commons)

7.1c The Arrival of Romanticism

The early American Republic witnessed a literary renaissance—in the form of an explosion of creative activity laced with excitement over human possibilities and a high regard for the individual—that became known as **romanticism**. This form of romanticism was uniquely American, as the writers struggled to understand what "American" could possibly mean—especially in terms of a literature that was distinctively American and not British. The struggle to achieve an American identity was more personal than nationalistic, as authors questioned their identity and place in society. Growing out of the Puritan heritage of salvation, sin, and guilt—and influenced by the wilderness reaches of the vast frontier and by the American ideals of democracy, freedom and equality—the American brand of romanticism developed its own character. The rise of romanticism disturbed the orderly patterns of the Age of Reason. During the latter years of the eighteenth century, philosophers and critics in America and Europe became increasingly uncomfortable within the framework of thought erected earlier by Newton, Locke, and Pope. They were no longer content with a rationalism and classicism that, it seemed to them, had hardened into traditionalism. Thinkers on both sides of the Atlantic began to seriously question some of the attitudes of the Enlightenment and to alter their conceptions of nature, human nature, and society.

Many of these romantic ideas were not new, nor were they ever assimilated into a unified system. Yet the climate of opinion that characterized the intellectual activity in both America and Europe from the closing decades of the eighteenth century to the middle of the nineteenth century was coherent and consistent enough to warrant calling the period the Age of Romanticism.

The romantic view of society rested on three general concepts. First, it rested on the idea of *organism*—of wholes, or units, with their own internal laws of governance and development. A society had a life of its own—a "national spirit," a "national destiny." Second, it rested on the idea of *dynamism,* of motion and growth. Institutions and beliefs were assumed to be fluid, changing, and capable of improvement and adaptation. The age had a dislike of finality. Third, it rested on the idea of *diversity*—the value of differences in opinions, cultures, tastes, societies, and characters—as opposed to the value of uniformity endorsed by the Enlightenment.

In the Age of Reason, conformity meant rationalism, and diversity meant irrationality, and therefore error. In the Age of Romanticism, consensus seemed less important than individual judgments. It was "natural" and "right" for things and people and ideas and societies *not* to be all alike.

Those who fought the Revolution and set the Republic on its way were largely products of the Age of Reason and derived their intellectual inspiration from it. The next generation of leaders was shaped less by the Enlightenment than by romanticism. What Americans thought about their country, their arts, and the organization of their political and social relationships, as well as about themselves and the natural world around them, was powerfully influenced in the early 1800s by this new set of ideas. By the time the nation unraveled into Civil War—which temporarily derailed the spirit of romanticism— American writers, influenced by romanticism, had produced masterpieces that included Ralph Waldo Emerson's *Representative Men*, Nathaniel Hawthorne's *The Scarlet Letter* and *The House of Seven Gables,* Herman Melville's *Moby-Dick* and *Pierre*, Henry David Thoreau's *Walden*, and Walt Whitman's *Leaves of Grass*.

7.10 Religious Change

At the time of the Revolution, there were approximately three thousand churches in the United States. The majority of these were Calvinist and belonged to the Presbyterians and Congregationalists, whose differences lay less in creed than in matters of church government. The Anglican Church was seriously divided by the Revolution, supplying, on the one hand, the largest number of Loyalists of any church, and on the other, the majority of the signers of the Declaration of Independence.

The Methodists, whose first missionaries had arrived in 1769, were growing rapidly, as were the Baptists; and both groups would explode in growth after the Revolution. Lutheran and Reformed church membership lay chiefly in German- and Dutch-settled areas, while the small Catholic population was concentrated primarily in Maryland. In 1782 there were still fewer than twenty-five Catholic priests in America. The first American Catholic bishop, Father John Carroll, was appointed in 1789.

During the Revolution, the states immediately set about establishing new relationships with the various churches. Each former colony had its own religious history, but it was plain that no single church could satisfy a diverse, expanding population that already worshipped under numerous different creeds. The legislatures began to allow "free enjoyment of the rights of conscience." The Continental Congress, and later the Constitutional Convention, reaffirmed the prevailing belief that religion, as Jefferson phrased it, was "a matter which lies solely between man and his God." Most of the state constitutions contained clauses or bills of rights guaranteeing freedom of worship on much the same terms as the federal Constitution.

In a time when over three thousand Protestant churches had been established in the United States while only a mere twenty-five Catholic priests resided in the new land. The first American Catholic bishop, Father John Carroll, was appointed. (Wikimedia Commons)

Also during the war years, each legislature (in one way or another) provided for a clear separation of the churches from state authority. The only exceptions to the "separation of church and state" model were New Hampshire, Connecticut, and Massachusetts—where the Congregationalists successfully resisted disestablishment for another thirty to fifty years. In Virginia, Jefferson authored the Statute for Religious Freedom in 1786, which separated church and state in Virginia. The primary principle of the Virginia Statute was that religion would be most free without government interference. The statute contained the provision that "no one shall be compelled to contribute to an opinion with which he disagrees." Though written by Jefferson, the Statute was ushered through the Virginia Legislature by James Madison. Jefferson personally counted the Virginia Statute to be among his proudest accomplishments.

Nevertheless, there was still widespread doubt whether religious freedom and toleration could be fully extended to everyone. For full civil and political rights, a number of states required religious tests or qualifications that discriminated against Catholics, Jews, and nonconformist Protestant sects. Most of these restrictions, however, had disappeared by 1830.

Ministers of the postwar years generally believed American Protestantism to be in a "low and declining state." The Presbyterian Assembly of 1798 noted "a general dereliction of religious principles and practice among our citizens." Congregations were often restive with authority and impatient with the old doctrines. In 1800, even the powerful Congregational and Presbyterian churches could count less than 10 percent of the people of New England and the Mid-Atlantic States as church members. All the major Protestant sects were split by argument and dissension. None of the older Calvinist groups, in fact, had been able to make the necessary adjustments to the great new surge of scientific information; and none had kept direct touch with the secular, optimistic, republican spirit of the time.

The churches also faced a threat in the form of a religious philosophical movement, transported from England and Europe during the latter decades of the eighteenth century under the name of *Deism*. Rooted in the Enlightenment's faith in reason and science—and closely in tune with the secular, rationalistic temper of the period—Deism had a strong appeal for intellectual and political leaders such as Franklin, Jefferson, Paine, and the poets Joel Barlow and Philip Freneau. Cutting away the intricacies of Calvinistic doctrine, the Deists proclaimed not only God's benevolence but also His detachment from the running of the Universe. They believed in human rationality, goodness, and free will, and in nature's order, harmony, and understandability. If people would but live by these beliefs, said Ethan Allen of Vermont, "they would ... rid themselves of blindness and superstition, gain more exalted ideas of God, and make better members of society."

Against the Deists, the orthodox theologians put up a sturdy defense, but against the inroads of another "heresy," Unitarianism, they had less success. Partly imported from England and partly the legacy of the Old Lights of Great Awakening fame, **Unitarianism** was so named because it rejected the idea of the Trinity and emphasized the human personality, rather than the divinity, of Jesus. "Liberal" Unitarian doctrines, which assumed that most persons possessed the ability to discern religious truth, interested more and more orthodox Calvinist parishioners and ministers after 1790.

Harvard College, the traditional fortress of New England Calvinism, surrendered to the "liberals" in 1805. The "Conference of Liberal Ministers"—called in 1820 to furnish leadership for those dissatisfied with Calvinistic orthodoxy—became the American Unitarian Association six years later. This association was a separate group of 125 churches, among them twenty of the oldest Calvinist churches in New England.

Unitarianism
Rejected the idea of the Trinity and emphasized the human personality, rather than the divinity, of Jesus; assumed that most individuals possessed the ability to discern religious truth

7.1e Frontier Evangelism

At the same time, there were indications, as early as the 1790s, that the religious fervor that had been embodied in the Great Awakening might once again provide a revitalizing force in American churches. The Methodists and Baptists, especially, produced a number of evangelist preachers—though revivalism was never really popular in Presbyterian and Congregational circles. On the frontier, in particular, the evangelists' simple, direct, and emotionally satisfying version of Christian faith was well suited to the needs of a pioneer community. There, the new institution of the camp meeting took on great importance; and by 1800 traveling preachers had spread revivalism through western Pennsylvania, Kentucky, Ohio, and Tennessee. Famous exhorters, such as James McGready and Barton Stone—preaching a vivid religion of hellfire, rigid morality, and salvation—attracted huge crowds.

At the great Cane Ridge camp meeting of 1801 in Kentucky, between ten thousand and twenty thousand people heard forty evangelists preach over a six-day period. Such meetings spread across the country—Methodist Bishop Francis Asbury counted four hundred of them in 1811, chiefly in the South and West—and continued through the 1850s.

While frontier evangelism sometimes encouraged emotional excess, it helped bring stability and order to new communities, increased church membership, and gave churches great influence in social and political affairs—especially valuable, given that the Revolution had disrupted traditional patterns of authority and destroyed earlier institutions. Calvinism was powerfully affected by the impact of this "second Great Awakening," which, in addition to exerting a strong democratizing force on religion, emphasized individual responsibility, morality, and social action. The new romanticism—by reason of its insistence on the individual, the validity of human emotions, and the ability of the individual to make things better—also contributed significantly to the impetus of revivalism. From the religious enthusiasm generated by this "Awakening," churches became involved in reform causes such as temperance, social welfare, prison reform, and eventually the abolition of slavery. Religious historian Mark Noll has characterized the evangelical developments of this era as "democratized Christianity."

7.1f Freedom and Equality: The Ideal

After the American Revolution, few foreign travelers failed to remark on the fluidity of American classes—much the result of the broad economic opportunities offered by an expanding society. Thomas Jefferson put into the Declaration the phrase "all men are created equal" (using the word *men* in the eighteenth-century sense of "human beings"). Those who signed the Declaration apparently agreed that this was part of that body of "self-evident" truth enumerated in the document and supported by natural law. Equality and liberty, the Declaration implied, were coexistent. *Liberty* was the more easily defined; *equality* was more difficult, yet the need for defining its meaning was imperative. Neither Puritans nor Virginians came to the colonies looking for equality. The company settlers were in search of more wealth, while the Puritans brought with them the elements of an aristocratic theology. Both carried to the new country many of the distinctions of the inegalitarian British social system.

Calvinism, however, in a number of ways pointed in an egalitarian direction. It rejected much of the church hierarchy, believed in the priesthood of all believers, and introduced elective methods into portions of church policy. Similarly, philosophers of the later Enlightenment included the principle of equality within their listings of "natural rights," and John Locke and Jean Jacques Rousseau added wider dimensions to the term's meaning.

More important, however, the idea of equality had a strong practical basis in the American colonial experience. The wilderness stripped away the distinctions of civilization and tended to put men on an equal footing. American Indians, disease, starvation, and other hazards of frontier life killed an earl's or a tinker's child with equal disregard. The lack of fixed organization in the new society made it possible for Americans to be both free and equal in an actual, visible sense. Social mobility allowed them to change their status, within limits, rather rapidly. The rough equality forced on American society by the endless frontier was the most compelling fact about American society.

7.1g The Social Problem

After 1783, when Americans faced the necessity of implementing the terms of the Declaration, almost every leader gave attention to the problem of equality and of how to make it an integral part of the new nation's life. Jefferson's "glittering generality," as John Adams called it, had provided an inspirational rallying cry for revolution but had not provided a practical definition for constructing a government in a disjointed postwar society. Some, like Fisher Ames, believed the doctrine "a pernicious tool of demagogues"; others, like Thomas Paine, thought it "one of the greatest of all truths" in political theory.

Franklin, while remarking that "Time, Chance, and Industry" created social and economic distinctions, believed that everyone was equal in "the personal securities of life and liberty." Jefferson and John Adams discussed the matter in their old age, concluding, in Jefferson's phrase, that there was a "natural aristocracy" of "virtue and talents," but that there was also an equality of rights belonging to all. (Or, as Nathaniel Ames said succinctly in his popular *Almanac*, "Men are by nature equal, but differ greatly in the sequel.")

Generally, the leaders of the postwar generation agreed that the new nation needed a government in which the better and more able governed, but also one in which the rights of all were equally protected and maintained. On this basis, the nation began to build its society, with the implications of the term *equality* still to be explored more fully by future generations.

Thoughtful Americans were well aware that it was inconsistent to have slavery in a society based on "natural rights" and to wage a revolution to free people who held others in bondage. There was no dearth of opposition to slavery. Between 1776 and 1804, seven states passed legislation for emancipating slaves. Jefferson—though he did not free his own slaves, purportedly for financial reasons—included an antislavery clause in his instructions to the Virginia delegates to the Continental Congress and tried, unsuccessfully, to place an antislavery provision in the Virginia constitution of 1776. Revolutionary leaders Charles Carroll and William Pinkney also unsuccessfully sponsored an antislavery bill in the Maryland legislature in 1789. Even though slavery was a matter of legal condition, it was also a matter of race—which made a great difference when emancipation legislation and the black slaves' future status in an overwhelmingly white society were discussed.

Americans now turned to the issue of interpreting the Constitution's terms for equality and implementing them into society. Thomas Paine considered the equality provision in the Constitution, "one of the greatest of all truths" in political theory. (Wikimedia Commons)

Theories of race were not well developed until the eighteenth century, when continuing contact with American Indians and blacks forced Europeans to speculate about the different kinds of human beings, their origins, and their qualities. Eighteenth-century scientists, who arranged all life forms in systems, considered the different races as varieties of one human *species*. That species, created by God to occupy a particular place in the design of nature, existed within fixed, unchangeable limits. The varieties of races were the result of geography, climate, and other factors, which produced differences within the species but did not alter its boundaries. Beginning with the Biblical account of the creation of Adam, scientists postulated that at one time all humans had been alike but that different environments had changed them into members of related races—differing in color, size, hair, and other characteristics. Though color was not a wholly satisfactory criterion for identifying these varieties of human beings, it provided the most visible and logical basis for classifying them.

There were also those who believed—claiming Biblical support—that the different races were the result not of environmental influence but of a second creation, or as the result of God's punishment for sin (the mark of Cain). Later, there were still others who believed that each race had originated in one of a series of separate creations. Whatever the theory, it was generally agreed that there were five biologically identifiable groups of humans: Caucasian or white, Mongolian or yellow, Malayan or brown, "American" or red, and Ethiopian or black. Whether these races were equal in abilities—or if not, whether they possessed the potential to be made so—became a question of major importance.

Some philosophers believed that since all people, whatever their color, were created as members of the same species, they had the same potentialities. Through education, favorable environment, and other means, they could reach equality. Among the American writers who belonged to this school, one of the most influential was professor (later president) **Samuel Stanhope Smith** of Princeton. Others disagreed, arguing that the races were separate and not necessarily equal. Thomas Jefferson, in *Notes on Virginia* (1786), took the view that certain races, particularly the "red" and the black, probably did not possess the proper potential for progressive change and that while their status might be improved, it was doubtful they could attain actual equality. He later modified his ideas, expressing the hope that blacks would someday be "on an equal footing with the other colors of the human family."

As the debate over race continued into the nineteenth century, Jefferson's hope seemed increasingly less likely to be realized. Philosophers and scientists on both sides of the Atlantic tended to assume that each race had inherent and separate traits. The dominant view was that the races were not equal, nor could they be made so. Most authorities ranked them in descending order as white, yellow, brown, red, and black—on the basis of pseudoscientific evidence subject to much debate. This theory of racial abilities dominated American thinking about race over the next half century. It both shaped and was used to justify the national policy toward Native Americans and blacks.

7.2 Shaping American Society

7.2a Feeding and Clothing the Republic

From the earliest settlement, soil and sea provided Americans with abundance. Nowhere else in the world did people have food in such quantity and variety as in the United States. A visitor to New York City in 1796 counted sixty-three kinds of fish, fourteen kinds of shellfish, fifty-two kinds of meat and fowl, and twenty-seven kinds of vegetables for sale. Contemporary accounts show that American appetites were impressively large: Count Volney—who was almost hospitalized during a tour of the United States by a breakfast of fish, steak, ham, sausage, salt beef, hot breads, and cider—wrote that Americans seemed to pass "the whole day ... in heaping indigestions upon one another."

Such abundance was unavailable, however, to the less affluent. Habit and ignorance of nutrition, as well as economic deprivation in many instances, made the average American meal ill-balanced and monotonous. Frontier diet leaned heavily on game, mush, molasses, beans, peas, and "hawg and hominy." The city laborer's diet was not much different, except that it had less game and fewer vegetables. Its staples were bread and meat—usually salt pork, pickled beef, salt fish, and sausage. For most slaves the diet was even worse—though on occasion a slave mother could smuggle food to her family from the "big house."

Meat was salted or smoked because preservation was a problem. A freshly killed chicken lasted only about eighteen hours in a city market. Neither country nor city people, unless they could afford it, consumed much fresh milk or fruit, or many vegetables. The diseases of vitamin deficiency, scurvy and rickets, were common in the lower walks of life.

DRESS OF MIDDLE AND LATER PERIOD UP TO 1880 (SEE DESCRIPTION FOLLOWING)

American men in the post-Revolutionary years dressed much the same as their British counterparts. American women followed the fashions of Paris, when such pricey luxuries could be indulged. (Wikimedia Commons)

A great change in diet came after 1820, when new methods of refrigeration and canning partially solved the ancient problem of food preservation. Commercial canning began in 1819, and the substitution of tin containers for glass in the 1830s made the process better and cheaper. Icehouses for storage had been common since the seventeenth century, and efficient home iceboxes came on the market as early as 1803. By 1840, according to *The New-York Mirror*, an icebox was as much a necessity as a kitchen table.

7.2b Fashion

Fashion for American men in 1800 resembled that in Britain. Periwigs were on their way out in 1800, and most men wore long hair tied in a queue. Madison, however, was the last president to wear a queue, and by the 1820s the style was gone. Beards did not appear until the 1830s, and they did not gain respectability until the Civil War (Lincoln was the first bearded President); they then flourished until the 1890s.

A well-to-do city man's attire in the 1790s might include a beaver hat, blue cutaway coat with high collar and broad lapels, striped waistcoat, white linen scarf, light-colored doeskin breeches buttoning below the knee, and high soft boots with turned-down tops. Gone were the gaudy colors, gold embroidery, and decorative ruffles of the 1770s. Colors were muted, the emphasis on quality cloth, skilled tailoring, and understated elegance.

By 1810, the full-length pantaloon had replaced knee breeches; and by the 1820s men wore tight-waisted, high-collared, wide-shouldered coats with rolled lapels, contrasting vests, shirts with wide collars, and colored cravats. The city laborer or artisan wore buckskin or ticking (heavy cotton) breeches, a thick shirt of linen (or deerskin or "linsey woolsey," a linen-wool mixture), a coat of "duroy" or coarse woolen cloth, and heavy boots. He probably also had a suit of broadcloth or dark corduroy for special occasions. Fustian, a cotton-flax combination, was used widely in the South for both men's and women's ordinary clothes. Jean, a wool-cotton mixture, was common in the North.

Improved spinning and looming machinery and the rise of the textile industry changed male clothing habits. A plentiful supply of cheap cloth and the appearance of factory-made, ready-to-wear clothing made class distinctions in style, cut, and fabric less obvious. Without close inspection, foreign travelers observed, it was often difficult on a Sunday to distinguish a mechanic from a clerk or even a banker.

As men's fashions followed London, so women's fashions followed Paris— at least among the upper classes. In the postwar period, the tremendous hair arrangements dictated for women during the preceding years (some had to be mounted on wire forms) gave way to shoulder-length curled hair, secured by ribbons and combs and sometimes lightly powdered. Rouge and "pearl powder" were common cosmetics. By 1800, hair was shorter, pomaded into tight curls. By 1812, it was longer again, curled into loose tendrils and decorated with leaves, flowers, jewels, and the like.

The trend in fashion at that time was toward sheer, clinging materials—the basic dress a straight narrow tube (almost always white) with drawn-in high waist, puffed sleeves, and a single petticoat or pink tights underneath. Over the next decade, there evolved the "Empire" style, patterned after that of Napoleonic Paris, with long narrow sleeves, plunging necklines, and sweepingly draped skirts, done in rich damasks, brocades, silks, and fine light wools or cottons. Fashions shifted dramatically in the 1820s toward bright colors, low waistlines, ankle-length skirts, wide sleeves, large collars, and ballet slippers or low shoes. In the 1830s came stays, stomach boards, French pantelettes, leg-of-mutton sleeves, and full skirts that were soon to give way to hoopskirts.

Dolley Madison, wife of President James Madison, was reported to have worn at home "a plain stuff dress protected by a large apron with a linen kerchief pinned about the neck," which would be considered somewhat casual for a woman of her station. (Wikimedia Commons)

All this, of course, was high style. The usual costume for housework was a no-nonsense, long-sleeved wool or cotton dress buttoned up to the neck, with lightweight knee-length linen or flannel underdrawers for protection against the chill of unheated houses. A visitor to the White House reported that, like most American women, Dolley Madison at home wore "a plain stuff dress protected by a large apron with a linen kerchief pinned about the neck."

7.2c Marriage, Morals, and Family Life

"Marriages in America," wrote Franklin in 1782, "are more general, and more generally early, than in Europe." With agriculture pushing westward and industry expanding in the cities, young couples did not need to wait for capital to marry—as in Europe they often had to do. In the newer settlements, young women—considerably outnumbered by the men—were in much demand as wives and had much greater freedom of choice.

American marriages tended to be not just early but also unusually productive. Families with six to eight surviving children were common, and South Carolina authorities recorded one woman with thirty-four living children. In America, in contrast to Europe, the delicate business of marriage agreements was either neglected or left to the principals.

BVT *Lab*

Visit www.BVTLab.com
to explore the student
resources available for
this chapter.

The "arranged" marriage never found wide acceptance in the United States; much of Europe's nuptial apparatus—the dowry or *dot,* the contract, banns, and the like—had disappeared by the turn of the century. Young men and women could, of course, recognize the advantages of a good match, but observers agreed that American partners paid less attention to economic benefits.

Attitudes toward divorce also differed from those current in Britain and Europe. Divorce seemed more frequent (except in Catholic and strict Anglican circles) and somewhat easier to obtain, especially for men. Laws varied from state to state, with cruelty and desertion, adultery, and nearly twenty other reasons recognized as grounds for divorce in America before they were recognized in Europe. In sparsely settled areas, where courts met infrequently, couples sometimes simply separated without legal formalities. Similarly, couples might live together for months or longer until a circuit-riding parson arrived. The frontier also accepted "left-handed" marriages, in which a militia captain, an unlicensed minister, or even the bride's father could perform the ceremony. As churches and organized government grew, of course, these more casual practices lost favor.

Foreign travelers often noted that American families lacked the unity and patriarchal structure of those found in Europe. Although the family still formed a strong social unit—with clear educative, religious, economic, and protective responsibilities—it was noticeably less tightly knit than its British and Continental counterparts. In the cities, as factories sprang up, young people soon became a vital component of the labor market, and on the farms of the West the same was true. Though they were shamefully exploited, mill girls could earn enough to be independent, while boys could find work at 11 or 12 years of age. Family wealth, social caste, and parental influence—matters of importance in European society—counted for less in a fluid society where sons and daughters, through hard work and a bit of luck, could outdo their parents. In America, a young man could easily own more land than his father; a young woman could easily marry, leave home, and set up her own household—one better than her mother's. Meanwhile, the spread of public schools meant that the family need no longer serve as the sole medium of education and culture. In sum, material conditions in the new nation, combined with the ethos of the American Revolution, produced a more democratic family on the western side of the Atlantic.

Travelers were particularly amazed at the lack of strict parental control, and at the responsibilities parents placed on children in the United States. One British visitor wrote that even at 13 years old, "female children rejoice in the appellation of 'Misses' and begin to enjoy all the privileges of self-management." Boys, it seemed to Europeans, were on their own much earlier in America than was true abroad. Some thought this was the result of lax discipline in an unformed society, while others attributed it to the American emphasis on equality. More probably, the fact was that in the new society—where population was scattered and opportunities were great—children necessarily took on greater responsibilities. In a frontier setting, boys and girls needed to make their own way as soon as they could and grew up quickly because they had to; they performed the same labor as adults in agricultural settings because their very existence demanded it.

American moral attitudes were much the same as those of England, but the powerful Calvinistic tradition (and more rigid Anglicanism) in the United States probably produced a stricter code of morals in small town and rural areas. French émigré Moreau St. Mèry found Philadelphia's morals no looser than Europe's, though he was continually surprised by American frankness about sex. The European custom of keeping mistresses, though uncommon in the United States, was not unknown in sophisticated circles. One traveler noted "young and pretty street walkers" in Philadelphia, saw a bevy of attractive "sailors' girls" in Baltimore, and found an entire section of New York, called "Holy Ground," set aside for prostitution.

Travelers rarely failed to comment on the freedom granted to American youth. A study of Massachusetts church records later indicated that of two hundred couples married over a fourteen-year span, sixty-six admitted to premarital relations. The practice of "bundling," or sharing the same bed, was a result of frontier housing conditions. Its innocence no doubt varied with the participants, but travelers also agreed that there was probably less extramarital activity in America than in Europe. It appears, however, that although American girls enjoyed "unlimited liberty before marriage," an American wife "lived only for her husband, to devote herself without surcease to the care of her household and her home."

7.2δ Women's Legal Status

The legal status of women during the later eighteenth century remained much as it had been in colonial days. Although the Revolution did provide some advancements for women—who ran the farms and family businesses while their husbands fought the British—within three decades the status of women had largely reverted back to where it had been prior to the war. Many of the earlier laws limiting women's rights were carried into the law books of the new states without substantial change. Unmarried women were considered the wards of relatives, married women their husband's chattels. Although they varied from state to state, a wife's rights to property were closely limited. She could not make a will, sign a contract, or witness a deed without her husband's permission, because most states upheld the old English common law doctrine of "coverture," whereby a married woman's legal identity was "covered" by her husband's. For a woman to get a divorce, no matter what the provocation, was so difficult in most states as to be next to impossible.

The growth of the textile industry enabled more women to work outside the home. (Library of Congress, LC-USZ62-73733)

Almost all professions and trades were closed to women. Generally they could not vote, serve on juries, or hold office—a handicap they shared with some nonpropertied males. In the eyes of the law, as Blackstone tersely put it (summarizing the essence of coverture), "The husband and wife are one, and that one is the husband." Not only the law but also the church supported this view. According to both Catholic and Protestant clergy, a woman's subordinate place in society was established by those intellectual and physical limitations placed upon her at her creation, as the Bible said, and forever fixed by her weaknesses as a daughter of Eve.

Nonetheless, the American woman held a higher status in this new and flexible society than it might appear. In the city or country, woman's work—spinning; weaving; sewing; making shoes, soap, candles, clothing; and much else—was absolutely necessary to the maintenance of the home and the functioning of society. Nor were such mundane tasks the extent of her obligations. The development of the child-centered family, which had begun in the Renaissance, powerfully influenced the position of the woman within the home during the eighteenth century. With it came the idea that the family—not society at large—had the crucial task of preparing the young (socially, intellectually, and spiritually) to enter society. This belief placed major responsibility on the woman as supervisor of home and teacher of children. By the early nineteenth century, men were ready to agree that—from this point of view—women's role in society was equal to their own. Herein lay the beginnings of a reevaluation of women's place in the world.

Women were not restricted to purely domestic duties. The system of household manufacturing provided opportunities for them to learn a craft and become part of the home labor market. They also helped their husbands in their work, ran the farm or shop when the men served in the militia or went to sea or hunted game, and often took over management of farms or shops when husbands died. Thus, Franklin's sister-in-law Ann ran her husband's print shop after his death, and John Singleton Copley's widowed mother managed her late husband's tobacco store.

The growth of the textile industry was particularly influential in opening the way to the employment of women outside the home. Extending them the privilege of working fourteen hours a day at a loom naturally raised some doubts about their presumed inferiority. Other trades began to accept women workers until, by the early 1830s, Harriet Martineau could list seven kinds of employment dominated by females—teaching, sewing, typesetting, bookbinding, domestic service, textile mill work, and running boardinghouses.

7.2e New Thoughts on Women's Rights

The Revolution itself encouraged new ways of thinking about women's status. The Daughters of Liberty, though not so well publicized as the Sons, aided in the boycott of British goods and the harassment of Loyalists. Not only did the departure of men to serve in the army and the government create vacancies that women had to fill, but the whole drift of the revolutionary argument worked to their benefit. If all human beings were endowed with natural and unalienable rights, why were women not granted them in full? Strong-minded women like Mercy Warren, Margaret Winthrop, and Abigail Adams (not to mention the legendary Molly Pitcher, who joined her husband's artillery crew at the Battle of Monmouth) were likely to ask such questions. Thus, Judith Sargent Murray demanded that an American woman be treated as "an intelligent being" with interests beyond "the mechanics of a pudding or the sewing of the seams in a garment." Enlightened men like Franklin, Paine, and Benjamin Rush joined her in asking for a reconsideration of women's rights.

The legendary Molly Pitcher joined her husband's artillery crew at the Battle of Monmouth. Pitcher and others like her encouraged a shift in views regarding women's equality and rights to opportunities. (Wikimedia Commons)

Meanwhile, the winds of feminist ideas abroad blew westward across the water. Americans read Godwin and Condorcet and especially **Mary Wollstonecraft** author of *Vindication of the Rights of Woman* (1792). Women's rights became a topic of discussion in magazines and drawing rooms, especially in Philadelphia, the new nation's largest city. *Alcuin*, a tract written in 1798 by the Philadelphia-born **Charles Brockden Brown**, was intended to serve as the American version of *Vindication:* several of Brown's novels, notably *Ormond*, explored issues raised by the debate about women's rights. Judith Sargent Murray could thus confidently predict, in 1798, the advent of "a new era in female history."

This was not soon in coming, however. Both in England and in the United States, distrust of "radical theories" after the French Revolution led once-enthusiastic reformers to revise their concepts of female rights and return to earlier, more conservative views of a woman's place in society. Part of the reaction derived from a revised concept of "motherhood" and of woman's "place in the home." In contrast to the Puritan and neo-Puritan emphasis on the father as chief agent in childrearing, the eighteenth century gradually shifted responsibility for family life to the mother. By 1800, the mother was considered uniquely qualified, by biological and spiritual design, for raising and educating the next generation. This idea of the woman's role in American life, with its stress on domesticity, was in a sense an elevation of a woman's status; however, it also served to rationalize a change in attitude toward her rights. If mothers played such a crucial social and moral role in determining the nation's future, their political and legal emancipation seemed of secondary importance, really. Their right to rule the home seemed of greater importance than their right to vote or hold property.

Since it was assumed that most would become wives and mothers, the position of the unmarried woman was not of great social concern. Those who did not marry often served as caretakers in a relative's household (as "maiden aunts") or followed careers in teaching or in one of the limited number of semi-skilled professions open to them.

The key to legal (and social) equality, most women's rights advocates believed, lay in the right of self-development through education. The struggle for equal education was hard, for women faced the old tradition of female inferiority, summarized in Rousseau's dictum that woman's "whole education ought to be relative to man." Although men like Jefferson and Burr believed in educating their daughters in something more than the polite and domestic arts, most Americans considered women's minds to be incapable of contending with subjects like law, philosophy, science, or theology.

The argument for domesticity proved useful. A mother must be well-educated in order to educate her children to be the citizens of a republic, with all of the responsibility that implies. Moreover, if she was to be in charge of maintaining a virtuous home—a key institution in the new nation—she obviously must be educated in such a way as to enable her do so effectively. Historian Linda Kerber has coined the term "republican motherhood" to characterize this way of thinking.

The thrust for female education gained momentum swiftly during the early decades of the century. Emma Hart Willard, herself an accomplished mathematician, first cracked the wall (with the help of Governor DeWitt Clinton and others) by establishing the first endowed school for women that was equal to those for men in 1821—Troy Female Seminary, in Troy, New York. A few others appeared during the twenties and thirties—notably Mt. Holyoke Seminary, opened at South Hadley, Massachusetts, in 1837 by Mary Lyon. It would be left to another generation, however, to give the women's rights movement measurable momentum.

Noah Webster wrote, "America must be as independent in literature as she is in politics." The modern Merriam-Webster dictionary was first published in 1828 by Noah Webster as An American Dictionary of the English Language. *(Wikimedia Commons)*

7.3 The Quest for American Art

7.3a A Native Literature

Having gained political independence, Americans sought their own culture as a way to express—in literature, drama, and the other arts—the fundamentals of their civilization. Critics, editors, and authors agreed on the need for native, original art. As Noah Webster wrote, "America must be independent in *literature* as she is in politics"—but it is easier to demand art than to produce it.

The first step toward artistic independence was to declare America's freedom from English and European domination. The second was to define the circumstances and standards by which the new nation could produce a distinguished literature of its own. The author must have something American to write about and a defined, recognizable, native manner of writing it. True, Timothy Dwight admitted, the United States lacked "ancient castles, ruined abbeys, and fine pictures." On the other hand, the American artist possessed a number of things that neither British nor other European artists possessed.

The American artist had the American Indian, the frontier, and a short but eminently usable history. After 1790, every author of note made at least one attempt to use the American frontier or American history in a major work. In addition, American artists possessed ample material for studies of manners—what dramatist James Nelson Baker called "the events, customs, opinions, and characters of American life."

7.3b Patterns in American Prose

The distinguishing development in literature during the period from 1783 to 1830 was the growing popularity of the novel, the poem, the essay, and the drama. This growth was accompanied by a decline of such once-popular forms of writing as the sermon, the journal, and the travel narrative. It reflected, in part, the higher level of appreciation and sophistication of American society, and in part a greater effort by American writers to enter into the mainstream of contemporary literary fashions.

The essay, modeled chiefly after the work of the great British essayists, attracted a number of talented Americans, among them **Washington Irving**, who became famous with the appearance of *The Sketch Book* (1819–1820). Although most critics did not consider the novel an art form worthy of serious effort, the popular demand for fiction increased rapidly. Magazines printed novels by the score, and libraries stocked greater numbers of them each year.

The most popular ones, such as William Hill Brown's *Power of Sympathy* (1789) and Susannah Rowson's *Charlotte Temple* (1791), copied the style of novels by English author Samuel Richardson. The Gothic novel of suspense and terror found a gifted American practitioner in Philadelphia's Charles Brockden Brown, whose *Wieland* (1798) and *Ormond* (1799) were uneven in quality but indicative of genuine talent.

Most popular of all, however, was the historical romance, patterned on the works of Sir Walter Scott, whose novels enjoyed a tremendous vogue in early nineteenth-century America. Dozens of American novelists imitated him, but none successfully fitted the Scott formula to the American scene—until **James Fenimore Cooper** wrote *The Spy* (1821), *The Pioneers* (1823), *The Last of the Mohicans* (1826), and thirty other novels. When Cooper's buckskin-clad hero, Natty Bumppo, walked into American fiction and leaned on his long rifle, the American novel came of age.

Meanwhile another American, the aforementioned Washington Irving, had included several pieces of short fiction in his *Sketch Book*. Two of these, "Rip Van Winkle" and "The Legend of Sleepy Hollow," provided a pattern for a new literary form—the short story—and their central characters quickly became a part of American cultural heritage. Irving's popularity, combined with Cooper's, furnished a decisive answer to English critic Sydney Smith's sneer in 1820, "Who reads an American book?"

"The Legend of Sleepy Hollow" was one of the pieces of short fiction contained in Washington Irving's The Sketch Book. *The story of the headless horseman pursuing Ichabod Crane has become an American classic. (Wikimedia Commons)*

7.3c Reading for the People

With a near doubling of population between 1790 and 1830, there was a new mass audience for books. At the close of the Revolution, Boston counted fifty bookstores, New York and Philadelphia thirty or more each. Peddlers and "book agents" hawked books—along with pots, ribbons, and liniments—up to the edge of the frontier. Subscription and rental libraries, developed in the mid-eighteenth century, swiftly multiplied. In 1825, the libraries of the five largest American cities had twenty times more books to *lend* than the entire country *owned* during Washington's day.

With this growing audience in mind, publishers, booksellers, and writers soon worked out better marketing and publication methods. New machinery for papermaking, typesetting, and printing increased production a hundredfold. The steam-powered cylinder press, perfected by the 1830s, turned out thousands of impressions an hour. Improved mail services and the expanding network of roads meant cheap, quick distribution of reading matter.

Fiction was a particularly lucrative field for writers and publishers alike. **Sentimental novels**, in which characters had to distinguish between "false" and "true" love and surmount heartrending domestic disaster, flooded the market. Written by and for women, these novels were the "true confessions" of the day. Often, the protagonist was an orphaned girl who had to learn how to grow into a skilled and virtuous housewife and mother. With this theme, these novels reinforced the cultural authority of women as household managers and mothers, and at the same time carried implicit messages of female pride and independence.

Of the approximately two hundred American novels published between 1790 and 1820, two-thirds were by female authors. While they tended to feature highly emotional and melodramatic plots—with names such as *The Coquette, The Beggar Girl*, or *Virtue Rewarded*—they nevertheless showed that women's concerns and values were legitimate literary subjects and emphasized the importance of women in the society of the new Republic.

Equally popular were tales of mystery, terror, and crime, such as *Adventures in a Castle* and *The Asylum*, patterned on the British Gothic novel. Popular, too, were stories of American Indians, war, and adventure, like *The Prisoners of Niagara*,

The Champions of Freedom, and *The Mysterious Chief*. Nearly as much fiction as fact, Parson Mason Weems' biographies of Francis Marion, Benjamin Franklin, and George Washington (including the hatchet-and-cherry-tree story) left indelible impressions on the American mind.

Spectacles

Pageants presented at theaters either as separate exhibitions or as portions of plays

7.3ᛞ Poetry in the New Republic

Poetry found hard going in the period after the Revolutionary War. Some talented writers, like Joel Barlow, tried their hands at "epics" only to retreat into politics; John Trumbull, one of the cleverest, went into law. Timothy Dwight—whose poetic aims were high but whose gifts were of doubtful quality—turned to theology and education.

This was not the case with Philip Freneau, the first authentic poetic voice to be heard in the new nation. His poems—dealing with nature, beauty, the past, and personal experience—show genuine talent. These early poets, however, belonged to the formal English tradition. Colonial Americans had imported the British broadside, a sheet of paper with ballad verses written on one side and sold for a penny by street hawkers. These remained popular after the turn of the century. Really a form of versified journalism, they dealt with crimes, battles, deaths of the famous, holidays, natural disasters, and anything else of public interest.

The Revolution and the War of 1812 elicited hundreds of such poems, many anonymous, printed either as broadsides or in magazines, with titles like "A Patriot's Prayer," "A Song for the Redcoats," and "Hale in the Bush." Similarly, funeral poetry—written to commemorate the passing of the famous and ordinary alike—constantly appeared in newspapers.

Philip Freneau's poems—dealing with nature, beauty, the past, and personal experience— were the first to provide a true poetic voice for the new nation. The delicacy and skill of his lyric verse were unmatched by any American poet of his day. (Wikimedia Commons)

7.3ȼ The Theater and Other Entertainments

Immediately after the Revolution, people flocked back to the theaters, which had been closed by the Continental Congress in 1774 (along with "horse racing, gambling, cockfighting … and other expensive diversions"). American dramatists tended to follow foreign models, using American materials. Royall Tyler's *The Contrast* (1787), patterned on Sheridan's comedy of manners, contrasted true-blue American Colonel Manly with Billy Dimple, an Anglicized fop, much to the latter's disadvantage. James Nelson Barker's *The Indian Princess, or La Belle Sauvage* (1808), focused on the Indian-white conflict, a persistent theme. John Howard Payne's *Clan* (1823) introduced the song, "Home, Sweet Home."

The growth of audiences stimulated a wave of theater building in American cities between 1790 and 1840—and they were big theaters, too, often seating as many as four thousand. Where theaters did not exist, companies played in tents, taverns, ballrooms, barns, and anywhere else that an audience could find seats. As audiences increased, prices decreased. Whereas a New York theater box cost $2 in 1800, most city theaters by 1820 had a 75¢ top price, with tickets for the gallery as low as 12½¢. Shakespeare, Goldsmith, and Sheridan—well acted and presented—were successful at the box office, but theatrical emphasis clearly began to shift to mass entertainment. Farces like *The Double-Bedded Room*, melodramas like *Metamora: The Last of the Wampanoags*, and roaring comedies like *The Lion of the West* gave the popular theater audience what it wanted.

Spectacles or pageants presented either as separate exhibitions or as portions of plays, were as popular as plays. *The Battle of Bunker Hill*, staged in Boston in 1793, reproduced the entire engagement—with troops, cannon, gunfire, burning houses, fireworks, and a parade. *The Young Carolinian* (1818) included a full-scale battle between the United States Navy and the Barbary pirates. *The Last Days of Pompeii*, presented in Philadelphia in 1830, had twenty-two spectacular scenes, the last one being the eruption of Vesuvius. An evening at the theater in 1820 might also include between-the-acts skits, afterpieces, comic routines, and parodies with names like *Hamlet and Egglet* and *Much Ado About Pocahontas*.

Another popular theatrical form featured the **panorama** or **diorama**. A panorama was a painting on the inner walls of a rotunda. To view it, the spectator stood in the middle and slowly turned full circle. A diorama was a continuous strip of painted canvas about twelve feet wide, cranked from one roller to another across a stage to make a moving picture. Both were often accompanied by music, a lecture, and program notes. Panoramic views of cities— Paris, Rome, London, Jerusalem—were particularly popular. One could take *A Trip to Niagara,* view *The Battle of Trenton,* or have *A Tour of the Pyramids* for a dollar or less. Probably the largest panorama displayed was the one shown in 1831, depicting the Battle of Waterloo, Napoleon at St. Helena, and Napoleon's funeral procession—all covering a total of twenty thousand square feet.

Animal shows, equestrian shows, jugglers, acrobats, puppeteers, and other itinerant entertainers traveled the countryside in America as they did in England. In 1815, Hachaliah Bailey of Somers, New York, took to the road with a few animals and an elephant named Old Bet. Within a few years, more and larger shows followed, some with clowns.

Quite logically, these shows teamed up with traveling acrobatic groups and horse shows to become "circuses," as we use the word today. Where roads did not go, circuses went by boat, down the Ohio and the Mississippi rivers in the 1820s, as far west as Detroit by 1830. The more prosperous shows began to use canvas walls, and later tents, to accommodate larger audiences.

Audiences for theatrics and circuses grew rapidly. With this new public demand, a wave of entertainers traveled the countryside spotlighting animal shows, clowns, jugglers, equestrian performers, and acrobats. (Wikimedia Commons)

The first circus to travel under "the big top" was probably the Turner show in 1826. A few years later, tents were standard for all but the smallest shows. Copying the stage "spectaculars," circuses introduced costumed parades and pageants. Well aware of the popularity of the city "dime museums," they also added "side shows."

The need soon arose for buildings to serve the new state and federal governments. From this demand, two distinct architectural traditions were formed—one being a modified Georgian style such as is exemplified in the architecture of Independence Hall in Philadelphia. (Wikimedia Commons)

7.3f Architecture

The Enlightenment, as befitting an Age of Reason, preferred spare, clean, harmonious designs derived from Greek and Roman buildings over the intricate and ornamental baroque and medieval styles inherited from the seventeenth century. There were very few professional architects in the United States at the time of independence, and most existing public buildings were copied from designs imported from Britain. The typical colonial style was, therefore, a modification of Georgian, made popular in England by Inigo Jones and the Adam brothers.

After the Revolution, there was an immediate demand for buildings to serve the new state and federal governments, and a corresponding need for professional architects. The current vogue for things Greek and Roman, as well as the prevailing English style, created two distinct architectural traditions: a modified Georgian style (exemplified in Philadelphia's State House, or Independence Hall) and a Romanized style characteristic of the Middle and Southern Colonies—best illustrated by Jefferson's Virginia State Capitol at Richmond.

The two greatest practitioners of these architectural styles were Charles Bulfinch of Boston and Thomas Jefferson of Virginia. Deeply impressed by the British style, Bulfinch developed an American version of it, called the Boston or "Federal" style. It emphasized simplicity and balance, with cleanly symmetrical brickwork, graceful doorways separating equal numbers of sash windows, white trim, and classical cupolas. He rebuilt Faneuil Hall in Boston, designed capitols for Boston; Hartford, and Augusta; built a number of churches; and served for a time as architect in charge of the national Capitol in Washington. His influence may still be seen in the small towns of Ohio, Michigan, and Illinois, or wherever the next generation of New Englanders migrated.

Jefferson believed that the United States needed to develop an architectural tradition of its own, free of British influence and worthy of a young, great nation. Perceiving an analogy between the grandeur of the classic past and the future of the Republic, he drew on his study of Roman remains in Europe, and of French and Italian adaptations of the Classical style, to create an American tradition well illustrated by his plans for the University of Virginia. His home at Monticello, on which he worked for forty years, was his crowning achievement and is one of the gems of American architecture.

After Jefferson, the Classical tradition was further modified by **Benjamin Latrobe**— whose source was Greek, not Roman, and who, with his followers, helped initiate what soon became the Greek Revival era in American architecture. The Federal, Classical, and Greek Revival styles—though they added grace, beauty, and charm to the American scene—could not yet be called wholly American architecture.

The laborer, farmer, and frontier settler, of course, could not afford a Monticello or a Boston townhouse. The early colonists quickly replaced the medieval gables, thatched roofs, and exposed timbers of the English cottage with shingles and clapboards, better suited to American weather. The result was the graceful, functional (and usually unpainted) Cape Cod cottage, translated into brick in the Middle Colonies and built with variations throughout the country. In the South, the "shotgun" cabins, introduced by Scandinavian settlers, were still built on the frontier; and in the growing settlements people preferred the plank-built, four-square cottage or two-story house.

Benjamin Latrobe

Helped initiate what soon became the Greek Revival era in American architecture

7.39 Musicians and Painters

The eighteenth-century colonists loved music as ardently as their English contemporaries. French and German immigrants, too, brought their musical tastes to America; and after 1800 such cities as New York, Philadelphia, Boston, and Charleston supported good orchestras, musical societies, studios, and academies. American composers and musicians, such as William Billings or James Hewitt, could hardly hope to match their powerful European contemporaries or to compete with the talented, trained immigrants who came to America from the finest European orchestras and schools.

As for popular music, eighteenth-century colonists imported large numbers of songbooks from England. "Singing meetings" were common diversions, and "singing schools" trained not only church choirs but secular choruses, some of professional skill. After the Revolution, publishers put together "songsters" or "musical miscellanies" by the hundreds, including such songs as "The Blue Bell of Scotland," "Drink to Me Only with Thine Eyes," "Yankee Doodle," "Auld Lang Syne," and many others that became enduring favorites. These collections (such as the 1808 *Missouri Songster*, which Lincoln remembered using as a boy) proliferated after the 1790s and served as the main source of American popular music over the next century.

Popular music in the eighteenth century came initially from imported songbooks from England. After the revolution, publishers put together new songs ,such as "Yankee Doodle" and "Auld Lang Syne," that became familiar favorites in the United States for the next century. (Wikipedia Commons)

Samuel Miller, in his *Retrospect of the Eighteenth Century* (1803), admitted apologetically that American art had as yet produced no great painters, though he could point with pride to **Benjamin West**, **John Singleton Copley**, **Charles Willson Peale**, **Gilbert Stuart**, and **John Trumbull**. These painters, all born into the prerevolutionary generation and rooted in an English and European tradition, looked to Paris, Rome, and especially London for instruction and inspiration. Because their work predated the Revolution, Miller viewed their work as European rather than American.

Leaving America, West became court painter to England's King George III and successor to Sir Joshua Reynolds as President of the British Royal Academy. A painter in the so-called grand style, he specialized in huge canvases of such famous events as *The Death of General Wolfe*. Copley, one of West's students, left also and became one of the best portrait painters in London. Peale not only painted well, he also founded the first museum in the United States (1786), organized the first public art exhibition in the country (1794), and in 1805 helped establish the Pennsylvania Academy of Fine Arts. He was friends with—as well as the portrayer of—many members of the founding generation, corresponding with Jefferson, for example, about their mutual interest in invention.

Gilbert Stuart, another pupil of West's, dominated American portrait art for nearly thirty years, producing the amazing total of 1,150 portraits. His realistic, luminous style and his feeling for the person behind the painting made him the best portrait painter of the period. His *Washington,* which appears on a well-known postage stamp, is an example of Stuart at his best. Trumbull, strongly affected by West's manner, became head of the American Academy of Arts in 1817 and exerted considerable influence on American taste and critical standards for many years.

Since the Romantic Age was intensely interested in the individual, the most popular form of painting was the portrait. The market for official portraits of businessmen, judges, legislators, militia officers, and the like was excellent—and the market for family portraits of ordinary folk was even better. From polished professionals to self-taught "limners," painters traveled the land taking commissions, while the better-known maintained thriving studios in the cities. There were so many that Gilbert Stuart grumbled in his old age that "you kick your feet against a dog kennel, and out will start a portrait painter." For those who could not afford the best, portrait painters would sometimes "paint in" customers' faces on prepainted figures. For even less, a silhouette cutter provided cheaper immortality.

There were limited opportunities for women to receive art training until after 1800, when female seminaries and art academies introduced studio instruction and a few male painters took female pupils. Nevertheless, there were a few notable women in this field traditionally dominated by men—Ellen and Rolinda Sharples, who came from England to do portraits; Jane Stuart, Gilbert's daughter; and Sara Goodrich, the miniaturist. There were also Angelica Kaufmann Peale and her cousins Sarah Miriam and Anna Claypoole of the "painting Peale family".

Sarah Peale and her sister, in fact, were both selected by the prestigious Pennsylvania Academy. Sarah, who had her own studio in Boston for twenty years and in St. Louis for thirty, was recognized as one of the more successful portrait painters of her time. She was the first professional woman painter in the United States, supporting herself entirely on her commissions.

In areas free of male competition, how-

Pictured is a self portrait of Sarah Miriam Peale. Peale was among the few woman selected to study painting at the prestigious Pennsylvania Academy. Later she went on to operate her own studios—supporting herself on commissions alone. (Wikipedia Commons)

ever, there developed a strong female aesthetic sense and a tradition of craftsmanship displayed in quilting rugs, lace, furniture decoration, homemade water colors, folk painting, and the like. Female academies and private teachers taught needlework, the best of which required great skill and years of training in technique and design. Though the sampler was the most common form of self-expression, the highest technical and artistic performance was the needlework picture done in silk embroidery, based on paintings or original sketches, which could take a year or so to complete. Only in recent years have art historians begun to take such early women's art seriously, and much work remains to be done.

7.3f Winning Artistic Independence

During the period from 1787 to 1830, art in the United States was for the most part derivative and imitative—dependent upon Britain and Europe for standards and inspirations. Literature showed much more of an American disposition than painting, architecture more than music. Artistic production on the whole was becoming increasingly nationalistic in spirit, though artists and writers still lacked confidence in their own tastes and ideas. They were fearful about not conforming to traditional, time-tested artistic norms.

What the United States wanted was a Golden Age of its own, built out of American materials and ideas but couched in artistic terms and derived from traditional esthetic theories. Real artistic independence was yet to come. At the popular level, however, there was already a sturdy, quite American tradition that would flourish and grow more independent in the half century ahead.

BVT *Lab*

Improve your test scores. Practice quizzes are available at www.BVTLab.com.

Timeline

1769	First Methodist missionaries arrive.
1776–1804	Seven states pass legislation emancipating slaves.
1786	Virginia Statute for Religious Freedom separates church and state in Virginia,
1789	First American Catholic bishop is appointed.
1790	First patent law goes into effect.
1792	Mary Wollstonecraft publishes *Vindication of the Rights of a Woman.*
1793	Eli Whitney invents the cotton gin.
1794	Charles Willson Peale organizes America's first public art exhibition.
1798	Charles Brockden Brown publishes *Alcuin.*
1803	Efficient home ice boxes are introduced.
1805	Pennsylvania Academy of Fine Arts is established.
1819	Commercial canning begins.
	Washington Irving publishes *The Sketch Book.*
1821	Troy Female Seminary is founded at Troy, New York.
1826	American Unitarian Association is formed.
	James Fenimore Cooper publishes *The Last of the Mohicans.*
	Turner's traveling big top circus tours America.
	America's first art museum is established by Willson Peale.
1830	Tin containers begin replacing glass in the marketplace.
1837	Mt. Holyoke Seminary opens in South Hadley, Massachusetts, in 1837.

CHAPTER SUMMARY

$\mathcal{T}$he two great intellectual movements at the time of the American Revolution were the Age of Reason and the Age of Romanticism. Under the influence of the Enlightenment (or the Age of Reason), the leaders of American thought—such at Thomas Jefferson—believed they might find solutions to the problems of human society through the application of scientific methods and reasoning. The scientific approach produced much ingenuity, and by 1830 the United States Patent Office was issuing, annually, four times as many patents as were being issued in England. As a result, a textile industry developed in New England while Eli Whitney's cotton gin transformed the South into a cotton-based export-led economy.

Simultaneously, however, the ideas of Romanticism influenced American culture and challenged the ideas of the Enlightenment. From the late eighteenth century to the mid-nineteenth century, the Romantic ideas prevalent in American society included the idea that society had a life of its own—a "national spirit," or a "national destiny"—and that destiny rested on the idea of *dynamism,* or motion and growth. Institutions and beliefs were assumed to be fluid, changing, and capable of improvement and adaptation. The idea of *diversity*—the value of differences in opinions, cultures, tastes, societies, and characters—also became prevalent, as opposed to the conformity of thought that characterized the Age of Reason.

Religion changed and became more diverse as a second Great Awakening in the early nineteenth century spawned the rise of the Methodists as America's largest denomination, and the new diversity brought separation of church and state. The expansion of the frontier brought frontier religion replete with camp revivals. Religion was also challenged by Deist ideas, or the idea that a Supreme Being created the Universe and the laws of nature, but then left humans to their own devices, no longer willing to intervene.

America's class structure was perhaps the most fluid in the world, but the dominant pattern was a great equality due to the frontier—a great leveler. The Revolution brought a movement against slavery, and further slave trade from Africa was illegal after 1808; yet slavery continued as varying theories on the idea of "race" developed.

America became a family society. Most people married young, and families tended to be large with more than six children per household. Families also tended to be more "democratic" in structure with less patriarchal control and more freedom for family members. Women, though still subordinate and without the franchise, experienced expanding opportunities in education and in employment outside the home in the textile industry.

In the arts, uniquely American literature developed, led by Washington Irving and James Fenimore Cooper, featuring American characters in American situations. Parson Weems contributed embellished biographies of real American heroes, such as George Washington and Ben Franklin, that helped shape American culture; and Philip Frenau became known as the first truly authentic American poet. Similarly, theater and other forms of entertainment developed American themes incorporating America's history and frontier culture. Architecture continued with Greek and Roman styles; however, other forms of art, such as painting, took on a more uniquely American character—notable in the focus on individuals through portraits, exemplified by Gilbert Stuart, reflecting America's Romanticism. Though real artistic independence was yet to come, an American artistic sensibility had been born.

KEY TERMS

BIBLIOGRAPHY

A

Ahlstrom, Sydney E. *A Religious History of the American People*. New Haven, CT: Yale University Press, 2004.

B

Boas, George. *Romanticism in America*. New York: Russell and Russell, 1968.

Burns, Sarah, and John Davis. *American Art to 1900: A Documentary History*. Berkeley, CA: University of California Press, 2009.

C

Chase, Gilbert. *America's Music: From the Pilgrims to the Present*. Champagne, IL: University of Illinois Press, 1992.

Craven, Wayne. *American Art: History and Culture*. New York: McGraw-Hill, 2002.

Crawford, Richard. *America's Musical Life: A History*. New York: W. W. Norton & Company, 2005.

F

Ferguson, Robert A. *The American Enlightenment, 1750–1820*. Cambridge, MA: Harvard University Press, 1997.

Finke, Roger, and Rodney Stark. *The Churching of America 1776–1990. Winners and Losers in Our Religious Economy*. Camden, NJ: Rutgers University Press, 1990.

G

Gerlernter, Mark. *A History of American Architecture: Buildings in their Cultural and Technological Context*. Lebanon, NH: University Press of New England, 2001.

H

Harris, Neil. *The Artist in American Society: The Formative Years, 1790–1860*. Chicago, IL: University of Chicago Press, 1982.

Hughes, Robert. *American Visions: The Epic History of Art in America*. New York: Alfred A. Knopf, 1999.

K

Kelly, Catherine E. *In the New England Fashion: Reshaping Women's Lives in the Nineteenth Century*. Ithaca, NY: Cornell University Press, 2002.

N

Noll, Mark. *A History of Christianity in the United States and Canada*. Grand Rapids, MI: William B. Eerdamans Publishing, 1992.

R

Rigal, Laura. *The Manufactory: Art, Labor, and the World of Things in the Early Republic*. Princeton, NJ: Princeton University Press, 1998.

Roth, Leland. *American Architecture: A History*. Boulder, CO: Westview Press, 2003.

S

Scheller, William. *America: A History in Art: The American Journey Told by Painters Sculptors, Photographers, and Architects*. New York: Black Dog and Leventhal, 2008.

Smith-Rosenberg, Carroll. *Disorderly Conduct: Visions of Gender in Victorian America*. New York: Oxford University Press, 1986.

T

Tompkins, Jane. *Sensational Designs: The Cultural Work of American Fiction, 1790–1860*. New York: Oxford University Press, 1986.

W

Wass, Ann Buerman, and Michelle Webb Fandrich. *Clothing Through American History: The Federal Era Through Antebellum, 1786–1860*. Westport, CT: Greenwood Publishing, 2010.

POP QUIZ

1. The intellectual impact of the Enlightenment manifested itself most clearly in America in _____:
   a. the expansion of religion in America in the late eighteenth century.
   b. the way the founding fathers began working with completely new ideas.
   c. the advancement of American science in the late eighteenth century.
   d. the expansion of Romanticism in the late eighteenth century.

2. The inventor of the cotton gin was _____.
   a. Cyrus McCormick
   b. Eli Whitney
   c. Samuel Morse
   d. Thomas Edison

3. Benjamin Franklin and Thomas Jefferson were _____.
   a. Deists
   b. Anglicans
   c. Atheists
   d. Calvinists

4. Famous exhorters, such as James McGready and Barton Stone, preached a religion of _____.
   a. hellfire, rigid morality, and salvation
   b. sinning to excess so that God's grace could abound
   c. individual study and intellectualism
   d. secularism

5. Eighteenth-century scientists thought there were _____ biological races.
   a. two
   b. three
   c. four
   d. five

6. The first bearded president was _____.
   a. Abraham Lincoln
   b. James Madison
   c. James Monroe
   d. Frank Beard

7. As compared to Europe, divorce in America was _____.
   a. much less frequent due to the predominance of religious belief
   b. much less frequent due to the large percentage of people who simply lived together rather than getting married
   c. much more frequent and somewhat easier to obtain
   d. much less frequent due to the frequency of spousal homicides

8. What does a study of Massachusetts church records on two hundred couples, over a fourteen-year span, reveal?
   a. that sixty-six ended up divorced
   b. that sixty-six stayed married
   c. that sixty-six admitted to premarital relations
   d. that sixty-six admitted to adultery

9. To what was Linda Kerber's term "republican motherhood" a reference?
   a. the idea that women should be educated only in things pertaining to men
   b. the idea that women should not be educated at all
   c. the idea that women should be educated in the things necessary to educate their own children and manage the household efficiently
   d. the idea that women should be educated in all the same things as men

10. The person described as the first authentic poetic voice to be heard in the new nation was _____.
    a. Philip Freneau
    b. Walt Whitman
    c. David Frost
    d. Parson Weems

11. The painter who dominated American portrait art, and who is famous for his portrait of George Washington, was _____.
    a. Gilbert O'Sullivan
    b. Gilbert Stuart
    c. Benjamin Moore
    d. Sherwin Williams

POP QUIZ

12. American families were less democratic than those in Europe. T   F

13. According to the doctrine of _____, a woman and her husband were _____.

14. The most popular type of literature from 1783 to 1830 was the _____ _____, such as *The Spy* by _____.

15. Although real artistic independence was yet to come, as of 1830 American artistic production on the whole was becoming increasingly _____ in spirit.

(Wikimedia Commons)

Chapter 8

The Jeffersonian Era, 1800–1824

CHAPTER OUTLINE

8.1 Jefferson in Power

8.1a "The Revolution of 1800"

Thomas Jefferson often referred to his presidential election victory as "the revolution of 1800," though it was hardly a revolution in the usual sense. It was, nonetheless, an important election, for it shifted national political authority toward the South and West and introduced a new emphasis on decentralized power and state sovereignty. It marked

Thomas Jefferson

Third president, principal author of the Declaration of Independence, author of the Virginia Statute for Religious Freedom, and sponsor of the Louisiana Purchase and the Lewis and Clark expedition the first successful alliance of the agrarian and urban forces that were later consolidated by President Andrew Jackson—and since it was also the first really hard-fought American political campaign, it set faction and partisanship firmly into the political process. In actual practice Jefferson did surprisingly little to erase what his predecessors had done, and there was much greater continuity from the Federalist decade into his own than appeared at first glance. Indeed, in his inaugural address he proclaimed, "We are all Republicans, we are all Federalists."

8.16 Thomas Jefferson

Thomas Jefferson, the third President of the United States and first Secretary of State, is viewed by historians as a bit of an enigma—a man of contradictions. Jefferson owned a tobacco plantation, but did not smoke. Jefferson drank little alcohol, but planted a vineyard and made wine at his Monticello estate. In a time where the rugged frontiersmen of Virginia tended to be familiar with guns and game, Jefferson did not hunt, ate little meat, and was concerned with the protection of the environment. Although Jefferson was a member of Virginia's elite class, yet he showed little respect for the position, even spending entire days in his housecoat, serving guests himself, and accepting visitors in the order that they arrived rather than in the order of importance. Jefferson was a slave owner who viewed blacks as inferior, and he favored the return of blacks to Africa. He also opposed inter-racial "mixing," yet he had sexual relations and children with at least one of his slaves, **Sally Hemmings**. Jefferson favored a balanced budget for the nation and a small military; yet he was generally known as a spendthrift in his personal life, and his personal debts usually exceeded his ability to pay them. He also violated his balanced budget principles when he borrowed $15 million from English bankers to purchase Louisiana. Jefferson believed the nation would be best served if it did not build great cities and remained a nation of small farms, yet he built a nail factory on his own plantation where he put slave children to work making nails for profit.

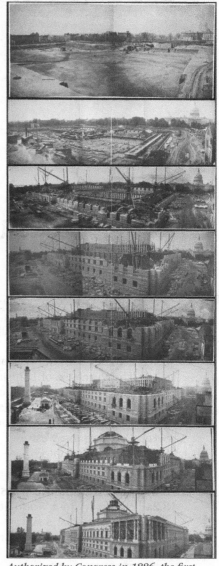

Authorized by Congress in 1886, the first separate Library of Congress building, the Jefferson Building, was opened to the public in 1897. (Wikimedia Commons)

Jefferson is considered one of America's "scholar-presidents," and few would doubt that he had an active and inquisitive mind. Jefferson wrote over thirty thousand personal letters in his lifetime, was very well-read, and his personal library became a major contribution to the beginnings of the Library of Congress after his death. Jefferson is also generally credited with founding the University of Virginia. Jefferson (primarily) wrote not only the Declaration of Independence but also the **Virginia Statute for Religious Freedom** in 1786, which essentially separated church and state in Virginia. Jefferson's religious views appear to lean toward Deism, as evidenced by his letter to his nephew Peter Carr in which Jefferson argues that one should "read the Bible as you would Livy or Tacitus." Jefferson also wrote his own gospel, in which he essentially assembled the words of Jesus and left out the miraculous deeds depicted in the New Testament.

Jeffersonian democracy began the long process of extending political participation to the common man. Jefferson is known as an advocate of states' rights and less government, stemming from his negative view of human nature. Jefferson believed that government was a necessary evil that by its very nature limits freedom. In spite of these beliefs, however, Jefferson expanded the power of the national government with his purchase of Louisiana. Jefferson espoused a strict interpretation of the Constitution and therefore opposed the Bank of the United States because the Constitution mentions nothing specifically about a bank, even though the power to purchase territory—as Jefferson did with the **Louisiana Purchase**—is not mentioned in the Constitution either.

Finally, Thomas Jefferson is credited with forming the first democratic opposition party, the Democratic-Republicans, counter to the policies of John Adams and Alexander Hamilton—though Jefferson himself denounced political parties. Jefferson's party would be so successful that it would dominate American politics for decades and eventually morph into the Democratic Party as it exists in the twenty-first century.

8.1c Conflict with the Barbary Corsairs

Jefferson's administration had hardly caught its breath before it was plunged into a vortex of swift-moving foreign affairs. The president's first problem involved the depredations of pirates from the Barbary states of North Africa (Tunis, Algiers, Morocco, and Tripoli), who had been preying on Mediterranean commerce for a quarter century—both enslaving seamen and levying tribute on shipping. During their administrations, Washington and Adams had paid out more than $2 million in ransom and bribes to the Barbary potentates, and Jefferson was determined to end the affair. Then the pirates announced an increase in the bounty. Jefferson refused to pay the increase; Tripoli responded by declaring war on the United States, launching what became known as the **Barbary Wars**. Tripoli captured an American ship, the USS *Philadelphia*, and in 1803 the United States responded. Jefferson dispatched to the Mediterranean four naval squadrons led by **Stephen Decatur**, who reclaimed the *Philadelphia* and in a series of brilliant actions finally forced some of the pirate states to sue for peace. Decatur quickly became an American hero and was famous for his unrestrained patriotism, exemplified by his statement, "My country right or wrong, but may she always be right."

Under a treaty signed in 1805, the U.S. agreed that it would continue to pay a bounty to the pirates, but at the previous, lower price. The U.S. also agreed to pay a ransom for the return of some captured U.S. seamen, and the pirates agreed to allow the U.S. unmolested passage in the Mediterranean. The U.S. Navy remained in the Mediterranean to protect American shipping, but was recalled in 1807 by President Jefferson due to conflict with Britain. All of the bounties were not ended until 1815, when Algiers declared war on the U.S. and resumed disruption of American shipping. The U.S. Navy returned to the Mediterranean and with help from European navies finally defeated the pirates and ended the payment of tributes and piracy.

8.1d The Purchase of Louisiana

In 1801 Napoleon Bonaparte recovered the territory of Louisiana, lost by France to Spain in 1763. Jefferson recognized the potential danger posed by this sudden shift in ownership of half the American continent from impotent Spain to imperial France. The United States could not afford to have New Orleans possessed by a foreign power. Jefferson wrote that whoever controlled New Orleans was "our natural and habitual enemy." Jefferson was a believer in Manifest Destiny and favored the expansion of the United States across the continent. French control of Louisiana was therefore counter to Jefferson's long-term goals. Jefferson reacted to the news of French ownership of Louisiana by securing the authorization for fifteen gunboats to patrol the Mississippi and the federalization of eighty thousand state militiamen for duty along the Mississippi. Jefferson also declared that "the day that France takes possession of New Orleans, we must marry ourselves to the British Navy." Jefferson's actions were, in actuality, little more than "saber rattling"—but the French well understood that they could not control the vast territory of Louisiana, and might be unable to prevent the United States from taking it by force.

Louisiana Purchase

The land between the Mississippi River and the Rocky Mountains purchased by the United States from France in 1803

Barbary Wars

Wars on the Mediterranean between the United States and Barbary pirates in the early nineteenth century

Stephen Decatur

America's patriotic hero of the war with the Barbary pirates

Lieutenant Stephen Decatur reclaimed the USS Philadelphia *from the Tripolitan pirates and burned her in the harbor. Decatur became an American hero, famous for his unrestrained patriotism. (Wikimedia Commons)*

In March 1801, Napoleon resumed war against England and could ill-afford to spare troops for the defense of Louisiana in North America. Napoleon had amassed an army for that purpose, but it had never made it to the New World because it was iced-in at port in the Netherlands for the winter of 1802–1803. Moreover, Napoleon had tried to reconquer Haiti (then called Saint-Domingue)—which had been lost to France after a rebellion of black slaves led by Toussaint L'Ouverture in 1793—but the venture had not been a success; and Napoleon was eager to cut his losses on the western side of the Atlantic. In 1802, a slave rebellion in Saint-Domingue cost Napoleon twenty-four thousand French soldiers, most of whom died from yellow fever. Despite the presence of fifty thousand French troops in Saint-Domingue, Napoleon's General Victor Leclerc suggested that seventy thousand more troops were needed and that every slave over 12 years of age had to be killed in order to quell the rebellion. Napoleon therefore gave up Saint-Domingue for lost in 1803, proclaiming, "Damn sugar, damn coffee, damn colonies."

In 1801, Napoleon Bonaparte recovered the territory of Louisiana for France. Thomas Jefferson sent James Monroe to negotiate purchasing New Orleans. Monroe returned having purchased New Orleans and the Louisiana Territory for $15 million. (Wikimedia Commons)

As Napoleon searched for solutions to his problems in the Western Hemisphere, Jefferson sent **James Monroe** to Paris to assist American minister to France Robert Livingston in discussing the possible purchase of New Orleans, and east and west Florida (the coastal bend between Baton Rouge and Pensacola). It was either buy now, Jefferson said, or fight for it later. Jefferson privately authorized Monroe to offer as much as $10 million for New Orleans and the Floridas. If France should refuse to negotiate, Monroe was instructed to depart to England and negotiate an alliance with the British (the type of Anglo-American alliance against France that the French greatly feared). The French emperor therefore decided to sell, and the French foreign minister, Talleyrand, asked Livingston if the U.S. would like to own all of Louisiana rather than just New Orleans. Two days later, Monroe arrived in Paris; and Livingston and Monroe agreed that the U.S. should buy all of Louisiana—even though they lacked the explicit authority to commit the U.S. to such an agreement. The United States offered to purchase the Louisiana territory and west Florida

Map 8.1 American Explorations of the Far West

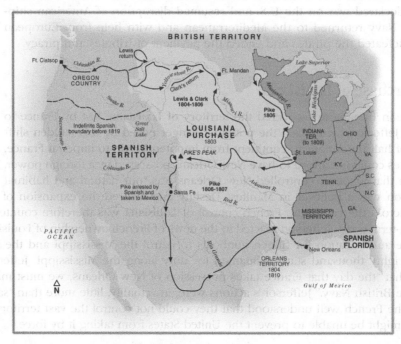

in April 1803 for $15 million. France accepted the American offer, and the agreement was signed on May 2, 1803. The purchase was financed by Baring Brothers of London.

Jefferson, though overjoyed at the bargain, was embarrassed by the fact that nowhere in the Constitution could he find presidential authority to purchase territory. He finally accepted Madison's view that the purchase could be made under a somewhat elastic interpretation of the treaty-making power—a view he had earlier rejected. Jefferson argued to the Senate that "strict observance to higher law was one of the high duties of a good citizen, but not the highest. The laws of necessity and of self-preservation when a country is in danger are of a higher obligation." The brilliance of the maneuver obscured the constitutional question involved, but the "strict constructionist" doctrine (that the government is limited to powers specifically stated in the Constitution) was never the same again since its most celebrated proponent had abandoned the principle when it became expedient.

The agreement was also problematic in that Spain claimed that, under the provisions of an earlier treaty, Louisiana was rightfully theirs because France had agreed that Louisiana could not fall to a third power when Spain transferred ownership of Louisiana to France. Furthermore, it was unclear whether or not the purchase included west Florida (Spain argued that it did not). Jefferson had also declared all of the inhabitants of Louisiana to be U.S. citizens, a power that is not granted to the president by the Constitution, once again contradicting Jefferson's own preference for a strict interpretation of the Constitution. It was also unclear at the time whether all of the residents of Louisiana, many of whom were of French heritage, would accept U.S. citizenship or control, placing the U.S. in a position similar to that of England when the British took control of French Canada.

Whatever its constitutionality, the Louisiana Purchase was one of the most important presidential decisions in American history. With one stroke, the United States became a continental power, master of the continent's navigation system, and owner of vast new resources that promised greater (and perhaps final) economic independence from Europe. The purchase also put an end to the likelihood that the American West could ever be split from the East Coast, and set a precedent for future territorial expansion.

8.1e The Problems of Political Patronage

In addition to the need for keeping a watchful eye on Europe and the Mediterranean, Jefferson had political problems at home. His cabinet, a particularly able group, included **James Madison** of Virginia as secretary of state and the brilliant Swiss from Pennsylvania, Albert Gallatin, as secretary of the treasury. Quite aware of the utility of patronage, Jefferson quietly replaced Federalist appointments with his own; thus before the close of his first term, he had responsible Democratic-Republicans in most positions of importance.

One of his thorniest problems, however, was that of the so-called "midnight judges" appointed by John Adams under the Judiciary Act of 1801. The act reduced the number of Supreme Court justices to five, created sixteen new circuit courts, and added a number of federal marshals and other officials. About a month before Jefferson's inauguration, Adams had nominated Secretary of State John Marshall as chief justice of the Supreme Court. Then, on the eve of the inauguration, Adams filled many of the new judicial posts with solid Federalist Party men—and under the Constitution (then as well as now) federal judges are appointed for life.

John Marshall was a stalwart Federalist, but beyond that he was a convinced nationalist who believed that the Constitution was the most sacred of all documents, "framed for ages to come … designed to approach immortality as nearly as human institutions can approach it." He did not trust the Jeffersonians, and he entered the Court determined that none should play fast and loose with the Constitution so long as he could prevent it.

8.1f Jefferson versus Marshall

Jefferson was sure that Marshall, that "crafty chief judge," would set as many obstacles as he could in the administration's path and that the "midnight judges" would undoubtedly follow his lead. In 1802, Jefferson launched what historians call the **war on the judiciary** when he

James Madison
Secretary of state under Thomas Jefferson and fourth president of the United States

War on the judiciary
Jefferson's conflict with the Federalist Supreme Court of John Marshall

Marbury v. Madison

Case where the Supreme Court asserted its right to judicial review

Chief Justice John Marshall

Chief Justice of the United States from 1801–1835

persuaded Congress to repeal the Judiciary Act of 1801; all of Adams' judges were left without salaries or duties. This, the Federalists claimed, was unconstitutional.

To test the constitutionality of Congress' repeal, William Marbury (one of the "midnight" appointments) asked Secretary of State Madison to give him his commission as justice of the peace of the District of Columbia. Madison refused, so Marbury petitioned the Supreme Court for a writ of mandamus ordering Madison to do so. In what became the case of *Marbury v. Madison*, **Chief Justice John Marshall** was presented with a problem: Although he desired to order Madison to deliver Marbury his commission as a federal judge, he knew that Madison would not do so if he (Marshall) issued such a ruling—and that the Court would lose prestige if it was seen that the president and secretary of state could ignore its rulings. Marshall found an out, however, that the Constitution established very limited jurisdiction for the Supreme Court; under the Constitution alone, the Court did not have jurisdiction in the case. The Judiciary Act of 1789 had expanded the Court's jurisdiction to include cases such as the petition filed by William Marbury, however. Marshall therefore ruled that the Judiciary Act of 1789, which gave the Court jurisdiction, was unconstitutional since it conflicted with the jurisdiction for the Court spelled out in the Constitution. In doing so, Marshall removed himself from the case because the Court did not have jurisdiction. By declaring part of an act of Congress to be unconstitutional, Chief Justice Marshall had just established the power of judicial review (the power of the courts to determine the constitutionality of statutes and actions).

The Constitution, wrote Marshall, is "the *supreme* law of the land, superior to any ordinary act of the legislative." "A legislative act contrary to the Constitution is not law," Marshall went on, "it is the province and duty of the judicial department to say what the law is." In saying this, Marshall had seized for the Court a power that had not been specifically granted to it in the Constitution—and thus elevated the judicial branch to coequal status with the legislative branch and the executive. William Marbury did not get his commission as a federal judge, but that was beside the point. Jefferson may have successfully derailed the "midnight judges," but the Court had taken for itself a far more important power.

The Jefferson administration then launched an attack directly on the Federalist-dominated judiciary itself, at one point leading Congress to cut off funding for the Court and effectively closing it for a year. Jefferson and the Democratic-Republican Congress then began using the constitutional power of impeachment for "high crimes and misdemeanors" against Federalist judges. The first target was John Pickering of the New Hampshire district court, who was apparently both insane and suffering from alcoholism. Pickering was impeached by the House, judged guilty by the Senate, and removed from office. Next, in 1804, the Democratic-Republicans picked Associate Justice Samuel Chase of the Supreme Court, a violently partisan Federalist who had presided over several trials of Jeffersonian editors under the Sedition Act of 1798. In 1805, when the Senate decided it could not convict Chase, Jefferson conceded that impeachment was ineffective as a political weapon. Congress gradually created a series of new judgeships and filled them with Democratic-Republicans.

Chief Justice John Marshall's court opinions helped lay the basis for American constitutional law and assumed the Court power to overrule Congress. Marshall was also the longest-serving chief justice of the United States. (Wikimedia Commons)

8.1g Marshall and Constitutional Law

Jefferson's differences with Marshall were temporarily settled, but Marshall's long tenure as chief justice was a most important influence on the rapid growth of the power of the federal government over the next three decades. Marshall served on the Court from 1801 to 1835, participated in more than a thousand opinions and decisions, and wrote some five hundred opinions himself. Whenever opportunity presented itself, as it often did, Marshall strove to affirm two principles: that the Supreme Court possessed the power to nullify state laws that were in conflict with the Constitution and that the Court alone had the right to interpret the Constitution, especially in regard to such broad grants of authority as might be contained in terms such as *commerce, general welfare, necessary and proper,* and so on. His opinion did not always become the final verdict on constitutional issues; however, the consistency of his attitudes, carried over an entire generation of legal interpretations, had much to do with the shaping of American constitutional law. Marshall's principles of judicial review and the broad interpretation of the necessary and proper clause of the Constitution, along with his affirmation of the supremacy of the Constitution and the national government in its sphere, remain cornerstones of constitutional law through the present.

Lewis and Clark expedition

Expedition from Missouri to the Pacific led by Meriwether Lewis and William Clark, 1804–1806

8.1ĥ Opening the West

After the Louisiana Purchase, there was great anxiety to find out about what the nation had bought, more or less, sight unseen. Jefferson, a respected scientist in addition to his many other achievements, had already made plans for the exploration of these newly acquired lands and persuaded Congress to finance an expedition up the Missouri River, across the Rocky Mountains, and if possible on to the Pacific. To lead it, Jefferson chose his private secretary, a young Virginian named Meriwether Lewis, and William Clark, brother of George Rogers Clark, the frontier soldier. Congress appropriated $2,500 for an expedition that eventually cost $38,000. The mission itself was political, scientific, and commercial, as Lewis and Clark were charged with making note of the landscape, finding natives with whom the U.S. could engage in profitable trade, and finding plants and animals that could be useful.

In the spring of 1804, Lewis and Clark's party of forty-eight (including several scientists) left St. Louis for the West. In one fifty-five foot keel boat and two pirogues (dugout canoes), the **Lewis and Clark expedition** went forth—mapping, gathering specimens of plants and animals, collecting data on soil and weather, and observing every pertinent detail that they could of the new country. They journeyed up the Missouri River and wintered in the Dakotas with the Mandan Indians, who welcomed the expedition for their usefulness as a security measure against their rivals, the Sioux Indians. The expedition

Map 8.2 Territorial Growth (1810)

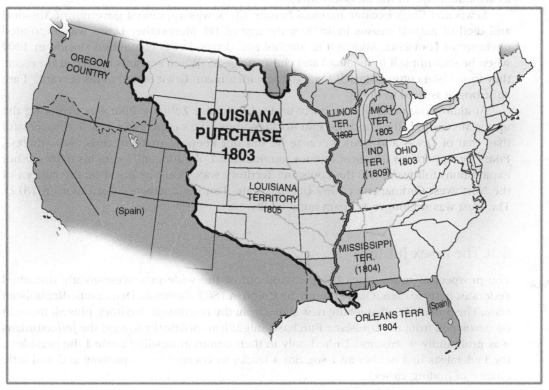

experienced tragedy when Sergeant Charles Floyd perished at Council Bluffs from appendicitis, the only death on the expedition.

Lewis and Clark were aided on their journey by a French fur trader, Toussaint Charbonneau, and his Shoshone Indian wife, Sacajawea. **Charbonneau and Sacajawea** served as language interpreters, rather than guides, since they did not know the way across the Rocky Mountains to the Pacific. Sacajawea was probably about 15 years old at the time and had been kidnapped in her youth by another Native American tribe, kept as a slave, and then sold as a wife to Charbonneau. Sacajawea's presence with the expedition may have been most helpful, in that other tribes viewed the presence of a woman as an indication that Lewis and Clark's group was not a war party. Sacajawea also may have saved the entire expedition from annihilation when Shoshone warriors aborted what appeared to be a staged attack because they recognized Sacajawea as a family member who had been kidnapped six years prior. Nevertheless, Lewis and Clark were unable to avoid problems with all native tribes along the way. On the return trip, one Blackfoot Indian was stabbed while attempting to steal a gun, and another was shot by Lewis for stealing a horse. As a consequence, the expedition traveled sixty miles, nonstop, over the next three days to escape the pursuing American Indians.

Lewis and Clark crossed the Rockies and followed the Columbia River to the Pacific, catching their first glimpse of the ocean in November 1805. In the Columbia River valley, Lewis and Clark encountered the Clatsop and Chinook Indians, who were very poor tribes that made their existence by spear fishing in the river. The males in these tribes were all blind by age 30, their retinas burned by the sun's reflection on the river. Lewis administered laudanum, an opiate, to the American Indians. Although Lewis wrote that the American Indians were not cured, he also stated that they "felt much better." Lewis, himself, would eventually become addicted to laudanum as a result of a wound he suffered on the expedition. Lewis and Peter Cruzatte went elk hunting wearing elkskins, and Cruzatte—whose vision was impaired by the fact that he had only one eye—accidentally mistook Lewis for an elk and shot him in the buttocks. Lewis took laudanum for the pain and developed an addiction that would plague him the rest of his life.

By autumn of 1806, the expedition was back in St. Louis. What they brought back was both scientific data and vivid accounts that fed the imagination of their fellow Americans, then and since. Lewis and Clark also returned with dozens of plant and animal species, including two bear cubs that President Jefferson kept in a pit on the White House lawn. In addition, the explorers made detailed and accurate drawings of other wildlife as well as accurate maps of the Missouri River.

Lewis and Clark became national heroes. Clark was appointed governor of Missouri and died of natural causes in 1838 at the age of 68. Meriwether Lewis was appointed governor of Louisiana. Addicted to alcohol and drugs, Lewis committed suicide in 1809 when he shot himself in the head and chest, at age 35. When servants arrived at his room, they found him cutting himself head to toe with a razor. Lewis stated to his servant, "I am so strong, it is hard to die."

At almost the same time, a party under Lieutenant Zebulon Pike was exploring the upper Mississippi River and the mid-Rockies—but Pike's expedition was less successful than that of Lewis and Clark because he did not keep accurate records. Nevertheless, Pike's Peak, perhaps the most famous mountain in Colorado, still bears his name. Other explorations followed, and the Louisiana Territory was soon organized on the pattern of the Northwest Ordinance of 1787 (its first state, Louisiana, entered the Union in 1812). The West was no longer a dream but a reality.

BVT Lab

Flashcards are available for this chapter at www.BVTLab.com.

8.1i The Essex Junto

The prospect of more states being carved out of the wide new West greatly disturbed Federalist Party leaders. Ohio entered the Union in 1803, a soundly Democratic-Republican state. The probability that all the new states from the Northwest Territory, plus all those to be developed from the Louisiana Purchase, might lean politically toward the Jeffersonians was profoundly worrisome. United only in their common hostility toward the president, the Federalists had neither an issue nor a leader to counter his popularity and had little chance of finding either.

The gloom was especially thick in New England, so much so that a small number of Federalists (nicknamed the **Essex Junto**) explored the possibilities of persuading the five New England states, plus New York and New Jersey, to secede from the Union to form a separate Federalist republic—a "Northern Confederacy," said Senator Timothy Pickering of Massachusetts, "exempt from the corrupt and corrupting influence and oppression of the aristocratic democrats of the South."

Alexander Hamilton of New York showed no inclination to join them, so the New Englanders approached **Aaron Burr**. Since Burr felt it unlikely that he would be nominated for vice president again, he consented to run for the governorship of New York, an office from which he might lead a secession movement.

Hamilton disliked the Jeffersonians but he considered Burr a dangerous man and campaigned against him. After Burr lost, he challenged Hamilton to a duel in July 1804—on the basis of certain slurs on Burr's character reported in the press (Hamilton had accused Burr of incest with his daughter, while Burr had accused Hamilton of adultery with his sister-in-law)—and killed him with the same gun that had been used to kill Hamilton's son Philip in a similar duel.

Alexander Hamilton died as he had lived, a controversial man who aroused strong feelings. His blunt distrust of "King Mob" and his frank preference for British-style constitutionalism had never endeared him to the public, but the leadership he provided for the country during the crucial postwar years had much to do with its successful transition from a provincial philosophy to a federal one. Above all, he had a rare ability to think in large terms about what it would take to create a powerful national economy. Thus, he made an invaluable contribution when it mattered most.

The duel ruined Burr's reputation and helped to complete the eclipse of the Federalist Party. Yet Burr himself was not quite finished. After the Democratic-Republicans passed him over as their vice-presidential candidate in 1804 in favor of George Clinton of New York, he apparently entered into a scheme to carve a great empire of his own out of the American West—a conspiracy that ended with his trial for treason in 1807. In 1806, Burr and General James Wilkinson, then governor of Louisiana, organized a force of about eighty men on Blennerhassett Island on the Ohio River for the purpose of militarily taking New Orleans from the United States. Wilkinson betrayed Burr to Jefferson, who issued a proclamation warning the nation and calling for Burr's arrest. Burr was brought to Richmond, in Jefferson's home state. Jefferson's nemesis, John Marshall, tainted the trial with instructions to the jury that were so narrow that Burr's attempt to militarily seize New Orleans from the U.S. did not fall under Marshall's definition of treason. Marshall stated to the jury that "organizing a military assemblage ... is not a levying of war." Furthermore, Marshall stated that "to advise or procure treason, is not treason itself." Jefferson, however, also tainted the trial by offering a pardon to any Burr associate who would testify against him.

Although Burr was acquitted, thanks to Marshall's narrow instructions to the jury, everyone drawn into his plan was ruined; and Burr was forced to flee to England to escape further prosecution for Hamilton's death and additional charges of treason in six states. Burr would eventually return to the U.S. in his old age, where he fathered two illegitimate children in his 70's and was divorced by his wife at age 80 on the grounds of adultery. Meanwhile, the Federalist Party approached the election of 1804 with its brilliant leader dead, its reputation tarnished, and neither candidates nor issues of any public value.

8.1j The Election of 1804

The election of 1804 was very nearly no contest. The Democratic-Republican caucus nominated Jefferson for a second time, with George Clinton of New York as his running mate. The Federalists ran the reliable Charles Cotesworth Pinckney and Rufus King of New York. Jefferson carried every state except Connecticut and Delaware, garnering 162 of the total 176 electoral votes and sweeping in an overwhelmingly Democratic-Republican Congress with him.

Essex Junto

A group of Federalists who attempted to persuade the New England states to secede

Aaron Burr

Running mate of Thomas Jefferson in 1800, slayer of Alexander Hamilton in 1804, and leader of insurrection conspiracy in New Orleans in 1806

Map 8.3 Presidential Election of 1804

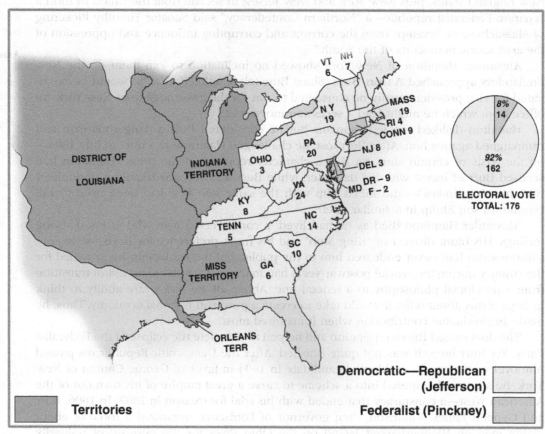

DISTRICT OF LOUISIANA

INDIANA TERRITORY

OHIO 3

VT 6

NH 7

N Y 19

MASS

RI 4

CONN 9

PA 20

NJ 8

DEL 3

MD DR – 9 F – 2

VA 24

KY 8

TENN 5

NC 14

SC 10

MISS TERRITORY

GA 6

ORLEANS TERR

8%
14

92%
162

ELECTORAL VOTE
TOTAL: 176

Democratic—Republican (Jefferson)

Territories

Federalist (Pinckney)

Jefferson's first administration ended on a high note of success. As John Randolph said later, the United States was "in the 'full tide of successful experiment.' Taxes repealed; the public debt amply provided for, both principal and interest; sinecures abolished; Louisiana acquired; public confidence unbounded." Unfortunately, it could not last.

8.2 America and the Woes of Europe

8.2a Neutrality in a World at War

Napoleon Bonaparte loomed large in the future of both America and Europe. Jefferson did not like him; to Jefferson and many other Americans, France was still the country of Lafayette, Rochambeau, De Grasse, and the great French philosophers of the Enlightenment. Against Napoleon stood England, whose aim Jefferson believed was "the permanent domination of the ocean and the monopoly of the trade of the world." He did not want war with either, nor did he wish to give aid to either in the war that flamed up between them in 1803.

It would be an oversimplification, of course, to assume that American foreign policy of the period was governed primarily by a like or dislike of France or England. The objectives of Jefferson's foreign policy, like those of Washington and Adams, were first, to protect American independence and second, to maintain as much diplomatic flexibility as possible without irrevocable commitment to any nation.

In the European power struggle between England and France that developed after 1790, Jefferson saw great advantages to the United States in playing one against the other without being drawn into the orbit of either. An American friendship with France would form a useful counterbalance against the influence of Britain and Spain, the chief colonial powers in North and South America. A British and Spanish defeat might well mean the end of their American empires.

Pictured is Emperor Napoleon Bonaparte at the Battle of Austerlitz in 1805. (Wikimedia Commons)

At the same time, Jefferson did not want to tie America's future to the fortunes of Napoleon, who might be an even greater threat to American freedom if he won. The wisest policy, therefore, lay in neutrality toward all and trade with anyone—or as the British wryly put it, America's best hope was "to gain fortune from Europe's misfortune."

America's major gain during the European war stemmed from American misuse of a naval doctrine known as the **doctrine of the "broken voyage."** Under this doctrine, if merchant ships broke a voyage from French or Spanish islands in the Caribbean by paying duties in an American port, the status of the cargo changed to American. Given that the U.S. was neutral in the war, the cargo shipped under American flags was not legally subject to seizure by the warring nations. As a result, a "re-export" business boomed in the U.S. In 1806 alone, the U.S. exported forty-seven million pounds of coffee, none of which was grown in the U.S.

Maintaining neutrality was as difficult for Jefferson as it had been for Washington and Adams before him. The British navy ruled the seas, and Napoleon, after the Battle of Austerlitz in 1805, ruled Europe. The war remained a stalemate while the two countries engaged in a battle of proclamations over wartime naval commerce. Each side set up a blockade of the other's ports. The British argued that the American **re-export business** was illegal because the U.S. often rebated 90 percent of the duties paid by a foreign power in its ports. As a consequence, the British argued that the voyages were not "broken" but rather "continuous"—and therefore subject to seizure by the British. The British stationed their warships near U.S. ports and then forced American ships carrying French and Spanish re-exports to Canada for trial in a British admiralty court where the cargo would be confiscated by the British.

In 1803, the British also angered the Americans by returning to their policy of **impressment** in an effort to meet the demand for sailors caused by the war against France. The demand for sailors was caused not only by the war but also by a high desertion rate (2,500 per year) among British sailors. Many of the deserters found work on American merchant ships, as American merchants were pleased to hire professionally trained sailors. The British, therefore, began stopping American ships and impressing sailors who could not prove American citizenship. The British seized over ten thousand men from American ships between 1803 and 1812, though 3,800 were released after they proved their American citizenship.

To make matters worse, the British did not recognize American naturalized citizens. England claimed that all persons born in England were forever English citizens—even if they had become recognized as naturalized citizens by the U.S. Americans exacerbated the situation by forging naturalization papers. In the words of Britain's Lord Vincent, "Every Englishman may be made an American for a dollar."

Doctrine of the "broken voyage"

If a ship traveling from one country to another interrupted its voyage by stopping in the port of a third country and paid a duty in the port of that third country, the ship's cargo changed its status to belonging to the third country.

Re-export business

Goods brought into an American port from a foreign port, and then "re-exported" from the American port to a different foreign port after the country of origination paid a duty

Impressment

The British practice of forcing British citizens into service in the Royal Navy

Orders in Council

Orders from the English King's Privy Council proclaiming a blockade of Europe

USS *Chesapeake*

Navy ship fired upon by the HMS *Leopard*

Embargo of 1807–1808

An act of Congress placing an embargo on all American exports to Europe

8.2b The British at Sea

In 1806, the British announced the first of a series of **Orders in Council** (orders from the King's Privy Council) that proclaimed a blockade of Europe. Napoleon retaliated with the Berlin Decree, which declared all British ports closed. The result was that the U.S. was caught between two warring nations, and American vessels were liable to confiscation by either one if they obeyed the rules of the other.

Finally, in the summer of 1807, the British warship *Leopard* stopped the United States navy's ***Chesapeake*** (a warship, not a merchant vessel), killed or wounded twenty-one men, and impressed four sailors (three of whom were Americans). The British sailor, Jenkin Ratford, was hanged; the three Americans languished in a British prison. The British action was an act of war under international law, as well as an insult to American honor. America burst out in a great roar of rage. Had Congress been in session, it almost certainly would have declared war on the spot; but Jefferson held his temper, demanded apologies and reparations, and ordered British ships out of American waters to prevent further incidents. Jefferson understood America's naval inferiority at the time and viewed nonmilitary options as preferable. Though the British apologized, they also reaffirmed their right to search American ships and seize deserters. The *Leopard-Chesapeake* affair rankled in American minds for years and had much to do with the drift toward war with Britain in 1812.

8.2c The "Obnoxious Embargo"

Jefferson and Secretary of State Madison bent every effort to avoid provocation that might lead to war. There were only two choices: war or some kind of economic substitute. The easier choice would have been war, for which Jefferson could have obtained public and congressional support. Instead he chose peace, pinning his hopes on "peaceful coercion," as he called it, by means of a boycott of British goods, and a set of nonimportation acts that Congress passed in 1806 and 1807.

Neither was sufficiently effective to do much good, however. As the situation between the two nations steadily deteriorated, Jefferson asked Congress for a full-scale embargo, a logical move since Britain needed American trade, especially foodstuffs, in increasing quantities as the war in Europe progressed. In late 1807 Congress passed the Embargo Act, which forbade American ships to leave the United States for any foreign port or even to engage in the American coastal trade without posting a heavy bond. Jefferson hoped that **Embargo of 1807–1808** would do two things: first, that it would discourage the British from seizing American ships and sailors and force them to greater regard for American rights; second, that it would encourage the growth of American industry by cutting off British imports.

England suffered shortages, but not enough to matter; France approved of the embargo since it helped at second hand to enforce Napoleon's own blockade of England. Meanwhile, American ships rotted at anchor along the eastern seaboard. Shipping merchants went bankrupt, and American farm surpluses piled up. In New York, one traveler wrote, "The streets near the waterside were almost deserted. The grass had begun to grow upon the wharves." American exports dropped 80 percent in 1808, and British exports to the U.S. dropped 50 percent. The negative impact of the Embargo Act on the American economy was exacerbated by the fact that the export business was the fastest growing segment of the American economy.

While the shipping interests suffered, however, New England and the Middle Atlantic port states did begin a transition to manufacturing that was soon to change their economic complexion. With foreign competition removed, capital previously invested in overseas trade was available for new factories and mills, which sprang up in profusion along the seaboard. These economic benefits, however, were difficult to see in the midst of the paralyzing effects of the embargo. American merchants in New England circumvented the act by smuggling goods into Canada and then "re-exporting" the goods to England. Some New Englanders even talked of secession, and violators of the Embargo Act were often found "not guilty" by New England jurors sympathetic to the smugglers. Jefferson was vociferously condemned in the taverns and counting houses, and finally

Congress repealed the Embargo Act. On March 1, 1809, three days before his successor Madison took office, Jefferson reluctantly signed the bill.

The end of Jefferson's second term came during the bitterest disputes over the embargo; and the president, who had wished for some time to retire to his beloved Monticello, was relieved to continue Washington's two-term precedent and announced his retirement. His eight years in the presidency, begun in such high confidence, ended on a much more equivocal note. Ironically, Jefferson, the believer in decentralized government, found himself (under the Embargo) wielding more power over American life than any Federalist would have dreamed. Though a believer in states' rights, he had coerced the New England states into an economic boycott that hurt their commerce badly.

Non-Intercourse Act

Act of Congress opening trade to all countries except England and France, but providing that trade would be opened to one or the other if that country would recognize American rights at sea

8.2b The Election of 1808

Jefferson trusted and admired James Madison and easily secured the Democratic-Republican nomination for him. The Federalists nominated the tireless Charles Cotesworth Pinckney, yet again. In spite of the embargo and divided Democratic-Republican sentiment, Madison won by 122 to 47 electoral votes.

James Madison, far from being a mere, graceful shadow of Jefferson, was very much his own man. His role in the formation of the Democratic-Republican Party was a decisive one, and the political philosophy of the Jeffersonian group owed much to his thinking. Madison wrote a number of the *Federalist Papers*, and without his persuasive arguments the Constitution might never have been ratified. Madison also took notes at the Constitutional Convention so that future generations would know what actually went on in Philadelphia that summer— though at the time the proceedings were kept secret so as to foster free and open debate. In addition, Madison is considered to be the principal author of the Bill of Rights, and the Constitution itself may reflect Madison's ideas as much as anyone's. In fact, the American system of government—with federalism, separation of powers, checks and balances, and multiple restrictions on concentrated power—is often referred to as the "Madisonian model." Madison, however, did not view the Constitution as sacred or perfect, and instead termed it as a political compromise that reflected the best that the men at the convention could forge together at the time. If changes to the Constitution would be expedient in the future to ensure better governance, Madison would expect the Constitution to be changed.

James Madison, who also wrote several of the Federalist Papers, *won the election of 1808 by a landslide. (Wikimedia Commons)*

8.2c The Drift to War

Madison was an astute practitioner of politics as well as a profound student of it. But when he succeeded Jefferson, he inherited a large bundle of thorny problems. The **Non-Intercourse Act**, with which Madison replaced the Embargo Act in 1809, allowed American ships to trade with any nations except France and England. The act also provided that the U.S. would resume trade with Britain or France if either would respect freedom of the seas. The Non-Intercourse Act was ineffective at remedying the economic problems, however, because the vast majority of American trade had been with England and France. Furthermore, the Non-Intercourse Act was unenforceable, in that no one could prevent ships from actually sailing to France or England once they had left American ports. When France began confiscating American cargo and seizing and imprisoning American sailors, Congress followed the Non-Intercourse Act with Macon's Bill No. 2 (named after the chairman of the House Foreign Affairs Committee), which relieved American shipping from all restrictions while ordering British and French naval vessels out of American waters. The bill stipulated, however, that if either Britain or France would recognize American rights at sea, the U.S. would reinstate the Non-Intercourse Act against the other.

The battle of the USS President, *an American ship, and* Little Belt, *a British ship, took place off the Virginian coast. The* Little Belt *incident was one of many that led to the War of 1812. (Wikimedia Commons)*

Napoleon announced that his government would lift restrictions on U.S. shipping, thus forcing Madison to invoke the Non-Intercourse Act against England in February 1811.

Map 8.4 Presidential Election of 1808

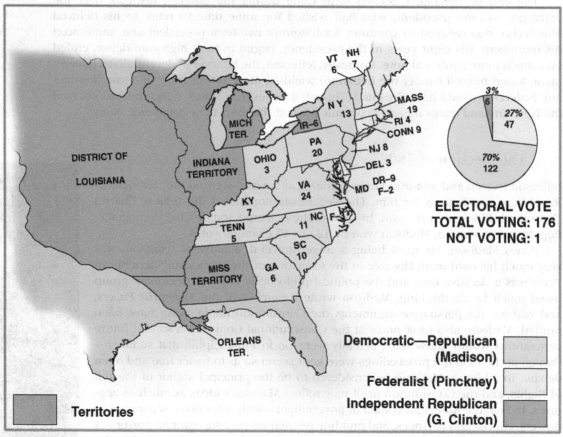

NH 7
VT 6
N.Y 13
MASS 19
RI 4
CONN 9
NJ 8
PA 20
DEL 3
MD DR-9 F-2
IR-6
MICH TER.
DISTRICT OF LOUISIANA
INDIANA TERRITORY
OHIO 3
VA 24
KY 7
NC F 11
TENN 5
SC 10
MISS TERRITORY
GA 6
ORLEANS TER.

3% 6
27% 47
70% 122

ELECTORAL VOTE
TOTAL VOTING: 176
NOT VOTING: 1

Democratic—Republican (Madison)

Federalist (Pinckney)

Independent Republican (G. Clinton)

Territories

Chief Tecumseh

American Indian chief who led a rebellion in the Ohio Valley in 1811

Three months later, tensions heightened when an American ship, the *President*, fired on the smaller British ship, *Little Belt*, off the Virginia coast. Nine British sailors were killed and twenty-three were wounded in the exchange. This failed to influence British policy, but "peaceable coercion" was beginning to hurt England more than the British admitted and more than Madison realized. Parliament was preparing to relax some of its restrictions even as Congress moved toward a declaration of war. In the summer of 1811, the British returned two of the impressed Americans from the USS *Chesapeake* (the third had died in prison) and made reparations to the United States for the incident. It simply did not happen soon enough to change the course of events.

8.2f The War Hawks

Jefferson's "peaceful coercion" policy was probably the best that could have been pursued under the circumstances. Except for some exceedingly clumsy diplomacy abroad and mounting pressures for war at home, it might have worked. Much of the pressure came from a group of aggressive, young congressmen, the first of the postrevolutionary generation of politicians—Henry Clay of Kentucky, John C. Calhoun and Langdon Cheves of western South Carolina, Peter B. Porter of western New York, Felix Grundy of Tennessee, and other so-called "buckskin boys." Intensely nationalist and violently anti-British, this group of "War Hawks," as John Randolph of Roanoke called them, clamored loudly for an attack on Britain via Canada and on the seas.

The regions from which these War Hawks came believed they had special reasons to dislike England. The West had fallen on hard times in the years from 1805 to 1809, and it blamed the British navy rather than the Embargo Act. More serious, however, was the charge that the British, from their Canadian posts, were stirring up the Native Americans and arming them for marauding raids across the American frontier. In 1811, there was a Native American uprising in the Ohio Valley led by **Chief Tecumseh** and his brother

"The Prophet." The Native Americans were defeated at the **Battle of Tippecanoe** by General William Henry Harrison, but the Americans discovered that the weapons used by the tribes in the uprising were purchased from the British.

8.2g "Mr. Madison's War"

The origins of war are rarely simple, and the **War of 1812** seems to have developed from a bewildering complexity of causes. Historians have advanced a number of explanations as to why the United States, after seven months of somewhat disordered debate in Congress, decided on June 18, 1812, to declare war on Great Britain. The vote was close in the Senate, 19 to 13, and not overwhelming in the House, 79 to 49. Simultaneously, Congress narrowly defeated a proposal for a Declaration of War against France as well.

Nineteenth-century historians tended to agree that the causes of the war were first, to "vindicate the national character" (as the House Foreign Affairs Committee said); and second, to retaliate against British violations of America's maritime rights. Yet the largest vote for war came from the South and West, where sea trade was less important. New England, the center of American sea trade, opposed the war. At the news, flags flew at half-mast in New England, and there were minor riots in some port cities.

The eastern Federalist press dubbed it "Mr. Madison's War," and so it remained. Some, too, regarded it as a stab in Britain's back when that nation stood alone against Napoleon, who in 1812 was on his way to Moscow for what seemed likely to be his last great conquest.

Later historians, noting the rhetoric of the Congressional debates and the distribution of the vote, concluded that the South and West hoped the war would lead to annexing Canada and Florida as room for expansion, an expression of what later became known as America's Manifest Destiny to occupy the continent. Some still favor this expansionist interpretation; other historians have suggested that fear of Britain's economic dominance—a reassertion of England's old imperial power over her former colonies—also played an important role. Whatever the motivations, it was a brief, confused, and—except for a few instances—not very heroic war, which nonetheless had a crucial role in the national development.

8.3 The War of 1812

8.3a War on Land: The First Phase

Many Americans believed that not only should Canada rightfully join the United States but that it wanted to do so. The Articles of Confederation had provided for Canada's admission to the Union, and the first Congress had called itself "Continental" by design. Some Americans believed that the only way to end their problems with the British in North America was to militarily expel them from Canada. Other Americans simply desired land in Canada and believed that Canada would be an easy military conquest. Henry Clay, for instance, argued that taking Canada was "a mere matter of marching." Secretary of War William Eustis wrote in 1812, "We have only to send officers into the Provinces and the people, already disaffected toward their own government, will rally to our standard."

There was, in fact, a good deal of pro-American sympathy in the western St. Lawrence region—then called Upper Canada, and later Ontario—but those loyal to Britain controlled both the Assembly and the Governor's Executive Council. As the Anglican Bishop of Upper Canada wrote, they and the British Canadians wanted no part of that "degenerate government … equally destitute of national honor and virtue," that lay to the south. French Quebec, with vivid memories of Revolutionary anti-Catholic propaganda, feared the loss of its language and its religion under American rule, whereas neither British nor French merchants in Montreal could see any advantage in a change.

In April 1812, Congress imposed a 90-day embargo on all ships in port—an action generally regarded as preparatory to war. That same month in England, disruption of trade and economic recession had spurred enough political unrest that the government announced that it would repeal the Orders in Council, under which the British had

Map 8.5 Northern Campaigns (1812–1814)

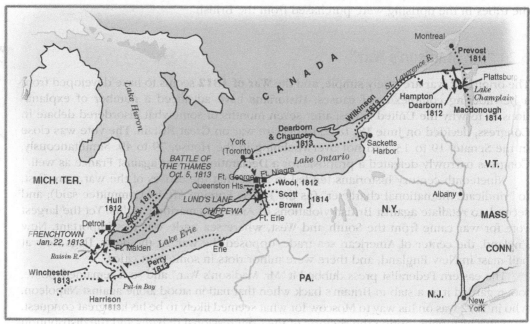

General William Hull

Tricked by the British at Detroit, surrendered without a shot

been seizing American shipping, if the Americans resumed normal trade and the French rescinded their restrictions on trade. Two months later, on June 16, the British announced that they would suspend the Orders in Council on the condition that the U.S. resume normal trade relations. Congress declared war two days later, on June 18, not knowing that England had agreed to suspend the Orders in Council.

Upon hearing of the American War Declaration, the British expected that Madison would suspend it as soon as he learned of the British suspension of the Orders in Council. Madison did not do so, however, because the British had not agreed to end impressment—which he viewed as an affront to American honor and sovereignty.

The War of 1812 was very unpopular in New England from the outset. New Englanders talked of secession, loaned money to the British, aided British soldiers moving through the country, and traded with Canada and England while the U.S. was at war. In return, the British allowed New England merchant ships to trade with England.

The United States was totally unprepared for war: its defenses outmoded, its army—reduced to about seven thousand men—badly equipped, scattered across the frontier, and poorly led. Madison called for one hundred thousand state militiamen, but only ten thousand reported for duty (even though state militia rolls contained seven hundred thousand names). The British situation was no better. Canada had a thousand miles of border, with six thousand scattered British regulars and a militia pool of perhaps sixty thousand to defend it. John C. Calhoun figured that a complete conquest of Canada might take a month. Henry Clay thought one company of Kentucky militia could do it. Both turned out to be overly optimistic.

The American strategy was threefold. First, take Montreal and seal off the St. Lawrence route to the interior. Second, invade the Niagara region and secure control of the central St. Lawrence Valley. Third, invade western Canada from Detroit, securing the Great Lakes and the Northwest.

None of it worked. The expedition into Canada failed at Crysler's Farm and at Châteauguay, due chiefly to the stubborn defense of the French-Canadian militia and the fact that some of the American militiamen refused to fight outside of their home states. **General William Hull**, the American commander at Detroit, crossed into Canada in July 1812, lost his courage, and quickly returned. British General Isaac Brock, with a smaller force, persuaded Hull (who was later court-martialed and sentenced to death, but pardoned by the president) into surrendering Detroit on August 14 with a fictitious report about the size of the Native American force allied with the British. Hull surrendered, without firing a shot, to a Native American force half the size of his own force. After

Fort Michilimackinac in upper Michigan and Fort Dearborn in Illinois fell, the British controlled the Northwest. Brock then rushed his army toward Niagara in 1813, where he defeated an American invasion at Queenston Heights in mid-October. Brock was killed in the battle, but he had saved western Canada for the British.

The British proclaimed a blockade of the entire United States, and the U.S. lacked the naval power to do anything about it. At the outset of the war, the U.S. had only sixteen sea-worthy ships and a fleet of 170 small gunboats that were fit only for harbor or river patrol.

In the middle of these military failures, Madison was nominated for another term. An eastern antiwar wing of the Democratic-Republicans, however, nominated De Witt Clinton of New York against him; and the Federalists added their support for Clinton. Madison won, 128 to 89 electoral votes—but significantly, Clinton carried all of New England and the Mid-Atlantic States except Vermont and Pennsylvania. At the same time, the Federalists doubled their delegation in Congress.

8.3b War on Land: The Second Phase

Despite its early disasters, the army kept trying to conquer Canada. American sailors, commanded by **Captain Oliver Hazard Perry**, built a small fleet and met and smashed the British lake squadron at the Battle of Lake Erie, near Sandusky, Ohio, in September 1813. Lake Erie was the scene for one of the most savage naval actions of the era (Perry's flagship suffered 80 percent casualties); after three hours of fighting, Perry dispatched his message to General William Henry Harrison commanding the forces near Detroit, "We have met the enemy and they are ours." Without control of Lake Erie, the British evacuated Detroit and fell back toward Niagara; however, Harrison's swiftly advancing force caught and defeated the British at the Battle of the Thames on October 5, 1813.

Pictured is Oliver Hazard Perry transferring from U.S. Brig Lawrence *to U.S. Brig* Niagara *during the battle. The United States' victory ensured American control of the lake for the rest of the war. The naval action on Lake Erie was considered one of the most savage of the era. (Wikimedia Commons)*

By reason of Perry's and Harrison's victories, the United States now commanded the Northwestern frontier. London, however, was sending more British regulars; and the Canadian militia was gaining experience. Two American invasions were turned back at Stoney Creek and Beaver Dam, and on July 25, 1814, a bitter battle at Lundy's Lane near Niagara Falls stopped a third attempt. The British then struck back at Buffalo, capturing and then burning the town. Later that year they took Fort Niagara.

8.3c War at Sea

The American navy entered the War of 1812 with sixteen ships. The British had ninety-seven in American waters alone. The out-numbered Americans, therefore, limited themselves to single-ship actions, in which they did surprisingly well. The **USS *Constitution*** ("Old Ironsides"), a forty-four gun frigate commanded by Yankee Isaac Hull, defeated the British frigate *Guerriere* on August 19, 1812, in one of the most famous sea fights in American history. The *Constitution's* victory proved that the American ships and sailors could compete with the British when their ships were of a similar class. The big frigate *United States,* commanded by Captain Stephen Decatur, captured the British *Macedonian* a few weeks later, but the American *Chesapeake* lost a bitter fight to the British *Shannon* in 1813.

The Constitution, *a forty-four gun frigate commanded by Yankee Isaac Hull, defeated the British frigate* Guerriere *in one of the most famous sea fights in history. (Wikimedia Commons)*

American privateers contributed most to the success of the war at sea. These swift ships sailed circles around the British, captured or destroyed 1,300 British merchantmen, and

Plattsburgh

Battle in the Lake Champlain Valley that was won by the Americans and induced the British into a negotiated settlement to the War of 1812

Francis Scott Key

Author of the lyrics of the "Star Spangled Banner"

even had the impudence to sack British shipping in the English Channel in full sight of the shore. They gave the American public something to crow about now and then, though the overall effect on the outcome of the conflict was negligible. The British naval blockade was quite effective, and by 1813 the majority of American ports were tightly bottled up. British naval captains even forced American cities to pay tribute in order to avoid bombardment.

8.30 War on Land: The Final Phase

Napoleon abdicated in April 1814 and was exiled to the isle of Elba in the Mediterranean. With Bonaparte gone and the French war finished, England turned its huge army of fourteen thousand veterans toward American shores. The strategy of the British general staff was to make three coordinated attacks: one from the north, from Canada down Lake Champlain into New York State; a second on the coast, through Chesapeake Bay, aimed at Baltimore, Washington, and Philadelphia; and a third up from the south, at New Orleans. The end was in sight, wrote the *London Times,* for this "ill-organized association" of states. Indeed, it looked that way.

The northern campaign began in July 1814. Since Lake Champlain in upstate New York was the vital link in the invasion route, British General Sir George Prevost wanted it cleared of American ships. Surprisingly, in September 1814 the American lake squadron under Captain Thomas Macdonough decisively defeated the British. Without control of the lake, the British drive stalled and eventually dissolved at **Plattsburgh**, New York, where the British army retreated from an American force it outnumbered 11,000 to 3,300.

The British were more successful at Chesapeake Bay, where in August 1814 General Robert Ross landed a strong force that marched on Washington. The American government fled into Virginia; and the British, in retaliation for the American burning of York (Toronto) in 1813, set fire to the White House and the Capitol before moving toward Baltimore. The British were stopped at Fort McHenry, where a spirited defense inspired **Francis Scott Key** to write "The Star-Spangled Banner"—putting patriotic words to an old English drinking song. Unable to crack the Baltimore defenses, the British set sail for the West Indies.

The third British offensive, aimed at New Orleans and commanded by General Edward Pakenham, sailed from Jamaica in November 1814 with 7,500 seasoned veterans.

Map 8.6 Southwest Campaigns (1813–1815)

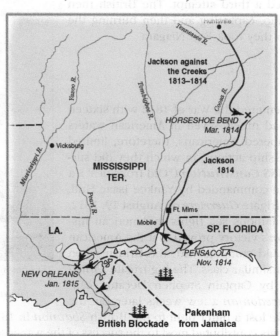

To oppose Pakenham, General Andrew Jackson took his frontier army on a forced march in December. Though neither Jackson nor Pakenham knew it, American and British representatives were already at work in Belgium on a treaty of peace. Two weeks after the **Treaty of Ghent** was signed, on December 24, 1814, Jackson's western riflemen almost annihilated Pakenham's army. The British lost two thousand men (including Pakenham), while Jackson's loss totaled only eight dead and thirteen wounded. In the end, the battle did not really affect the war or the peace.

The signing of the Treaty of Ghent ended the War of 1812 between the United States and Great Britain. Though celebration was quickly widespread among Americans, "Mr. Madison's War" had actually accomplished very little in the military or political sense. (Wikimedia Commons)

8.3e The Hartford Convention

In 1814, when American prospects seemed darkest, the Federalist Massachusetts legislature called a convention at Hartford, Connecticut, to discuss "public grievances and concerns"—that is, the Democratic-Republican conduct of the war. Some of the delegates—who came primarily from the Massachusetts, Connecticut, and Rhode Island legislatures—advocated amending the Constitution to clip Congress' war-making powers. Others suggested negotiating a separate peace with England.

Curiously enough, the delegates, all Federalists, appealed to the doctrine of states' rights—the same doctrine that the Jeffersonians had used against Federalist centralization during Adams' administration. They argued that since the Democratic-Republican Congress had violated the Constitution by declaring an unwanted war, those states that did not approve had the right to override congressional action. At the conclusion of the meeting, Massachusetts and Connecticut sent commissioners to Washington to place their protests before Congress. When the commissioners arrived, the war was over; whatever they had to say was moot. It is likely that the biggest accomplishment of the **Hartford Convention** was to weaken the Federalist Party even further.

8.3f A Welcome Peace

In August 1814, American and British representatives met in Ghent, Belgium, to negotiate peace. As the meetings dragged on, it became clear that the British could not successfully invade the United States—nor could the United States successfully take Canada. The defeat at Plattsburgh convinced the British that the Americans were determined to hold on to their land and continue fighting. Public opposition in Britain to the "worthless" war in the Americas coupled, with fears that Napoleon could return to power, pushed the British to genuinely seek a negotiated settlement. Both British and Americans were war-weary and wanted to finish it, and on December 24, 1814, the commissioners signed a peace treaty. The British had originally demanded American land in the area of the Great Lakes, and the U.S. had demanded the cession of Canada to the U.S. Both sides reduced their demands to "status quo ante bellum," or a return to how things were before the war. The Treaty of Ghent was signed by both sides based on this principle. Interestingly, the treaty did not mention impressment—Madison's reason for not rescinding the Declaration of War in the summer of 1812, after Britain rescinded the Orders in Council—nor did it mention the British blockades, seizures at sea, or any of the major disputes that seemed to have precipitated the war.

Treaty of Ghent
Treaty with England in Ghent, Belgium, that officially ended the War of 1812

Hartford Convention
Meeting where New England Federalists opposed the War of 1812, citing states' rights

BVT *Lab*

Visit www.BVTLab.com
to explore the student
resources available for
this chapter.

8.3g The Results of the War

The reaction of war-weary Americans to the news of the Treaty of Ghent—which arrived in the United States in February, 1815—was swift. Bells rang, parades formed, and newspapers broke out in headlines to proclaim the "passage from gloom to glory." Yet "Mr. Madison's War" had accomplished very little in a military or political sense. In short, Madison had fought the war to end impressment and did not achieve his goal.

The most that can be said is that the treaty opened the way for future settlements to be worked out over the next decade with Britain, Spain, and France. The war dislocated business and foreign trade, deranged currency values, and exposed glaring cracks in the national political organization.

To the American people, the outcome (ambiguous as it was) marked a turning point in patriotic self-esteem. True, the war might have been avoided by better statesmanship, and it might even have been fought with France on equally reasonable grounds. Yet from the American point of view, the War of 1812 gave notice to the rest of the world that the United States had arrived as a nation. Henceforth, the powers of Europe would tread on American sovereignty only at a price. "Who would not be an American?" crowed the *Niles' Register*. "Long live the Republic! All Hail!"

Madison had also used the war to seize both east and west Florida for the United States. Madison had Congress officially annex west Florida (the Gulf Coast from Pensacola to Baton Rouge) in the spring of 1812 and sent troops into west Florida to defend American control of the area. American troops, under General James Wilkinson, took Mobile from the Spanish in 1813; and Americans under Andrew Jackson took Pensacola from the Spanish in 1814—though the U.S. returned east Florida (current day Florida) to Spain at the conclusion of the war.

8.3h The War and Canada

The War of 1812 marked the first step in creating the country of Canada, which was to emerge a half-century later as a sovereign nation. In the conflict between England and the United States, British and French Canadians alike were caught in the middle—just as they had been in the American Revolution. For England to strike at the United States, the route lay through Canada. For the United States to strike at England, the only vulnerable point was Canada.

However, to the average Canadian, whether British or French, the war's causes meant little; and they had small stake in it. Canada's problem was simply survival, and survive it did. Whatever their differences, French, British, and Loyalist Canadians joined in common cause to outlast a long, hard war and preserve their part of the British Empire.

America's attempted invasions intensified already strong anti-American feelings, while Canada's repulse of them was understandably a source of growing national pride. Opposition to the United States and wariness of its motives thus became continuing factors in subsequent Canadian-American relations. The war strengthened Canada's "Britishness," and at the same time gave Canada the beginnings of its own sense of identity.

8.4 America Makes a New Start

8.4a A Confident Nation

The War of 1812 marked the end of America's lingering sense of colonial inferiority. It was hardly a "second war of independence," as some called it—but from it there did stem a new spirit of national consciousness. Albert Gallatin wrote, "It has renewed and reinstated the national feeling and character which the Revolution had given, and which were daily lessening. The people now have more general objects of attachment … They are more Americans, they feel and act more as a nation."

After the Treaty of Ghent, the United States turned toward the great, hazy West, where half a continent lay virtually empty. America could now concentrate on its domestic problems with less concern for European standards, ideals, and entanglements. Indifference to foreign affairs after 1814 was so great that even Napoleon's escape from Elba, his return to France, and his final defeat at Waterloo in June 1815 excited little attention in the American press. American indifference to foreign affairs, however, was in part made possible by the conclusion of the Napoleonic wars and the **Congress of Vienna** in 1815, which brought peace to the great powers of Europe. With Europe at peace and the United States no longer caught between the warring powers, the interest of the United States centered on perfecting and expanding the nation it had constructed out of two wars and a generation of experimentation. In other words, its chief task lay in developing modern America.

Congress of Vienna
Meeting of European countries at the conclusion of the Napoleonic wars that brought lasting peace in Europe

8.4b The Aftermath of War

The most persistent postwar American problems were economic. Finances during the war had been handled almost as ineptly as military affairs, and banks had multiplied profusely and without proper control. As a result, the country was flooded with depreciating paper money, and prices were at the most inflated level in America's brief history. Furthermore, the shipping industry had been badly hurt by war and blockade. On the other hand, the value of manufacturing had increased tremendously—the total capital investment in American industry in 1816, it was estimated, was somewhat more than $100 million. The West, now producing foodstuffs and raw materials in abundance, balanced on the verge of a tremendous boom. As soon as peace was established, the Democratic-Republican Congress began to consider a three-point program for economic expansion: a tariff to protect infant American industry; a second Bank of the United States, since the charter of Hamilton's original Bank had expired in 1811; and a system of roads, waterways, and canals to provide internal routes of communication and trade.

8.4c A Protective Tariff

The protection of America's infant industries was a matter of first priority. New factories, encouraged by the war, had grown in great numbers, especially in the textile industry— where for the first time the workforce was comprised of young women. As soon as the wartime blockade ended, British-made products streamed toward the United States. Young industries that had flourished under conditions of embargo and war found it quite another matter to compete in an open, peacetime market. Whereas the total value of United States imports in 1813 had been $13 million, by 1816 it had leaped to $147 million—and American manufacturers begged for protection.

Congress, in 1816, passed a tariff to protect the new factories—the first United States tariff passed, not to raise revenue, but to encourage and support home industry. The argument over this protective tariff exposed some potentially serious sectional economic conflicts and marked the first appearance of a perennial political issue. Southern producers and New England shippers opposed the tariff; the growing factory towns of New England supported it, however, as did some of the younger Southern cotton politicians— who hoped to encourage industrial development in the South. The Middle Atlantic States and the West favored it, and the Southwest divided on the issue.

8.4d Renewing the Bank of the United States

In 1816 Congress turned its attention to the national bank. The charter of the first Bank of the United States had been allowed to expire because the Democratic-Republicans believed that, as Jefferson originally claimed, banking powers properly belonged to the states and Hamilton's centralized bank was therefore unconstitutional. In contrast, the new contingent of Western congressmen was much less interested in the Bank's constitutionality than in its usefulness. Henry Clay, who had opposed renewal of the first Bank in 1811 on constitutional grounds, now supported the second, he explained, because it was necessary for the national (especially Western) interest to have a stable, uniform currency and sound national credit. Therefore, Congress in 1816 gave the second Bank of the United States a twenty-year charter, on much the same terms as before but with about three and a half times more capital than the first and substantially greater control over state banks.

8.4c Building Better Connecting Links

The British wartime blockade and the westward movement had exposed a critical need for roads, improved waterways, and canals. When coastal shipping was reduced to a trickle by British offshore naval patrols, forcing American goods to move over inland routes, the roads and rivers were soon choked with traffic. The Democratic-Republican program of improved internal communications was especially popular in the West. However, more conservative easterners, including President Madison, doubted the constitutionality of federal assistance for roads and canals unless an amendment to the Constitution was adopted for the purpose.

John C. Calhoun of South Carolina introduced a "bonus bill" into Congress in 1816, empowering the use of federal funds for internal improvements. It cited the "general welfare" clause of the Constitution as providing authority for such action. The bill was passed, but Madison vetoed it on his last day of office in 1817. Many of the states began digging canals and building roads themselves. Madison's successor, President James Monroe, later agreed that the federal government did have the authority to fund such internal improvements, thus inaugurating the great canal and turnpike era of the 1820s.

8.5 America Moves West

The Treaty of Ghent released a pent-up flood of migration toward the West. In 1790 a little more than 2 percent of the population lived west of the Appalachian mountain chain. By 1810 it was 14 percent; and in 1820, 23 percent—with the proportion still rising. The stream of migration moved west in two branches following the east-west roads and rivers—one from the South through Cumberland Gap into the Southwest, the other from the northeastern states through the Hudson River system into the Northwest Territory (the Ohio River valley and Great Lakes area).

There were a number of reasons for this great westerly movement. One was America's soaring population, which almost doubled in the first two decades of the nineteenth century, from 5.3 million in 1800 to over 9.6 million in 1820. Another was the discharge of war veterans, accompanied by a rush of immigrants from Europe, who moved west to look for new opportunities. Still another was improved transportation. Whereas there had been few good routes to the West, the number of roads and turnpikes now grew, while the Great Lakes–Ohio River waterway provided an excellent route for settlers to move into the Northwest.

The most compelling force behind the westward migration, however, was land—the rich, black bottom lands of the Southwest, and the fertile forest and prairie lands of the Northwest. Governor William Henry Harrison of Indiana Territory persuaded Congress, in 1800, to reduce the minimum requirement for the sale of land to a half section at $2 an acre, with four years to pay. In 1804, Congress reduced the minimum to a quarter section, and in 1820 to eighty acres at a base price of $1.25 an acre. This was the great magnet that drew settlers west as more and more people could afford cheap land in the West as prices were reduced. Unfortunately for all involved, the land was sometimes already occupied by Native Americans.

8.5a Land Hunger versus Native American Rights

In 1789, Congress had assured the Native Americans that their "land and property shall never be taken from them without their consent." In appropriating funds to pay certain tribes for land claims, Congress had tacitly recognized, as Secretary of War Henry Knox said, the Indians' right to ownership as "prior occupants." Even at the time, however, George Washington had remarked that despite the government's good intentions, he doubted that "anything short of a Chinese wall" would ever keep land-hungry settlers out of the American Indians' lands.

Washington would prove to be correct. The Native Americans, reported Thomas Forsyth from frontier country in 1818, "complain about the sale of their lands more than anything

Map 8.7 New Boundaries Established by Treaties

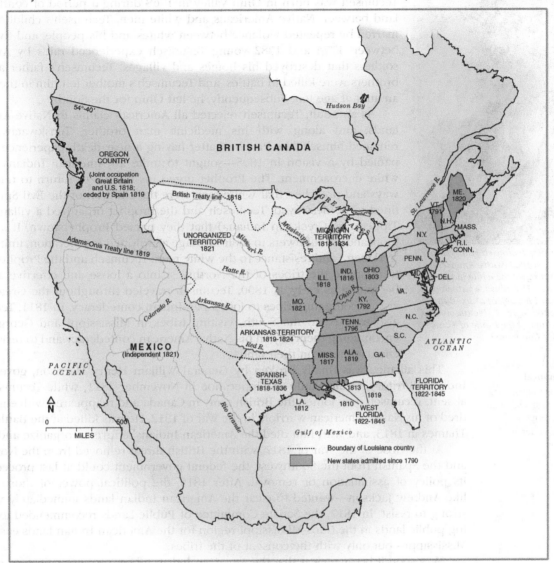

else." The settler, he wrote, "tells the Indian that that land, with all that is on it, is his," and, treaty or not, "to go away or he will kill him, etc." Such constant clashes between Native Americans and settlers had forced the natives to surrender much of their land, yet Congress' American Indian policy was neither sufficiently definite nor sufficiently aggressive to satisfy impatient settlers, traders, land speculators, or the Native Americans.

8.56 Resistance to Federal Policy

The possibility that the two races might live together in "perpetual peace and affectionate attachment," as Jefferson had hoped, quickly faded. Particularly in the South, state governments resisted federal American Indian policy, while on the frontier few paid attention to boundaries or treaties. For their part, Native Americans proved unwilling to give up more and more land, whether treaties had been signed or not. Not unsurprisingly, each advancing encroachment by whites brought resentment and retaliation from Native Americans. Under the best of circumstances, the task of converting hunters and warriors into farmers is not easy—and American frontiersmen were much more interested in getting land from the Native Americans than in teaching them how to farm it.

Native Americans, of course, were expected by whites to relinquish their lands at once. Predictably, conflicts between settlers and Native Americans became increasingly

Shawnee Chief Tecumseh gathered a following of united Native Americans to resist and reject the white man and his ways. His alliance gathered strength until his defeat at the Battle of Tippecanoe in 1811. Tecumseh died two years later at the Battle of Thames. (Wikimedia Commons)

Indian removal

The U.S. policy of removing American Indian tribes from the Southeastern United States to Indian Territory (Oklahoma)

violent and frequent; and the emergence of a remarkable Native American leader, the Shawnee Chief Tecumseh, crystallized Native American resistance. Tecumseh was born in Ohio Valley in 1768 during a period of conflict over land between Native Americans and white men. Tecumseh's childhood was marred by repeated violence between whites and his people, and five times between 1774 and 1782 young Tecumseh experienced raids by American soldiers that destroyed his homes and villages. Tecumseh's father and two brothers were killed in battles, and Tecumseh's mother left him in the care of an aunt at age ten. Subsequently, he left Ohio for the South.

As an adult, Tecumseh rejected all American claims to Native American lands, and along with his medicine man brother, Tenskwatawa—who renamed himself "the Prophet" after having a near death experience accompanied by a vision in 1805—sought to unite all American Indians against white encroachment. The Prophet urged his people to return to traditional ways and preached that white men were the children of the Evil Spirit, destined to be destroyed. Tecumseh and the Prophet organized a village along Tippecanoe Creek (in Indiana) that they named Prophetstown. It attracted thousands of followers to their message of spiritual regeneration, unity of the "red men," and resistance to the white men. Tecumseh and the Prophet began to organize the tribes of the Northwest into a loose and effective alliance, beginning as early as 1800. Tecumseh traveled throughout the Great Lakes area encouraging tribes to join a pan-Indian confederacy. In 1811, Tecumseh also traveled to the South, visiting tribes in Mississippi and Georgia, and encouraging them to join his Native American confederacy and to resist white encroachment on their lands.

This alliance was finally broken by General William Henry Harrison, governor of Indiana Territory, at the Battle of Tippecanoe in November 1811, while Tecumseh was absent. Tecumseh then joined the British army in Canada and reappeared with eight hundred of his Native American warriors in the War of 1812. He was killed at the Battle of the Thames in 1813, and with him died the American Indians' efforts to organize and resist.

At the close of the War of 1812, with the British threat removed from the Northwest and the Spanish from the Southwest, the federal government could at last proceed with its policy of assimilation or removal. After 1815, the political power of those who—like Andrew Jackson—wanted to clear the American Indian lands immediately was too strong to resist. In 1817, the Senate Committee of Public Lands recommended exchanging public lands in the trans-Mississippi region for the American Indian lands east of the Mississippi—but only with the consent of the tribes.

Very soon it became clear that the American Indian tribes were not willing to consent. The only remedy, John C. Calhoun wrote in 1820, was to place them "gradually under our authority and laws." "Our opinions, and not theirs," he continued, "ought to prevail, in measures intended for their civilization and happiness." In 1825 then Secretary of War Calhoun and President Monroe presented Congress with a plan to remove the eastern tribes into the region beyond Missouri and Arkansas—a plan opposed by those who felt such an act to be a betrayal of the national honor. The opposition to **Indian removal** was inadequate; and by the 1830s the tribes were removed—many to present-day Oklahoma and Kansas. By 1848, twelve new states had been created from what had once been American Indian country.

8.6 Growing Pains

8.6a The Election of 1816

Madison selected James Monroe of Virginia as his successor in the presidential election of 1816. Although some Democratic-Republicans favored William H. Crawford of Georgia, the party caucus agreed to choose the third Virginian in succession for the presidency. The Federalists, disheartened by the Hartford Convention, failed to nominate an official candidate, though in some states they supported Rufus King of New York.

Map 8.8 Presidential Election of 1816

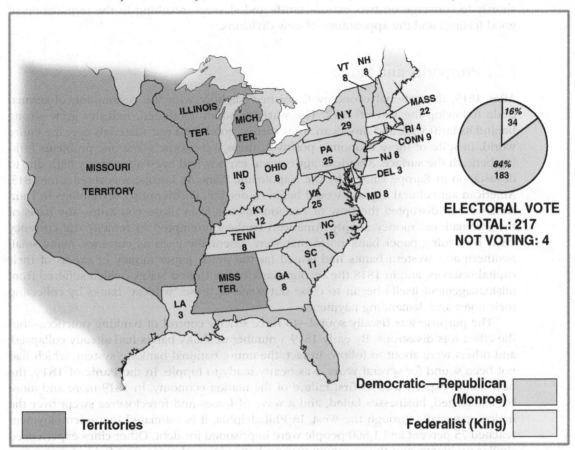

VT 8
NH 8
MASS 22
N Y 29
RI 4
CONN 9
ILLINOIS
MICH. TER.
PA 25
NJ 8
DEL 3
MISSOURI TERRITORY
IND 3
OHIO 8
VA 25
MD 8
KY 12
NC 15
TENN 8
SC 11
MISS TER.
GA 8
LA 3

16% 34
84% 183

ELECTORAL VOTE
TOTAL: 217
NOT VOTING: 4

Democratic—Republican (Monroe)

Federalist (King)

Territories

King received only the votes of Massachusetts, Connecticut, and Delaware; and Monroe won easily by 183 to 34 electoral votes.

A tall, distinguished, and quiet man, James Monroe had studied law with Jefferson and was the older statesman's close friend and disciple. He drew his advisers impartially from different sections of the country, choosing John Quincy Adams (son of John and Abigail Adams) of Massachusetts as secretary of state, William H. Crawford of Georgia as secretary of the treasury, John C. Calhoun of South Carolina as secretary of war, and William Wirt of Maryland as attorney general. Henry Clay of Kentucky, the Speaker of the House, and others of the western group dominated Congress, with Daniel Webster of New Hampshire and other New Englanders furnishing the opposition.

Era of Good Feelings
The period following the War of 1812, between 1815 and 1819, when the country experienced robust economic growth and peace at home and abroad

8.66 The Era of Good Feelings

Because of the virtually unchallenged Democratic-Republican control of political life until 1824, and a robust economy following the war of 1812, these years have been labeled the **Era of Good Feelings**. The Federalist Party was dead, and it seemed for a time that the two-party system itself was ending. There were no European wars of consequence during the period to involve the United States, nor any other crucial issues in foreign affairs. President Monroe contributed to the "good feelings" in that he possessed a personality that seemed to bring people together. Monroe toured New England—an area that had been fraught with secessionist discontent during the War of 1812—espousing a position of nationalism to enthusiastic crowds. Of course, to call it the "Era of Good Feelings" is an oversimplification: Feelings may hav been "good," but subterranean conflicts were soon to destroy the political peace.

Underneath the "good feelings," sectional interests and aspirations were growing and changing. The new Northwest, as it gained stature and stability, demanded greater influence in national policy. The South, tied more and more to cotton, and New England, changing from an agricultural to a manufacturing economy, were both undergoing inner stresses that took outward political form. Specifically, these sectionalized rivals were shortly to converge on two issues—tariffs and slavery—resulting in the termination of good feelings and the appearance of new divisions.

8.6c Prosperity and Panic

After 1815, the national economy flourished mightily with the resumption of normal trade following the War of 1812. The wartime boom continued, industry grew strong behind its tariff wall, and American ships carried goods and raw materials over the entire world. In spite of these economic positives, there were some economic problems lurking beneath the surface. American agricultural exports had been abnormally high due to devastation in Europe caused by the Napoleonic Wars. As Europe recovered after 1815, American agricultural exports would begin to decline. Furthermore, revolutions in Latin America had disrupted the flow of precious metals from those countries—the basis of the international money supply. American bankers attempted to remedy the currency crisis by issuing paper bank notes that were essentially used as currency. Many small Southern and Western banks had issued far too much paper money in excess of their capital reserves, and in 1818 the second Bank of the United States (which suffered from mismanagement itself) began to close out some of these "wildcat" banks by collecting their notes and demanding payment.

The purpose was fiscally sound—to force stricter control of banking practices—but the effect was disastrous. By early 1819 a number of shaky banks had already collapsed, and others were about to follow. In fact, the entire national banking system, which had not been sound for several years, was nearly ready to topple. In the **Panic of 1819**, the new nation experienced its first failure of the market economy. In 1819 more and more banks crashed, businesses failed, and a wave of losses and foreclosures swept over the nation, especially through the West. In Philadelphia, it is estimated that unemployment reached 75 percent and 1,800 people were imprisoned for debt. Other cities experienced similar problems, and the economy was no better in rural areas. The field of macroeconomics did not yet exist, and generally the people did not understand the reasons for their plight; thus, the Bank of the U.S. became the nation's scapegoat. The consequences of the 1819 crisis continued to be felt until 1832, when President Andrew Jackson would do away with the Bank.

8.7 "Fire Bell in the Night"

8.7a Sectionalism and Slavery

As the tariff issue of 1816 had exposed some of the sectional economic tensions beneath the surface of "good feelings," so the Panic of 1819 revealed more. The second great issue—the question of the existence and extension of the institution of slavery—was also projected onto the national stage in 1819, coming before Congress that year because of Missouri's impending statehood.

Slavery had been a submerged issue in national politics since Washington's time. In 1793, during his administration, Congress had passed a fugitive slave law and later forbade the further importation of slaves, beginning in 1808, without unduly arousing sentiment in North or South. In fact, there were many in both sections who hoped that the 1808 act might lead to the eventual extinction of the entire system. In the North, where slavery was unprofitable and unnecessary, all the states had legally abolished it by 1804 (as the Ordinance of 1787 already had abolished it from the Northwest Territory). Even in the South, antislavery societies actively campaigned against it. Still, after 1816 there was growing harshness in Northern and Southern discussions of the slavery question.

The most important area of disagreement over slavery concerned its economic relationship to Southern cotton culture. Eli Whitney's invention of the cotton gin, the introduction of new strains of cotton, the expanding postwar textile market at home and abroad, and the opening to production of the rich "Black Belt" lands of the Southwest—all combined to make cotton an extremely profitable cash crop. Cotton was on the way to becoming "king" in the South—and it required a large, steady supply of cheap (and not necessarily skilled) labor. Many believed that black slaves best filled this need. At the same time, it was found that the delta lands of Louisiana and Mississippi were ideal for sugar cane, while tobacco culture moved from the coastal South into Kentucky and Tennessee. These, too, required manual labor and were viewed as conducive to slavery.

In 1800 there were about 894,000 blacks in the United States—almost wholly concentrated in the eastern portion of the South. In 1808, when the importation of slaves ceased, the figure stood at over one million; and by 1820 the South's investment in slaves was estimated to be nearly $500 million. It was perfectly clear that slavery and cotton provided the foundation of Southern society and would continue to do so.

8.76 The Missouri Compromise

Missouri Compromise
Viewed as the "final solution" to the slavery dispute, it stated that Missouri was to be admitted as a slave state, but that no slavery would be permitted west of Missouri in any of the territories north of Missouri's southern border.

Early in 1819 Missouri, carved out of the territory acquired in the Louisiana Purchase, counted sixty thousand persons and applied for entry to the Union as a slave state. No doubt the bill for its admission would have passed without appreciable comment, had not James Tallmadge, Jr. of New York introduced in the House an amendment requiring the gradual abolition of slavery in the new state as a condition of its admission. This amendment immediately exposed the heart of the issue.

As the nation moved west, the tendency had been to maintain a rough balance of power between slave- and free-state blocs in Washington. The North and Northwest, however, had gained a million more persons than the South and Southwest since the 1790 census, thereby proportionately increasing their congressional representation. The slave states were already outvoted in the House; only in the Senate were the sections equally represented, a situation that might not continue for long.

Of the original thirteen colonies, seven became free states and six slave. Between 1791 and 1819, four more free states were admitted and five slave. Thus, when Missouri applied for entrance to the Union in 1819, the balance was even—and Tallmadge's amendment involved far more than Missouri's admission alone.

Slavery was already barred from the Northwest Territory, but not from those lands acquired through the Louisiana Purchase. Should Missouri and all other states subsequently admitted from the Louisiana Purchase lands be admitted as slave states, the balance of federal political power would be tipped toward the South and slavery. If they were to be free states, their entry favored the North and emancipation.

At stake lay political control, present and future, of the Union. "It is political power that the northern folk are in pursuit of," Judge Charles Tait of Alabama wrote to a friend concerning the Missouri question, "and if they succeed, the management of the Gen'l Gov't will pass into their hands with all its power and patronage." Most Northerners were not, at this time, opposed to slavery on moral grounds, but they believed that the Three-Fifths Compromise gave Southern states disproportionate strength in Congress since they could count three-fifths of their growing slave population for purposes of representation in the U.S. House of Representatives. Thus, Northerners opposed the admittance of Missouri as a slave state for the advantage it would give to Southerners in Congress.

Nevertheless, Tallmadge's bill finally passed the House in February, after hot and protracted debate. Congress adjourned, however, until December; and during the interval, Maine—long attached to Massachusetts—applied for statehood. Sensing compromise, the Senate originated a bill accepting Maine as a free state and Missouri as slave, thereby preserving the balance. The House accepted it, but added a proviso that slavery be banned forever from the Louisiana Purchase lands above the line of 36°30′ (Missouri's southern border).

The bill was passed and signed in March 1820, but this so-called **Missouri Compromise** merely delayed the ultimate confrontation of the problem of slavery—and everyone knew it. The "momentous question," wrote Jefferson from Monticello, "like a fire-bell in the night, awakened me and filled me with terror." The debates over Missouri sparked the first protracted public discussion of the contradiction between the ideals expressed in the Declaration of Independence and the institution of slavery—thus foreshadowing the decades of sectional conflict to come, hence the aging Jefferson's alarm.

Map 8.9 The Missouri Compromise (1820)

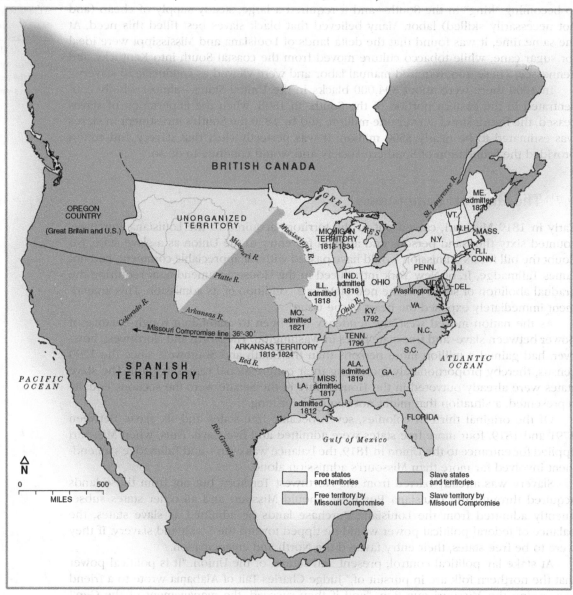

BRITISH CANADA

OREGON COUNTRY
(Great Britain and U.S.)

UNORGANIZED TERRITORY

Missouri R.

Platte R.

Colorado R.

Arkansas R.

Missouri Compromise line 36°-30'

Red R.

SPANISH TERRITORY

PACIFIC OCEAN

Rio Grande

Gulf of Mexico

MICHIGAN TERRITORY 1818-1834

ILL. admitted 1818

IND. admitted 1816

OHIO

MO. admitted 1821

KY. 1792

Ohio R.

ARKANSAS TERRITORY 1819-1824

TENN. 1796

N.C.

S.C.

ALA. admitted 1819

GA.

MISS. admitted 1817

LA. admitted 1812

FLORIDA

ME. admitted 1820

VT. N.H. MASS.

N.Y.

R.I. CONN.

PENN. N.J.

MD. DEL.

Washington

VA.

St. Lawrence R.

ATLANTIC OCEAN

N
0   500
MILES

Free states and territories

Free territory by Missouri Compromise

Slave states and territories

Slave territory by Missouri Compromise

Convention of 1818

Treaty with England that granted U.S. nationals fishing rights off the coasts of Labrador and Newfoundland, established the northern boundary of the Louisiana Purchase at the 49th parallel, and left the Oregon country—which both countries claimed—under joint occupation for ten years

8.8 Evolving a Foreign Policy

8.8a Catching Up on Old Problems

Following the Treaty of Ghent, the United States and Britain gradually worked out their differences one by one. In 1815, the U.S. and England signed a commercial convention which established a reciprocity agreement in trade. Nevertheless, the U.S. and England still distrusted each other, and each began fortifying its possessions around the Great Lakes. The Rush-Bagehot Agreement of 1817 demilitarized the Great Lakes, but both countries retained land fortifications and the U.S.-Canadian border remained a guarded border until 1871. The next year, the **Convention of 1818** gave U.S. nationals fishing rights off the coasts of Labrador and Newfoundland, established the northern boundary of the Louisiana Purchase at the 49th parallel, and left the Oregon country, which both claimed, under joint occupation for ten years.

America and Spain, too, settled some old disputes. The United States took one section of Florida (west Florida) from Spain during the War of 1812, and Secretary of State John Quincy Adams continued negotiations for the rest of the territory. His diplomacy,

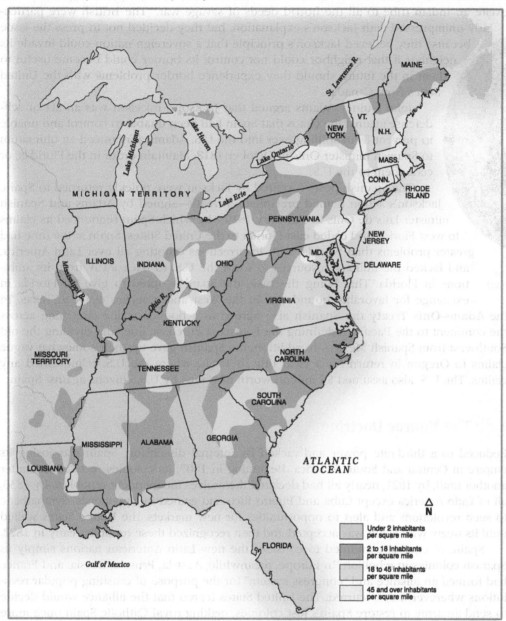

Map 8.10 Population Density (1820)

Legend:
- Under 2 inhabitants per square mile
- 2 to 18 inhabitants per square mile
- 18 to 45 inhabitants per square mile
- 45 and over inhabitants per square mile

however, was disturbed by Florida's Seminole Indians, who kept up raids (with Spanish and British assistance) on the Georgia border. In 1818, General Andrew Jackson raised an army and marched into Florida, claiming that he had received a letter from President Monroe authorizing the invasion. Monroe denied that he had given his approval; and Jackson claimed that he burned the letter, so any evidence that Monroe ordered the invasion was destroyed, if it existed. Jackson led three thousand Americans and two thousand Native American allies into Florida, captured two Spanish forts, and executed two suspected British agents in what is known as the First Seminole War.

Americans were divided over Jackson's actions. Secretary of War John C. Calhoun called for Jackson's court-martial since Jackson had acted without authority from Calhoun's War Department. Congressman Henry Clay introduced a motion of censure in Congress which failed to pass. Meanwhile, local governments in New York and Philadelphia praised Jackson's actions. Britain viewed Jackson's invasion as a violation of international law and demanded an explanation for the execution of two British citizens. Jackson replied, "the execution of these two unprincipled villains will prove an awful example to the world and convince the government of Great Britain that certain though slow retribution awaits those unchristian wretches who, by false promises, delude and excite an Indian tribe to all the horrid deeds of savage war." The British were particularly unimpressed with Jackson's explanation, but they decided not to press the issue because they believed Jackson's principle that a sovereign nation could invade its neighbor if that neighbor could not control its border could become useful to them in the future should they experience border problems with the United States from Canada.

John Quincy Adams argued that Jackson's invasion was an act of self-defense against the chaos that Spain had been unable to control and unable to prevent from spilling over into the U.S. Adams announced an ultimatum to Spanish minister Onís in October 1818: Maintain order in the Floridas, or cede them to the U.S.

The Spanish posts captured by Jackson were quickly returned to Spain. Jackson's action helped precipitate a treaty—signed by Adams and Spanish minister Luis de Onís in February 1819—by which Spain renounced its claims to west Florida and ceded east Florida to the United States. Spain at the time had greater problems than Florida, with insurrections erupting all over Latin America, and lacked the military resources to force the U.S. to back away from its ambitions in Florida. That being the case, the Spanish opted to give up Florida in exchange for favorable boundaries in the West and a secure claim to Texas. In the **Adams-Onís Treaty** the Spanish also agreed to a boundary line stretching across the continent to the Pacific, redefining the Louisiana Purchase line, and dividing the old Southwest from Spanish Mexico. In addition, the Spanish gave up their somewhat vague claims to Oregon in return for a clear title to Texas, where the U.S. relinquished any claims. The U.S. also assumed $5 million worth of claims by U.S. citizens against Spain.

John Quincy Adams (Wikimedia Commons)

Adams-Onís Treaty

Also known as the Transcontinental Treaty with Spain, the U.S. gained east and west Florida in exchange for renunciation of any claims to Texas.

Monroe Doctrine

Articulated by James Monroe, stating that the U.S. would view any European interference in the Western Hemisphere as unfriendly to the U.S. and that the U.S. would stay out of European affairs

8.86 The Monroe Doctrine

Reduced to a third-rate power and racked by internal dissension, Spain was losing its empire in Central and South America. Beginning in 1807, its colonies revolted one after another until, by 1821, nearly all had declared themselves independent republics. By 1830, all of Latin America except Cuba and Puerto Rico had gained independence. Sympathetic to such revolutions and alert to opportunities for new markets, the United States waited until its treaty with Spain was accepted and then recognized these republics early in 1822.

Spain, of course, continued to consider the new Latin American nations simply as Spanish colonies in rebellion. In Europe, meanwhile, Austria, Prussia, Russia, and France had formed an alliance and "congress system" for the purpose of crushing popular revolutions wherever they occurred. The United States feared that the alliance would decide to send an army to restore Spain's lost colonies, making royal Catholic Spain once more a power in the New World. Nor was the alliance the only threat to the Americas. Russia had already established trading posts in California, and in 1821 Czar Alexander's edict claimed part of the Oregon country for Alaska and barred foreign ships from a large area of the northwest Pacific.

The British—who had no desire to see Spain regain its empire or Russia expand its colonial holdings—offered to join with the United States in a declaration against any interference in the Americas on the part of the alliance. In response, Secretary of State John Quincy Adams convinced President Monroe and the cabinet that the United States should handle the problem alone. For one thing, Adams did not want his country to "come in as a cockboat in the wake of the British man-of-war." Furthermore, Adams and others recognized the potential value of the new Latin American republics as markets. Lastly, no one wanted to write off the possibility of American expansion southward if one or more of the new republics asked to be annexed to the United States.

President Monroe, in his annual message to Congress on December 2, 1823, stated the official attitude of the United States on the issue. The **Monroe Doctrine**, as it came to be called, rested on two main principles—noncolonization and nonintervention.

Concerning the first, Monroe stated that any portions of the Americas were "henceforth not to be considered as subjects for future colonization by any European power." In regard to the second, he drew a sharp line of political demarcation between Europe and America. "The political system of the allied powers is essentially different … from that of America," he said. "We should consider any attempt to extend their system to any portion of this hemisphere as dangerous to our peace and safety." At the same time, Monroe promised that the United States would not attempt to interfere with the internal affairs of European nations or with any of their existing colonies in the New World, such as Cuba.

These ideas had been implicit in all American foreign policy since Washington's Farewell Address, but Monroe's message restated in precise terms the classic American principles of hemispheric separation and avoidance of foreign entanglements that had motivated the diplomacy of his predecessors. His enunciation of American domination over half the globe seemed "arrogant" and "haughty" to European statesmen, and the Latin American republics were not particularly pleased with such doubtful protection. What both knew, however—whether Monroe or the American public cared to admit it—was that it was the British navy and not the Monroe Doctrine that barred European expansion into the Americas.

8.8c The Triumph of Isolation

The Monroe Doctrine simply articulated what Americans had believed since the beginnings of their foreign policy—that there were two worlds, old and new, contrasted and separate. The Old World of England and Europe seemed to Americans regressive, corrupted, and plagued by wars and ancient hatreds. The New World was thought to be democratic, free, progressive, and hopeful. The objective of the United States, reflecting these attitudes, was to keep these worlds apart, lest the "taint" of the old besmirch the "fresh future" of the new.

The first generation of American statesmen, from Washington to Monroe, unanimously insisted that the United States should, whenever possible, avoid entanglements in Old World politics or problems. At the same time, it was perfectly clear to them that the United States could not exist without European trade and that, since the major European powers still held territorial possessions in the New World, it would be extremely difficult to avoid some sort of implication in their almost continuous wars. The foreign policy of every president from Washington to John Quincy Adams was shaped by this constant tension between the dream of isolation and the reality of involvement. Still, there were certain accepted positions on foreign affairs that the United States throughout the period believed it must maintain—freedom of the seas, freedom of trade, neutrality in European disputes, national integrity, and, above all others, the promotion of the cause of liberty throughout the world. In practice, American diplomats found it hard to work out solutions within this somewhat rigid framework. Did maintenance of freedom of the seas, for example, justify involvement in a European war? Would American assistance to other nations' revolutions justify entanglement in European affairs, even for the best of motives? Should American policy, when it coincided with that of a European power, be pursued jointly? Ought the United States to assume responsibility for internal affairs of democracy in other American republics?

In attempting to answer these and similar questions, the makers of American foreign policy during the early years of the Republic followed rather closely the principles laid down by Washington and the first generation. Fortunately for them, Europe was so preoccupied with its own power conflicts that American diplomacy had time to temporize and room to make a few mistakes. Still, every statement about foreign affairs in the early decades of the nineteenth century derived from the American assumption that the United States was detached from Europe and must remain so, always free to pursue its special ends.

Timeline

1800	Thomas Jefferson is elected president in what he called the "Revolution of 1800."
1801	France regains possession of Louisiana.
1802	Slave revolt on Saint-Domingue leads to the death of twenty-four thousand French troops.
1803	Jefferson sends the U.S. Navy to confront the Barbary Pirates.
	The U.S. purchases Louisiana from France for $15 million.
	The U.S. Supreme Court claims the right of judicial review in *Marbury v. Madison.*
	A group of federalists, known as the Essex Junto, attempts to persuade New England states to secede.
	War between England and France under Napoleon causes England to renew impressments of American sailors.
1804	Aaron Burr kills Alexander Hamilton in a duel.
	Thomas Jefferson is reelected president.
1804–1805	The House impeaches Supreme Court Justice Samuel Chase; however, the Senate does not convict, and Chase stays on the Court.
1805	Treaty with Barbary Pirates ends hostilities and returns bounties paid to pirates to the previous lower level.
1806	Aaron Burr attempts, and fails, to conquer New Orleans.
	British Orders in Council effectively blockade Europe.
	Lewis and Clark expedition reaches the Pacific and returns to Missouri.
1807	Jefferson recalls the navy from the Mediterranean due to antagonism with Britain.
	The USS *Chesapeake* is fired upon by HMS *Leopard.*
	Embargo Act is passed, placing a ban on American Exports.
1808	James Madison is elected President.

Timeline

1809	Embargo Act is lifted.
1810	Non-Intercourse Act and Macon's Bill #2 are passed, opening trade with everyone except France and England.
1811	Chief Tecumseh's Native American Confederation is defeated.
1812	Congress declares war on England on June 18, and the War of 1812 begins.
1814	The British burn Washington D.C.
	Francis Scott Key pens "The Star Spangled Banner" based on events at Fort McHenry.
	The Treaty of Ghent is signed December 24, officially ending the War of 1812.
1815	Americans, under Andrew Jackson, defeat the British in the Battle of New Orleans in January after the signing of the Treaty of Ghent.
	The U.S. Navy, with help from European navies, defeats Barbary Pirates and puts an end to bounties.
	Napoleon's final defeat at Waterloo
	Congress of Vienna
1815–1819	Era of Good Feelings
1816	James Monroe is elected president.
1818	Andrew Jackson invades Florida in the First Seminole War.
1819	Transcontinental Treaty with Spain
	The Panic of 1819
1820	The Missouri Compromise
1823	James Monroe announces the Monroe Doctrine.

CHAPTER SUMMARY

𝔍n 1800 Thomas Jefferson was elected President, representing a shift from the Northern and urban based Federalists to Jefferson's more Southern and agrarian Democratic-Republicans. Jefferson also represented the expansion of democracy to common men and a shift to a more states' rights centric orientation—though he would also expand the power of the national government as president, one of Jefferson's many contradictions.

Almost immediately, Jefferson was confronted with a foreign policy challenge from the Barbary Pirates, who increased the bounty they charged merchant ships to operate in the Mediterranean. Jefferson, who had opposed a large military, sent the U.S. Navy to the Mediterranean to defeat the pirates; the U.S. would continue paying bounties, however, until 1815. Simultaneously, Jefferson (who had opposed a national debt) borrowed much of the $15 million from Baring Brothers of London at 6 percent interest from Baring Brothers of London to purchase Louisiana from France—even though this was not a power given to the president by the Constitution, and he was a self-proclaimed proponent of a strict interpretation of the venerable document.

Jefferson then commissioned the Lewis and Clark expedition to explore Louisiana, departing from Missouri in 1804; the successful expedition reached the Pacific coast at Oregon and then returned to Missouri with samples of exotic flora and fauna in 1806.

Domestically, Jefferson did battle with the federalist Supreme Court under Chief Justice John Marshall with the result that the Court claimed for itself the power of judicial review in *Marbury v. Madison* in 1803. Jefferson attempted to rid the courts of Federalist judges through cutting off funding to the Supreme Court and impeaching judges. Nevertheless, Marshall would stay on the Court until 1835, exerting great influence on American constitutional law.

The Napoleonic Wars in Europe (beginning in 1803) resulted in disruption of American trade by both England and France, and eventually in the War of 1812 with England over American sovereignty rights and freedom of the seas. President James Madison, elected in 1808, waged war with the British primarily to end the British practice of impressment after embargoes against the English had not achieved the desired results. The war resulted in a British invasion of America and the burning of the American Capitol—but a decisive victory by the Americans at Plattsburgh caused the British to seek a negotiated peace, ending the costly war. The Treaty of Ghent ended the war on the principle of "status quo antebellum," and the British did not cease their impressments; nevertheless, America had proven that Europeans who tread on American sovereignty do so only at a price.

The War of 1812 was followed by an "Era of Good Feelings" where America was at peace and the economy was robust under the popular President James Monroe. The "good feelings" would be shattered, however, by a major economic panic in 1819 followed by a slavery dispute. The next year, Congress forged the Compromise of 1820, which was viewed as the "final solution" to slavery. Missouri was admitted as a slave state, but slavery was to be prohibited west of Missouri in all of the territories north of Missouri's southern border. Meanwhile, Native Americans in the Southeastern United States were slated for removal to Indian Territory in the West (Oklahoma).

Finally, all of Latin America would revolt against Spain in the second decade of the nineteenth century. Spain ceded Florida to the U.S. in 1819, a year after Andrew Jackson's invasion, with the stipulation that the U.S. would give up any future claims to Texas. By 1823, all of Latin America would achieve independence from Spain, prompting James Monroe to declare that the Western Hemisphere was now closed to European colonization and that European interference in the Western Hemisphere would be viewed as unfriendly toward the U.S. In return, the U.S. would stay out of European affairs.

KEY TERMS

BIBLIOGRAPHY

B

Bemis, Samuel F. *John Quincy Adams and the Foundations of American Foreign Policy*. New York: W. W. Norton & Company, 1973.

———. *John Quincy Adams and the Union*. Westport, CT: Greenwood Press, 1980.

Benson, Lee. *The Concept of Jeffersonian Democracy: New York: A Test Case*. Princeton, NJ: Princeton University Press, 1961.

Bernstein, R. B. *Thomas Jefferson*. New York: Oxford University Press, 2003.

Brodie, Fawn M. *Thomas Jefferson: An Intimate History*. New York: W. W. Norton & Company, 2010.

C

Chernow, Ron. *Alexander Hamilton*. New York: Penguin-Putnam, 2004.

Cross, Barbara, ed. *The Autobiography of Lyman Beecher*. Cambridge, MA: Harvard University Press, 1961.

Current, Richard N. *Daniel Webster and the Rise of National Conservatism*. Boston, MA: Little, Brown, 1955.

D

Dangerfield, George. *The Era of Good Feelings*. San Diego, CA: Harcourt Brace, 1963.

E

Egan, Clifford L. *Neither Peace Nor War: Franco-American Relations, 1803–1812*. Baton Rouge, LA: Louisiana State University Press, 1983.

Ellis, Richard E. *The Jeffersonian Crisis: Courts and Politics in the Young Republic*. New York: Oxford University Press, 1971.

F

Ferguson, James E. *Power of the Purse: A History of American Public Finance*. Chapel Hill, NC: University of North Carolina Press, 1961.

Fischer, David Hackett. *The Revolution of American Conservatism*. Chicago, IL: University of Chicago Press, 1975.

G

Garraty, John A., and Robert McCaughey. *The American Nation: A History of the United States Since 1865*. 6th ed. New York: HarperCollins, 1987.

H

Hickey, Donald R. *The War of 1812: A Forgotten Conflict*. Champaign, IL: University of Illinois Press, 2012.

Hofstadter, Richard. *The Rise of Legitimate Opposition in the United States 1780–1840*. Berkeley, CA: University of California Press, 1970.

Horsman, Reginald. *The Diplomacy of the New Republic, 1776–1815*. New York: Harlan Davidson, 1985.

J

Jacoby, Susan. *Freethinkers: A History of American Secularism*. New York: Henry Holt, 2004.

K

Ketcham, Ralph. *Presidents Above Party: The First American Presidency, 1789–1829*. Chapel Hill, NC: University of North Carolina Press, 1987.

Kerber, Linda. *Federalists in Dissent: Imagery and Ideology in Jeffersonian America*. Ithaca, NY: Cornell University Press, 1980.

Koch, Adolf G. *Republican Religion: The American Revolution and the Cult of Reason*. New York: Henry Holt, 1933.

Kohn, Richard H. *Eagle and the Sword: The Federalists and the Creation of the Military Establishment in America, 1783–1802*. New York: Free Press, 1985.

L

Lipset, Seymour Martin, and Earl Raab. *The Politics of Unreason: Right-Wing Extremism in America, 1790–1970*. New York: Harper and Row, 1970.

M

Madison, James. "The Federalist No. 51." In Edward Mead Earle, ed., *The Federalist*. New York: Modern Library College Editions, 1987.

McCollough, David. *John Adams*. New York: Simon and Schuster, 2001.

McCoy, Drew R. *The Elusive Republic: Political Economy in Jeffersonian America*. Chapel Hill, NC: University of North Carolina Press, 1996.

———. *The Last of the Fathers: James Madison and the Republican Legacy*. New York: Cambridge University Press, 1989.

Miller, John C. *The Federalist Era, 1789–1801*. Charleston, SC: Nabu Press, 2011.

Miner, Brad. *The Concise Conservative Encyclopedia*. New York: Simon and Schuster, 1996.

Moore, Glover. *The Missouri Controversy, 1819–1821*. Lexington, KY: University of Kentucky Press, 1953.

Muccigrosso, Robert. *Basic History of Conservatism*. Melbourne, FL Krieger, 2003.

Muller, Jerry Z. *Conservatism: An Anthology of Social and Political Thought from David Hume to the Present*. Princeton, NJ: Princeton University Press, 1997.

BIBLIOGRAPHY

N

Nelson, John R., Jr. *Liberty and Property: Political Economy and Policymaking in the New Republic: 1789–1812*. Baltimore, MD: Johns Hopkins University Press, 1987.

Newmyer, R. Kent. *The Supreme Court Under Marshall and Taney*. New York: Harlan Davidson, 2006.

O

Oren, Michael B. *Power, Faith, and Fantasy: America in the Middle East 1776 to the Present*. New York: W. W. Norton & Company, 2007.

P

Palmer, Robert. *The Age of Democratic Revolution: The Struggle*. Princeton, NJ: Princeton University Press, 1964.

Perkins, Bradford. *The First Rapprochement: England and the United States 1795–1805*. Berkeley, CA: University of California Press, 1967.

———. *Prologue to War: England and the United States 1805–1812*. Berkeley, CA: University of California Press, 1961.

R

Risjord, Norman K. *The Old Republicans: Southern Conservatism in the Age of Jefferson*. New York: Columbia University Press, 1965.

S

Schlesinger, Arthur, Jr. *The Age of Jackson*. New York: Little, Brown, 1945.

Schlesinger, Arthur, Jr., Gil Troy and Fred L. Israel. *History of American Presidential Elections, 1789–2008*. New York: Facts on File, 2011.

Sellers, Charles. *The Market Revolution: Jacksonian America 1815–1846*. New York: Oxford University Press, 1993.

Sharp, James R. *American Politics in the Early Republic: The New Nation in Crisis*. New Haven, CT: Yale University Press, 1993.

Smelser, Marshall. *The Democratic Republic, 1801–1815*. Long Grove, IL: Waveland Press, 1992.

Stagg, J. C. A. *Politics, Diplomacy, and Warfare in the Early Republic*. Princeton, NJ: Princeton University Press, 1983.

W

White, Leonard B. *The Jeffersonians: A Study in Administrative History, 1801–1829*. New York: Macmillan, 1961.

POP QUIZ

1. For what was Stephen Decatur known?
   a. his heroism in the war with the Barbary pirates
   b. his unrestrained patriotism
   c. ending the bounties to the Barbary pirates
   d. both a and b

2. Which of the following were problems for Jefferson in the purchase of Louisiana?
   a. The Constitution did not explicitly authorize the President to purchase territory.
   b. A treaty between France and Spain stated that Louisiana could not be possessed by a power other than France or Spain.
   c. It was unclear that all of the inhabitants of Louisiana would accept American rule.
   d. All of the above

3. What was the purpose of the Lewis and Clark expedition?
   a. to explore the land of the Louisiana Purchase
   b. to secure profitable trade with Indians
   c. to make note of exotic plants and animals
   d. all of the above

4. Which of the following occurred in the Election of 1804?
   a. Jefferson defeated Aaron Burr.
   b. The Federalists did not run a presidential candidate.
   c. Jefferson defeated Charles Cotesworth Pinckney by a narrow margin in an election decided by the House of Representatives.
   d. Jefferson defeated Pinckney by a very wide margin.

5. Under the doctrine of the "broken voyage," if merchant ships in the Caribbean "broke a voyage" by paying duties in a U.S. port, what occurred?
   a. It was considered status quo.
   b. It was considered an act of war against the U.S.
   c. The status of the cargo changed to "American."
   d. The status of the ship became that of an illegal slave ship.

6. Under the Non-Intercourse Act, the U.S. declared that it would resume normal trade with either Britain or France if which of the following occurred?
   a. that country would cease all re-export business
   b. that country would recognize the doctrine of continuous voyage
   c. that country would recognize American rights at sea
   d. that country would remove all of the British illegal aliens from American merchant ships

7. Captain Oliver Hazard Perry is famous for _____.
   a. taking military risks
   b. defeating the British navy on Lake Erie
   c. surrendering without a shot at Detroit
   d. ending British impressments

8. The Battle of New Orleans _____.
   a. was the deciding battle of the War of 1812
   b. caused the British to decide to negotiate peace
   c. ended two weeks after the signing of the Treaty of Ghent
   d. both a and b

9. Reasons for westward expansion in the early nineteenth century included _____.
   a. rapid population growth
   b. the discharge of war veterans after the War of 1812
   c. improved transportation
   d. all of the above

10. What was a major cause of the Panic of 1819?
    a. the collapse of the Bank of the United States
    b. too many small western banks issued too many paper notes, in excess of their capital reserves
    c. excessive government spending on roads and canals
    d. the flooding of American markets with cheap British goods

11. The Barbary Wars were fought after Thomas Jefferson refused to pay a higher bounty imposed by the pirates for safe passage in the Mediterranean. T F

12. In 1808, Congress banned future importation of slaves. T F

13. The Barbary States included _____, _____, _____, and _____.

14. Supporters of the War of 1812 were called _____ _____.

15. The Hartford Convention had delegates primarily from _____ states in _____ _____.

Chapter 9

(Wikimedia Commons)

The Growth of Democratic Government, 1824–1844

CHAPTER OUTLINE

9.1 The Election of 1824

9.1a Four Political Factions

The sands of political allegiance never shifted more swiftly than in the last year and a half of James Monroe's administration, when the "good feelings" in the immediate aftermath of the War of 1812 degenerated into feuding so intense that the historian Sean Wilentz has recently labeled the period "The Era of Bad Feelings." Yet, for practical purposes, there was still only one political party. Although the Federalist Party continued to exist for a while in enclaves like Delaware, most citizens called themselves Democratic-Republicans, including the four leading candidates for the presidency in 1824.

Henry Clay, Speaker of the House of Representatives, chose to support Adams in his presidential campaign. Once Adams was elected, Clay was appointed his secretary of state. (Wikimedia Commons)

Caucus system

The system of nominating presidential candidates through informal votes in Congress

John Quincy Adams

Son of second president John Adams and the sixth president of the United States, elected in 1824

"Old Hickory"

Nickname for Andrew Jackson because it was the "hardest wood"

Andrew Jackson

Seventh president of the United States, first elected in 1828 and credited with bringing mass politics and the spoils system to American politics

John C. Calhoun

Ardent states' rights supporter and vice president under Andrew Jackson

"Corrupt bargain"

So-called by the supporters of Andrew Jackson; the supposed political bargain between John Quincy Adams and Henry Clay, in which Clay was given the position of secretary of state in return for his support of Adams as president

Before 1824, the congressional caucus of the Democratic-Republican majority had chosen the party's presidential candidates; during Monroe's second administration, however, the **caucus system** as a means of choosing presidential candidates met with increasing opposition. The public looked on the caucus system as undemocratic and sought reforms that would be more democratic in character. Moreover, since the launching of the new nation, there had been an increasing groundswell of democratic organization that had found its chief expression at the local and state levels—as Wilentz brilliantly demonstrates in *The Rise of American Democracy*—but which was poised to make itself felt at the national level in the mid-1820s.

There was also a growing conviction that it was not in the country's best interest for a newly elected president to feel that he owed his office to Congress. This provides an excellent example of the evolution of the American party system; criticism of the caucus system eventually led to the establishment of national party conventions in the 1830s.

Politicians, impressed by the strenuous objections against the caucus, moved to dissociate themselves from it. In a number of states, ether the legislature or state conventions tended to nominate their own favorite sons. The result was that when the Democratic-Republican caucus was held in February 1824 only 66 of the 216 Democratic-Republican congressmen even attended.

The caucus chose Secretary of the Treasury William H. Crawford, a Georgian, as their candidate. Most of Crawford's support came from the Southeast, and his rivals and their many followers scorned his selection. New England supported **John Quincy Adams** of Massachusetts, son of John Adams and secretary of state in Monroe's cabinet. Kentucky, Missouri, and Ohio looked to Speaker of the House Henry Clay of Kentucky. Meanwhile, Pennsylvania, most of the West, and some of the Southeast rallied behind **"Old Hickory,"** General **Andrew Jackson** of Tennessee, the famous hero of New Orleans. Secretary of War **John C. Calhoun** of South Carolina also had supporters, but finding his support to be insufficient to win, dropped out of the race early, seeking the vice-presidency instead.

9.16 Adams Defeats Jackson

The real contest in the presidential election of 1824 was between Jackson and Adams. Jackson received approximately 153,000 popular votes to Adams' 108,000, and ninety-nine electoral votes to Adams' eighty-four. But Crawford and Clay, with forty-one and thirty-seven electoral votes respectively, split the total sufficiently that neither Jackson nor Adams received a majority of the electoral vote.

Constitutional procedure in such cases called for the decision to be referred to the House of Representatives. Here each state had one vote, and the three candidates with the most electoral votes—Jackson, Adams, and Crawford—remained in the running.

House Speaker Clay, no longer a presidential candidate, held the balance of power in the House decision. Although earlier he had instigated an anti-Adams campaign in the West, Clay personally disliked Jackson more than Adams and feared him as a future rival for the support of the West. As a consequence, Clay made amends with his former adversary and decided to support Adams.

With Clay's support in the House, Adams was elected on the first ballot on February 9, 1825. The new president promptly appointed Clay his secretary of state. Just as promptly, Jacksonians angrily charged that a **"corrupt bargain"** accounted for both Adams' election and Clay's appointment. There probably was an implicit (if not explicit) understanding between Adams and Clay that the latter would receive the cabinet post in exchange for his support. No evidence exists to demonstrate such corruption—in fact whether or not such a bargain is corrupt at all, or just good democratic politics, remains a matter of debate. Nevertheless, the appointment of Clay turned out to be an enormous political problem for the Adams administration because it saddled both men with tarnished reputations and ensured that the new administration would commence under a cloud.

Map 9.1 Presidential Election of 1824

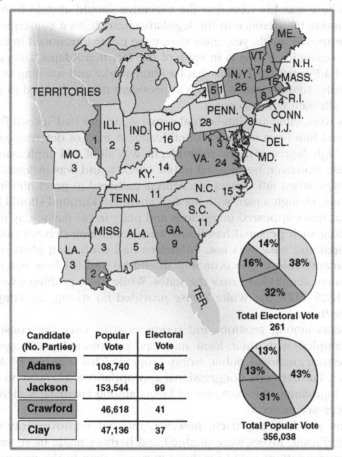

Candidate (No. Parties)	Popular Vote	Electoral Vote
Adams	108,740	84
Jackson	153,544	99
Crawford	46,618	41
Clay	47,136	37

Total Electoral Vote 261

Total Popular Vote 356,038

In the minds of Jackson supporters, that the man who won a plurality of both the popular vote and the electoral vote would not be president was an injustice.

One of the often-unseen pivots of history is discernible in the election of 1824. Adams was almost exclusively a New England candidate until the New York General Assembly gave him twenty-six of New York's thirty-six electors. This resulted from tricky maneuvering by Adams' Albany managers, who were able to divert from Clay several of the electoral votes he had counted on. In addition, if Clay instead of Crawford had been the third candidate, it is possible that the popular Speaker of the House would have appealed to his fellow representatives more than either Adams or Jackson.

9.2 The J. Q. Adams Interlude

9.2a Adams in the White House

President Adams projected a bold domestic program. An intellectual like his father before him, in his first annual message he called for laws creating a national university (as was first proposed by Washington), a naval academy, and a national astronomical observatory. Adams likewise advocated a uniform national militia law; a uniform bankruptcy law; an orderly, federally financed system of internal improvements; and a Department of the Interior to manage America's vast public land holdings. Most of these ideas were highly imaginative; and had his program gone into effect, the second Adams would have been well known today as a remarkable forward thinker.

Such accomplishments, however, were simply not forthcoming. From the outset, Adams made little effort to push his policies once he had enunciated them. A principal cause of this failure was his view that the executive should abstain from what he considered to be undue interference in the legislative branch. As a consequence, numerous White House proposals, made year after year, were never introduced in Congress as legislative bills or resolutions. This is in spite of the fact that Adams was endowed with a sharp mind and a Puritan work ethic that had him awake and working at four o'clock in the morning, daily. Adams wrote so much as president that he learned to write with both hands so as to alleviate writer's cramp.

Despite his work ethic and intellectual prowess, Adams had several flaws in particular that prevented him from being a natural leader. A man of determined character and possessed of a high degree of moral rectitude, he was aloof and unpleasant toward many of his associates. Moreover, he disliked public contact, and was incapable of appearing to good advantage when little knots of admirers gathered to greet him in the course of his limited travels. Though a man with his diplomatic background should have overcome such traits, he at times appeared ungracious and petty in his day-to-day interactions.

Compounding such personal handicaps were continuing debates over exactly what was constitutional and what was not. Politicians had conflicting ideas on (1) what the federal government's role in the economy should be and (2) how much authority the federal government should have over the states. While these problems were not peculiar to the period 1825–1829, the White House provided no strong, directing force toward helping to solve them.

Disagreements among senators and representatives over the construction of the Constitution, coupled with their local interests, contributed to Congress' refusal to develop a systematic, national public works program. This was one of Adams' greatest disappointments. Furthermore, Congressional appropriations followed no logical pattern; and legislative logrolling—the exchange of favors among lawmakers—left undone some of the most necessary projects.

Despite this slapdash approach, however, internal improvements during Adams' tenure were significant. Rivers were dredged and harbors made more serviceable, with more federal appropriations voted for those purposes than in the previous thirty years. Lack of funds had halted work on the National Road in 1818, but new federal money permitted construction to resume in 1825. By mid-century this important highway stretched from Cumberland, Maryland, to Vandalia, Illinois.

9.26 Democratic-Republicans, National Republicans

Off to an inauspicious start in the first half of his term, Adams was hopelessly beset after 1826 by a congressional coalition fighting him at every turn. Increasingly, Jacksonians were known as Democratic-Republicans, and Adams-Clay supporters as **National Republicans**. Jacksonians would not forget that a "deal" had made Adams president, despite the electorate's clear preference for Jackson. Sectional hostilities were increasing, and states' rights adherents opposed Adams' bold plans to expand federal authority. Political idealists might praise Adams for being one of the least domineering of all our chief executives, but his effectiveness suffered for this very reason. His opponents played politics to the hilt, especially after they came to control Congress.

Sectionalism and partisanship in the 1820s were most flagrant in the area of tariff debates and tariff votes. One reason for the passage of the Tariff of 1824, enacted while President Monroe was still in office, had been its inclusion of duties on raw wool and other farm products. These schedules were attractive to the West, but eastern manufacturers of woolen textiles complained that their profits diminished because raw materials were so expensive. Yet in 1827, a bill containing a compromise that was supposedly acceptable to both the Northeast and Northwest was defeated in the Senate by Vice President Calhoun's tie-breaking vote.

The next year, a tariff crisis occurred that would lead to further disputes. In drafting the tariff bill of that year, Jacksonians in Congress gave top priority to the protectionist features desired by Middle Atlantic States, where Jackson hoped to find strong support in the next presidential election. His congressional friends virtually ignored New England interests, assuming that Adams' fellow New Englanders could not avoid voting for a high tariff in any case—but the measure was offensive to a wide variety of individuals and sections, especially the Southeast.

Martin Van Buren
Andrew Jackson's hand-picked successor and eighth president of the U.S.

Painted into a corner by the shrewd strategy, Adams signed the bill with loathing. Then, because of his signature, he—not the Jacksonians—bore the brunt of the blame for it. Thereafter his name was associated with what critics appropriately labeled the "Tariff of Abominations."

9.2c Foreign Relations

Adams' background in diplomacy had led his supporters to believe he would leave a memorable record in foreign affairs. Yet he achieved nothing as president on a par with his earlier success as secretary of state. During his presidency, the United States failed to obtain from England the right of free navigation of the St. Lawrence River. Furthermore, American shippers had to resort to a roundabout trade when the ports of the British West Indies were closed to American merchantmen as tightly as they had ever been, in 1826. Adams retaliated by closing American ports to England, with the result that American trade with England diminished precipitously and the American economy sagged.

Other diplomatic problems also went unsolved during the Adams years. Old claims against France for damages arising out of the wars of the French Revolution were no nearer settlement in 1829 than they had been in 1825. Additionally, though delegates were sent to the Congress of Panama in 1826—called for the purpose of establishing cooperation among the republics of the Western Hemisphere—one died en route to Panama, and the other arrived too late. The mission accomplished nothing.

In the entire field of foreign relations, Adams could point with pride only to an unprecedented number of minor treaties and to the renewal in 1827 of the Anglo-American agreement covering joint occupation of Oregon. With these exceptions, his administration was a negative interlude in diplomatic history.

9.3 Jackson Triumphant

9.3a The Election of 1828

The election of 1828 has long been seen as a watershed in American political history, owing partially to the vastly increased voter turnout that year. It also marked the beginning of a new era because it was the first presidential election after two momentous deaths that occurred on July 4, 1826. On that day—exactly fifty years after the Declaration of Independence—both Thomas Jefferson and John Adams died. Since Washington had died in 1799, the country had now lost its first three presidents—its most important living links to the Revolution. Moreover, his awe-inspiring father would no longer be around to challenge—and sometimes torment—John Quincy Adams.

Even if Adams' personality had been more attractive, his attitude more gracious, and his leadership more compelling, he would have had trouble in any contest with the forces arrayed against him. As early as 1825, the general assembly of Tennessee placed Andrew Jackson on the track for the 1828 presidential race. Moreover, except in New England, enthusiasm for Jackson appeared everywhere. From New York to Illinois and from Pennsylvania to Louisiana, acclaim for Jackson reverberated. Furthermore, Jackson had impressive allies. Vice President Calhoun, an outstanding South Carolinian who had been Monroe's secretary of war, did little to conceal his antipathy toward Adams. Another important addition to the Jackson high command was Senator **Martin Van Buren** of New York. Formerly a Crawford lieutenant, the ingratiating Van Buren worked dexterously with Calhoun and others to weld a powerful combination of Southerners and Northerners opposing Adams and favoring Jackson. The combination was especially powerful in that it included both established men and those representing popular democratic movements.

Map 9.2 Presidential Election of 1828

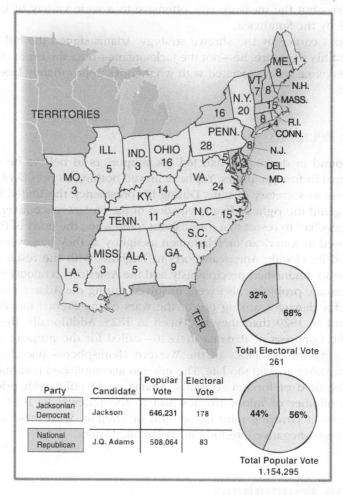

Party	Candidate	Popular Vote	Electoral Vote
Jacksonian Democrat	Jackson	646,231	178
National Republican	J.Q. Adams	508,064	83

Total Electoral Vote 261

32% 68%

Total Popular Vote 1,154,295

44% 56%

The election of 1828 is also noteworthy for the fact that during the campaign backers of both Adams and Jackson indulged in disreputable tactics. Pro-Adams journalists made much of Jackson's reputation for military highhandedness. They dragged the name of Mrs. Jackson through the gutters of partisan filth by reminding voters that her divorce from another man had not been final in the 1790s when she became Jackson's wife. Furthermore, Jackson's detractors pointed out that there was no record of Jackson's actual marriage to Rachel and argued that he was therefore "living in sin." This infuriated Jackson, and some have claimed that it may have had something to do with Mrs. Jackson's death from a heart attack soon after the election. Jackson "remarried" Rachel during the campaign so as to satisfy the critics. Pro-Jackson editors, however, were no innocent bystanders when the mud was slung and pilloried Adams as a billiards-playing aristocrat who was out of touch with the common people. That Jackson himself was a wealthy plantation owner was beside the point.

During the election of 1828, pro-Adams journalists made a scandal of Andrew Jackson's marriage to Rachel Jackson, claiming she had not been legally divorced when Jackson married her in the 1790s. An angry Jackson remarried his wife during the campaign to satisfy the public's concern. (Wikimedia Commons)

Substantive issues were not entirely ignored, however. Since the country had not yet reached the period of national conventions and platforms, there was no formal enunciation of principles. Nevertheless, in many minds Jackson was linked with proposals for tariff reform, and Adams—fairly or unfairly—with the Tariff of Abominations. Critics of the Second Bank of the United States hoped that Jackson, as president, would oppose it. Some advocates of the federally funded construction of roads and canals and the dredging of rivers and harbors preferred Adams because he had spoken out in favor of federal appropriations for these purposes. Nevertheless, there was no unanimity even on this issue, as others believed that Jackson would support federal funding for internal improvements more heartily than Adams.

If serious citizens held serious opinions, a simple "Hurrah for Jackson!" was the rallying cry that appealed to most Americans. About three times as many people voted in 1828 as had four years before, and the results were recorded with more care. Jackson, the Democratic candidate, scored a clear triumph with approximately 647,000 popular votes to 508,000 for Adams. In the Electoral College, the margin was two to one, with 178 votes for Jackson and 83 for Adams. This growth in the size of the electorate reflected population growth, an increased turnout of eligible voters, *and* a growth in the size of the pool of those eligible to vote—as property qualifications for voting had been more or less eliminated by this time in a number of states.

"King Mob"

A reference to unruly Jackson supporters who vandalized the White House after Jackson's inauguration in 1828

9.3b "King Mob"

Jackson's inauguration in March 1829 was accompanied by a demonstration unparalleled in American history. The thousands of people assembled in Washington behaved well outside the Capitol while Jackson read his inaugural address—but when the time came for the White House reception, **"King Mob"** took over. Men, women, and children crashed, trampled, and crushed their way in muddy boots and shoes into and through the White House. Only when someone thought of placing refreshments on the White House lawn did the crowd move outdoors.

The "King Mob" incident occurred at the reception for Andrew Jackson's inaugural address. In muddy boots and shoes, men, women, and children crashed, trampled, and crushed their way into and through the White House. The drunken mob left the White House a great mess, with several thousand dollars worth of damage. (Wikimedia Commons)

Jackson's political enemies were shocked by this public demonstration and talked darkly of a reenactment of the French Revolution's excesses on American soil. Actually, the scene had been more a matter of bad manners and an explosion of pent-up energy than anything else. The base of governmental support had broadened appreciably in the several years preceding the election, but no excesses other than social ones upset the evolutionary development of an increasingly democratic state. Nevertheless, when the multitude faded away shortly after inauguration day, the symbol of "King Mob" remained as a counterweight to "King Caucus" of old, when candidates were chosen through Congressional caucuses and the common people were largely shut out of the process.

9.3c Andrew Jackson: Man of the People

Andrew Jackson resonated with the common people partially because of his humble roots. Though Jackson was a wealthy planter at the time of his election, he was born in a log cabin in North Carolina and made his reputation as the hero of the Battle of New Orleans and as one of the country's greatest Indian fighters. Jackson also connected with the common people through his speech, which was laden with incorrect grammar like that of the uneducated masses. Jackson had little formal education, was a poor writer, and an atrocious speller. Like the common people who loved him, Jackson chewed tobacco incessantly and spit tobacco juice into spittoons while entertaining guests at the White House.

Jackson also had a deserved reputation as a real-life tough guy. In the words of one of Jackson's fellow law students, he was the "most roaring, rollicking, game-cocking, horse racing, card playing, mischievous fellow." His nickname was "Old Hickory" because hickory was such a hard wood and Jackson was such a hard man. Jackson also had a very Southern sense of honor, which he said that he got from his mother, who instructed him to "never lie, cheat, steal, or sue anyone at law for insults. Handle insults to one's honor yourself." As a consequence, Jackson was twice wounded by gunshot defending his honor: once in the shoulder in a bar fight and once in the chest during a duel in 1806. The bullet from the duel lodged in Jackson's ribs (Jackson allowed his opponent to shoot first) and caused Jackson pain the rest of his life.

Americans identified with their new president. Jackson came from humble beginnings, had little formal education, chewed tobacco like the common people, was a real-life tough guy, and had a very Southern sense of honor that he attributed to his mother. (Wikimedia Commons)

9.3ᵈ Reorganization of the Cabinet

The Democratic Party of sixty-two-year-old President Jackson charted its administrative course in an atmosphere of confusion. Although Jackson's close associate Martin Van Buren became secretary of state, several cabinet members were more closely identified with Vice President John C. Calhoun than with either Jackson or Van Buren.

Almost at once, there erupted one of those odd controversies that have occasionally influenced American political history—a controversy whose ramifications played themselves out over a course of two years. Secretary of War John H. Eaton, a Jackson appointee who had long been on intimate terms with the new president, had recently married a young widow whose comeliness was said to have attracted him even before her first husband's death. The story goes that Mrs. Calhoun and the wives of Calhoun's cabinet friends took the lead in snubbing Mrs. Peggy Eaton. Jackson resented the social chill, associating it with the shameful treatment of his own late wife during the campaign.

Van Buren—who endeared himself to Jackson by siding with the Eatons (and who, being a widower, had no wife to consult on the matter)—offered to resign from his cabinet post in May, knowing that a cabinet reorganization would enable Jackson to be rid of the problem. Jackson demanded the resignations of Calhoun supporters Samuel Ingham and John Branch; and by the summer of 1831, he would have resignations from all the remaining cabinet members. Calhoun's supporters were excluded from the next cabinet, while Van Buren retained the confidence of Jackson, who promptly named him minister to Britain. Looked at one way, the Eaton affair was a tempest in a teapot. On the other hand, it demonstrates the increasing social power and moral authority of women at the time—even when, as in this case, this power was deployed in a snobbish cause. John Eaton resigned from the cabinet in August in an attempt to put an end to the affair, as women in Washington continued to snub his wife, Peggy. Almost as if to validate the behavior of the Washington wives, Peggy would later return to Washington after the death of her husband and marry, at age fifty-nine, a nineteen-year-old dance instructor.

9.3ᵉ Changing Problems, Changing Arguments

Meanwhile, a more fundamental division between Jackson and Vice President Calhoun developed over two more serious issues. First, the president was greatly disturbed by the discovery that, years before, Calhoun had recommended that Jackson be court-martialed for his conduct during the Seminole War of 1818. Second, and more significant, Jackson hotly disapproved of Calhoun's contention that a state had the right to nullify a federal statute within its borders. It was this **"nullification"** question that caused the smoldering antipathies of the two top-ranking officials in the country to flare into the open.

The nullification stance of the vice president and his fellow South Carolinian, Senator Robert Y. Hayne, resulted from their state's opposition to the tariff policies of the United States—especially the Tariff of Abominations. They believed that while the industrial Northeast benefited from the higher tariffs, the agricultural South was damaged by the rising customs duties.

Economic conditions in the Southeast in the early 1830s were steadily worsening. The extension of cotton planting to the rich bottomlands of Alabama, Mississippi, and Louisiana (then the Southwest) had expanded production of the staple, and cotton prices consequently dropped. Many planters in the Southeast, threatened with ruin by their inability to compete on relatively poor soil, pulled stakes and took their slaves to the Southwest for a fresh start. The consequent loss of population compounded the Southeast's financial difficulties. There were also political reverberations since fewer people would mean smaller representation in Congress for South Carolina and similarly affected states.

Webster–Hayne Debate

Famous 1830 congressional debate over nationalism versus sectionalism and states' rights

Calhoun had lately joined Hayne and other South Carolina politicians in the conviction that most of their state's troubles could be traced to the tariff. In 1828, while running for reelection to the vice presidency as a Jackson adherent, Calhoun had secretly written the "South Carolina Exposition." This document, published without his name, declared protective tariffs unconstitutional. It went on to assert the right of any state to nullify or prevent the enforcement within its boundaries of what it deemed to be an unconstitutional act of Congress. Calhoun's authorship of the "Exposition" was not generally known in 1830, but his new position was becoming clear in some minds—including Jackson's.

In 1830, the vice president carefully coached the less brilliant Hayne to eloquently defend the extreme states' rights position in a dramatic Senate debate with Senator Daniel Webster of Massachusetts in what would become known as the **Webster–Hayne Debate**. As Massachusetts had become more industrialized, and accordingly adopted a high tariff policy, Webster had abandoned his low-tariff convictions (he had opposed the Tariff of 1824). By 1830 he was a high-tariff advocate. Moreover, Webster identified Massachusetts' changed economic attitude with a political nationalism that contrasted with the growing sectionalism of South Carolina. In so doing, he sought to equate the North's economic interest with patriotic virtue.

The famous Senate debate of 1830 arose as the result of a resolution by Connecticut Senator Samuel A. Foot, which had as one aim a restriction of the sale of public land. The land question was a vital matter to congressmen from the West. Current land laws, in effect since the early 1820s, provided for (1) a minimum purchase of eighty acres; (2) a minimum price of $1.25 an acre; (3) a no credit system; and (4) exceptions which recognized but did not wholly satisfy western insistence on lower land prices, and on the preemption principle (by which genuine settlers would have the first chance to buy at the minimum price). Already in the air were proposals for liberalizing land policies. Eastern laborers joined western farmers in favoring such liberalization, and Southerners saw an advantage in linking western land desires to Southern low-tariff hopes. Thus the opposition to Foot's restrictive resolution was not limited to any single section.

Senator Thomas H. Benton of Missouri resoundingly assailed the Foot Resolution. Benton saw it as a scheme of New England manufacturers, fearful of losing factory operatives to the lure of the West, to make cheap land inaccessible and so keep their workers in the east. Hayne took the issue to Benton's supporters, but took a different approach. If Foot's proposition were put into effect, he said, future prices of western land would be high. The income would then constitute "a fund for corruption," adding to the power of the federal government and endangering the independence of the states. Thereupon Webster launched his first reply to Hayne. Denying that the east was illiberal toward the West, the erstwhile sectionalist from Boston proclaimed his nationalism.

Hayne again spoke, reminding his listeners of New England's anti-Union attitude during the War of 1812. Where, he asked, were New England nationalists then? Had not residents of Webster's section, plotters of the Hartford Convention, favored the same constitutional arguments contained in the "South Carolina Exposition"? The northeastern sectionalists of old, Hayne insisted, currently championed theories that they formerly had decried. Their sincerity, he implied, was open to grave doubts and their past words and tactics hovered as reminders of appalling inconsistencies.

9.3f Webster's "Second Reply to Hayne"

After Hayne spiritedly elaborated on the extreme states' rights point of view, Webster answered him in what is widely regarded as the greatest speech ever delivered in Congress. In New England, he said, what Hayne had discussed was consigned to a bygone time. New Englanders were thinking, not of the past, but of the present and the future.

American System

A plan supported by Henry Clay which encompassed a national bank, high tariffs, and federal aid for internal improvements

Vital now was the wellbeing of America as a whole. Nothing could be more preposterous than the idea that twenty-four states could interpret the Constitution as each of them saw fit. The Union should not be "dissevered, discordant, belligerent." The country should not be "rent with civil feuds, or drenched … in fraternal blood." It was delusion and folly to think of "Liberty first, and Union afterwards." Instead, "dear to every true American heart" was that blazing sentiment—"Liberty *and* Union, now and forever, one and inseparable!"

In bygone days, countless young Americans memorized the peroration of Webster's "Second Reply to Hayne," regarded at the time and throughout the nineteenth century as a particularly eloquent statement of democratic nationalism. Calhoun, the idea man for Hayne, had morphed from an ardent defender of a strong central government to a defender of states' rights in order to protect his key constituency, the South Carolina planters, while Webster had gone in the other direction.

Calhoun and Jackson succeeded Hayne and Webster in the public spotlight during the spring of the same year, 1830, when a Jefferson birthday banquet was held in Washington's Indian Queen Hotel. Jackson offered fellow Democratic-Republicans a toast: "The Federal Union, it must be preserved!" Calhoun countered with a toast of his own: "The Union, next to our liberty, most dear!" The disparate sentiments were not lost upon the diners. The president had hurled down the gauntlet, and the vice president had picked it up. After that, their relations became ever more strained; and before Jackson's first term ended, Calhoun had resigned the vice presidency.

9.39 Two Controversial Vetoes

Jackson sternly opposed the Bank of the United States and objected to most proposals to use federal funds for internal improvements. The improvements question loomed large in 1830, when Congress passed a bill authorizing subscription of stock in a private company constructing a road between Maysville and Lexington, Kentucky. Jackson vetoed the proposition on the grounds that the Maysville Road lay wholly in one state and therefore was not entitled to financial support from Washington.

Jackson's controversial veto seemed tyrannical to many, and enemies dubbed him "King Andrew." Henry Clay and other transportation-minded Americans charged the president with being an impediment in the march of progress. Clay, it should be noted, was the prime advocate of the so-called **American System**, a plan that encompassed a national bank, high tariffs, and federal aid for internal improvements. The veto, however, was well received by Southern strict constructionists and by others resentful of what they deemed undue interference by the federal government in purely state affairs. Moreover, Jackson's selection of a western road as a target of his disapproval pleased those in New York and Pennsylvania who had financed their own projects locally and saw no reason why people in other regions should get the kind of Washington help they themselves had failed to obtain.

Jackson was hostile to the Bank of the United States for several reasons. First, he held the Jeffersonian strict-construction view, maintaining that Congress was not empowered by the Constitution to incorporate a bank outside the District of Columbia (in spite of the fact that the Supreme Court had ruled the Bank constitutional in 1819 along with the doctrine of Implied Powers from the Necessary and Proper Clause in *McCulloch v. Maryland*). Jackson also doubted that the Bank would serve the nation's welfare and accused it of not having established a sound and uniform currency. His third objection was that the Bank played politics in election campaigns and influenced congressmen by lending them money or placing them on its payroll. Furthermore, Old Hickory had an ingrained suspicion of the note issues of all banks (trusting only gold and silver)—with the Bank of the United States being the most notorious offender because it was far and away the most powerful. Finally, Jackson erroneously argued that foreigners controlled the bank; in truth, 80 percent of the bank's stock was held by domestic entities.

Moreover, it should be noted that there was a political payoff to the antibank stance: one of the key elements of the Jacksonian constituency, the urban workingmen, tended to see the Bank of the United States as an undemocratic monopoly; and these workers were organizing into parties in cities such as New York and Philadelphia.

To be fair, under Nicholas Biddle's leadership, the Bank of the United States had made important contributions to American economic stability. Regardless of what Jackson said, it did provide a sound currency; and its monetary standards and the financial power it wielded often exerted a salutary effect on the fluctuating currencies of state banks—many of which were dangerously weak. Jackson's charge against the Bank of political activity and legislative influence was, for the most part, warranted. Jackson came to consider the Bank a monopoly—but though government deposits were exclusively entrusted to it, the Bank was not a monopolistic enterprise in the customary sense of the term. Instead, there were many competing private banks.

The Bank's charter had four years to run in 1832. Clay, now a United States senator, was in full accord, however, with bank president Biddle's desire to see the institution rechartered long in advance of the legal deadline. Consequently, Clay pushed a Bank bill through both houses of Congress. Then, chosen by the National Republicans as their standard bearer in opposition to Jackson, he strove to make the Bank of the United States the main issue in the campaign of 1832. Jackson lost no time in vetoing the rechartering act in July 1832.

Anti-Masonic Party

Minor, xenophobic political party that subscribed to a grand conspiracy theory that Masons were attempting to take over American politics

9.3ʃ The Election of 1832

It can be argued that Clay was handicapped in his presidential race by the existence of a third party, the **Anti-Masonic Party**, that considered the Masonic fraternity an aristocratic threat to democratic institutions and objected to both Jackson and Clay because they were Masons.

Map 9.3 Presidential Election of 1832

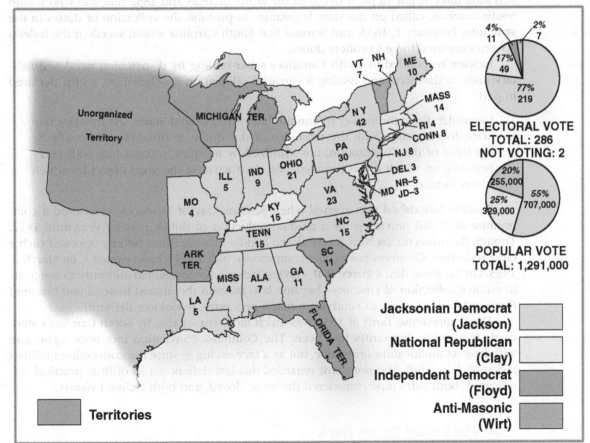

ELECTORAL VOTE
TOTAL: 286
NOT VOTING: 2

POPULAR VOTE
TOTAL: 1,291,000

Jacksonian Democrat (Jackson)
National Republican (Clay)
Independent Democrat (Floyd)
Anti-Masonic (Wirt)

Territories

Force Bill

Passed in 1833, gave Jackson
congressional authority
to use arms to enforce
collection of customs

The Anti-Masons nominated William Wirt of Maryland, ironically also a Mason and for twelve years attorney general under Monroe and Adams. They chose their candidate by a party convention, foreshadowing the method soon to be adopted by all the parties. The National Republicans' choice was Clay, while the Democratic-Republicans (now beginning to be called Democrats) were for Jackson, of course, with Van Buren as his running mate. In most states the anti-Jackson following was concentrated behind either Clay or Wirt, with the other man staying out of the contest within that state. Even with this tactical advantage, however, neither Clay nor Wirt had a very good chance to oust the popular Jackson. Furthermore, the Bank of the United States issue did not aid Clay as he had anticipated it might.

Not all historians agree on the exact size of the popular vote. It is clear, however, that Jackson won easily; his popular vote was approximately 687,500 against 530,000 for Clay and Wirt combined. Jackson was victorious in nearly the entire South and West, plus the "big" states of New York and Pennsylvania. In the Electoral College, Jackson scored 219 to Clay's 49 and Wirt's 7. South Carolina, still voting through its legislature, refused to back any of the regular candidates and cast eleven protest ballots for John Floyd of Virginia.

9.4 "King Andrew"

9.4a Crisis Over Nullification

No sooner was the 1832 election decided than South Carolina brought the nullification controversy to a head. The issue immediately in question was the Tariff of 1832, which lowered customs duties, but not enough to satisfy critics in the Palmetto State. The newly elected state legislature, composed predominantly of "nullifiers," ordered a special state convention to deal with the problem. The convention met in Columbia in November and took three major steps: It declared the tariffs of 1828 and 1832 null and void within South Carolina; called on the state legislature to prohibit the collection of duties in the state after February 1, 1833; and warned that South Carolina would secede if the federal government used force to collect duties.

Jackson responded to South Carolina's saber-rattling by dispatching naval and military units to that state and issuing a stirring Nullification Proclamation, which declared in part:

> I consider, then, the power to annul a law of the United States, assumed by one State, incompatible with the existence of the Union, contradicted expressly by the letter of the Constitution, unauthorized by its spirit, inconsistent with every principle on which it was founded, and destructive of the great object for which it was formed.

Possible bloodshed was averted when Senator Clay of Kentucky sponsored a compromise tariff bill providing for a gradual reduction of duties year by year until 1842. Though the protectionist New England and Middle Atlantic States bitterly opposed such a tariff reduction, Congress passed the compromise bill; and Jackson signed it on March 2, 1833. On the same day, a **Force Bill**—giving Jackson congressional authority to use arms to enforce collection of customs—became law. Jackson threatened to send two hundred thousand federal troops to South Carolina, if necessary, to enforce the tariff.

The Compromise Tariff of 1833 was much more reasonable by South Carolina's standards than preceding tariffs had been. The Columbia convention met once again and withdrew its nullification ordinance, but as a face-saving gesture the convention nullified Jackson's Force Bill. The president regarded this last defiant act as of little practical significance. Both sides now considered the issue closed, and both claimed victory.

9.4b The United States Bank

Jackson, interpreting his success in the 1832 election as a mandate from the voters to continue action against the Bank of the United States, decided to remove federal deposits from the Bank gradually and deposit them in selected state banks. An order to this effect was issued on September 26, 1833. When Secretary of the Treasury Duane refused to carry it out, Jackson replaced him with **Roger B. Taney**, until then attorney general. By the end of the year, twenty-three state banks—dubbed **"pet banks"** by anti-Jacksonians—had been selected as depositories.

Jackson's move against the Bank met with considerable political opposition, and his policy was attacked in Congress. In December 1833 Henry Clay introduced Senate resolutions to censure both the treasury action and the president for having "assumed upon himself authority and power not conferred by the constitution and laws, but in derogation of both." By the spring of 1834, President Jackson's opponents even had a new name: the Whig Party. This name played off of the idea that Jackson was acting as if he were "King Andrew" because it was the Whig party in Britain that espoused the limiting of royal power.

When the Senate resolutions were adopted, Jackson formally protested that that body had charged him with an impeachable offense but denied him an opportunity to defend himself. The Senate, however, rejected Jackson's protest and would not approve Taney's nomination as secretary of treasury, as a further measure of Senate defiance. Only after a three-year Senate battle did Jackson's supporters succeed in having the resolution of censure expunged from the Senate record. Nevertheless, in eliminating the Bank of the U.S., Jackson had eliminated a security measure against a banking crisis and rendered the entire American banking system more volatile.

9.4c Hard Money and Land

Jackson's bank policy contributed to a series of severe nationwide economic reverses. Even though the administration withdrew federal funds from the United States Bank only gradually, using them to meet current expenses while depositing new revenue in "pet banks," the Bank's decline was sharp enough to touch off an economic recession in 1833–1834. Nicholas Biddle's actions aggravated the situation. To make up for the lost federal deposits and to force congressional reconsideration of the Bank's charter, Biddle took the unnecessarily harsh step of calling in outstanding loans, thus creating demands for credit from state banks which they could not meet. Only under strong pressure from businessmen and from the governor of Pennsylvania did Biddle, at last, reverse his policy.

The country quickly pulled out of the economic doldrums by the end of 1834 and almost immediately headed into a dangerous inflationary spiral. States chartered hundreds of new private banks, each issuing its own banknotes and each setting its own interest rates, typically much higher than rates had been prior to Jackson's veto. These factors, along with an influx of silver from Mexican mines, caused prices to rise 50 percent between 1834 and 1837. State banks also used their newly acquired federal funds for speculative purposes. At the same time, the federal government greatly increased its sale of public land, inadvertently encouraging the most reckless speculators.

Although political leaders were divided in their reaction to the inflationary trend, Jackson agreed with Senator Benton's prediction that "the present bloat in the paper system" could foreshadow another depression. On July 11, 1836, Jackson chose to issue a Specie Circular, which provided that after August 15 all public lands purchased from the federal government were to be paid for only in gold or silver, with one exception: until December 15, people actually settling on the land were permitted to use state bank notes to purchase parcels of land up to 320 acres. The impact of Jackson's action was to greatly diminish the value of the money supply since paper banknotes could not be used to purchase federal land. Jackson's sudden policy reversal sharply curtailed western land sales and weakened public confidence in the state banks. It also encouraged the hoarding of specie (hard money) and was a factor in bringing on the **Panic of 1837**—a severe economic recession that would last through 1843.

The western land problem figured repeatedly in congressional debates from Jackson's day to Lincoln's and beyond. Benton and other westerners favored the policy of "graduation," by which prices for the less desirable portions of the public domain would be reduced from $1.25 an acre to $1.00, 50¢, or less, depending on the length of time they had been for sale. Westerners also wanted the policy of preemption, which favored squatters (who lived on the land) rather than speculators (who bought the land for the purpose of resale at a profit).

Roger B. Taney
Attorney general and then secretary of the treasury under Andrew Jackson and later chief justice of the Supreme Court, who issued the *Dred Scott* decision in 1857

"Pet banks"
A reference by Jackson's opponents to the twenty-three banks that Jackson deposited federal funds into after he dissolved the Bank of the U.S.

Panic of 1837
Severe economic recession resulting from a real estate and financial collapse that followed Jackson's Specie Circular

Although Congress passed no graduation bill until 1854, a temporary Preemption Act in 1830 authorized settlers to buy up to 160 acres of public land at a minimum price of $1.25 an acre. The act was renewed regularly and remained in force until 1842.

Not to be confused with preemption, Henry Clay advocated "distribution." In 1833, the Kentuckian drove through both the House and Senate a bill stipulating that most of the revenue derived from public-land sales be distributed among all the states, with a smaller fraction earmarked for states where the sales took place. That was a typical example of Clay's desire to appeal politically to two sections at once. Jackson, however, pocket-vetoed the bill—thwarting his adversary and identifying himself further with the actual settlers of the Northwest and Southwest. Jackson was the first president to use the **pocket veto**, whereby any bill passed by Congress during the last ten days of a session does not pass without the president's signature. Since Clay's distribution bill was passed during the last ten days of a Congressional session, Jackson did not have to formally veto the bill to kill it but merely did not sign it, and thus accomplished the same result.

9.4b Jackson's Foreign Policy

Jackson's handling of foreign affairs was at times as headstrong and unconventional as one might expect of an old border captain. The only real diplomatic crisis of his two terms concerned claims against France for seizures of American ships during the Napoleonic wars. Adams and preceding presidents had failed to collect; at Jackson's urging, however, France agreed to pay $5 million in a series of indemnity installments. The first $1 million was due in 1833. When the French made no payment then or the following year, but made payment to England who they also owed, Jackson viewed it as an insult to American honor and favored war with France. Jackson was poised to take coercive action, uttering, "I know them French—They won't pay unless they're made to." In December 1834, Jackson requested congressional support for an ultimatum to France in demand of payment. Jackson also urged Congress to authorize reprisals on French property unless the money was speedily sent. The French responded with a demand for a "satisfactory explanation" of Jackson's ultimatum, which they viewed as an insult to French honor. For a few months there appeared to be danger of war, but the British offered mediation of the dispute and persuaded the French to accept Jackson's address to Congress asking for an ultimatum as an "explanation." The French desired to avoid war and accepted the British solution. French payment of the debt began in 1836.

Jackson also faced the problem of whether to recognize the independence of Texas from Mexico—established as a republic by the Treaty of Velasco after the Texans defeated the Mexican army under Santa Anna at the Battle of San Jacinto in April 1836. The people of the new Republic of Texas quickly held an election and voted overwhelmingly for annexation to the United States. Because it was a potential slave state, Jackson trod carefully in order not to inflame the American people over the slavery issue and possibly jeopardize Van Buren's presidential hopes in the election of November 1836. Jackson was fearful also of angering Mexico, which insisted that Texas was still a Mexican State in rebellion and that any American interference with Texas could mean a war with Mexico, which Jackson sought to avoid. Though there was no question about Jackson's personal sentiment—his sympathy for the Texan revolutionists was strong—he withheld recognition from the Texas republic until the very day he left office in 1837.

9.4c The Supreme Court

Andrew Jackson's most enduring influence on the Supreme Court came indirectly through the justices he elevated to the bench. When he retired, five of the sitting judges were his appointees. The number included slavery advocate Roger B. Taney, who had succeeded John Marshall as chief justice on the latter's death in 1835.

Among the principal early decisions under Taney was *Briscoe v. The Bank of Kentucky* (1837), which reduced the application of constitutional limitations on state banking and currency matters. This decision held that it was not unconstitutional for a state that owned stock to issue bank notes. More famous is *Charles River Bridge v. Warren Bridge*

(1837), which stressed community responsibilities of private property and modified the contract doctrines of Marshall. In *Bank of Augusta v. Earle* (1839), the Chief Justice denied that corporations had all legal rights of natural persons. He also held that while corporations could take part in interstate commerce, any state had the right to exclude another state's corporations.

In later cases, there sometimes was a lack of agreement or consistency regarding federal power to regulate commerce on the one hand and the states' internal police power on the other. This is traceable, in part, to the Court's changing personnel after Jackson's presidency, and in part to the alterations in Taney's own ideas.

For many years, it was the fashion among historians to be hypercritical of Taney's Supreme Court record. Continuing on the tribunal until he died during the Civil War, he became very unpopular in the North because of his position in favor of states' rights and because of the infamous *Dred Scott* decision in 1857, in which he declared slaves to be property and without rights, including standing to sue. Actually, the judicial philosophies and influences of Marshall and Taney had many similarities. Taney and most of his associates believed that the growing power of corporations needed supervision by states in the public interest, but they were not unsympathetic toward property rights as such; and modern authorities on judicial history see no sharp break between most constitutional interpretations made by the two jurists.

Supreme Court Justice Roger B. Taney, appointed by Andrew Jackson, was in favor of slavery. In the famous Dred Scott *decision, Taney declared that slaves had no rights and that they were no more than property. (Wikimedia Commons)*

9.5 Jacksonian Democracy—A Look Back

9.5a The Influence of Economic Factors

In Jackson's time, as now, political changes were often tied to economic changes, and alliances formed and reformed over economic issues. What had been the Democratic-Republican Party had, by 1836, split into two parties known as Democrats and **Whigs**, with opposing views on government and its proper role in the economy. In what historians refer to as the **Second Party System**, Democrats and Whigs would be the dominant forces in American politics until the demise of the Whigs and rise of the Republican Party in the 1850s during the unrest that led up to the Civil War.

To find consistency in the political actions of Democrats and Whigs is difficult, chiefly because of shifts brought about by economic factors. Daniel Webster, for example, had begun his career as a champion of New England shipping interests and free trade. Then, after the War of 1812, when domestic manufacturing was growing, Webster caught the spirit of industrial progress. He and other Whigs felt that the fledgling industries needed all the government protection they could get. Thus, by the late 1820s Webster had become an aggressive advocate of protective tariffs that would foster American industry. Besides a protected market, he and his fellow Whigs felt that industry also needed a sound banking system, which would provide a stable currency and ample credit.

Henry Clay, too, had changed his political convictions with changing times. Reared in the Virginia of Jeffersonian agrarianism, he migrated to Kentucky and was awakened to new western economic ambitions. A spokesman for western Whigs, Clay believed in a nationalistic program—his American System. Through federally funded internal improvements, a liberal policy of public-land sales, a central bank, and tariffs, the aim of this system was to reduce American dependence on foreign trade and provide a home market for the exchange of the North's manufactured goods and the West's agricultural products.

The Whigs felt that government aid to business would promote the economic progress and wellbeing of all Americans. The Whig party, however, also contained prominent Southern planters, though their reliance on cotton exports and low-cost imports caused them to oppose the protective tariffs advocated by the Northern Whigs. Like the leaders in other sections, those in the South took anguished turns in their search for adjustment.

Whigs

The political party supported by Daniel Webster and Henry Clay that opposed the policies of the Jacksonian Democrats and supported higher tariffs

Second Party System

The party system that developed in the 1830s with the dominant two parties being the Democrats and the Whigs

Bank Veto

Jackson's veto of the renewal of the charter of the Bank of the U.S.

Jacksonian democracy

Democracy built on mass politics and the spoils system

John C. Calhoun of South Carolina began as a "War Hawk" nationalist during the days of Jefferson and Madison. Later, he became a defender of states' rights in defiance of federal "authoritarianism." Politically, he shifted from the Democrats to the Whigs and back to the Democrats.

Jackson was able to cope with these shifting factions. With a military hero reputation that aided him in politics, he was looked upon as a champion of the plain people and an enemy of "privilege" to any one class or section. Often arbitrary in method, Jackson was at times headstrong and uncompromising, such as in the case of the **Bank Veto**. He did, however, try to find a middle ground at times, favoring a "judicious" tariff and avoiding the annexation of Texas so as to prevent a heightening of sectional tensions. He approved or opposed federal funding for internal improvements on the merits of each individual case, and he and his Democratic followers were more aware than the Whigs of the potential dangers of monopolies.

9.5b Characteristics of Jacksonian Democracy

The policies identified with **Jacksonian democracy** have been associated with five major trends. First, Jacksonian democracy represented a trend toward equality and expansion of democracy, with more men participating more fully in the political process. While Jackson drew support from persons in many walks of life, common people were most inclined to identify themselves with Jackson and his policies. Second, Jacksonian democracy marked a departure from the domination of bankers and merchants, even though some bankers and merchants were steadfast Jacksonians. Third, Jacksonians were expansionists, committed to making room for white settlers on what had been American Indian lands. Fourth, as seen in the South Carolina controversy, Jacksonian democrats resolutely opposed weakening the Federal union. Fifth, Jackson's followers approved Jackson's exercise of federal authority over the American economy.

To understand Jackson's influence, it is essential to understand why Jackson was so popular and what caused him to retain his popularity. The War of 1812, as we have seen, involved no other military victory on a par with Jackson's brilliant one. Fervidly admired because of his achievement, he intrigued fellow-Americans who found in him no mere child of luck but a man of iron will and ingenious battlefield prowess. Also (and this was nearly as important), he seemed to symbolize the "outs" or non-establishment people in contrast with the "ins" of Washington. He had come up in the world on his own and was a leader of forcefulness and determination—the very sort of dynamic figure who makes enemies and yet attracts hosts of followers and friends. No understanding of Jacksonian democracy can be complete without awareness of the charismatic Jackson image.

9.5c Evaluation of Jackson's Administration

As president, the active and dominant Jackson continued both to arouse strong adverse criticism and to inspire praise bordering on idolatry. The Tennessean's enemies did not hesitate to call him every unpleasant name in the book. They depicted him as "King Andrew," a would-be tyrant with slight regard for the ways of free people and with a ruthless intent to impose his will on the country. On the other hand, Jackson's friends (and they were a majority) loved him personally and held his political talents in the highest esteem.

In the perspective of the years, Jackson's record shows marked differences from issue to issue. Although moderation is not traditionally considered a trait of Jackson's, he was essentially a moderate on the tariff, and his attitude toward land policy was generally temperate. Though he did not block all internal improvements financed with federal funds, he was apt to be conservative or reactionary (depending on one's point of view) on projects in that category.

Many scholars have argued that Jackson's greatest mistake was his hostility to the Bank of the United States, and that his Specie Circular reflected a miscalculation in timing if not in principle. On the other hand, Jackson's foreign policy was successful, and his nationalism was tellingly asserted in opposition to the nullifiers.

A slaveholder with the manners and tastes of a Southern planter, Jackson had, nonetheless, an acute awareness of public preferences and the public interest. He also had an instinct for reaching the "common" people and for identifying their desires with his own. A simple man with a fighting heart, Jackson lived in constant pain, owing to injuries he had received in the duels he had fought. The pain likely contributed to his irascibility. That said, it could still be concluded that Jackson judged each issue on its merits—as he understood them—and contributed vigorous leadership to every cause he championed.

Historians' opinions of Jackson, like their judgments of Jefferson and other presidents, have changed from generation to generation. The principal recent charges against Jackson are that his American Indian policy, which included the removal of tribes in the Southeast to Indian Territory (Oklahoma), was too harsh. Regardless of opinion, Jackson indisputably brought major, long-lasting changes to American politics. He ushered in the era of mass partisan politics, with more people involved in the political process than ever before and the emergence of mass-based political parties as the driving force of politics. Jackson also strengthened the power of the executive in a number of ways, among them his use of the veto for something other than "unconstitutional" legislation and his use of the pocket veto. Prior to Jackson, the veto had been used only nine times in American history, all on legislation that the vetoing presidents viewed as unconstitutional. Jackson alone used the veto twelve times—more than all previous presidents combined—and used the veto on bills that he simply opposed, that were not considered unconstitutional.

William Henry Harrison

Hero of the Battle of Tippecanoe in 1811, who won the presidency in 1840 only to die a month after giving his inaugural speech on a cold day and wearing no coat or hat

9.6 Democrats and Whigs

9.6a The Election of 1836

As Jackson's second term neared its end, Vice President Martin Van Buren was the Democratic presidential nominee and received the endorsement of Andrew Jackson. The Whig opposition tried to throw the contest into the House of Representatives by sponsoring several candidates on a regional basis. Van Buren faced Daniel Webster in the Northeast, Ohio's **William Henry Harrison** in the Northwest, and Tennessee's Hugh L. White in the South. These three Whigs won fourteen, seventy-three, and twenty-six electoral votes respectively. South Carolina gave its eleven votes to the anti-Jacksonian Willie P. Mangum of North Carolina. Even so, their combined total of 124 was well under Van Buren's figure of 170—and the Whig popular vote of 739,000 failed to match Van Buren's 765,000. So while the Whigs made gains, the 1836 regional scheme fell apart and again the Democrats were victors.

9.6b The Panic of 1837

The "Little Magician" or "Red Fox of Kinderhook," as Van Buren was nicknamed, proved to be an unlucky president. A New York lawyer of ability and a politician who, up to that point, had proved himself adroit in difficult situations, Van Buren found himself confronted by an economic disaster beyond his control. In May 1837, only two months after his inauguration, a New York bank panic signaled the start of one of America's deepest depressions. In part, the trouble stemmed from an English financial crisis during which many British creditors canceled their American investments. Yet Jackson and Van Buren drew much of the blame because the panic began shortly after Jackson's Specie Circular caused a rapid decline in land sales, and some of Jackson's "pet banks" were among those that failed. Furthermore, while the Specie Circular checked speculation in western lands, it curtailed the activities of financiers who had been supplying funds to speculators. Jackson's bank veto proved to make the banking system more fragile by eliminating the possibility of loans from the Bank of the U.S. to other banks that were short on capital.

The depression affected the lives and fortunes of people in every part of the country. Widespread unemployment developed in seaboard cities of the Northeast, spreading into interior communities and fanning out to the South and West. Bread lines and soup

Martin Van Buren was elected president in 1836. Unfortunately, two months after his inauguration the country fell victim to one of its deepest financial depressions, and Van Buren was blamed. (Wikimedia Commons)

Map 9.4 Presidential Election of 1836

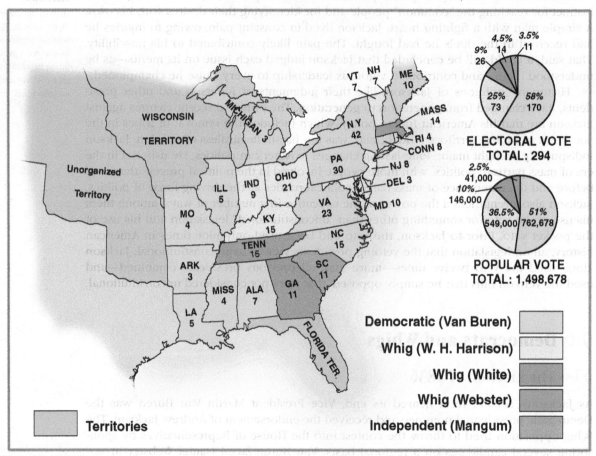

ELECTORAL VOTE TOTAL: 294

4.5% 14
3.5% 11
9% 26
25% 73
58% 170

POPULAR VOTE TOTAL: 1,498,678

2.5% 41,000
10% 146,000
36.5% 549,000
51% 762,678

Democratic (Van Buren)
Whig (W. H. Harrison)
Whig (White)
Whig (Webster)
Independent (Mangum)
Territories

State labels on map:
WISCONSIN TERRITORY
Unorganized Territory
MICHIGAN 3
VT 7
NH 7
ME 10
NY 42
MASS 14
RI 4
CONN 8
PA 30
NJ 8
DEL 3
MD 10
OHIO 21
IND 9
ILL 5
VA 23
KY 15
MO 4
TENN 15
NC 15
SC 11
GA 11
ARK 3
MISS 4
ALA 7
LA 5
FLORIDA TER.

kitchens struggled to relieve the hunger of poor families, including thousands of recent immigrants. Farmers received low prices for their crops, factories closed, and laborers walked the streets. Canal and railroad projects were halted as capital for investment evaporated. In 1839, the worst of the depression seemed to be over, but another decline occurred later that same year due to cotton overproduction and falling agricultural prices. Good times would not return to America as a whole until 1843.

In the meantime, Van Buren's fine display of statesmanship belied his reputation as a crafty politician. Beginning in 1837, he induced Congress to agree to a temporary issue of short-term treasury notes. These amounted to $47 million in the next six years and enabled the government to meet its obligations. He also advocated an independent treasury, where federal funds could be safely retained without either running pet-bank style risks or resorting to another Bank of the United States.

Most Whigs and some Democrats opposed the banking bill on the grounds that removal of federal funds from the state banks where they were deposited would restrict credit at a time when credit was sorely needed. The Independent Treasury Act finally was passed in 1840, but Van Buren's victory was short-lived. The next year, under the Tyler administration, the act was repealed; and for the next five years the Whig majority in Congress defeated Democratic efforts to reestablish this "subtreasury system."

9.6c Indian Removal

In 1830 the nation's land and water area covered more than 1,780,000 square miles. In addition, more than twelve thousand square miles in the far Northeast and approximately half a million square miles in the far Northwest (Oregon Territory) were claimed by both Washington and London. Substantial numbers of Americans had spilled over into Texas, which then was still part of Mexico, on land that the Mexican government had granted to Moses Austin and his son, Stephen F. Austin.

Most pioneers, however, were less concerned with Mexican Texas or with Anglo-American boundary differences than they were with the nearby Native Americans. From the Native Americans' points of view, it was utterly wrong for them to be forced out of their ancestral lands in order to make places for white settlers. Most whites had a very different attitude, considering Native Americans to be inferior and looking on them as obstacles that were simply in the way.

During this period, the pressure of frontiersmen and their families pushed tens of thousands of Native Americans west of the Mississippi River. In ninety treaties signed during Jackson's presidency—some less honorable than others—Native Americans reluctantly accepted new western lands in lieu of their old homes.

North of the Ohio River there was relatively little trouble for the white Americans when what was left of the Shawnees, Wyandots, Delawares, and Miamis were moved to western reservations. Although the move was a difficult one, the northern tribes were to suffer less in the process of relocation than the tribes of the South.

The most dramatic example of resistance by northern Indians in the 1830s was an exception to the rule. This involved a resolute Sauk, Black Hawk by name, who believed that a treaty ceding the Rock River region of southern Wisconsin and northwestern Illinois to the hated whites had been signed under conditions of trickery. Black Hawk reluctantly moved his people to the west bank of the Mississippi, but in 1832 he led them back to southern Wisconsin in search of fertile farm land. The ensuing **Black Hawk War**, won by the whites that summer, marked the end of organized Native American resistance in the old Northwest. Westward migration of Sauk, Fox, Winnebago, and other tribes increased. Within six years, both Wisconsin and Iowa became territories; within sixteen years they became states, as settlers from the east populated the land while the Native Americans were again dispossessed.

Beginning in 1819, Congress began an **assimilationist policy** under which they granted $10,000 annually to a number of missionary associations for the purpose of "civilizing" Native Americans by converting them to Christianity. The program included teaching the English language and English literacy to Native Americans, as well as the teaching of traditional gender roles favored by whites. Not everyone agreed with the assimilationist policy. Andrew Jackson, for instance, stated to Congress in his 1833 address that the Native Americans had "neither the intelligence, the industry, the moral habits, nor the desire of improvement which are essential."

In the judgment of many whites, however, southern Native Americans generally were making more progress toward "civilization" than those being prodded westward north of the Ohio. Sequoya, inventor of a set of characters for Cherokee syllables, enabled thousands of Cherokee adults and children to read and write. Because by white standards they were more advanced than other Native Americans, the Cherokees, Chickasaws, Choctaws, Creeks, and Seminoles are known in American history as the Five Civilized Tribes. Some of them, notably the Seminoles and the Creeks, did not always prove civilized if placidity is a criterion—but it is small wonder that enlightened leaders could not invariably remain placid in light of the whites' tricks and treachery.

The Indian Springs Treaty of 1825, involving Creek land in southern Georgia, was so unfair to the Creeks that the U. S. Senate rejected it. Often, treaties were said to be the result of corrupt deals in which Native American leaders sold out to the whites in return for handsome rewards. In any case, the treaties secured the land for the whites. The Treaty of Dancing Rabbit (1830) relinquished nearly eight million Choctaw acres in Alabama and Mississippi, and in the next decade other substantial cessions were made. Many Cherokees and other Native Americans in the Southeast were forced to move west. Thousands died along the way on what has been called the **Trail of Tears**, between their traditional homes in the Southeast and Indian Territory (present-day Oklahoma). Suffering not only indignities but also agonies on the 1,200-mile trek, an estimated four thousand of fifteen thousand Cherokees, Choctaws and Chickasaws perished from the elements before they could reach their new homes. Because Andrew Jackson was president during the period in which the legal basis for removal was enacted, it is he, more than any other political leader, who is held responsible for this

Black Hawk War

War against the American Indians, who were led by Black Hawk, to expel the American Indians from southern Wisconsin and northwestern Illinois in 1832

Assimilationist policy

The U.S. government policy toward Native Americans that required them to adopt the language and culture of whites

Trail of Tears

The trail from the Southeast to Indian Territory, along which four thousand Native Americans died

dark page in American history. In Jackson's first annual message to Congress in 1829, he declared that moving the American Indians to territory west of the Mississippi River was the only way to "save" them from extinction. Jackson repeated this message in his next seven annual addresses to Congress. It was also under Jackson, in 1830, that Congress passed the **Indian Removal Act** of 1830 that appropriated $500,000 to relocate American Indian tribes living on over one hundred million acres in the east to land west of the Mississippi, as Jackson had suggested the previous year.

Not all southern tribes submitted passively to the whites' intrusions. Osceola, a Florida Seminole sub-chief, so resented the Treaty of Payne's Landing, which authorized removal of the Seminoles to west of the Mississippi, that he is said to have plunged his knife into the document when he was expected to sign it with his "X."

Resistance on the part of Micanopy, Alligator, Osceola, and other Native Americans—supported by some runaway slaves—culminated in the **Second Seminole War**. In 1835 the Seminoles ambushed and massacred 107 of the 110 officers and men fighting with Major Francis L. Dade. Taking full advantage of Florida's maze of inland rivers and swamps to hide their women and children, they harassed United States troops and then rushed back to cover. Osceola was seized and imprisoned when, under a flag of truce, he came for an interview with an American general. He died in a military prison, with the war—the bloodiest and most expensive of all American conflicts with American Indians—continuing until 1842. Although there are Seminoles in Florida in our own time, most of the original tribesmen were forced to surrender or were tricked into capture by the whites. Usually they settled in Indian Territory.

The Cherokee tribe of Georgia mounted a legal challenge to their removal. The Cherokees, perhaps more than any other tribe, had attempted to pacify whites through assimilationist policies, adopted their own written constitution based on the American model, and adopted white ways in terms of clothing, housing, and cotton plantation agriculture—including the ownership of a thousand slaves. In 1832 in **Worcester v. Georgia**, the U.S. Supreme Court recognized the Cherokee nation as a sovereign entity with its own territory in which the laws of Georgia had no force. Andrew Jackson—understanding that it was the executive branch, not the judiciary, which had enforcement powers—simply ignored the ruling and pressed the Cherokees to move west.

In 1835, Jackson's side received a break when a small, unrepresentative group of Cherokees signed a treaty ceding all tribal land in exchange for $5 million and equal acreage west of Arkansas. Cherokee Chief John Ross petitioned the U.S. to ignore the unrepresentative treaty, but Georgia rapidly sold the Cherokee's land to whites. Most Cherokees refused to vacate their land until President Martin Van Buren sent federal troops to Georgia to force their evacuation. Many Americans opposed the brutal treatment of Native Americans—including such prominent Northern Whigs as John Quincy Adams and Daniel Webster. Unfortunately, they were unable to prevail. One such man, whose troubled conscience about Native Americans led him down the unusual path not of protest but of the artistic rendering of Native Americans, was the artist **George Catlin**. Giving up his career as a Philadelphia lawyer, he made five trips into the Great Plains during the 1830s, so as to paint the Plains Indians—in the days before photography. Self-taught, Catlin was a man on a mission. When he completed his vast body of portraiture and scenes of daily life, he tried, unsuccessfully, to sell his paintings to Congress. In the end he had to travel to Europe to get the recognition he craved. Modern Americans are indebted to him because he left an invaluable record—in some instances, such as with the Mandans, of tribes that subsequently would be wiped out by the white people's pathogens. Over time, the paintings found their way into American museums, and today hundreds of them are in the collection of the Smithsonian Institution in Washington, D.C., among other repositories.

George Catlin gave up his career as a lawyer and instead made five trips into the Great Plains during the 1830s to paint the Plains Indians. Though he received little fame in his day, today hundreds of his paintings—such as the one above—are in the collection of the Smithsonian Institution. (Wikimedia Commons)

9.6ᵈ The *Caroline* Affair

Another problem of the Van Buren regime concerned a spat with England along the Canadian border. In 1837 Canadian insurgents, dissatisfied with London's rule, fled to an island in the Niagara River, where American Anglophobes reinforced insurgents with recruits and arms. The American steamer *Caroline* was employed in the supply service.

Canadian soldiers, crossing to the American side of the Niagara, set the *Caroline* afire and turned her adrift. Because of the high state of excitement, there was danger of mob invasions in either direction; and the slaying of an American citizen, **Amos Durfee**, on the night the vessel burned seriously complicated the situation. The citizens of Buffalo placed Durfee's body, with a bullet hole in his forehead and blood still in his hair, on display in the town square. New York newspapers called for war against England in the name of national honor and demanded an apology from Britain. No apology was forthcoming from Britain, however, because they argued that Durfee's death was an act of self-defense.

Three years later, a Canadian deputy sheriff named **Alexander McLeod** was arrested in Lockport, New York, and indicted for murder and arson in connection with the ***Caroline* affair** after he had publicly boasted of killing Durfee in a Buffalo tavern. The British demanded the release of McLeod on the basis that if he had killed Durfee, it was a military action and he was acting under orders to defend a British territory (Canada) against insurgents. Furthermore, President Martin Van Buren had declared American neutrality in the Canadian rebellion; consequently, it was illegal under international law for the United States to aid Canadian rebels in the conflict or the U.S. would be violating its own neutrality. Although the Americans involved in aiding the Canadian rebels on the *Caroline* were doing so with private funds, the British pointed out that the U.S. had claimed the right to invade a country on its borders that did not sufficiently secure its own border, as in Andrew Jackson's invasion of Florida in 1818. The British threatened war if McLeod was not released, and on both sides of the border additional sums were appropriated for the strengthening of boundary defenses. Even after McLeod was acquitted by a New York court in 1841 (his claim that he had killed Amos Durfee proved to be nothing more than drunken bravado), the case seemed an unpromising preliminary to the Webster-Ashburton negotiations on border disputes that were to take place the next year.

In the Caroline *incident, Canadian soldiers seized the American Steamer* Caroline, *towed her into the current, set her on fire, and turned her adrift over Niagara Falls. American citizen Amos Durfee was killed in the process, sparking more anger between the U.S. and Britain. (Wikimedia Commons)*

Amos Durfee

American killed by the British in the attack on the *Caroline*

Alexander McLeod

British subject who boasted of killing Amos Durfee in a Buffalo tavern and almost caused war between England and the U.S.

***Caroline* affair**

During the Canadian revolt against England, the British attacked, on the American side of the Niagara River, the American ship, *Caroline*, which was carrying men and arms for the Canadian insurgents.

9.6ᵉ Tippecanoe and Tyler Too

During Van Buren's presidency, Webster and Clay continued to be prominent in the senatorial spotlight. Webster's oratorical ability was as outstanding as ever, and Clay distinguished himself as a parliamentary leader, thus helping to keep the Whig party in the spotlight.

Northern Whigs favored the creation of a new national bank and advocated a high tariff and federally financed internal improvements. If their anti-Jackson and anti-Van Buren confréres of the South did not agree about the tariff and the bank, the common bond linking all Whigs was the issue of "executive tyranny." Less domination by the president and more authority vested in Congress were aims that Southern and Northern Whigs shared. They also capitalized on the country's economic distress, which had occurred under Van Buren's watch, and were as one in their criticism of Van Buren as the 1840 election approached.

The Whigs played their cards cannily in the 1840 test of skill. In the first place, their standard-bearer was neither Clay nor Webster—able men who had many friends and also many enemies—but William Henry Harrison of Ohio. Harrison had run well as a regional Whig candidate in 1836 and had won a measure

THE TIPPECANOE QUICK STEP
Published by SAMᴸ CARUSI *Baltimore*

For the presidential election of 1840, the Whigs chose William Henry Harrison of Ohio. Harrison had run well as a regional Whig candidate in 1836 and had won a measure of military glory in the dim past at the Battle of Tippecanoe. (Library of Congress, LC-USZ62-89290)

Map 9.5 Presidential Election of 1840

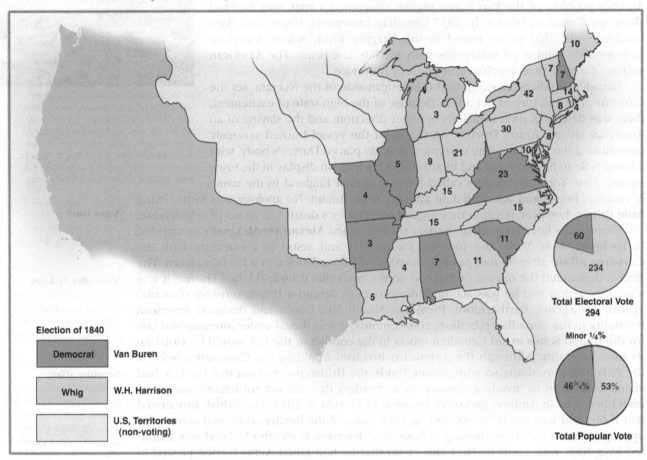

Election of 1840

Democrat — Van Buren

Whig — W.H. Harrison

U.S. Territories (non-voting)

10
7
7
42
14
8
4
30
8
10
5
9
21
23
4
15
15
3
15
15
11
4
7
11
5

60
234

Total Electoral Vote 294

Minor 1/4%

46³/₄% | 53%

Total Popular Vote

of military glory in the dim past at the American Indian Battle of Tippecanoe. Second, the Whigs turned to their advantage a journalist's taunt that Harrison was unfit for the presidency. "Give him a barrel of hard cider, and settle a pension of two thousand a year on him," the newsman sneered, "and [take] my word for it, he will sit the remainder of his days in his log cabin by the side of a 'sea coal' fire, and study moral philosophy."

Yes, the Whigs replied, their nominee was a man of the people who preferred a log cabin and hard cider to the frippery of red-whiskered Van Buren. In reality, Harrison dwelt in a mansion near Cincinnati and was an aristocratic Virginian by birth and rearing—but log cabins, barrels of cider, coonskin caps, and even live raccoons became Harrison's symbols in the campaign.

For the vice presidency, the Whigs had chosen **John Tyler** of Virginia—a former states' rights Democrat who was now a spokesman for the minority Southern element within the Whig party. The Whigs' most typical campaign verse contained the best known of all jingles associated with elections:

What has caused the great commotion,
motion, motion,
Our country through?
It is the ball a rolling on
For **Tippecanoe and Tyler too**—
Tippecanoe and Tyler too,
And with them we'll beat
little Van, Van, Van.
Van is a used up man.

As expected, the Whigs were victorious in 1840. Harrison's Electoral College showing was impressive (234 to Van Buren's 60), and his popular vote was 1,274,000 to 1,127,000 for the Democrat. Although the Whig margin was not vast in a number of critical states, it was large enough. North of the Mason-Dixon line, Van Buren carried only New Hampshire and Illinois.

The 1840 election was not a critical or realigning one like those of 1800 and 1828, as no permanent party changes stemmed from it. Nevertheless, the Tippecanoe campaign did have importance as it (1) showed how adroitly Whigs could play the Democrats' game and (2) served as a model for presidential contests that would last for more than a century.

9.6f President Without a Party

The sweet taste of triumph, however, soon turned bitter in Whig mouths. Inaugurated in March 1841, the sixty-eight-year-old Harrison gave his inaugural address on a cold day in Washington with no hat and no coat and died of pneumonia after a single month in office. Tyler, the first man to reach the presidency through the death of his predecessor, shared few of the ideas of the dominant Whig group in Congress and was voted out of the party at the end of summer, 1841. Twice he vetoed attempts to revive the Bank of the United States, and twice he vetoed Clay-sponsored tariffs. Thrice he defeated distribution to the states of proceeds from public-land sales. All members of Harrison's cabinet, which Tyler inherited, resigned after six months—with the exception of Secretary of State Webster, who stayed on only long enough to complete ongoing negotiations over the border with Canada.

TYLER RECEIVING THE NEWS OF HARRISON'S DEATH.

This illustration depicts Vice President John Tyler receiving news of President Harrison's death. Tyler was the first president to succeed to the presidency through the event of the elected president's death. (Wikimedia Commons)

John Tyler found himself in the unenviable position of a president without a party. He did agree with Northern Whigs that the Independent Treasury law should be repealed, and this was accomplished in 1841—but his vetoes of Clay's tariff measures made him a deserter in their eyes. The Tariff of 1842, which Congress reluctantly passed and Tyler signed, was only mildly protective. Tyler also approved a General Preemption Act and cooperated more and more with Democrats, whose nomination he hoped to obtain in 1844. Northern Whigs and "border-staters" like Clay rued the day when "Tyler too" had been tapped to run with "Tippecanoe."

9.6g Features of American Democratic Growth

The years 1824–1844 were characterized by an increase in the number of elected office-holders, by a relative decrease in appointed officials at the state and local levels, and by some reflection of the popular will by the Supreme Court. There was, also, far greater participation in government than had been the case in prior eras. By the time the period was well launched, all states except one chose presidential electors by popular vote. The popular vote itself steadily increased from campaign to campaign, not only because the population was greater, but because such barriers as religious and property qualifications were gradually lowered on a state-by-state basis. Jacksonians regarded changes of these kinds as desirable reforms, whose democratizing purposes and spirit bore resemblances to the era's social reforms.

The development of democratic government was not without its growing pains. One of the most criticized aspects of the political scene was the **spoils system**, by which governmental posts were allotted as "spoils" of victory to members of the party triumphant at the polls. Under Monroe and Adams, a small coterie of federal clerks and minor administrators had held offices on what amounted to a lifetime good-conduct basis. Jackson removed a number of these perennials because they had played the partisan game against him, because they were corrupt and inefficient, or because he wanted to make room for partisans of his own. In 1832 when Senator William L. Marcy, a Jackson adherent, had remarked, "To the victor belong the spoils of the enemy." Jackson's enemies applied the phrase "spoils system" to Jackson's program of rewarding his political supporters with public office. Although the spoils system clearly leads to corruption and appointment of incompetent government officials, Jackson believed that most government jobs were so simple that they required little intellectual capacity and the damage was therefore mitigated.

Furthermore, during his entire presidency Jackson removed only a fifth of those holding office. Nevertheless, he did take a decisive step toward perpetuating an undesirable system. Jacksonians defended the policy as the quickest and surest path to reform. Yet for every Adams man like embezzler Tobias Watkins who was removed, Jackson's party contributed a scamp of its own—such as collector Samuel Swartwout of the port of New York, who embezzled more than $1 million.

National party conventions, which came into being with the Anti-Masonic assembly held in 1831, were thoroughly established in the political structure by the end of Jackson's second term. Sometimes they have resulted in the choice of second-rate candidates for first-rate posts, but in the main the decisions of conventions have been sound. They were, and are, more directly representative and democratic than "King Caucus" ever was. After momentarily striking a pose of aloofness from Jacksonian electioneering tactics, Whigs imitated their rivals by adopting slogans and symbols similar to Democratic ones. For over a century, styles of campaigning were patterned, to an appreciable degree, on the 1840 ballyhoo techniques that promoted "Tippecanoe and Tyler Too!"

During Jackson's administration the personal advisers on whom the president relied came to be known as the "kitchen cabinet" because they ostensibly conferred with Jackson more intimately than did members of his official cabinet. Later chief executives have followed Jackson's example by surrounding themselves with capable but unofficial counselors whose advice has supplemented, or even at times supplanted, that of department heads. It is doubtful that the "kitchen cabinet" would have originated as, and when, it did if Jackson had not owed his election in part to Calhounite Deep South support—which at least two cabinet members personified, but on which he chose not to rely once his administration was underway.

It would be a mistake to minimize the role of the West in the period 1824–1844. Public lands, the tariff, internal improvements, the United States Bank, and almost all other issues were of interest to westerners. The West had its own viewpoint, or viewpoints, of a predominantly sectional variety—yet it also exerted a nationalizing influence. The Southwest had much in common with the Northwest, and Jackson the Southwesterner proved himself a foremost nationalist who was supported as consistently in the Northwest as in any other portion of the country. Truly national political parties and affiliations had emerged and were here to stay.

Timeline

1819 — Supreme Court upholds the constitutionality of the Bank of the U.S. in *McCulloch v. Maryland.*

1824 — John Quincy Adams wins the presidential election in the House of Representatives with the "Corrupt Bargain" of 1824.

1826 — England closes the British West Indies to U.S. shipping.

Both John Adams and Thomas Jefferson die on July 4.

1828 — Andrew Jackson defeats John Quincy Adams in the presidential election.

John C. Calhoun writes the "South Carolina Exposition," claiming the right of states to nullify the federal tariff.

1829 — "King Mob," a group of unruly Jackson supporters, vandalizes the White House in the rain after Jackson's inauguration in March.

1830 — Webster-Hayne Debate

Congress passes the Indian Removal Act.

1831 — Eaton Affair disrupts Andrew Jackson's cabinet.

1832 — Andrew Jackson vetoes the renewal of the Bank of the United States.

Andrew Jackson wins reelection.

South Carolina legislature nullifies the federal tariff.

1834 — Jackson's opponents become the Whig Party.

Jackson issues an ultimatum to France to pay debts to the United States.

1835–1842 — Second Seminole War in Florida

1836 — Jackson's Specie Circular requires that all federal land be purchased with specie (gold or silver).

Martin Van Buren is elected president.

1837 — Andrew Jackson recognizes the Republic of Texas.

Panic of 1837 follows the real estate crash caused by Jackson's Specie Circular and the New York bank collapse.

The *Caroline* Affair and death of Amos Durfee

1840–41 — William Henry Harrison defeats Martin Van Buren for the presidency, but dies a month after his inauguration.

1841 — John Tyler assumes the presidency after the death of Harrison.

CHAPTER SUMMARY

new era of politics began to take shape in 1824 as support coalesced around Andrew Jackson, who won the most electoral votes. No candidate won a majority of the electoral votes in 1824, however; and John Quincy Adams was able to win the White House by making a "corrupt bargain" with Henry Clay, whereby Clay threw his support to Adams in return for being named secretary of state. Though a brilliant man and a hard worker, Adams would only serve one term, as the American economy sagged due to trade restrictions with Britain. The masses then swept General Andrew Jackson into the White House. Jackson's supporters, however, were quickly denounced as "King Mob" when they vandalized the White House while celebrating after Jackson's inaugural.

Jackson was a poorly educated, battle-hardened general, who used poor grammar, chewed tobacco, and drank; perhaps for these reasons, he related well with common Americans. Jackson brought numerous innovations to American politics, including party conventions as a way of nominating candidates, more liberal use of the veto, the pocket veto, the spoils system, and the removal of Native American tribes from the Southeast to Indian Territory (Oklahoma). Jackson and his supporters were typically advocates of states' rights; however, when South Carolina nullified the federal tariff within its borders in 1832, Jackson threatened to send two hundred thousand troops to South Carolina to enforce the tariff (though he simultaneously pushed Congress to lower it).

In economic policy, Jackson vetoed the renewal of the charter for the Bank of the U.S. in 1832, and then in 1836 decreed that federal land could only be purchased with specie (silver or gold). Jackson's actions led to a real estate and finance crash—followed by bank failures, unemployment, and a severe economic recession that would last into the 1840s and thus doom the presidency of his hand-picked successor, Martin Van Buren.

In foreign affairs, the impetuous Jackson almost caused war with France in 1834 over French nonpayment of debts. War was averted, essentially, because the French backed down and did not desire it. Meanwhile, Jackson delayed recognition of the Republic of Texas until his last day in office so as to avoid provoking a war with Mexico.

Shortly after Jackson left office, a Canadian rebellion against England almost dragged the U.S. into a war with England when the British attacked an American ship on the American side of the Niagara River and killed an American, Amos Durfee. When a British subject, Alexander McLeod, boasted of killing Durfee, he was arrested—but Britain threatened war if he was not released. War was averted when McLeod was acquitted because his boast had been false.

By 1840, opponents of Jacksonian politics coalesced into the Whig Party and nominated sixty-eight-year-old hero of the Battle of Tippecanoe, William Henry Harrison, for president. Harrison and his running mate John Tyler defeated Martin Van Buren during the continued economic recession, but Harrison died of pneumonia one month after his inauguration (after giving his inaugural speech with no coat and no hat on a cold day in Washington). John Tyler then assumed the presidency for the Whigs, but the patterns of mass politics and the spoils system ushered in by the Democrats under Andrew Jackson were here to stay.

KEY TERMS

BIBLIOGRAPHY

B

Bemis, Samuel F. *John Quincy Adams and the Foundations of American Foreign Policy*. New York: W. W. Norton & Company, 1973.

———. *John Quincy Adams and the Union*. Westport, CT: Greenwood Press, 1980.

Benson, Lee. *The Concept of Jeffersonian Democracy: New York: A Test Case*. Princeton, NJ: Princeton University Press, 1961.

Billington, Ray Allen. *The Protestant Crusade 1800–1860*. New York: Rinehart, 1938.

Brinkley, Alan. *American History: A Survey*. 11th ed. Boston, MA: McGraw-Hill, 2003.

C

Cash, W. J. *The Mind of the South*. New York: Knopf, 1941.

Craven, Avery. *The Coming of the Civil War*. New York: Scribner, 1942.

Crenson, Matthew A. *The Federal Machine: Beginnings of Bureaucracy in Jacksonian America*. Baltimore, MD: Johns Hopkins University Press, 1975.

Cross, Barbara ed. *The Autobiography of Lyman Beecher*. Cambridge, MA: Harvard University Press, 1961.

Current, Richard N. *Daniel Webster and the Rise of National Conservatism*. Boston, MA: Little, Brown, 1955.

D

Davis, David Brian. "Some Themes of Counter-Subversion: An Analysis of Anti-Masonic, Anti-Catholic and Anti-Mormon Literature." *Mississippi Valley Historical Review*. XLVII, 1960.

Donald, David. *Lincoln Reconsidered*. New York: Vintage, 1961.

F

Farquhar, Michael. *Great American Scandals*. New York: Penguin, 2003.

Ferguson, James E. *Power of the Purse: A History of American Public Finance*. Chapel Hill, NC: University of North Carolina Press, 1961.

Fischer, David Hackett. *The Revolution of American Conservatism*. Chicago, IL: University of Chicago Press, 1975.

Freehling, William W. *Prelude to Civil War: The Nullification Controversy in South Carolina 1816–1836*. New York: Oxford University Press, 1992.

G

Garraty, John A., and Robert McCaughey. *The American Nation: A History of the United States Since 1865*. 6th ed. New York: HarperCollins, 1987.

Gould, Lewis L. *Grand Old Party: A History of Republicans*. New York: Random House, 2003.

H

Hammond, Bray. *Banks and Politics in America from the Revolution to the Civil War*. Princeton, NJ: Princeton University Press, 1991.

Hofstadter, Richard. *The Rise of Legitimate Opposition in the United States 1780–1840*. Berkeley, CA: University of California Press, 1970.

Howe, Daniel Walker. *The Political Culture of the American Whigs*. Chicago, IL: University of Chicago Press, 1979.

J

Jacoby, Susan. *Freethinkers: A History of American Secularism*. New York: Henry Holt, 2004.

Jones, Howard. *Crucible of Power: A History of American Foreign Relations to 1913*. Lanham, MD: Rowman and Littlefield, 2009.

K

Ketcham, Ralph. *Presidents Above Party: The First American Presidency, 1789–1829*. Chapel Hill, NC: University of North Carolina Press, 1987.

L

Lence, Ross M., ed. *Union and Liberty: The Political Philosophy of John C. Calhoun*. Indianapolis, IN: Liberty Fund, 1995.

Lipset, Seymour Martin, and Earl Raab. *The Politics of Unreason: Right-Wing Extremism in America, 1790–1970*. New York: Harper and Row, 1970.

M

Meacham, John. *American Lion: Andrew Jackson in the White House*. New York: Random House, 2009.

Miner, Brad. *The Concise Conservative Encyclopedia*. New York: Simon and Schuster, 1996.

Muccigrosso, Robert. *Basic History of Conservatism*. Melbourne, FL: Krieger, 2003.

Muller, Jerry Z. *Conservatism: An Anthology of Social and Political Thought from David Hume to the Present*. Princeton, NJ: Princeton University Press, 1997.

BIBLIOGRAPHY

A

Nagel, Paul C. *John Quincy Adams: A Public Life, A Private Life*. Cambridge, MA: Harvard University Press, 1999.

Nagle, Robert. *American Conservatism: An Illustrated History*. New York: Allied Books, 1988.

Newmyer, R. Kent. *The Supreme Court Under Marshall and Taney*. New York: Harlan Davidson, 2006.

Nichols, Roy F. *The Disruption of American Democracy*. New York: Collier, 1962.

O

Oren, Michael B. *Power, Faith, and Fantasy: America in the Middle East 1776 to the Present*. New York: W. W. Norton & Company, 2007.

P

Perdue, Theda, and Michael Green. *The Cherokee Removal: A Brief History with Documents*. 2nd ed. Boston, MA: Bedford/St. Martin's 2005.

R

Remini, Robert V. *Andrew Jackson and His Indian Wars*. New York: Penguin, 2002.

S

Schlesinger, Arthur, Jr. *The Age of Jackson*. New York: Little, Brown, 1945.

Schlesinger, Arthur, Jr., Gil Troy and Fred L. Israel. *History of American Presidential Elections, 1789–2008*. New York: Facts on File, 2011.

Sellers, Charles. *The Market Revolution: Jacksonian America 1815–1846*. New York: Oxford University Press, 1993.

Sharp, James R. *American Politics in the Early Republic: The New Nation in Crisis*. New Haven, CT: Yale University Press, 1993.

Stagg, J. C. A. *Politics, Diplomacy, and Warfare in the Early Republic*. Princeton, NJ: Princeton University Press, 1983.

W

White, Leonard B. *The Jeffersonians: A Study in Administrative History, 1801–1829*. New York: Macmillan, 1961.

POP QUIZ

1. The candidate who won the most votes before the election went to the House of Representatives in 1824 was _____.
   a. Andrew Jackson
   b. John Quincy Adams
   c. William Crawford
   d. Henry Clay

2. In 1828, what claim did Andrew Jackson's political opponents make?
   a. that Jackson was living with his wife Rachel before her divorce from her husband was final
   b. that Jackson was an intellectual elite
   c. that Jackson was a billiard-playing aristocrat
   d. that Jackson was a draft dodger in the War of 1812

3. In 1831, why did Andrew Jackson ask for the resignation of several cabinet members?
   a. They were disloyal to Andrew Jackson.
   b. They were disloyal to America.
   c. Their wives socially snubbed the wife of Secretary of War John Eaton.
   d. They had lied under oath before Congress.

4. Which of the following arguments did Jackson make against the Bank of the United States?
   a. It was unconstitutional.
   b. It influenced congressmen by loaning them money or placing them on its payroll.
   c. It was controlled by foreigners.
   d. All of the above

5. Why did the Whigs choose that particular party name?
   a. They favored the wearing of periwigs.
   b. They supported "King Andrew" Jackson as the "Whigs" in England had supported the King.
   c. They opposed "King Andrew" Jackson, and the "Whigs" in England had favored limiting the King's power.
   d. They opposed the wearing of periwigs.

6. Andrew Jackson was the first president to use the pocket veto. What did the pocket veto allow?
   a. During the last ten days of a congressional session, if the president does not sign a bill, the bill dies.
   b. The president may veto specific lines in appropriations bills.
   c. The president may protest a bill by not signing it, but it becomes a law in ten days without his signature.

   d. The president can nullify acts of Congress within the District of Columbia.

7. Characteristics of Jacksonian democracy included which of the following?
   a. the expansion of democracy with more men participating fully in the democratic process
   b. equal rights for Native Americans
   c. states rights and nullification
   d. all of the above

8. Which of the following is true of the congressional assimilationist policy toward the Indians in 1819?
   a. Congress granted $10,000 annually to missionary associations in an attempt to convert the American Indians to Christianity.
   b. The program included a campaign to teach the American Indians the English language.
   c. The program included the teaching of traditional gender roles.
   d. All of the above

9. Which of the following is true of the Supreme Court ruling in *Worcester v. Georgia*?
   a. The Cherokee nation was recognized as a sovereign entity with its own territory in which the laws of Georgia had no force.
   b. The ruling was ignored by President Andrew Jackson.
   c. The Court's decision allowed the Cherokees to evade removal to Oklahoma.
   d. Both a and b

10. The British claimed the right to attack the *Caroline* in U.S. waters based on _____.
    a. the Doctrine of Continuous Voyage
    b. the "rule of 56"
    c. the principle established by Jackson's invasion of Florida in 1818
    d. the rule of preemption

11. Clay's American System called for more money for the military. T F

12. Jackson's veto of the Bank bill had little impact on the economy. T F

13. In the 1836 election, three Whigs ran for the presidency. T F

14. Martin Van Buren wanted an _____ _____ to replace the Bank of the United States.

15. _____ _____ died only one month after his inauguration.

ANSWER KEY:
1.a 2.a 3.c 4.d 5.c 6.a 7.a 8.d 9.d 10.c 11.F 12.F 13.T 14. Independent treasury 15. William Henry Harrison

Chapter 10

(Wikimedia Commons)

American Culture Comes of Age

10.1 Laying the Groundwork

10.1a The Excitement of Progress

In the half-century preceding 1830, the United States had made great progress in establishing itself as a viable nation. The victory at Yorktown, the Constitution, the Bill of Rights, the Louisiana Purchase, the Battle of New Orleans, the Missouri Compromise, and the Monroe Doctrine—all were landmarks that had been passed within the memory of many citizens still living in 1830. The increase in the population, the growth of the national domain, and the development of cities and industries were only a few reasons for Americans' sense of gratification.

The wonder was that one could see such substantial cultural growth in so short a time. At the close of the Jacksonian Era, only about six decades had elapsed since the eventful months of the ratification of the Constitution—yet distinctive intellectual, artistic, and scientific progress had been made, especially during the most recent twenty years. Authors, artists, and scientists already were giving eloquent and sustained proof of the richness and variety of American life and thought. Ordinary Americans were participating and they and their descendants reaped the benefits.

10.16 Technological Change and Economic Development

Such heady developments should not obscure the fact that the majority of Americans lived simple lives. In the decades before the Civil War, most Americans were still farmers, and most farms were still small—but, subtly or abruptly, what happened on them from dawn to dusk was changing.

Since the arrival of Europeans in the New World, the amount of physical labor required to convert wild land into cultivated fields had limited agricultural productivity. The agriculturalists of the eastern United States had spent countless hours swinging axes against trees, removing stumps, and digging rocks out of their fields. As Americans claimed land further into the West, rainfall declined—but so did the number of trees. Also, much of the soil in the West was less rocky than that in the east, especially when compared to rocky New England. In 1813, **Richard B. Chenaworth** developed a cast iron plow made in three separate pieces that made the replacement of broken parts. possible. The plow was used with success in the east; however, the heavy western soils would stick to the cast-iron plow, which then proved too brittle to break the ground of the western prairies. In 1837, **John Deere** patented a steel plow that provided a solution for breaking western land.

In 1834, **Cyrus McCormick** patented the mechanical reaper, which greatly reduced the labor involved in harvesting grain. Prior to McCormick's invention, farmers still cut grain by hand, swinging cradles that cut swathes through the grain. The cut grain was then gathered in sheaves and hauled away for threshing. The mechanization of this process through the use of McCormick's reaper greatly increased agricultural production. With the coming of the cast-iron plow, the steel plow, and the mechanical reaper, more food and fiber could be produced on the same amount of land. This led many farmers to acquire and cultivate more soil. It also meant that increasing numbers of them, no longer essential agriculturally, would be free to move to cities—mainly in the Northeast—where mills and factories were springing up.

No invention wrought more changes in everyday living than the steam engine, invented by **Oliver Evans** in 1802. Machines found their way into diverse settings, most importantly the new factories that were located in towns and small cities in the eastern United States, thereby transforming rural people into urbanized workers with year-around income. Prior to the steam engine, it was virtually impossible for anyone to build a factory away from a river because factories were powered by water wheels attached to interconnected systems of wheels and belts. The steam engine provided a power source that allowed the construction of factories in locations never before possible. Steam-propelled riverboats, with their cheap and smooth transportation, sped the expansion of river cities like Cincinnati and St. Louis. Railways, from the 1830s and 1840s on, were to have a similar impact on inland communities. One of the most amazing changes, barely beginning in this period, was the coming together of ship and rail traffic, notably at a spot where a small village named Chicago was incorporated in 1837.

In 1830, the first steam locomotive was built in America. By 1860, thirty thousand miles of rail had been laid—more miles of track than in all the rest of the world combined. (Wikimedia Commons)

The first steam locomotive (a European invention) built in America was that of **Peter Cooper** in 1830. By 1850, nine thousand miles of rail had been laid, most of it on the eastern seaboard. By 1860, thirty thousand miles of rail had been laid—more than had been laid in the rest of the world combined. Railroads also made tremendous ripples in the American economy at large. Trains traveling at twenty miles per hour allowed farmers in far-flung locations to get their produce to market before it spoiled. The railroads also allowed areal agricultural specialization, as different places could import a variety of agricultural products rather than growing everything themselves. Railroads stimulated western movement and the development of frontier towns as water stops for the trains. The railroads also stimulated the production of iron, steel, coal, and timber to meet the needs of the trains. Railroads aided in the development of the telegraph industry as telegraph lines were built alongside railroad tracks, so the railroad men could signal by telegraph from any location as to whether or not there were problems with tracks or anything else.

The railroads were essentially financed by federal land grants to private railroad corporations. The federal government granted to the railroads up to six square miles of land for every mile of track laid by the railroad corporation. The railroads then sold their land to settlers for profits, thus both financing the railroad operation and spurring settlement of the American West. By 1860, Congress had granted twenty million acres of federal land to the railroads, thus providing great wealth to the railroads that would last for decades.

The railroads also stimulated the American banking system because the building of the railroads required large amounts of capital. There were less than a hundred state chartered banks in the U.S. at the close of the War of 1812, but by 1830 there were over three hundred. Banks stimulated the economy by making loans to railroads, manufacturers, and merchants, thus expanding the money supply and enabling the expansion of America's rail, manufacturing, and commerce.

Other scientific thought and technological action had similar economic and social impact. **Samuel F. B. Morse**, an admirable portrait painter, invented the telegraph and sent his first message in 1844. For the first time in human history, communication over long distances became instantaneous. **Charles Goodyear** discovered the process known as the **vulcanization** of rubber, which made rubber much more useful by preventing it from sticking and melting in hot weather. Goodyear's process made possible the manufacture of a wide array of rubber products, most notably the overshoe. From the mind and skill of **Samuel Colt** came the first practical firearm with a revolving chamber, and Elias Howe is given credit for the first sewing machine. Indeed, the sewing machine reminds us that during this period there were countless other inventions of a more humble nature that changed the nature of housework, such as the first appearance of the cast iron stove for cooking—as opposed to cooking over an open hearth.

During this period, too, medical and dental pioneers in Georgia and New England helped ease the suffering of future millions by applying anesthesia during surgery. In 1842 Crawford Long was the first to administer ether in surgery, thus reducing both pain and the risk of patients going into shock. William Beaumont, an American army doctor on the Michigan frontier, was the first student of gastric digestion in a living patient; and Oliver Wendell Holmes, the Massachusetts poet-physician, saved the lives of countless mothers and babies by showing that antiseptics could prevent puerperal ("child-bed") fever.

Because of these technological changes, the growth of industrial production, and improved transportation, more and more goods that previously had been produced at home began to be commercially available—including soap, textiles, and men's clothing. This, in turn, meant that the women who had traditionally produced them could now fill their days with other activities: they had more time to read, for example, and more time for needlework of an aesthetic nature. They also began to join a variety of new organizations—some church affiliated, and others of an explicitly reformist nature.

Samuel F. B. Morse
Invented the telegraph

Charles Goodyear
Discovered the process known as vulcanization of rubber

Vulcanization
Makes rubber more useful by preventing it from becoming too sticky in hot weather

Samuel Colt
Invented the pistol revolver

The invention of the telegraph (a replica of the first telegraph is shown here) enabled instantaneous communication over long distances for the first time in human history. (Associated Press)

10.2 The Role of Reformers

10.2a American Women

By twenty-first-century standards, white women in the early nineteenth century endured a harsh existence with very inequitable treatment. Most of them spent their lives at hard, repetitious labor, whether in frontier cabins, isolated farm houses, or urban dwellings—though their work was being somewhat lightened by the availability of new commercial goods. Some left farms and villages to tend machines in such new "mill towns" as Lowell and Lawrence, Massachusetts, where the primary form of employment was in textile mills. Recently arrived immigrant girls took menial jobs—often as domestic servants—in Atlantic seaboard cities and interior communities.

Certain legal restrictions on women carried over from earlier periods into the Jacksonian Era and even into the twentieth century. Women still could not vote, and property rights of wives were circumscribed at best. Often, wives were prevented by law from controlling their own inheritances. With rare exceptions, women—no matter how talented or ambitious—found themselves excluded from most professions. Yet in these years, amid the legal and social limitations, women began to lay the groundwork for considerable progress.

The 1820s, 1830s, and 1840s marked the start of major reforms, many of them spearheaded by women. Fundamental to these efforts was the improved education being extended to girls in hundreds of private female academies that had emerged all over the United States. Beginning in the 1830s, states began to open teacher training academies (known as **normal schools**) exclusively for female students. Many noteworthy female reformers—women's rights advocate **Elizabeth Cady Stanton** being the prime example—had attended one of the new academies.

Oberlin College in Ohio began admitting white women and black men in 1851, and graduated its first women in 1855. No other colleges admitted women until after the Civil War, but several private "female seminaries" were established to provide college-equivalent education to women. Emma Willard, who founded Troy Seminary in New York in 1821, and Mary Lyon, who founded Mount Holyoke in Massachusetts in 1837, were the two most well-known pioneer educators. Mention should also be made of Catherine Beecher, sister of the novelist **Harriet Beecher Stowe**, who founded the Hartford Seminary in Connecticut. Harriet Beecher Stowe, who taught at the Hartford Seminary, argued that women are better teachers than men. In the words of Stowe, "If men have more knowledge, they have less talent at communicating it. Nor have they the patience, the long-suffering, and gentleness necessary to superintend the formation of character."

Women also became involved in the abolitionist movement. Sarah and Angelina Grimké, of a prominent South Carolina family, were among many who crusaded in the North for the abolition of slavery—and thereby challenged the taboo against respectable women speaking in public. The Grimkés were among the first, but they would be followed by many other courageous women, white and black alike. **Dorothea Dix** founded facilities to help the mentally ill. Many women were also widely known as writers and editors. It was an augury of the future when Elizabeth Blackwell entered medical school in the 1840s, becoming the first woman to receive a Doctor of Medicine degree (M.D.) in 1849.

Above all, these years were distinguished by the first appearance of a women's suffrage movement, launched at the **Seneca Falls Conference** in New York in 1848. The two women who called the meeting, Elizabeth Cady Stanton and Lucretia Mott, had first met at an anti-slavery convention in London in 1840. There they had been denied the right of full participation because of their gender. This slight rankled both women. When they met again in the upstate New York town where Stanton lived with her husband and four children, they decided to call a meeting for a week hence—the first national women's rights convention in the United States—and thereby inaugurated what would become a revolution in gender mores. Stanton drew up a document, modeled on the Declaration of Independence, to present to the approximately three hundred people who attended the meeting. In this "Declaration of Sentiments," she announced that "all men *and women* are created equal" and cited eighteen specific injuries that women suffered at the hands of men (as Jefferson had adduced evidence against George III), including the denial of access to the professions and to higher education. Stanton stated, "the history of mankind is a history of repeated injuries and usurpations on the part of man toward woman, having in direct object the establishment of an absolute tyranny over her." Stanton added that through the doctrine of male supremacy men had "endeavored in every way they could to destroy her confidence in her own powers, to lessen her self-respect, and to make her willing to lead a dependent and abject life." Stanton demanded that women be granted all the rights and privileges that men had as U.S. citizens, including, most radical of all, the vote—then seen as belonging entirely to "the male sphere."

The great black abolitionist, **Frederick Douglass**, was in attendance; and he spoke on behalf of women's suffrage, which the delegates voted to support after a lively debate. It would be decades before suffrage was attained; yet many of the other items on the list, such as a married woman's right to control her own property, began to be redressed in that era. From 1848 forward, through the perseverance of many, a network of women's rights advocates emerged. Over twenty other women's rights conventions would be assembled before the Civil War, each also calling for the franchise. It was not yet a social movement, and its progress would be interrupted by the Civil War, but it was the beginning of one.

Frederick Douglass

African American former slave who became an abolitionist orator and writer, published *Narrative of the Life of Frederick Douglass* (1845), and published an abolitionist newspaper, *The North Star*

10.26 Fighting Ills, Woes, and Evils

That so much humanitarian reform was taking place in the mid-nineteenth century was in many ways due to religious changes. In brief, the older emphasis on original sin and human depravity was giving way to a more optimistic set of beliefs in human possibility—doctrines that were appearing in many sectors of American Protestantism. The theory and practice of democracy, when carried to their logical conclusions, likewise led humanitarians to devote days, years, and even lifetimes to helping unfortunates. Numerous reformers were motivated, also, by the desire to impose order on the fast-changing society of which they were a part. Finally, we should consider the influence of the Romantic Movement, with its emphasis on the individual's insights, intuitions, and personal responsibilities.

Sylvester Graham

Inventor of the graham cracker, who favored better living through celibacy and better diet, hygiene, and exercise

Just as not everyone was politically active, the number of steadfast participants in some of these reforms was small, but with enough Americans believing in human perfectibility to make reform a key characteristic of this period. The zeal of reformers, both men and women, found many targets in the very nation where so many opportunities for improvement and advancement beckoned. The number of people arriving from Europe, particularly from the 1840s on, was larger than America could neatly accommodate. Many immigrants, poor and uneducated, crowded into port cities where they received low wages for long hours and lived in squalor in what came to be known as slums.

Attempts to cope with such problems in 1824–1854 proved rudimentary and unsuccessful, on the whole. Most of the effort to improve the lot of urban workers came from the relatively weak labor unions. The unions consisted mainly of skilled artisans, who were primarily interested principally in bettering their own lot—not that of the unskilled newcomers. In general, the chief gain for both groups stemmed from workers' demands for free public schools, which were established in New York in 1832 and Philadelphia two years later.

Both urban and rural Americans ate too much fatty meat, too many fried foods, and too few fruits and vegetables. Reformers like **Sylvester Graham**, for whom Graham bread and graham crackers were named, did their best to promote dietary change. In the 1830s, Graham argued that the keys to better health could be found through proper diet, exercise, and hygiene. Graham also argued, however, that celibacy was essential to proper health and that women should have intercourse only for procreation. A medical doctor and associate of Graham's added that women ought not to be educated because the blood needed for procreation would be diverted to the head, thus breeding "puny men." As for men, Graham's associate argued that semen was not to be expelled, but should be saved for reproductive purposes and should not be used for pleasure either in masturbation or in intercourse. Such use of semen, the doctor argued, would lead to "enervation, disease, insanity, and death." Furthermore, the doctor argued that expenditure of sperm would mean a loss of needed energy from the economy and that such a diversion of energy from business to sex was wasteful and a contributor to social disorder.

Heavy drinking in America, by children and teenagers as well as by adults, had been appalling (by modern standards) ever since colonial times. In the words of one historian, "A house could not be raised, a field of wheat cut down, nor could there be a log-rolling, husking, quilting, a wedding, or a funeral, without alcohol." The early nineteenth century witnessed the beginning of a movement against the abuse of alcohol. Many men, women, and children "took the pledge" that they would drink no more alcoholic beverages. Then as now, of course, there was cynicism as to how well such pledges would be kept; vast improvements in drinking habits did occur, however, in the Jacksonian period—far more than with respect to eating.

Horace Mann

The leading proponent
of public education in
Massachusetts in the
1820s and secretary of the
Massachusetts State Board of
Education (1837–1849)

Reformers similarly progressed substantially in many other areas. One was the struggle to eliminate imprisonment for debt. Headway was also made in the movement to end the traditional flogging of wayward sailors. The horrors of war anywhere and everywhere led Elihu Burritt, the learned blacksmith of Connecticut, to champion the cause of pacifism. Thomas H. Gallaudet labored ably on behalf of the deaf. Samuel G. Howe, with equal dedication, educated the deaf and the blind. Finally, **Horace Mann** was an effective crusader for public education in Massachusetts.

10.2c Progress in Education

Among the most striking reforms of the Jacksonian period were those in the field of education. If some citizens objected to paying for the instruction of other people's children, most of them—at least in the Northeast—endorsed the drive for public schools below the college level. The impetus came from sources as contrasting as Harvard graduates and New York union members. Parents from all spheres wanted their sons and daughters to have the educational exposure they themselves had lacked.

As a member of the Massachusetts legislature in the 1830s, Horace Mann persuaded the legislature to provide support for the schools in the form of taxation and to establish a state board of education, of which he became the head. Mann argued that private property was actually held in trust for the good of the community and therefore "is pledged for the education of all its youth up to such a point as will save them from poverty and vice, and prepare them for the adequate performance of their social and civil duties." Mann's argument for public education as a means to teach morality, discipline, and order to potential ruffians and revolutionaries convinced the middle and upper classes to support the funding of education with tax money. As a consequence, the public schools of the nineteenth century taught not only math, English, and science but also the Protestant values of industry, punctuality, sobriety, and frugality stressed in William Holmes McGuffey's *McGuffey's Eclectic Readers* (1836). Millions of American children learned to read while also learning of the terrible consequences of sloth, drunkenness,

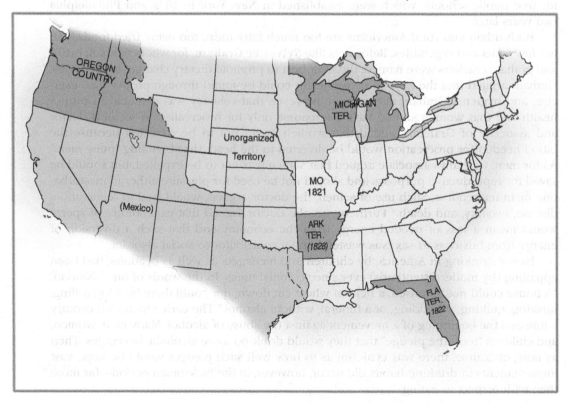

Map 10.1 Territorial Growth (1830)

or wastefulness, taught in McGuffey's parables. Critical thinking, however, was largely ignored. More and more children grew familiar with Noah Webster's excellent grammar and speller, young Americans read and memorized the offerings of McGuffey, and some of the finest literature of the ages became part of their consciousness.

Public grade and high schools did not spread evenly across the face of the land, however. Primary and secondary education in rural regions was handicapped by the long distances separating farm families, with the resultant problem of assembling students under one roof. As there were more situations of this sort in the South and West than in the Northeast, it was Southern and Western girls and boys living outside towns and cities who were most frequently deprived of the advantages of public education. Wealthy parents tried to compensate by sending their children to private academies or by hiring tutors for them, but this practice was of no help to any but the well-to-do.

In higher education, prestige continued to be identified with Harvard, Yale, and Princeton. The University of Virginia admitted its first students in 1825. Generally, however, small denominational colleges were more typical, making Latin, Greek, and mathematics available in out-of-the-way places. Such institutions received marginal support from their respective churches.

There were few medical schools, and fewer still in engineering. Most young lawyers got their training in older attorneys' offices. Nevertheless, sons of farm and village families had opportunities denied their fathers—even though few state universities thrived. The era also provided a beginning for the higher education of women when coeducation was inaugurated at Ohio's Oberlin College in the 1830s.

10.2b Communitarianism

For some idealists, devotion to reforms *within* established society could not suffice. A small minority of American men and women looked upon the current social order—in which the majority toiled and suffered so many privations and indignities—as so utterly harsh and materialistic that it should be forsaken in favor of communitarianism. The communitarians' idea was for a limited number of people to live together in a little community, wholly or mainly self-sufficient and more or less apart from the general society surrounding it.

These communities could be either religious or secular. Among the Christian **communitarians** were the Shakers, who believed in separation from the cruel and wicked world, in simplicity of language, and in celibacy. The Shakers founded settlements in New England, New York, Kentucky, and elsewhere. Religious communities were also sponsored by the Mormons and by several Adventist sects.

Secular communities resembled the Christian communities in that the purpose was to join people together so as to face collectively the challenge of the frontier or to confront collectively the trends toward industrialization. Many secular communities had their philosophical bases in the social contract theories of the eighteenth century. Among the secular experiments were New Harmony in Indiana, the North American Phalanx in New Jersey, and Fruitlands in Massachusetts.

A number of free thinkers inaugurated a Massachusetts community named Brook Farm, known for its intellectually talented members that included George and Sophia Ripley. Though Brook Farm was a communitarian working farm where women and men were all paid equally, Sophia Ripley opened a private school that became so successful that it became the community's most important source of income. One Brook Farm resident, a French theorist named Charles Fourier, published a journal, the *Harbinger,* in which he expounded on his socialist ideas. Unfortunately, Brook Farm was devastated by a fire in 1847 and forced to close.

10.2c Oneida Community

One of the longest-lived religious communities was Oneida, founded in upstate New York by **John Humphrey Noyes**. Deeply religious, Noyes also believed in a system of "complex marriage," which was a rejection of monogamy. Noyes argued that the root of evil was in marriage and in "men's conviction that women are their private property." Noyes also argued that when the will of God is done on earth as it is in heaven, there

Communitarians
Those who believed in the sharing of income and property in small, (mostly) self-sufficient communities

John Humphrey Noyes
Founded a community in Oneida, New York, based on "complete sharing" and "complex marriage"

BVT Lab

Flashcards are available for this chapter at www.BVTLab.com.

will be no marriage on earth because Jesus stated that in heaven people do not marry. In order to reproduce this vision of heaven on earth, Noyes advocated complete sharing in family relationships as a step toward what he called "perfect cooperation." That being the case, Noyes and his fifty-one followers shared everything, both economically and sexually. Child rearing was the responsibility of the entire community and there was no differentiation of gender roles in work. All private property was relinquished to the community.

In Noyes' "complex marriage," every "saved" man was married to every "saved" woman. All who were "saved" were considered to be without sin. Although Noyes preached complete sharing of everything, he also decreed that only certain "spiritually advanced" males were allowed to have sex and father children. Noyes also taught that women could become "spiritually advanced" through sex with "spiritually advanced" males; he considered himself to be "first husband," helping many women to "spiritual advancement." One Oneida community woman, Mary Cragin, appears to have been one of Noyes' favorite partners; she described her sexual experiences with Noyes as spiritual experiences as well. In the words of Cragin,

> In view of God's goodness to me and of his desire that I should let him fill me with himself, I yield and offer myself, to be penetrated by his spirit, and desire that love and gratitude may inspire my heart so that I shall sympathize with his pleasure in the thing, before my personal pleasure begins, knowing that it will increase my capability for happiness.

JOHN HUMPHREY NOYES
About 1850

John Humphrey Noyes founded the Oneida community, which rejected traditional Christian beliefs, including monogamy, and lived as a community who shared everything—both economically and sexually. Noyes and his followers believed that sharing in family relationships was a step toward "perfect cooperation." (Wikimedia Commons)

Noyes also argued that sex should be a public act that could be performed in public to the pleasure of all, much like music or dancing. Noyes even argued that watching such public sex would give pleasure to "older people who have nothing to do in the matter." To his credit, in addition to these oddities, Noyes also tried a number of expedients to give women more freedom, such as communal nurseries. Oneida lasted from 1848 to 1879, when Noyes fled to Canada to avoid prosecution for adultery. After that, his followers abandoned complex marriage and set up an animal trap, silverware, and kitchenware manufacturing enterprise that has survived into the present.

The Oneida community was consistent with other religious and secular communitarian groups in that it had such features as vegetarianism, prohibition of alcoholic beverages, equitable division of labor, and community ownership and control of property.

Most secular experiments did not last long, perhaps owing to an absence of explicitly Christian zeal that, in the case of the Mormons and the Shakers, proved a reliable source of community strength. In all, only a few thousand people committed themselves to communitarianism—but this handful of communities has received much attention, then and since, because they embodied visionary goals of social justice perhaps inspired by Charles Fourier at Brook Farm, or in the case of New Harmony, by the ideas of the British thinker, Robert Owen.

10.2f Religion and the People

Religion played an important part in the lives of average Americans. While the Baptist and Methodist churches had more members than any others, the Presbyterian, Congregational, Episcopal, and other denominations also appealed to substantial segments of the population. Sunday schools constituted a standard medium for indoctrinating the young, and Methodists and Baptists were successful in developing black congregations.

Religious diversity should likewise be stressed. With the influx of Irish and German immigrants by the hundreds of thousands during the 1840s and 1850s, growing numbers of Americans adhered to the Roman Catholic and Lutheran faiths. Supplementing churches with European origins were indigenous ones like the Disciples of Christ, Mormons, and Seventh Day Adventists.

Widespread evangelistic endeavors also characterized the era. Especially in the South and West, the example of Bishop Francis Asbury inspired his Methodist successors to "ride the circuit" and present in graphic language the punishments for sin and the rewards of salvation. In the East and then in Ohio and Indiana, Lyman Beecher and his sons preached powerful Calvinistic sermons and attacked such social ills as dueling and alcoholic indulgence.

More popular than any other evangelist in the West and North, Charles Grandison Finney, in countless revival meetings, emphasized the individual's ability to repent. Salvation, Finney believed, represented only the start of a useful life—the person saved should then save others. Finney's theology, lacking the orthodox Calvinistic tenet of predestination, won converts by the tens of thousands.

No longer were clergymen as apt as in the past to bewail a "low state" of American Protestantism. No longer did religion—as in the 1790s—appear to be removed from the masses in Middle Atlantic and other communities, with church memberships declining and the dissensions and arguments of ministers severely damaging their sects. If—as the French traveler **Alexis de Tocqueville** thought in the 1830s—religion was the foremost American institution, there were solid reasons for its number one rank. The **Second Great Awakening**, which had begun with the turn of the century, continued into the time of de Tocqueville's visit; and its spiritual force was felt long after that.

The evangelists of the Second Great Awakening did much of their preaching and exhorting outside the doors of churches, reaching the people at huge camp meetings in the countryside or at medium-sized revivals. Nevertheless, a significant part of their ultimate effect was to lead zealous converts into Baptist and other church folds, where continuing inspiration, strength, and comfort could be found.

There was also a close relationship between the assailing and reforming of social sins and the Protestant Ethic concept of hard work as a glorification of God. The excitement of economic progress and the challenge of technology had an undeniable identification with thrift, industry, and self-discipline. So it was not accidental that Christianity was far from being a Sunday-only affair in the Jacksonian period. Both rural and urban faithful attended prayer meetings on week nights. Grace was said before meals in innumerable homes, and devotional services were held in family circles with parents and children devoutly kneeling.

Alexis de Tocqueville

Frenchman who toured America and published his observations in *Democracy in America* in 1835

Second Great Awakening

Religious revival in the early- to mid-nineteenth century

William Miller

Founder of the Seventh Day Adventists who predicted that Jesus would return on March 21, 1843

Charles Grandison Finney was a Presbyterian evangelist and the most popular preacher in the West and North. Finney emphasized a sinner's ability to repent and won tens of thousands of converts. (Wikimedia Commons)

10.2g William Miller and the Millerites

A preoccupation with the expected return of Christ also experienced a boost in the mid-nineteenth century when **William Miller**, a farmer from upstate New York, claimed in 1842 that he had mathematically calculated the exact time of the second coming of Christ as March 21, 1843. According to Miller, the correct meaning of Daniel 8:14—which states that "the sanctuary will be cleansed after 2,300 days"—was that the earth would be destroyed by fire 2,300 years after the prophecy, thus mandating Christ's return in 1843. Miller also concluded that the earth would be six thousand years old on that date.

Miller published his conclusions in the 1830s and began preaching at churches and camp meetings, rapidly building a following. It is estimated that by 1843 some fifty thousand Americans believed Miller's predictions and that an estimated million more expected "something" to happen. Miller and his followers gave away their worldly belongings in March 1843, donned white robes, and flocked to the hills and tops of buildings to wait for Jesus' return. March 21, 1843, passed without incident, however, causing Miller to recalculate several times—but each time Christ did not return.

Miller died in 1848 as a discredited prophet. His followers continued to adhere to his teaching that Christians must still "Remember the Sabbath and Keep it Holy," and therefore must worship on Saturday (instead of Sunday) and perform no work on that day. Miller's followers eventually became known as the Seventh Day Adventists, who continue in the twenty-first century to honor the Sabbath as Miller instructed.

William Miller's prophetic time chart from 1843 about the prophecies of Daniel and Revelation. Miller claimed, in 1842, that he had mathematically calculated the exact time of the second coming of Christ as March 21, 1843. Miller began the movement that developed into the religious denomination, the Seventh-day Adventists. (Wikimedia Commons)

10.2f] Mormons

Joseph Smith
Founder of the Mormon Church who dictated the *Book of Mormon*

Perhaps no new religious group of the early nineteenth century has placed a greater stamp on America than the Mormons, founded by **Joseph Smith** of Palmyra, New York, in the 1820s. Smith claimed to have been visited by the Angel Moroni, who along with his horoscope led Smith to dig on a particular day for some golden plates buried in the ground near his home. Written on the plates in an indecipherable language Smith described as "reformed Egyptian" were more than five hundred pages of the *Book of the Mormon*. Smith also uncovered two sacred stones, Urim and Thummim, with which he could interpret the plates.

Smith then went about the business of interpreting the plates and dictated the *Book of Mormon* to a scribe who wrote down what Smith interpreted from behind a curtain. Some witnesses were amazed that Smith could interpret the plates using the sacred stones while the plates themselves remained under a sheet. At least eight other people testified, however, that they had personally seen the plates before Smith returned them to the Angel Moroni.

The plates described the one true church and a "lost tribe of Israel" that had been missing for centuries. The *Book of Mormon* essentially provided an explanation for something that had bewildered Christians everywhere for centuries: how the Native Americans had come to be in the Western Hemisphere. The Native Americans were explained in the *Book of Mormon* to be the lost tribe of Israel, and it was explained that Jesus Christ had come to America after his Resurrection and preached to the American Indians. Independence, Missouri, was identified as the original sight of the Garden of Eden. The *Book* also contained the prediction of the appearance of a prophet in America who would establish a new, pure kingdom of Christ in the United States, and a prediction of the coming of the Civil War—proof to many that Smith was a true prophet of God and that the *Book of Mormon* was God's Word.

Blood atonement

A way for excommunicated Mormons to return to the Mormon Church by killing the enemies of the Church

Skeptics point out, however, that the *Book* also mentions the presence of horses, steel, and wheat in the Western Hemisphere prior to the arrival of Columbus. Furthermore, in 1835 Smith purchased and translated Egyptian papyruses that he claimed were written by Abraham. Twentieth-century Egyptologists, however, contend that Smith's papyruses were not written by Abraham, but are copies of the Egyptian *Book of the Dead*.

Theologically speaking, Smith's Mormonism is a Protestant Christian religion. The teachings of Smith's Mormonism include not only belief in the one true God of Christianity but also in Jesus Christ as the Son of God and savior of all humanity. Smith's Mormonism also taught that human life on earth is part of human progress toward an eventual status in heaven essentially equivalent to that of God in the Old Testament. The logic, in essence, is that if humans are God's children, then when humans "grow up" in the afterlife, they will be "Gods"—residing on a distant planet orbiting the star Kolob. While in heaven, human males will be sexually active with the heavenly mother and other wives in a paradise of jewels and gold. In Mormonism, marriage is eternal and people will be reunited in the afterlife.

Joseph Smith founded the Latter Day Saints movement. Smith published what he said was an English translation of the Book of Mormon *from gold plates he found buried near his home. (Wikimedia Commons)*

While on earth, Mormons should avoid strong drinks, including alcohol, coffee, and tea. Mormonism also teaches that prosperity is a path to Godliness; thus, the Mormons stress work. Mormonism is also hierarchical ;and the Church is headed by a "First President" and twelve Apostles. At first, Mormonism also taught that converts must give all their property to the Church; but when Joseph Smith found that the wealthy rebelled against the practice, he changed the requirement from "all property" to a tithe. This alteration is an early example of the doctrine of "continuous Revelation," which allows doctrine to evolve with changing times. Famously, Mormonism also allowed polygamy, and Joseph Smith himself had twenty-eight wives; the Mormon Church abandoned the practice in 1890, after it was struck down as unconstitutional by the U.S. Supreme Court.

Polygamy, of course, was controversial and caused the Mormons to be persecuted by the larger communities around them. Mormonism also requires evangelism—which aids in the growth of Mormonism, but also alienates those who do not care to be evangelized. Thus, Smith and his followers were forced to migrate from Palmyra, New York, to Kirtland, Ohio, then to Missouri, and then to Nauvoo, Illinois. In spite of the migrations, Nauvoo had a Mormon population of fifteen thousand by 1844. Smith petitioned Congress for separate territorial status and even ran for president. The entire Mormon population at the time of Smith's untimely death (at the hands of an angry mob in 1844) is estimated to have been twenty-six thousand.

Smith's Mormonism contained the idea of "blood atonement," whereby Mormon believers could justify killing the enemies of the church or those who had fallen away from the church—such as was demonstrated in 1857 at Mountain Meadows, Utah. Mormons slaughtered 140 men, women, and children from Arkansas who were in the process of crossing Utah in a wagon train. (Wikimedia Commons)

The persecution of Mormons by the larger community was undoubtedly severe, thus leading to the multiple migrations. But Smith's (and later Brigham Young's) Mormonism itself was not entirely pacific, and the Mormons at times lashed back at their persecutors. Smith's Mormonism endorsed the idea of **blood atonement**, whereby enemies of the Church or those who had fallen away from the Church could be justly killed by Mormon believers. Those who had fallen away and desired to return to the Church could regain their salvation by killing the enemies of the Church. The espoused method was for the throats of the victims to be slit, and it was required that their blood be spilled on the ground. At Haun's Mill near Kirtland, Ohio, in 1838, seventeen people were killed in this manner when they refused to migrate with the rest of the Mormon community. Even more horrific, in 1857 at Mountain Meadows, Utah, Mormons slaughtered 140 men, women, and children from Arkansas who were in the process of crossing Utah in a wagon train. Twenty children ages 7 and under were spared as "innocents," adopted by the Mormons, and later as adults lived to tell the true story of the massacre. If it were not for the coming of the Civil War, the U.S. government might have invaded Utah and arrested **Brigham Young** for his responsibility in the **Mountain Meadows massacre**. The magnitude of the sectional crisis in the U.S. at the time, however, forced the government to direct its energy elsewhere.

10.2i The Unitarian Influence

For the Mormons whose ardor and faith have just been depicted, God the Son and God the Holy Ghost were as integral to a conception of the Deity as God the Father. Concurrently spreading in New England, however, was the influence of Unitarians, who rejected the doctrine of the trinity, believing that God exists in only one Being.

Unitarians accepted Christian revelation, but only so far as it accorded with what they conceived to be human reason. The Calvinistic belief in the doctrine of election was not for them because it implied an arbitrary God. Instead, Unitarians underscored the Deity's benevolence and declared that Jesus was Divine in the sense that all people are Divine. To a degree, they were reacting against both the creed and the formalism of Congregationalists and the fire-and-brimstone evangelism of the Great Awakenings—although one also finds links between the latter and Unitarian individualism. To Unitarians, the life of Jesus represented an example to be emulated by persons who were already innately good and spiritually free.

A spokesman for Unitarian thought and action was the Boston clergyman William Ellery Channing. Implicit in his ideas was the prominence of the individual—independent, yet spiritually obliged to "transcend" the individualistic self through intimate identification with the Deity. Though Channing had been reared in the creed of Calvinism, he came to deny the doctrine of original sin and to believe firmly in freedom of will. Many of the era's reformers and intellectuals were Unitarian in their beliefs.

10.2j Romanticism Revisited

It is not difficult to understand why Channing and other Unitarian thinkers appealed to young scholars and writers who had been impressed by the ideas of romanticism because the belief in human possibility was very congruent with romanticism. Romanticism had already had an important influence on the thinking of the young republic. From 1824–1854, romanticism's influence was, if anything, even more pervasive.

Romantic writers and artists had as their goal the "liberation" of the individual—the full realization of the human potential. To accomplish this, they felt that individuals should give free rein to imagination and emotion, experimenting with new ways and new ideas. The emphasis was on informality, the picturesque, the exotic, and the sensuous as ways of appreciating external nature and capturing the transient aspects of life. They shunned tradition, feeling that human intuition and poetic sensibility were best qualified to lead people to truth.

The growth of democratic government during the Jacksonian period also reflected this new emphasis on the value of the individual and faith in the ability of the common person. This individualism was not necessarily "nonconformist"—most Americans still took their cue for behavior from the majority—but people did tend to admire the rugged individualists among them, whether in life or in literature (such as the heroes of James Fenimore Cooper's *The Last of the Mohicans*).

The ultimate liberated men were those who invaded the wilderness, drove the American Indians out, and established settlements in the West. These men saw themselves as economically self-reliant and capable of almost any achievement, and developed versatility, robustness, and resilience, along with the physical courage and (sometimes) moral obtuseness that was required of them.

The romantics felt that society was a growing organism that could be changed and improved. Thus, romanticism as well as Christianity nourished the reform movements of the period. Most American romanticists thought their country already had the political foundations it needed and concerned themselves largely with social and humanitarian reforms.

10.3 The Golden Age of Literature

10.3a Emerson and Transcendentalism

The period from the triumph of Jacksonian democracy to the Civil War was one of the greatest eras in American literary history. It has been called "The Golden Day," "The New England Renaissance," and "The Flowering of New England." We begin with **Ralph Waldo Emerson**, Margaret Fuller, and **Henry David Thoreau**, who were among the leading proponents of the Boston-based transcendentalist movement—into which the two intellectual streams we have just observed, Unitarianism and romanticism, flowed.

Transcendentalism has been defined philosophically as "recognition in man of the capacity of knowing truth intuitively, or attaining knowledge transcending the reach of the senses." Transcendentalists believed that the power of the solitary individual was limitless and that people should not conform to the materialistic world. Instead, people should look within themselves and within the natural world for guidance.

In his first little book, *Nature,* published in 1836, Emerson asked penetrating questions:

> Foregoing generations beheld God and nature face to face; we, through their eyes. Why should not we also enjoy an original relation to the universe? Why should not we have a poetry and philosophy of insight and not of tradition, and a religion by revelation to us, and not the history of theirs?

Emerson pointed out that Jesus "spoke of miracles," for Jesus felt "man's life was a miracle" and man's "daily miracle shines, as the character ascends," whereas the churches' interpretation of the word miracle gave a false impression and was "not one with the blowing clover and the falling rain."

The depiction of clover and rain as miracles is an expression of the transcendentalists' search for revelations of divinity in external nature as well as in the individual's own nature. Emerson viewed the different aspects of the universe as diverse manifestations of a central spirit, which he called the Over-Soul. Man and woman, according to Emerson, could be channels for the higher truths of the Over-Soul by developing their intuitive powers to the fullest. Emerson's doctrine of the Over-Soul also implied a belief in self-reliance, as expounded in his famous essay of that name. When he wrote about self-reliance, Emerson's meaning was that the human being could reach a direct, exalted relationship with the universal spirit.

Emerson's philosophy was essentially a variety of philosophical idealism, as distinct from materialism. Broadly speaking, an idealist is one who sees basic reality as spiritual; the materialist is one who sees it as physical or material. Emerson's idealism was concerned ultimately with the conduct of life. For this he felt that men and women have the capacity to draw upon a power greater than their own.

One of Emerson's chief allies in the transcendentalist project was Margaret Fuller, America's first great female intellectual. A few years younger than Emerson, Fuller was unable to attend Harvard as so many of her male colleagues had—but she pursued a ferociously ambitious program of reading and was able to hold her own with any and all of

Ralph Waldo Emerson believed that a human being could reach a direct, exalted relationship with the universal spirit. (Wikimedia Commons)

Ralph Waldo Emerson
Leading transcendentalist and author of *Nature*

Henry David Thoreau
Leading transcendentalist and author of *Walden*

Transcendentalism
The idea that humans should look within themselves, and to nature, for guidance

Margaret Fuller was America's first recognized female intellectual and a close friend of Ralph Waldo Emerson. Unable to attend Harvard University due to her gender, Fuller read extensively and was able to hold her own with any and all of the other transcendentalists. (Wikimedia Commons)

Nathaniel Hawthorne
Author of *The House of Seven Gables* and *The Scarlet Letter*

Herman Melville
Author of *Moby Dick*

the other transcendentalists. In the fall of 1836, a number of these Boston intellectuals began meeting informally in what evolved into the Transcendentalist Club. For a brief period they published a journal, the *Dial*, of which Fuller was the editor. A brilliant conversationalist, Fuller would visit the Emerson household in Concord where she and her host would talk by the hour. After her untimely death in 1850, Emerson wrote a memoir about her.

10.3b Thoreau

Although Emerson published many volumes of poetry and essays, he was more widely known in his lifetime as the most popular lecturer of his day; Fuller was known best for her journalism. In contrast, Henry David Thoreau was not well known in his time. Very few bought or read his *A Week on the Concord and Merrimack Rivers* (1849) or even his now-celebrated *Walden* (1854), both of which related his experience and thinking in the 1840s.

Today Thoreau is considered one of the greatest American writers of all time. Emerson recognized the younger man's greatness as a stylist, testifying that "Thoreau illustrates with excellent images that which I convey in a sleepy generality." An erstwhile schoolteacher and local handyman, Thoreau spent the years 1845–1847 in a shack on the edge of Walden Pond near Concord, where he dwelt among the birds and beasts, reading and writing with few distractions. "I went to the woods because I wished to live deliberately," he explained, "to front only the essential facts of life."

Any romanticist, any fellow-transcendentalist, would have no trouble grasping the logic of what Thoreau said: "I had not lived there a week before my feet wore a path from my door to the pondside … How worn and dusty, then, must be the highways of the world, how deep the ruts of tradition and conformity."

Independence and self-reliance dominated Thoreau's life. He actively helped the "underground railroad" to convey runaway slaves to the freedom of Canada. He spent a night in jail rather than pay a tiny tax to support a government then prosecuting what he considered an unjust war against Mexico.

Out of the latter experience came *Civil Disobedience,* a highly influential political essay that the modern author and critic Henry S. Canby referred to as "Gandhi's textbook in his campaign of passive resistance" against the British in twentieth-century India. Later, Thoreau and Mahatma Gandhi both would greatly influence the nonviolent resistance of Martin Luther King, Jr. Thoreau declared it the duty of citizens to deny allegiance to a government that they feel is wrong.

Such an attitude is essential to the health of a democracy. It is the opposite of that apathy which prevents citizens from taking a stand, allowing important contests to be decided by default. Thoreau was not antisocial. He merely took his duties as a citizen more seriously than most Americans.

10.3c The Boston Brahmins

In his own day, Thoreau was not nearly so well known as Henry Wadsworth Longfellow, James Russell Lowell, or Oliver Wendell Holmes. Each of these was an admired poet (and Holmes, somewhat later, the author of well-regarded prose). Although Lowell and Longfellow attacked slavery in verse, all three were primarily literary aristocrats. Holmes applied the label "Brahmin caste of New England" to the cultivated, exclusive class he typified.

These "Brahmins" were inclined to view literature as something lofty and ennobling. Much of the time in their writing, they erected barriers against unpleasant or perplexing social and philosophic questions. The dreamy utopias of Emerson and the back-to-nature living of Thoreau were not for them in the 1830s and 1840s—nor were the portrayals of evil that characterized the books of **Nathaniel Hawthorne** and **Herman Melville**. Benevolent toward others, the "Brahmins" were usually satisfied to savor the pleasant intellectual life of Boston and Harvard—where all three were professors. Although (or perhaps because) he had a sense of humor, Holmes considered Boston "the thinking center of the continent, and therefore of the planet."

10.3b Hawthorne

The writer who most brilliantly opposed transcendentalist tendencies was Nathaniel Hawthorne of Salem, Massachusetts. He was the chief inheritor, in literature, of the old Puritan tradition; and his works—particularly his novel *The Scarlet Letter* (1850)—embodied Puritan ideas. His ancestors had been Puritan magistrates charged with persecuting Quakers and condemning "witches" at Salem court. While disapproving of their bigotry and cruelty, he recognized the ancestral tie: "Strong traits of their nature," he said, "have intertwined themselves with mine."

Hawthorne rejected both the optimism inherent in transcendentalism and the reform movements abetted by it. He held the Puritan beliefs that people are innately sinful, that evil is an ever present reality (not an illusion to be brushed aside), and that self-reliant individualism alone cannot save a person from destruction. In Hawthorne, we see the persistence of the Puritan point of view into the Jacksonian Era.

Unlike Emerson, who denied that evil existed in an ultimate form, Hawthorne made evil central in his stories and novels. *The Scarlet Letter* deals with secret guilt, the effects of crime on man and woman, and the need for expiation through confession or love. In *The House of the Seven Gables* (1851), evil appears as a hereditary taint visiting the sins of the fathers on the children in a study of degeneration and decay. *The Blithedale Romance* (1852) is, in part, a satire on the secular community Brook Farm—the villain showing how a reformer's zealotry can mesh with unconscionable ambition and thus serve evil rather than good.

Pictured is Nathaniel Hawthorne, author of the famous 1850 novel, The Scarlet Letter. *(Wikimedia Commons)*

10.3c Melville

A writer close to Hawthorne—both in his concern with the "deep mystery of sin" and in his aversion to Emersonian currents of optimism—was Herman Melville. Born in New York, reared there and in the Berkshires of Massachusetts, Melville as a youth shipped as a sailor on a merchantman plying the Atlantic and later on a whaler bound for the South Seas. On these voyages he saw first-hand a world of violence, crime, and misery.

Such early Melville books as *Typee* and *Omoo* were popular, but his increased pessimism caused the novelist to be neglected after the 1840s. He was "rediscovered" in the 1920s by post-World War I readers—for whom, in their mood of disillusionment, *Moby Dick* (1851) held a powerful appeal.

Although Melville, like Hawthorne, was a philosophical pessimist, he arrived at his pessimism along intellectual avenues differing from Hawthorne's in three ways. First, Hawthorne still cherished Calvinist values though he was critical of them and all others, whereas Melville rebelled against the religious conservatism he had known as a boy. Second, in Liverpool and in the South Seas, Melville was shocked by the roughness and cruelty of "civilized" men—brutalities that neither Hawthorne nor Emerson experienced. Finally, just as he lacked Emerson's optimism, he lacked Hawthorne's resignation.

Said Hawthorne in reference to an 1856 meeting with Melville in England:

> Melville, as he always does, began to reason of providence and futurity, and of everything that lies beyond human

" Both jaws, like enormous shears, bit the craft completely in twain."

—*Page 510.*

Herman Melville wrote the great American classic Moby Dick. *(Wikimedia Commons)*

ken, and informed me that he had "pretty much made up his mind to be annihilated";
but still he does not seem to rest in that anticipation; and, I think, will never rest
until he gets hold of a definite belief. It is strange how he persists—and has persisted
ever since I knew him, and probably long before—in wandering to-and-fro over these
deserts, as dismal and monotonous as the sand hills amid which we were sitting.
He can neither believe, nor be comfortable in his unbelief; and he is too honest and
courageous not to try to do one or the other.

Modern literary critics give Melville high ratings and are fascinated by his imagery.
Sometimes they remind us that we should not forget his love of the exotic, the sensually
attractive, and the humorous—for Melville was a many-sided man. While the dilemma
of understanding the author of *Moby Dick* has been variously approached, it is probable
that Hawthorne's interpretation was not wide of the mark.

10.3f James Fenimore Cooper

The disparity between the dream of a peaceful, democratic society in the virgin wilderness and the reality of frontier life was frequently reflected in the thought and literature
of this period. The real Western frontier posed many problems of adjustment for its
settlers. Land speculation, political corruption, and immorality were common in the
poorly organized towns. In short, the real frontier bore little resemblance to the
literary legend or to the popular tall tale.

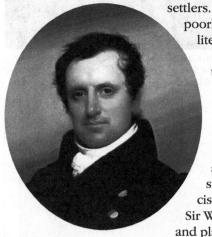

The first major writer of fiction to exploit the literary potential of the frontier was James Fenimore Cooper, whose series of *Leatherstocking Tales* both
romanticized the wilderness and conveyed the loss many Americans felt when
they became aware of the crude fashion in which the frontier was being settled. For instance, Cooper convincingly expressed the tragedy of the American
Indian, pushed out of ancestral lands by the advancing white settler.

Although it is easy to lampoon his didacticism, stock characters,
and strained and starchy dialogue, at his best Cooper was a captivating
storyteller with a talent for both description and perceptive social criticism. *Leatherstocking Tales* represents a romantic view of the West, just as
Sir Walter Scott's novels and ballads romanticized with charm and skill the people
and places of a lost Europe. Cooper's real life "West," however, was confined mainly
to upper New York State before 1800. He himself never saw the prairie, never
neared the Rocky Mountains—in fact never even crossed the Mississippi River.

James Fenimore Cooper
(Wikimedia Commons)

10.3g Southern Romanticism

The South produced numerous authors before the Civil War, yet there were few direct
literary connections with New England. Sectional interests influenced literature, just as
they influenced politics. With many Southerners convinced that slavery must be maintained and allowed to spread, Southerners liked to idealize their plantations as happy
feudal domains where blacks benefited from the most humane treatment. Southern writers praised Greek democracy, where *inequality,* rather than *equality,* had prevailed.
There as in the American South, they held, competent individuals directed and cared for
the less competent—acting in the interest of all.

Because of the feudal emphasis, the dominant influence on romantic Southern literature prior to the Civil War was the British author Sir Walter Scott. Scott's fictional recreation of the Middle Ages—his knights in shining armor, his defenders of glamorous ladies
in distress, and his heroes' exemplary characters—fit with notions of Southern chivalry
far better than Northern commercialism and reformism.

A number of American writers attempted to romanticize the "feudal" South in works
of fiction. One of the best examples was John P. Kennedy's *Swallow Barn* (1832), which
depicted rural Virginia in the 1820s. A resident of Baltimore, Kennedy strung together
sketches of idealized plantation aristocracy with a minimal plot. In it, the master of the
estate in *Swallow Barn* is genial and generous, his relatives and friends are virtuous, their
hospitality is bountiful, and the blacks are cheerful.

10.3ϝ Edgar Allan Poe

Reared as a foster child in Virginia, **Edgar Allan Poe** nevertheless can be treated only partly as a Southerner. Although in his personal life he was—or wanted to be—a conservative Southerner, and although he supported the works of other Southern authors and praised the Southern defense of slavery, Poe's writings rarely reveal a Southern tone or setting. In his tales he was more influenced by the "gothic" tradition in English fiction—the kind of fiction that used certain stock properties like old castles, decayed houses, dungeons, secret passages, ancient wrongs, and supernatural phenomena.

Poe was not concerned with portraying contemporary scenes or providing moral reflections on life. He believed that poetry, for example, should exist for its own sake, never as an instrument of instruction. It may be that no other American has maintained more consistently that literature exists primarily and perhaps solely to entertain. But Poe did not take this function lightly. In his own poetry and prose, he applied the theories of literary technique that he expounded in his critical writings. There was a great deal of originality in Poe's writing, particularly in his short stories and detective stories. Both his poetry and his prose were enormously admired abroad, especially in France.

Edgar Allan Poe
(Wikimedia Commons)

10.4 **Journalism and Popular Culture**

10.4ɑ **Writing for the People**

> **Edgar Allan Poe**
> Author of *The Raven* and numerous other classic and sometimes chilling tales

Americans of the time read newspapers more avidly than even the most exciting fiction. New York City produced some of the best journalism in Horace Greeley's *Tribune* and poet-editor William Cullen Bryant's *Post*. James Gordon Bennett's New York *Herald*, a pioneer in the "penny press" field, presented national and world news alongside lurid accounts of murders and sex scandals. Nowhere else had there ever been so many newspapers as there were then in America. While quality varied from town to town, Americans knew more about what was going on than any other general population anywhere.

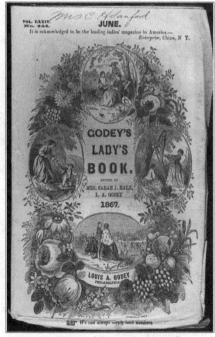

After stereotyping began in 1811 and electrotyping in 1841, the influence of technology on popular culture was evident. Printers used steam presses to mass-produce books which, cheaply bound and extensively distributed, sold for as little as 25¢. Intellectuals read such magazines as the *North American Review* and the *Southern Literary Messenger*. Tillers of the soil preferred the *American Farmer*, the *American Agriculturist*, and the *Southern Cultivator*. In addition to agricultural articles, these offered fiction and verse to farm families.

Religious periodicals abounded—notably the *Biblical Repertory* (Presbyterian), the *Biblical Repository* (Congregationalist), the *Christian Review* (Baptist), the *Christian Examiner* (Unitarian), the *Methodist Magazine,* and the *United States Catholic Magazine*. Carrying theological arguments and sectarian messages, many of them also disseminated miscellaneous culture. "Of all the reading of the people," a commentator observed in 1840, "three fourths is purely religious." In 1848, fifty-two religious journals were published in New York City alone.

10.4ɓ **Magazines and Books for Women**

Discerning innovators discovered that women could comprise one of the most dependable magazine markets. From 1830 on, a Philadelphia periodical called *Godey's Lady's Book* enjoyed an enviable circulation, helped along by the efforts of its gifted editor, Sarah Josepha Hale. By the 1850s, its subscription list reached 150,000. Eventually, its publisher amassed a million-dollar fortune. *Graham's Magazine,*

Godey's Lady's Book was a highly influential women's magazine that reinforced the values of the Cult of Domesticity. "True women" were supposed to possess four cardinal virtues: piety, purity, domesticity, and submissiveness. (Wikipedia Commons)

which made its bow in 1841, instantly appealed to both women and men. Soon it had forty thousand subscribers and a $50,000 annual profit. Its contents? Short stories, essays, poetry, colored fashion plates, book reviews, and a department on fine arts. Bryant, Cooper, Lowell, and Longfellow contributed to *Graham's*. For a time Poe was literary editor, and some of his best work graced its pages. Combining the insipid and sentimental with better things, *Graham's* and *Godey's* provided exactly what their readers wanted.

Women writers were widely published during the period. Authorship lent opportunity to women when most other vocational doors were shut. Mrs. Ann Stephens, co-editor of the *Ladies' National Magazine,* sent florid but thrilling tales to the *Lady's Wreath* and similar media. Poems (often lachrymose by modern standards) and articles by Mrs. Lydia Sigourney won acceptance in countless journals. Among women authors with large followings were Catharine M. Sedgwick and Mrs. Anna Mowatt. Mrs. Caroline Lee Hentz and Mrs. E.D.E.N. Southworth, popular novelists of the 1850s, got their start in the previous decade. Margaret Fuller edited the *Dial* in Boston (as we have noted) and later, in New York on Greeley's *Tribune,* gained more admirers of her astute criticism. Her volume, *Women in the Nineteenth Century,* drawn from her writings for the *Tribune,* projected advanced views on women's rights.

New York's periodical, Spirit of the Times, *featured sports and pastimes like horse racing, boxing, hunting, shooting, and fishing. (Wikimedia Commons)*

10.4c Sports, Humor, and Realism

One of the liveliest periodicals was New York's *Spirit of the Times*. Its editor featured sports and pastimes like horse racing, boxing, hunting, shooting, and fishing. He also had an eye for realism and amusing exaggeration in fiction. In the *Spirit* and in books, small farmers and reckless frontiersmen of the Old Southwest—from Georgia to Arkansas—became subjects of wildly humorous yarns by such frontier writers as Thomas B. Thorpe, William T. Thompson, Augustus B. Longstreet, J. J. Hooper, and George W. Harris. Authentically depicting the speech, customs, and scenery of their region, they produced comedy combined with realism.

Harris, who wrote for the *Spirit* in the 1840s, created his fictional character Sut Livingood a bit later. There is no better example of the breed of men inhabiting these humorists' stories. A lanky mountaineer and self-confessed "nat-ral-born durn'd fool," Sut loves liquor and women but hates Yankees and circuit-riding preachers, whom he describes as "durn'd, infurnel, hiperkritical, potbellied, scaley-hided," and "whiskey-wastin'." These storytellers delighted in the boast and brag of the "tall tale":

> I'm that same David Crockett, fresh from the backwoods, half-horse, half-alligator, a little touched with the snapping-turtle; can wade the Mississippi, leap the Ohio, ride upon a streak of lightning, and slip without a scratch down a honey locust; can whip my weight in wild-cats—and if any gentleman pleases, for a ten-dollar bill, he may throw in a panther …

Chauvinism, boastfulness, and exaggeration—all reflected the influence of the West and Southwest on thinking and reading tastes. There are historians who believe that the "starting point of a truly American literature" can be located on the frontier, in just such tales, more logically than in the east.

10.5 Arts, Sciences, and Popular Taste

10.5a The "Higher Culture"

As in literature, so in other arts: Americans valued both the light and the serious. Classical music had numerous appreciators, particularly in urban centers with their orchestras and choral societies. No actor won more plaudits than Edwin Forrest, who played major Shakespearean parts like Brutus and King Lear. No lecturer was more respected than Emerson, who discoursed on intellectual topics annually from New England westward. Margaret Fuller's "conversations," in Boston, attracted audiences of women—eager participants—hungry for mental stimulation. And in 1826 in Millbury, Massachusetts, Josiah Holbrook organized a series of public lectures that were to form the basis of the National American Lyceum movement. This movement, which was dedicated to the spread of information about the arts, sciences, history, and public affairs, spread to other states and became an important force in adult education and social reform.

Despite the fact that serious research was beyond the reach of most teachers, the period witnessed advances along scientific lines. There was keen public interest in science, and young and older people crowded scientific exhibitions and marveled at scientific experiments. Benjamin Silliman, professor at Yale, published *Elements of Chemistry* in 1830 and wrote learnedly on subjects ranging from gold deposits to sugar planting. Other scientific pioneers were Elisha Mitchell, geologist and botanist at the University of North Carolina; Edmund Ruffin, Virginia soil chemist; and Matthew F. Maury of the U.S. Navy, his generation's expert in navigation and oceanography. George Ticknor at Harvard was the American trailblazer in the study and teaching of modern foreign languages. In the historical field, William H. Prescott was publishing his monumental works on Mexico and Peru; and another first-rate historian, Francis Parkman, was writing *The Oregon Trail* and *The Conspiracy of Pontiac*.

In some of the arts and sciences, America still leaned on Europe for much of its leadership. Thus, John James Audubon—the ornithologist and painter whose *Birds of America* is a classic—was born in the West Indies and reared in France. Duncan Phyfe, famous for the furniture he produced in New York, came to America from Scotland. Louis Agassiz of Switzerland, who joined the Harvard faculty, did as much as anyone to arouse American interest in zoology and geology. Young Americans of promise went to Germany and France for graduate study. In philanthropy, too, the Old World pointed the way: Washington's Smithsonian Institution was endowed by an Englishman.

Among highly regarded performing artists appearing in the United States were many Europeans, including an Austrian ballet dancer, a Norwegian violinist, and countless British actors and actresses. The Swedish soprano Jenny Lind—the "Swedish Nightingale"—was one of the most beloved performers of her day. Presented by the famed impresario, P.T. Barnum, Lind packed concert halls in several American cities. Objects ranging from a style of crib to a locomotive were named in her honor.

Pictured is sheet music for "Home, Sweet Home"—a well-known, 150-year-old American folk song originally adapted by Henry Bishop. (Wikimedia Commons)

10.56 Popular Music and Drama

Americans by no means depended exclusively on Europe for their culture. Much folk art and folk craft (the beautiful furniture of the Shakers, for example) was far from being purely derivative, although many of songs that Americans hummed—"Home, Sweet Home," as an illustration—were at least partly of European origin. Well-loved ballads, fiddle tunes, and folk songs fused the native and the imported. The same was true of hymns, work songs, political chants, and comic airs. Some were totally native. All were intimately integrated into the lives, worship, and fun of average people.

On the stage, light plays and musicals competed with the classical—though even the plays of Shakespeare might well have been presented in so rollicking a fashion as to constitute popular entertainment. With low admission prices, the urban theater boomed. Rowdy comedies and farces played to rowdy audiences. The versatile James H. Hackett helped make Rip Van Winkle famous and ridiculed

Minstrel show

A kind of show that often featured white men wearing blackface make-up as both a racist spectacle, deriding black people, and a vehicle for calling attention to aspects of African American folk culture

"high society" in *The Moderns, or A Trip to the Springs*. The lighter side of cultural life developed with zest in rural areas as well. Heroes were applauded and villains hissed and booed in smaller cities and towns—even in barns and log houses and on boats on western waters.

Among indigenous American entertainments was the **minstrel show** with its interlocutor and end men, banjos, bones, and tambourines. The minstrel show often featured white men wearing blackface make-up—both a racist spectacle deriding black people, and a vehicle for calling attention to aspects of African American folk culture. Audiences cheered minstrels like Ohio's Daniel Emmett, the singer and composer who subsequently gave "Dixie" to the South. Enchanting were the tunes of Stephen Collins Foster, the Pennsylvanian who immortalized Florida's "Swanee" River and evoked tears with the strains of "My Old Kentucky Home." Love of the spectacular as well as good music—in the case of Jenny Lind—led multitudes to line the pockets of Phineas T. Barnum, who amazed gaping compatriots with his museum of curios—from the woolly horse and bearded lady to the midget "General Tom Thumb."

10.5c Sculpture, Architecture, Painting

American sculptors had a remarkable vogue. Among the most celebrated were Hiram Powers, whose "Greek Slave" Londoners greeted with admiration, and Thomas Crawford, whose "Armed Freedom" surmounts the Capitol in Washington, D.C. Pseudoclassical portrait busts were produced by the thousands. Average Americans took pride in this art form, although the nude "Greek Slave" did not please the prudish, and Horatio Greenough's "George Washington"—partly draped in a Roman toga—drew its share of outraged criticism.

The Jefferson-Latrobe influence remained strong in Greek Revival architecture. But in the 1830s and 1840s, young architects considered classical columns and porticos too formal and artificial. Devotees of romantic theories, they stressed the organic in plan and construction. A multiplicity of styles, especially the Gothic, characterized the work of Alexander J. Davis and of Richard Upjohn, who designed Trinity Church in New York City. While most Americans did not employ architects, thousands of houses showed the influence of architectural handbooks.

Although the most successful portrait painter, Thomas Sully, had come to the United States from England (like Upjohn), the canvases of the American-born artists John Neagle and Henry Inman were also popular. "Storytelling" or anecdotal painting—in which common human situations were depicted nostalgically or humorously—was likewise growing in public favor. Scenes of life on the farm, of raftsmen poling their flatboats upstream, or of prairie schooners and American Indians appeared in the work of George Caleb Bingham, William Sidney Mount, and Alfred Jacob Miller. Romanticism and American pride in the land combined to inspire a group of painters known as the Hudson River School, who romantically portrayed the wilderness of forests, mountains, and streams.

10.6 Slavery and Democracy

African slavery played an indispensable part in settlement and development of the United States. The institution of slavery was no abnormality in human history, but the distinctive features of American slavery were its racial basis and its thoroughly economic character. As the American Republic developed, the stark contrast between America as the home of freedom and opportunity and America as the home of bondage for African Americans became glaringly evident. It was only on the backs of slaves that many Americans—especially in the southern United States—became free to take control of their destiny and to enjoy the American dream of liberty and equality.

Unlike previous forms of slavery, the American version would not decline over a long period of time, but would come to an abrupt and violent end. The struggle for emancipation began in 1776 with the first antislavery society in Philadelphia, and ended on the American Civil War battlefield in 1865. An institution that had been accepted for thousands of years in Europe and elsewhere disappeared in the United States in less than a century. Significant credit for this momentous achievement must be given to the unprecedented novelty and speed of the American abolitionist movement.

William Lloyd Garrison
Founder of *The Liberator*, an abolitionist newspaper

The Liberator
Abolitionist newspaper founded by William Lloyd Garrison

10.6a Garrison and Abolition

For all the progress and all the pride in the white American of the antebellum period—for all the artistry of the gifted, the technology of the inventive, and the fun and frolic and misery and strivings and achievements of the masses of people—the dark cloud of slavery deeply troubled first the few and then the many.

In the 1820s, the ranks of abolitionists tended to be filled by Quakers, such as Philadelphian Benjamin Lundy. Then in Boston in 1831, a journeyman printer named **William Lloyd Garrison** founded *The Liberator*, a new kind of abolitionist paper—new because it carried an unprecedented tone of moral urgency. Garrison could see no good in the legal sanctions protecting slavery in half the country. Constitutionalism meant far less to him than securing freedom for his fellow human beings. It was no happenstance that Garrison's insistence on this reform occurred at the very time when other movers and shakers were spurring other reforms—both religious and secular.

According to Garrison's concept of Christianity, slavery was sinful. As *The Liberator's* editor, he was motivated primarily by this sinfulness. Fervent in his conviction, he attacked the Constitution as "a covenant with death and an agreement with hell" and called for an immediate end to slavery. It was hardly surprising that most "respectable" northerners would not subscribe to what was seen as extremism in a day when John Quincy Adams—himself against slavery but no Garrisonian—described the abolitionist faction as small and shallow.

But Garrison was persistent. In 1843, he began the first of twenty-two terms as president of the American Anti-Slavery Society. The seed nourished by Garrison and fellow abolitionists eventually flowered in the emancipation of blacks from bondage. Long depicted in historical writing as a fanatic, Garrison is now regarded as one of the era's most influential reformers—primarily but not exclusively for his abolitionism. He also espoused women's rights and pacifism.

Yet it must be stated that the possibility of slavery's westward extension—rather than the existence of slavery in states where it was legal—would be what millions of Northerners would strenuously object to from the outbreak of the Mexican War forward. Abraham Lincoln and other political leaders would approach slavery from a very different angle than had Garrison.

Second only to Garrison in national fame among abolitionists, perhaps, was Frederick Douglass: an African American who had escaped from slavery and become an agent of the Massachusetts Anti-Slavery Society. Of commanding appearance and a gifted orator, Douglass established an antislavery paper—the *North Star*—and was well-received by both American and British audiences. Another well-known black abolitionist was the eloquent Charles L. Remond, born free, who for a time rivaled Douglass on abolitionist platforms. Black clergymen also had significant parts in the antislavery cause. Presbyterian Henry H. Garnet and Congregationalist Samuel R. Ward both held pastorates in upstate New York, but were known chiefly as abolition spokesmen. Finally, there were a number of clubs composed of black women abolitionists—including Frances Watkins Harper and the former slave, Sojourner Truth, who toured as anti-slavery lecturers.

10.6b The Literary Antecedents to Civil War

From 1833 on, the New England Quaker John Greenleaf Whittier contributed poems and prose to the abolitionists' campaign. Longfellow, in 1842, published a few antislavery poems but never became a Garrison adherent. James Russell Lowell wrote for the *National Anti-Slavery Standard*. Other younger authors—Thoreau, Melville, and Walt Whitman among them—were repulsed by slavery and openly said so. Then—while Holmes and Hawthorne continued to abstain from the agitation—Emerson swung around in the 1850s to laud the abolitionist crusader John Brown, likening Brown's gallows

BVT Lab

Improve your test scores. Practice quizzes are available at www.BVTLab.com.

Harriet Beecher Stowe authored Uncle Tom's Cabin, *which depicted the separation of families, maternal loss, and other evils inherent in slavery. It turned out to be the greatest work of propaganda ever written by an American. (Library of Congress, LC-USZ62-11212)*

(Brown was executed after being captured in an attempt to lead a slave revolt in 1859) to the cross of Jesus.

It was a powerful novel, however, that proved to be the most effective tool deployed by any of slavery's opponents. Written by Harriet Beecher Stowe—daughter, wife, and sister of Calvinist ministers and a woman abundantly aware of her own New England conscience—*Uncle Tom's Cabin* (1852) provided a searing indictment of "the peculiar institution." Stowe contended that the book—which depicted the separation of families, maternal loss, and other evils inherent in slavery—was inspired by God. Inspired or not, it turned out to be the greatest work of propaganda ever written by an American, selling hundreds of thousands of copies and imbuing the anti-slavery crusade with a moral fervor that captured Northern attention and sympathy in an unprecedented way. Truly, it changed the nature of the discourse. Stowe's treatment of slavery caused many Americans to, for the first time, see blacks as human and face the inhumanity of slavery. Southern fiction produced by way of reply had no comparable punch, though it is noteworthy that the sectional conflict was fought with words before it was fought with bullets.

The ablest Southern arguments were in essay form and came mostly from politicians and educators. Many slaveholders agreed with John C. Calhoun and William Harper of South Carolina, and with Thomas R. Dew of Virginia that, far from being harmful, slavery was a positive practice. Other Southerners merely saw—or thought they saw—a practical necessity for retaining the slave labor system.

When *The Impending Crisis of the South* was published in 1857 (attacking slavery on economic grounds), its author, Hinton R. Helper of North Carolina, was bitterly assailed by Southerners. On the other hand, the writings of a Virginian, George Fitzhugh, were warmly praised in the 1850s by those who denounced Helper. In *Sociology for the South,* Fitzhugh said slavery was a social, political, and economic blessing—and avowed that people trying to eliminate it were blind to Southern realities.

10.6c Alexis de Tocqueville's America

Alexis de Tocqueville, the young French magistrate who spent nine months in the United States in 1831 and 1832, has been mentioned previously for his views on life in America. His noteworthy contribution to political science, sociology, and history was *Democracy in America* (1835). He concluded that American democracy was functioning successfully, that its success depended chiefly on separation of church and state and on the absence of centralization, that American political morality was important, and that the exportation of American democracy to Europe would not work until such time as Europeans elevated their standards of governmental morality.

The Frenchman was particularly struck by what he saw as an American tendency toward the practical, an avoidance of traditions, and an optimistic hope that in the new social system people would be able to progress rapidly toward perfection. One of his principal theses was that the American system of government derived from a dominant principle—the will of the people—which had been felt all during the nation's history.

UNCLE TOM'S CABIN;

OR,

LIFE AMONG THE LOWLY.

BY

HARRIET BEECHER STOWE.

VOL. I.

ONE HUNDRED AND FIFTH THOUSAND.

BOSTON:
JOHN P. JEWETT & COMPANY
CLEVELAND, OHIO:
JEWETT, PROCTOR & WORTHINGTON.
1852.

Pictured is a print of Harriet Beecher Stowe's novel, Uncle Tom's Cabin. *The book sold hundreds of thousands of copies. Without a doubt it changed Americans' views of slavery, caused many Americans to view blacks as human, and ultimately, to face the inhumanity of slavery. (Wikimedia Commons)*

The French magistrate, who stayed long enough to look around thoroughly and to reflect on what he saw and heard, was by no means oblivious to problems involved in the questions of slavery and race. "The most formidable of all the ills which threaten the future existence of the Union," he wrote, "arises from the presence of a black population upon its territory; and in contemplating the cause of the present embarrassments or of the future dangers of the United States, the observer is invariably led to consider this as a primary fact."

Social mobility was a feature of American life that intrigued de Tocqueville. He believed that, with one exception, such mobility would prevent both class stratification and the extreme social conflict resulting from it. The exception could be found in black-white relationships. If and when Southern blacks "are raised to the level of freemen," he predicted, "they will soon revolt at being deprived of almost all their civil rights; and as they cannot become the equals of the whites, they will speedily show themselves as enemies." Northern whites, he observed, "avoided the Negroes with increasing care in proportion as the legal barriers of separation are removed."

The French observer was not without other doubts concerning the American experiment. He saw a potential danger to freedom of the individual in the possibility that majorities would crush minorities or nibble away at minority rights. He also thought he discerned a trend toward mediocrity in popular leaders and in American culture—this, in a country where Emerson, Fuller, Thoreau, Hawthorne, Melville, Stowe, and Lincoln all were living when de Tocqueville's book went to press. Still, while the French visitor guessed wrong at times, he was remarkably correct in the aggregate.

Alexis de Tocqueville, a young French magistrate, spent nine months in the United States between 1831 and 1832. De Tocqueville reported back about the nature of the new country's democracy, morality, and revolutionary ideas regarding the separation of church and state. (Wikimedia Commons)

Timeline

1802	Oliver Evans invents the steam engine.
1813	Richard B. Chenaworth develops a cast iron plow made in three separate pieces, making possible the replacement of broken parts.
1821	Emma Willard founds Troy Seminary, a private female seminary in New York.
1826	Josiah Holbrook organizes a series of public lectures that were to form the basis of the National American Lyceum movement.
1830	Benjamin Silliman, professor at Yale, publishes *Elements of Chemistry*.
	Peter Cooper builds the first American locomotive.
	Joseph Smith publishes the *Book of Mormon*.
1831	William Lloyd Garrison founds *The Liberator*.
1832	Free public schools established in New York.
	John P. Kennedy publishes *Swallow Barn*.
1834	Cyrus McCormick patents the mechanical reaper, which greatly reduced the labor involved in harvesting grain.
1835	Alexis de Toqueville publishes *Democracy in America*.
1836	Ralph Waldo Emerson publishes *Nature*.
1837	John Deere patents a steel plow, providing the solution to breaking the western land.
	Chicago becomes an incorporated municipality.
	Mary Lyons founds Mount Holyoke, a private women's seminary, in Massachusetts.
1842	Crawford Long administers ether in surgery.
	William Miller predicts that Jesus will return on March 21, 1843.
1843	To the disappointment of the Millerites, Jesus does not return on March 21.
1844	Samuel Morse sends his first telegraph message.
	Joseph Smith is murdered by an angry mob.
1847	Brook Farm is destroyed by fire.

Timeline

1848
Elizabeth Cady Stanton and Lucretia Mott begin the women's suffrage movement at Seneca Falls, New York.

John Noyes founds the Oneida Community.

1849
Elizabeth Blackwell becomes the first woman to be granted a Doctor of Medicine (M.D.) degree

1850
Nathaniel Hawthorne publishes *The Scarlet Letter*.

1851
Oberlin College begins admitting white women and black men.

Herman Melville publishes *Moby Dick*.

1852
Harriet Beecher Stowe publishes *Uncle Tom's Cabin*.

1854
Henry David Thoreau publishes *Walden*.

1857
One hundred and forty persons from an Arkansas wagon train are massacred by Mormons at Mountain Meadows, Utah.

CHAPTER SUMMARY

$\mathcal{T}$he first half of the nineteenth century was a time of great advancement in terms of economic growth and invention as well as in the growth of American democracy. It was also a time that witnessed the flowering of American culture in literature, magazines, and architecture. Furthermore, the period was one of social experimentation, featuring attempts at utopian societies and the founding of new religions. It was a time of social progress as temperance, women's suffrage, and abolitionist movements all gained strength.

The economic growth was boosted by the opening of the West—which was made possible by the steam locomotive, John Deere's steel plow, and Cyrus McCormick's reaper. Samuel Morse's telegraph allowed Americans to build a communication network that would eventually connect the entire nation.

While these men's inventions would transform the nation, women worked to reform the nation so that they could have full participation in it. The first convention on women's rights was held in Seneca Falls, New York, in 1848. Simultaneously, women's seminaries were founded to educate women, and Oberlin College in Ohio first accepted women as students in 1851.

Education in general received a boost when Horace Mann led the fight for the first publicly supported schools in Massachusetts. Others would follow, and the first free public schools in New York opened in 1832.

The more educated society would quickly become a more well-read society and great American authors—including Nathaniel Hawthorne, Herman Melville, and James Fenimore Cooper—turned out masterpieces of literature that remain classics in the twenty-first century. Americans were also treated to literature with a purpose, such as Harriet Beecher Stowe's *Uncle Tom's Cabin* and William Lloyd Garrison's abolitionist newspaper, *The Liberator.* Ralph Waldo Emerson and Henry David Thoreau wrote transcendentalist essays, while Joseph Smith of Palmyra, New York, dictated the *Book of Mormon* and founded the Mormon religion. After Smith's death at the hands of an angry mob in 1844, Brigham Young would lead Smith's followers to Utah where Mormonism remains the largest religion to date.

As Alexander de Tocqueville observed, American democracy flourished in the first half of the nineteenth century based on social mobility, decentralization, an optimistic vision, and the will of the people. Tocqueville did see a danger, however, in the possibility that the majority could crush minority rights. In fact, since slavery remained, the rights of a significant minority were already crushed. Tocqueville warned, however, that if the slaves were freed, they would be likely to revolt because they would still be denied full citizenship rights and would therefore remain without social mobility, unhappy in their plight. Although Tocqueville was not always right, in this case it appears that he accurately foresaw the American future.

KEY TERMS

BIBLIOGRAPHY

B

Billington, Ray Allen. *The Protestant Crusade 1800–1860*. New York: Rinehart, 1938.

Brinkley, Alan. *American History: A Survey*. 11th ed. Boston, MA: McGraw-Hill, 2003.

Brooke, John L. *The Making of Mormon Cosmology, 1644–1844*. New York: Cambridge University Press, 1996.

C

Cash, W. J. *The Mind of the South*. New York: Knopf, 1941.

Collins, Gail. *America's Women. 400 Years of Dolls, Drudges, Helpmates, and Heroines*. New York: William Morrow, 2007.

Craven, Avery. *The Coming of the Civil War*. New York: Scribner, 1942.

Cross, Barbara, ed. *The Autobiography of Lyman Beecher*. Cambridge, MA: Harvard University Press, 1961.

Cross, Whitney R. *The Burned Over District: The Social and Intellectual History of Enthusiastic Religion in Western New York, 1800–1850*. Ithaca, NY: Cornell University Press, 1981.

Current, Richard N. *Daniel Webster and the Rise of National Conservatism*. Boston, MA: Little, Brown, 1955.

D

Davis, David Brian. "Some Themes of Counter-Subversion: An Analysis of Anti-Masonic, Anti-Catholic and Anti-Mormon Literature." *Mississippi Valley Historical Review*. XLVII, 1960.

Denton, Sally. *American Massacre: The Tragedy at Mountain Meadows, September 1857*. New York: Alfred A. Knopf, 2003.

G

Garraty, John A., and Robert McCaughey. *The American Nation: A History of the United States Since 1865*. 6th ed. New York: HarperCollins, 1987.

Gems, Gerald, Linda Borish and Gertrud Pfister. *Sports in American History: From Colonization to Globalization*. Champaign, IL: Human Kinetics Publishing, 2008.

Gura, Philip F. *American Transcendentalism: A History*. New York: Hill and Wang, 2008.

H

Harris, Neil. *The Artist in America: The Formative Years 1790–1860*. Chicago, IL: University of Chicago Press, 1982.

Hofstadter, Richard. *The Rise of Legitimate Opposition in the United States 1780–1840*. Berkeley, CA: University of California Press, 1970.

Hughes, Jonathan, and Louis P. Cain. *American Economic History*. 8th ed. Englewood Cliffs, NJ: Pearson Prentice-Hall, 2010.

J

Jacoby, Susan. *Freethinkers: A History of American Secularism*. New York: Henry Holt, 2004.

Johnson, Curtis D. *Redeeming America: Evangelicals and the Road to Civil War*. Lanham, MD: Ivan R. Dee, 1993.

Johnson, Paul E., and Sean Wilentz. *The Kingdom of Matthias: A Story of Sex and Salvation in 19th-Century America*. New York: Oxford University Press, 1995.

K

Kolchin, Peter. *American Slavery: 1619–1877*. New York: Hill and Wang, 2003.

L

Lipset, Seymour Martin, and Earl Raab. *The Politics of Unreason: Right-Wing Extremism in America, 1790–1970*. New York: Harper and Row, 1970.

M

Meacham, John. *American Lion: Andrew Jackson in the White House*. New York: Random House, 2009.

N

Nichols, Roy F. *The Disruption of American Democracy*. New York: Collier, 1962.

Novak, Barbara. *Nature and Culture: American Landscape and Painting, 1825–1875*. New York: Oxford University Press, 1981.

O

Oren, Michael B. *Power, Faith, and Fantasy: America in the Middle East 1776 to the Present*. New York: W. W. Norton & Company, 2007.

BIBLIOGRAPHY

Parrington, Vernon Louis. *Main Currents in American Thought,* II. New York: Harcourt Brace Jovanovich, Inc., 1927.

Phillips, Jerry, and Andrew Ladd. *Romanticism and Transcendentalism (1800–1860).* New York: Facts on File, 2005.

Schlesinger, Arthur Jr. *The Age of Jackson.* New York: Little, Brown, 1945.

Smith-Rosenberg, Carroll. *Disorderly Conduct: Visions of Gender in Victorian America.* New York: Oxford University Press, 1986.

Stewart, James Brewer. *Holy Warriors: The Abolitionist and American Slavery.* New York: Hill and Wang, 1997.

Tocqueville, Alexis de. *Democracy in America.* New York: Penguin, 2003.

Tompkins, Jane. *Sensational Designs: The Cultural Work of American Fiction, 1790–1860.* New York: Oxford University Press, 1986.

POP QUIZ

1. The building of the railroads was essentially financed through _____.
   a. private charity
   b. a second mortgage on Peter Cooper's house
   c. private entrepreneurship without government intervention
   d. federal land grants to the railroads for each mile of track

2. The only coeducational college that admitted women before the Civil War was _____.
   a. Texas Women's University
   b. Texas A&M University
   c. Oberlin College in Ohio
   d. Radcliff

3. John Henry Noyes founded this community and championed "complex marriage."
   a. Fruitlands
   b. New Harmony
   c. Brooke Farm
   d. Oneida

4. Emerson believed in _____.
   a. self-reliance
   b. the "Over-Soul"
   c. the idea that reality was spiritual not material
   d. all of the above

5. Enemies of the Mormon Church were killed under the doctrine of _____.
   a. the land of Canaan
   b. blood atonement
   c. righteous anger
   d. turn the other cheek

6. Who wrote "Civil Disobedience"?
   a. Ralph W. Emerson
   b. Henry D. Thoreau
   c. Herman Melville
   d. Edgar A. Poe

7. The dominant influence on Southern romantic literature in the early nineteenth century was _____.
   a. Sir Walter Scott
   b. Sir Walter Raleigh
   c. William Shakespeare
   d. Jane Austen

8. The form of entertainment that featured white men wearing blackface was _____.
   a. the minstrel show
   b. jazz
   c. the toga party
   d. vaudeville

9. Alexis de Tocqueville believed that the greatest problem faced by Americans was _____.
   a. slavery
   b. maintaining separation of church and state
   c. political corruption
   d. the lack of social and economic mobility

10. In general, access to higher education was denied to women in the early period of American history.
    T F

11. Southern romantic novelists depicted slave life as happy and contented. T F

12. Alexis de Tocqueville believed that separation of church and state was a factor in America's success as a nation. T F

13. _____ believed that people could live together in peace.

14. According to Henry David Thoreau, individuals had a duty to _____ a government they felt was _____.

15. Nathaniel Hawthorne and Herman Melville both took a _____ view of life.

(Wikimedia Commons)

Chapter 11

Westward Expansion, 1824–1854

11.1 The Background of Expansion

11.1a Manifest Destiny

New York magazine editor John L. O'Sullivan proclaimed in 1845 that it was "the fulfillment of our manifest destiny to overspread the continent allotted by Providence for the free development of our yearly multiplying millions." O'Sullivan's exuberant words reflected the optimism of fervid nationalists that the American banner soon would wave over all of North America and beyond. For the exponents of **Manifest Destiny**, even the addition of Texas, New Mexico, California, and the Oregon country to the nation would not be enough: God had destined the United States to extend its sovereignty over Canada, Alaska, Mexico, Cuba, other islands in the West Indies, and Hawaii. Related to this outlook was the fact that millions of Americans firmly believed that God had singled out their country to play a special role in human history.

The dream of Manifest Destiny should be placed in the context of America's impressive achievements and realized dreams since 1776: nearly anything seemed possible in the next half century. In 1803 the Louisiana Purchase had doubled the area of the American republic, and in May the following year, Lewis and Clark had left on their historic expedition. When they returned two and a half years later, they brought back not only hard data about the flora and fauna of the upper Missouri and the Columbia watersheds, but also

Manifest Destiny
The idea that it was God's will that Americans overspread the continent bringing freedom, democracy, Christianity, and the American way wherever they went

Pictured is a book cover for
Two Years Before the Mast.
(Wikimedia Commons)

food for potent dreams about the West. By 1830 commerce with Europe was flourishing, and trade with Asia was burgeoning, with adventurers extracting fortunes from China. Wealthy speculators were willing to invest in almost any feasible enterprise. Americans thus had a sense of themselves as risk-takers. Moreover, in 1840 Bostonian Richard Henry Dana published a vivid description of the California coast in *Two Years Before the Mast,* thereby feeding the imaginations of his fellow Americans about that then remote region.

Dreams of Manifest Destiny were both concomitant with the westward expansion actually taking place between 1824 and 1848, and an augury of future hemispheric expansion. During this period, American Indians were moved out of the way of the conquering whites, and immense areas of the new Southwest and the far West were added to the United States. It was a period that saw a rapid influx of European immigrants into the United States. Between 1830 and 1850 more than two million Europeans—most of them impoverished farmers or manual workers—crossed the Atlantic. Many were of the new German and Irish wave of immigrants. Between 1830 and 1850 the population of the United States as a whole almost doubled, from nearly thirteen million to over twenty-three million. Though immigration was very significant, natural increase accounted for most of the growth, as these figures make clear.

Progress made possible by new technological breakthroughs—such as steam engines, locomotives, steel plows, reapers, and the cotton gin—helped instill in Americans the belief that they could conquer the frontier and produce material wealth from it. More expansion of America would translate into a wealthier, more prosperous country, and would allow opportunity for there to be more wealthy and prosperous individuals. Thus, much of the emphasis on expansion was frankly materialistic—and by today's standards racist, due to the belief that white Americans were God's chosen people—but idealistic motives for expansion were present, too. Protestant and Catholic missionaries, active in Oregon and elsewhere, hoped for numerous American Indian converts—though it should also be pointed out that most of them were quite culturally insensitive. Many Americans took pride in the contrast between freedoms flourishing in their own country and oppressions evident in foreign lands—often flattering their own country by exaggerating the contrasts. In fact, there was widespread concern that the intrigues of European imperialists would endanger the opportunities and liberties of ordinary Americans. Rumors spread that Britain and other powers were scheming to influence the internal and diplomatic policies of the Republic of Texas, to acquire Hawaii, and to control the bays of San Francisco and San Diego as well as Puget Sound. (Some of the rumors had more substance than skeptics realized.) Would not encroachments of

Map 11.1 Immigration (1840–1860)

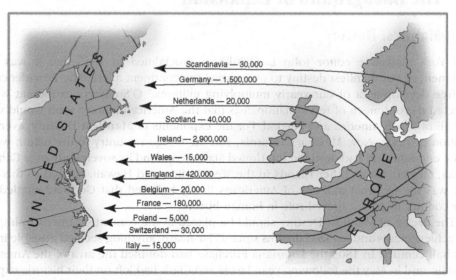

inimical courts and kings imperil the future of American democracy? Might they not also limit areas otherwise available for millions of oppressed Europeans, still hoping to come to American shores? Surely, it was God's and America's way to counter and remove the threat through a constructive program of rapid expansion. This was the sincere conviction of idealistic believers in Manifest Destiny.

The realization of America's Manifest Destiny, however, would come at a great cost. Native Americans would be systematically slaughtered and removed from their land; Mexico would lose approximately a third of its territory and fifty thousand people in a war with the U.S. that would also kill thirteen thousand Americans; and American pioneers would suffer great hardships as they traversed the continent in search of the American dream. Finally, Manifest Destiny led to significant degradation of the environment (for example, mining companies cut down every tree at Lake Tahoe to build mine shafts at Virginia City).

Maine border dispute
Dispute between the U.S. and Great Britain over the border between Maine and New Brunswick, culminating in a border clash in 1839 followed by the Webster-Ashburton Treaty

11.16 The Webster-Ashburton Treaty

Before Webster entered the State Department, the *Caroline* affair was not the only border incident fanning the flames of international misunderstanding. In addition there was the **Maine border dispute**, also known as the undeclared Aroostook War, caused by conflicting claims to the Aroostook River region on the undefined Maine-New Brunswick boundary. England and the U.S. had disputed the actual boundaries since the Peace of Paris in 1783 when the map used by the negotiators turned out to be flawed. In 1827, the King of the Netherlands mediated the dispute and drew a compromise border in 1831 that the English accepted and the U.S. rejected. Eight years later, the government of New Brunswick granted land titles to its subjects in areas that were north of the border drawn in 1831, but nevertheless still claimed by the U.S. When Canadian lumberjacks moved into what Americans claimed was American territory in Maine, the Maine legislature authorized the Maine militia

Map 11.2 Webster-Ashburton Treaty and Treaty of Paris Boundaries

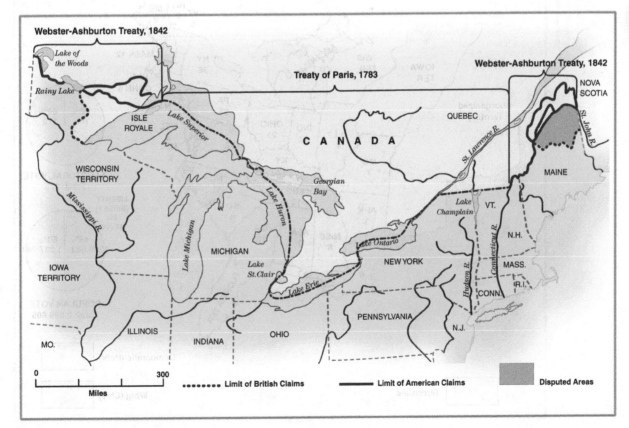

Webster-Ashburton Treaty

Set the border between Maine and New Brunswick and awarded the U.S. upper Minnesota

Election of 1844

Won by James Polk over Henry Clay on a platform of Manifest Destiny

to expel the "Warriors of Waterloo." The Canadian lumberjacks clashed with the Maine militia and captured fifty American militiamen. In response, General Winfield Scott and ten thousand Maine troops were committed in 1839 to the defense of the area subject to dispute. Instead of waging war with the Canadians, however, Scott arranged a truce that awarded land ownership according to the areas already occupied by each side at the time.

As the crisis eased, Secretary of State Daniel Webster met in a series of conferences with England's envoy, Lord Ashburton, to settle all items in dispute. In their treaty of 1842, Webster accepted a border very similar to the one drawn by the King of the Netherlands in 1831 after the British produced an old Ben Franklin map with the line drawn much further south than the 1831 border. New Brunswick received five thousand square miles out of the twelve thousand in dispute, and the U.S. gained the area around Thunder Bay, Minnesota. In spite of U.S. gains, the treaty was resented and Webster's popularity forever damaged in Maine, which felt itself shortchanged. Nevertheless, the **Webster-Ashburton Treaty** did help to achieve order and peace.

11.1c Return of the Democrats

Fresh issues had a vital impact on the **election of 1844**. Some had to do with the West, others with chattel slavery. Texans had won independence from Mexico in 1836, and now there was considerable sentiment for the annexation of the Republic of Texas by the United States. Southerners particularly favored such a step, while expansion-minded Northerners hoped that Americans would wholly occupy Oregon instead of being divided between the United States and Britain.

Henry Clay's nomination for president by the Whigs in 1844 came as no surprise—but former president Martin Van Buren was shunted aside by the Democrats because he

Map 11.3 Presidential Election of 1844

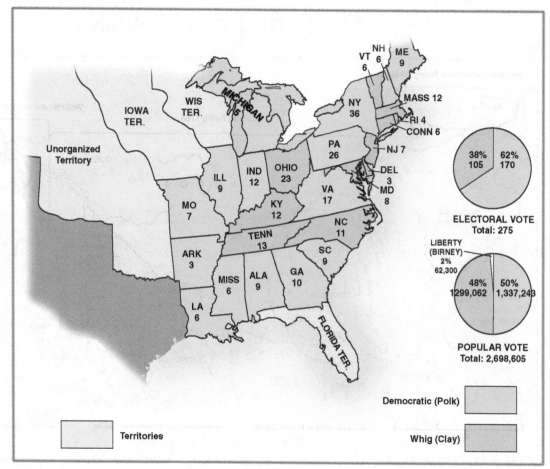

was thought to be anti-Texas, and little attention was paid to Tyler as a candidate since he was not a reliable party man. Instead, delegates to the Democratic National Convention nominated James K. Polk, a former governor of Tennessee and Speaker of the House of Representatives. Polk seemed thoroughly at home on the Democratic platform, which euphoniously but none too accurately described the desired Western policy as "the reannexation of Texas" and "the reoccupation of Oregon." Whigs made light of Polk's qualifications. "Who *is* James K. Polk?" they asked. But Polk's campaign strategy proved more effective than that of Clay, who tried to straddle the Texas dilemma and was impaled on the horns of equivocation.

Into the close contest came James G. Birney, heading the first partisan political expression of antislavery sentiment, the **Liberty Party**. Birney siphoned off Clay votes in New York, causing the state's electors to go to Polk and thus providing the difference. Polk received 170 electoral votes to Clay's 105. The popular outcome, however, favored the Tennessean much more narrowly. Polk's 1,338,000 supporters outnumbered Clay's by only 38,000.

Liberty Party

Antislavery party in 1844 that siphoned enough votes from Henry Clay that James Polk won both New York and the presidency

11.10 The Pathfinders

By the 1830s, with the removal of the American Indians, the trans-Appalachian West was a great complex of newly admitted states, and already people were moving beyond the Mississippi River. Missouri had been admitted as a state as early as 1821, and Arkansas followed in 1836. The wilderness beyond the Mississippi provided attractive commercial opportunities for aggressive American frontiersmen. The lucrative fur trade in the Northwest, for example, had drawn rugged trappers and traders to that area.

The most successful of the early fur traders was German-born John Jacob Astor, who organized the American Fur Company in 1808 with the intention of establishing a monopoly on the fur trade throughout the West. Astor's acquisitiveness, ruthlessness, enormous capital, and efficient administration helped him take over Great Lakes and Mississippi valley trading posts that originally had belonged to other companies. In the 1820s he pushed west and northwest, absorbing the Columbia Fur Company in the Oregon country and ruthlessly crushing rival trappers and traders.

Astor's business methods met with severe criticism on the frontier. An army officer had this to say: "Take the American Fur Company in the aggregate, and they are the greatest scoundrels the world ever knew." But Astor, undaunted by criticism, continued to prosper. In 1834, he withdrew from the fur business to concentrate on New York City real estate.

William Henry Ashley of St. Louis was another who made a fortune from furs in the Northwest. Ashley's Rocky Mountain Fur Company originated the revolutionary "rendezvous" method of fur trading, by which company agents, instead of trading with the American Indians, bought furs directly from white trappers at an annual "rendezvous" in the mountains. From 1822 to 1826, Ashley and the rugged trappers on his payroll pushed north and west, penetrating the country of hostile tribes and trapping beaver there.

When Ashley retired, he sold his Rocky Mountain Fur Company to Jedediah S. Smith, the "Knight in Buckskin" whose explorations greatly fostered American interest in the far West. In the autumn of 1826 Smith led the first American overland expedition from Missouri to California. He carved an amazing career as "mountain man" and plainsman, accomplishing the daunting task of survival through self-reliance in the harsh elements of the Rocky Mountains, while using the methods and technology of Native Americans.

Another fabulous character and "mountain man" was Jim Bridger, who may have been the first white man to see Salt Lake. Still another was Thomas Fitzpatrick, the noted guide and a genuine friend to the Native Americans.

Smith, Ashley, Bridger, Fitzpatrick, and the employees of Astor all were experts with the knife, the rifle, and the trap, but more important, they contributed significantly to frontier expansion and marked the paths for others. They had much to do with the development of communities like St. Louis and of future states in what is now the western part of the Midwest. Accounts of their exploits as men at one with nature while surviving the elements turned easterners' eyes and imaginations to the Rockies and beyond.

BVT *Lab*

Flashcards are available for this chapter at www.BVTLab.com.

Map 11.4 Settlement of the Mississippi Valley

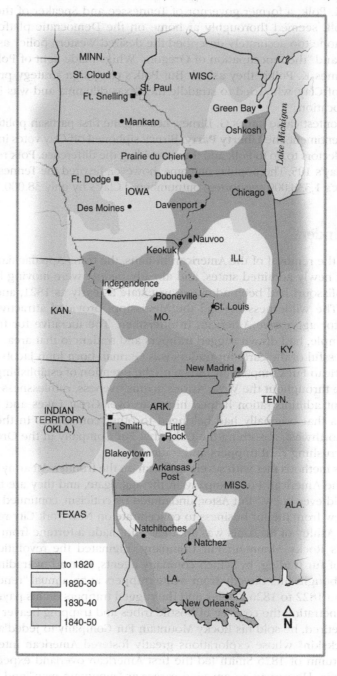

MINN.
St. Cloud
St. Paul
Ft. Snelling
Mankato

WISC.
Green Bay
Oshkosh

Lake Michigan

Prairie du Chien
Dubuque
Ft. Dodge
IOWA
Chicago
Des Moines
Davenport

Nauvoo
Keokuk
ILL.

Independence
Booneville
St. Louis

KAN.
MO.

KY.

New Madrid

TENN.
ARK.
INDIAN
TERRITORY
(OKLA.)
Ft. Smith
Little
Rock

Blakeytown
Arkansas
Post
MISS.
ALA.

TEXAS
Natchitoches
Natchez

LA.

New Orleans

N

to 1820
1820-30
1830-40
1840-50

John C. Frémont

Explorer who led several
expeditions to the West in
the 1840s—exploring the
Oregon Trail, the Sierra
Nevada, California, the
Colorado River, and the Rio
Grande—and whose well-
written reports, avidly read
in the East, stimulated further
immigration to the West

Oregon Trail

Opened to wagon trains in
1836, the route stretched
from Independence,
Missouri, to Oregon

Perhaps the most famous explorer among his contemporaries—so famous that he
was known as the "Pathfinder" and won the Republican nomination for president in
1856—was **John C. Frémont**. Son of a French émigré schoolteacher, Frémont formed
a strong taste for meeting and mastering wilderness challenges early in life. It was
in 1838–1839, when employed on a survey of the broad plateau between the upper
Mississippi and upper Missouri Rivers, that this army officer got his real start as a
geological observer, mapmaker, and scientific reporter. In the 1840s, he led several
expeditions to the West, exploring the **Oregon Trail**, the Sierra Nevada, California, the
Colorado River, and the Rio Grande. His well-written reports, avidly read in the east,
stimulated further immigration to the West.

11.1e The Santa Fe Trail

Santa Fe, in the Mexican territory of New Mexico, also provided attractive commercial opportunities for enterprising Americans. Though the volume of American trade in Santa Fe was never large, it was economically significant because American merchants were able to dispose of goods at handsome profit and because they brought away silver in an era when silver was at a premium.

William Becknell of Arrow Rock, Missouri, initiated the Santa Fe trade in 1821, when he sold his goods for ten to twenty times what they would have brought on the banks of the Mississippi. Venturesome American merchants and farmers followed Becknell's example, carrying goods along the eight hundred mile **Santa Fe Trail** from Independence, Missouri, to the great bend of the Arkansas and into New Mexico. Though the trip was arduous—confronting caravans with the dangers of rattlesnakes, heat, and storms—only eleven whites are reported to have been slain by American Indians on the trail before 1843, illustrating that the Santa Fe Trail was less dangerous than it is sometimes depicted to have been.

Santa Fe Trail
Opened in 1821, an eight hundred mile trade route from Independence, Missouri, to Santa Fe, New Mexico, where Americans would trade their goods for silver at exorbitant prices

11.1f The Oregon Trail

Mention of the Oregon Trail also conjures up visions of caravans moving west, but in this case the wagon trains carried not merely merchants but also farmers and other permanent settlers. Back in Jefferson's time, Lewis and Clark had traversed part of what was to become the celebrated route to the Pacific Northwest. Other hardy spirits followed, adding discoveries of their own.

The Oregon idea was not difficult to sell to land-hungry Americans—even though at that time Oregon was jointly occupied by the United States and Britain. The Hudson's Bay Company, an English economic interest, had long been established on the Columbia River in the business of beaver pelts. Church interest heightened when such American Protestant missionaries as Jason Lee, Samuel Parker, and Dr. Marcus Whitman and his wife Narcissa went out to Oregon to convert American Indians. Thus national pride, missionary zeal, the lure of cheap land, and the favorable reputation of the region all played a part in enticing thousands to Oregon.

John C. Frémont, known as the "Pathfinder" for his fame as an explorer, won the Republican nomination for president in 1856. (Wikimedia Commons)

As in the case of the Santa Fe Trail, Missouri towns like Independence and St. Joseph were takeoff spots for the Oregon-bound. For a couple of days of travel, the two routes even coincided. Then, as one went south, the other bent north. Out across various rivers including the Platte, and beyond to Fort Laramie, the covered wagons and pack trains of those seeking homes in the Northwest wound their way in the 1840s. On to Fort Bridger and along the Snake River they proceeded to Whitman Mission. At last they saw the storied Columbia and reached Astoria on the Pacific Coast, or wherever they were going. The Oregon Trail stretched two thousand miles—two and a half times the length of the Santa Fe journey.

11.1g Western Army Posts

The exploits of the mountain trappers, the Santa Fe traders, and the Oregon pioneers should not tempt us to overlook the role of the professional soldiers. From the 1820s well into the 1840s, the United States Army was not large, but its role in aiding the settlement of the West can hardly be exaggerated. Speculators and homesteaders were more likely to bring their families to areas when the military was nearby. Army posts in time became villages, towns, and cities. It was not unusual for a retired officer to become a respected civilian in a new community. Soldiers brought steamboats to Western rivers, constructed

Map 11.5 Trails of the Old West

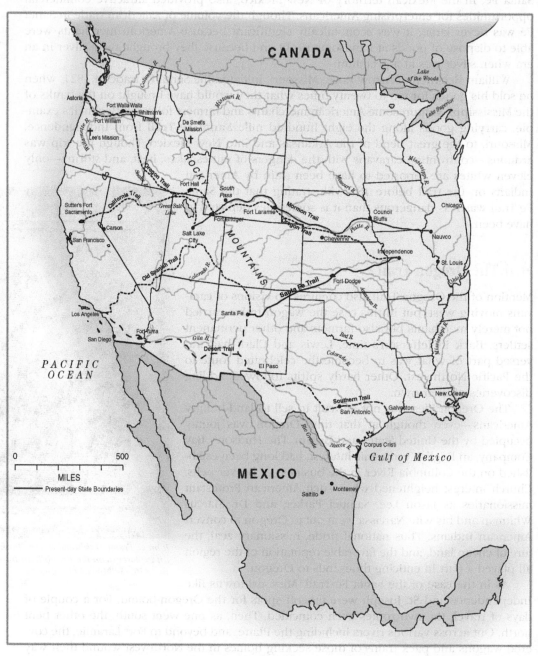

Stephen S. Long

Surveyed parts of the Great Plains and Rocky Mountains in 1819–1820; described the Great Plains as the "Great American Desert"

sawmills, and built their own forts. They farmed adjacent fields, introduced cattle, and disproved the widely credited legend that a "Great American Desert" existed between the Mississippi and the Rockies.

When it came to exploration, the army also played its part. In general, the information provided by military expeditions was better documented and more useful than the stories from the mountain men. Although these military expeditions were not so colorful as the exploits of a Jim Bridger or of the famous trapper, Indian fighter, and scout Kit Carson, they were nevertheless essential in opening up the previously unknown West. Perhaps most important was the expedition of **Stephen S. Long** (1819–1820) who surveyed parts of the Great Plains and Rocky Mountains. Long, however, described the Great Plains as the "Great American Desert," fit only for the American Indians and the buffalo, not for cultivation or white settlement. As a consequence, many maps of North America would label the area between the Mississippi River and the Rocky Mountains as the "Great American Desert" for decades.

11.2 Conquering the West

11.2a A National Question

As long as the westward movement was confined to a few explorers and commercial adventurers, Washington could act indecisively and put off any attempt to reach terms with London and Mexico City in connection with territorial disputes in the West. As American settlers poured into the far West and the Southwest, setting up communities and then local governments, the United States government could no longer hesitate. The dispute with Britain over the boundaries of the Oregon country had to be settled and the aspirations of fellow Americans living in Texas had to be heeded. What had been social and economic developments in the West had by the 1840s risen to the level of national political questions.

11.2b The Oregon Dispute

The "Oregon country" was a great deal larger than the present state of Oregon, and included what are now the states of Idaho, Oregon, and Washington as well as much of British Columbia. It was bounded roughly by the "Great Stony" Mountains to the east, the Pacific to the west, California to the south, and Alaska (then Russian) to the north. When informed men chatted about Oregon in the era after the War of 1812, they referred to a wondrously varied land with towering mountains and fertile valleys, swift-coursing rivers and magnificent forests. Details, however, eluded even the best-informed of commentators; lack of surveys made it impossible to define its area precisely.

Early in the nineteenth century both Russia and Spain laid claim to sections of Oregon, but Spain bowed out of the picture in 1819, and Russia in the next decade acknowledged 54°40′ as Alaska's southern border. Britain and the United States were left in contention over the Oregon country between Russian Alaska and Spanish California.

The principal area involved in the **Oregon dispute** was the territory between the Columbia River and the line of 49° latitude to the Pacific—the northwestern two thirds

Oregon dispute

Dispute between England and the United States over control of Oregon, eventually settled in 1846 at the 49th parallel during the Polk presidency

Map 11.6 The Oregon Controversy

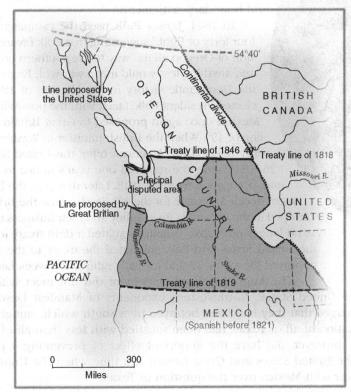

James Polk

Eleventh president of the
United States, elected in
1844 on a Manifest Destiny
platform

of the present state of Washington. Britain based its claims on the exploration, discovery, and occupation of the region by British subjects, and British fur trapping operations in the Columbia River Valley. American claims also were based on exploration and occupation, including Captain Gray's original discovery of the Columbia River in 1792, the Lewis and Clark expedition of 1804–1806, and the presence of American missionaries and settlers in the area in the 1830s and 1840s.

During Anglo-American negotiations in 1818, the United States proposed the boundary line of 49° to the Pacific Ocean. Britain agreed except for the part north and west of the Columbia River; it was unwilling to relinquish its claims to the Columbia River—the "St. Lawrence of the West," and home to British beaver trapping operations. Unable to reach a satisfactory agreement, in 1818 the two nations settled upon a treaty of ten year joint occupation of the area "on the northwest coast of America, westward of the Stony Mountains." In 1827 the treaty was renewed for an indefinite period, with the provision that either party could terminate it on a year's notice.

Neither in 1818 nor at any other time until 1845 did the United States or Britain provide for civil government in Oregon. No marshal, no sheriff, no jury, no judge was empowered to carry out legal procedures. No laws could be executed because none had been enacted, there being no enacting authority. As a consequence, men often took justice—or what they deemed was justice—into their own hands. A missionary, without the shadow of authority, might name a constable or a magistrate, and there were times when American traders and trappers tried alleged culprits for murder and other crimes—but maintenance of order, while frequently successful, was unofficial at best. American Indians in the Oregon territory did not become subject to the slightest American official authority until 1843, when President Tyler appointed Oregon's first Indian agent.

That was the year when the first large body of American immigrants arduously entered the Willamette valley in western Oregon. It was also then that a committee, composed of American pioneers and their French-Canadian neighbors, met in Champoeg and formed a provisional government. Once the government came into being, it was almost immediately effective. People of stamina and initiative determined to do in Oregon what Washington agencies had not done.

Soon the "Oregon fever" had hit the eastern United States, and British settlers in Oregon began to find themselves vastly outnumbered. This rapid influx of Americans prompted both Britain and the United States to try once again for a peaceful boundary settlement.

In 1844, **James Polk** used the campaign slogan "fifty-four forty or fight," suggesting that Polk favored U.S. possession of Oregon all the way to the southern border of Alaska and anything less would mean war with England. Soon after the Democratic victory in the election of 1844, the newly elected President Polk, faced with the possibility of war with Mexico, once again proposed to Great Britain the boundary line of 49°. When the British minister in Washington peremptorily rejected the American offer, the United States, on April 26, 1846, gave the required one year's notice to terminate the joint-occupation treaty of 1818. Later that year, the British government decided to settle for the 49° line because the British had over-trapped in the Columbia River valley and their business in beaver pelts was no longer profitable. Britain submitted a draft treaty to this effect to the United States and Polk submitted the treaty to the Senate, which approved it on June 12 and formally ratified it a week later.

President James Polk, 1844
(Wikimedia Commons)

The Anglo-American settlement did not meet with unanimous approval in the United States: Northwestern exponents of Manifest Destiny and anti-slavery men charged that they had been betrayed by a South which, smugly complacent over the annexation of all of Texas, had been satisfied with less than all of Oregon. The Oregon Treaty, however, did have the important effect of preventing a possible third war between the United States and Great Britain at a time when the United States was involved in a war with Mexico over the question of Texas.

11.2c Settlement of Texas

BVT Lab

Visit www.BVTLab.com to explore the student resources available for this chapter.

In the 1820s and 1830s a number of Americans—mostly Southerners—took Mexico's liberal colonization law, offering cheap land to settlers, at face value and migrated to Texas. With the help of slaves and cotton gins they farmed the fertile soil and conducted business under the aegis of Stephen Austin and other *empresarios* who had contracted with the Mexican government to settle a certain number of families in Texas in return for large grants of land.

In three centuries, the Spanish government had brought only four thousand subjects to Texas. Now the population of the Austin communities alone expanded from 2,000 in 1828 to more than 5,500 three years later. By 1836, more than twenty-five thousand white men, women, and children were scattered between the Sabine River and San Antonio de Bexar. Colonists from the United States far outnumbered those of Spanish ancestry.

Friction between Mexicans and Americans in Texas was probably inevitable. Mexicans, long accustomed to Spanish procedures, were naturally unprepared for the expectations of the Anglo-style administrative and legislative procedures introduced by the immigrants. Blunt and self-assertive, Americans in Texas were certain that their way of life was freer, healthier, happier, and in all ways superior to that of the Mexicans. They looked upon themselves individually and collectively as proper agents to impose reform and progress on what they deemed to be a benighted society, handicapped for generations by superstition and sloth. The average newcomer failed to recognize the spirituality and

Map 11.7 The Texas Revolution

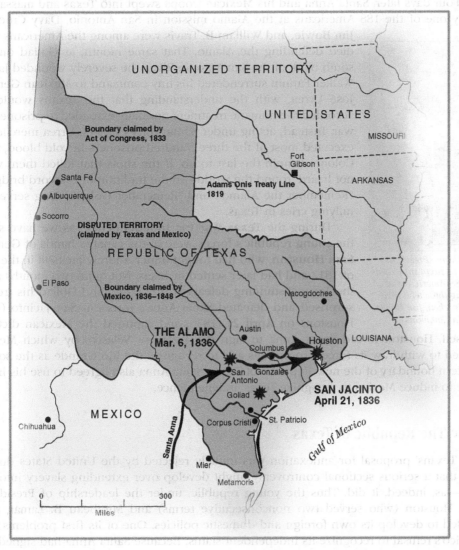

Texas War for Independence

Texans defeated a Mexican Army under Santa Anna at San Jacinto near Houston and won their independence from Mexico in 1836

Sam Houston

Tennessean and Jacksonian Democrat who became the head of the Texas army in the Texas Revolution and the first president of the Republic of Texas

gentility of Spanish culture and criticized the Mexican peasants for being illiterate and ignorant. Americans also overlooked the equally pertinent truth that both Mexican peasants and their grandee overlords were sensitive and proud.

Americans in Texas were distressed by fluctuations in Mexican policy and the uncertainty of their own status. The Mexican government appeared indifferent to educational needs and law enforcement, and it did nothing to meet the Americans' request for the separation of Texas from the state of Coahuila, to which it had been joined. This neglect, as well as the government's pressure to force the Roman Catholic religion on the settlers, impose taxes, impose centralized rule from Mexico City, and to abolish slavery, contributed to a drift that widened the gulf between the native Mexicans and the settlers who had emigrated from the north.

11.2b War for Independence

In Mexico City, meanwhile, a growing trend toward dictatorial rule reduced the likelihood of conciliation. The master spirit of despotism was Antonio Lopez de Santa Anna, who became president of Mexico in 1833. Santa Anna, "the Napoleon of the West," was ambitious, adept at intrigue, and an able field commander as long as fate favored him. As president, he ruthlessly crushed every semblance of liberalism in Mexico's central government and then turned his attention to Texas, where Americans were vehemently protesting his abandonment of the eleven-year-old, "enlightened" Mexican federal constitution of 1824. The Texans' protests culminated in a proclamation of independence from Mexico on March 2, 1836.

Four days later, Santa Anna and his Mexican troops swept into Texas and massacred every one of the 188 Americans at the Alamo mission in San Antonio. Davy Crockett, Jim Bowie, and William B. Travis were among the Americans who died defending the Alamo. That same month, at Goliad on the south bank of the San Antonio River, the severely wounded James Walker Fannin surrendered his tiny command to Mexican General José Urrea, with the understanding that the Texans would be accorded the humane treatment normally extended to prisoners of war. Instead, acting under Santa Anna's orders, Urrea mercilessly executed most of the three hundred prisoners in cold blood, with Colonel Fannin the last to go. If the shots that killed them were not heard 'round the world—in the tradition of Concord bridge— "Remember the Alamo!" and "Remember Goliad!" long served as rallying cries in Texas.

In the infamous massacre at the Alamo, President Santa Anna and his Mexican troops swept into Texas and massacred every one of the 188 Americans at the mission in San Antonio. Among those who died defending the Alamo were Davy Crockett, Jim Bowie, and William B. Travis. (Wikimedia Commons)

During the **Texas War for Independence**, as we have seen, the young republic's forces were in the capable hands of General **Sam Houston**, who had fought under Andrew Jackson in the War of 1812 and had later settled in Texas. Not quite two months after the Texans' stunning defeats at the Alamo and Goliad his troops surprised and defeated Santa Anna's forces at San Jacinto (near Houston) on April 21, 1836, and captured the Mexican dictator himself. Houston forced Santa Anna to sign the Treaty of Velasco, by which Mexico agreed to withdraw its forces from Texas and to recognize the Rio Grande as the southwestern boundary of the new Republic of Texas. Santa Anna also agreed to use his influence to induce Mexico to recognize Texas' independence.

11.2c The Republic of Texas

The Texans' proposal for annexation was initially rejected by the United States due to fear that a serious sectional controversy might develop over extending slavery into the area—as, indeed, it did. Thus the young republic, under the leadership of Presidents Sam Houston (who served two nonconsecutive terms) and Mirabeau B. Lamar, proceeded to develop its own foreign and domestic policies. One of its first problems was Mexico's refusal to recognize its independent status. Because Santa Anna had signed the

Treaty of Velasco under duress while a prisoner of war and Mexico had never ratified the treaty, the Mexicans denied its validity. Thus, though both Europe and the United States officially recognized Texas' independence, Mexico withheld recognition and continued to consider Texas to be a Mexican state in rebellion.

Though the sizable volunteer army of the San Jacinto campaign was disbanded in 1837, Texas maintained armed troops against the danger of another military campaign by Mexico. The Texas Rangers, loosely organized until then, were further developed to fight American Indian raids and border incursions by Mexican cattle rustlers; at the same time, the Texas navy made itself felt in the Gulf of Mexico. As late as 1843, Texan sailors were fighting against Mexican steam warships in the Gulf.

Maintenance of the navy and defenses against marauding American Indians and banditos—as well as a Mexican army that twice invaded Texas and took over the town of San Antonio in 1842—demanded more money than Texas had. Texan troops unsuccessfully invaded the Mexican towns of Mier and Santa Fe in 1842, with the result that some five hundred Texans were either dead or imprisoned in Mexico after the failed expeditions. The republic's civil government desperately needed financial support. Though bond issues were floated with varying degrees of success, the fiscal structure was never very solid in the period of the republic, which was experiencing inflation, currency devaluation, and massive debt.

Nevertheless, Texas prospered in terms of population, which grew rapidly due to immigration; most of the immigrants continued to be Americans. Large in territory and rich in untapped resources, Texas was regarded with covetous eyes by those American politicians who viewed it as a promising field for expansion, exploitation, and the extension of slavery.

11.2f Annexation of Texas

Presidents Jackson and Van Buren had been concerned about the North's opposition to the **annexation of Texas** due to the numerical balance between slave states and free states. Jackson favored annexation and was more outspoken about it after he retired from the presidency. In fact, Jackson had recognized Texas' independence on his last day in office in 1837. Hamstrung by the Panic of 1837, Van Buren marked time. His successors Tyler and Polk had no qualms about working toward annexation, however. Although both were slaveholders, neither seemed to have been thinking primarily about slavery while they were pushing for Texas' annexation (Polk's diary gives abundant evidence to this effect). Instead, both couched their motives in terms of expansion: Would it be to the country's advantage to *limit* expansion of the federal domain? This was substantially the same question Jefferson had asked himself in 1803 with reference to the Louisiana Purchase. Like Jefferson, Tyler and Polk answered with a ringing "No!"

Antislavery elements in the North, however, viewed the situation differently. Most Northerners—excluding the tiny minority of abolitionists—agreed with their Southern brothers that the Constitution protected slavery where slavery then existed. Extension of slavery into the West, however, was something of which they strongly disapproved. Thus, many citizens north of the Mason-Dixon line opposed the addition of Texas as a slave state.

Early in 1844 President Tyler, anticipating the presidential campaign of that year, sent a treaty for the annexation of Texas to the Senate. When the Senate rejected it by a vote of thirty-five to sixteen, Tyler recommended that Texas be annexed by joint resolution of both houses of Congress, since a joint resolution could be passed by a simple majority in both houses plus the president's signature, in contrast to the two-thirds Senate majority needed for treaty ratification. Congress adjourned before the measure could be brought to a vote, but when the second session convened on December 2, 1844, Tyler again urged a joint resolution to annex Texas.

Momentum gained for the measure in the fall of 1844, partially due to the election of James Polk, who had campaigned for president on a Manifest Destiny platform that included the annexation of both Texas and Oregon. Many in Congress viewed Polk's election as a public mandate for expansion. Therefore the resolution passed in both House and Senate this time, and Tyler signed it on March 1, 1845. Under the terms of the

John Slidell

John Slidell was sent to Mexico in 1846 to attempt to purchase the American Southwest from Mexico and to settle the Texas border at the Rio Grande; Slidell's offer was rejected by Mexico.

"Spotty Lincoln"

The nickname given to Congressman Abraham Lincoln for demanding to know "the spot" where blood was shed on American soil before the American war with Mexico in 1846

resolution, Texas was offered statehood with the understanding that its territory might be subdivided into not more than four additional states. The Missouri Compromise line of 36°30' was extended westward, permitting slavery in Texas but not in its territories north of the Missouri Compromise line. Texas was also allowed to retain its public lands so that it could sell the land and address the $10 million in public debt the state had incurred during its years as a republic.

Before the annexation resolution was passed, there had been hints and fears of British involvement in the fate of the Texas Republic. It was to England's, as well as to Mexico's, interest to see that Texas stayed out of the United States. A pending arrangement whereby Texas would ship cotton directly to Liverpool, for example, would mean the tightening of mutually advantageous Anglo-Texas economic ties.

The London government tried to induce Mexico to recognize Texas independence on the condition that the Lone Star republic would not become part of the United States. Mexico did assent to this proposal in May, 1845, and Texans had a choice of being annexed to the United States or negotiating such a treaty with Mexico. The Mexican offer had come too late, however. Now that annexation to the United States was theirs for the taking, Texans—most of whom were recent emigrants from the United States—found this alternative the more desirable.

11.2g War with Mexico

Already irate over Texas' independence, the Mexican government became exceedingly resentful when, in 1845, its erstwhile possession was formally annexed by the United States. Mexico had threatened to declare war on the United States if Texas was annexed. Now it withdrew its minister to the United States and severed official relations with the American government.

Mexico and the United States also disputed the official border between Texas and Mexico. The United States claimed that the border was the Rio Grande, based on the Treaty of Velasco signed by Santa Anna under duress and never ratified by Mexico. Mexico claimed that the border was the Nueces River (about 150 miles north of the Rio Grande) based on a border drawn by Spain in 1775 when Texas was part of New Spain, prior to Mexican independence. In June, 1845, President Polk ordered General Zachary Taylor and his troops into Texas to defend the territory. Taylor set up camp on the south bank of the Nueces River. In November, Polk dispatched **John Slidell** to Mexico on a special mission to discuss the outstanding issues between Mexico and the United States. Slidell was to propose that the United States assume the $2 million in claims of American citizens against the government of Mexico, in return for Mexico's recognition of the Rio Grande as the southwestern boundary of Texas. Polk also authorized Slidell to offer $5 million for New Mexico, or $25 million for both New Mexico and California (whose port of San Francisco seemed highly desirable to a people now committed to the China trade).

When the new Mexican government under President José I. Herrera refused to receive Slidell because public sentiment in Mexico was against the sale of territory to the United States, Slidell wrote to President Polk and argued that "nothing is to be done with these people until they have been chastised. War is desirable and we can never get along with them until we have given them a good drubbing." Polk ordered Taylor to proceed to the Rio Grande—a movement of troops that was bound to be taken as provocative, since Mexico claimed that the area was Mexican soil. Polk also sent the U.S. navy to the coast of California so that the U.S. could easily take over the ports of California if Mexico attacked American troops in Texas.

On April 12, Mexico warned Taylor to withdraw to the Nueces River, but Taylor refused and instead instituted a blockade of the Port of Matamoros, an act of war under international law. On April 25, 1846, Taylor's troops were attacked by Mexican troops, and eleven men were killed. Congress declared war on the Republic of Mexico after Polk declared to congress on May 11 that Mexico had "shed American blood on the American soil" and that "War exists" between the United States and Mexico. One young congressman from Illinois opposed the War Declaration on the grounds that the spot where blood was shed might not have been American soil. For demanding to know the "spot" on which American blood had been shed, Congressman Abraham Lincoln gained the nickname **"Spotty Lincoln."**

Map 11.8 Mexican War Campaigns

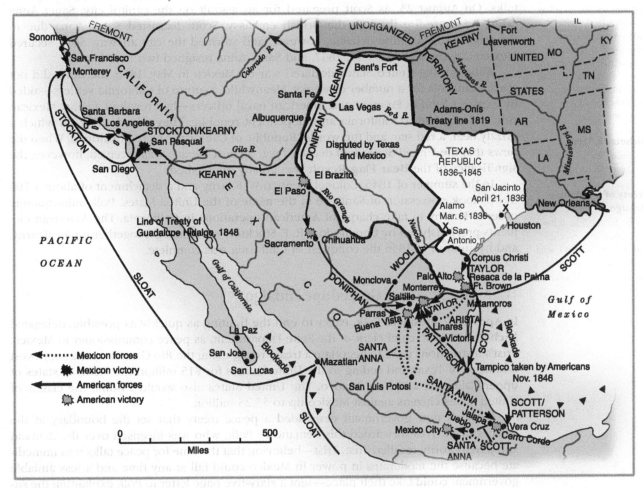

President Polk aided the return of the exiled Santa Anna to power in Mexico, believing that Santa Anna would quickly negotiate peace in return. Instead, Santa Anna raised a twenty-five thousand man army and moved north to meet Taylor's forces. The battles of Palo Alto and Resaca de la Palma followed; the first was an inconclusive artillery duel, the second a smashing American victory. These opening engagements of May, 1846 were followed by the major encounters of Monterrey the next September, and Buena Vista in February, 1847. General Zachary Taylor, bearing battlefield and theater responsibility in the Monterrey area, displayed great gallantry and was popular with his men—however, he did not make much progress in the direction of Mexico City, partly because Polk transferred most of the seasoned soldiers from Taylor's command to that of Major General Winfield Scott on the southeastern Mexican coast.

The battle at Buena Vista was General Zachary Taylor's greatest battle of the war. His success at Buena Vista helped him win the presidential election in 1848. (Wikimedia Commons)

It was Scott who, landing at Vera Cruz in March 1847, made that Gulf port his supply base and advanced inland to the mountain pass of Cerro Gordo, where he routed Mexican General Santa Anna. Other battles took place in 1847, and all were American victories. Scott entered Mexico City in September—but it was blood-soaked Buena Vista, more than half a year before, that would make Taylor the next president. Before Scott entered Mexico City, Santa Anna offered (through the British Minister in Mexico City) to accept peace on the receipt of $10,000 up front and $1 million

Bear Flag Revolt

In 1846, a group of
California settlers—aided by
explorer John C. Frémont
and by American naval
officers—revolted against
Mexican rule and raised a
flag on which a grizzly bear,
a red star, and the words
"Republic of California" were
positioned.

Nicholas P. Trist

Negotiated the Treaty of
Guadalupe Hidalgo

**Treaty of Guadalupe
Hidalgo**

Set the Texas border at the
Rio Grande, and ceded the
current Southwestern United
States to the U.S. provided
that the U.S. pay $18.25
million

to be paid after a treaty was ratified. Scott made the $10,000 payment through a secret service fund, but Santa Anna then announced that the Mexican legislature opposed peace talks. On August 23, as Scott prepared for an assault on the capitol city, Santa Anna offered a cease-fire through the British embassy. Scott distrusted Santa Anna due to the failed $10,000 bribe debacle, however, and stormed the city anyway. Scott secured Mexico City on September 14, 1847, and Santa Anna resigned two days later.

Although the United States declared war on Mexico in May, 1846, the news did not reach California for a number of weeks. Meanwhile, a group of California settlers—aided by explorer John C. Frémont and American naval officers—had revolted against Mexican rule and proclaimed California an independent republic. They raised a flag on which a grizzly bear, a red star, and the words "Republic of California" were positioned. When the news that the United States had declared war against Mexico was received, however, the significance of the **Bear Flag Revolt** was greatly diminished.

In the summer of 1846, Colonel Stephen W. Kearny and a detachment of about 1,700 troops took possession of Santa Fe in the name of the United States. Polk subsequently ordered Kearny to take charge of American operations in California. The American elements previously led by Commodore R. F. Stockton were brought together under Kearny, and by autumn of 1846 the conquest of California was complete.

11.2h The Treaty of Guadalupe Hidalgo

In April 1847 President Polk, eager to end the fighting as quickly as possible, delegated **Nicholas P. Trist**, chief clerk of the State Department, as peace commissioner to Mexico. Trist's instructions were to negotiate a treaty recognizing the Rio Grande as the southwest boundary of Texas and ceding to the United States for $15 million the Mexican states of upper California and New Mexico. The United States also would assume the claims of United States citizens against Mexico up to $3.25 million.

Mexico's new government demanded a peace treaty that set the boundary at the Nueces River. Trist forwarded this demand to Polk, who was incensed over the demand and peremptorily recalled Trist. Trist—believing that the time for peace talks was immediate because the moderates in power in Mexico could fall at any time and a less amiable government could take their place—sent a sixty-five page letter to Polk explaining the situation, and refused to return to Washington. With no official authority, he signed a treaty on February 2, 1848, that incorporated all the provisions of his annulled instructions. Polk was furious at Trist's disobedience, declaring that Trist had acted "worse than any man in the public employ whom I have ever known," but he immediately sent the treaty to the Senate for ratification. Though the **Treaty of Guadalupe Hidalgo** was denounced by two vocal minorities—those who had demanded the cession of all of Mexico and those who wanted none of the southwestern territory—the Senate ratified it on March 10, 1848. The United States now found itself in possession of the mammoth region that includes the present states of California, Nevada, and Utah, most of Arizona and New Mexico, and parts of Colorado and Wyoming. It also found itself with a considerable number of Spanish-speaking residents, many of whom belonged to families that had lived there for generations. According to the treaty, they became U. S. citizens, and their property rights were entitled to respect.

The territory, however, had come at a great cost. The U.S. lost 13,000 men (11,550 from disease) from its army of 105,000—the highest death rate of any foreign war in U.S. history. The cost was even greater for Mexico, which lost 50,000 men and approximately half its territory. The war also created ill will toward the U.S. in Mexico that lasted for generations.

11.2i Gadsden Purchase

Santa Anna returned to power in Mexico in the 1850s and his government was desperate for money. Santa Anna knew that the United States coveted land in the Mexican northwest for the construction of a railroad from Texas to California. Santa Anna therefore let President Franklin Pierce, elected in 1852, know that he would be willing to give up more desert borderland in the Mexican northwest in exchange for a generous offer. To avoid political dissent in Mexico, however, Santa Anna required that the U.S. amass its army near the Mexican border and appear to threaten another military incursion. President Pierce dutifully sent the U.S. military to the Rio Grande in a charade of force, and U.S. Minister to Mexico James Gadsden secured fifty-four thousand square miles of what is now southern Arizona and New Mexico for $10 million.

11.2j Filling Out the West

While settlement of Texas and the Oregon country was proceeding, other areas were luring pioneers westward in search of land or mineral wealth. Some who had started out on the Oregon Trail bound for the Northwest changed their destination to California. The path to California followed the Oregon Trail to the Continental Divide where, turning southwestward, it became the California Trail and led through the Sierra Nevada into California.

Before 1840, only fur traders penetrated to California, though whaling ships stopped there for supplies occasionally. In the early 1840s, some farmers began to move into the Pacific Coast valleys, but when war with Mexico broke out in 1846, there were only about seven hundred Americans in California. The discovery of gold at Sutter's Mill near Sacramento in 1848 started the gold rush, which brought the total population of the area to ninety thousand by 1850, when California became a state. The gold seekers came by sea around Cape Horn, by sea after an overland crossing of Mexico or Central America, or by various overland routes across the North American continent. The transcontinental journey was chosen by most immigrants—an estimated forty thousand traversing it in 1849 alone. The California gold rush brought people—a disproportionate share of them male in the first years—from all over the world and left an imprint on the region that is, arguably, felt to this day: California is one of the most ethnically diverse regions of the country. As New Mexico continues to be regionally distinct because it was the most populous region in the Mexican domain before being sold to the United States in 1848; as New Orleans and Louisiana still show many traces of the French and creole cultures that preceded the Louisiana Purchase; so San Francisco and northern California are different today because "the world rushed in" in 1849. Two-thirds of the adult males in Oregon quickly immigrated to California in search of gold. Some thirteen thousand immigrants arrived in California from Mexico, South America, and Europe.

By the 1850s, there were two frontiers in America: one moving westward beyond the Mississippi and the other moving eastward from California and Oregon into the Rocky Mountain area. The first settlement to fill the gap between them was established by the Mormons, who moved to Utah in 1847 (another region that continues to bear a strong imprint of its original settlement patterns). To escape persecution, and under the leadership of Brigham Young, the Mormons decided to move to a desert valley around the Great Salt Lake in 1846, where they hoped to find peace. The Mormons had chosen Utah because no one else wanted the barren territory and they believed that they would be left alone. Thousands of Mormons migrated along the Mormon Trail—some 1,300 miles from Iowa to Utah—using handcarts. In one great exodus, a thousand Mormons and their handcarts got stuck in the Rocky Mountain snow and Brigham Young sent an entourage of Mormons with mules to save eight hundred of the stranded pilgrims. They had some misfortunes and near disasters in the first few years, but eventually became prosperous due to their ingenious canal irrigation using the Rocky Mountain snowmelt. Throughout this time they continued to practice polygamy. Brigham Young installed himself as president of the Mormon Church, and considered Utah to be an independent country. Young was prone to self-aggrandizement, however, and claimed his own death and resurrection; he also had twenty-three wives.

With the close of the **Mexican-American War**, the Mormons lost the nominal Mexican jurisdiction under which they had been free to do as they pleased. Congress organized the Mormon lands into Utah Territory in 1850, naming Brigham Young as territorial governor. By 1860, there were forty thousand people living in Utah—but it was not admitted as a state until 1896 because the Mormon Church did not renounce the practice of polygamy until 1890. For a few years after 1849, the Mormons profited substantially from the sale of supplies to gold seekers on the way to California.

Mexican-American War
Began with the U.S. invasion of Mexico in 1846 to secure the Texas border at the Rio Grande (Thirteen thousand Americans and fifty thousand Mexicans died in the war.)

BVT Lab

Improve your test scores. Practice quizzes are available at www.BVTLab.com.

The treaty ending the war with Mexico filled out the present continental limits of the United States with the exception of a strip of land in what later became southern New Mexico and Arizona. This was purchased from Mexico in 1853 because it was thought to provide the best route for a railroad to California. With the **Gadsden Purchase**, the American "empire" was complete from Atlantic to Pacific.

11.2ꝶ Growing Sectionalism

While the economic bonds were tightening between Northeast and Northwest, the South depended increasingly on exporting cotton and other plantation products to the European market. Although there were notable exceptions, Southerners were basically pulling away from their earlier common interests with other parts of the country. The South's growing identification with an international market economy was natural for the specialized producer of seven-eighths of the world's cotton fiber.

Certain financial obstacles, however, prevented the South from completely freeing itself from dependence on the North. A growing demand for slaves meant continually rising prices for them. To buy land and slaves for the expansion of cultivation required new increments of capital, which the planter class—a leisure-loving economic aristocracy—simply could not provide for itself. The new capital, therefore, had to be acquired in the financial markets of the North and Europe, in competition with an expanding and increasingly productive mechanized industry.

Likewise, the shipping and sale of cotton tended to be handled by mercantile agencies in the principal Northeastern seaports, because the highly specialized shipping requirements of the Southern economy could not be met efficiently except in conjunction with the more general trade of the major ports. Southern ports did not offer such possibilities of pooling cargo and warehouse space. Southerners complained that their industry was being taken away from them, as Northern merchants who obtained the profits of the cotton trade kept the Southern planters dependent upon them for mercantile credit.

Nevertheless, the South continued to follow its policy of determined divergence from the economies of the other sections of the nation and continued to seek a free world market. Not all whites living in the South were in agreement on means and methods, but the most extreme elements felt that there was only one way in which their section could escape economic submission to the North and West: Only through secession from the Union, they were convinced, could the Southern states avoid being damaged by future economic policies that would destroy slavery and the plantation system. Ultimately, the South would indeed choose the path of secession—a path that would lead not only to the end of the institutions they had sought to save but also to the most destructive event in our national history: the Civil War.

Timeline

1803	Louisiana Purchase adds land between the Mississippi River and Rocky Mountains
1808	Jacob Astor organizes American Fur Company
1818	U.S. and England agree on joint occupation of Oregon
1819	Stephen S. Long surveys the Great Plains and declares them a "Great American Desert"
1821	William Becknell of Arrow Rock, Missouri, initiates the Santa Fe trade
	Missouri is admitted as a state
1826	Jedediah S. Smith leads the first American overland expedition from Missouri to California
1831	The king of the Netherlands draws a border between Maine and New Brunswick that is accepted by England, but rejected by the U.S.
1836	Arkansas is admitted as a state
	Texas wins its independence from Mexico
	The first Oregon wagon trains are organized at Independence, Missouri
1838	John C. Frémont surveys the plateau between the Mississippi and Missouri Rivers
1839	Border clash between Maine militia and Canadian lumberjacks
1840	Richard Henry Dana publishes a vivid description of the California coast in *Two Years Before the Mast*
1842	Webster-Ashburton Treaty settles Maine border and grants upper Minnesota to the U.S.
1844	James Polk is elected president on an expansionist platform
1845	John L. O'Sullivan proclaims it "the fulfillment of our manifest destiny to overspread the continent allotted by Providence for the free development of our yearly multiplying millions"
	The U.S. officially annexes Texas on December 29
1846	The U.S. gains sole occupation of Oregon, south of the 49th parallel, in a treaty with England
	The U.S. invades Mexico in a border dispute
1847	Brigham Young leads the Mormons to Utah
1848	Treaty of Guadalupe Hidalgo sets the Texas border at the Rio Grande and grants the American Southwest to the United States
	Gold is discovered at Sutter's Mill near Sacramento
1854	Gadsden Purchase: the U.S. purchases fifty-four thousand square miles of what is now southern Arizona and New Mexico

CHAPTER SUMMARY

etween 1824 and 1854, Americans spread across the North American continent, subscribing to the belief in Manifest Destiny—or that American control of the continent was part of God's Divine plan. In 1803, Thomas Jefferson had purchased the vast area between the Rocky Mountains and the Mississippi River from France, and in 1804 he commissioned Lewis and Clark to explore it. Lewis and Clark made it all the way to the Pacific Ocean on the Columbia River—but England had also claimed the area and America agreed to joint occupation of the Oregon Territory with the British in 1818.

In 1831, the king of the Netherlands drew a border between the U.S. and Canada in northern Maine, but the U.S. rejected the new border. When Canada granted land to lumberjacks in an area south of the new border, an armed border clash followed between the Maine militia and the Canadian lumberjacks. The Maine border dispute was finally settled by the Webster-Ashburton Treaty, which set the border at the James River and awarded upper Minnesota to the U.S.

In 1819–1820, Stephen S. Long explored the Great Plains and labeled it the Great American Desert; consequently, Americans would settle the Continent by bypassing the "desert" and heading further west. In 1821, the Santa Fe Trail opened a trade route from Independence, Missouri, to Santa Fe. In 1836, the Oregon Trail opened to wagon trains traveling from Independence, Missouri, to Oregon.

In 1844, James Polk won the presidency on a Manifest Destiny platform. Polk then waged war with Mexico to gain placement of the Texas border at the Rio Grande, and the Southwestern United States, from Mexico. Polk negotiated the division of Oregon with the British and the Canada-United States border was set at the 49th parallel. In 1854, the U.S. would purchase fifty-four thousand square miles of southern Arizona and southern New Mexico from Mexico in the Gadsden Purchase. Meanwhile, Brigham Young led his Mormon followers to Utah in 1847, and gold was discovered at Sutter's Mill near Sacramento in 1848 leading to a westward rush of settlers to California. Unfortunately, just as "Manifest Destiny" was coming together, sectionalism threatened to rip the country apart.

KEY TERMS

BIBLIOGRAPHY

A

Arrington, Leonard J., and David Bitton. *The Mormon Experience: A History of the Latter Day Saints*. Champaign, IL: University of Illinois Press, 1992.

B

Billington, Ray Allen. *The Protestant Crusade 1800–1860*. New York: Rinehart, 1938.

———. *The Far Western Frontier, 1830–1860*. Albuquerque, NM: University of New Mexico Press, 1995.

Brinkley, Alan. *American History: A Survey*. 11th ed. Boston, MA: McGraw-Hill, 2003.

C

Calvert, Robert A., Arnoldo De Leon, and Gregg Cantrell. *The History of Texas*. 4th ed. Hoboken, NJ: Wiley-Blackwell, 2007.

Campbell, Randolph. *Gone to Texas*. New York: Oxford University Press, 2003.

Clark, Malcolm, Jr. *Eden Seekers: The Settlement of Oregon 1818–1862*. Boston, MA: Houghton Mifflin, 1981.

Craven, Avery. *The Coming of the Civil War*. New York: Scribner, 1942.

Cummings, Bruce. *Dominion from Sea to Sea. Pacific Ascendancy and American Power*. New Haven, CT: Yale University Press, 2011.

F

Fehrenbach, T. R. *Lone Star: A History of Texas and the Texans*. Cambridge, MA: Da Capo Press, 2000.

G

Garraty, John A., and Robert McCaughey. *The American Nation: A History of the United States Since 1865*. 6th ed. New York: HarperCollins, 1987.

H

Hughes, Jonathan, and Louis P. Cain. *American Economic History*. 8th ed. Englewood Cliffs, NJ: Pearson Prentice-Hall, 2010.

J

Johnson, Curtis D. *Redeeming America: Evangelicals and the Road to Civil War*. Lanham, MD: Ivan R. Dee, 1993.

Jones, Howard. *Quest for Security: A History of U.S. Foreign Relations*. New York: McGraw-Hill, 1996.

K

Kolchin, Peter. *American Slavery: 1619–1877*. New York: Hill and Wang, 2003.

L

Lipset, Seymour Martin, and Earl Raab. *The Politics of Unreason: Right-Wing Extremism in America, 1790–1970*. New York: Harper and Row, 1970.

M

Meacham, John. *American Lion: Andrew Jackson in the White House*. New York: Random House, 2009.

Merk, Frederick. *Manifest Destiny and Mission in American History*. Cambridge, MA: Harvard University Press, 1995.

N

Nichols, Roy F. *The Disruption of American Democracy*. New York: Collier, 1962.

O

Oren, Michael B. *Power, Faith, and Fantasy: America in the Middle East 1776 to the Present*. New York: W. W. Norton & Company, 2007.

P

Paul, Rodman. *California Gold: The Beginning of Mining in the Far West*. Lincoln, NE: University of Nebraska Press, 1967.

Potter, David M. *The Impending Crisis: American before the Civil War 1848–1861*. New York: Harper Perennial, 1977.

R

Rohrbough, Malcom J. *The Trans-Appalachian Frontier: People, Societies, and Institutions 1775–1850*. Bloomington, IN: Indiana University Press, 2008.

S

Schlesinger, Arthur Jr. *The Age of Jackson*. New York: Little, Brown, 1945.

Schroeder, John H. *Mr. Polk's War: American Opposition and Dissent, 1846–1848*. Madison, WI: University of Wisconsin Press, 1973.

Stegner, Wallace. *The Gathering of Zion: The Story of the Mormon Trail*. Lincoln, NE: Bison Books, 1992.

Stewart, James Brewer. *Holy Warriors: The Abolitionist and American Slavery*. New York: Hill and Wang, 1997.

BIBLIOGRAPHY

T

Tocqueville, Alexis de. *Democracy in America*. New York: Penguin, 2003.

U

Unruh, John D. *The Plains Across: The Overland Emigrants and the Trans-Mississippi West 1840–1860*. Champaign, IL: University of Illinois Press, 1993.

W

Weeks, Philip. *Farewell, My Nation: The American Indian and the United States in the Nineteenth Century*. New York: Harlan Davidson, 2000.

POP QUIZ

1. John L. O'Sullivan argued that the fulfillment of America's "manifest destiny" was to _____ "allotted by Providence."
   a. end slavery
   b. achieve equality for all
   c. overspread the North American continent
   d. bring freedom to the Middle East

2. What was the result of the undeclared "Aroostook War"?
   a. Canadian lumberjacks defeated the Maine militia and captured fifty Americans.
   b. The Maine militia gained territory in New Brunswick.
   c. The Maine militia gained territory in Nova Scotia.
   d. Americans briefly took over Prince Edward Island.

3. The most successful of the early fur traders who organized the American Fur Company in 1808 was _____.
   a. John Jacob Astor
   b. John Jacob Jingleheimerschmidt
   c. Joseph Sterling
   d. Richard Montgomery

4. The British Hudson's Bay Company's interest in Oregon was primarily in _____.
   a. gold
   b. silver
   c. beaver pelts
   d. timber

5. The claims to Oregon were based on _____.
   a. British Manifest Destiny
   b. the Treaty of Tordesillas
   c. a Treaty with Russia
   d. British discovery, exploration, and occupation of the region

6. The Mexican Army massacred hundreds of Texans at _____.
   a. the Alamo
   b. Goliad
   c. San Jacinto
   d. both a and b

7. The congressman who protested the war with Mexico by demanding to know "the spot" where American blood had been shed was _____.
   a. Henry Clay
   b. Daniel Webster
   c. Abraham Lincoln
   d. Bill Richardson

8. What happened at Sutter's Mill near Sacramento in 1848?
   a. Gold was discovered.
   b. Seventeen people were killed in an apparent blood atonement murder.
   c. Sutter discovered a way to spin straw into gold.
   d. The angel Moroni appeared to Joseph Smith.

9. Why wasn't Utah admitted as a state until 1896?
   a. A wagon train was massacred at Mountain Meadows.
   b. Not enough people lived in Utah until 1890.
   c. The Mormon Church did not renounce polygamy until 1896.
   d. The U.S. government did not know that Utah was inhabited until 1896.

10. More than one thousand whites were killed by Indians on the Santa Fe Trail. T F

11. When Texas was annexed to the U.S., the federal government assumed ownership of its public lands. T F

12. The South's major market for its cotton was Europe. T F

13. The belief that God wanted Americans to bring their way of life to the world is called _____ _____.

14. _____ was the first president of Texas.

15. The _____ from Mexico in 1853 provided the best railroad route to _____.

Chapter 12

(Wikimedia Commons)

The Nation at Mid-Century

12.1 The Modernization of the United States

12.1a Characteristics of Modernization

Many scholars have used the concept of "modernization" to describe and analyze the rapid change experienced by Americans in the North in the middle decades of the nineteenth century. According to this thinking—which can provide a useful way of organizing information about such a transformative period—modernization is characterized by four factors—all of which were present in the mid-century North. The first is a heavy investment in social overhead capital, or improved transportation and communication infrastructure. This produces a transition from a localized subsistence economy to a regionally or nationally integrated market economy. The second factor is a rapid increase in the output per man-hour that results from technological innovation and the substitution of machines for human labor. The third factor is the evolution from decentralized handcraft manufacturing to centralized industries that produce standardized, interchangeable parts.

With the modernization movement in the United States came the substitution of technology for human labor. Slavery was on its way out in the north as machines were used more commonly. (Wikimedia Commons)

Last is the accelerated growth of the industrial sector as compared with other sectors of the economy.

Socially, modernization is marked by a growth in education, literacy, and mass communication and by a transition from a static, predominantly rural populace to an urbanizing population in which farms and villages become cultural as well as economic satellites of the urban/industrial market. Politically, modernization is accompanied by the rise of nationalism and centralized authority and by increased popular participation in government. Ideologically, modernization is characterized by an outlook that emphasizes change rather than tradition. In sum, modernization is the transition from a rural, village-oriented system of traditional personal and family ties to a dynamic, urban, market-oriented system of impersonal relationships. Once again, this set of descriptions fits the North in the mid-nineteenth century very well.

Modernization was both a cause and effect of the growing differences between North and South. The causes of antagonism between North and South are complex, but one source of stress was that Southerners feared the encroachment of modernization on their more traditional agrarian society. Furthermore, the Southern economy was a labor-intensive system, tying up large amounts of capital in the ownership of human beings—thus, slavery undoubtedly did inhibit technological innovation. Capital was diverted in the South from investment in factories and other innovations to investment in human inventory, stunting both technological advancement and economic growth. Landless Southerners and small landed farmers lacked the capital necessary to finance industrialization, and the capital that planters could have used to further develop the Southern economy was spent on goods manufactured in the North or overseas. The concentration of Southern capital into few hands depressed consumption and hindered the development of an indigenous Southern market and industry. Ideologically, the South feared change while the North both welcomed it and came increasingly to see slavery and the South's conservatism as obstacles to the progress and greatness of America.

12.16 American Modernization

This period marked the transition of America—with the partial yet significant exception of the South—from a pre-modern to a modern society. In the 1850s, middle-aged Americans could look back upon unprecedented changes in their own lifetimes. Since 1815, the development of steamboats, canals, macadamized roads, and railroads had radically increased the speed of inland transportation and reduced its cost. Whereas in 1815 the average cost of shipping freight had been 40¢ per ton-mile by wagon and 6¢ by water, in 1855 it was less than 3¢ by rail and 1¢ by water. Goods sent from Cincinnati to New York in 1817 took more than fifty days to reach their destination; by the early 1850s they required only six days. The same trip for passengers was reduced from three weeks to less than two days.

A few simple statistics will illustrate the pace of change in other indices of modernization as well. While all sectors of the economy grew rapidly from 1840 to 1880, the rate of growth in the manufacturing sector was more than twice that of agriculture. The percentage of the labor force engaged in manufacturing nearly doubled during the same period, and the proportion of the population living in urban areas increased more than two and a half times. As measures of the increased efficiency and higher standard of living produced by a modernizing economy, the per capita commodity output increased 72 percent and per capita income doubled during the same years.

This growth was a mixed blessing. The industrial working class did not share equally in the rising prosperity, for the real wages of blue-collar workers rose less than the income of other groups. Furthermore, no one can measure the human consequences of the transition from a craft-oriented system of manufacturing (in which skilled journeymen and apprentices worked alongside master craftsmen in small shops) to a factory system (in which unskilled or semiskilled workers performed repetitive tasks at a machine).

The loss of skills and of pride in craftsmanship, the growing separation of a working class from its employers, and the sense of relative deprivation caused by unequal distribution of increasing national wealth lay behind much of the labor unrest of this period.

In contrast with Europe, however, wages in America were high because of a relative shortage of labor. Despite rapid population growth, the supply of workers was never sufficient to meet the demand. This labor shortage, in turn, continued to stimulate technological innovation. New machines and new methods of production had to compensate for labor scarcity. Eli Whitney's attempt in 1798 to manufacture interchangeable rifle parts was sparked by the lack of skilled labor to make rifles in the traditional way. Although making interchangeable parts by machine was not exclusively an American development, it became known as the **"American system" of manufacturing**. By the 1850s, according to a team of visiting British industrialists, the American system was used for the production of a wide variety of goods—including "doors, furniture, and other woodwork; boots and shoes; ploughs and mowing machines; wood screws, files, and nails; biscuits; locks, clocks, small arms, nuts and bolts."

American system of manufacturing
A manufacturing system based on interchangeable parts

Robert Fulton
Constructed a successful commercial steam boat in 1807

12.2 The Economics of Expansion

12.2a The West and the Transportation Revolution

From the beginning of human life on earth, people have lived in close association with rivers and streams. Waterways were the natural routes over which travelers moved both themselves and their goods, for rivers cut through wildernesses travelers could not penetrate in other ways. Therefore, when the settlers moving into the American frontier were forced to return to the most primitive conditions of living, rivers naturally became their first important means of inland transportation.

One of the great drawbacks to river transportation is that the river does not always go where the traffic needs to go. This became true in the United States as soon as the territory west of the Appalachian Mountains was opened for settlement. Rivers descended eastward from the Appalachian watersheds to the Atlantic or westward to meet the Ohio and Mississippi, but no waterway directly connected the East Coast with the West. Thus, the great enthusiasm for building national roads during the "Turnpike Era," from 1800 to 1830, was occasioned partly by the fact that roads were needed to connect the Ohio River system with the Atlantic coastal rivers.

Transportation of goods over these road and river routes, however, was prohibitively expensive except in the case of light and very valuable merchandise. The best outlet for the bulky western produce was not eastward but southward on flatboats down the Ohio and Mississippi Rivers to New Orleans. Any attempt to try to propel flatboats back up the river against the current was still impractical, however. Manufactured products needed by western settlers—such as guns, ammunition, traps, axes, plows, tools, and even shoes and cloth—still had to come in overland from the east.

Pictured is a preserved flatboat. Flatboats were propelled southward down river to transport bulky produce. (Wikimedia Commons, Thomas R. Machnitzki)

Because America's immediate economic problem was the need to move goods over great distances inexpensively, the new steam power developed in England in the eighteenth century was applied in America to water transportation even earlier than it was applied to industry. Beginning with John Fitch in 1786, a series of American inventors worked on the problem of driving a boat with steam, culminating with **Robert Fulton** and his commercial success in powering his *Clermont* up the Hudson River in 1807. In the following decade steamboats were successfully tried on the Ohio and Mississippi rivers. By 1829 there were two hundred steamboats in operation on the western rivers, and by 1842 the number had reached 450. A decade later, there were well over a thousand. Partly because of the special needs of the West and partly because early steamboats were too fragile for ocean use (trans-Atlantic steamer service was not frequent until mid-century),

Map 12.1 Territorial Growth 1840

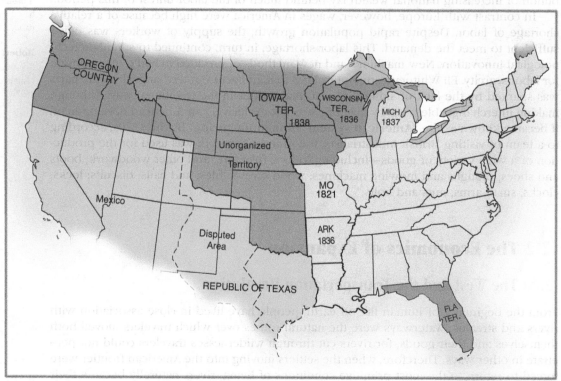

Erie Canal

Commercial canal and waterway from Buffalo to New York City completed in 1825

more steamboats were in service on the Mississippi River system than anywhere else in the world. Pittsburgh, Cincinnati, and Louisville began as river towns, while New Orleans became one of America's greatest ports.

Meanwhile, in an attempt to avoid the roundabout route through New Orleans, Northerners turned their attention to canal building, which had been so successful in England in the 1760s and 1770s. The first such waterway of great importance was New York's **Erie Canal**, connecting the Great Lakes with the Hudson River—and thus to the port of New York). Upon its completion in 1825, freight charges from Buffalo to New York City were cut from $100 to $10 a ton, and the time of the trip was reduced from twenty days to six. Migrants began to use the canal to gain access to the West. Buffalo, Cleveland, Detroit, Chicago, and other cities began to sprout around the Great Lakes; and the area began to fill up with settlers just as the Ohio valley had earlier. As a result of the canal trade, New York City grew rapidly in wealth and population, becoming the greatest port on the Atlantic seaboard. The nation was propelled into the Canal Era (1825–1840), with other sections from Illinois to Massachusetts trying to imitate the success of New York.

Yet rivers and canals had their shortcomings. During winter, frozen waterways could not be used in the North. Rivers followed inconvenient courses, and canals could not be built in rough or hilly country. The development of the railroads would overcome all of these limitations.

Steam-powered rail locomotives had already won success in England when the Baltimore and Ohio Railroad started the first few miles of American rail service in 1830. Soon other short lines were built in other locations, and by 1840 2,808 miles of track had been laid. Ten years later, the mileage had more than tripled to 9,029 miles, and by 1860 it had tripled again to 30,626 miles (as compared to industrial Britain's 10,410 miles). The railroads—which connected the Atlantic coast with Chicago and St. Louis by the 1850s—provided the West with exactly the kind of transportation it needed for the first time. Western products, no matter what their bulk, could now be moved regardless of weather or terrain directly to eastern markets for overseas shipment. Manufactures from the east and abroad could come in freely. Simultaneously, traffic on the rivers and canals declined. With the coming of the rails, the commercial and industrial Northeast and the agricultural Northwest were tied more closely together by common economic bonds.

Map 12.2 The Railroad Network (1850 and 1860)

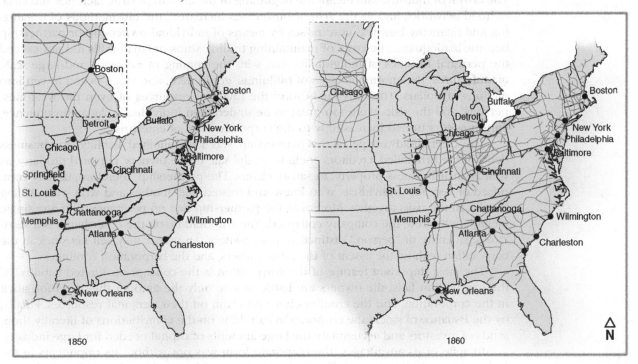

1850

1860

12.26 The Northeast and the Industrial Revolution

Under the impact of continually expanding trade, each section of the country underwent a characteristic economic evolution of its own. For example, New England—the section that had achieved the lead in population in the colonial era—was the first to pass from agriculture to commerce and industry. The absence of good soil for agriculture, combined with its good harbors adjacent to ample supplies of pine and hardwood, had turned New Englanders to shipbuilding, fishing, and overseas commerce in colonial days. It was no accident, then, that industrialism should have entered America through New England—for towns well located for commerce were also attractive for manufacturers. Mills and factories need to be near shipping points, markets, and sources of raw materials. The Northeast provided shipping points, with its excellent harbors, and a market, with its burgeoning population.

Industrial Revolution
The great explosion of manufacturing in the nineteenth century

Other circumstances contributed to the growth of industrialism in the Northeast. In the early stages, streams were still a must for turning the water wheels that drove the machinery of mills and factories, and the Northeast was favorably endowed with water power. The Embargo Act and the War of 1812, in restricting overseas trade, had driven idle commercial capital into investment in domestic industry. The tremendous potentialities of trade with the West, facilitated first by the Erie Canal and then by the railroads, provided further incentive for the manufacture of industrial products. Finally, even after steam had replaced water power in industry, manufacturing continued for a time to be located where capital and labor were already concentrated—in the Northeast.

The Erie Canal was a bustling western trading route during the Industrial Revolution in the United States. (Wikimedia Commons)

The rise of industrialism in the northern United States had economic and social consequences of such a revolutionary character that it has been called—as in England—the **Industrial Revolution**. It revolutionized the nature of business organization, of labor, of population distribution, and of the life and welfare of all Americans.

12.2c The Corporate Revolution

The arrival of industrialism meant the beginning of the growth of large factories and large railroad networks; and as the size of businesses increased, the old methods of organizing and financing business enterprises by means of individual ownership or partnership became inadequate. The costs of maintaining trading ships or small mills did not exceed the personal fortunes of individuals—but with the coming of railroads and large-scale manufactures, the enormous costs of buildings, equipment, and stock began to run into millions of dollars. This was far beyond the financial resources of even the wealthiest persons, and the risks were too great to be undertaken individually. As a consequence, entrepreneurs turned increasingly to the corporate form of enterprise.

The chief disadvantage of the partnership was its "unlimited liability" for business debts. If the firm failed, creditors could force the sale of the owners' personal property, as well as their business property, to satisfy claims. The partnership, therefore, usually comprised of very few individuals who knew and trusted one another and who were willing to take on the risks together. Moreover, the partnership had no permanence. If any single member withdrew, the company collapsed. The corporation, on the other hand, is a separate legal entity or "person," distinct from its owners. An owner may sell his stock in the corporation without the assent of the other owners, and the corporation continues.

The most important feature of the corporation is the concept of "limited liability." If the corporation fails, the owners are liable to lose only the amount they paid for stock in the corporation, and the creditors have no claim on their personal resources. Finally, by the issuance of stock, the corporation can draw on the contributions of literally thousands of investors and accumulate the large amounts of capital needed for large industry.

In spite of its advantages, the corporate form was not without its opponents in the Jacksonian period. Jackson, Jefferson before him—and even the father of *laissez faire* or free enterprise, the English economist Adam Smith—had attacked corporations as awarding "exclusive privilege" to some and limiting "free competition." In addition, Abraham Lincoln later warned that the power of corporations could subvert American democracy. What they were all attacking, really, was the kind of incorporation that was known before the 1830s. Prior to that point, corporate charters had been granted only through special legislation and only for some specific enterprise that had to be run as a monopoly in order to be profitable. Thus, **turnpikes**, canals, bridges, and banks—enterprises of a semipublic character—were often conducted under charters granting exclusive privileges. Part of Jackson's hostility toward the Bank of the United States can be traced to what he viewed as its monopolistic charter. Even less clearly beneficial to all the public was the construction of industrial establishments.

Many thought that the government should have no authority over the economy—but wider markets in the West and new technical processes made increased capital so necessary to industry that corporate charters were sought more and more frequently in spite of possible public opposition. To make incorporation democratic and consonant with Jacksonian equal-rights principles, Whigs and like-minded Democrats urged "general incorporation laws" (as distinct from special legislative grants) which would make corporate charters available to all who could meet certain legal requirements. Beginning in the 1830s and continuing into the 40s and 50s, corporations began to proliferate under the new system of general laws.

The Whig Party, which generally favored business interests (as would its successor, the Republican Party), had advocated free incorporation as a method of inaugurating a kind of "democratic" capitalism. That is, business would no longer be dependent upon rich men but could gather the combined resources of countless small investors. This multiplication of ownership, however, eventually resulted in a revolutionary change in the nature of business organization. As the number of stockholders or owners in a corporation rose into the thousands, and as they were dispersed about the country, actual management or "control" of the company fell into the hands of individuals who were not dominant owners or perhaps not even stockholders at all.

Under the system of individual proprietorship or partnership, ownership and control had been in the hands of the same person. The corporate system began the process of divorcing ownership from control and of creating a vast class of investors dependent, insofar as their profits were concerned, on the actions of others—the corporate managers. The inherent danger was that the managers might not act in the interests of the owners. In the days when owners managed their own businesses, owners who defrauded the company defrauded themselves. With the separation of ownership and control, the "insiders" or managers could systematically loot a company for their own profit. Said a contemporary observer concerning the stock market scandals of 1854:

> The spring trade of '54 opened gloomily … In June it was discovered that the Parker Vein Company had flooded the market with an immense and unauthorized issue of stock. The first of the next month New York was startled by the intelligence that Robert Schuyler, President of the New York and New Haven Railroad, had been selling some 20,000 illegal shares at par—and was now a defaulter for two millions. Almost simultaneously it was ascertained that Alexander Kyle, Secretary of the Harlem Railroad Company, had made an issue of forged stock to the amount of $300,000. Other developments of breaches of trust came flocking from the inland cities.

Scandals, very fortunately, represented only one phase of America's part in the Industrial Revolution. Another phase, at least equally significant, was the entirely new evaluation of the forces that affected the location of industry.

12.20 The Rise of Industrial Populations

Slater's Mill
The first textile mill in America at Pawtucket, Rhode Island

Lowell, Massachusetts
Location of textile mills that primarily employed women

Before the steam engine was developed, the almost complete reliance on water power resulted in scattering manufacturing among a large number of small or medium-sized towns, for the capacity of any given dam site was limited. The first American factory, **Slater's Mill**, was built in Pawtucket, Rhode Island, in the 1790s by British immigrant Samuel Slater, who designed his textile mill from memory based on those with which he was familiar in England. At the time, it was illegal to take a written blueprint of a textile mill out of England. By 1815, New England had over 150 textile mills producing thread and yarn from raw materials. All the mills worked on water power from water wheels in New England streams. This pattern would change, however, when the triumph of steam made it feasible for manufacturing to concentrate in large cities with locations off of riverbanks.

Industrial employment brought with it new problems that had not been imaginable in the previous handicraft period of individual workshops. In America, as in England, people did not know how to cope with the problems of health and safety in the new factories because never before had such problems existed. (Even in England, factory laws were not introduced until the 1840s.) Moreover, congested living quarters in the growing industrial cities of New England and the Mid-Atlantic often resulted in deplorable lack, not only of sanitation, but also of the minimum requirements for decent human existence. Hours of work were usually long, wages low, and schools for the children of workers inadequate. Workers could afford little for housing. The idea of public transportation had not been developed, so employees had to live within walking distance of their place of employment. All these conditions worked together to produce housing for industrial workers that would become slums of the worst sort.

Unlike the earlier handcraft industries, the new steam-driven machines did not require workers with great skill or physical strength. Increasingly, women and even children were hired to perform the simple but arduous and monotonous tasks of factory work. The best-known early textile mills were in **Lowell, Massachusetts**, where the workers were young, unmarried, New England farm women. By 1830, eight textile mills in Lowell employed over five thousand women, most of whom were between 16 and 25 years of age. The young women lived in company owned boarding houses with company housemothers and slept with four to six women in each bed. Company rules provided for curfews at ten o'clock at night and prohibitions against alcohol, gambling, and unsupervised courtship. There were soon several other mills in Massachusetts and New Hampshire, so that by the 1830s there were some forty thousand women working

At a time when it was illegal to take a building blueprint of a textile mill out of England, Samuel Slater built the first American factory from memory. Slater's Mill still stands in Pawtucket, Rhode Island. (Wikimedia Commons)

Map 12.3 Distribution of United States Population (1840)

DISTRIBUTION OF POPULATION
1840
★ **Center of Population**

LEGEND

Under 2 inhab. to the Sq. Mile

2 - 6 " " " "	I
6 - 18 " " " "	II
18 - 45 " " " "	III
45 - 90 " " " "	IV
90 and over " " " "	V

*Cities over 8000 inhabitants in solid color
in circles proportionate to population.*

Lowell Offering

A literary magazine published by women working in the textile mills of Lowell, Massachusetts

in New England textile production. Scholars have tried to assess how much their work represented opportunity—for most, this was their first chance to earn money—and how much it involved exploitation. What is certain is that the work day was long and arduous; the women worked in hot and humid conditions; and the power looms they tended—along with all the spinning gears and whizzing belts—created an extremely noisy atmosphere. Nonetheless, the Lowell women found the energy to publish a literary magazine, the **Lowell Offering**; and when employers tried to cut wages in the 1830s, the women twice went on strike. It has been suggested that the fact that they lived in dormitories together (so as to reassure their parents that they were being supervised) may actually have promoted solidarity among them. For most of them, after a stint in the mills, they married—having been able to put some money aside for household necessities out of their wages. Research has disclosed that they also sent money home to help educate their brothers or for other needs of their families of origin. Once Irish immigrants began to arrive in large numbers in the 1840s, the newcomers supplanted the native-born women as textile workers.

Urban industrialism resulted not only from new production techniques and new western markets but also from increased efficiency in agriculture. Improved farm methods and farm machinery permitted more people to be siphoned off into industrial production. In addition, a good many immigrants settled immediately in the cities. As a result, between 1820 and 1850 the cities grew much faster than the population as a whole. In 1820, only one person in fourteen lived in a city of 2,500 or more. By 1850, nearly one person in six lived in such a city. This meant an increase of more than fivefold in the population of cities, while the whole population had increased just over twofold during those years.

The great majority of Americans were still rural, still untouched by conditions developing in the Northeast—but those who watched the cities fill with immigrants and develop slums, vice, and crime were deeply disturbed. Many associated crowded cities and the factory grind with a Europe of decadence and oppression. The traditional Jeffersonian vision of America—the land of democratic simplicity—seemed to be threatened by new problems of industrial complexity.

12.2c The Rise of Labor

Among the first to react to these unsatisfactory conditions were the workers themselves. Although workers were influential in contributing to trends toward better education, their moves in the direction of unionization were in the main separate and distinct from most other reforms of the period.

The oldest labor organizations in America date back to the late eighteenth century, when various skilled craftsmen banded together to obtain higher wages, shorter hours, and other benefits from their merchant-artisan employers. It was not until the late 1820s and 30s that aggressive union activity began, with the establishment of strong craft unions in Philadelphia, Boston, New York, Providence, and other cities. An attempt was made in 1834 to form a National Trades Union; but even though the group held conventions for several years, the effort failed to achieve an enduring result.

The most successful of the early unions were local groups that were primarily political in their objectives, working especially hard for various social reforms like free public schools. Aided by favorable public opinion, they were able to make substantial gains through legislative action. By the middle of the nineteenth century, the idea of free public education, at least through the primary grades, was pretty generally accepted.

Nowhere was the political presence of workingmen more visible than in New York City. There, they organized as the short-lived New York Workingmen's Party in 1829 and again made their presence felt as the radical, anti-bank wing of the Democratic Party, the Loco Focos (so-called after a type of match that they struck at meetings), in the 1830s. With so much democratic ferment taking place, there was also an audience for radical lectures and a radical press. Perhaps the most colorful of the lecturers was the Scottish-born **Fanny Wright**, a woman who defied the taboo against women speaking in public—and then defied it even more thoroughly by advocating a number of reforms for workers. In addition, she advocated the reform of marriage laws in the direction of more freedom, even to the extent of "free love." Sean Wilentz suggests that her advent in January 1829, marked the beginning of worker insurgency in New York City.

Beginning in the late 1840s, a number of important states began to establish the ten-hour day as the legal maximum workday, even though it was usually possible for workers to make a special contract with their employers to work longer. Economic necessity frequently drove them to do so, thus nullifying the effect of the statutory provision. Nevertheless, such laws represented a gain for labor since they helped to establish the idea of a ten-hour limit.

Finally, in the 1850s, unions less interested in political activity than in "bread-and-butter" (wages, hours, and working conditions) issues gathered momentum. During this period, the first permanent national unions of separate trades were set up, beginning with the **National Typographical Union** in 1852.

The appearance of solid and enduring national unions was a sign of the end of America's industrial adolescence. Many more decades were to pass before economic conditions would convince even a substantial minority of American workers or employers

Fanny Wright

A woman who defied the taboo against women speaking in public and advocated reform for workers and marriage laws, along with "free love," in 1829

National Typographical Union

First permanent trade union in America in 1852

BVT Lab

Visit www.BVTLab.com
to explore the student
resources available for
this chapter.

that unions were a good and permanent element in industrial relations. The individualistic tradition and conditioning of both workers and employers, and an excess of labor, prevented that result sooner. National unions were here to stay—and their very existence testified to the arrival of a new period in American economic history.

12.2f Education and Innovation

A high level of literacy, an openness to change, and that intangible quality known as "Yankee ingenuity" also contributed to American technological progress. Economists consider education to be an investment in "human capital" that is vital to economic growth. The United States (with the exception of the South) had a higher percentage of its population in school than any other country in 1850. Literacy in the North—and especially in New England—was nearly universal. It was no accident that most technological advances came out of New England, as it was the most industrialized and modernized section of the country. As one observer wrote in 1829: "From the habits of early life and the diffusion of knowledge by free schools there exists generally among the mechanics of New England a vivacity in inquiring into the first principles of the science to which they are practically devoted. They thus frequently acquire a theoretical knowledge of the processes of the useful arts, which the English laborers may commonly be found to possess only after a long apprenticeship."

Although Prussia and France were far ahead of the United States in basic science, and Britain had a clear lead in engineering and machine-tool capacity, American entrepreneurs and engineers—much like those of Asian countries today—had a knack for adapting foreign technology to their own needs and improving it through dozens of incremental changes. Thus, while the basic inventions of textile machinery were British, most of the important improvements in such machinery in the 1820s and 30s were American. "Everything new is quickly introduced here," wrote a German visitor. "There is no clinging to old ways, the moment an American hears the word 'invention' he pricks up his ears."

Moreover, in some ways we can trace the dawning of today's "Information Revolution" to this period, because as transportation became faster and cheaper, both the ideas and the people disseminating them could circulate more widely. As a case in point, once it became possible to travel from Cincinnati to New York in two days, it also became possible for leading Northeastern intellectuals and reformers to appear on lecture platforms in a wider geographical area.

12.2g Technology and Agriculture

Although industrial and urban growth outpaced that of farms and villages during this period, farming remained the principal occupation of Americans and the backbone of the economy. Farming provided most of the exports that earned foreign exchange, and this helped provide the capital to launch America's industrial growth. Yet in most elements of husbandry, American farmers were incomparably careless and wasteful. Crop rotation was only occasionally practiced, fallow lands were not plowed to preserve fertility, and millions of tons of manure were allowed to wash away unused each year. Not until after the Civil War did most American farmers begin to approach the careful, scientific farming practiced in Europe.

The reason for such wastefulness, of course, was the existence of seemingly limitless, fertile, virgin land. It was cheaper to exhaust the soil in one area and move westward than to nourish the fertility of eastern land. The constant extension of the frontier was the main reason for the abundance of American agriculture; and after 1830 the mechanization of farming—especially the harvesting process—became an increasingly important cause of rising productivity. Insofar as the substitution of machines for human muscles is an index of modernization, Northern agriculture (there was little mechanization in the South, with its supply of slave labor) was at the forefront of this process before the war.

For centuries there had been little improvement in farm implements. Plows were hardly better than those used by pre-Christian Egyptians: "In culture, harvesting and threshing of grains," writes one historian, "the colonists were not much advanced beyond Biblical times." Suspicion of "newfangled" ideas was stronger among farmers than among other groups. But the same problem that stimulated innovation in manufacturing—a shortage of labor—overcame this conservatism on the expanding frontier. The first improvements came with the development of an iron plow by **Jethro Wood** of New York in the 1810s, and of a steel plow by John Deere of Illinois in the 1830s (further improved by **James Oliver** of Indiana in the 1850s). Drills for faster planting of seed also came into use during the early nineteenth century. These implements, which increased the acreage a farmer could plow and plant, actually made worse the chief bottleneck of farming—the harvest. A farmer could grow more grain than he and his family could reap.

The reaping process was vastly improved with the invention of horse-drawn reapers by Cyrus McCormick of Virginia and Obed Hussey of Maine in the 1830s—the most revolutionary development in nineteenth-century agriculture. Two workers and a horse could now harvest as much grain in a day as twenty workers had been able to with sickles. Of course, even this quantum leap in productivity would have meant little had not similar improvements in threshing come along at the same time. Here, the principal invention was a combined threshing and fanning machine patented by John and Hiram Pitts of Maine in 1834. These inventions—and the continued expansion of grain farming onto the prairies—enabled wheat farmers to double their productivity per man-hour between 1835 and 1880, and to multiply the total wheat harvest sixfold. **McCormick's reaper** even made it possible for Northern farms to increase the production and export of wheat during the Civil War, despite the military enlistment of nearly a million farmers.

Jethro Wood

Invented an iron plow in New York in the 1810s

James Oliver

Made improvements on the steel plow in the 1850s

McCormick's reaper

Mechanized the harvesting of grain

Elias Howe

Inventor of the sewing machine

Isaac M. Singer

Major manufacturer of the sewing machine

Map 12.4 Wheat Production

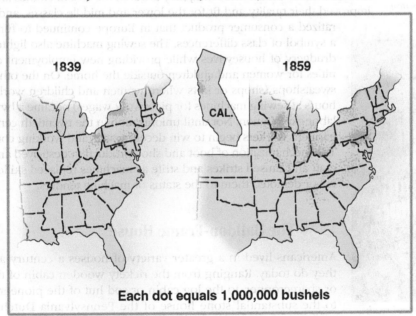

1839

1859

CAL.

Each dot equals 1,000,000 bushels

12.3 The Social Impact

12.3a Ready-Made Clothing

Although crude sewing machines had been developed in France and America during the 1830s, the first patented machine with the crucial capacity to sew interlocking stitches was perfected by **Elias Howe** of Massachusetts in 1846. Howe exhibited his machine at the Quincy Hall Clothing Manufactory in Boston, where amazed visitors watched him sew 250 stitches in a minute—seven times the speed of a fast seamstress. In the next few years, several other technicians made improvements on Howe's original machine. One of them, **Isaac M. Singer** of upstate New York, began to sell sewing machines without paying Howe a royalty. Howe finally won the resulting patent suit in 1854. To avoid more patent battles, several manufacturers merged in 1856 to form the Great Sewing Machine Combination, the first monopoly in American industrial history. By the 1870s nearly a million sewing machines were manufactured each year, three quarters of them by I. M. Singer Company, heir of the 1856 merger.

The Civil War was the catalyst for the ready-made clothing industry. The demand for millions of uniforms was a powerful spur to standardized production. When the Union government supplied manufacturers with a series of graduated measurements for soldiers, producers developed the concept of "sizing" and soon began to make clothes in regular sizes. By the end of the century, nine-tenths of the men's clothing in the United States was ready-made. Although a smaller percentage of women's clothes were commercially manufactured, the development of standardized dress patterns helped democratize female fashions as well.

Technological changes and the Civil War also profoundly affected the shoemaking industry. In the 1850s, adaptation of the sewing machine to work on leather hastened the trend to standardized production; the sewing of uppers to soles remained handwork until 1862, however, when Gordon McKay—a Massachusetts entrepreneur—patented an improved sewing machine that mechanized this process. This invention and later ones not only enabled manufacturers to fill government contracts for army boots but laid the groundwork for a mechanized, mass-production shoe industry after the war. By the century's end, factory shoes (like ready-made clothing) dominated the market.

In 1856 several sewing machine manufacturers merged to form the Great Sewing Machine Combination—the first monopoly in American industrial history. (Library of Congress, Prints & Photographs Division, Horydczak Collection, LC-H814-T-2403)

These developments illustrate both the positive and negative impacts of mechanization. On the one hand, they lowered the cost of clothes and shoes, improved their quality and fit for the lower and middle classes, and democratized a consumer product that in Europe continued to function as a symbol of class differences. The sewing machine also lightened the drudgery of housewives while providing new employment opportunities for women and children outside the home. On the other hand, sweatshops (shops or lofts where women and children worked long hours at sewing machines for piecework wages) became a byword for labor exploitation. Not until unionization in the twentieth century did garment workers begin to win decent wages and working conditions. The mechanization of boot and shoe production destroyed an ancient craft and caused strikes and strife as machines replaced skilled workers or demoted them to the status of machine tenders.

12.36 The Balloon-Frame House

Americans lived in a greater variety of houses a century ago than they do today. Ranging from the rickety wooden cabin of the slave or sharecropper, to the log cabin or sod hut of the pioneer farmer, to the substantial stone house of the Pennsylvania Dutch farmer, to the Georgian or neoclassical mansion of the rich—these structures had the virtues of variety and individuality. In an era of rapid growth, however, they also had disadvantages. Stone or brick construction was slow and required many skilled workmen. The same was true of substantial wooden houses, which for centuries had been built with thick timbers joined by mortise and tenon and fastened by wooden pegs. The skilled carpenters necessary for this kind of construction were in short supply in the mushrooming Midwestern cities of the period.

By the end of the century, factory shoes and ready-made clothing produced from the textile industry dominated the market. (Library of Congress, Prints & Photographs Division, LC-USZ62-59520)

Balloon-frame house
The now familiar combination of machine-sawed boards (two-by-fours, two-by-sixes, etc.) nailed together as wall plates, studs, floor joists, and roof rafters to form the skeleton of a house

The lack of skilled workers inspired a new technique of inexpensive, speedy, standardized home construction—the **balloon-frame house**. This was the now-familiar combination of machine-sawed boards (two-by-fours, two-by-sixes, etc.) nailed together as wall plates, studs, floor joists, and roof rafters to form the skeleton of a frame house. A Connecticut Yankee, Augustine Taylor, who in 1833 moved to the boomtown of Chicago, probably invented the technique. A severe housing shortage was solved by these balloon-frame structures, so-called by skeptics who sneered that the first strong wind would blow them away. In fact they were remarkably strong, for the boards were nailed together in such a way that every strain went against the grain of the wood. Such houses could be built in a fraction of the time and at a fraction of the cost of a traditional house. So successful was the "Chicago construction" that it spread to all parts of the country. By the end of the nineteenth century at least half of all American homes were built in this fashion.

The balloon-frame house would not have been possible without a related revolution in the manufacture of nails. New England factories pioneered in the mechanization of the handcraft methods of nail making in the 1820s, cutting the price of nails by two-thirds and creating another mass-production industry.

Titusville, Pennsylvania
Site of the first commercial oil well

Frederic Tudor
The "Ice King" of Boston, who perfected an ice-cutting machine

12.3c Plumbing, Lighting, and Heating

Changes inside homes also had a large impact on the way middle-class urban Americans lived. Bathing was a once-a-week occurrence at best when water had to be pumped by hand, heated in an open fireplace, carried to a tin tub, and drained by bailing after the bath. Before midcentury, wealthier homeowners and better hotels had installed tubs with running water heated by pipes passing through a boiler—but such contrivances were rare in modest urban homes and virtually nonexistent for the majority who lived in rural areas. The same was true of toilets, which first appeared in the 1830s but made little headway at a time when relatively few cities had municipal water systems (about one hundred places had them by 1860) and even fewer had sewer systems. By the 1880s, many middle-class urban homes had hot and cold running water and "modern" bathroom equipment. Nevertheless, the outdoor privy and the Saturday night, hand-filled bathtub remained standard for rural Americans. Even as late as 1900, Baltimore had ninety thousand outdoor privies.

Improvements in lighting, cooking, and heating spread more widely than improvements in plumbing. For light, most houses before 1860 used candles or lamps that burned one of several kinds of animal or vegetable oil. Whale oil was the cleanest and safest fuel, but it was expensive. Even though coal, oil, lard, and camphene (turpentine and alcohol) were cheaper, the first two were dirty and the last dangerous. Gas derived from coal had been used for lighting as early as 1806. While most cities had piped-in gas supplies by the time of the Civil War, this form of lighting was confined mainly to streets, public places, and a few wealthy homes. After the discovery that petroleum could be used as a fuel, and the drilling of the first commercial oil well at **Titusville, Pennsylvania**, in 1859, kerosene lamps became the ubiquitous source of home lighting—persisting long after Thomas A. Edison perfected the incandescent electric light bulb in 1879.

As late as 1840 in most homes, food was still cooked in an open fireplace. In 1834, Philo P. Stewart—a Connecticut-born abolitionist, missionary to the American Indians, founder of Oberlin College, and inveterate tinkerer—patented a stove that, with subsequent improvements, became the standard wood- or coal-burning kitchen appliance for the second half of the nineteenth century.

Another Connecticut Yankee, Eliphalet Nott, president of Union College, patented several improvements on the basic Franklin heating stove and invented the first stove to burn anthracite coal. By the 1840s, these stoves heated many homes, and European visitors were already complaining that Americans kept their houses too warm. Central heating with hot air first made its appearance in the 1830s. The "radiator," heated by steam or hot water piped from a basement boiler, became common in the last three decades of the century.

12.3d The Icebox

The use of ice to preserve food was mainly a nineteenth-century development. The icebox was entirely so. Nothing better illustrated Yankee ingenuity and enterprise than the career of **Frederic Tudor** of Boston, the "Ice King." A passing remark at a party in 1805 gave him the idea of exploiting one of New England's few natural resources—the ice on its ponds. By 1825, Tudor and his Cambridge partner Nathaniel Wyeth had perfected an ice-cutting machine that mechanized the "harvesting" process, and through trial and error had worked out the best methods for building and insulating ships to transport the ice as well as icehouses to store it. The old underground icehouses had suffered a seasonal loss from melting of at least 60 percent. Inside Tudor's heavy-timbered double walls with sawdust insulation, the loss was only 8 percent.

In 1833, Tudor sent one of his ships with 180 tons of ice from Boston to Calcutta, crossing the equator twice in a voyage of four months and arriving with the cargo intact. Although the main markets for ice were the American South and the West Indies, Tudor shipped his product all over the world. In the 1850s, Boston exported up to 150,000 tons of ice per year.

Tudor's achievements helped make possible the "icebox" (an American word), which by 1860 was a common feature of American households. These large wooden boxes on legs, lined with tin and zinc and interlined with charcoal, improved the American diet and extended the season for fresh fruits and vegetables. Meat could be preserved longer without salting. Ice cream became a widely enjoyed pleasure instead of a rare luxury. Americans began to put ice in their drinks, to the consternation of European visitors. Even that abomination in British eyes, iced tea, made its appearance before the Civil War. After the war, the development of refrigerated railroad cars further improved the quality and variety of fresh fruits and vegetables available in all parts of the country. It also permitted the meat-packing industry to become centralized in Chicago and to serve a national market with its products.

12.3e The Emergence of the Modern Family

Scholars have identified a new type of family that was coming into being in these years under the impact of such rapid economic change. In the traditional family, men and women both worked at home—though their chores were probably gender-specific. Industrialization removed male work from the home—except in rural areas—and it also made having a large number of children less economically valuable since their work was no longer required on a farm. Further, more women were gaining more education. For all of these reasons, the birth rate began to drop in the early nineteenth century, and the family began to become a more democratic institution. Scholars have called this new style "the modern family."

12.4 Modernization and Reform

12.4a The Protestant Ethic and Reform

Economic growth and a rising standard of living depend not only on material factors but also on intangibles such as social values. The openness to change and the emphasis on education in Northern states have already been mentioned as important contributors to economic development. Equally important were attitudes toward work. There is universal agreement that nineteenth-century Americans (at least those in the North, and especially those in New England) were infused with a strong work ethic. "The national motto," wrote a British observer of the United States, "should be 'All work and no play.'" This produced some unlovely habits—such as the tendency of Americans to bolt their food in order to lose little time from labor—but it also reinforced a value system that was well adapted to a modernizing society.

This value system was more or less synonymous with what is generally called the **Protestant ethic**, or sometimes the Puritan ethic, since it descended from Puritan attitudes toward work as a glorification of God and idleness as an instrument of Satan. Emphasizing hard work, thrift, sobriety, reliability, self-discipline, self-reliance, and the postponement of immediate gratification for the sake of long-range goals, the Protestant ethic reinforced precisely those values best suited to capitalist development. There was also a close relationship between the Protestant ethic and many of the reform movements. These movements grew out of the evangelical enthusiasm of the Second Great Awakening (1800–1830) and the radical idealism of transcendentalism. In addition to urging Christians to stop committing such social sins as fornication, drunkenness, violation of the Sabbath, and enslavement of other human beings, reformers sought to instill in the poor, the idle, the depraved, and the intemperate "the virtues of true Protestantism—industry, sobriety, thrift and piety"—to enable them to reform themselves.

The voluntary associations that carried on reform activities provided another link between reform and modernization. The social network of pre-modern societies was confined mainly to kin and village. An essential element of modernization is the transcendence of these localized and prescriptive ties by supralocal voluntary organizations formed for a specific purpose—trade unions, missionary societies, reform associations, pressure groups, and the like. This was precisely what happened in the United States. There were only a few such associations in the eighteenth century, but by 1832 their number and variety astonished the French visitor, Alexis de Tocqueville. "Americans of all ages, all conditions, and all dispositions constantly form associations," he wrote in *Democracy in America*, "associations to give entertainments, to found seminaries, to build inns, to construct churches, to diffuse books, to send missionaries to the antipodes … to found hospitals, prisons, and schools … Wherever at the head of some new undertaking you see the government in France, or a man of rank in England, in the United States you will be sure to find an association."

Four of the reform movements, all related to the modernization process (though it would be too limiting simply to see them in those terms), had a crucial impact on American society after 1848: the movements for **temperance**, improved education, women's rights, and abolition.

Temperance
A social movement urging reduction in the consumption of alcohol

Lyman Beecher
Founder of the American Temperance Society

12.46 Temperance

In the early nineteenth century, Americans consumed an extraordinary amount of liquor. The average annual intake of spirituous and distilled alcohol per person of drinking age in the 1820s, for example, was seven to ten gallons—at least five times today's average. In addition, the average person consumed thirty gallons of some combination of hard cider, beer, and wine each year. The most common distilled liquor in New England and other coastal regions was rum; in the rest of the country, it was usually whiskey. Beer and wine were drunk everywhere, but the most popular fermented drink in those days was hard cider (about 20 proof). No social occasion, whether a corn-husking bee or the installation of a clergyman, was complete without heavy drinking. Whiskey was a form of money on the frontier, and even church subscriptions were payable in liquid coin. Wretched transportation facilities before the 1820s meant that grain could only be marketed over long distances in distilled form. Liquor was cheap, untaxed in most areas, and constituted a considerable portion of people's daily calorie intake. Many men greeted each day with a gill (four fluid ounces) of grog. John Adams regularly drank a pint of hard cider before breakfast. European visitors were astonished by the "universal practice of sipping a little at a time … [every] half an hour to a couple of hours." Rum was included in the standard daily rations for members of the American army and navy, and colleges typically served ale by the pint to students with their meals.

Pictured is a comic about a "temperance man," or one who abstained from alcohol. (Wikimedia Commons)

The temperance movement arose partly as a reaction to excessive consumption. Beginning as a local religious and moral reform led by ministers, doctors, and women, the movement had expanded by the 1830s into a well-organized national crusade. In 1826, Connecticut minister **Lyman Beecher** founded the American Temperance Society, dedicated to the reduction of the consumption of alcohol because of its deleterious effects on society. Beecher argued that drunkenness led to crime, unemployment, poverty, and domestic violence. Following Beecher's example, temperance lecturers rode from town to town lecturing on the damaging effects of alcohol. At the height of its power in 1836, the American Temperance Union—a federation of eight thousand local and regional societies—claimed a membership of one and a half million. The Union fragmented, however, as members divided over the question of temperance versus prohibition. At first, the movement had been for *moderation* in drinking—urging the elimination only of distilled spirits, while still endorsing temperate consumption of beer, wine, or cider. But by the 1830s, temperance advocates became more militant, taking on the character of Christian perfectionism and moral regeneration that characterized other reform crusades of the decade. Like the abolitionists, who demanded universal emancipation, prohibitionists began to call for the total abolition of *all* alcoholic beverages. The requirement that members pledge total abstinence caused a dramatic drop in the membership of the American Temperance Union by 1840.

Up to this time, temperance had been primarily a middle-class, Protestant movement. Its goal was to impose the values of the Protestant Ethic, especially sobriety, upon the whole society. It was here that temperance intersected with modernization. Work patterns in pre-modern society were task-oriented rather than time-oriented. Artisans typically worked in bursts of effort until a particular job was completed and then took several days off, perhaps to spend their wages in heavy drinking. This irregularity was unsuitable to mechanized factories in which successful operation of complex and dangerous machinery required punctuality, reliability, and sobriety. Work became time-oriented rather than task-oriented.

This Temperance Society certificate and pledge to abstain from alcohol, tobacco, and profanity was signed in 1866. Many employers began requiring their employees to take a temperance pledge, where employees "volunteered" to cease alcohol consumption as a condition of their employment. (CORBIS/© Bettmann)

It was no coincidence that the temperance movement in both Britain and America coincided with the Industrial Revolution in those countries. As part of the effort to instill the values of reliability and self-discipline in the working classes, employers supported the temperance movement and often forbade their workers to drink on *or* off the job. Many employers began requiring their employees to take a temperance pledge, where employees "volunteered" to cease alcohol consumption as a condition of their employment.

Many workers, especially Irish and German immigrants, did not take kindly to such discipline. Nevertheless, in 1840 Protestant workingmen began to organize the Washington Temperance Societies. The first such society was founded in Baltimore, ironically by six heavy-drinking workmen (who had been converted by a temperance lecture). Proudly declaring themselves "reformed drunkards," they moved with missionary zeal to organize societies all over the Northern and western states. Native-born workers pointed to their endorsement of temperance as evidence of their superior dependability as compared to immigrant laborers.

The Washingtonian movement rejuvenated the temperance crusade. It was this period that produced an outpouring of sentimental songs with such titles as "Father, Dear Father, Come Home with Me Now" and the play *Ten Nights in a Bar Room*, which did for temperance what *Uncle Tom's Cabin* did for the antislavery movement.

The alliance of middle-class prohibitionists and Washingtonians helped push prohibition laws through fifteen state legislatures in the decade after 1846, when Maine passed the first. In a dress rehearsal for the national prohibition of the 1920s, these state laws were widely evaded and most were eventually repealed. Whatever success the temperance cause enjoyed was the result of other factors, especially the evangelical revivals of the Second Great Awakening. In any case, the per capita consumption of alcohol appears to have declined sharply, perhaps as much as fivefold in the two decades before 1850. It never again approached the earlier level, and rum and hard cider almost disappeared as American drinks.

12.4c Public Education

Traditional histories of education emphasize the great reforms inspired by Horace Mann, secretary of the Massachusetts State Board of Education from 1837 to 1849. Before then, so the story goes, the New England common schools had fallen into decay. The few public schools elsewhere were "pauper" schools to which self-respecting parents would not send their children, and teachers were semiliterate; thus most children outside New England grew up with scarcely any formal schooling. Although this picture contains some truth, historians have recently uncovered evidence of a vigorous and growing educational system in the generation before 1837. It now appears that in New England and New York at least three-quarters of the school-age children were in school; and in 1830 the average adult in those states had completed eight or nine years of schooling (though the typical school term was only three or four months each year).

Pictured is an early school room. (Library of Congress, Prints & Photographs Division, LC-USZ62-54037)

Elsewhere the picture was less bright, although a mixture of public, private, and church schools provided some education for well over half the white population (except on the frontier and in parts of the South). If this had not been true, one would have difficulty explaining the 95 percent literacy rate for Americans in the North.

In some respects, however, things were as bad as the reformers of the 1840s painted them to be. Formal teacher training was almost nonexistent; educational standards varied widely; schools were generally ungraded; with rare exceptions, no public school system worthy of the name existed in the Deep South; and the white illiteracy rate in slave states was above 20 percent. Black illiteracy was close to 90 percent. Pennsylvania, New Jersey, and the western states had little in the way of public school systems before 1835.

What Horace Mann and his fellow New England reformers did was to rationalize and centralize the existing patchwork pattern of public schools, to professionalize the calling of teacher, and—by force of example and crusading zeal—to spread this system through most of the North by 1860. Mann founded the first "normal" school for training teachers at Lexington, Massachusetts, in 1839. During the next two decades, such institutions were established in several states and half a century later they evolved into teachers' colleges.

Massachusetts also pioneered in other reforms: a standardized graded curriculum, extension of public education to the secondary level, and the first compulsory attendance law (1852). Indeed, Mann did his work so well that some revisionist historians have criticized him for inaugurating a bureaucratic educational establishment that they regard as rigid and reactionary.

Revisionists have also condemned the school reformers for creating a system designed to impose Protestant, middle-class values on all children, in order to perpetuate the class structure through repression of ethnic minorities and the poor. It is true that the schools tried to teach the values of the Protestant ethic. An essential task of education, wrote the Massachusetts Superintendent of Schools in 1857, was "by moral and religious instruction daily given" to "inculcate habits of regularity, punctuality, constancy and industry." *McGuffey's Readers* and the various readers and spellers of Noah Webster, which taught hundreds of millions of nineteenth-century children to read, reiterated these lessons. But the reformers of the time considered this progressive, not reactionary. The purpose of reform, after all, was not to keep the poor content in their humble station but to lift them out of poverty by equipping them with the skills and values they needed to function and hold their own in a modernizing, fluid, competitive, capitalist economy. "Nothing but Universal education can counterwork this tendency to the domination of capital and the servility of labor," wrote Horace Mann in 1848. Education "does better than to disarm the poor of their hostility toward the rich; it prevents being poor." If this was unrealistic, it nevertheless spoke to the faith that all classes of Americans have placed in education.

12.4⬭ Higher Education

Ever since the founding of Harvard College in 1636, higher education had been associated primarily with the churches. In 1860, of the 207 colleges existing, churches had founded 180—most of them during the previous generation, as population flowed westward and the Protestant denominations struggled to educate a ministry and a lay leadership that would preserve and expand the faith on the frontier.

Many of the six thousand "academies" (with only twelve thousand teachers combined) that provided nearly all the country's secondary education were also church-supported. In 1860, there were only 321 public high schools, nearly a third of them in Massachusetts.

After the Civil War, higher education became more secular and more broadly available. By 1890 twenty-five states outside the South had followed the lead of Massachusetts and passed compulsory school attendance laws. By 1900, there were six thousand public high schools. The need for technical and scientific training to keep pace with rapid advances in these fields led to the founding of several schools modeled on the earlier examples of Rensselaer Polytechnic Institute (1824) and Massachusetts Institute of Technology (1865). In 1862, the Morrill Act created the land-grant colleges by setting aside public lands to support universities that emphasized "agriculture and mechanical arts." Eventually, universities would develop—such as Texas A&M and Alabama A&M—that would encapsulate the spirit of the Morrill Act in their very names.

In the postwar decades, the modern university outgrew the confines of the old Christian college. In 1869 Charles W. Eliot became the first nonclergyman president of Harvard and proceeded to liberalize the curriculum. Men who may not have had church affiliations dominated boards of regents, and students were recruited and donations were solicited from persons of all faiths. In 1868 Andrew D. White launched another university with a similarly liberalized curriculum at Cornell, and in 1876 Daniel Coit Gilman started America's first true research university at Johns Hopkins.

12.4e The Media

Not all education took place in schools, of course. In addition to such institutions as the family, church, and voluntary associations, many channels existed for the dissemination of information and ideas. One of the most important was the public lecture. Abolitionists, temperance workers, and other reformers found lecturing to be the most effective means of spreading their message, with women having won the right to appear on the lecture stage by the 1850s. Debating societies, literary associations, and the like grew up in almost every crossroads village. In 1826 Josiah Holbrook, a Massachusetts educator and friend of Horace Mann, founded the **American Lyceum of Science and the Arts**. The Lyceum was the first national agency for adult education, bringing lecturers on almost every conceivable subject to cities and hamlets throughout the nation. In 1838, young Abraham Lincoln spoke at the Springfield, Illinois, Lyceum on "The Perpetuation of Our Political Institutions." Lyceums and debating societies fostered independent thought and new ideas in addition to providing lecture forums for well-known thinkers such as Ralph Waldo Emerson.

Overshadowing all other means of communication, however, was the popular press. America was a newspaper culture. Technological advances in printing brought explosive growth to newspaper circulation after 1830. The expansion of the railroad network enabled urban dailies to print weekly editions specifically for rural areas. By 1860, the weekly edition of Horace Greeley's New York *Tribune* had an unprecedented circulation of two hundred thousand copies. Samuel F. B. Morse's invention of the telegraph in 1844 made possible the instantaneous transmission of news over long distances and led to the formation of the Associated Press in 1846. The number of newspapers, which had doubled between 1825 and 1840, doubled again by 1860, reaching a total of 3,300. Widespread literacy, the highly partisan nature of American journalism, and universal white male suffrage help explain the remarkable politicization of the population—an important factor in the emotionally-charged controversies that led to the Civil War. Though women could not vote, the print culture gave them the opportunity to weigh in on issues related to the sectional conflict—*Uncle Tom's Cabin* being the outstanding (but not unique) example of this phenomenon.

Popular magazines such as *Godey's Lady's Book* (started 1830), *Harper's Monthly* (1850), and the New York *Ledger* (1851) also enjoyed an expanding readership. Prominent features in newspapers, as well as magazines, were sentimental poetry and moralistic fiction. Most novels were serialized in weeklies before appearing between hard covers, often focusing on domestic situations revolving around such themes as marriage, home, family, religion, and death. Most of the authors were women, who poured forth serialized novels year after year, reaching a huge audience—also mostly women—through mass-circulation magazines and inexpensive books. Susan Warner's *Wide, Wide World* (1850) and Maria Susanna Cummins' *The Lamplighter* (1854), for example, were two of the best-sellers. Marion Harland's first novel, *Alone* (1854), sold half a million copies. She wrote dozens more, the last one in 1919. Mary Jane Holmes produced a book a year from 1854 to 1907.

By all estimations, the leader of this school was Mrs. E. D. E. N. Southworth, who wrote her first novel, *Retribution* (two hundred thousand copies), in 1849 after her husband had deserted her. She followed with sixty-one more in the next four decades. Serialization of her books lifted the *Ledger's* circulation to four hundred thousand by 1860. Not surprisingly, given her personal history, many of her novels—such as *The Deserted Wife* (1850)—were highly critical of the gender norms of her day. Indeed, many modern critics have discerned an underlying political strain in the domestic novels, in general, because so many of them featured women trying to establish their autonomy under difficult conditions, using the moral authority of the home and the housewife to do so.

A particularly noteworthy work of fiction by a woman during these years was *Our Nig* by **Harriet Wilson** (1850), the first known novel by an African American woman. Wilson, who had herself been a servant, wrote a narrative that inverts many of the conventions of the domestic novel because it depicts the home, not as the site of female empowerment a la *The Wide, Wide World,* but rather as the site of the oppression of a free black servant in a Northern state.

12.4f Women's Rights

The preeminence of women in popular literature was only one sign of the growing achievements of, and opportunities available to, women by mid-century. Yet there was a certain ambivalence to these achievements. Literary themes and popular culture reinforced the tenets of domesticity and the sexual double standard that tied women to home, marriage, and family—while men continued to manage affairs in the outside world. At the same time, however, economic modernization was taking many women out of the home and putting them into the wage-earning labor force. The textile and garment industries were large-scale employers of women (and children). The inventions of the telegraph (1844), typewriter (1874), and telephone (1876) created new white-collar jobs for women.

The expansion of public education and the professionalization of teaching also opened a major career opportunity for women—though female teachers were paid less than their male counterparts. By the 1850s the "schoolmarm" was a familiar figure, especially in the Northeast. In the decades after Oberlin, which had been an exclusively male university, opened its doors to women in 1837, several other colleges followed suit. Three decades later after the Civil War, beginning with Vassar (1865) and Wellesley and Smith (1875), numerous colleges built exclusively for women were founded. (Mount Holyoke, a school for women founded in 1837, did not become a full-fledged college until 1888.)

The spirit generated by antebellum reform movements spurred demands for an end to women's inferior legal and political status. Female abolitionists began to speak out against sexual as well as racial slavery. As we have seen, the first women's rights convention was organized by Elizabeth Cady Stanton and Lucretia Mott and held at Seneca Falls, New York, in 1848. The movement's first priority was abolition of laws that treated unmarried women as minors and forced married women to turn over all property to their husbands. By 1861, more than half the states had taken steps toward ending such legal inequalities.

After the war, feminist leaders decided to concentrate on winning the right to vote, believing that the ballot was the key to open other doors to sexual equality. By 1890 women had won the right to vote in school-board elections in seventeen states and territories. Wyoming territory granted women general suffrage in 1869, and with its admission to statehood in 1890 became the first state to have done so. Colorado followed in 1893, Utah and Idaho in 1896. Although no other states enfranchised women until 1910, the nineteenth century movement laid the groundwork for the passage of the Nineteenth Amendment in 1920.

Harriet Wilson
Author of *Our Nig* in 1850, the first known novel by an African American woman

Amistad

Slave ship and court case that resulted in the freeing and return to Africa of fifty-three slaves, illegally imported from Africa, who had managed to take over the ship

12.4g The Broadening Antislavery Movement

In 1831 in Boston, William Lloyd Garrison began his publication, *The Liberator,* with the uncompromising goal of immediate and complete abolition of slavery. The next year, Garrison's supporters began the New England Antislavery Society, and New York and Philadelphia followed with similar groups in 1833. In the late 1830s and 1840s, the antislavery movement began to reach out to—and convince—more Northerners, with 1,300 local antislavery societies comprised of some 250,000 members in existence by 1837. Similarly, abolitionist newspapers and antislavery lecturers began to permeate the Northern states.

One of the key elements in this growth of the anti-slavery movement was the so-called "gag rule" in the House of Representatives and the battle against it by the one-term president and subsequent House member, John Quincy Adams. Antislavery advocates were circulating petitions attacking the "peculiar institution" of slavery, as it existed in the District of Columbia itself, and sending them to Northerners in Congress. In 1836, Southerners in the House succeeded in enacting the gag rule—whereby the petitions were tabled without being officially acknowledged. Adams's battle took eight years, but he ultimately managed to get the rule overturned. During those eight years, many people began to see the antislavery effort as involving the defense of free speech as well as the opposition to slavery itself, and this broadened its appeal.

From 1839–1841 there was another important issue in which Adams—known as "Old Man Eloquent"—played a crucial role: the **Amistad** case. The *Amistad* was a Spanish slave ship, carrying fifty-three slaves, on which there had been a mutiny before it could reach its destination in Cuba. Slaves picked the lock to their hold with a nail and took over the ship. Understanding that they had sailed away from the morning sun on their way from Africa to Cuba, the slaves ordered the Spanish sailors to sail into the morning sun. The Spanish therefore sailed east by day, but west and north by night—zigzagging their way up the North American coast. In August 1839 some of the mutineers came ashore in Long Island, New York, with the ship just off-shore. Over the next two years there was a sustained legal dispute, in which the Spanish "owners" were trying to get the slaves back, while the slaves were in American custody. Going against the Spanish was the fact that the Spaniards had been engaged in the slave trade in violation of a treaty made in 1817 between their country and Britain—a treaty which had prohibited the importation of slaves into Spanish colonies. The crucial evidence in the case was that none of the slaves seemed to be able to speak Spanish—though the Spaniards claimed they were all born in Cuba—and none would answer to their Spanish names. If the slaves had been born in Cuba, they were legally the property of their Spanish slave owners. If they were from Africa, then they were imported to the Western Hemisphere in violation of the 1817 treaty and would be given their freedom. Adams successfully proved that the slaves were recent imports from Africa and argued for the slaves' freedom before the U.S. Supreme Court. The Spanish then tried for compensation, to no avail.

With so much ferment going on, the antislavery movement entered politics in 1840 with the founding of the Liberty Party. The only previous antislavery organization had been the American Colonization Society, founded in 1817 by Southern planters who favored gradual, individual emancipation, and the return of the slaves to Africa. The Colonization Society failed to take hold—even though several thousand slaves were repatriated to Liberia in the 1820s—because of the enormous cost of repatriation and the fact that most American slaves in the 1820s were born in the U.S. and had no knowledge whatsoever of Africa.

Some Liberty Party men insisted that the Constitution empowered the federal government to abolish slavery. Officially, however, the party stood only for the exclusion of slavery from new territories and states, for its abolition in the District of Columbia, and for prohibition of the interstate slave trade. In 1848, the Liberty Party was absorbed by the more broad-gauged Free Soil Party—which adopted a similar platform (omitting reference to the slave trade), but which also attracted many members who were more opposed to Southern political power than to slavery, as such.

Genuine abolitionists watched these and subsequent developments, leading to the founding of the Republican Party in 1854, with mixed feelings. While they welcomed the growth of antislavery sentiment in the North, they were well aware that it was often based on a dislike of both slavery *and* blacks. Moreover, Garrison and his adherents advocated nonresistance, rather than political parties, as the means of ending slavery. Hence, abolitionists kept their societies alive and continued to work for the equal rights and education of Northern blacks.

Women played prominent roles in the abolition movement, forming women's auxiliaries and raising funds to support abolitionist lecturers. William Lloyd Garrison published a letter by Angelina Grimke in *The Liberator* that made her an overnight celebrity among abolitionists. Grimke and her sister Sarah then quickly became in-demand lecturers on the abolitionist lecture circuit. The **Grimke sisters**, however, also wrote and spoke about women's rights, thus sewing discord among the abolitionists themselves—though some abolitionists, such as Garrison, favored women's rights as well.

By the 1850s there was a robust antislavery discourse, fed most importantly by the publication of *Uncle Tom's Cabin* in 1852, but also by the writings and lectures of many former slaves, Frederick Douglass being the best known. In 1845, Douglass published his *Narrative of the Life of Frederick Douglass*. He also began publishing an abolitionist newspaper, *The North Star*. Another former slave who became well known in the antebellum United States was **Sojourner Truth**. Born a slave in New York in 1797, Isabella van Wagenen began to call herself "Sojourner Truth" after a religious conversion. She was a familiar presence on the lecture platform in the North, and in 1850 appeared the first version of her autobiography, as dictated to Olive Gilbert.

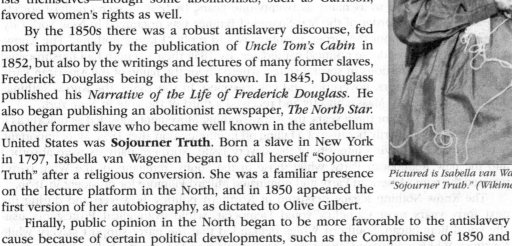

Pictured is Isabella van Wagenen, who called herself "Sojourner Truth." (Wikimedia Commons)

Finally, public opinion in the North began to be more favorable to the antislavery cause because of certain political developments, such as the Compromise of 1850 and the Kansas-Nebraska Act (both of which will be more fully discussed in Chapter 13). For now, what is important to point out is the fact that the Compromise of 1850 contained, as one of its key elements, a new and tougher fugitive slave law. After its passage, as we will see in the next chapter, there were a number of notorious cases that kept the issue of slavery in the public eye.

12.5 Prejudices, Politics, and Polarization

12.5a The New Immigration

In the first forty years of the Republic, immigrants did not come in large numbers. As late as the 1820s, the number of immigrants averaged less than thirteen thousand per year. But rapid population growth, land shortages, and labor surpluses in northern Europe—combined with cheap land, labor shortages, and higher wages in America—brought a quadrupling of this average in the 1830s. During the decade from 1845 through 1854, the number of immigrants averaged nearly three hundred thousand annually.

Although these newcomers provided much of the labor force necessary for rapid economic growth, many of them received a cold welcome in the United States. Actually, anti-immigrant sentiment (or **nativism**) was not directed primarily against immigrants in general, but specifically against *Catholic* immigrants. Nearly 40 percent of the immigrants to America during these years were Irish Catholics, driven to emigrate by the potato famine. Another 12 or 13 percent were German Catholics.

Settling mainly in cities, the Irish were the most concentrated and visible of the immigrant groups. They were poor, clannish, fiercely loyal to their church, hostile toward abolitionists and toward free blacks (with whom they competed for jobs)—and therefore looked favorably on slavery and the Democratic Party. This aroused a nativist anti-Irish movement that strongly influenced the politics of several states in the 1840s and 1850s.

Grimke sisters
Wrote and lectured in favor of both abolition of slavery and women's rights

Sojourner Truth
A former slave who became well known on the abolitionist lecture circuit and whose first version of her autobiography, as dictated to Olive Gilbert, appeared in 1850

Nativism
The ideological perspective that opposed immigration and anything "foreign" and favored rule by whites of English heritage

The movement was fueled by traditional Protestant anti-Catholicism and by temperance reformers, abolitionists, proponents of public schools, and Protestant workingmen—who saw the Irish influx as a threat to their reforms, values, and status. In the 1840s there were numerous anti-Catholic riots and some pitched battles between Protestant and Catholic workingmen. In Philadelphia in 1844, a Catholic church was burned, thirteen people were killed, and the state militia had to be called in to restore order.

In 1843, nativists in New York established the American Republican Party, which won 23 percent of the vote in New York City that year. The next year, the Whigs made an alliance with the nativists, supporting their local candidates in return for American Republican support of the Whig presidential candidate, Henry Clay. Though the nativist-laden Whigs were unsuccessful in the presidential race, they won six Congressional races in New York City and Philadelphia, and won the mayor's offices of New York and Boston.

Nativism reached its height in the **Know-Nothing Movement**, which had as its main goal the exclusion of "foreigners" from political power by lengthening the naturalization period from five to as many as twenty-one years. In 1849, a secret nativist society called the Supreme Order of the Star-Spangled Banner was organized in New York City. When questioned about the Order, members would reply, "I know nothing." The Know-Nothings began to endorse political candidates. By 1854 their strength had mushroomed to formidable proportions in several states, where under the name of the American Party they elected legislators, governors, and congressmen. In the 1850s, the Know-Nothings dominated politics in Massachusetts and received a third of the vote in New York.

Then, within two or three years, the Know-Nothing Movement subsided as quickly as it had risen. This was partly because of a falling off in immigration after 1854. More important, however, was the blazing intensity of the slavery issue. Northern nativists were absorbed into the new Republican Party, while those in the South (remnants of the Whig party) retained the name American Party and nominated Millard Fillmore for president in 1856.

The Know-Nothing legacy persisted in Northern politics, however; and during the next forty years most Catholics voted Democrat, while evangelical Protestants usually voted Republican. Southern Whigs demanded that the party support slavery while Northern Whigs demanded abolition. The result was the eventual dissolution of the Whigs, and the rise of the Republicans as the Northern party that opposed the expansion of slavery. Local and state elections often turned on such issues as temperance, parochial schools, and the like. The animosities expressed by the Know-Nothings flared up again in the American Protective Association (APA) of the 1880s and 1890s and in continuing patterns of prejudice against Catholics and immigrants.

The Know-Nothings were a party that had a brief, if significant, heyday. The other new party born in the heat of sectional conflict in these years, the Republican Party, is with us still today. To that dramatic chapter in American history we now turn.

Timeline

1793	Samuel Slater opens the nation's first textile mill in Pawtucket, Rhode Island.
1798	Eli Whitney's interchangeable parts for rifles, made by machines, spawn the "American system" of manufacturing.
1807	Robert Fulton's steamboat *Clermont* steams up the Hudson River.
1825	Erie Canal and Waterway is completed connecting Buffalo to New York City.
	Frederic Tudor begins harvesting ice.
1826	Josiah Holbrook, a Massachusetts educator and friend of Horace Mann, founds the American Lyceum of Science and the Arts.
	Lyman Beecher founds the American Temperance Society.
1829	The New York Workingmen's Party organizes.
1830	Baltimore and Ohio Railroad begins rail service.
1833	Augustine Taylor brings balloon-frame housing structures to Chicago.
1834	A combined threshing and fanning machine is patented by John and Hiram Pitts of Maine.
	Philo P. Stewart patents a wood burning stove.
1839	Horace Mann founds the first "normal" school for training teachers in Lexington, Massachusetts.
1839–1841	The *Amistad* case
1840	The Liberty Party is founded.
1843	Nativist American Republican Party wins 23 percent of the vote in New York.
1846	Maine passes alcohol prohibition law.
	A sewing machine, with the crucial capacity to sew interlocking stitches, is perfected by Elias Howe.
	The formation of the Associated Press

1849	Know-Nothings is founded in New York City.
1852	Massachusetts passes the first mandatory school attendance law.
	National Typographical Union is founded.
1854	Republican Party is founded.
	Several manufacturers merge to form the "Great Sewing Machine Combination," the first monopoly in American industrial history.
1859	First commercial oil well is drilled at Titusville, Pennsylvania.
1862	The Morrill Act creates the land-grant colleges, which emphasize agriculture and mechanical arts.
	Gordon McKay patents an improved sewing machine that mechanizes shoe manufacturing.
1869	Charles Eliot becomes the first nonclergyman president of Harvard.
	Wyoming grants women general suffrage.
1876	Daniel Coit Gilman starts America's first true research university at Johns Hopkins.
1879	Edison perfects the incandescent light bulb.

CHAPTER SUMMARY

$\mathcal{A}$merica experienced rapid modernization during the middle decades of the nineteenth century—especially in the North—characterized by investment in transportation and communication, which led to a nationally integrated market economy. The invention of Robert Fulton's steamboat in 1807 aided greatly in river navigation, the completion of the Erie Canal connected the Hudson River system to the Great Lakes, and the opening of the Baltimore and Ohio Railroad in 1830 began a new era of rail transportation. All of these advances in transportation helped create a national economy.

Simultaneously, there was an increase in the output per man-hour that resulted from technological innovation and mechanization; and manufacturing changed from artisanship to centralized industry utilizing Eli Whitney's system of standardized, interchangeable parts. The result was accelerated growth of the industrial sector as compared with other sectors of the economy. Income inequality, however, increased as many skilled workers found themselves replaced by machines.

Industrialization in the North also brought a corporate revolution because large amounts of capital were needed to build railroads and factories. Sole proprietorships, in most cases, were therefore infeasible. The corporations provided the stockholders with limited liability so that bankruptcy of the corporation would cause owners to lose only what they held in stock.

Industrialization also brought population concentration to the manufacturing centers of the Northeast, beginning with the development of the textile industry in New England. Factories in manufacturing towns such as Lowell, Massachusetts, employed thousands of workers. People had to live near their places of employment, and the resulting concentration of population was accompanied by problems in health and sanitation in the factories; worker exploitation was also a serious concern, and led to the development of an organized labor movement and labor unions.

Meanwhile, the country experienced growth in education as Horace Mann pioneered public schools and other states followed suit. Educational opportunities expanded for women, and by 1850 the United States had the highest percentage of persons in school in the world. Higher education also blossomed with the passage of the Morrill Act, which provided for land-grant universities and an explosion in college growth.

Modernization also led to advancement in agriculture with John Deere's steel plow and Cyrus McCormick's reaper. Other technological innovations that changed the American economy and culture included ready-made clothing, balloon-frame housing, advancements in plumbing (with running water and toilets), advancement in lighting (with coal oil lamps), and in refrigeration (with the icebox).

With these advancements came social change, including a temperance movement, advances in women's rights and the beginnings of a women's suffrage movement, and the rise of an abolitionist movement. As such, modernization contributed to antagonism between North and South as Southerners attempted to retain their system of human slavery. Finally, industrialization attracted new immigrant laborers, which led to a significant nativist movement in the Unites States that was directed primarily against Catholicism and immigration.

KEY TERMS

BIBLIOGRAPHY

A

Ahlstrom, Sydney. *A Religious History of the American People.* New Haven, CT: Yale University Press, 2004.

B

Billington, Ray Allen. *The Far Western Frontier, 1830–1860.* Albuquerque, NM: University of New Mexico Press, 1995.

Blackford, Mandsel, and Austin Kerr. *Business Enterprise in American History.* Stamford, CT: Wadsworth, 1993.

Blocker, Jack S. *American Temperance Movements: Cycles of Reform.* Farmington Hills, MI: Twayne Publishing, 1989.

Brinkley, Alan. *American History: A Survey.* 11th ed. Boston, MA: McGraw-Hill, 2003.

Burns, Eric. *A Social History of Alcohol.* Philadelphia: Temple University Press, 2004.

C

Calvert, Robert A., Arnoldo De Leon, and Gregg Cantrell. *The History of Texas.* 4th ed. Hoboken, NJ: Wiley-Blackwell, 2007.

Campbell, Randolph. *Gone to Texas.* New York: Oxford University Press, 2003.

Clark, Malcolm, Jr. *Eden Seekers: The Settlement of Oregon 1818–1862.* Boston, MA: Houghton Mifflin, 1981.

Collins, Gail. *America's Women: 400 Years of Dolls, Drudges, Helpmates, and Heroines.* New York: William Morrow, 2007.

Craven, Avery. *The Coming of the Civil War.* New York: Scribner, 1942.

Cummings, Bruce. *Dominion from Sea to Sea. Pacific Ascendancy and American Power.* New Haven, CT: Yale University Press, 2011.

D

Daly, Christopher B. *A Narrative History of a Nation's Journalism.* Amherst, MA: University of Massachusetts Press, 2012.

Daniels, Roger: *Coming to America: A History of Immigration and Ethnicity in American Life.* New York: Harper Perennials, 2002.

Dray, Philip. *There Is Power in a Union: The Epic Story of Labor in America.* New York: Anchor Books, 2011.

E

Engerman, Stanley L. and Robert E. Gallman. *The Cambridge Economic History of the United States, Vol. 2: The Long Nineteenth Century.* New York: Cambridge University Press, 2000.

F

Fehrenbach, T. R. *Lone Star: A History of Texas and the Texans.* Cambridge, MA: Da Capo Press, 2000.

G

Garraty, John A., and Robert McCaughey. *The American Nation: A History of the United States Since 1865.* 6th ed. New York: HarperCollins, 1987.

Godman, Paul. *Of One Blood: Abolitionism and the Origins of Racial Equality.* Berkeley, CA: University of California Press, 2000.

H

Hughes, Jonathan, and Louis P. Cain. *American Economic History.* 8th ed. Englewood Cliffs, NJ: Pearson Prentice-Hall, 2010.

J

Jones, Howard. *Quest for Security: A History of U.S. Foreign Relations.* New York: McGraw-Hill, 1996.

K

Kolchin, Peter. *American Slavery: 1619–1877.* New York: Hill and Wang, 2003.

L

Lipset, Seymour Martin, and Earl Raab. *The Politics of Unreason: Right-Wing Extremism in America, 1790–1970.* New York: Harper & Row, 1970.

M

Medbery, James K. *Men and Mysteries of Wall Street.* Boston, MA: Fields, Osgood, & Co., 1870.

Merk, Frederick. *Manifest Destiny and Mission in American History.* Cambridge, MA: Harvard University Press, 1995.

Mintz, Steven, and Susan Kellogg. *Domestic Revolutions: A Social History of American Family Life.* New York: Free Press, 1989.

BIBLIOGRAPHY

N

Nichols, Roy F. *The Disruption of American Democracy.* New York: Collier, 1962.

O

Olson, James S. *Encyclopedia of the Industrial Revolution in America.* Westport, CT: Greenwood Press, 2001.

Oren, Michael B. *Power, Faith, and Fantasy: America in the Middle East 1776 to the Present.* New York: W. W. Norton & Company, 2007.

P

Potter, David M. *The Impending Crisis: America before the Civil War 1848–1861.* New York: Harper Perennial, 1977.

Pursell, Carroll. *The Machine in America: A Social History of Technology.* Baltimore, MD: Johns Hopkins University Press, 2007.

R

Rohrbough, Malcom J. *The Trans-Appalachian Frontier: People, Societies, and Institutions 1775–1850.* Bloomington, IN: Indiana University Press, 2008.

S

Schlesinger, Arthur Jr. *The Age of Jackson.* New York: Little, Brown and Company, 1945.

Schroeder, John H. *Mr. Polk's War: American Opposition and Dissent, 1846–1848.* Madison, WI: University of Wisconsin Press, 1973.

Stegner, Wallace. *The Gathering of Zion: The Story of the Mormon Trail.* Lincoln, NE: Bison Books, 1992.

Stewart, James Brewer. *Holy Warriors: The Abolitionist and American Slavery.* New York: Hill and Wang, 1997.

T

Tocqueville, Alexis de. *Democracy in America.* New York: Penguin, 2003.

U

Unruh, John D. *The Plains Across: The Overland Emigrants and the Trans-Mississippi West 1840–1860.* Champaign, IL: University of Illinois Press, 1993.

Urban, Wayne J., and Jennings L. Wagoner, Jr. *American Education: A History.* New York: Routledge, 2008.

W

Weeks, Philip. *Farewell, My Nation: The American Indian and the United States in the Nineteenth Century.* New York: Harlan Davidson, 2000.

POP QUIZ

1. In spite of the fact that the factory system reduced the percentage of skilled labor in the workforce, wages in America did not decline as in Europe because of _____.
   a. strong labor unions in America
   b. the absence of labor unions in America
   c. the relative shortage of labor in America
   d. the amount of menial work that was performed by slaves (leaving more money for wage laborers)

2. The first permanent national trade union in 1852 was the _____.
   a. American Federation of Labor
   b. Knights of Labor
   c. National Typographical Union
   d. Congress of Industrial Organizations

3. The shortcomings of rivers and canals included which of the following?
   a. Waterways in the North often froze over in winter.
   b. Rivers often followed inconvenient routes.
   c. Canals could not be built in hilly country.
   d. All of the above

4. Abraham Lincoln argued that corporations could _____.
   a. be the salvation of America
   b. subvert democracy
   c. be the engines of economic growth
   d. be a positive force in the economy only if they are not unionized

5. Which of the following negatives was associated with the development of ready-made clothing?
   a. Workers were exploited in "sweatshops."
   b. Skilled laborers were often put out of business.
   c. People were forced to buy "one size fits all" clothing.
   d. Both a and b

6. Which of the following was a characteristic of the modern family?
   a. Industrialization removed male work from the home.
   b. Women gained more education.
   c. The birth rate dropped, and the family became more democratic.
   d. All of the above

7. The American Temperance Society was founded by _____.
   a. Lyman Beecher
   b. Harriet Beecher Stowe
   c. Jack Daniels
   d. Jim Beam

8. The individual who founded the first "normal" school for training teachers was _____.
   a. Abbie Normal
   b. Lyman Beecher
   c. Jonathan Boucher
   d. Horace Mann

9. The first known novel by an African American woman was _____.
   a. *Our Nig* by Harriet Wilson
   b. *Uncle Tom's Cabin* by Harriet Beecher Stowe
   c. *The Underground Railroad* by Harriet Tubman
   d. *Father Knows Best* by Harriet Nelson

10. The nativist party established in New York in 1843 was the _____.
    a. American Republican Party
    b. John Birch Society
    c. Libertarian Party
    d. American Democratic Party

11. Numerous women's colleges existed in the U.S. before the Civil War. T   F

12. Irish immigrants generally supported the Know Nothing Party. T   F

13. The American Lyceum was a women's college in Boston. T   F

14. The first monopoly in the U.S. was the _____ _____ _____.

15. Female abolitionists called for freedom from _____ _____.

Chapter 13

(Wikimedia Commons, CORBIS/© Bettmann)

The Sectional Crisis, 1848–1861

13.1 The Origins of Sectionalism

13.1a The Transcontinental Republic

Between 1846 and 1854, with the settlement of the Oregon question, the Treaty of Guadalupe Hidalgo, and the Gadsden Purchase, the United States became a two-ocean transcontinental republic, in the full sense. The contiguous United States had, for the most part, reached its present territorial limits. In one sense, the acquisition of the Southwest marked a fulfillment of American nationalism. No other nation on earth had grown so rapidly, and no people were prouder of their nation than the Americans—who boasted incessantly of the superiority of republican institutions. Yet ironically, the climax of national growth also brought with it a crisis of national unity, for it precipitated a bitter rivalry between two dissimilar sections of the country—areas divided by the Mason-Dixon line and the Ohio River.

The problem of geographical rivalries was not a new one in the United States. In a country larger than all of western Europe, with immense diversity of soil, terrain, and climate, conflicts had arisen more than once between the economic interests of one area and those of another. In fact, American history has been full of such conflicts, and they have often been marked by a division between east and west. This was true, for instance, in the contest over the Bank of the United States at the time of Jackson, and later in the battle between the advocates of the coinage of silver and the defenders of the gold standard in 1896. The theme of sectional rivalry has been so persistent that historians sometimes dispute whether the deepest antagonisms in American history have been between conflicting social classes, ethnic groups, or religious denominations, or between conflicting geographic sections.

Thus, the sectional crisis between North and South, which approached its climax between 1848 and 1860, was in no sense unique—but it did reach a unique pitch of intensity. Usually, competing sectional forces had sought only to gain advantage over one another within a union which both accepted, but on this occasion the South became so alienated that it made a titanic effort to withdraw from the Union entirely.

13.16 The Southern Way of Life

Historians have never been able to agree on any one factor as the primary cause of this division, but they do agree in recognizing a cluster of contributing factors. As far back as the seventeenth century, North and South had developed along dissimilar lines. Virginia, Maryland, and other colonies to the South had based their economy on crops that were limited to latitudes of warm climate and a long growing season. Tobacco, the first of these to be introduced in the colonies, was followed by rice and indigo in Carolina and sugar in

Map 13.1 Cotton-Growing Areas

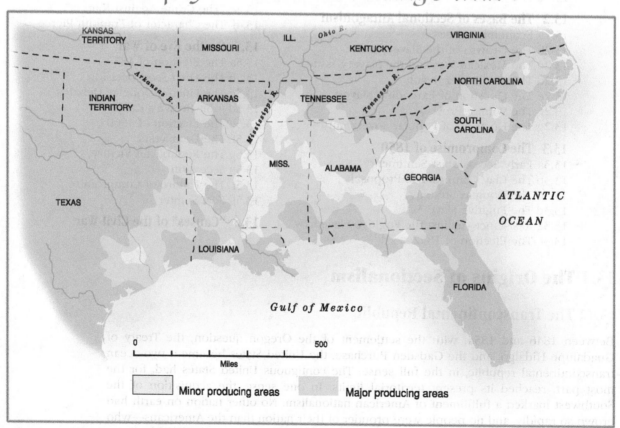

Louisiana, and most important, by cotton throughout the lower South after the invention of the cotton gin in 1793. For the cultivation of these crops, the plantation had evolved as the economic unit of production. Within the plantation system the labor supply had evolved to consist primarily of black slaves.

Actually, slave labor did not become dominant until the eighteenth century, but by the time of the American Revolution slaves had come to outnumber free persons in many plantation districts. In 1850, 32 percent of the South's total population was held in slavery. In South Carolina and Mississippi, a majority of the population consisted of slaves.

13.1c Slavery

Slavery presented a supreme paradox; while slaves were human beings, they were also considered property. The complex relationships between masters and slaves reflected this paradox. On the one hand, most white Christians recognized the slaves' humanity and believed that they had immortal souls to be saved (of course the idea of a better life after death could also be useful in converting slave unrest into religious zeal). The law viewed slaves as human beings to the extent of making them liable to punishment for serious crimes. Some masters permitted a wedding service for slave couples even though they could not legally be married. On plantations where blacks and whites mingled closely in everyday life, relations of intimacy and affection often developed. Even the proslavery stereotype of the "happy and carefree" slave—a reflection more of the whites' wishful thinking than of reality—was a backhanded way of admitting the slave's right to human happiness.

On the other hand, slaves were chattels—pieces of property. They could be bought, sold, mortgaged, bequeathed by will, or taken in payment for debt if their owners became bankrupt. They could not legally marry or own property, or in most states even be taught to read or write. Owners might let them have a family, earn money, and even buy their freedom; yet until slaves were free, their money, spouse, and children could be taken away at any moment.

The evils of slavery can be looked at in several ways. Many abolitionists condemned slavery primarily for its physical harshness—the flogging and branding of slaves, the separation of mothers from children at the auction block, the brutal labor conditions, especially for slaves who had been "sold down the river" to work in the sugarcane fields—and for the low standard of diet, clothing, and housing. Slaves experienced much cruelty and hardship no doubt, but in some instances slaves may have been kindly treated.

The worst feature of slavery may well have been its social and cultural impact on both slave and master. The slave's powerlessness tended to create a sense of dependency and to discourage self-reliance. Stable family life was difficult in situations where parents and children might be sold away from each other, white men could sexually exploit female slaves, and a slave father was legally unable to protect his wife and children. The master's power over fellow human beings tended to create feelings of superiority and domination, often in regard to

Pictured is a group of slaves on a South Carolina plantation. Slaves were seen as pieces of property. They could be bought, sold, mortgaged, bequeathed by will, or taken in payment for debt if their owners became bankrupt. (Library of Congress, LC-USZ62-67819)

his wife as well as his slaves. The racial theories that bolstered slavery bred in most white people a belief in black inferiority. Some blacks themselves subscribed to this notion.

Of course, this does not mean that all or even most slaves carried the psychological scars of dependence and inferiority. On many plantations, the black driver, rather than the overseer, exercised authority in day-to-day operations. As a sort of labor leader as well as "boss," the driver could do much to win better working conditions for the slaves. Drivers, slave artisans, highly-skilled cooks, and other blacks with critical skills played important roles in Southern life and provided other slaves with role models of self-respect and limited power *within* a system from which few could hope to escape.

Moreover, despite repression the slaves sustained a vigorous black culture largely independent from surrounding white institutions. Natural leaders in the slave quarters often became eloquent preachers in the "invisible institution" of the black church, whose congregations worshipped apart from whites (sometimes secretly) in spite of laws against separate worship. Some of these preachers, especially Gabriel Prosser in 1800 and **Nat Turner** in 1831, plotted armed insurrections to strike for freedom. The slaves created the most original and moving music in antebellum America—the spirituals—to express their longing for freedom as well as their resignation to sorrow; this evolved after the Civil War into blues and eventually jazz.

Recent research suggests that while slavery made stable family life difficult—and sometimes made family life brutal—a majority of slaves nevertheless formed strong ties of kinship and family. Thus, although slavery's impact on black people could be repressive, the countervailing force of a positive black culture provides an impressive example of survival in the face of adversity.

Furthermore, there were many mechanisms for resistance, some more successful than others. Some slaves—predominantly male—managed to run away. Others succeeded in being truant for a short while, though they may have faced severe punishment upon their return. Scholars have suggested that slaves may have deliberately broken farm

Map 13.2 Slavery and Agricultural Production

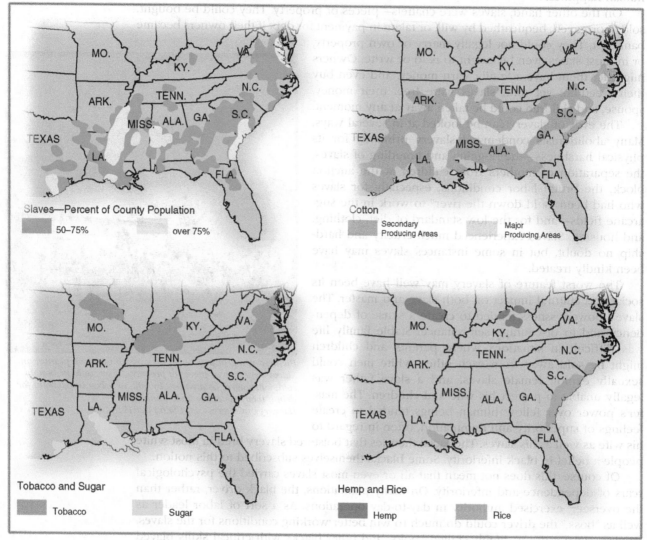

Slaves—Percent of County Population
- 50–75%
- over 75%

Cotton
- Secondary Producing Areas
- Major Producing Areas

Tobacco and Sugar
- Tobacco
- Sugar

Hemp and Rice
- Hemp
- Rice

implements or worked at a relatively slow pace by way of proving to themselves their independence from the master's interests—or maybe even to punish the master. For women, a recent book by Stephanie Camp suggests, one form of assertion of self may have been putting together party clothes out of whatever materials they could cobble together so that they could then sneak away from the quarters at night for an unauthorized good time. The slaves' freedom of movement was constantly at risk due to the monitoring of slave patrols, so the bondspeople had to be prudent in order to carve out time and space for either surreptitious religious services or for "frolics."

Slavery also put Southern whites on the defensive, ever fearful of slave insurrection and ever conscious that slavery was condemned throughout most of the Western world. As a result, they isolated themselves more and more, imposing an "intellectual blockade" to keep out not only abolitionist ideas but any social ideas implying freedom or change. To defend their system, they idealized their society as romantic and chivalric. At best, they realized their ideal in the attainment of a real aristocracy—but the tradition was maintained at a high cost.

By 1850 the Southern system, with its rural life and slave labor, had led to the development of a somewhat conservative temper, a marked stratification of social orders, and a paternalistic type of society. The power of all landowners to rule their own workers on their own plantations had prevented the growth of a strong public authority. As a result, violence was frequent, and qualities of personal courage and physical prowess were especially valued. For instance, the practice of dueling—which had died out in the North—still prevailed. The taboo against women working outside the home was far stronger than in the North, and in general, gender norms were far more conservative. Even women schoolteachers in the South were often Northerners by birth.

13.1b The Northern Way of Life

It would be a mistake to think of the North as presenting a total contrast, for the majority of people in the free states also engaged in agriculture and lived a rural life—the key difference being that the Northern economy and culture were more diversified. In the absence of a valuable export crop such as tobacco or cotton, many New Englanders had turned early to commerce as a means of securing money to buy the imports they needed. During the Napoleonic wars, when their commerce was disrupted and the supply of imported manufactures was cut off, they had begun a manufacturing industry. As manufacturing grew, cities grew with it.

Prosperity and rapid economic growth in the North fostered a belief in progress and innovation quite different from the more traditional (or static) attitudes of the South. Although the factory system brought with it a certain amount of exploitation of laborers through low wages, the fact that all men were free made for greater mobility, greater equality, more democracy, and less sharply defined social stratification than in the South. The modernizing North grew to value the commercial virtues of thrift, enterprise, and hard work—in contrast to the more traditional and militaristic virtues that held priority in the South.

Such differences as these can easily be exaggerated, for a great deal of frontier Americanism prevailed in both the North and the South. Similarly, evangelical Protestantism was the dominant religion of both sections. The materialistic pursuit of wealth motivated cotton planters as well as northern industrialists. To a European, all Americans seemed bumptiously democratic; and in the South, the Whig Party—favored by most planter aristocrats—could not have competed against the Democratic Party at all unless it had adopted the democratic symbols of the log cabin, the coonskin hat, and the cider barrel.

13.2 The Bases of Sectional Antagonism

Regional dissimilarity, however, need not lead to conflict. In the United States today there are profound differences between the red states and the blue states, the rural and the urban regions. And yet, no one is talking about secession—let alone war. The antagonism that drove North and South to war in the mid-nineteenth century, therefore, needs to be explained.

BVT Lab

Flashcards are available
for this chapter at
www.BVTLab.com.

13.2a Economic Causes

In one sense, the antagonism was economic: the dissimilar economic interests of the North and the South caused them to favor opposite economic policies and therefore to clash politically. Essentially, the South, with its cotton economy, produced raw materials for a textile industry centered in Britain. Accordingly, the South sold on the world market, and in return it needed to buy its manufactured goods where they were cheapest—which was also in the world market—and to keep down taxes and governmental costs as much as possible.

For the more diversified Northern economy, the needs were different. Northern manufacturers and workers wanted tariffs to protect them from the competition of low-priced goods produced by cheaper labor abroad. Manufacturers and farmers alike needed improved transportation facilities ("internal improvements") in the form of roads, canals, and railroads to foster inter-regional exchanges of goods. Northern economic groups and their congressional representatives, therefore, supported state and federal appropriations to build better roads and to assist canal and railroad construction.

Some of the states in the upper South (like Kentucky and Maryland) with urban and manufacturing centers of their own supported appropriations for these purposes, but the cotton-growing South did not fit into this scheme. Most of the cotton and tobacco crop was shipped by river or by short, locally built railroads to river or coastal port cities for export abroad. Internal improvements to the country, in general, meant only that the South would be paying part of the governmental cost of programs from which it did not benefit. Indeed, the new transportation routes diverted trade *away* from the South's own Mississippi River system, drawing trade southward toward New Orleans. In addition, tariffs meant that the South would be prevented from buying its manufactures from those who bought its raw materials and would be forced by law to pay a higher, tariff-supported price for its manufactures. As Virginian John Randolph, of Roanoke, angrily declared, "we shall only pay more for worse goods." Because of these economic factors, North and South tended to vote against each other on questions of tariff, internal improvements, and other extensions of the power of the central government. Their rivalry had reached a crisis at the time of the Nullification Controversy in 1833, when South Carolina was ready to defy federal law due to their opposition to what they viewed as too high a federal tariff. The crisis was averted when other Southern states would not commit to taking up arms in support of South Carolina. The South as a whole had resented federal economic policies but had never opposed them to the point of breaking up the Union, toward which most Southerners still felt strong patriotic loyalty.

13.2b The Growth of the Slavery Issue

A deeper cause of division was the institution of slavery. Until the 1770s, slavery had scarcely been regarded as a moral question at all, except by the Quakers. In one form or another, the institution had existed in other lands for thousands of years, and the slave trade had been essential to the colonization of the Western Hemisphere. As late as 1780, there was no division into slave states and free states; slaves were held in every state of the Union. They were simply less numerous in the North, and only because they were less profitable there. But in the late eighteenth century (during the Age of Reason, or the Enlightenment), slavery came under attack by believers in natural law, human equality, and human rights. At the same time, emphasis in the churches shifted from a limited concern with the personal salvation of the individual to a fuller application of Christian teaching in relation to human society. Thus, the savage penal code of earlier times was modified, various social reforms were adopted, and slavery was reconsidered on moral grounds.

States from Pennsylvania northward shared in this movement against slavery. By 1804, all of them had adopted laws for the gradual or immediate emancipation of their slaves; and Congress had prohibited the importation of any more slaves from Africa after 1808. For a time it appeared that the South might also participate in this movement. Southern Enlightenment leaders like Jefferson condemned slavery in the abstract, and antislavery societies were active in the South. Furthermore, slavery was restricted to the rice and tobacco economy, which was static and no longer very profitable. This meant that the Southern economy as a whole did not depend on slave labor.

Jefferson, however, never freed more than a handful of his own slaves since his exorbitant spending habits rendered him in a state of indebtedness virtually all of his life; slaves were his primary assets that not only could be sold at any time to pay debts but that also multiplied naturally. The Southern antislavery societies devoted their efforts mainly to encouraging the emigration of free blacks. The tenor of antislavery sentiment among Southerners, apart from the Quakers and the early Methodists, was one of anguished hand-wringing over an inherited evil, rather than vigorous action for its abolition.

The introduction of cotton and the cotton gin injected greater vitality into the slave system. In one generation, the cultivation of short-staple cotton spread across the lower South from middle Georgia to the banks of the Brazos in Texas. Every decade from 1800 to 1860, the value and the volume of the crop doubled. In this dynamic and expanding economy, the price of slaves rose and fell with the price of cotton. Slavery accompanied cotton as it expanded into new areas. By 1820, both slavery and cotton were completely interwoven into the whole Southern system.

With the introduction of cotton and the cotton gin, the market for cotton grew drastically, as did the demand for slave labor. During every decade from 1800 to 1860, the value and the volume of cotton doubled. (Wikimedia Commons)

While this was happening, the humanitarian crusade against slavery in Great Britain (which abolished slavery in the West Indies in 1833), in France (which abolished slavery throughout the British Empire in 1833), and in the Northern states (where the abolitionists became increasingly militant in their denunciations) caused the South to take a defensive stance. By 1830 Southern leaders were no longer saying—as some had earlier—that slavery was an evil, but one too deeply rooted to be abolished at once. Instead, they were beginning to assert that slavery was a positive institution. They defended it with claims that it had been sanctioned in the Bible and that the Negro was biologically inferior to the white. They argued that the exploitation of Negro workers by the slavery system was not so harsh as the exploitation of white workers by the wage system, in which the worker received only a bare subsistence when he was working and no subsistence at all when he was not. They held that, since social divisions were inevitable, assigning leadership to one class and subordination to another was better than having an endless struggle between classes.

These clashing arguments polarized the two sections more and more with each decade after 1830. As the abolitionists became more militant in their crusade against the "sin of slavery," the South became so defensive that it would not tolerate any expression of antislavery opinion.

In spite of this disagreement on the ethics of slavery, several factors prevented a legal or physical clash over the question. To begin with, slavery was widely regarded as a matter for the states to handle locally rather than for the federal government to regulate nationally (South Carolina's attempt at nullification was actually a challenge to the government's authority in this area, as well as its authority to set tariffs). At that time, people regarded the federal system more as a loose association of states and less as a consolidated nation—and they were willing to leave many important questions to state action. Further, it was generally understood that the Constitution (in its "three-fifths" and fugitive slave clauses) protected the South's right to practice slavery. It was on the basis of such provisions that the Southern states had agreed to join the Union.

Apart from the question of legal or constitutional obligation, many Americans took the position that the harmony of the Union was simply more important than the ethics of slavery—that the slave question must not be permitted to weaken the Union and that the abolitionists were wrong to keep up constant agitation on an issue that caused sectional antagonism. The abolitionists, who were in the minority, felt that the Union was not worth saving unless it was based upon freedom.

13.2c The Mexican War and the Slavery Issue

Northern reactions to the War with Mexico were even more intense than Northern reactions to Texas' annexation. No matter how moderate they previously had been, anti-extension Northerners began to heed the abolitionists' arguments that the South's "slave power" must be checked. According to this version of affairs, the South—having dominated the federal government since its establishment—was now afraid that population growth in the North and the proliferation of free states in the Northwest would destroy its political advantage; therefore, it sought to strengthen itself by spreading an evil that enlightened folk deplored. The threat would affect the Southwest (as a result of the Mexican War), the West as a whole, and Northern states as well. The "slave power," the argument continued, would try to annex every square mile in Mexico, as well as Central America and the West Indies.

At the same time, many Southerners blamed the North as the aggressor. The pamphlets of abolitionists stirred up blacks, they asserted. Slave insurrections had resulted and would continue to result from the "senseless" agitation. As an example, Southerners pointed to the Nat Turner Revolt of 1831, which Southerners blamed on Northern agitators. Most notably, David Walker—a freeborn black man living in Boston—published his *Appeal to the Coloured Citizens of the World,* which was an open invitation to all slaves to rebel. Walker's work was found in the hands of Virginia slaves, the state where Nat Turner launched his bloody revolt. Coincidentally, William Lloyd Garrison of Boston published his first issue of *The Liberator,* an abolitionist publication, the same year as Nat Turner's revolt.

Pictured is a depiction of Nat Turner being captured after hiding out for ten weeks. During Nat Turner's revolt, a total of fifty-seven whites were killed—including slave masters and their wives and children—by Turner and his followers. All of Turner's followers were eventually caught and killed, along with Turner himself. (Wikimedia Commons)

13.2d The Nat Turner Revolt

Nat Turner was a Virginia slave who, in his 20s, claimed to receive the Spirit of God, who appointed him as a Divine instrument against slavery. On August 22, 1831, Turner and six of his fellow slaves attacked their master and all of the white people on their plantation, beheading the slave master and his wife with an axe in front of their children. Turner and his followers visited ten other plantations by noon, killing all of the white men, women, and children they encountered. By the end of the day, fifty-seven white men, women, and children were dead; and Turner's following had grown to at least fifty slaves. The next day, the whites raised a militia and killed all of Turner's followers. Turner successfully hid for ten weeks before being captured, after which he was tried, convicted, and executed. Twenty other slaves were also executed for aiding Turner in his revolt, the most deadly in American history.

Antislavery rhetoric had long been limited to a few Northern hotheads, but now they saw the zealotry as epidemic. Northerners had petitioned to do away with slavery in the District of Columbia and on federal property in the South, and the same "intolerance" had been manifested in opposition to annexing Texas. Furthermore, Southerners asked, did not Northern states abysmally fail to live up to their constitutional commitments when they repeatedly refused to enforce the Fugitive Slave Law of 1793? So ran the Southern arguments.

As the world has often seen, in situations where emotion interferes with reason, there were exaggerations on both sides though rarely complete departures from truth. On the one hand, there simply was no "slave power" in the abolitionist sense of the term. There was no unanimity of Southern opinion as to policies. From Jefferson's day through Jackson's to Polk's, not all Southern officeholders in high places had been of one political mind. Contrary to what was charged, there was no widespread Southern *or* Northern conspiracy.

In the 1840s, the issues of slavery versus antislavery and expansion versus containment became intermeshed. If the Civil War had never taken place, we might not now be inclined to stress North-South antipathies respecting the West. But since the war did occur, it is evident that the relationship of the slavery question to the West was loaded with political dynamite. In the North, the Mexican War sparked opposition from the young, one-term Congressman from Illinois, Abraham Lincoln, as well as from the New Englander, Henry David Thoreau—and countless others who were not destined to be so famous. The War of 1812 had triggered domestic opposition in the North on the basis of sectional self-interest. The Mexican War triggered opposition by principled opponents of slavery, and some of the arguments deployed by these opponents have inspired subsequent anti-war activists down to the twenty-first century.

"Fifty-four forty or fight"
James Polk's 1844 campaign slogan regarding the dispute with Britain over Oregon

13.2e The Question of Extending Slavery

All of this meant that as long as the institution of slavery was confined to the existing slave states, few Northerners were willing to act against it—and it was not an explosive question politically. When the question of extending slavery to new areas arose, however, the opposition was far more determined. As early as the Ordinance of 1787, the old Congress (under the Articles of Confederation) had agreed to exclude slavery from the region north of the Ohio River. Some people, motivated by sincere antislavery sentiments, were determined to "contain" slavery. Others cared nothing about the evils of slavery but wanted to reserve unsettled areas for white residents only. Furthermore, many people wanted to bring these new areas to the support of the North in the economic struggle between North and South. The South, conversely, was equally convinced that the growth of the country should not be all on the side of the North, reducing the South to a defenseless minority. This feeling made the South unwilling to concede even the areas where there was little prospect of extending slavery.

Because of these attitudes, the acquisition of any new area, the organization of any new territory, and the admission of any new state had always involved a possible flare-up over the slavery question. There had been such a crisis in 1819, when Missouri applied for admission to statehood as the first state (except Louisiana) to be formed out of the Louisiana Purchase. In the same way, the prospect of the acquisition of territory from Mexico—as a result of the Mexican War—brought on a more protracted and more serious crisis beginning in 1846.

A few months into the Mexican War, President Polk asked Congress to appropriate $2 million to be used in negotiating for land to be acquired from Mexico at the termination of the war. Many Northern Democrats were at this time angry with Polk, partly because he had vetoed a rivers and harbors bill important to Midwestern economic development and partly because they felt he had violated the expansionist promises on which he had been elected. His platform had called for the "reoccupation" of Oregon and the "reannexation" of Texas, and for "all of Oregon or none." In fact, a Polk campaign slogan had been **"fifty-four forty or fight,"** suggesting that Polk would prefer to go to war with England rather than to settle for a Canada-Oregon border that did not include much of what is now British Columbia, all the way to the southern tip of Alaska. This had put the question of expansion on a bisectional basis by promising Oregon, sure to be a free territory, to the North, and Texas, which already had slavery, to the South. After becoming president, however, Polk had compromised on Oregon, accepting the boundary at the 49th parallel instead of at 54°40′ and thus avoiding confrontation with England. Meanwhile, he had also pushed expansion in the Southwest to the fullest extent by waging war with Mexico.

13.2f The Wilmot Proviso

This was the state of affairs when David Wilmot, a Democrat from Pennsylvania, introduced a resolution in the House of Representatives that slavery should be prohibited in any territory acquired from Mexico with the $2 million Polk had requested. This Free-Soil resolution passed the House, where the North was stronger, but failed to pass in the Senate, where the South had equal strength. The disagreement between Senate and

House marked a deadlock in Congress that lasted for four years, blocking the organization of governments in the newly acquired areas. The result was a steady increase in sectional tension.

In 1848, at the end of the Mexican War, the victorious United States acquired territory encompassing the present states of Nevada, California, and Utah, most of Arizona and New Mexico, and parts of Colorado and Wyoming. Mexico also relinquished all claims to Texas above the Rio Grande. In the same year, gold was discovered in California; and by 1849 the gold rush was in full swing.

The need for organizing the new land was urgent, and the territorial question became the foremost issue in public life. At one extreme on this question stood Wilmot and the **Free-Soilers**, comprised of both Whigs and Democrats who demanded the exclusion of slavery from the new areas by act of Congress. At the other extreme, Southern Whigs and Democrats alike adopted the position of John C. Calhoun, who argued that the territories were owned in common by all the states (rather than by the federal government, which was only a joint agent for the states) and that all citizens had an equal right to take their property (including slaves) to the common territory. Therefore, in Calhoun's logic, Congress had no power under the Constitution to exclude slavery from any territory.

13.29 The Doctrine of Popular Sovereignty

Political leaders who wanted some kind of adjustment or middle ground were not satisfied with either Wilmot's or Calhoun's alternative, one of which conceded nothing to the South, the other nothing to the North. They sought a more "moderate" position, and some of them advocated an extension of the Missouri Compromise line of 36°30′ to the Pacific. Most of them, however, were more attracted by a proposal sponsored by **Lewis Cass**, senator from Michigan, for what was called **popular sovereignty** or "squatter sovereignty." Cass contended that the fairest and most democratic solution would be to let the people in the territories decide for themselves whether they would have slavery, just as the people in the states had already decided. Cass' proposal offered an attractive means for keeping the slavery question out of federal politics, but it contained one ambiguity that he adroitly refused to clarify. It did not specify *when* the people in the territories should make the decision. If they could make the decision as soon as the territory was organized, free soil could be attained by popular vote as easily as by congressional vote. According to Calhoun, popular exclusion at this stage would be just as wrong as congressional exclusion, for it would mean that Congress was giving to the territory a power which Congress did not have and therefore could not give. If, however, the voters in a territory could decide on slavery only when they applied for statehood, this would mean that the territories would have been left open to slavery quite as much as by Calhoun's position.

Far from reducing the amount of support for popular sovereignty, however, this ambiguity actually added to the attractiveness of the doctrine. Antislavery people argued that popular sovereignty would result in free territories, while proslavery advocates contended that it guaranteed slavery a fair chance to establish itself during the period before statehood.

Military hero Zachary Taylor won the presidential election of 1848. (Wikimedia Commons)

13.3 The Compromise of 1850

While these various positions on the territorial extension of slavery were being developed, the impasse in Congress continued. For three entire sessions, covering most of the Polk administration, nothing could be voted on regarding California or the Southwest. It was only after long delay that an act to organize Oregon Territory without slavery was adopted.

In 1848, when the two national parties faced this question in a presidential election, both of them evaded it. The Democrats nominated Cass, whose reputation was based on the idea of popular sovereignty, on a platform that still did not say *when* the people of a territory could vote on slavery. The Whigs nominated a military hero, **Zachary Taylor**,

Map 13.3 Presidential Election of 1848

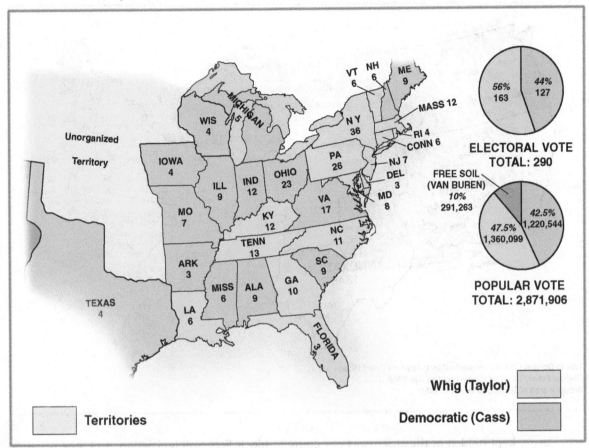

ELECTORAL VOTE TOTAL: 290

- 56% 163
- 44% 127

POPULAR VOTE TOTAL: 2,871,906

- FREE SOIL (VAN BUREN) 10% 291,263
- 47.5% 1,360,099
- 42.5% 1,220,544

Whig (Taylor)

Democratic (Cass)

Territories

who had never been in politics, without any platform whatever. Further muddying the waters was the development of the Free Soil Party, which held its inaugural convention in Buffalo. The Free Soil Party nominated former president and Jacksonian Democrat Martin Van Buren for president and Charles Francis Adams of the Whig Party for vice president on a platform of "free soil, free speech, free labor, and free men." In the election campaign the Free Soilers were successful in making slavery the main issue of the campaign, but they did not carry a single state. In the main contest between Taylor and Cass, however—which turned out to be a contest between frank evasion and concealed evasion—Taylor, who owned over one hundred slaves on plantations in Mississippi and Louisiana, was triumphant. He was inaugurated as president in 1849.

13.3a Early Secessionist Sentiment

Meanwhile, the House of Representatives had repeatedly voted in favor of Wilmot's principle of free soil by congressional action. The seeming possibility of a Free-Soil victory had, in turn, aroused bitter resentment in the South. For the first time, many Southerners began to think of withdrawing from the Union if Congress voted to prevent them from taking their slaves into areas they had helped to win and to pay for. By 1848, Southerners in Congress were beginning to speak rather freely of disunion. After Taylor was elected, he sent envoys to California and New Mexico to persuade settlers in the newly acquired territories to draft constitutions and apply for admission to the Union as states, rather than as territories. The inhabitants of both territories were predominantly anti-slavery. In California, gold rushers did not want to have to compete with gangs of slave labor in gold prospecting. In New Mexico, the climate was simply too arid to grow cotton and slave, labor was not necessary on the open range. Southerners realized that Taylor—though a Louisiana slaveholder who had brought slaves with him to the White House whom he

Map 13.4 Territorial Growth (1850)

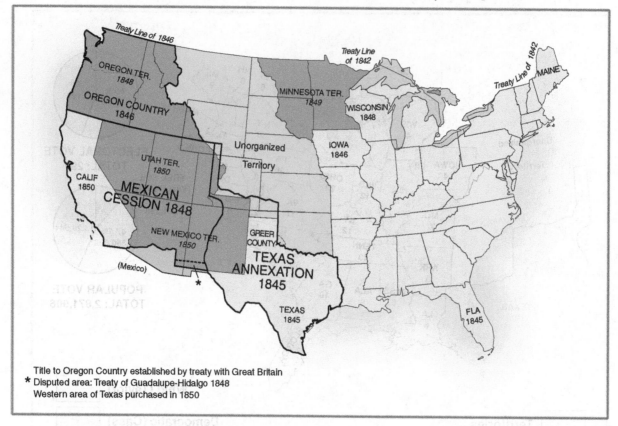

Title to Oregon Country established by treaty with Great Britain
* Disputed area: Treaty of Guadalupe-Hidalgo 1848
Western area of Texas purchased in 1850

kept hidden in the attic—was not going to block Free-Soil legislation; and they began to organize Southern resistance. Jefferson Davis of Mississippi argued, "we are about permanently to destroy the balance of power between the sections."

In October 1849 a state convention in Mississippi called for a convention of Southern state delegates to meet at Nashville, Tennessee, the following June to work out a united Southern position. Five Southern states officially elected delegates to such a convention, and representatives were unofficially chosen from four others.

Thus, when Taylor's first Congress met in December 1849, the need for organizing the area acquired from Mexico was urgent; and the relations between North and South were at a crisis. This crisis became more acute when Taylor announced his support for admitting California directly to statehood, without going through a territorial stage, and his intention to support the same plan for New Mexico in due course. Technically, this plan bypassed the question of congressional exclusion from the decision on slavery; in substance, however, it would represent a Free-Soil victory—for the proposed states seemed fairly certain to be free states. At this prospect Southern protests intensified. Though historians today disagree as to whether the country was actually close to disunion, many prominent leaders at the time certainly feared that it was.

A separate issue threatening disunion at the time was a border dispute between the United States and the new state of Texas. According to the 1836 Treaty of Velasco, under which Texas had staked its claim to independence, the Texas southern and western border was the Rio Grande. Texans sent envoys to the upper Rio Grande Valley (present day Albuquerque) and Santa Fe to organize county governments, but they were rebuffed by the residents. At Santa Fe, the Texan envoys were ordered to "cease and desist at every peril" by U.S. Army General Kearney, who exercised political authority in Santa Fe in the aftermath of the War with Mexico. Nevertheless, Texans still claimed their rights to the territory; and Peter Hansborough Bell won the Texas gubernatorial election of 1849 on a platform of retaining Santa Fe by force. Though Texas had fought for a decade to join the Union and had not been an American state for even four years, the

Texans were threatening war with the U.S. over Santa Fe. Under Texas' Articles of Annexation, however, a provision stated that Congress would settle border disputes. Northerners opposed Texas possession of Santa Fe primarily because they viewed it as an extension of slave territory into New Mexico. The Santa Fe issue would, therefore, become connected to the entire sectional debate.

13.3b The Clay Compromise Proposals

One of those leaders fearing disunion was Senator Henry Clay of Kentucky. As a spokesman of the border states—which were always anxious to promote sectional harmony—and as one who had played a leading part in arranging the compromises of 1820 (Missouri) and 1833 (Nullification), Clay was a natural leader of compromise. Although a Whig, he was at odds with President Taylor. Accordingly, Clay came forward early in the congressional session of 1850 with an elaborate compromise designed to cover the slavery question in all its national aspects. Clay's plan called for the following: (1) admitting California as a free state; (2) organizing the rest of the Mexican cession into two territories, Utah and New Mexico, which were to decide for themselves whether slavery should be permitted or abolished; (3) awarding New Mexico part of the area on the upper Rio Grande claimed by Texas, including Santa Fe, but compensating Texas through federal payment of the $10 million in debt Texas had contracted before annexation; (4) abolishing the sale of slaves in the District of Columbia but guaranteeing slavery itself in the District; (5) enacting an effective law to compel the return of fugitive slaves who had escaped into the free states.

Clay's proposal brought on a long, brilliant, and famous series of debates in Congress. Clay himself made an immensely eloquent appeal for his plan as a means of saving the Union, giving seventy speeches urging its passage. Calhoun, who did not support the compromise directly, helped it indirectly by coming into the Senate almost in a dying condition to warn solemnly of the danger to the Union and the determination of the South to maintain its rights. The most important speech of the session was made by Daniel Webster, who was Clay's only peer as an orator and who was generally regarded as an antislavery man. On March 7, Webster announced his support of the compromise and made a powerful argument that slavery was naturally excluded from the West by climatic, physical, and agricultural conditions and that there was no need to bring on a crisis by adopting an antislavery law, such as the **Wilmot Proviso**, to accomplish what had already been settled by physical environment. "I would not re-enact a law of God," said Webster, impressively, "I would not reaffirm an ordinance of nature."

Despite great oratorical support, Clay's "omnibus bill," incorporating all his proposals in one measure, faced heavy opposition. President Taylor was waiting to veto it, and in July it was cut to pieces on the floor by a process of amendment in which Northern and Southern extremists voted together to prevent its passage. Clay—old, worn out, and badly discouraged—went off to Newport for a rest.

13.3c The Douglas Strategy

Even before this vote was taken, however, the tide had turned. President Taylor died, and his successor, **Millard Fillmore**, favored the compromise and immediately began to exert presidential influence to support it.

Meanwhile, **Stephen A. Douglas**, a young and vigorous senator from Illinois, took over the management of the compromise forces in Congress. Douglas was not a great orator; he was, however, a supremely effective, rough-and-tumble debater, a man of immense energy ("a steam engine in breeches" was the phrase), and a most sagacious political tactician. He perceived that there was not a clear majority in favor of the compromise and that it could not be passed in the form in which Clay had presented it. He also realized that if Clay's proposals were taken up one by one, they could be passed by a combination of those who favored the compromise as a whole and those who favored each particular measure. For instance, California would be admitted by a majority composed of compromise men and antislavery men, while the **Fugitive Slave Act** would be adopted by a combination

Senator Henry Clay of Kentucky proposed a compromise that would cover the slavery question in its national aspects, and ultimately save the Union. (Wikimedia Commons)

Wilmot Proviso
This Free Soil resolution was introduced in the House of Representatives by David Wilson and proposed that slavery should be prohibited in any territory acquired from Mexico. The resolution passed the House, where the North was stronger, but failed to pass in the Senate, where the South had equal strength.

Millard Fillmore
Became president in 1850 after Zachary Taylor died in office

Stephen A. Douglas
Introduced the Kansas-Nebraska Bill in 1854 with a provision for popular sovereignty in the territories; defeated Lincoln for a seat in the U.S. Senate after a famous debate in 1858

Fugitive Slave Act
Unpopular law that required that Northerners help Southerners capture fugitive slaves in the North and return them to enslavement in the South

of compromise men and proslavery men. Douglas applied this strategy so effectively that within a few weeks Clay's entire program was enacted into law.

The adoption of the **Compromise of 1850** ended the crisis. It also broke the long deadlock and gave badly needed political organization to California and the Southwest. Because it brought a great sense of relief to those who had feared for the safety of the Union, it was hailed as the great and final settlement that defused the slavery issue, once and for all, as a source of discord in the Union. Free-Soiler Salmon Chase, however, drew the ominous conclusion that "the question of slavery in the territories has been avoided. It has not been settled." Unfortunately for the nation, Chase's conclusion would prove to be correct.

13.30 The Fugitive Slave Act

In fact, the Compromise of 1850 settled far less than it appeared to settle. For Utah and New Mexico, the Compromise of 1850 admitted them to the Union as territories with "popular sovereignty" to determine the status of slavery within their own borders. These provisions left open the explosive question Lewis Cass had so carefully avoided: Could the citizens of the territory outlaw slavery in the territory? More important, while laying to rest the explosive issue of the Wilmot Proviso, it brought to life the even more explosive issue of the fugitive slave. The question of the slave in the territories was a legal and abstract question—a question of what was later called "an imaginary Negro in an impossible place." But the question of the runaway slave was dramatic and real, involving a human creature on a quest for freedom, who was actively being hunted down by his fellow men.

For a time, the fugitive slave question raised a terrific furor. To appreciate the uproar, one must understand that the law contained a number of very extreme features. The general idea was that when slaves successfully escaped their captors in the South and fled to territory in the North where black persons could be free, Northerners were obligated to help the Southerners apprehend the runaway slaves and return them to their masters. Additionally, the Fugitive Slave Act denied trial by jury in the case of alleged fugitives and provided for their cases to be decided by a special federal commissioner. Those accused of being fugitives could not testify in their own defense; hence, if anyone were captured in a case of mistaken identity, he or she would not be able to say so in court. Further, the Act paid the commissioner a fee that was higher in cases where the alleged fugitive was returned to slavery than in cases where the fugitive was set free. Though this arrangement was defended on the ground that there was much more paper work in one case than the other, it led to severe criticism. Still further, the law stipulated that any citizen could be called upon to participate in the enforcement process, which meant that those who opposed slavery must not only permit the capture of fugitives but might possibly be made to help in their capture. Those Northern citizens who failed to assist in the capture of a slave when they were able to do so could be subject to both fines and imprisonment. The very idea that Northerners would have to assist Southern slave masters in recovering their "property" was abhorrent to Northern abolitionists, but to be jailed or fined for failing to do so was a double indignity.

Apart from these features of the law itself, the act aroused criticism because in operation it applied not only to slaves who were then running away but also to any slaves who had ever run away. There were many fugitives who had lived quietly in the North for many years and who had been quite safe from arrest under the relatively ineffectual Fugitive Slave Law of 1793. Now, under the act of 1850, they found themselves in real danger. Some Southerners went north, rounding up black people with little consideration of how long they had been free, or in some cases if they, in fact, had ever been slaves. For example, in 1851 a black man who had lived in Indiana for nineteen years was torn from his family and sent into slavery. Throughout the North, the law terrorized blacks, for those who were not fugitives had reason to fear being kidnapped quite as much as actual runaways had reason to fear being arrested. Consequently, a wave of migration to Canada set in, and several thousand blacks moved to Ontario. Northern abolitionists added fuel to the fire of sectional tensions over the Act by impeding the capture of fugitives, even when there was no question that the person was a recent runaway.

The problems with the Fugitive Slave Act reflect the fact that the 1850 Compromise had never commanded a real majority and had been enacted only by finesse. The Southern states accepted it somewhat reluctantly; Georgia spoke for the rest of them, however, its legislature voted on resolutions stating that if the compromise were not fully enforced, Georgia would withdraw from the Union. In fact, while the Southern disunionists were agreeing not to demand **secession** at this time, the Southern unionists were almost forced to agree to the *principle* of secession in order to get the secessionists to agree not to exercise it at that time. Meanwhile in the North, the antislavery forces were pouring their denunciations upon the Fugitive Slave Act and upon Daniel Webster for supporting it. Perhaps never before in American politics had political invective been so bitter.

Secession

Action led by South Carolina in December 1860, in opposition to Lincoln's election and the Republican platform that opposed slavery in the territories

Underground railroad

System of safe houses and contacts that helped slaves flee to freedom in the North

13.3c Resistance Against the Fugitive Slave Law

A series of fugitive slave episodes followed which kept the country at a high pitch of excitement. In Boston, leading citizens openly asserted their intention to violate the law. In October a "vigilance committee," headed by one of the foremost citizens of Boston, the Reverend Theodore Parker, smuggled two undoubted slaves out of the country. Four months later, a crowd (mostly black) seized a prisoner, Shadrach, from the courtroom and spirited him away to Canada. Finally in April 1851, the government succeeded in returning a slave from Boston, from which city it was boasted that no slave had ever been returned. This was accomplished only after mobs had surrounded the courthouse for several days. Only one other time was a slave—Anthony Burns—returned from Boston. In his case, a mob stormed the courthouse in an effort to rescue him, and a large military force was required in order to prevent his rescue.

In other cities, also, rescues and attempted rescues kept the pot boiling; and the fugitive slave question became, for a time, the foremost issue of the day. Yet the excitement and emotion that the issue generated have made it hard to get at the facts about whether the escape of slaves from the South was numerically significant. On the one hand, Northern antislavery advocates boasted of their resistance to the law and claimed that they were operating a vast **"underground railroad"** which had helped eighty thousand slaves to escape their pursuers. On the other, spokesmen of the South, indignant at the open violation of the law, complained bitterly that one hundred thousand slaves had been abducted over a forty-year period. These were probably inflated figures. The underground railroad was probably more extensive in legend than in reality and more important as a weapon of psychological warfare than as an escape route for slaves. It also appears that in many parts of the North, the Fugitive Slave Act had public support and was well enforced.

There is no doubt that the fugitive question dramatized the issue of slavery to a spectacular degree. The human being in search of freedom, trying to escape from bloodthirsty pursuers, was an immensely moving figure. By changing the focus of the slavery question from the legal status of an imaginary chattel in a remote territory to the human plight of an individual human being on a nearby street, the Compromise of 1850 had, perhaps, created more tension than it relieved. In the final analysis, the Fugitive Slave Act was largely an unenforceable failure as evidenced by the fact that in the decade between the passage of the Act and the Civil War, only three hundred slaves were returned to their masters under the Act. Given that a major fear of some Northern whites was still that blacks would leave the Southern plantations and move north, one might have expected at least as many slaves to be returned to their masters during this period even if the Act had never been passed.

Anthony Burns (Wikimedia Commons)

It is by no means an accident that *Uncle Tom's Cabin* (1852), the classic literary protest against slavery, was published less than a year after the enactment of the fugitive law. In fact, **Harriet Beecher Stowe** was encouraged by her sister-in-law to write something in response to the new law, and the novel was the result. The book's most dramatic scene was that of the fugitive slave woman, Eliza, crossing the icebound Ohio River with her son in her arms as she was being pursued by a slave trader. This book, one of America's all-time best sellers, forced readers to see the humanity of the slaves and wrung sympathy and tears from countless people who had never previously been moved by the abolitionists.

Pictured is a dramatic scene from Harriet Beecher Stowe's novel, Uncle Tom's Cabin, *in which the fugitive slave woman, Eliza, is crossing the icebound Ohio River with her son in her arms as a slave trader is pursuing her. (Wikimedia Commons)*

13.3f The Election of 1852

If the fugitive slave law dramatized the issue of slavery, the crisis preceding the Compromise of 1850 had dramatized the issue of the Union. Many Northerners who thoroughly disapproved of slavery felt that the question of the Union was more important and must have priority. Consequently, despite fugitive slave episodes, the Compromise received strong support throughout much of the country. Although there had not been a clear majority in favor of adopting it, there was certainly a clear majority in favor of maintaining it.

The firmness of public support for the Compromise showed up clearly in the election of 1852. As it approached, Millard Fillmore, who had signed the compromise acts while serving out the term of Zachary Taylor, aspired to a term of his own. At the party convention, however, Northern Whigs blocked the effort of Southern Whigs to nominate Fillmore and forced the nomination instead of General Winfield Scott, who had captured Mexico City in the Mexican War. Scott was the Whigs' third military hero; and they hoped that, like Harrison and Taylor, he would win the White House on his military record.

The adoption of a platform revealed a deep division among the Whigs. The majority secured the adoption of a plank accepting the Compromise of 1850, including the Fugitive Slave Act, as a final settlement. But there was strong opposition, consisting mostly of delegates who supported Scott. Scott, who was pompous and politically clumsy, tried to get out of this dilemma by saying merely, "I accept the nomination with the resolutions attached." It was clear, however, that he was not a thoroughgoing supporter of the Compromise.

The Democrats settled their differences between rival candidates by agreeing on a dark horse, **Franklin Pierce** of New Hampshire, who had served with gallantry in the Mexican War. Pierce later proved a weak man with a serious alcohol addiction (later, as president, even being arrested in Washington for recklessly trampling a woman with his horse while intoxicated) and a depressed wife (Jane, who wrote letters to their dead son). Nonetheless, Pierce was an attractive candidate—handsome and pleasing in his manner—and the Democrats gave him united support on a platform that proclaimed the finality of the Compromise.

Presidential candidate Franklin Pierce was expected to be a compromise for the Democrats. Though attractive as a candidate, Pierce was later found to be a reckless man and an alcoholic. (Wikimedia Commons)

The position of the two parties gave the voters a fairly clear choice on the question of compromise—Pierce and his party were united on it, the Whigs were not. The voters exercised their option in a decisive way. Pierce carried all but four states—two in the North, and two in the South.

The defeat smashed the Whig Party, which was already badly divided between the "Cotton Whigs" of the South and the "Conscience Whigs" of the North. Though many important figures—including Abraham Lincoln—remained in the Whig organization

Map 13.5 Presidential Election of 1852

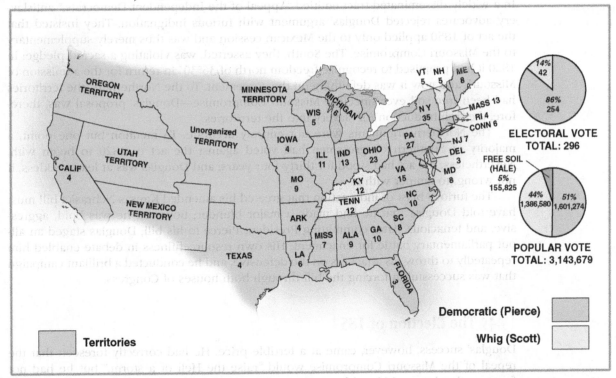

ELECTORAL VOTE
TOTAL: 296

14% 42

86% 254

FREE SOIL (HALE) 5% 155,825

44% 1,386,580

51% 1,601,274

POPULAR VOTE
TOTAL: 3,143,679

Democratic (Pierce)

Whig (Scott)

Territories

somewhat longer, it was never a national party after 1852. This meant that only one national party—the Democratic—was left, which in turn meant that there was now only one remaining political organization in which Northern and Southern leaders were still seeking to smooth out sectional disagreements for the sake of party victory.

13.4 Kansas and Nebraska

13.4a The Douglas Bill

Pierce's campaign had promised harmony for the Union and finality for the Compromise, but his administration brought just the opposite. His first Congress had barely met in December 1853, when the territorial question arose again in a new form. Stephen A. Douglas wanted to organize territorial government for the region west of Iowa and Missouri. This area lay within the Louisiana Purchase. Since it was north of 36°30′, it had been closed to slavery by the Missouri Compromise of 1820. Douglas, therefore, at first introduced a bill to organize free territories.

Southern senators voted against his legislation and thus blocked it. They did this in part because they knew that Douglas wanted to promote a transcontinental railroad west from Chicago, or some other Northern terminus, to the Pacific; and they were equally eager to run such a road west from New Orleans. There was simply no reason for them to give their votes to organize another Free-Soil territory for the purpose of facilitating a Northern railroad.

Douglas felt that he had to have their votes. Thus, in January 1854, he was led to take the fatal step of agreeing to change his bill so that it would repeal the Missouri Compromise line and would leave the status of slavery in the Kansas-Nebraska region to be settled by popular sovereignty. Douglas made the plausible argument that what he advocated was nothing new and that the legislation of 1850 had already replaced the principle of geographical division with the principle of popular sovereignty.

Republican Party

Arose to replace the Whigs
in 1856 in opposition to
slavery in the territories

13.4b "Appeal of the Independent Democrats"

In a widely disseminated tract entitled "Appeal of the Independent Democrats," antislavery advocates rejected Douglas' argument with furious indignation. They insisted that the act of 1850 applied only to the Mexican cession and was thus merely supplementary to the Missouri Compromise. The South, they asserted, was violating a sacred pledge; in 1820 it had promised to recognize freedom north of 36°30′ in return for the admission of Missouri, and now it was defaulting on the agreement. To the Northerners, the territories had been free soil ever since the Missouri Compromise—Douglas' proposal was, therefore, the "reintroduction" of slavery into the territories.

The Northern arguments were not entirely accurate. To mention but one point, a majority of Southern congressmen had voted against the act of 1820 to begin with. Nevertheless, the act had stood for thirty-four years; and Douglas was at least reckless, if not wrong, to tamper with it.

The furious blast of indignation that greeted his amended Kansas-Nebraska bill must have told Douglas that he had made a major blunder; however, he was bold, aggressive, and tenacious. After committing President Pierce to his bill, Douglas staged an all-out parliamentary battle for enactment. His own resourcefulness in debate enabled him repeatedly to throw his attackers on the defensive, and he conducted a brilliant campaign that was successful in forcing the bill through both houses of Congress.

13.4c The Election of 1854

Douglas' success, however, came at a terrible price. He had correctly foreseen that the repeal of the Missouri Compromise would "raise the Hell of a storm," but he had not foreseen that he would be able to travel to Chicago by the light of his own burning effigies, as he later put it. Six months after the act was adopted, the congressional elections of 1854 took place. All over the North "anti-Nebraska" parties sprang up to capitalize on Free-Soil anger at the Kansas-Nebraska Act. In Wisconsin and Michigan these parties took the name "Republican," and this name soon spread to other states. In the Northeast, however, the main beneficiary of the voter uprising in 1854 was not the newborn **Republican Party** but rather the anti-Catholic Know-Nothings, who shared the Republicans' hostility to the extension of slavery but were even more concerned about the apparent threat of Catholic immigrants. The Know-Nothings won enough votes to gain forty seats in the House of Representatives.

Whatever the name of their opponents, the Democrats suffered a stunning setback in the Northern congressional elections. The number of Northern Democrats in the House fell from ninety-one to twenty-five, and the Northern congressional Democrats functioned thereafter as the tail to the Southern Democratic dog. From 1854 forward, the Democratic Party would function as a Southern, sectional, proslavery party.

In the long run, however, the Republicans rather than the Know-Nothings proved to be the main beneficiaries of the 1854 electoral revolution, gaining one hundred seats in the House of Representatives. Northern opposition to the expansion of slavery proved deeper and more intense than Protestant dislike for Catholic immigrants. By the end of 1855, the Republican Party had emerged as the successor to the Whigs as the country's second major party. Unlike the Whigs, however, the Republicans were entirely a sectional party with no strength at all in the slave states.

13.4d "Bleeding Kansas"

The worst thing about the new Kansas-Nebraska Act was that even with the high price of causing the bitterest kind of sectional hostility, it failed to create a real basis for stability in the new territory. Instead, it merely changed the terms of the contest—for Douglas and many Northern Democrats believed that popular sovereignty could make Kansas and Nebraska free territories just as well as congressional action could, whereas proslavery leaders took the repeal of the Missouri Compromise to mean that slavery should prevail in at least one of the two new territories.

Both antislavery and proslavery groups prepared to rush supporters into Kansas to defend their respective positions there. In New England, antislavery advocates organized an **Emigrant Aid Society** to send Free-Soil settlers to Kansas. In 1854 and 1855 the society sponsored 1,240 settlers. Though the society never officially purchased weapons for these settlers, the leaders of the society bought rifles with separate funds to arm the emigrants against the proslavery groups.

From Missouri, proslavery advocates—known as border ruffians—had a way of riding over into Kansas on election day to vote and intimidate the Free-Soilers before riding back to Missouri. Missouri Senator David Rice Atchison publicly encouraged the election fraud. Atchison proclaimed, "there are eleven hundred coming over from Platte County to vote, and if that ain't enough, we can send five thousand to kill every God-damned abolitionist in the territory." Atchison himself led a contingent of armed men from Missouri to vote and frighten away Free-Soil voters. On the other side, Senator William H. Seward of New York retorted, "Come on then, Gentlemen of the Slave States ... since there is no escaping your challenge, I accept it in behalf of the cause of freedom. We will engage in competition for the virgin soil of Kansas, and God give the victory to the side which is stronger in numbers as it is in right."

In March 1855, an election was held in Kansas to elect a territorial legislature. Of the 2,905 eligible voters, somehow 6,307 votes were cast. Kansas quickly assembled a proslavery legislature elected through fraud primarily by proslavery zealots from

Emigrant Aid Society

Organized in New England in 1854 by antislavery advocates to send Free-Soil settlers to Kansas

Map 13.6 The United States in 1854

Free states and territories

Open to slavery by principle of popular sovereignty

Slave states and territories

John Brown

Antislavery fanatic who murdered five proslavery citizens in Kansas in 1856, took over a federal arsenal in 1859, and was executed for treason

"Bleeding Kansas"

Political unrest over slavery in Kansas in 1856 that led to the death of two hundred persons

Missouri. The new proslavery legislature quickly passed a law outlawing the abolition of slavery—a position that was opposed by a strong majority of the people who actually lived in Kansas.

It would have taken a strong president to keep order in Kansas, and Pierce was not strong enough. He appointed a succession of able governors for the territory, but he would not vigorously support them when they needed his backing. Affairs, therefore, went from bad to worse. After the proslavery faction had stolen an election, and Pierce had given recognition to the government thus elected—even replacing the Kansas governor who had objected to the election fraud—the Free-Soil advocates formed another government of their own. Kansas then had two governments: a proslavery one at Pawnee that was legal but not honest, and an antislavery one at Topeka that was honest but not legal. The antislavery legislature not only passed resolutions that would have banned slavery from the state but also passed a measure banning all blacks from the state, enslaved or free.

It is a great mistake to think of frontier Kansas as inhabited entirely by people who went there as missionaries for slavery or for freedom. Many settlers were simply land-hungry pioneers like those who swarmed into all new territories. Such settlers were often quick to violence, and not all the shooting that took place in Kansas was over the issue of slavery; however, the slavery issue did accentuate the violence and give a pattern to the lawlessness of the frontier.

With President Pierce denouncing the Free-Soil government for its illegality, the proslavery forces secured an indictment of the Free-Soilers by a grand jury that was, of course, of the proslavery men's own choosing. With this indictment an armed mob (or "posse," as they called themselves), led by a proslavery federal marshal, marched on the Free-Soil headquarters at Lawrence. There they shot cannon balls into the Free State Hotel, destroyed the printing press of the free soil newspaper, and burned or looted a good deal of property—both shops and private homes—while taking over the Free-Soil government buildings.

Four days later in May 1856, **John Brown**—a Free-Soiler who carried his views to fanatical lengths—and six companions (four of them his sons) avenged the sacking of Lawrence and the killing of several Free-Soil settlers by leading a body of men to Pottawatomie Creek, where they took five unarmed proslavery settlers from their homes in the dead of night and murdered them. Brown argued that his action was just, stating that "it was better that a score of bad men should die than that one man who came here to make Kansas a free state should be driven out."

These events were part of the ensuing escalation of terror and violence known as **"Bleeding Kansas."** Both Brown and proslavery groups roamed the countryside shooting and looting for their causes. Probably two hundred people met violent deaths before a new territorial government used federal troops to restore order four months later. Brown was neither captured nor killed by the federal troops, but forced to flee Kansas and go into hiding in October 1856.

Though things in Kansas were surely bad enough, exaggerated reports of the violence in the nation's newspapers made them even worse, further heightening sectional tensions. For example, one editor of a proslavery newspaper claimed that abolitionists came to Kansas "for the express purpose of stealing, running off and hiding runaway negroes from Missouri, and taking to their own bed … a stinking negro wench." Rumors circulated in Missouri that twenty thousand abolitionist migrants were coming to Kansas, a gross exaggeration that was nevertheless believed by many. The reality was that most Kansas residents were migrants from Missouri who came to Kansas for land ownership. The vast majority was against slavery, but they were not for racial equality and opposed the presence of free blacks in Kansas as well. In the words of one Kansas clergyman, "I kem to Kansas to live in a free state and I don't want niggers a-trampin' over my grave."

13.4e "The Crime Against Kansas"

Meanwhile, the intensity of sectional ill will was both illustrated and heightened by an occurrence in Washington. Charles Sumner, an antislavery senator from Massachusetts, delivered an oration entitled "The Crime Against Kansas" in which—in addition to castigating the slave power as bitterly as he could and denouncing those he termed "murderous robbers" and "assassins"—he spoke in extremely personal terms about elderly Senator Andrew P. Butler of South Carolina, accusing him of "cavorting with the harlot, slavery." He also alluded to "the loose expectoration" of the elderly Butler's speech. A nephew of Butler's in the House of Representatives, **Preston Brooks**, went to the Senate chamber when the Senate was not in session, found Sumner seated at his desk, and beat him severely with a cane. In the words of Brooks, "I gave him forty first-rate stripes."

For several years after the assault, Sumner was incapacitated, either by the blows that he received or by his psychological reaction to the assault, as is modern medical opinion. The public significance of this affair, however, lay less in the attack itself than in the fact that a large part of the Northern press made a martyr of Sumner and pictured all Southerners as barbarians, whereas the South made a hero of Brooks and typed all Yankees as rabid fanatics.

Senator Charles Sumner was an antislavery Republican from Massachusetts. After making a speech denouncing the Kansas-Nebraska Act, Sumner was brutally attacked by an opposing representative, Preston Brooks, in the empty Senate chamber. (Wikimedia Commons)

13.4f The Character of Franklin Pierce

By this time the Pierce administration was ending as a disaster because of the weakness of the president and the extent to which he let himself be dominated by Southern influence. After failing to prevent repeal of the Missouri Compromise, Pierce might still have saved the peace of the country if he had stood firm for real popular sovereignty in Kansas. Instead, he had backed a proslavery regime that was palpably fraudulent, had allowed violence to go unrestrained, and had finally given his support to the idea of statehood with a proslavery government. At this point, Stephen A. Douglas had broken with the administration and was fighting hard in Congress to defeat this proslavery government. Thus the political division now was less between Free-Soil and proslavery forces than between the honest application of popular sovereignty and the perversion of it.

Indeed, Pierce had backed the South at almost every point. He had negotiated the Gadsden Purchase (1854) with Mexico for what is now the southernmost part of Arizona and New Mexico because the land in question was strategic for the construction of a transcontinental railroad traveling the southern route from New Orleans. He had permitted three of his diplomatic emissaries in Europe to meet at Ostend, Belgium, in October 1854, to propose American annexation of Cuba by purchase, or if that failed, by "wresting it from Spain." Cuba had almost four hundred thousand slaves and would strengthen the power of slavery. This **Ostend Manifesto** aroused such worldwide indignation, however, that the administration was forced to repudiate it.

Moreover, the administration did nothing effective to prevent expeditions by adventurers, called *filibusterers*, who invaded Latin countries from American shores. One such expedition from New Orleans against Cuba failed. Another, against Nicaragua, was temporarily successful, installing American William Walker as the leader of the country. These efforts to acquire new slave territory for the United States sparked Northern anger and brought new recruits into the Republican Party. As for Pierce, he would sink even deeper into alcoholism and die of what historians believe to be cirrhosis of the liver. Pierce once explained his alcohol addiction by stating, "After the presidency, what is there to do but drink?"

Preston Brooks

South Carolina congressman who beat Massachusetts Senator Charles Sumner with his cane on the floor of the Senate

Ostend Manifesto

Proposal by three American emissaries in Ostend, Belgium, in October 1854, stating that America should annex Cuba by purchase, or if that failed, by "wresting it from Spain"

13.5 On the Eve of War

13.5a The Election of 1856

At the end of Pierce's term even the Southern Democrats knew that he could not be reelected. The Democrats nominated **James Buchanan** of Pennsylvania who, as minister to England, had been out of the country at the time of the Kansas-Nebraska Act. As one of three authors of the Ostend Manifesto, he was particularly acceptable to the South. Buchanan had been secretary of state under Polk and was a veteran of American politics—an old "public functionary," as he called himself.

Buchanan was also a bachelor—making him a bit out of the ordinary for an American president—and thus reliant on close friends as his confidants, instead of a wife. Buchanan's closest confidant, with whom he had roomed for a number of years, was Alabama senator Rufus King—whom Andrew Jackson referred to as "Miss Nancy" (a common term of the era for a man with effeminate mannerisms). Clearly, Buchanan relied on King, and the two had a close enough relationship that Congressman Aaron Brown of Tennessee referred to King as Buchanan's "better half and wife" in a letter Brown wrote to Mrs. James Polk. In 1844, when King was appointed ambassador to France, Buchanan wrote a friend that he was now "solitary and alone," adding that "I have gone wooing to several gentlemen, but have not succeeded with any of them." Buchanan would have even less success in keeping the country from falling apart.

To run against him, a remnant of the Know-Nothings and Southern Whigs calling themselves the American Party nominated Millard Fillmore—but Buchanan's principal opposition came from the new Republican Party. The Republicans passed over their most prominent leaders to nominate the dashing but politically inexperienced young explorer of the Rocky Mountains and the Far West, John C. Fremont.

Map 13.7 Presidential Election of 1856

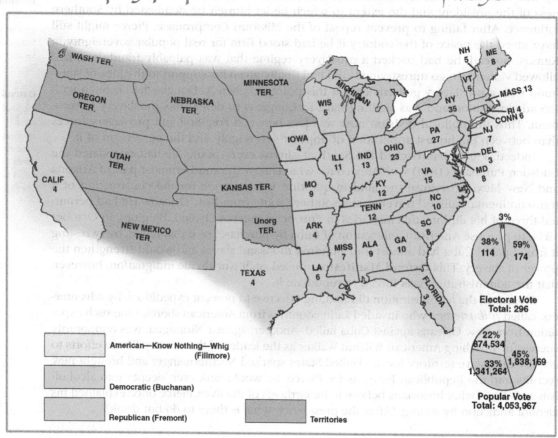

In the election that followed, Buchanan carried all of the slave states (except Maryland, which voted for Fillmore) and four free states, thus winning the election. The majority of the North was now backing the Republican Party, which denounced slavery as a "relic of barbarism." However, the party had no organization whatsoever throughout the southern half of the Union.

It is questionable whether, by this time, anyone could have brought the disruptive forces of sectional antagonism under control. Certainly Buchanan could not do it. His cabinet, like Pierce's, was dominated by Southern Democrats. In February 1858, he forfeited his claim to impartial leadership by recommending admission of Kansas to statehood under a proslavery constitution fraudulently adopted by a rump convention that met at Lecompton, Kansas. Free-Soil forces, suspecting a sham, had boycotted the Lecompton constitutional convention, so conventioneers had been able to draft a proslavery constitution without opposition and refused to allow Kansas voters to ratify the document.

Stephen Douglas and other Northern Democrats resisted the **Lecompton constitution** and rejected the bill to admit Kansas unless Kansas voters could ratify the Lecompton constitution. In January 1858, in spite of the fact that slavery advocates from Missouri again stuffed the ballot boxes, the voters of Kansas rejected the Lecompton constitution by a 2–1 margin. A second referendum was held at the insistent urging of President Buchanan; and this time fewer proslavery voters were able to cross the border, and the Lecompton constitution was voted down by an even larger 6–1 margin. Stephen Douglas' role in opposing the Lecompton constitution lost him the Southern support that he had won in 1854, and the Democratic Party became deeply divided. Douglas would defeat Abraham Lincoln in 1858 to retain his Illinois Senate seat, but it would be the last victory of his political career.

Lecompton constitution

A proslavery constitution voted down by Kansas voters in 1858

Dred Scott

Supreme Court decision in 1857 that struck down the power of Congress to prohibit slavery because slaves were property that could not be denied to any property owner, according to the Fifth Amendment

13.56 The *Dred Scott* Decision

Meanwhile, in 1857 the Supreme Court had handed down a decision that may have been intended to restore sectional peace but that had exactly the opposite effect. This ruling concerned a Missouri slave, Dred Scott, who had been taken by his master first to the free state of Illinois and then into Wisconsin Territory—which was within the Louisiana Purchase north of 36°30´, and therefore was free territory under the Missouri Compromise. After he had been taken back to Missouri, Scott sued for his freedom in Missouri. The case was eventually carried up on appeal to the Supreme Court, where justices divided in various ways on several questions that were involved. Essentially, the five justices from slave states held that Scott was still a slave, while the four from the free states divided two and two.

The principal opinion was rendered by eighty-year-old former slaveholder, Chief Justice Roger B. Taney. He stated that, during colonial times, blacks had "been regarded as beings so far inferior that they had no rights that the white man was bound to respect." Following Taney, the majority of the court held that a person born a slave or the descendant of slaves was not a citizen and therefore could not bring suit in federal courts. In strict logic, therefore, the court need not have ruled on the other questions Scott raised; but they went on to state that even if he could have sued, he still would not have been free because the Missouri Compromise was unconstitutional since Congress had no power to exclude slavery from the territories.

In a sense, the *Dred Scott* decision added nothing new to the debate about the extension of slavery, for it merely declared void a law which had already been repealed by the Kansas-Nebraska Act three years earlier. In another sense, however, it had a shattering effect in that it strengthened a conviction in the North that an evil "slave power," bent on spreading slavery throughout the land, was in control of the government and must be checked. It justified Southerners, on the other hand, in believing that the Free-Soilers were trying to rob them of their legal rights.

It even struck a deadly blow to the one moderate position—that of popular sovereignty, which lay between the extremes of Free-Soil and proslavery contentions: If, as the Court ruled, Congress had no power to exclude slavery from a territory by its own act, certainly it could not give a power that it did not possess to the territorial legislatures; and without such power

BVT Lab

Visit www.BVTLab.com to explore the student resources available for this chapter.

there could be no effective popular sovereignty. It made compromise by act of Congress almost impossible. Slavery, which had been illegal north of the Missouri Compromise line since 1820, was now legal everywhere unless state legislatures passed laws against it. Slaves could now be brought into Northern territories such as Oregon or Minnesota.

As for African Americans, the decision was devastating. It convinced many free blacks that they had no future in a country that denied them citizenship. Further, it intensified the growing mood of black nationalism and spurred movements for immigration to Haiti or Africa.

13.5c The Lincoln-Douglas Debates

The effect of the *Dred Scott* decision in polarizing sectional extremism showed up clearly in 1858, when Stephen A. Douglas ran for reelection to the Senate from Illinois and was challenged to a series of debates by his Republican opponent, Abraham Lincoln. Lincoln, a former Whig, was deeply opposed to slavery. He regarded it as morally wrong—"if slavery is not wrong then nothing is wrong"—and he insisted that the *Dred Scott* decision be reversed. Slavery must be kept out of the territories and placed "in the course of ultimate extinction."

But Lincoln was by no means an abolitionist. He did not advocate racial equality, stating clearly in the debates that "I am not, nor ever have been, in favor of bringing about the social and political equality of the white and black races." Lincoln also opposed black suffrage, interracial marriage, black citizenship, the repeal of the Fugitive Slave Act, and allowing blacks to serve on juries. Lincoln even predicted that slavery would last another hundred years, though he personally favored the repatriation of slaves to Africa.

Lincoln recognized, however, both the complexity of the slavery question and the fact that slavery was protected by constitutional guarantees which he proposed to respect—even to the enforcement of the Fugitive Slave Law. Lincoln defined the dilemma the *Dred Scott* decision had created for Douglas and for all moderates: If slavery could not be legally excluded from the territories, how could the people of the territory, under popular sovereignty, exclude it? Of the Southerners, Lincoln said, "They are merely what we would be in their situation."

Abraham Lincoln did not advocate racial equality, and opposed black suffrage, interracial marriage, black citizenship, the repeal of the Fugitive Slave Act, and allowing blacks to serve on juries. Despite these opinions, Lincoln strongly believed slavery to be morally wrong. (CORBIS/© Bettmann)

Douglas replied at Freeport, Illinois (the "Freeport Doctrine"), that unless a territory adopted positive laws to protect slavery by local police regulations, slavery could not establish itself. Thus by merely refraining from legislation, lawmakers could keep a territory free. This answer was enough to gain reelection for Douglas, but it cost him what was left of his reputation as a national leader with strong bisectional support. At one time, Southerners had applauded him for repealing the slavery exclusion of the Missouri Compromise. Now they saw him as a man who was supporting the Free-Soilers in Kansas and who was advocating a theory that would deprive the South of rights guaranteed by a decision of the Supreme Court.

Although Lincoln lost the election for Senate, he came to the attention of people throughout the country with his careful exposition of the issues raised by the *Dred Scott* decision. He consolidated his growing reputation with a speech given at Cooper Union in New York City on February 27, 1860. No doubt aware of the opportunity provided by this forum, Lincoln conducted extensive research on the opinions of signers of the Constitution on the question of slavery in the territories and dazzled his audience with his logic and his erudition. The historian Harold Holzer calls it "the speech that made Abraham Lincoln president."

13.5d John Brown's Raid

If the *Dred Scott* decision brought to a climax the Northern feeling that freedom was being dangerously threatened by a sinister conspiracy of the "slave power," John Brown's raid on **Harpers Ferry** created an even more intense feeling below the Mason-Dixon line that abolitionist fanaticism posed an immediate danger to the social order and even to human life in the South. After the "Pottawatomie Massacre" in Kansas, Brown had dropped out of sight. Then during the night of October 16, 1859, he suddenly descended, with a band of eighteen men (including five blacks), on the town of Harpers Ferry, Virginia, seized the federal arsenal there, and called upon the slaves to rise and claim their freedom.

Brown's plan was to arm the slaves. He expected that they would flock to his side for a massive revolt, after which a black republic would be established in the Virginia mountains; and then he and his supporters would wage a war against the slaveholding South. Exactly how Brown expected droves of slaves to hear of his actions, get away from their plantations, and join his rebellion is a mystery known only to Brown. Instead, no slaves arrived to join the revolt, and within thirty-six hours Brown was captured by federal troops under the command of Robert E. Lee. Ten of Brown's men were killed in the gun battle; and Brown was charged with treason, conspiracy, and murder. Later he was tried and hanged, but not before playing the role of the perfect martyr for Northern abolitionists. Brown proclaimed, "If it is deemed necessary that I should forfeit my life for the furtherance of the ends of justice … I say let it be done."

Brown's action had touched the South differently, however, and at its most sensitive nerve—its fear of the kind of slave insurrection that had caused immense slaughter at Santo Domingo at the beginning of the century and had periodically threatened to erupt in the South itself. Southern alarm and resentment would perhaps have been less great if more people in the North had denounced Brown's act—as some Northerners, including Lincoln, did. But the fact soon came out that Brown had received financial backing from some of the most respected figures in Boston, and the day of his execution became one of public mourning in New England. Brown was called Saint John the Just, and Henry David Thoreau publicly spoke in support of Brown. Similarly, Ralph Waldo Emerson wrote an essay about Brown entitled **"Courage,"** in which Emerson argued that Brown would "make the gallows as glorious as the cross."

13.5e The Election of 1860

By the **election of 1860**, developments were rapidly moving toward a showdown. For more than a decade, sectional dissension had been destroying the institutions that held the American people together in national unity. In 1844, it had split the Methodist Church, and in 1845 the Baptist Church also divided into separate Northern and Southern bodies. Between 1852 and 1856, **sectionalism** had split the Whig Party, and as matters now stood, the Democratic Party was the only remaining major national institution, outside of the government itself. In 1860, with another presidential election at hand, the Democratic organization—already strained by the tension between the Buchanan and the Douglas wings—also broke apart.

13.5f The Democrats

Meeting at Charleston, the Democratic convention divided on the question of the platform. Douglas Democrats wanted a plank that promised, in general terms, to abide by the decisions of the Supreme Court—but which avoided explicit expression of support for slavery in the territories. Southern Democrats, led by William L. Yancey (a famous orator from Alabama), wanted a categorical affirmation that slavery would be protected in the territories. When the Douglas forces secured the adoption of their plank, Yancey and most of the delegates from the cotton states walked out of the convention.

The accusation was later made that they did this as part of a deliberate plan or conspiracy to break up the Union by splitting the Democratic Party, letting the Republicans win, and thus creating a situation that would inspire the South to secede. In truth, many

Harpers Ferry
Site of federal arsenal raided by John Brown and his followers

"Courage"
Essay by Ralph Waldo Emerson extolling John Brown as a martyr for abolition and claiming that Brown would make the gallows as glorious as the cross

Election of 1860
Won by Republican Abraham Lincoln, though he won no Southern states

Sectionalism
Antagonism between the Northern and Southern states

Map 13.8 Presidential Election of 1860

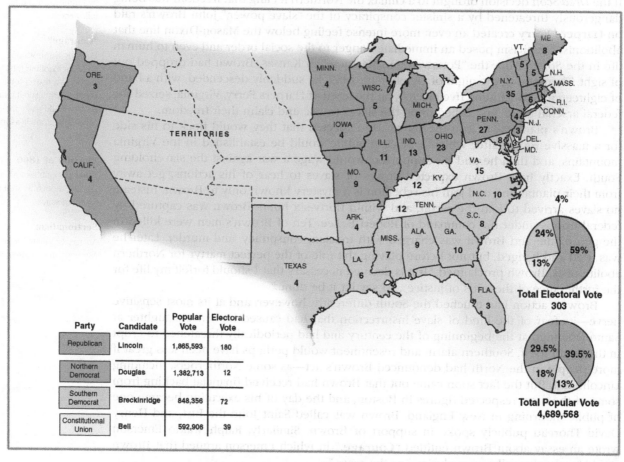

Party	Candidate	Popular Vote	Electoral Vote
Republican	Lincoln	1,865,593	180
Northern Democrat	Douglas	1,382,713	12
Southern Democrat	Breckinridge	848,356	72
Constitutional Union	Bell	592,906	39

of those who walked were hoping to force Northern Democrats to come to terms or to throw the election to Congress, where there was a chance that the South might have won. For weeks, desperate efforts were made to reunite the Democrats—but in the end, the Northern wing of the party nominated Douglas and the Southern wing nominated John C. Breckinridge of Kentucky, vice president under Buchanan.

Some of the conservative successors of the Whigs, now calling themselves Constitutional Unionists, nominated John Bell of Tennessee for president and Edward Everett for vice president on a platform that said nothing about the territorial question, and called only for "the Constitution, the Union, and the enforcement of the laws."

13.59 The Republican Victory

The principal opposition to Douglas, it was understood, would come from the Republicans, whose convention was meeting at a new building called the Wigwam in Chicago. The leading candidate before the convention was William H. Seward, a U.S. senator from New York who had been the foremost Republican for some years. But his talent for coining memorable phrases—"a higher law than the Constitution" and "the irrepressible conflict between freedom and slavery"—had won him a reputation for extremism. The Republicans, seeing a good chance of victory after the Democratic split, decided to move in a conservative direction in order not to jeopardize their prospects. Accordingly, they nominated Abraham Lincoln, who had made his reputation in the debates with Douglas, but who had never been militant on the slavery question. To balance this nomination they made Hannibal Hamlin, a former Democrat from Maine, their vice-presidential candidate.

To win, the Republicans needed only to hold what they had won in 1856 and to capture Pennsylvania and either Illinois or Indiana, which Buchanan had carried. As the

Map 13.9 Territorial Growth of 1860

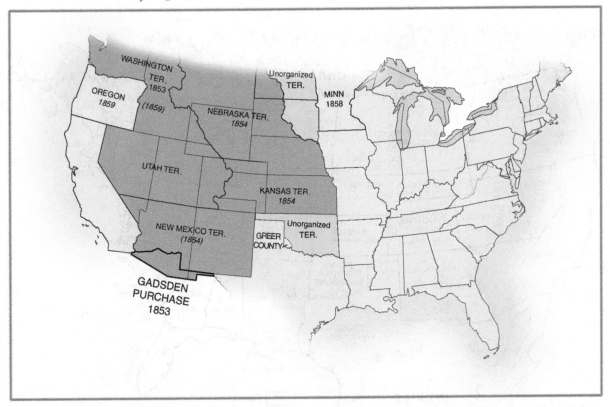

election turned out, they won every free state except New Jersey (part of which went to Douglas), while Breckinridge won all the slave states except Virginia, Kentucky, and Tennessee (which went to Bell) and Missouri (which went to Douglas). Douglas ran a strong second in popular votes but a poor fourth in electoral votes, while Lincoln was in the curious position of winning the election with only 40 percent of the popular vote. His victory resulted not from the division of his opponents, however, but from the fact that his strength was strategically distributed. His victories in many of the free states were narrow, and he received no votes at all in ten Southern states. Thus, the distribution of his popular votes had maximum effectiveness in winning electoral votes.

13.5h Secession

Lincoln's victory at last precipitated the sectional split that had been brewing for so long. As we can now see in the light of later events, Lincoln was moderate-minded and would have respected the legal rights of the South even though he deplored slavery. However to the South—fearful of Northern aggression—his victory was a signal of imminent danger. Here was a man who had said that a house divided against itself could not stand and that the Union could not continue permanently half slave and half free. To the South he denied rights that the Supreme Court had upheld. He was supported by swarms of militant antislavery men, and his victory clearly represented the imposition of a president by one section upon the other—since 99 percent of votes for Lincoln had come from the free states.

Southerners had controlled the United States government for most of the time since its founding. Although, as we have already seen, there was some diversity in their political opinion (especially before 1845), their prominence had been a matter of pride in the South and—increasingly—a matter of concern in the North. From 1789 to 1861, twenty-five of the thirty-six presidents pro tem of the Senate and twenty-four of the thirty-six Speakers of the House were Southerners. Twenty of the thirty-five Supreme Court justices were from the South. A Southerner was chief justice during all but twelve of these years,

Map 13.10 The United States on the Eve of the Civil War

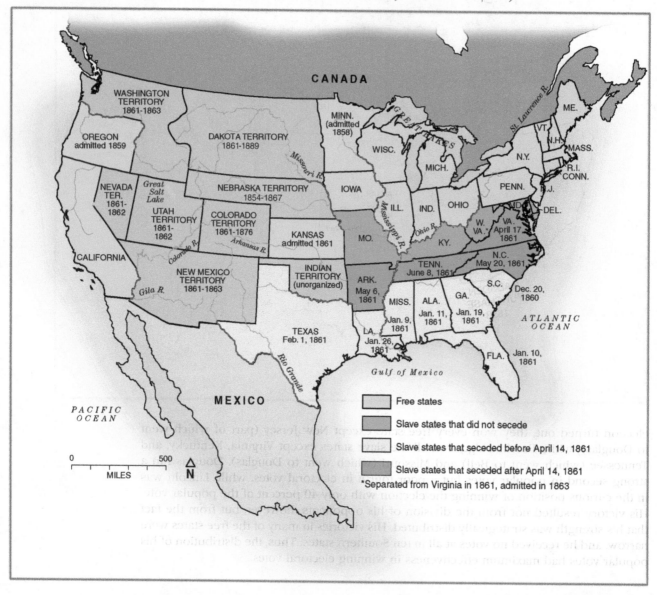

and at all times the South had a majority on the Court. During forty-nine of these seventy-two years the president of the United States had been a Southerner—and a slaveholder, as well. In addition, during twelve additional years—including most of the crucial 1850s—the presidents had been Northern Democratic "doughfaces," who were often more pro-South than even Southerners themselves dared to be.

Thus, when the news of Lincoln's election came in 1860, Charles Francis Adams—the son and grandson, respectively, of two truly Northern presidents, and himself a founder of the Republican party—wrote jubilantly: "The great revolution has taken place ... The country has once and for all thrown off the domination of the slave-holders."

The slaveholders, too, regarded the 1860 election as a political revolution that foreshadowed a future dominated by the ideology and institutions of the North. To the Old South, this would be disaster, and a counterrevolution of independence seemed the only answer.

Proponents of secession invoked the doctrine that each state had retained its sovereignty when it joined the federal Union. Thus, in the exercise of this sovereignty, each state, acting through a special convention like the conventions that had ratified the Constitution, might secede from the Union. As soon as they learned of Lincoln's election, the South Carolina legislature called a convention to take the state out of the Union. Within six weeks, the six other states of the lower South—Mississippi, Florida,

Alabama, Georgia, Louisiana, and Texas—also called conventions. Delegates were elected by popular vote after short but intensive campaigns. Each convention voted by a substantial—in most cases even overwhelming—majority to secede. By February 9, 1861, three months after Lincoln's election but almost a month before his inauguration, delegates from the seven seceded states had met in Montgomery, Alabama, to adopt a provisional Constitution for the **Confederate States of America** and to elect Jefferson Davis and Alexander Stephens as provisional president and vice president of the new republic.

13.5i The Failure of Compromise

The actual arrival of disunion, which had been dreaded for so long, evoked strenuous efforts at compromise—especially by leaders in the border slave states, where loyalty to the Union was combined with sympathy for the South. From Kentucky, Senator John J. Crittenden, heir to the compromise tradition of Henry Clay, introduced proposals in Congress to revise and extend the Missouri Compromise line by constitutional amendment. Virginia took the lead in organizing delegates from twenty-one states for a peace convention that met in Washington in February. Congress actually adopted a proposed amendment that would have guaranteed slavery in the states that wanted to keep it. This amendment was even submitted to the states for ratification, but then the war came and made it obsolete.

President Buchanan, still in office until Lincoln's inauguration, professed himself powerless to prevent secession. Buchanan denounced the action as illegal, but as a lame duck president did not want to commit his successor to any course of action. In the meantime, the nation waited to see if the incoming President Lincoln would attempt to preserve the Union by force or peacefully allow secession.

Unlike Buchanan, Lincoln was unwilling to make any concessions that would compromise the basic Republican principle of excluding slavery from the territories. The Crittenden Compromise would have permitted slavery in all territories south of 36°30′ "now held, *or hereafter acquired*." In view of the South's appetite for the acquisition of new slave territory in the Caribbean and Central America, Republicans feared that adoption of such a compromise "would amount to a perpetual covenant of war against every people, tribe, and State owning a foot of land between here and Terra del Fuego" and turn the United States into "a great slave breeding and slave extending empire." Therefore they defeated the Crittenden Compromise. In any case, it is unlikely that adoption of this or any other compromise would have stemmed the tide of secession in the lower South where, by February 1861, the Confederacy was a *fait accompli*.

13.5j Fort Sumter

Thus, when Lincoln was inaugurated on March 4, 1861, he was faced with a new Southern republic where seven states of the Union had once been. This new Confederacy had seized federal post offices, customs houses, arsenals, and even federal forts, with the exceptions of **Fort Sumter** in Charleston Harbor and Fort Pickens in Pensacola Harbor. The federal forts in the South were, by and large, manned by Southerners and commanded by Southerners in the U.S. army who turned over their forts to the Confederates without a shot. In Texas alone, eighteen federal forts and all of their provisions were handed to the Confederates without a fight. From North Carolina to the Rio Grande, Forts Sumter and Pickens were the only two places where the Stars and Stripes still flew. There was great speculation at the time as to what position Lincoln would take, and there has been great dispute among historians since then as to what position he actually *did* take.

Certainly, he made it absolutely clear that he denied the right of any state to secede and that he intended to preserve the Union. In his inaugural address, Lincoln denounced secession as illegal; however, whether he intended to wage war in order to preserve the Union is not so clear. Lincoln also proclaimed that the North and South were not enemies, but friends. Furthermore, there were eight slave states (Virginia, North Carolina, Kentucky, Tennessee, Missouri, Arkansas, Maryland, and Delaware) still in the Union; and Lincoln was extremely eager to keep them loyal. As long as they remained in the Union,

Confederate States of America

South Carolina and ten other Southern states that seceded from the U.S.

Fort Sumter

Site of the first shots of the Civil War, where Southerners fired on a Union fort that refused to turn over possession to the Confederacy

there was at least the possibility that they might help to bring the other slave states back. This split among the slave states represented a failure on the part of the secessionists to create a united South. Thus, Lincoln had every reason to refrain from hasty action.

If he had been able to maintain the federal position at Fort Pickens and Fort Sumter, or even at one of them, he might have been prepared to play a waiting game. This changed less than twenty-four hours after becoming president when he learned that Major Robert Anderson, commander at Fort Sumter, was running out of supplies and would soon have to surrender unless food was sent to him. Lincoln apparently gave serious consideration to the possibility of surrendering Sumter, and he might have done so if he had been able to reinforce Fort Pickens and make it the symbol of an unbroken Union. Attempts to reinforce Pickens, however, were delayed; and on April 6, Lincoln sent a message to the governor of South Carolina that supplies would be sent to Sumter. If the Southerners allowed the supplies to reach the Union fort in Southern territory, Lincoln promised that no military reinforcement would be attempted.

The Confederates attacked Fort Sumter at dawn. Bombarded with Confederate battery, the Union fort surrendered after twenty-six hours of furious shelling. The battle of Fort Sumter marked the beginning of a war that lasted four years and was one of the greatest military conflicts the world had seen up to that time. (Wikimedia Commons)

Historians have disputed whether this was a promise not to start shooting if supplies were allowed, or a threat to start shooting if they were not allowed. In any event, the Confederate government decided that the supplies could not be allowed. On April 12, 1861, after Major Anderson had rejected a formal demand for surrender, Confederate batteries opened a bombardment before dawn that forced Fort Sumter to surrender without casualties after twenty-six hours of furious shelling.

On April 15, Lincoln issued a call for the loyal states to furnish seventy-five thousand militia to suppress the Southern "insurrection." All the free states responded with alacrity and enthusiasm. The four slave states of Virginia, North Carolina, Tennessee, and Arkansas responded by seceding and joining the Confederacy, as they had promised they would. The other four slave states—Maryland, Delaware, Kentucky, and Missouri—remained uneasily in the Union, though many of their men went South to fight for the Confederacy. The bombardment of Fort Sumter marked the beginning of a four-year war and which, with the exception of the Napoleonic wars, was the greatest military conflict the world had seen up to that time.

13.6 "Causes" of the Civil War

Ever since 1861, writers have disputed what caused the Civil War and whether or not it was an "irrepressible conflict" in the sense of being inevitable. Southerners have argued that the war was fought not over slavery but over the question of states' rights. Several of the Confederate states, they point out, seceded only when the others had been attacked. Economic determinists have contended that the Northern public would never have supported the abolitionists on any direct question, that Lincoln did not even venture to issue the Emancipation Proclamation until the war had been in progress for a year and five months, and that the conflict was really between an industrial interest that wanted one kind of future for America and an agrarian interest that wanted another. Other historians, going a step beyond this, have pictured the North and the South as two "diverse civilizations," so dissimilar in their culture and their values that union between them was artificial and unnatural.

In the 1940s another group of writers, known as revisionists, emphasized the idea that Northerners and Southerners had formed distorted and false concepts of each other and that they went to war against these images rather than against the people they were really fighting. The war, they argued, grew out of emotions, not out of realities.

Abraham Lincoln had no intention of leading a crusade against slavery in the South. The Southerners perceived that he did, however; and that perception, though unsupported by facts, became their reality.

Every one of these points of view has something to be said for it. The causes of the Civil War were certainly not simple. It should also be noted that, although each of the explanations points to something other than slavery as the major cause, slavery was identified as an involved factor in all of them. It is true that the South believed in the right of the states to secede whereas the North did not, but this belief would have remained an abstraction and never been acted upon if the Republican crusade against extending slavery had not impelled the South to use the secession weapon. Southerners were steadfast in their claim to states' rights, but it could be argued that the primary right that the Southern states claimed was the right to keep their slaves. At least to a degree, the states' rights argument remained very much an argument about slavery. Evidence in support of this fact is present in the "Declaration of Causes" for secession of many Southern states in which slavery was mentioned prominently. For example, the declared "causes" passed at the Secessionist Convention in Texas in 1861 included the following:

- The general government of the United States had administered the common territory so as to exclude Southern people from it (in other words, Congress had attempted to ban slavery in the Western territories).

- The Northern people had become inimical to the South and to their beneficent and patriarchal system of African slavery, preaching the debasing doctrine of the equality of all men, irrespective of race or color.

- The slaveholding states had become a minority, unable to defend themselves against Northern aggression against slavery.

- The extremists of the North had elected as president and vice president two men whose chief claims to such high positions were the approval of the above wrongs, and these men were pledged to the final ruin of the slaveholding South.

Texans mentioned two more causes: blaming the U.S. government for the carnage in Kansas (which was, of course, also related to slavery), and for failing to defend Texans against raiding Indians and Mexican banditos. Taken together, the Texans' statements suggest that the states' rights argument may have been at least partly Southern propaganda to aid the South in their struggle to gain European (especially British) support for their cause, whereas the real cause was simply slavery. England was decidedly abolitionist and could not violate its own collective moral conscience to aid the South in a war to retain slavery. Aiding the South in its struggle for "states' rights," however, was much more palatable to the English sense of morality.

Slavery was clearly important as a moral issue; yet it was also important as an economic institution that divided two different—and in many ways antagonistic—societies. Both of these societies—the modernizing, free-labor, capitalist North and the conservative, agrarian, slave-labor South—were expansionist. Each believed that its social system must expand into the new territories in order to survive. Each saw the expansion of the other as a threat to its own future.

It is hard to imagine that, without slavery, the general dissimilarities between North and South—even their social and cultural separateness—would have been brought into such sharp focus as to precipitate a war. It is true that in the 1850s extremist leaders came to the fore and that each section formed an emotional stereotype rather than a realistic picture of the other, but this is a process that typically occurs as antagonism deepens.

The point is that slavery furnished the emotional voltage that led to deep distrust and dislike in each section for the people of the other. In his second inaugural, Abraham Lincoln said, "All know that slavery was somehow the cause of the war." The operative word in his statement was "somehow," for the war was not in any simple sense a fight between crusaders for freedom all on one side and believers in slavery all on the other. Robert E. Lee, to name but one Southerner, did not believe in slavery at all; and many a Northern soldier who was willing to die, if need be, for the Union was deeply opposed to making slavery an issue of the war. It is also true, however, that both antislavery Southerners and proslavery Northerners were caught in the web woven by the issue of slavery.

Could this issue have been settled without war? Was the crisis artificial? Was the territorial question a contest over "an imaginary Negro in an impossible place"? Was war really necessary in a situation where it seems doubtful that a majority of Southerners wanted to secede (only seven out of fifteen slave states seceded before the firing on Fort Sumter) or that a majority of Northerners wanted to make an issue of slavery? (Lincoln had only 40 percent of the popular vote, and he promised security for slavery where it was already established.) Were the American people, both North and South, so much alike in their religion (overwhelmingly evangelical Protestant), their speech (American variants of English), their ethnic descent (mostly from British, Irish, and German stock), their democratic beliefs, their pioneering ways, their emphasis upon the values of self-reliance and hard work, their veneration for the Constitution, and even their bumptious Americanism—were they so much alike that a war between them could and should have been avoided? This, in turn, raises the question of whether disagreements are any less bitter among parties who have much in common.

What was happening in America was that the center of gravity was gradually shifting from a loosely organized agricultural society to a modern industrial society with much greater concentration of power. As this happened, the United States was being transformed from a loose association of separately powerful states to a consolidated nation in which the states would be little more than political subdivisions. In America's startling growth the North had outstripped the South, and the equilibrium that previously existed between them had been destroyed. The proposal of the victorious Republicans to confine slavery—and in this sense, to exclude the South from further participation in the nation's growth—dramatized this shift in equilibrium. It seems most unlikely that the South would ever have accepted the political consequences of this basic change without a crisis—especially since Southern whites greatly feared the possibility that a preponderant North, once in control of the federal government, might ultimately use its power to abolish slavery. Southerners well understood that if the entire frontier west of Missouri eventually came into the Union as free territory, slavery would exist only in the southeastern geographic quarter of the continent; and the Free-Soilers would eventually have the votes in Congress to eliminate slavery democratically.

The brooding presence of race permeated this issue. Slavery was more than an institution to exploit cheap labor. It was a means of controlling a large and potentially threatening black population and of maintaining white supremacy. Any hint of a threat to the "Southern way of life," which was based on the subordination of a race both scorned and feared, was bound to arouse deep and irrational phobias and to create a crisis. Whether this crisis had to take the form of armed conflict, and whether this phase of armed force had to occur precisely when it did, would seem to be a matter for endless speculation.

Timeline

1808	Congress prohibits the importation of slaves from Africa.
1831	Nat Turner's Revolt
1833	Great Britain abolishes slavery in the British Empire.
1848	France abolishes slavery.
	Treaty of Guadalupe Hidalgo is ratified.
1849	Gold rush in California
1850	The Compromise of 1850 admits California as a free state and settles the border dispute with Texas, but includes the Fugitive Slave Act.
1852	Harriet Beecher Stowe publishes *Uncle Tom's Cabin*.
	Franklin Pierce is elected president.
1854	Stephen Douglas proposes "popular sovereignty" as a solution to the slavery question in the territories in his Kansas-Nebraska Bill.
	Gadsden Purchase
1855	Fraudulent election for Kansas legislature
1856	John Brown murders five proslavery citizens in Kansas, and two hundred more die in "bleeding Kansas" in the six months that follow.
1857	*Dred Scott* decision is issued by the Supreme Court.
1858	Kansas voters reject the Lecompton Constitution.
	Lincoln-Douglas debates
1859	John Brown's Raid
1860	Abraham Lincoln is elected president.
	South Carolina secedes in December.
1861	Seven seceded states create the Confederate States of America.
	April 12, Confederates fire first shots of the Civil War at Fort Sumter.

CHAPTER SUMMARY

$\mathscr{B}$y the mid-nineteenth century, America had spread across the continent and essentially fulfilled its "Manifest Destiny" (after a war with Mexico had secured the Southwestern United States, and Oregon Territory had been gained from England by treaty). Yet the nation remained divided sectionally between North and South, each with its own unique cultural features. In the South, the economy was dominated by plantation agriculture built on slave labor whereas in the North—though most people still engaged in agriculture—a manufacturing economy was quickly developing. The two sections had different economic interests (higher tariffs in the North to protect manufacturing and lower tariffs in the South to help boost agricultural exports) and were suspicious of each other. The Three-Fifths Compromise gave the Southern states disproportionate strength in Congress, which caused the Northerners to oppose the extension of slavery into the Western territories in an effort to check Southern slave power.

The issue boiled over in 1854, when Illinois senator Stephen Douglas proposed that popular sovereignty should settle the slavery question in the territory of Kansas. Proslavery citizens from Missouri poured into Kansas and voted illegally, establishing a fraudulent proslavery government and a proslavery constitution that was eventually rejected by Kansas voters. Meanwhile, John Brown touched off a wave of violence that led to the gruesome deaths of two hundred citizens after he and his followers lynched five proslavery citizens at Pottawatomie Creek.

The Supreme Court added fuel to the fire in 1857 with its ruling in the *Dred Scott* case. The Court ruled that Dred Scott (a former slave) was property and that the part of the Missouri Compromise that prohibited slavery in the territories was unconstitutional under the Fifth Amendment because Congress could not deny anyone their property.

John Brown stirred up more controversy in 1859 after he and his followers attempted to take over a federal arsenal at Harpers Ferry, Virginia, in an effort to instigate a slave revolt. Abolitionists, such as Ralph Waldo Emerson, praised Brown as the "perfect martyr" before Brown was sent to the gallows.

Abraham Lincoln was elected president in 1860 on the Republican Party ticket without winning any Southern states. Given that Republicans opposed the extension of slavery in the territories, Southern states, led by South Carolina, viewed his election as a threat to slavery and the "Southern way of life" and seceded from the Union. When Fort Sumter in Charleston Harbor refused to capitulate, and Lincoln gave an order to resupply the fort, Southerners shelled the fort until it surrendered. The Civil War had begun.

KEY TERMS

BIBLIOGRAPHY

A

Ahlstrom, Sydney. *A Religious History of the American People*. New Haven, CT: Yale University Press, 2004.

Angle, Paul. *The Complete Lincoln-Douglas Debates of 1858*. Chicago, IL: University of Chicago Press, 1991.

B

Baker, Jean H., and Arthur M. Schlesinger. *The 15th President, 1857–1861*. New York: Times Books, 2004.

Billington, Ray Allen. *The Far Western Frontier, 1830–1860*. Albuquerque, NM: University of New Mexico Press, 1995.

Blackford, Mandsel, and Austin Kerr. *Business Enterprise in American History*. Stamford, CT: Wadsworth, 1993.

Blue, Frederick J. *The Free Soilers: Third Party Politics, 1848–1854*. Champaign, IL: University of Illinois Press, 1974.

Brinkley, Alan. *American History: A Survey*. 11th ed. Boston, MA: McGraw-Hill, 2003.

C

Calvert, Robert A., Arnoldo De Leon, and Gregg Cantrell. *The History of Texas*. 4th ed. Hoboken, NJ: Wiley-Blackwell, 2007.

Campbell, Randolph. *Gone to Texas*. New York: Oxford University Press, 2003.

Campbell, Stanley W. *The Slave Catchers: Enforcement of the Fugitive Slave Law 1850–1860*. Chapel Hill, NC: University of North Carolina Press, 2011.

Cash, W. J. *The Mind of the South*. New York: Knopf, 1941.

Clark, Malcolm, Jr. *Eden Seekers: The Settlement of Oregon 1818–1862*. Boston, MA: Houghton Mifflin, 1981.

Cooper, William J. and Thomas E. Terrill. *The American South: A History*. New York: McGraw-Hill, 1991.

———. *The South and the Politics of Slavery 1828–1856*. Baton Rouge, LA: Louisiana State University Press, 1980.

Craven, Avery. *The Coming of the Civil War*. New York: Scribner, 1942.

Cummings, Bruce. *Dominion from Sea to Sea. Pacific Ascendancy and American Power*. New Haven, CT: Yale University Press, 2011.

D

Donald, David Herbert. *Lincoln*. New York: Simon and Schuster, 1996.

Donald, David. *Lincoln Reconsidered*. New York: Vintage, 1961.

Dray, Philip. *There Is Power in a Union: The Epic Story of Labor in America*. New York: Anchor Books, 2011.

Dumond, Dwight L. *Secessionist Movement: 1860–1861*. London: Octagon Books, 1973.

E

Engerman, Stanley L. and Robert E. Gallman. *The Cambridge Economic History of the United States, Vol. 2: The Long Nineteenth Century*. New York: Cambridge University Press, 2000.

F

Fehrenbach, T. R. *Lone Star: A History of Texas and the Texans*. Cambridge, MA: Da Capo Press, 2000.

Fehrenbacher, Don E. *The Dred Scott Case: Its Significance in American Law and Politics*. New York: Oxford University Press, 2001.

Freehling, William W. *The Road to Disunion: Secessionists at Bay, 1776–1854 Volume I*. New York: Oxford University Press, 1991.

Fite, Emerson David. *The Presidential Campaign of 1860*. Ithaca, NY: Cornell University Press, 2009.

G

Gara, Larry. *The Liberty Line: The Legend of the Underground Railroad*. Lexington, KY: University of Kentucky Press, 1996.

———. *The Presidency of Franklin Pierce*. Lawrence, KS: University of Kansas Press, 1991.

Garraty, John A., and Robert McCaughey. *The American Nation: A History of the United States Since 1865*. 6th ed. New York: HarperCollins, 1987.

Godman, Paul. *Of One Blood: Abolitionism and the Origins of Racial Equality*. Berkeley, CA: University of California Press, 2000.

Gould, Lewis L. *Grand Old Party: A History of Republicans*. New York: Random House, 2003.

Greeenberg, Kenneth S. *Nat Turner: A Slave Rebellion in History and Memory*. New York: Oxford University Press, 2004.

H

Hamilton, Holman. *Prologue to Conflict: The Crisis and Compromise of 1850*. Lexington, KY: University of Kentucky Press, 2005.

Hughes, Jonathan, and Louis P. Cain. *American Economic History*. 8th ed. Englewood Cliffs, NJ: Pearson Prentice-Hall, 2010.

J

Johannsen, Robert W. *Stephen A. Douglas*. Champaigne, IL: University of Illinois Press, 1997.

Jones, Howard. *Quest for Security: A History of U.S. Foreign Relations*. New York: McGraw-Hill, 1996.

BIBLIOGRAPHY

R

Klein, Maury. *Days of Defiance: Sumter, Secession, and the Coming of the Civil War.* New York: Vintage, 1999.

Kolchin, Peter. *American Slavery: 1619–1877.* New York: Hill and Wang, 2003.

L

Lipset, Seymour Martin, and Earl Raab. *The Politics of Unreason: Right-Wing Extremism in America, 1790–1970.* New York: Harper and Row, 1970.

M

McPherson, James M. *Battle Cry of Freedom: The Civil War Era.* New York: Oxford University Press, 2003.

Morrison, Chaplain. *Democratic Politics and Sectionalism: The Wilmot Proviso Controversy.* Chapel Hill, NC: University of North Carolina Press, 1967.

Muccigrosso, Robert. *Basic History of Conservatism.* Melbourne, FL: Krieger, 2001.

N

Nichols, Alice. *Bleeding Kansas.* New York: Oxford University Press, 1954.

Nichols, Roy F. *The Disruption of American Democracy.* New York: Collier, 1962.

Niebuhr, Reinhold. *The Irony of American History.* Chicago, IL: University of Chicago Press, 2008.

O

Oates, Stephen B. *To Purge this Land with Blood: A Biography of John Brown.* Amhurst, MA: University of Massachusetts Press, 1984.

Olson, James S. *Encyclopedia of the Industrial Revolution in America.* Westport, CT: Greenwood Press, 2001.

Oren, Michael B. *Power, Faith, and Fantasy: America in the Middle East 1776 to the Present.* New York: W. W. Norton & Company, 2007.

P

Peterson, Merrill D. *The Great Triumvirate: Webster, Clay, and Calhoun.* New York: Oxford University Press, 1988.

Porter, Kirk H., and Donald Bruce Johnson eds. *National Party Platforms 1840–1968.* Urbana, IL: University of Illinois Press, 1972.

Potter, David M. *The Impending Crisis: America before the Civil War 1848–1861.* New York: Harper Perennial, 1977.

R

Rawley, James A. *Race and Politics: "Bleeding Kansas" and the Coming of the Civil War.* Lincoln, NE: University of Nebraska Press, 1979.

S

Sewell, Richard H. *Ballots for Freedom: Antislavery Politics in the United States 1837–1860.* New York: W. W. Norton & Company, 1980.

Stewart, James Brewer. *Holy Warriors: The Abolitionist and American Slavery.* New York: Hill and Wang, 1997.

W

Wooster, Ralph. *The Secessionist Conventions of the South.* Princeton, NJ: Princeton University Press, 1962.

POP QUIZ

1. By 1850, the Southern system and its slave labor had led to the development of a _____.
   a. somewhat conservative temper
   b. society based on equality
   c. society based on maternalism
   d. society based on a strong public authority

2. As late as 1780, why were slaves less numerous in the North?
   a. Africans tended to suffer from high mortality rates in the northern winters.
   b. Northerners were morally opposed to slavery.
   c. Slaves were less profitable in the North (due to its shorter growing season and grain crops).
   d. Slaves were much more prone to escape in the heavily wooded North.

3. Which of the following did John C. Calhoun argue?
   a. that the national government was supreme over the states according to the Constitution
   b. that Congress had no power to exclude slavery from any territory
   c. that Congress had complete authority over the territories
   d. Both a and c

4. In 1849, on what platform was Peter Hansborough Bell elected governor of Texas?
   a. peace with the U.S. at any price
   b. "retaining" Santa Fe for Texas, by force if necessary
   c. "fifty-four forty or fight"
   d. abolition of slavery

5. Problems under the Fugitive Slave Act included which of the following?
   a. Southerners roamed Northern territory capturing blacks, many of whom had never been slaves.
   b. Northerners actually helped fugitive slaves escape from Southern masters.
   c. Many blacks in the North fled to Canada to avoid enslavement by marauding Southerners.
   d. All of the above

6. Stephen Douglas started a political firestorm in 1854 when he included a provision in his Kansas-Nebraska bill that called for _____.
   a. the continuation of slavery in the territories
   b. the abolition of slavery in the territories
   c. popular sovereignty to determine slavery in the territories
   d. a railroad built by slaves in the territories

7. Historians believe that a contributing factor in President Franklin Pierce's death was _____.
   a. alcoholism
   b. a gunshot wound suffered in the civil war
   c. mercury poisoning
   d. bloodletting by doctors

8. Why did John Brown raid the federal armory at Harper's Ferry?
   a. to become the American "Don Quixote"
   b. to become a martyr for the cause of emancipation
   c. to arm a slave rebellion and wage a war of emancipation against the South
   d. to take over the federal government in Washington

9. What would the Crittenden Compromise have permitted?
   a. slavery in states where it already existed, but nowhere else
   b. slavery only where people voted for slavery
   c. slavery everywhere south of 36°30' (the Missouri Compromise line)
   d. slavery only in the Caribbean

10. In his second inaugural address, Abraham Lincoln stated which of the following?
    a. "All know that slavery was somehow the cause of the war."
    b. "All know that states rights were the cause of the war."
    c. "All know that the dispute over tariffs was the cause of the war."
    d. "All know that the dispute over Kansas was the cause of the war."

11. The South preferred high tariffs to protect its economy. T F

12. According to the Supreme Court, slaves had no right to use federal courts because they were property not citizens. T F

13. The doctrine of popular sovereignty was promoted by Senator _____ _____ of Michigan in the _____ presidential election.

14. Harriet Beecher Stowe wrote _____ _____ _____.

15. In the Lincoln-Douglas Debates, Douglas's argument on slavery was called the _____ _____.

Chapter 14

(Wikimedia Commons)

Civil War, 1861–1865

CHAPTER OUTLINE

14.1 The Blue and The Gray

14.1a The "American" War

The American Civil War lasted four years, from April 1861, to April 1865. It was fought in more than half of the United States, with battles taking place in every slave state except Delaware (a slave state that did not secede) and Confederate forces making incursions into Pennsylvania, Ohio, West Virginia, Kansas, even Vermont (by raiding from Canada).

From a total of fourteen million white males, nearly three million were in uniform—just over two million for the Union and eight hundred thousand for the Confederacy.

This was more than 20 percent of all white males—a higher proportion than in any other American war. The highest participation rate of any state was from Texas, where a staggering 75 percent of men between the ages of 18 and 45 served in the Confederate army. The Union total included 180,000 black soldiers and perhaps 20,000 black sailors, nearly one tenth of the men in the Northern armed forces. Either as battle casualties or as victims of camp maladies, 618,000 men died in service (360,000 Union troops and 258,000 Confederates). More than one soldier in five lost his life—a far heavier ratio of losses than in any other war in American history. For the Confederate soldiers, the ratio was one in three.

Partly because the cost was proportionately so heavy, and partly because the Civil War was distinctly an American war, this conflict has occupied a place in the American memory and the American imagination that other wars—even more recent, more destructive, and more global wars—have never held. On both sides, men were fighting for what they deeply believed to be American values.

Southerners were convinced that their right to form a Confederacy was based on a principle of the Declaration of Independence—that governments derive their just powers from the consent of the governed. They were also fighting to defend their states from invasion. "All we ask is to be let alone," said **Jefferson Davis** in his first war message to the Confederate Congress. Early in the war some Union soldiers captured a Southern soldier who, from his tattered homespun butternut uniform, was obviously not a member of the planter class. They asked him why he, a nonslaveholder, was fighting to uphold slavery. "I'm fighting because y'all are down here," was his reply.

The North was fighting to defend the flag and to prove that a democracy was not too weak to hold together. Secession was the "essence of anarchy," said Lincoln. "The central

Map 14.1 Population Density (1860)

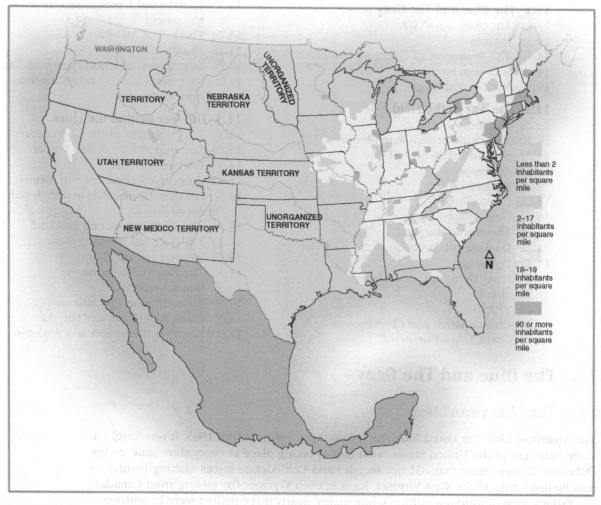

idea pervading this struggle is the necessity of proving that popular government is not an absurdity. We must settle this question now, whether in a free government the minority have the right to break up the government whenever they choose." Abolition of slavery was not at all a motivation for most people in the North at the outset of the war. Instead, the abolition of slavery became a purpose in 1863 when Abraham Lincoln believed that the North needed a greater moral motivation. Until that time, preserving the Union was the primary Northern motive, but Lincoln found it insufficient to stir the masses by the end of 1862. Thus, the greater moral purpose was added.

14.16 Lincoln

Long after these events, people who had grown up with an oversimplified image of Lincoln as a Great Emancipator became disillusioned by this record. In the ensuing century and a half, some critics have sought to tear down his reputation, but he remains a figure of immense stature; and scholars and popular biographers continue to find nuances of his personality and achievements to explore.

Born in 1809 in a log cabin in Kentucky, Lincoln grew up on the frontier in Indiana and Illinois, doing rough work as a rail splitter and a plowboy and receiving only a meager education. Lincoln's early life was filled with tragedy. His grandfather (the senior Abraham Lincoln) bequeathed none of his 5,544 acres to Abraham's father (**Thomas Lincoln**), instead leaving it all to Abraham's uncle Mordecai. Thomas Lincoln was then cheated out of the land he owned in Kentucky by land speculators who paid off crooked surveyors to allow those speculators to stake claims to Lincoln's land. The family moved to Indiana in 1816 where tragedy struck again when Abraham's mother, Nancy, died of "milk sickness" after drinking milk from cows that had eaten the poisonous white snakeroot plant. Thomas remarried **Sarah Bush**, with whom Abe had a good relationship, but she too died in 1829.

Young Abraham spent two years on a flatboat on the Mississippi River and then managed a general store in New Salem, Illinois. When the store failed in 1834, Lincoln began his political career by becoming postmaster of New Salem. That same year, Lincoln ran and won a seat in the Illinois State legislature at age 25—primarily because he needed the pay. After becoming a legislator, Lincoln realized that he would benefit from studying law; he did so on his own and passed the bar. Later he practiced law with a partner in Springfield and rode the circuit on horseback to follow the sessions of the court.

Lincoln's personal life, however, continued to be filled with tragedy. In 1835, Lincoln fell in love with a short, plump woman named **Ann Rutledge**, who tragically died of "brain fever." Lincoln unfortunately sank into a fit of depression, and would suffer from recurring bouts of depression for much of his adult life. Later, in 1844, Lincoln wrote, "I am now the most miserable man living. If what I felt were equally distributed to the whole human race, there would not be one cheerful face on earth." Lincoln refused to carry a penknife out of fear that he might become self-destructive in a fit of depression, and on numerous occasions he cleared his house of all sharp objects so as to help eliminate any self-destructive temptations. Lincoln's law partner blamed his depression on chronic constipation; however, it was more likely related to the medicine he took for his depression known as "**blue mass**," the ingredients of which included licorice, rose water, dead rose petals, honey, sugar, and mercury. Symptoms of mercury poisoning include insomnia, tremors, and rage attacks—all symptoms from which Lincoln suffered. Lincoln himself eventually made that connection and quit taking blue mass a few months into his presidency because it made him "cross."

After the death of Rutledge, Lincoln had another failed relationship with a woman named Mary Owens, whom Lincoln described as "pleasingly stout, weighing between 150 and 180 pounds." Owens, however, ended the relationship, stating that Lincoln was "deficient in those little links which make up the chain of a woman's happiness." After the relationship failed, Lincoln wrote to Mr. O. H. Browning: "I can never be satisfied with anyone who would be blockhead enough to have me."

In 1837, Lincoln met **Mary Todd**, who at age 22 was "just short of being an old maid." Lincoln married Mary Todd in 1842. Mary was a Southern woman born of privilege, but

Thomas Lincoln
Abraham Lincoln's father

Sarah Bush
Abraham Lincoln's stepmother

Ann Rutledge
Abraham Lincoln's romantic interest who died of an illness

"Blue mass"
Medication, which contained mercury, that was taken by Abraham Lincoln for depression

Mary Todd
Abraham Lincoln's wife, and First Lady of the United States

Mary Lincoln, First Lady and wife of Abraham Lincoln, was known for being a volatile woman. On one occasion, Mary chased Abe out of the house with a butcher knife. She also spent extravagantly and racked up sizeable debt without Abe's knowledge. (Wikimedia Commons)

Willie and Eddie Lincoln

Abraham Lincoln's two sons who died in childhood

Tad Lincoln

Lincoln's son with behavioral problems

Robert Lincoln

Lincoln's oldest son, who attended Harvard

Mary's sisters dropped her from their social circle because of her low-status choice of a husband. Unfortunately, Mary was also known for a bad temper; suffered from headaches; was highly emotional; was terrified of storms, dogs, and robbers; and was prone to panic. On one occasion, Mary chased Abe out of the house with a butcher knife. On another, she struck him on the nose with a piece of firewood. Her temperament was well known; and although she was the first president's wife to be regularly called "First Lady," members of Lincoln's cabinet frequently referred to her as "Hell-Cat."

While in the White House, Mary spent extravagantly, accepted gifts from office-seekers and those seeking favors, and ran up debts without Abe's knowledge. Mary sold furniture from the White House and manure from the White House stables to pay her debts. When that wasn't enough, she fired the White House steward and kept the salary, and then presented Congress with fake vouchers for nonexistent purchases. At one point, the House Judiciary Committee even investigated Mary for passing sensitive information to the South during the Civil War.

The Lincolns had four children, but **Willie and Eddie Lincoln** died of childhood diseases. Another son, **Tad Lincoln**, evidently suffered from a hyperactivity disorder and was wholly undisciplined, unable to dress himself at age 9, and remained illiterate even by the time of Lincoln's death.

The deaths of their two boys, along with a head injury she suffered from a fall from a carriage, may have contributed to mental illness in Mary Lincoln by the time of her husband's death. Mary held eight séances in the White House to speak with the spirits of her deceased children, one of which was attended by the president himself. Mary reportedly told Abe that her deceased son Willie often came to visit her at night, and often little Eddie (who died at age 4) was with him. In 1875, their son **Robert Lincoln** had Mary committed to a mental institution where she lived the rest of her life.

Lincoln was very much the frontiersman and rarely went east, except for his one term in Congress (1847–1849). He was relatively unknown until the debates with Douglas, which gained him a reputation in 1858. In many ways, it is surprising that Lincoln became the greatest contributor to the end of slavery. In the 1840s, Lincoln opposed the annexation of Texas, formerly a territory of Mexico, partially because he thought of the Mexicans as "greasers." Lincoln also viewed Native Americans as a "barbarous barrier to progress" and allowed the execution of thirty-eight American Indians by a military tribunal during the Civil War, after the Indians had killed 350 whites because they had not been paid for their land. This was the largest mass execution in American history. Concerning the slaves, Lincoln thought blacks to be inferior and opposed black suffrage, black equality, interracial marriage, blacks on juries, and the repeal of the Fugitive Slave Act. Lincoln also favored the repatriation of blacks to Africa as late as his debates with Stephen Douglas in 1858. Nevertheless, in 1861, at a moment of crisis, this tall, gangling, plain-looking man—whose qualities of greatness were still unsuspected—became president.

Lincoln's relaxed and unpretentious manner masked remarkable powers of decision and qualities of leadership. Completely lacking in self-importance, he seemed humble to some observers, but he acted with the patience and forbearance of a man who was sure of what he was doing. He refused to let the abolitionists push him into an antislavery war which would antagonize Union men who did not care about slavery, and he refused to let the Union men separate him from the antislavery contingent by restricting war aims too narrowly. He saw that the causes of union and emancipation must support each other instead of opposing each other, or both would be defeated.

Patiently, he worked to fuse the idea of union with those of freedom and equality ("a new nation conceived in liberty and dedicated to the proposition that all men are created equal"). Thus, he reaffirmed for American nationalism the ideal of freedom and gave to the ideal of freedom the strength of an undivided union. Knowing that, in a democracy, a man must win political success in order to gain a chance for statesmanship, he moved patiently and indirectly to his goals. His opportunism offended many abolitionists, but in the end he succeeded in striking down slavery with a fatal blow.

Once the war started, Lincoln was very forceful in support of his goals. Lincoln closed newspapers that were too critical of his administration and arrested their editors and proprietors. He also allowed the arrest of preachers who delivered sermons against the war and allowed the arrest, trial, and conviction for treason by a military tribunal of former Ohio congressman Clement L. Vallandigham, who had spoken out strongly against the war. Lincoln then commuted Vallandigham's sentence from imprisonment to banishment to the Confederacy.

14.1c The Resources of North and South

In later years, after the Confederacy had gone down in defeat, men said that the "Lost Cause" (as Southerners called it) had been lost from the beginning and that the South had been fighting against the census returns. In many respects this seems true, for the South was completely outnumbered in almost all the factors of manpower and economic strength that make up the sinews of modern war. The eleven Confederate states had a white population of 5,450,000, while the nineteen free states had 18,950,000. (These figures leave out both the population of the four border slave states of Missouri, Kentucky, Maryland, and Delaware and the slave population of the Confederate states.) Greater population, of course, translated into more soldiers. At its peak in 1863, the Union army had 690,000 soldiers, as compared to 270,000 for the Confederates.

The four **border states** were divided, but most of their people and resources supported the Union side. Slaves strengthened the Confederate war effort in an important way, however, for they constituted a majority of the South's labor force and thereby enabled most white men to leave home to fight in the army.

The Union was far ahead of the Confederacy in financial and economic strength. It had a bank capital more than four times as great as that of the South. It led the South in the number of manufacturing enterprises by 6.5 to 1, in the number of industrial workers by 12 to 1, and in the value of its manufactures by 11 to 1. In railroad mileage, it led by more than 2 to 1. The Union also had a serious naval advantage, in that the South possessed almost no warships at the beginning of the war. This deficiency would allow the Union to **blockade** the South; this was particularly damaging to the Southern economy, which was dependent upon cotton exports for its revenue and upon foreign trade for its manufactured goods.

Against these ratios of strength must be placed the fact that the Union was undertaking a vastly more difficult military objective. It should be noted that virtually every advantage enjoyed by the Union during the Civil War was also enjoyed by the British during the American Revolution—yet the British still lost. Much like the British during the American Revolution, the Union was seeking to occupy and subdue an area larger than all of western Europe. This meant that armies had to be sent hundreds of miles into hostile territory and be maintained in these distant operations. This necessity involved the gigantic tasks of transporting the immense volume of supplies required by an army in the field and defending long lines of supply and communication, the longest in American history, which would be worthless if they were cut even at a single point. In wars prior to the Civil War, armies had depended upon the use of great wagon trains to bring supplies. As the supply lines lengthened, the horses ate up in fodder a steadily increasing proportion of the amount they could haul, until there was scarcely any margin left between what the supply lines carried and what they consumed in carrying it.

During the Civil War, for the first time in the history of warfare, railroads played a major part in the supply services. If these more efficient carriers of goods had not changed the whole nature of war, it is questionable whether invading armies could ever have marched from the Ohio River to the Gulf of Mexico. Ten years earlier, the United States had not possessed the railroad network that supplied the Union armies between 1861 and 1865. Therefore, at an earlier time the defensive position of the South would have been far stronger.

President Abraham Lincoln allowed the arrest of preachers who preached sermons against the war. Former Ohio Congressman, Clement L. Vallandigham (who had spoken out strongly against the war) was arrested, tried, and convicted—but Lincoln later commuted Vallandigham's sentence from imprisonment to banishment to the Confederacy. (Wikimedia Commons)

Border states
Slave states (Maryland, Delaware, Kentucky, and Missouri) that did not secede

Blockade
The closing of Southern ports by the Union navy

Even with railroads, superior munitions, and superior industrial facilities, the military tasks of the Union were most formidable. America was a profoundly civilian country. The peacetime army numbered only sixteen thousand, and few people on either side had any conception of the vast problems involved in recruiting, mobilizing, equipping, training, and maintaining large armies. It was an amateur's war on both sides, and many of its features seem inconceivable today.

Most of the troops were recruited as volunteers rather than drafted. At the outset of the war, Lincoln called for seventy-five thousand 90-day volunteers, reflecting a bit of naivety in Lincoln's inability to foresee a protracted conflict. In defense of Lincoln, his own war experience had consisted of the Blackhawk War in 1832 where, by his own admission, he survived "bloody encounters with mosquitoes and led raids on wild onion patches." Even the larger war against Mexico that Lincoln had experienced as a young congressman had ended after little more than a year of actual fighting, and that war involved the invasion of a country farther away and with more territory than the Confederacy.

Nevertheless, by July 1861, Lincoln's call for seventy-five thousand 90-day volunteers had in fact raised 186,000; the South had simultaneously raised 112,000 volunteers. The massive recruitment effort simply overwhelmed organizational and supply capacities on both sides.

Southerners quickly began building new factories to supply their soldiers with uniforms and arms, but Southern manufacturing and transportation capacities would never be sufficient. Although by April 1864 Josiah Gorgas—the head of the Confederacy's Ordnance Bureau—boasted that the South was making enough guns and ammunition to meet the needs of its soldiers, at the outset of the war there were no factories in the South that made guns, swords, shells, or powder; and the Confederate army would remain under-equipped throughout the war. Even in those areas where the production capacity of the South was sufficient, such as in food production, the available products often did not make it to the troops in the field due to a lack of rail transportation.

Both the Union and the Confederacy sold war bonds, raised taxes, and issued paper currency to fund the war. Much like the American Revolution, however, the increased taxation and borrowing were not enough to completely fund the war effort—and Americans on both sides essentially paid for the war through the depletion of their savings, caused by the rapid inflation that accompanied the issuing of paper currency. Prices in the North increased approximately 80 percent during the war; even worse, in the South—where the costs of the war per capita were far greater—inflation reached 9,000 percent by the end of the war.

The Confederacy enacted **conscription** in April 1862, and the Union followed suit in March 1863. The real purpose of these laws, however, was to stimulate volunteering rather than to institute a genuine draft. Both the North and the South allowed drafted men to hire substitutes, until the Confederacy abolished this privilege in December 1863. The Union government also exempted a drafted man upon payment of a $300 commutation fee, until this privilege was abolished in July 1864, due to popular discontent. In the North, the $300 commutation fee gave the common people reason to denounce the war as a "rich man's war, poor man's fight." In the South, the idea that a central authority could force anyone, anywhere, to do anything against their will was a violation of the very "states' rights" principles that the South was fighting for in the first place.

Union conscription was applied only in localities that failed to meet their quotas. Thus, communities were impelled to pay "bounties" to encourage men to volunteer. This resulted in the practice of "bounty-jumping." A man would enlist, collect his bounty, desert, enlist again in some other locality, collect another bounty, and desert again.

Volunteers enlisted for specified periods, normally three years. The Confederacy's draft laws compelled them to reenlist even when their enlistment terms were up. On the Union side, by contrast, volunteers could not be compelled to reenlist; and in 1864 the North had to rely on bounties and patriotic persuasion to induce more than half of its three-year volunteers to reenlist.

Volunteer regiments at first elected their own officers up to the rank of captain, and they frequently preferred officers who were not strict in matters of discipline. This was to handicap them in battle, however. Men without prior training as officers were placed in positions of command, and recruits were often thrown into combat with little basic training as soldiers. Even physical examinations for recruits were often a farce. It was, to a considerable extent, a do-it-yourself war because the machinery of the modern state was in its infancy even in the North.

Cotton clads

Confederate ships draped with cotton bales for protection

William Seward

Secretary of state under Abraham Lincoln

14.10 Southern Strategy

Southerners believed that they would win the war because of their "just cause," superior character, and of course, because God was on their side. With foolhardy bravado, the Southerners believed that their rugged country outdoorsmen with their frontier mentality would easily defeat the city boys from the North, whom they viewed as soft, flabby, and unprincipled. Southerners compared their position to that of the colonists in 1776—who had triumphed against insurmountable odds over the more powerful British.

Southerners also believed that the North would collapse without Southern cotton, and that without the Southern market, Northern manufacturing would collapse in over-production with no Southerners to purchase their goods. Southerners also believed that the Europeans, especially the British, would be on their side because of the need for Southern cotton. The British imported 900 million pounds of cotton annually, three-fourths of which came from the American South. Of Britain's workforce, 20 percent was involved in the textile industry; by this reasoning, Britain would collapse without Southern cotton and would therefore want to ensure their supply using what was still the world's largest navy. If England could be persuaded to join the Southern cause because of their need for cotton, then victory would be assured.

Confederate President Jefferson Davis termed the Southern strategy as an "offensive-defensive" strategy. Southerners recognized that a Union victory would require that they invade, defeat, and subjugate the South on its own soil (the same challenge that had been faced by the British in the American Revolution); a Confederate victory, on the other hand, only required that the South avoid annihilation until the North exhausted its resources and will to fight (the feat that had been accomplished by the colonists in the American Revolution). This was the "defensive" part of the Southern strategy. The "offensive" part of the strategy called for Southern campaigns (preferably into Northern territory) that would produce shocking, "decisive victories," intended to break the Northern will to fight and convince the Europeans to support the Southern cause as allies. In short, the Southerners sought a Civil War version of Saratoga, where a decisive victory by the colonists brought France into the American Revolution as an ally, and a "Yorktown," where a decisive victory by the colonists convinced the British that the fight was too costly, inducing them to negotiate peace and accept the independence of their former possession.

To combat the Union navy, the Southerners armed their merchant ships, often draping them with bales of cotton to provide protection from Union guns. These **cotton clads** seized Union merchant ships and cargo, not only disrupting Union trade, but also confiscating goods for the South. The Confederates also constructed the beginnings of a navy, purchasing ships from England.

14.1¢ Northern Strategy

President Lincoln's primary objective in the war was to preserve the Union and his primary means was military subjugation of the South through a massive land invasion and naval blockade. In order to accomplish his goals, Lincoln needed to keep the war domestic and prevent European intervention on the behalf of the South. Direct European military intervention on the behalf of the South would tip the balance and secure Southern independence, so it had to be avoided at all costs. Massive economic aid from Europe to the South could perhaps tip the balance in the favor of the South as well, so Secretary of State **William Seward** advised a blockade on all Southern ports, which Lincoln announced on April 19, 1861. In the beginning, the blockade was really merely a paper blockade since the U.S. had fewer than a hundred ships to guard 185 Southern ports and 3,500 miles of coastline. Furthermore, only forty-two of the Union's ships were considered seaworthy in 1861, and only eight were in U.S. waters at the time of the proclamation. The Union would build more ships, however, with the result that the blockade effectively crippled Southern international trade by the end of the War.

BVT Lab

Flashcards are available for this chapter at www.BVTLab.com.

The blockade also presented a problem for the Union because a "blockade" under international law was considered an act of war. Therefore, Lincoln's blockade inferred that the South was an independent nation (a point disputed by the Union) and that the Civil War was actually a war between two independent nations, rather than an insurrection or a domestic dispute. The rules of international law were different for wars between belligerents (two independent, warring nations) than they were for insurrections or domestic disputes. As a belligerent in a war between nations, the South could obtain loans and purchase war materials in Europe. Furthermore, European nations would have the right to trade nonmilitary goods with both warring nations—the same rights that the U.S. had claimed and fought for in the War of 1812. When Lincoln declared the blockade, he essentially inferred that the South was an independent warring nation and that the Europeans would have those rights. England immediately declared neutrality, therefore at least demonstrating that they were asserting their rights as neutrals to trade nonmilitary goods in Southern ports. If Lincoln interrupted this trade, he risked war with England, which would doom Union prospects in the conflict with the South.

Lincoln's other option would have been to allow the Europeans unlimited trade with the South under the premise that the South was not independent and was still part of the U.S. The advantage would be that the European powers would not be able to aid the South as an "independent country." But if the South were not independent—as England's Lord Lyons explained to Secretary of State Seward—then a blockade would not be binding because blockades under international law applied only to two nations at war. Lincoln essentially attempted to skirt international law and do both: treating the war as a domestic dispute and denying European aid to the South, while imposing a blockade (thus inferring that the South was independent) and shutting off European trade with the South. The results would be legal disputes with England over the seizure of ships at sea that would be settled after the war, and a continual risk of bringing England into the war on the side of the South over Union violations of international law.

Instead of the long protracted war of attrition and annihilation that the Civil War eventually became, Lincoln and his generals envisioned a quick strike invasion into the South that would provide a stunning and decisive victory that would quickly quell the rebellion by proving to Southerners that their insurrection had no chance in the face of Northern superiority. Given that Richmond was only one hundred miles from Washington, D.C., many Northern generals evidently believed that a quick strike on the Southern capitol could produce the decisive Union victory necessary to cause the South to abandon the rebellion before it was even underway.

Instead, it was the Union strategy that was derailed before it even began. On April 19, the 6th Massachusetts Regiment that had been mobilized for an assault on Virginia arrived in Baltimore, Maryland—a city in a slave state that had chosen not to secede. Sentiments in Maryland were divided and tensions were high. In Baltimore, the Massachusetts Regiment had to change railroad lines, forcing the soldiers to cross the city on foot. As they marched through the streets, a mob of some ten thousand Confederate sympathizers flying Confederate flags attacked them at first with rocks, then bullets. Under orders from their commander, the Union troops returned fire—and the city of Baltimore erupted into riotous violence. Twelve citizens of Baltimore and four Union soldiers were killed before the riot could be ended by military force. Secessionists cut the telegraph wires and burned the railroad bridges connecting Baltimore to both North and South, cutting off the town not only from the Confederacy but also from the rest of the Union. The destruction of the rail bridges also cut off Washington (south of Baltimore) from the rest of the Union. To prevent the nation's capitol from being surrounded by hostile enemy territory, Lincoln ordered that federal forces turn Maryland into an occupied state.

In order to prevent further bloodshed, Lincoln ordered that troops be routed around Baltimore. Lincoln then suspended habeas corpus and ordered the arrest of Confederate sympathizers, with the result that Baltimore's mayor, police chief, a judge, and nineteen Maryland state legislators were imprisoned without trial. Chief Justice Roger Taney, who had penned the *Dred Scott* decision, challenged the president's action and issued a writ of habeas corpus for the release of a Southern sympathizer, John Merryman. In *Ex parte Merryman,* Taney ruled that if the public's safety were endangered, only Congress had the right to suspend the writ of habeas corpus. Lincoln, however, essentially ignored the ruling throughout the war and imprisoned, without charges or trials, whomever he saw fit.

Many Confederate sympathizers from Maryland fled to Virginia, formed a Confederate Maryland government in exile, and joined up with the Confederate army or simply launched guerrilla raids back into Maryland. Unionists won the Maryland state elections and gained firm control of the Maryland legislature in the fall of 1861, but Maryland would remain a battleground for invading armies throughout the war.

The situation in Missouri essentially mirrored that in Maryland. St. Louis erupted into a full-scale riot and pitched battle between Union and Confederate militias on May 10–11, 1861, in which thirty-six people were killed. Union commander Nathaniel Lyon led his troops in a summer campaign that drove the Confederate militia, along with Missouri's governor and pro-Confederate legislators, into Arkansas, where they formed a Missouri Confederate government in exile.

While in Arkansas, the Missouri Confederates recruited Arkansas comrades to help them invade back into Missouri in August. On August 10, the Union commander in Missouri, Nathaniel Lyon, was killed at Wilson's Creek in southwest Missouri. The Confederates then marched northward along the Missouri River and captured a Union garrison, at Lexington, Missouri—forty miles east of Kansas City—on September 20, 1861. This early victory was the South's high water-mark in Missouri, but the Union would officially control the state throughout the war. Nevertheless, Confederate **bushwhackers** and Unionist **jayhawkers** would launch hit and run raids and ambushes against each other throughout the war. Notorious postwar outlaws Jesse and Frank James and Cole and Jim Younger rode with the Confederate bushwhackers. Over the course of the war, perhaps more so than any other state, Missouri suffered through a "civil war" within the Civil War.

Kentucky Confederates, outnumbered approximately 2 to 1 in Kentucky, also fled to the Confederacy and formed a state government in exile—but the state of Kentucky remained solidly in the Union. Union sentiments were also strong in the western mountain portion of Virginia, west of the Shenandoah Valley where most of Virginia's delegates had voted against secession. In fact, part of the reason for placing the Southern capital in Richmond was to shore up Confederate support in the state. Western Virginia, however, was a mountainous, agricultural area of small farms where family labor sufficed and slaves were few in number. Western Virginia's economy had much stronger ties to Ohio and Pennsylvania than to the rest of Virginia or the South at large. Western Virginia's largest city, Wheeling, was 330 miles away—over rugged mountain terrain—from Richmond, but only 60 miles from Pittsburgh. With the help of Union troops (who crossed the Ohio River and won several minor battles against Confederate forces in western Virginia in the summer of 1861), the people of western Virginia withdrew from the Confederacy and created the state of West Virginia, which was officially added to the Union in 1863.

The James Boys and the Younger Brothers

Notable outlaws were Confederate "bushwhackers" Jesse and Frank James, and Bob and Cole Younger, who together formed the James-Younger gang. Among other acts, they robbed banks and trains, and murdered. The gang gained fame throughout the "Confederate frontier." (© CORBIS)

The Civil War in the border states even spread into American Indian Territory, and Confederate sympathizers manning Union forts turned over the facilities to Confederates from Texas without a shot. Several American Indian tribes were coaxed into signing treaties of alliance with the Confederacy, including the five "civilized tribes" (Cherokees, Creeks, Seminoles, Chickasaws, and Choctaws). However, other American Indian tribes sided with the Union, and aided by Union regiments from Kansas and Missouri eventually gained control of American Indian Territory for the Union.

14.2 The War in the Field

14.2a The Virginia Front

From the very outset of the war, attention was focused on the Virginia front. After fighting had begun at Fort Sumter and the states of the upper South had joined the Confederacy, the Confederate government moved its capital to Richmond, Virginia—about one hundred miles south of Washington. With the two seats of government so close together, the war in the east became a struggle on the part of the Union to capture Richmond, and on the part of the South to defend it.

Between Washington and Richmond a number of broad rivers—the Potomac, the Rappahannock, the York, the Chickahominy, and other tributaries—flow more or less parallel with one another from the Allegheny Mountains in the west to Chesapeake Bay in the east. This grid of rivers afforded a natural system of defense to the South and presented an obstacle course to the North. Southern armies on the defensive could lie in wait for their attackers on the south banks of these streams, as they did at Bull Run, **Fredericksburg**, **Chancellorsville**, and the Wilderness. When the Southern army was driven back after going on the offensive, it could recross to safety, reorganize, and recoup, as it did after **Antietam** (Sharpsburg), and **Gettysburg**.

For four years, the principal army of the North (the Army of the Potomac) struggled against the principal army of the South (the Army of Northern Virginia) over this terrain. Each side placed its foremost commander here. **Robert E. Lee** headed the Army of Northern Virginia after Joseph E. Johnston was wounded in 1862, and Ulysses S. Grant was brought east to take overall command of Union armies in 1864 after his great successes in the West. Public attention centered primarily upon these campaigns, and they have continued to receive more than their share of attention in history.

14.2b The Battle of Bull Run (Manassas)

During the first half of the war, the Union met with a long succession of disappointments and defeats on the Virginia front. In July 1861, when both armies were still raw and unseasoned, the Union sent **General Irvin McDowell** south with the slogan "Forward to Richmond" and with expectations of an easy victory—in spite of the fact that General Winfield Scott and his field commander, General McDowell, both had misgivings about the ability of their green, poorly trained, ninety-day volunteers to fight a real battle. In fact, Scott had argued for a cautious, long-term strategy known as the **Anaconda Plan**, in which the North would weaken the South gradually through blockades on land and sea until the Northern army was strong enough to move forward and crush the weakened

Map 14.2 First Battle of Bull Run (1861)

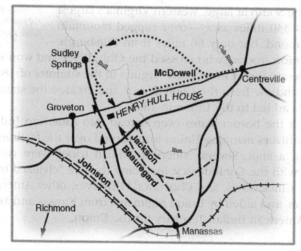

Fredericksburg
Site where Union army under General Ambrose E. Burnside is repulsed by Confederates under Robert E. Lee, December 11–15, 1862

Chancellorsville
Battle in May 1863, where a smaller force of Confederates under Robert E. Lee defeated a larger Union army under General Joseph E. Hooker, but lost General Thomas "Stonewall" Jackson, who was accidentally shot by his own men

Antietam
Confederate defeat on September 17, 1862, that ended General Lee's best attempt at bringing a decisive victory in a Northern offensive

Gettysburg
Decisive Union victory in the North on July 1–3, 1863, normally viewed as the turning point in the Civil War

Robert E. Lee
Commander of the Confederate Army of Virginia

General Irvin McDowell
Union general who suffered defeat at the First Battle of Bull Run

Anaconda Plan
Union strategy where the North would weaken the South gradually through blockades on land and sea until the Northern army was strong enough to move forward and crush the weakened South

South. The public, however, demanded bold, quick action—as did Scott's commander-in-chief, Abraham Lincoln. Thus, McDowell and his army marched into Virginia against the military judgment of the Union's most experienced general. Twenty-five miles southwest of Washington, McDowell encountered the Confederate armies of Generals Pierre G. T. Beauregard (a West Point classmate of McDowell's known as the "Napoleon of the South") and Joseph E. Johnston; together they were twenty-five thousand strong and had been deployed at Manassas, Virginia, to defend a key rail junction. In the Confederacy, the battle would be known as the Battle of Manassas. In the Union, the battle was named after the creek that crossed the battlefield, the **First Battle of Bull Run**.

First Battle of Bull Run
Won by the Confederates, July 21, 1861

Thomas J. Jackson
Confederate general who earned the name "Stonewall" for his stand at Bull Run, was accidentally shot by his own men at Chancellorsville, and later died from complications

On July 21, the Union army forded Bull Run—a sluggish branch of the Potomac River—and engaged the Confederate troops on the Confederate left flank, at first driving them back. By early afternoon, the Union army appeared to be on the verge of breaking Southern lines, but a Virginia brigade commanded by **Thomas J. Jackson** stood their ground. A South Carolina general, seeking to inspire his own troops, pointed to Jackson and his men, standing like a "stone wall" in repelling the Union troops. Afterwards, Thomas Jackson would be affectionately referred to in the South as "Stonewall Jackson."

Jackson's stand, combined with the arrival of his 2,300 fresh Confederate reinforcements from the Shenandoah Valley (who hit the battlefield with a famed "rebel yell"), drove the green Union troops into a disorganized retreat. Union troops broke ranks and fled in a panic, trampling spectators who had foolishly arrived on the battlefield with parasols and picnic baskets to witness the romantic struggle of courage. Fleeing Union soldiers abandoned their weapons and stumbled past their abandoned supply wagons on their way back to Washington.

The inexperienced Southern troops lacked the organization and supply capacity necessary to press their advantage and therefore failed to pursue the fleeing Union army. Casualties on both sides were light by Civil War standards (2,800 for the Union and 2,000 for the Confederates), but the battle boosted Southern confidence while simultaneously proving to Lincoln and the Union that victory would not be swift and that a broader strategy for winning the war would be necessary. In fact, for the South the victory

Pictured is the first battle of Bull Run, also known as the Battle of Manassas. (Wikimedia Commons)

may have engendered overconfidence—as some Southerners mistakenly believed that the war was won. In contrast, the Union became more realistic, and Congress authorized the enlistment of up to a million three-year volunteers. Union men answered the call by the hundreds of thousands, and Lincoln and the Union settled in for a long, hard fight.

McDowell was replaced by thirty-four-year-old George Brinton McClellan, who had campaigned successfully in West Virginia. A little man of supremely self-confident manner, he had gained the nickname "The Young Napoleon"—but McClellan was much less like Napoleon than he appeared. In truth, real resistance in West Virginia had been light, and McClellan and the Union press had overplayed the significance of his victories. Boldness in battle, which was the commodity Lincoln sought, would not prove to be McClellan's strongest suit after all.

McClellan was the child of wealthy parents in Philadelphia, had been educated in the best schools, and was a graduate of West Point where he finished second in his class, and then served as an army engineer. McClellan possessed real ability as an organizer, and he had the good sense to realize that he must make his troops into an army before he took them campaigning. McClellan was a perfectionist, however; he refused to mount an offensive until his army was trained to his own exacting requirements. Every commander has essentially two responsibilities: to win when engaged in military conflict, and to keep as many of his own men alive as possible in the process. McClellan clearly believed that latter goal to be the more important of the two and sought every means by which he could avoid unnecessary loss of life and destruction of property. McClellan even stated that he expected to win by "maneuvering rather than fighting." McClellan was averse to risk, and of course no military conflict can be waged completely absent of risk.

Map 14.3 Peninsula Campaign (1862)

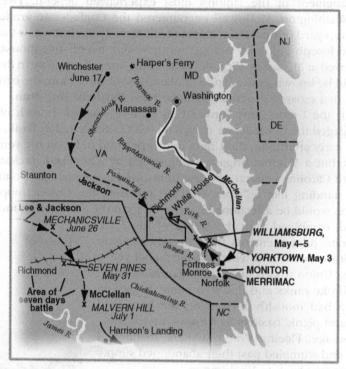

The president prodded McClellan to speed up the process and become more aggressive, at one point stating, "If General McClellan does not want to use the army, I would like to borrow it." McClellan, however, was confident in his own abilities and had little respect for Lincoln, once referring to him as "the original gorilla." Consequently, there was no more major fighting on the Virginia front for almost a year.

When McClellan did at last move in April 1862, with an army of 150,000 strong, he persuaded President Lincoln to let him transport his troops by ship to Fort Monroe—a point on the Virginia coast within striking distance of Richmond. From this point he proposed to move up the peninsula between the York and James Rivers (hence it was called the Peninsula Campaign) to capture the Confederate capitol.

McClellan's plan was a brilliant solution to the difficult problem of supply, for he could now bring provisions for his army by ship without fear of Confederate raiders getting to his rear and cutting his lines, The plan had one important drawback, however, in that it left, or appeared to leave, Washington exposed to the Confederates. Therefore, for the defense of the capitol, President Lincoln insisted on withholding 30,000 of the troops that McClellan wanted, leaving McClellan with an invasion force of 120,000. So although McClellan launched his invasion from Fort Monroe toward Richmond, he failed to push his offensive with the vigor the North expected. McClellan also moved with methodical precision—so methodical in fact, that it took him over ten weeks to advance sixty-five miles. A small Confederate blocking force at Yorktown delayed McClellan for the entire month of April. McClellan insisted on bringing siege guns to the front to blast his way through an infantry that his immense army should have been able to crush on foot in a matter of days. Finally, McClellan and his men were within six miles of Richmond—close enough to hear the town's church bells.

While these developments were in progress, the Confederate commander, Joseph E. Johnston, launched a counterattack on May 31 to June 1 in what has become known as the Battle of Seven Pines. The battle was indecisive, although the Confederates suffered six thousand casualties and the Union five thousand. Johnston was badly wounded in the shoulder during the assault and was replaced by Robert E. Lee.

Lee—a Virginia aristocrat, mild of speech and gentle of manner but gifted with a daring that was terrible to his adversaries—quickly perceived that he could play upon the Union's fear that Washington was too exposed. Accordingly, he sent his brilliant subordinate,

Thomas "Stonewall" Jackson, on a raid up the Shenandoah Valley, appearing to threaten Washington and causing the administration to hold the defensive troops (approximately thirty thousand) that had previously been promised to McClellan. In the month between May 4 and June 9, 1862, Stonewall Jackson's Confederates, with only seventeen thousand men, marched over 350 miles, defeating three separate Union armies in four engagements. Furthermore, the number of Union troops Jackson and his men defeated was more than twice that of Jackson's army.

Once Jackson had returned from his raid with phenomenal speed, Lee's reunited forces (numbering eighty-five thousand) took the offensive against McClellan's one hundred thousand original troops south and east of Richmond in a series of engagements known as the Seven Days' Battles (spanning June 25 to July 1, 1862). McClellan fought hard and was not decisively defeated; however, he lost his nerve, moved back to a base on the James River, and sent Washington a series of frantic messages claiming that the government had deserted him. By the time McClellan had reached the water and the safety of Union naval support, the Union had suffered sixteen thousand casualties and the South twenty thousand. Although the South had suffered greater casualties, Lee had saved Richmond, forced the Union to retreat, and at least temporarily reversed the Union's momentum.

McClellan's retreat convinced Lincoln that the peninsula campaign would not work and that McClellan was not the right man to lead the Union army. Thus, on July 11, Lincoln appointed General Henry W. Halleck—who had been the overall commander in the western theater where the Union had experienced greater success—to be the new general in chief.

14.2c Second Battle of Bull Run

Second Battle of Bull Run

Battle of August 28–30, 1862, at which Confederates forced Union general John Pope to retreat

Lincoln (who had never fully accepted the basic idea of operating by sea), through Halleck, withdrew McClellan's troops from the peninsula to northern Virginia where they joined a smaller force under the command of General John Pope, who had gained a reputation for aggressiveness in the West. The president hoped to launch another assault against Richmond via the overland route that he had preferred. As McClellan departed from the peninsula by water, Lee quickly took advantage of the opportunity that was provided him by the separation of the two Union armies, and moved north with his Army of Northern Virginia to engage Pope's troops before McClellan could arrive. In what is known as the **Second Battle of Bull Run**, Lee sent Stonewall Jackson to attack Pope from the rear, provoking Pope to launch a counterattack against the Confederate contingency under Stonewall Jackson. Lee then hurled the main thrust of his army against Pope's flank before McClellan and the Army of the Potomac could arrive. An exasperated Lincoln then removed Pope from command and reassigned him to the American Indian conflict in Minnesota. McClellan was restored to command and given a second chance.

14.2d Antietam

When Lee marched north, crossed the Potomac, and advanced into Maryland, he believed that a decisive victory in Maryland could win the state for the Confederacy and influence the Union congressional elections in November to an anti-war stance. Perhaps a decisive victory in Maryland could also bring recognition by, or intervention from, England and thus win the war. Lee's movement into Maryland was fraught with difficulties from the start, however, as Lee was greatly outnumbered (fifty thousand to eight-five thousand), poorly supplied, and exhausted from the Richmond campaigns. Again Lee divided his forces, sending part of his army under Stonewall Jackson to capture Harpers Ferry, which lay along Lee's supply route from the Shenandoah Valley. Lee held the other part of his army on watch in the mountain passes west of Frederick, Maryland.

Union forces under McClellan had a stroke of good luck when they found a copy of Lee's battle plans, wrapped in three cigars, at Frederick—evidently dropped by a Southern officer. McClellan proclaimed, "here is a paper … with which if I cannot whip Bobbie Lee, I will be willing to go home." Even with a copy of Lee's secret orders in his hands—so that the Union general knew exactly what to expect—McClellan did not move quickly or decisively. Twelve thousand of McClellan's men surrendered to Stonewall Jackson's

Confederates at Harper's Ferry on September 15, 1862. McClellan's delay allowed Lee the time he needed to assume a position behind Antietam Creek near Sharpsburg on September 17. McClellan threw his seventy-five thousand men at Lee's forty thousand Confederates (though McClellan, as was his nature, thought the Union was outnumbered). After a supremely hard-fought engagement at Antietam (Sharpsburg), Lee withdrew; it had been the deadliest single-day battle of the war. Lee's forces—bloodied, but not crushed—retreated to the south bank of the Potomac. A total of six thousand men were killed, and seventeen thousand more were wounded in that one day. McClellan's army almost broke through the Confederate lines on a road northeast of Sharpsburg (known afterwards as Bloody Lane); fearing counterattacks from reserves that Lee did not have, however, McClelland held twenty thousand of his troops in reserve. McClellan received reinforcements the next day and Lee did not, but even so McClellan did not renew his attack. The next night, the Confederates retreated back across the Potomac to Virginia.

Although the battle had been a Union victory, in that the Southern offensive was halted and Lee was forced to retreat, the victory was not complete because McClellan failed to press his advantage and allowed Lee's troops to return to Virginia to rebuild. Lincoln again replaced McClellan on November 7—this time with **Ambrose E. Burnside**. Britain and France, who had been considering intervention or recognition of the Confederacy, decided to withhold that recognition. Four days later on September 22, Lincoln issued his preliminary **Emancipation Proclamation**.

At the battle at Antietam Creek a total of six thousand men were killed, and seventeen thousand wounded, in one day. (Wikimedia Commons)

14.2e Fredericksburg

Ambrose E. Burnside was most certainly a more aggressive general than McClellan, but he also proved to be a less-than-brilliant battlefield tactician. In December 1862, Burnside made an unimaginative frontal attack across the Rappahannock at Fredericksburg, Virginia, against prepared Confederate defenses. Fighting the Confederates on ground of their own choosing, Burnside launched his troops on an uphill charge; he sustained terrible losses—more than twice the casualty rate of the Confederates—and was promptly replaced by **Joseph Hooker**. After Lincoln heard the bad news from the battlefield, the president reportedly groaned, "If there is a worse place than hell, I am in it." Other than his failed frontal assault at Fredericksburg, Burnside is perhaps most noteworthy for his distinctive whiskers—from which the term "sideburns" became part of the English language.

Morale in the Union, both among the troops and among the public, reached a new low in the winter of 1862–1863—as did Lincoln's popularity. The army was suffering from high desertion rates, and the bleak outlook is what caused Lincoln to turn to "Fighting Joe" Hooker to lead the troops. Hooker was described as ill-tempered, vindictive, and deviously in favor of a military dictator for the United States. In his letter appointing Hooker to lead the army, Lincoln acknowledged that Hooker favored a dictatorship (while he did not) but said that he was appointing Hooker to lead his army in spite of this fact. Lincoln did, however, believe Hooker to be a bold general—though he cautioned him against "rashness."

14.2f Chancellorsville

Thus, Hooker seemed a man of boldness and decision, in command of 120,000 well-trained troops north of the Rappahannock River, opposite Fredericksburg. In May 1863, in what became known as the battle of Chancellorsville, Hooker crossed the Rappahannock north of Fredericksburg and moved his army toward the town and the Confederate army. After executing an excellent flanking march to maneuver Lee into battle on unfavorable terms, Hooker evidently lost his poise and drew his army back to what he thought was a defensive position in a desolate area of scrub trees known as the "Wilderness." Hooker allowed Jackson's corps to roll up the Union right flank in a surprise attack that rocked the Federals and eventually drove them back across the Rappahannock—in spite of the fact that the Confederates were outnumbered 2 to 1. Although a great Confederate victory, the South paid a fearful price for Chancellorsville. Confederate casualties exceeded twelve thousand, and General Stonewall Jackson was accidentally wounded by his own troops; he died a few days later.

14.2g Gettysburg

Hooker remained in command until Lee launched a second offensive against the North, this time into Pennsylvania. Lee understood that the South would lose in a war of attrition, which favored the North; so he set his sights on scoring a decisive victory in the North that could break the morale of the Union and perhaps bring European intervention and recognition. When Lee escaped from Hooker with seventy-five thousand troops on the northward march, Lincoln again changed commanders, turning this time to George Gordon Meade. By late June 1863, Lee's army had fanned out across southern Pennsylvania in a fifty-mile arc from Harrisburg almost to Baltimore. Meade's army and Lee's army met at Gettysburg, though neither had planned it that way. On July 1, Confederate troops in search of shoes in the town of Gettysburg clashed with a Union cavalry unit west of Gettysburg. Both sides sent out calls for reinforcement, and the two armies converged. For the first three days of July 1863, the South made its supreme effort—and the little town in Pennsylvania became the scene of the greatest battle ever fought in North America. Confederates broke the Union lines on the afternoon of July 1, driving the Union to a

Map 14.4 Fredericksburg to Gettysburg (1862–1863)

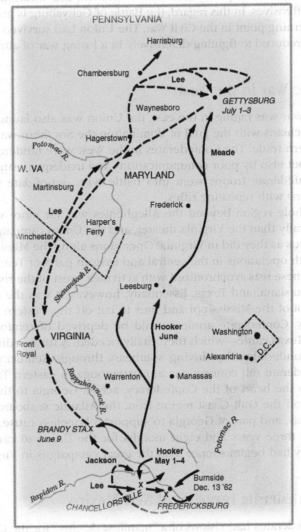

Pickett's Charge

Failed Confederate charge under General George Pickett at Gettysburg that was the turning point in the battle and therefore the war

defensive position on Cemetery Ridge south of town. General Richard Ewell, Stonewall Jackson's successor, judged the Union position too strong to defeat and chose not to attack further as darkness fell on July 1. The next morning, Lee and the Confederates occupied Seminary Ridge, facing Meade to the south on the high ground at Cemetery Ridge. General James Longstreet argued against a frontal assault, instead favoring a maneuver to the south toward Washington, D.C.—in an attempt to get the Union to attack the Confederates when they occupied a strong defensive position. Lee, however, reportedly pointed to the Union lines and said, "the enemy is there, and I am going to attack him there." Across a valley between the two ridges, on July 2, Lee threw his troops against the Union positions in a series of bold attacks on the Union flanks. Though the Union army withstood the attacks, Lee believed that the center of the Union lines might be weak; so on July 3, Lee ordered an assault on the Union center on Cemetery Ridge, where Meade's troops were dug-in with almost a mile of clear vision. After a two-hour Confederate artillery bombardment, in an assault known as **Pickett's Charge**, General George Pickett and fifteen thousand Confederates charged into Union cannon and rifle fire—but Meade's forces were too strong to be dislodged. Pickett's assault was almost successful in that it actually broke the Union lines on the afternoon of July 3, but Union reinforcements drove the Confederates back before they could secure their positions. Approximately half of Pickett's men did not survive, and Lee lost over a third of his forces at Gettysburg overall. Lee realized his mistake and was heard to state, "It's all my fault." Nevertheless, Lee and his decimated army waited for more than a day to receive a counterattack that never came, and then marched south. Meade did not pursue until too late, and ten days after the battle Lee recrossed the Potomac unmolested. The Army of Northern Virginia had still never been driven from a battlefield, but its great offensive power was forever broken. Lee would be able to mount no more Northern offensives. In this regard, the Battle of Gettysburg is generally considered to have been the turning point in the Civil War. The Union had survived its greatest threat, and the South was reduced to fighting defensively in a losing war of attrition.

14.2ḥ The War in the West

While the war was raging in the east, the Union was also launching an offensive west of the Appalachians with the goal of dominating the Southern waterways and thus controlling Southern trade. The Confederates in the West were hindered not only by poor transportation but also by poor communications and inadequate supplies. For instance, many of the Confederate troops went into battle with out-of-date flintlock muskets against Union troops with repeating rifles.

The whole region beyond the Alleghenies was far more vast and more broken up geographically than the Virginia theater, and the Union campaigns in the West never had a single focus as they did in Virginia. Operations along the Mississippi were scarcely coordinated with operations in the central and eastern parts of Tennessee and Kentucky; and neither of these was synchronized with activities "west of the river" in Missouri, Arkansas, most of Louisiana, and Texas. Essentially, however, it was the objective of the Union to gain control of the Mississippi and thus to cut off the western wing of the Confederacy. In this way, Confederate armies would be deprived of reinforcements and supplies—especially Texas cattle—which they vitally needed. A further division of the Confederacy would be undertaken by driving southeast through Kentucky and Tennessee, cutting vital Confederate rail connections at Chattanooga in eastern Tennessee, and continuing thence into the heart of the Confederacy, across Georgia to the sea. Such an operation would cut off the Gulf Coast region from the Atlantic seaboard and leave only Virginia, the Carolinas, and part of Georgia to support a hopeless cause.

It took three years and eight months for the Union to carry out these plans, even though they had begun sooner than the great campaigns in Virginia.

14.2i Confederate Invasion of New Mexico

Some Confederates had visions of a "manifest destiny" for the Confederacy that included expanding the Confederacy across the Mexican cession of the Southwestern United States.

Map 14.5 War in the West (1862)

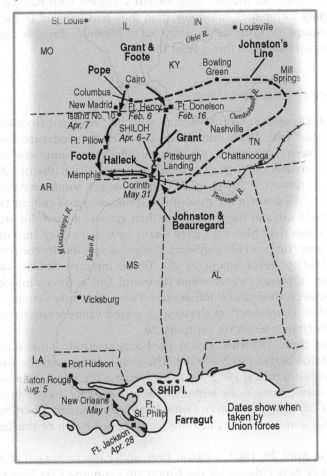

Dates show when taken by Union forces

Some Southerners even envisioned a Confederate slave empire expanding throughout all of Latin America. In furtherance of these grandiose goals, and with the specific objectives of securing the upper Rio Grande Valley (Albuquerque and Santa Fe) for the Confederacy and of establishing a Confederate Pacific port at the Gulf of California at the mouth of the Colorado River (an area that through the twenty-first century remains under Mexican sovereignty), Confederate Colonel John R. Baylor issued a proclamation on August 1, 1861, establishing the "Confederate Territory of Arizona," comprised of present-day New Mexico and Arizona south of the 43° north latitude. Baylor rode west with a Confederate force all the way to Tucson, where he captured the federal garrison there from its unenthusiastic Union defenders. Baylor established a Confederate government in Tucson, and he was made governor of the new Confederate territory.

In January 1862, three regiments of Confederate Texans under H. H. Sibley marched on the upper Rio Grande Valley. They defeated a New Mexican militia and a group of Union army regulars at Valverde in February 1862, thus securing Albuquerque and Santa Fe for the Confederacy. The Confederate expansion was short-lived, however, as a Union regiment of Colorado miners who had marched over the Rocky Mountains in winter defeated the Confederate Texans at Glorieta Pass on March 26–28, forcing the Confederates to retreat all the way back to Texas. Of the 3,700 Confederates who had launched the New Mexico campaign, only 2,000 made it back to Texas—due not only to battlefield losses but also to insufficient food supplies and the harshness of the elements as well.

14.2j Pea Ridge

Before the Union army could march on Tennessee, they believed they had to secure Missouri; consequently, in March 1862, Union troops under General Samuel R. Curtis advanced across

Pea Ridge

Confederate defeat in
Arkansas on March 8, 1862,
that secured Union control of
Missouri

**General
Ulysses S. Grant**

Conqueror of Vicksburg, and
the Union commander for
the duration of the war

**Confederate Forts
Henry and Donelson**

The capture of these two
Confederate forts by the
Union, on February 6 and
February 16, 1863, gave
the Union control of the
Cumberland River.

David Farragut

Captured New Orleans for
the Union on April 29, 1862,
and was rewarded with
the rank of admiral; also
remembered in popular
culture for his order at the
Battle of Mobile Bay on
August 5, 1864, usually
paraphrased: "Damn the
torpedoes, full speed ahead!"

Shiloh

Major battle on
April 6–7, 1862, that resulted
in twenty-three thousand
combined Union and
Confederate casualties and
is generally credited with
destroying the notion that
the war was a romantic test
of courage

Missouri into northwestern Arkansas where they engaged and defeated sixteen thousand Confederates under General Earl Van Dorn at **Pea Ridge**. The Confederate army included three regiments of American Indians from Indian Territory, who had joined up with the Confederates hoping for greater autonomy than they had enjoyed in the Union. Though Curtis' campaign swept the Confederate army out of Missouri, the state remained a hotbed of guerrilla activity and violence throughout the war.

14.2k Forts Henry and Donelson

In February 1862, **Ulysses S. Grant**—a man who had resigned from the army in 1854 as a failure and had later been reinstated—captured **Confederate Forts Henry and Donelson** (in western Tennessee), which controlled the Tennessee and Cumberland rivers. Unlike the streams of Virginia, which cut across the paths of advancing armies, each of these rivers flowed in a U-shaped course from the southern Appalachians southward into northern Alabama (in the case of the Tennessee) and central Tennessee (in the case of the Cumberland), and then, reversing their course, almost due north to the Ohio River. Control of these river highways gave Grant easy entry deep into the South.

The Union's new "timberclad" gunboats, designed specifically for river warfare, took out Fort Henry without involvement by the Union infantry. At Fort Donelson on the Cumberland River, however, twenty-seven thousand Union forces under General Grant clashed with seventeen thousand Confederates. Grant famously demanded the "immediate and unconditional surrender" of thirteen thousand Confederate troops who, lacking options, agreed to Grant's terms on February 16.

As a result of these victories, Union gunboats controlled the Tennessee River to Alabama and the Cumberland to Nashville. The Union army used the rivers to transport its troops, and on February 25, 1862, Nashville became the first Southern state capitol to surrender. Confederate army units withdrew from Kentucky and Tennessee to Corinth, Mississippi. From Corinth, the western Confederate commander, Albert Sydney Johnston, planned to attack Grant's army at Pittsburg Landing just north of the Tennessee border with Mississippi.

Meanwhile, on April 29, 1862, a Union fleet under the command of **David Farragut** captured the port of New Orleans for the Union after running past forts south of the city. Besides securing and occupying New Orleans, Farragut proceeded to blockade the Gulf of Mexico and control traffic on the lower Mississippi. Farragut's exploits were so important to the Union that, in 1866, Congress created the rank of admiral specifically for Farragut.

14.2l Shiloh

On April 6, Johnston and forty thousand Confederates attacked thirty-five thousand Union troops under General Grant near a church called **Shiloh**. The attack caught Grant and his men off-guard. Many of Grant's men were half-dressed, some were asleep, and others were brewing their morning coffee. Grant's army was pushed back, but was holding its ground by the end of the first day. The Confederates lost Johnston, who bled to death from a shot to the leg. Grant received reinforcements overnight from a Union army of twenty-five thousand under the command of General Don Carlos Buell; and the Union counterattacked the next day, driving the Confederates back to Corinth, Mississippi.

A total of thirteen thousand Union and ten thousand Confederate troops were lost at Shiloh—more deaths than in all the battles of the American Revolution, the War of 1812, and the War with Mexico combined. A full day after the battle, 90 percent of the wounded were still lying on the battlefield in heavy rain. Many of the wounded died of exposure, and some of them actually drowned in the downpour. The massive casualty rates and gruesome battlefield proved to citizens in both the North and South that the war was not to be viewed as simply a romantic test of courage. Even Grant later stated that after Shiloh he "gave up all idea of saving the Union except by complete conquest." For Grant, personally, the high casualties and the fact that he had been caught by surprise—plus the fact that he had allowed the battered Confederate army to escape—damaged his reputation and temporarily cost him his command.

After Shiloh, however, Union victories continued in the West. The Union armies under the general command of Henry W. Halleck expelled the Confederates from Corinth—the hub of several important railroads—by the end of May, while the Union gunboat fleet wiped out the Confederate fleet at Memphis on June 6. Moving north from New Orleans, Farragut captured Baton Rouge and Natchez before meeting up with Union gunboats from the North at **Vicksburg**. The Union fleet, however, was unable to subdue the heavily fortified Confederate position at Vicksburg; even so, the series of Northern victories after Shiloh had many in the North believing that the war was won in the West by the summer of 1862. Union victories in the spring of 1862 had brought over fifty thousand square miles of Confederate territory under Union control.

However the new Confederate commander in the West, General Braxton Bragg, consolidated his troops in Chattanooga with plans to launch an offensive to retake Tennessee and Kentucky in the winter of 1862. Bragg and the Confederates were countered by a Union army under the command of Don Carlos Buell, and later William Rosecrans, whose goal was to capture Chattanooga. The Confederates pushed north into Kentucky and had almost reached the Ohio River by September, but they were defeated at Perryville on October 8 and forced to retreat back to Tennessee. After several months of maneuvering, the two armies clashed again on December 31, 1862, at Murfreesboro (or Stones River), where the Confederates were again forced to retreat and abandon their Tennessee offensive.

Problems for the Union in the western theater persisted, however. Occupying and administering vast areas of territory in the South proved difficult and costly as soldiers for occupation had to be drawn from combat forces elsewhere. Furthermore, Union soldiers in the West were far from the Union infrastructure and at the end of long supply lines. The occupying Union soldiers therefore dangled in front of Confederate guerrillas as easy targets. During the last half of 1862, Southern cavalrymen under Nathan Bedford Forrest and John Hunt Morgan staged repeated guerrilla raids and sabotage in which they burned bridges, blew up tunnels, destroyed railroad tracks, and stole Union supplies. The Southern guerrillas in the West very quickly reinforced the lessons learned by the British in the American Revolution: It is easier to defeat an inferior enemy in a frontal assault than to occupy and control a vast hostile country thousands of miles from home.

14.2m Vicksburg

During the winter of 1862–1863, Grant began a campaign against the Confederate stronghold at Vicksburg, where towering bluffs command the Mississippi. Deep in enemy country, Vicksburg was rendered almost impregnable by vast swamps, a succession of steep hills, and the river itself. After making a series of unsuccessful moves against this natural fortress, Grant at last hit on the bold and unorthodox plan of moving down the west side of the river, crossing below Vicksburg, abandoning his lines of communication, and living off of the country during a final drive against the Confederate defenses. In furtherance of his plan, Grant first ran his ironclad river fleet downriver past the Confederate guns overlooking the river from Vicksburg. Grant's troops then marched down the Mississippi's west bank to a point forty miles south of Vicksburg, where they were ferried across the river into the state of Mississippi. Grant then deceptively marched his army east toward Jackson, Mississippi, instead of marching directly to Vicksburg. Grant's purpose was to scatter the Confederate forces, which were concentrated at Vicksburg, by making it appear that Jackson, the Mississippi state capitol, was his primary goal. Grant defeated the Confederate army at Jackson commanded by General Joseph Johnston and then turned his full attention toward Vicksburg. Grant also sought to destroy the Southern rails so that they would be hindered in attacking him from the rear when he turned his forces toward Vicksburg. During the first three weeks of May 1863, Grant fought and won five engagements with the Confederates in Mississippi and surrounded the Confederate troops at Vicksburg—pinning them between the Union gunboats on the river and his army to their east. Grant launched assaults on the Confederate lines on May 19 and May 22, but was repulsed. Grant then settled down to lay an old fashioned siege to the city with his army that now numbered over seventy thousand. After more than a month of siege warfare, the Confederates were running out of supplies, and on

Vicksburg

Major Confederate stronghold on the Mississippi River, captured by the Union under General Ulysses S. Grant on July 4, 1863

BVT Lab

Visit www.BVTLab.com to explore the student resources available for this chapter.

In the battle of Vicksburg, General Ulysses S. Grant and his Union army crossed the Mississippi River and drove the Confederate army of General John C. Pemberton into the fortress city of Vicksburg, Mississippi. Pemberton surrendered an army of about thirty thousand men—the largest that has ever been captured in North America. (Wikimedia Commons)

Chickamauga and Chattanooga

The battle of September 19–20, 1863, at which combined casualties were thirty-six thousand—the most of any battle at that point except for Gettysburg—and after which the Union was forced to retreat from Chickamauga

July 4, 1863—the day on which Lee began his uncontested withdrawal from Gettysburg—another Confederate general, John C. Pemberton, surrendered an army of about thirty thousand men at Vicksburg. It was the largest force to ever be captured in North America. The man to whom he surrendered was Ulysses S. Grant, and the event marked the culmination of a series of campaigns in the West which had been much more decisive in their results than the eastern campaigns. After the battle, an impressed Abraham Lincoln stated, "Grant is my man, and I am his the rest of the war." After over two years of searching, Lincoln had finally found his general. Five days later, the Confederate garrison at Port Hudson (two hundred miles south of Vicksburg) also surrendered to the Union army, giving the Union control of the entire Mississippi.

14.2n Chickamauga and Chattanooga

After the battle of Murfreesboro (Stones River), lasting from December 31, 1862 to January 3, 1863, William Rosecrans' Union Army of the Cumberland and Braxton Bragg's Confederate Army of Tennessee maneuvered against each other for six months without major engagements. Finally, on June 24, 1863, Rosecrans launched an offensive designed to dislodge the Confederates from Eastern Tennessee, resulting in decisive victories at **Chickamauga and Chattanooga**. Rosecrans' offensive forced the Confederates to retreat to Chattanooga. Rosecrans paused to take on supplies, and then connected with another Union army commanded by Ambrose Burnside and drove the Confederates out of Knoxville on September 2, and Chattanooga on September 9, thus severing the South's only direct east-west railway. With the capture of Chattanooga, the Union was in position to launch an invasion of Georgia.

On September 19, however, the Confederates counterattacked Rosecrans army in the valley of Chickamauga Creek. Over the next two days of fierce fighting, the two armies suffered thirty-six thousand combined casualties—the most of any battle up to that point except for Gettysburg. On September 20, Confederates under James Longstreet broke the Union lines and forced a segment of the Union army to retreat to Chattanooga.

After the battle Lincoln replaced Rosecrans, whom the president described as "confused and stunned like a duck hit on the head," with George H. Thomas, who gained the nickname "Rock of Chickamauga" for his firm stand against the Confederate assault. Lincoln then reinforced Thomas at Chattanooga with two Union armies from Virginia under "Fightin' Joe" Hooker and William Tecumseh Sherman. Lincoln also ordered General Grant to Chattanooga and appointed him to take overall command of the Union forces. By November 24, the tide had turned again in the Union's favor. On that day, Hooker's troops drove Confederates from Lookout Mountain; the next day, Union forces broke the Confederate lines at Missionary Ridge in Georgia, east of Chattanooga.

14.20 Grant Takes Command

In March 1864, Lincoln brought Grant east to serve as general in chief and to take personal charge of the Army of the Potomac (Meade was not removed but was under Grant's command). By this time the Confederacy, outnumbered from the beginning, was fearfully handicapped by the loss of men who could not be replaced, as Union losses could. Grant, recognizing this handicap, settled upon a plan that while less brilliant than his operations in the West, was no less decisive. By steadily extending his flanks, he forced the Confederacy to extend also and to make its lines very thin. By continuing pressure, he gave his adversaries no rest. The Confederates no longer had the manpower to launch invasions into the North in an effort to score the decisive victory that would cause the North to quit or the Europeans to intervene—but the Southerners could still fight a guerrilla war of attrition on their own soil as

Pictured is General Ulysses S. Grant. Impressed with the general, Abraham Lincoln stated, "Grant is my man, and I am his the rest of the war." (Wikimedia Commons)

the Americans had done against the British in the American Revolution in the hopes of eventually exhausting the Union's will to sacrifice its children in the interest of stopping the secession. In fact, by the summer of 1864, Lincoln's popularity may have been at an all-time low. The Union Democrats nominated **General George B. McClellan** on a peace platform. There was a strong possibility that Lincoln and the Unionists would lose the election of 1864 and that Lincoln's successor would end the war to satisfy the popular will, and thus the Union would be lost and the secession successful.

In the spring of 1864, Grant placed himself in command in Virginia and **General William Tecumseh Sherman** in Georgia. Grant opted for an all-out offensive on all fronts, so that the South could not shift troops to where the fighting was the hottest. Lee resisted with immense skill, attacking Grant in the Wilderness in early May where Union artillery and superiority in numbers were greatly mitigated. In the **Battle of the Tangled Wilderness**, the Confederates inflicted eighteen thousand casualties on the Union, while suffering twelve thousand themselves. Many soldiers were burned to death by fires started by exploding shells in the dry Virginia brush.

Grant, however, simply moved his army to the east toward **Spotsylvania Court House**, ten miles closer to Richmond. Lee blocked the road junction between Grant's army and Richmond, which resulted in another eighteen thousand Union soldiers and twelve thousand Confederates being killed, wounded, or captured in between May 8 and 19, 1864. Ahead of his time, Lee engaged in the trench warfare tactics that would dominate WWI some fifty years later.

Repulsed at Spotsylvania, Grant moved south in an effort to outflank Lee's forces; but Lee confronted him near the crossroads inn of **Cold Harbor**, ten miles northeast of Richmond. Grant opted for an assault on Lee's entrenched forces at Cold Harbor on June 3, only to lose seven thousand men in less than an hour. Grant again tried to outflank Lee and moved his army to the James River at Petersburg, twenty miles south of Richmond. Lee again blocked Grant's troops; and in four days of fighting from June 15 to 18, 1864, Grant's forces suffered another eleven thousand casualties.

Map 14.6 War in the East (1864)

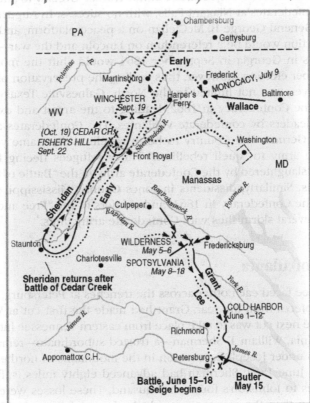

General George B. McClellan

Union General who had been twice sacked by Lincoln for his lack of aggressiveness, but was chosen to campaign for president on a peace platform in 1864

General William Tecumseh Sherman

Union general who captured Atlanta and marched from Atlanta to Savannah, Georgia, destroying everything in his path while waging "total war"

Battle of the Tangled Wilderness

The battle of May 5–7, 1864, at which Confederates inflicted eighteen thousand casualties on the Union, while suffering twelve thousand themselves

Spotsylvania Court House

Lee blocked the road junction between Grant's army and Richmond with the result that another eighteen thousand Union soldiers and twelve thousand Confederates were either killed, wounded, or captured in the days between May 8–19, 1864.

Cold Harbor

The site of one of General Grant's worst defeats where Grant lost eighteen thousand men between June 3 and June 18—and gained no advantage

Grant sacrificed men so freely between May 5 and June 18, 1864, in the Virginia campaign that his losses (sixty-five thousand) almost equaled the total number of men in Lee's army and earned Grant the disparaging title, "Butcher Grant." During the same six weeks, the South had suffered thirty-seven thousand casualties, however—a number they could ill-afford to lose. Lee was winning the battles, but Grant was winning the war.

Unable to break the Confederate lines, Grant finally settled down for a siege along the Petersburg-Richmond front like he had done at Vicksburg. With Lee no longer mobile, it was only a question of time; Lee held on for nine long months, during which time Richmond remained the Confederate capitol.

Meanwhile, Confederates also thwarted other Union efforts in Virginia. Union general Benjamin Butler attempted an attack up the James River against Richmond but was stopped by a rag-tag Confederate army under General Beauregard. A Union offensive in the Shenandoah Valley was stopped at Lynchburg by Stonewall Jackson's old troops under the command of Jubal Early. Early then led a daring raid across the Potomac almost to Washington, D.C., on July 11–12 before being driven back to Virginia.

14.2p Presidential Election and the Peace Movement

With the Southerners reaching the outskirts of Washington, the high casualties, and the fact that Richmond was still in Southern hands, the mood of the public in the North was decidedly antiwar and anti-Lincoln. If an election had been held in August 1864, many historians believe that Lincoln would have lost to an anti-war candidate and the fate of the United States might have been forever altered. Lincoln told a friend, in August, "I am going to be beaten, and unless some great change takes place, badly beaten." Democrats called for Lincoln to drop the issue of emancipation and negotiate peace with the South with the understanding that slavery could continue if the South would return to the Union, but Lincoln refused.

Union casualties in just three months (May–July) of 1864 had reached a staggering 110,000—double the casualty rate for any other three-month period of the war—and newspaper headlines boldly shouted to "STOP THE WAR!" Lincoln understood the public sentiments and even sent New York Tribune editor Horace Greeley to attempt to negotiate peace with the Confederates at Niagara Falls, with no success. In August, the Democratic Party nominated General George B. McClellan on a peace platform, and it appeared that the November election would be a referendum on Lincoln and the war—and that Lincoln would lose. Events in Georgia in September 1864 would shift the mood of the public before the November election, however, thus sealing the preservation of the Union.

Dissent, however, was not limited to the North. Gainesville Texas announced their withdrawal from the Confederacy in 1862, leading to the arrest and execution of forty-four of the rebel leaders by confederate vigilantes. The Confederates also declared six counties in Texas German Hill Country to be in rebellion that same year and sent the Texas Confederate army to "quell rebellion." Thirty refugees fleeing for Mexico were tracked down and slaughtered by the Confederate army in the "Battle of the Nueces" near Brackettville, Texas. Similarly, dissidents in Jones County, Mississippi, announced their withdrawal from the Confederacy in 1863, and soldiers of the "Free and Sovereign State of Jones" fought several skirmishes with Confederate army units.

14.2q The Fall of Atlanta

While Grant and Lee faced each other across the trenches at Petersburg, the Confederacy was being cut to pieces from the rear. Grant had made the first cut at Vicksburg on the Mississippi, and the next cut was to take place from eastern Tennessee into Georgia. When Grant left for Virginia, William T. Sherman—a trusted subordinate—remained to face the Confederate forces under Joseph E. Johnston in the mountains of northern Georgia.

By the end of June 1864, Sherman had advanced eighty miles, suffering seventeen thousand casualties to Johnston's fourteen thousand. These losses were immense, to be sure, but far less so than the carnage wrought by Lee and Grant in Virginia. Johnston, a "retreating general" but a resourceful obstructionist, blocked and delayed Sherman

Map 14.7 Final Campaigns of the Civil War (1864–1865)

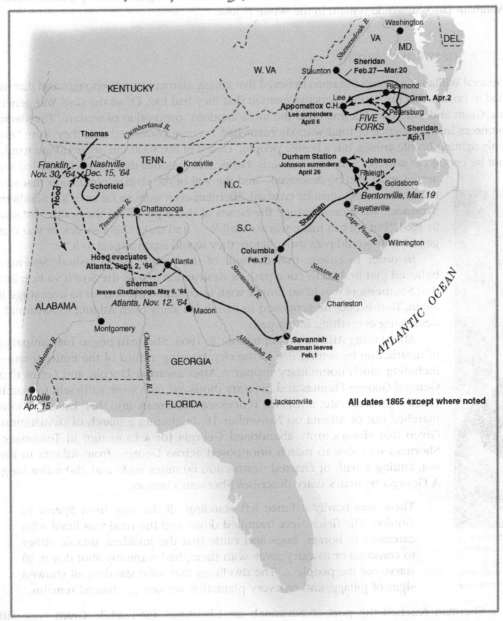

at every step, all the way to Atlanta. At Peachtree Creek just outside Atlanta, however, Confederate President Jefferson Davis removed Johnston because of his unwillingness to take the offensive; John B. Hood was put in his place. Hood made the mistake of challenging Sherman in a series of direct attacks at Peachtree Creek and Ezra Church, and was so badly defeated (suffering fifteen thousand casualties to six thousand for Sherman) that he had to settle down into a purely defensive position by July 28.

After a month of stalemate, Sherman moved to attack the last rail link into Atlanta from the south at Jonesboro on August 31. On September 1, Sherman's men captured the railroad, and Hood abandoned Atlanta. Sherman moved his troops into the symbolic city on September 2. The news that Atlanta had fallen sent shockwaves throughout the South and waves of jubilation throughout the North. Southerners had believed that Lincoln would lose the election in November and his successor would quickly negotiate an end to the war that would result in Confederate independence and the retention of Southern slavery. The fall of Atlanta, however, shifted public sentiments in the North back in favor of Lincoln and his

Sherman's March

General William Tecumseh
Sherman's destructive march
from Atlanta to Savanna
where he destroyed a swath
through Georgia sixty miles
wide

policies of emancipation and military subjugation of the South. To most Northerners, the fall of Atlanta proved that the North had won. Similarly, the fall of Atlanta was a devastating blow to the morale of the South. Many Southerners now understood that they had lost; they also understood that the man who had waged the irrepressible war against slavery and the South, Abraham Lincoln, would remain in the White House.

14.2r Sherman's March

General William Tecumseh Sherman believed that taking Atlanta was not enough, and that he had to ensure that the Southerners understood that they had lost. Of all the Civil War generals, Grant and especially Sherman had the most "modern" conception of warfare. They were pioneers in the practice of total war. Sherman had become convinced that they were "not only fighting hostile armies, but a hostile people." Defeat of the Southern armies alone would not be enough to win this war. The railroads, farms, and factories that fed and supplied the armies must also be destroyed—and the will of the civilian population that sustained the armies must be crushed. Sherman even went so far as to kill Southern livestock. "We cannot change the hearts of those people of the South," he said in 1864, "but we can make war so terrible … and make them so sick of war that generations would pass away before they would again appeal to it."

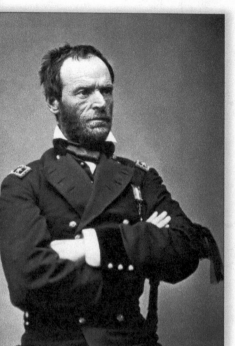

General William Tecumseh Sherman led his army across Georgia, burning, killing off livestock, and leaving a swath of destruction 60 miles wide and 280 miles long. (Wikimedia Commons)

In order to ensure that the will of the people was crushed, Sherman believed that he had to cut a path of destruction across the South so horrible that Southerners would no longer wish to continue the war, or to ever wage it again. To this end, he proposed to march his army from Atlanta to Savannah, destroying everything in his path.

After taking Atlanta on September 2, 1864, Sherman began his campaign of destruction by setting fire to the city, burning a third of the entire town—including much nonmilitary property. After assuring Lincoln and Grant that General George Thomas and his sixty thousand men were sufficient to match Hood's Confederate army in Tennessee, Sherman and his Union troops marched out of Atlanta on November 16, beginning a march of devastation. Given that Hood's army abandoned Georgia for a campaign in Tennessee, Sherman was able to march unopposed across Georgia from Atlanta to the sea, cutting a path of charred destruction 60 miles wide and 280 miles long. A Georgia woman's diary describes Sherman's impact:

> There was hardly a fence left standing all the way from Sparta to Gordon. The fields were trampled down and the road was lined with carcasses of horses, hogs and cattle that the invaders, unable either to consume or to carry away with them, had wantonly shot down, to starve out the people … The dwellings that were standing all showed signs of pillage, and on every plantation we saw … charred remains.

Sherman reached the port of Savannah on Christmas 1864 while Grant was still outside Petersburg. The march of his army from Atlanta to the sea not only destroyed Confederate resources but also functioned as a form of psychological warfare. "It is a demonstration to the world," wrote Sherman, "that we have a power which Jefferson Davis cannot resist. This may not be war but rather statesmanship."

14.2s Destruction of Hood's Army of Tennessee

Hood's attempt to retake Tennessee rather than engage Sherman in Georgia turned out little better for the Southerners than **Sherman's March**. On November 30, 1864, the Confederates attacked the Union army at Franklin—twenty miles south of Nashville—but were badly defeated. Hood then attempted to move on to Nashville, where his army was almost wiped out by Union troops under General George Thomas. Of the fifty thousand men under his command in July, only fifteen thousand remained after the defeat at Nashville. With no real army left to lead and a record only of defeat, Hood resigned in January 1865. The South's western army, for all practical purposes, was no more.

14.2t Sherman's March in the Carolinas

Appomattox
Courthouse in Virginia where Robert E. Lee surrendered to Ulysses S. Grant, April 9, 1865

At the end of January 1865, Sherman's army of "total warriors" moved north from Savannah into South Carolina, destroying everything in their path as they had in Georgia. Sherman left even less standing in Columbia, South Carolina, than he had in Atlanta. Sherman then continued his march all the way into North Carolina where he defeated a Confederate force under Joseph E. Johnston. Just as Sherman had intended, Southern morale was effectively destroyed everywhere he went. One South Carolina physician wrote, "All is gloom, despondency, and inactivity … Our army is demoralized and the people panic stricken. To fight longer seems to be madness."

14.2u Appomattox

From this time forward, the South was completely fragmented and the Confederacy's cause was hopeless. But Johnston, having returned to his command in the southeast, held together a force that retreated across the Carolinas, with Sherman pursuing and wreaking havoc in South Carolina as he went. Lee, meanwhile, held against steadily increasing odds against him at Petersburg. By April 1865, however, the inevitable defeat could be put off no longer. Petersburg fell and Richmond was evacuated. As the Confederates fled their capitol, they set fire to all of the military stores they could not carry—with the result that the fires spread out of control and destroyed more of Richmond than Sherman had destroyed of Atlanta or Columbia. Lee and his army headed west, hoping to join the remnants of Johnston's army in North Carolina, but the Union army under Philip Sheridan cut them off at **Appomattox**, ninety miles from Petersburg, on April 8. The next morning, Lee realized that his position against the superior Union army was hopeless. Lee stated, "There is nothing left for me to do, but to go and see General Grant, and I would rather die a thousand deaths."

General Robert E. Lee met Lt. General Ulysses S. Grant at a farmhouse near the Appomattox Court House. Upon realizing that the Union cavalry was backed up by two corps of infantry, Lee had no choice but to surrender the Army of Northern Virginia to Grant. (Wikipedia Commons)

Lee met Grant on April 9 at a farmhouse near Appomattox Court House. In a moving scene, Lee surrendered the Army of Northern Virginia to Grant, who accorded generous terms and told his troops not to cheer because, he said, "the rebels are our countrymen again." Southern leaders were not arrested, and Jefferson Davis was not to be "hanged from a sour apple tree" as Union newspapers had suggested. Instead, Southerners were to merely lay down their arms and go home. After Lee's surrender, General Johnston also surrendered at Greensboro, North Carolina, before the end of the month; and the Confederate government, which had fled south after the fall of Petersburg, simply evaporated.

14.3 The War Behind the Lines

14.3a The Problems of the Confederacy

Writers on the Civil War have piled up a vast literature—one of the largest bodies of literature on any historical subject—detailing the military aspects of the war: the battles and leaders, the campaigns and maneuvers, the strategies and tactics. This military record, however, does not fully explain the outcome of the war. In terms of strategy and tactics, the Confederate performance equaled that of the Union, and on the Virginia front surpassed it until the last year of the war. The final result was registered on the battlefield, but the basic factors that caused the Confederate defeat lay behind the lines. Essentially, the Confederacy failed to solve the problems of organizing its society and its economy for war. It faced these problems in a particularly difficult form; and when it proved unable to solve them, it went down in defeat.

One basic handicap of the Confederacy lay in the fact that, while the North had a balanced agricultural and industrial economy that was invigorated by war, the Southern economy was based primarily on cotton production, which was dislocated and almost paralyzed by the war. In the North, war stimulated employment; and while wages failed to keep pace with inflation, civilian morale was generally high except among the underpaid urban poor. In the South, economic conditions deteriorated so badly that what may be called economic morale declined even while fighting morale remained good. During the spring of 1863, "bread riots" occurred in Richmond and several other Southern cities. Indeed, Drew Gilpin Faust has argued that because women's interests were so little represented in the way the South publicly defined the war's meaning, Southern women lost heart and in so doing contributed substantially to the collapse of morale.

Essentially, the Confederacy—with its rural, agricultural society—needed two things. First, it needed access to the products of European (especially British) industries. Second, it needed to stimulate production of food, of horses, and of strategic supplies within the South. Ultimately, it was unable to meet most of those needs.

In order to be able to draw on British industry, the Confederacy needed to have buying power in the European market and to be able to ship goods freely to and fro across the Atlantic. But once war broke out, Lincoln proclaimed a blockade, which meant that federal naval vessels would try to seize the merchant vessels of any neutral country bringing goods to Confederate ports.

Southerners thought that the blockade would not work, partly because there were too few Union ships to enforce it—but even more so because they believed in what has been called the "King Cotton delusion." They were firmly convinced that their cotton was an absolute economic necessity to Britain because textiles were the heart of British industry. Without cotton, they were sure this industry would be prostrated. Britain's factories would stand idle, and its workers would be unemployed and would literally starve. When this started happening, the British government would decide to intervene to regain access to Southern cotton. The British navy, which still dominated the seas, would break the blockade.

Southerners were so confident in this idea that they were quite willing to see the British supply of cotton cut off for a while. In the first months of the blockade, while it was still largely ineffective, they deliberately kept their cotton at home rather than sending a part of it abroad to be held in British warehouses for later sale—a move that would have given them funds for the later purchase of supplies. Unfortunately for the South, they had miscalculated; the bumper crops of the previous two years had produced such a surplus of cotton that British manufacturers were able to operate without interruption for nearly a year after the war broke out.

14.36 The Importance of Sea Power

For this and other reasons, Southern faith in cotton ultimately proved to be a fallacy. Britain increased its supplies of cotton from Egypt and India. Also, British antislavery sentiment generated strong resistance in Parliament to taking steps that would help the Confederacy. Britain was also pleased to see America adopting a doctrine of international law concerning the right of blockade, which it had always advocated and which was bound to be favorable to a nation with large naval power. But most of all, British industry was not paralyzed because Northern wartime purchases stimulated it. Britain, as a neutral, enjoyed an economic boom from supplying war materials to the Union—a boom very similar to those the United States later enjoyed in 1914–1917 and 1939–1941 as a neutral supplying war materials to Britain.

Consequently, Britain and France (which was following Britain's lead) never did give diplomatic recognition to the Confederate government, although they did recognize the existence of a state of war in which they would be neutral. This meant that they would treat Confederate naval vessels as warships and not as pirates.

The British recognition of belligerency was much resented in the United States. But in fact, the real danger for the Union cause lay in the possibility of diplomatic recognition of the Confederacy—which would probably have resulted in efforts by the British to break the blockade. Such efforts would, in turn, have led to war with Britain. Yet this recognition, for which the Confederacy waited so anxiously, never came.

In November 1861, Confederate hopes were high when an eager Union naval officer, Charles Wilkes, stopped the British ship *Trent* on the high seas and took off two Confederate envoys to Britain, James Mason and John Slidell. Britain, at this point, actually prepared to fight—and an emergency British cabinet meeting demanded a formal apology to the British flag, reparations, and the release of Mason and Slidell. The British then put their navy on alert and sent eleven thousand troops to Canada, who departed England with a band playing "Dixie." President Lincoln, however, wisely admitted the error and set the envoys free, thus avoiding the possibility of war with England. Meanwhile, the blockade steadily grew tighter. One Confederate port after another was sealed off. Small Confederate vessels, built for speed and based in the islands of the Bahamas, continued to delight the South by running the blockade and bringing in cargoes with high value in proportion to their bulk. Even so, their volume was small; they did not, in any sense, provide the flow of goods that the Confederacy so vitally needed.

In addition to depending on British naval might, the Confederacy made two important efforts to establish sea power of its own. To begin with, it fitted out the first, large ironclad vessel ever to put to sea. A powerful steam frigate, the U.S.S. *Merrimac,* which the federals had scuttled in the Norfolk Navy Yard, was raised, renamed the *Virginia,* covered with armor plate, and sent out in March, 1862—an iron giant against the wooden vessels of the Union navy. In its first day at sea it destroyed two large Union vessels with ease.

The entire Union navy appeared to be in acute danger, and there was panic in Northern coastal cities. However, the Union had been preparing a metal-clad vessel of its own—a small craft that lay low in the water, with a revolving gun turret. The *Monitor,* as it was called, challenged the *Virginia* on March 9, 1862. The historic battle between the **Merrimac** and the **Monitor** ended in a draw, but with *Monitor* class vessels the Union navy was again safe.

The Confederacy's second major endeavor at sea was to buy vessels and equipment in England. Unarmed ships built in England by private companies were sent to the Azores Islands, outside of British Sovereignty, and outfitted with weaponry to produce fighting ships without violating Britain's neutrality. Such vessels could then raid merchant vessels flying the Union flag.

There were several of these raiders, the most famous of which was the *Alabama*. This great marauder, commanded by Admiral Raphael Semmes, roamed the seas for two years, from Newfoundland to Singapore, capturing sixty-two merchant ships (most of which were burned, after careful attention to the safety of their crews and passengers). It also sank the U.S.S. *Hatteras* in a major naval battle. It was at last cornered and sunk off Cherbourg, France, by the U.S.S. *Kearsarge,* but its career had made the American flag so unsafe on the high seas that prohibitive insurance costs caused more than seven hundred American vessels to transfer to British registry. The American merchant marine never again during the war attained the place in the world's carrying trade that it had held before the *Alabama* put to sea.

Pictured is the USS Monitor *versus the CSS* Virginia *in the Civil War's Battle of Hampton Roads on March 9, 1862. (Wikimedia Commons)*

The Confederacy sought to have additional raiders built in British shipyards; and two immensely formidable vessels—the Laird rams—were actually constructed. There were vigorous protests from Charles Francis Adams, the American minister to England, however; and the British were aware that, in spite of technicalities, this was really a violation of neutrality. The British did not desire war with the Union. With this in mind, the British government purchased the ships from the private contractors who had built them at a higher price than what had been paid by the Confederates in September 1863. After this the Confederate cause was lost at sea as well as on land, and the federal blockade tightened like a noose to strangle the Confederacy economically.

Andersonville Prison

Notorious Confederate prison where sanitation was poor, disease was rampant, and thirteen thousand prisoners died during the war

Henry Wirz

Commander at Andersonville Prison, the only Confederate soldier executed by the Union after the war

14.3c Prisoners of War

The issue of prisoners of war was one of the bitterest of the war, especially in the North, because the conditions in Southern prison camps were notoriously deplorable. After all, if Southern soldiers in the field had insufficient rations, what could one expect for Northern POWs in Southern prison camps? In 1862, the two sides had solved the problem by agreeing to the exchange of prisoners captured in battle, thus eliminating the need for large, long-term POW camps. This all changed, however, when the Union began enlisting former slaves in its army. The Confederate government then announced that it would refuse to treat former slaves in Union uniforms as legitimate soldiers and would execute them when captured, along with their white Union officers for the crime of fomenting slave insurrections.

In reality, the Southerners did not implement the official policy, and Lincoln warned that he would retaliate against Confederate POWs held in the North if they id. Nevertheless, Confederate troops did sometimes murder black Union soldiers and their white commanders on the battlefield when they tried to surrender. Other captured black soldiers were returned to slavery or put into forced labor for the Confederate army. Because of these practices, Lincoln suspended the exchange of prisoners in 1863 until the Confederates agreed to treat white and black prisoners alike. The South, of course, refused, leading to the growth of large POW camps on both sides with squalid conditions, especially in the South. Of all Union POWs held by the South, 16 percent died while 12 percent of the Confederates held by the North also died.

The most notorious POW camp on either side was the Confederate's **Andersonville Prison**, commanded by **Henry Wirz**—the only person executed by the Union after the war. Andersonville was a stockade with no cover that held thirty-three thousand Union prisoners by the end of the war. Altogether, thirteen thousand Union soldiers died at Andersonville at a rate of one hundred per day. The Southerners lacked the manpower to tend to all of the bodies, with the result that an entire range of vermin invaded the prison. It is said that the ground essentially moved at Andersonville with all of the rats, roaches, flies, maggots, etc. that crawled amid the rotting flesh and human waste. The horrors of Andersonville would remain a symbol to the North of Southern barbarism for decades after the war.

It should be mentioned, however, that treatment of the civilian populations by the marauding armies was extremely mild by war standards. Although much Southern property was destroyed—especially during Sherman's March—rape, murder, and the general terrorizing of civilians were less common. Although Northerners had sworn that they would execute Jefferson Davis, when he was finally captured in May 1865, he was imprisoned on charges of treason and murder instead, and was eventually released in 1867 and never brought to trial.

14.3d Economic Failures of the South

Meanwhile, on the home front, the Confederacy failed economically because it was caught between the need to stimulate production and the need to keep down prices and control inflation. The Southern government began with few financial assets other than land and slaves, neither of which could be readily transformed into negotiable currency. It faced a dilemma. It could encourage production by buying goods in the open market at an uncontrolled price, in which case inflation would mushroom. Or it could control inflation by a system of requisitioning goods for its armies at arbitrarily fixed prices, in which case production would be discouraged rather than stimulated. In addition, help in reducing this problem would have required a program of heavy taxation, by which the government would take back the inflationary dollars that had been spent. But the Confederacy was afraid to use its taxing power. It raised less than 5 percent of its revenue from taxes—a smaller proportion than any other nation in a modern war. Its bond drives to raise funds by borrowing also fell short of hopes.

The South's main source of money was the printing press—the most inflationary method of all. Prices rose by 9,000 percent in the four years of war. Goods grew scarcer while money grew more plentiful. It was grimly said that at the beginning of the war people took their money to market in a purse and brought their goods home in a basket, but that by the end they took the money in a basket and brought their purchases home in a purse.

In short, the Confederacy died of economic starvation—an insufficiency of goods. Its government was too weak to cope with the nearly insoluble economic problems the war had caused. President Jefferson Davis was a bureaucrat who thought in legalistic rather than in dynamic terms. He was not an innovator, but rather a conservative miscast as a revolutionist. The state governments also competed against the Confederate government for the control of manpower and supplies. They insisted upon their sovereign status so strenuously that it has been said that the Confederacy was born of states' rights and died of states' rights.

The best chance the Confederacy ever had—and it was perhaps a fairly good one—was to win a short war before the results of economic malnutrition set in. Once that failed, the cause was hopeless. A few Confederates, like Josiah Gorgas in the Ordinance Department, improvised brilliantly—and others did so desperately. But in a country where a vitally necessary rail line could be laid only by tearing up the rails somewhere else and re-laying them, a long war against a dynamic adversary could have but one end.

Morrill Tariff

A tariff increase in February 1861

Transcontinental Railroad

Railroad connecting east and west from Council Bluffs, Iowa, to Sacramento, California that was completed in 1869

14.3e Northern Industrialism and Republican Ascendancy

The problems and limitations of the Confederacy—problems of localism and decentralization, of an agricultural economy, and of small-scale economic activities—were characteristic features of the kind of folk society the Confederacy was defending. While the South was making a last stand against the forces of the modern mechanized world, however, the war was rushing the North along the path toward industrial domination. Before the Southern states withdrew from the Union, they had blocked some of the governmental measures most conducive to the new industrial economy. Southern secession, however, left the new Republican Party in control. The Republicans combined a free-soil, antislavery ideology with the traditional Whig policy of using the government to stimulate economic growth. While this program was designed to promote the mutual interests of capital and free labor, Republican economic legislation, in practice, usually helped the former more than the latter.

Thus, secession and the war enabled the Republicans to enact what one historian has called their "blueprint for modern America." In February 1861, while the empty seats of the departing Southern congressmen were still warm—and even before President Lincoln took office—Congress adopted the **Morrill Tariff**, which, though not very high, was higher than the existing tariff of 1857. This was the first of many tariff increases. There was not another perceptible reduction until 1913. Meanwhile Congress repeatedly strengthened the measures by which it gave American industrial producers more exclusive control in the American market, even if this forced American consumers to pay higher prices than they would have had to pay on the world market.

Pictured are the beginnings of the Union Pacific Railroad, which is still operational today and remains the largest railroad network in the country. The ceremony for the driving of the golden spike took place at Promontory Summit, Utah, on May 10, 1869, marking the completion of the First Transcontinental Railroad. At center left, Samuel S. Montague, Central Pacific Railroad, shakes hands with Grenville M. Dodge, Union Pacific Railroad (center right). (Wikimedia Commons)

14.3f The Transcontinental Railroad

In 1862 Congress broke the long deadlock the sectional conflict had created over the building of the **Transcontinental Railroad** from Omaha to the Pacific. For a decade, advocates of a southern route and supporters of a northern route had blocked each other. Now, with the Southerners absent, Congress created the Union Pacific Railroad Company, incorporated with a federal charter, to build westward from Omaha and to meet another railroad, the Central Pacific—a California corporation, building eastward from Sacramento. To encourage this enterprise, Congress placed very large resources at the disposal of the railroads. For each mile of track built, it gave to the roads ten square miles of land, running back in alternate blocks from the tracks; and it granted loans (not gifts) of between $16,000 and $48,000 a mile—according to the difficulty of the terrain where construction took place.

Even though the value of the lands at that time was not great, and the munificence of this largesse has often been exaggerated, the point is that the government was paying most of the costs of construction, whereas it might well have controlled or even owned the railroad. Instead, it placed these resources in the hands of private operators—who, if they succeeded, would become owners of the world's greatest railroad, and if they lost, would be losing the government's money rather than their own. It was "venture capitalism," as it is now called—but the government was doing most of the venturing, and the private interests that constructed the road were getting most of the capital. Furthermore, the railroads committed fraud against the government by presenting surveys that showed more mountainous terrain than actually existed (the government paid more per mile of track for mountainous terrain than for flatlands) and by needlessly zigzagging in their track construction so as to increase mileage, for which the government also paid.

In 1869, four years after the war ended, the Union Pacific and the Central Pacific met at Promontory Point in Utah; and a golden spike was driven to mark the event. Travelers to California no longer were obliged to go by wagon train or by a lengthy sea voyage. The United States was a long step closer to being a transcontinental, two-ocean republic in an operative sense as well as in a purely geographical one.

14.39 The National Banking System

One other major economic measure resulting from Republican ascendancy was the creation of a new and far more centralized system of banking and money. Ever since Andrew Jackson's overthrow of the Bank of the United States in 1832, the country had had a decentralized, loose-jointed financial system—one that today it is difficult even to imagine. The United States, of course, issued coins and also bills. For each bill in circulation, a corresponding value of precious metal was held in the Treasury and could be claimed by the holder of the bill. The government handled all its own transactions in such currency and was thus on a "hard money" basis.

This kind of money, however, was not nearly sufficient to meet the economic needs of the country as a circulating medium. The principal circulating medium, therefore, had been provided by notes issued by banks operating under charters from the various states. State laws governing the incorporation of banks naturally varied, which meant that the financial soundness of the various banks also varied. This, in turn, meant that some of the notes circulated at face value, while others circulated at various degrees of discount from face value. So although the government was on a hard money basis, the economy of the country was not; and the federal government exercised no control whatever over the principal component in the monetary system of the country.

The Legal Tender Act of 1862 and the National Banking Act of 1863 changed all this. They grew out of the government's need to raise the immense sums required to fight the war. The Legal Tender Act authorized the issuance of Treasury notes—the famous **greenbacks**— that circulated as authorized money, but without a backing in metal held in the Treasury.

Primarily, however, the Treasury relied upon borrowing—that is, upon selling bonds. To borrow it had to make the bonds attractive as holdings for the banks. Accordingly, the National Banking Act provided that a bank which purchased government bonds to the amount of one third of its paid-in capital might issue federally guaranteed notes, known as national bank notes, in an amount equal to 90 percent of its bond holdings.

In 1865, a tax was laid on the notes issued under state authority by state-chartered banks. The tax had the effect of making these notes unprofitable and thus driving them out of circulation. As a result of government borrowing policy, therefore, the United States acquired a new, uniform, federally sanctioned circulating medium of national bank notes.

These notes became the principal form of money for the next fifty years, but they had a great defect—they made the amount of money dependent upon the volume of federal debt rather than upon the economic needs of the country. They were inflexible, and in 1913 they were largely replaced by Federal Reserve notes as a result of the establishment of the Federal Reserve System. But the principles that the United States should have a uniform currency in use throughout the nation, and that the federal government should be responsible for this currency, had come to stay.

Women and the War

Although the Civil War brought suffering and loss to hundreds of thousands of American women, the war meant progress toward independence and equality for women as a group. It meant new opportunities for employment, broadened social and political interests, and demonstrations of competence in activities previously reserved for men. Some women went to war as nurses, spies—even as soldiers (most often masquerading as men). But it was the vast majority who served at home—including those who stayed in the home—who did the most damage to the myth of the "helpless female."

It is estimated that almost four hundred women posed as men to join the Union and Confederate armies during the Civil War, and this may be an underestimate because there may have been many more who were simply never discovered. So many smooth-faced and slightly built young boys joined both armies that many women could have easily passed as young boys. Physical examinations on both sides were almost nonexistent; thus women only needed to cut their hair, bind their breasts close to their body, and show enthusiasm for the conflict. Sarah Emma Evelyn Edmonds, who joined the 2nd Michigan Volunteers as "Franklin Thompson," stated in her memoirs that her physical examination consisted only of a firm handshake. Although Edmonds' true identity was eventually discovered, she remained in service afterwards as a nurse and a spy. Many women managed to keep their true identities secret throughout the war. Albert D. J. Cashier, who served in an Illinois regiment in the Vicksburg campaign, was only discovered years later when "he" was hospitalized as a war veteran and doctors discovered that he was really Jennie Hodges. Others, such as Lyons Wakeman, who is buried at Chalmette National Cemetery in St. Bernard Parish, Louisiana, were only discovered in death. Wakeman, whose real identity was **Sarah Rosetta Wakeman** of Afton, New York, fought with General Nathaniel P. Banks in a battle the Union lost at Mansfield, and also at Pleasant Hill, before dying of dysentery.

Sarah Emma Evelyn Edmonds joined the Second Michigan Volunteers as "Franklin Thompson." Edmonds' true identity was eventually discovered, but she remained in service afterwards as a nurse and a spy. (Wikimedia Commons)

Other women accompanied their husbands as **camp followers**. These women not only tended to their husbands' laundry and sewing but also served as field nurses, kept weapons loaded, and carried water to cool both weapons and throats. One **Rose Rooney**, however, openly enlisted with the Crescent Blues Volunteers in the Confederate army at New Orleans in 1861. Her assigned duty was to serve as a cook and a laundress, but she eventually did much more than that. At the First Battle of Bull Run, she is credited with running through a field of heavy fire to tear down a rail fence so as to allow a battery of Confederate artillery to advance forward and help halt a Union charge. Rooney served in Lee's Army of Northern Virginia for virtually the entire war and remained in the ranks when Lee surrendered in 1865.

Aside from their roles on the battlefield—as in earlier wars, but in much greater numbers—women during the Civil War had to take their husbands' places as heads of households, running shops, managing farms and plantations, and finding jobs to earn food for their families. In the South, many had to do housework—and field work—for the first time. Some had to face armed, hostile blacks as well as enemy soldiers. In Minnesota and elsewhere on the frontier, women had to survive American Indian uprisings.

Job opportunities for women multiplied as men went off to fight or quit old occupations for better-paying ones. The war quickened the movement of women into school teaching, a profession once dominated by men. Many Northern women also went South to teach in schools for freed slaves. In both the Union and the Confederacy, women also went to work for the government. Many were employed, and some were killed, in government arsenals. By the end of the war, thousands held government office jobs. Here, too, the change was permanent: Washington, D.C., would never again be without its corps of women workers.

When the war began, women dominated the work force in the mills and factories of New England, while in the South women industrial workers were a small minority—another situation that favored the Union war effort. As men joined the service, women took their places in industry and helped produce military equipment and supplies.

Sarah Rosetta Wakeman
Woman who fought with General Nathaniel P. Banks in the Union's loss at Mansfield and also at Pleasant Hill before dying of dysentery

Camp followers
Women who followed their husbands into battle and played support roles

Rose Rooney
Woman who openly enlisted in the Confederate army and served in Lee's Army of Northern Virginia for virtually the entire war

The demand for what was considered women's work also expanded. Sewing women were hired by the thousands, and brutally exploited. In self-protection, the women organized, protested, and went out on strikes.

In addition to work for pay, there was a tremendous amount of unpaid activity by women in both South and North—though there was more in the North, because women in that region had a tradition of public activism lacking in the more conservative South. Women volunteered to nurse; and some of them—above all **Clara Barton**—became famous. They joined aid societies and organized activities to raise funds. They wrote and spoke for the causes they believed in and even, in a few cases, comprised part of the attendance at riots, North and South. Overall, many women demonstrated talents for efficiency and leadership.

In the North, women took the initiative to found the United States Sanitary Commission, which did valuable work in raising money and gathering materials for wounded soldiers. Their initial enthusiasm was somewhat alarming to the military authorities—who were anxious about good-natured female busybodies—hence, men were put officially in charge of the organization. Nevertheless, women supplied much of the energy. Over time, the women did so much good work that even the doubters came around. In an era when married women could not sign contracts (owing to the tenets of coverture), women raised hundreds of thousands of much-needed dollars for humanitarian relief.

The Civil War gave American women a chance to enter many new areas and prove themselves quite as capable as men. When the war ended, many lost their jobs to returning veterans. Some returned gratefully to domesticity, but there was no turning back the clock.

14.3i **The Road to Reunion**

Wars always bring results not intended by those who fight them. The Civil War accelerated the growth of mass production and economic centralization in the North while it destroyed much of the economic plant in the South and convinced the rising generation of Southern leaders that future regional prosperity would depend upon industrialization. The war also caused an increase in federal power at the expense of the states—for no government could spend the funds, organize the forces, and wield the strength the federal government did without increasing its power. The main purpose of the war, however, was to reunite a broken union of states—and there was the question of whether the abolition of slavery was necessary to the objective of reunion. Some Republicans wanted to make emancipation one of the objects of the war, simply because they deplored slavery and did not believe that a Union which had slavery in it was worth saving. Others (who were relatively indifferent to the welfare of the blacks) believed that the slaveholding class, which they called the "slave power," was guilty of causing disunion; that to make the Union safe, this power had to be destroyed; and that the way to destroy it was to abolish slavery. Still others—including many of the "War Democrats" and the Unionists in the border states—regarded the war as one against secession, having nothing to do with slavery.

14.3j **Emancipation**

For his part, Abraham Lincoln had stated his belief, long before he became president, that the Union could not endure permanently half-slave and half-free. He knew, however, that he could not free any slaves unless he won the war, and that he could not win the war if he antagonized all the Unionists in the slave states of Delaware, Maryland, Kentucky (his own birthplace), and Missouri. As a result, he moved very slowly on the slavery question; and when two of his generals tried to move more quickly by emancipating slaves in the areas they had occupied, he countermanded their orders.

14.3k **Emancipation Proclamation**

Few people realize it today, but the war had raged for seventeen months and was more than a third over before Lincoln moved to free the slaves in the Confederacy. In July 1862, he made up his mind to proclaim the freedom of slaves in the insurrectionary states—but he decided to wait for a victory before doing so. The Battle of Antietam (Sharpsburg) in September was not a great victory, but it sufficed. In that month, Lincoln issued a proclamation that after January 1, 1863, all slaves in areas that were at that time in rebellion should be "forever free." This still did nothing about slaves in places like New Orleans, which was occupied by federal forces, or in the border slave states, because those areas were not in rebellion; therefore, the slaves in those areas were not free. The Emancipation Proclamation also did not free the slaves in areas under rebellion because those areas were obviously not under Union control and any proclamation by the president—whether concerning emancipation or otherwise—would without a doubt be completely ignored. The Emancipation Proclamation also gave all the states of the Confederacy one hundred days time during which they could save slavery by coming back into the Union. Clearly, the principle of the Emancipation Proclamation was not that one could not own slaves, but rather that one could not own slaves and secede from the Union.

Strongly believing in persuasion rather than force, in December 1862, Lincoln proposed a constitutional amendment for the gradual emancipation of slaves in the border states by the year 1900, with compensation to the owners. But this proposal was overtaken by other events as the escalating impact of the war accelerated the destruction of slavery. On January 1, 1863, Lincoln issued the Emancipation Proclamation, to apply in all areas under Confederate control. Although it would require Northern victory to become a reality, the Emancipation Proclamation announced a new Union war aim—freedom for the slaves as well as restoration of the Union. Enthusiasm for the war in the North was already on the decline in late 1862; and Lincoln sought a greater moral cause for the war than merely the preservation of the Union—which by the end of 1862 was simply an insufficient cause for too many people North of the Mason-Dixon line. Lincoln also surmised that

the emancipation cause would help prevent English intervention on the side of the South. As the self-appointed world leader of the abolition movement, England could hardly join the war on the side of slavery once the Union had made abolition one of its goals.

The caution with which Lincoln had proceeded with emancipation reflects his own scruples about the Constitution and the prudence of his own temperament, but it also reflects the fierceness of the divisions within the North and the dangers that these divisions held for the administration. On one flank, Lincoln was assailed by the Democrats. And although a minority of "War Democrats" gave him vigorous support, a majority of the Democrats, known as **Copperheads**, constantly called for a negotiated peace and especially assailed any move against slavery—believing that any move against slavery would force the South to fight rather than negotiate. Democratic propagandists helped convince white workingmen that they were being used in a war to free blacks who would then take their jobs away. It was this conviction that turned the **draft riots** of New York, in July 1863, into mob assaults on blacks. More than a hundred people were killed in these assaults, most of them white rioters shot down by police and troops. The riots were so tumultuous that the draft was suspended in New York City for the remainder of the war.

This painting depicts Abraham Lincoln presenting the first draft of the Emancipation Proclamation to his cabinet. Though the legislation did not free all slaves everywhere, it was a step in that direction. (Wikimedia Commons)

On the other flank, pressure was coming from many sources—including from women and the black community. **Susan B. Anthony** and **Elizabeth Cady Stanton** organized their fellow suffragists into the **Women's National Loyal League** and gathered hundreds of thousands of signatures on an antislavery petition. Further, the more militant antislavery men in the Republican Party denounced Lincoln because he did not instantly take drastic action to end slavery. These "Radical Republicans" hoped to dominate the administration by forcing all moderates on the slavery question out of the cabinet—and in 1864, some of them sought to prevent Lincoln's nomination for a second term. By unrivaled

Copperheads
Northern Democrats who favored a negotiated peace and opposed any move against slavery

Draft riots
Riots in opposition to the draft in 1863, most famously in New York City

Susan B. Anthony
Suffragette who opposed slavery

Elizabeth Cady Stanton
Worked with Susan B. Anthony for women's suffrage and against slavery

Women's National Loyal League
Women's group for suffrage and the abolition of slavery founded by Susan B. Anthony and Elizabeth Cady Stanton

political dexterity and skill, Lincoln frustrated these attacks from both directions and maintained a broad base of support for the war among abolitionists.

As late as 1864, however, the House of Representatives defeated a constitutional amendment for the abolition of slavery. The Thirteenth Amendment abolishing slavery was not passed by Congress and submitted to the states until January 31, 1865. Maryland, Tennessee, and Missouri abolished slavery by state action at about this same time, but slavery was still legal in Kentucky and Delaware when the Civil War ended—and the amendment was not ratified until eight months after Lincoln's death.

14.3 Black Americans and the War

For black Americans, the Civil War years were a time of elation and rejoicing, as well as frustration and despair. Black men and women alike worked hard for the Union cause. Black intellectuals wrote and lectured, both at home and abroad. Blacks organized their own aid and relief societies for the great numbers of freed slaves and went to them as teachers. Black women volunteered their services as nurses and hospital aids. Black men by the hundreds of thousands went to war for the Union as sailors in the navy and as servants, cooks, and laborers with the army. When they were finally allowed to do so, they also went as soldiers.

For a long time, however, blacks were not allowed to serve in the army. Not until the autumn of 1862 were blacks officially permitted to enlist, and it was another year before the bravery of black regiments in battle began to change the scornful attitude of whites in and out of the service. Most instrumental in this shift was the heroic, if doomed, assault on Fort Wagner, South Carolina, by a black regiment—the **54th Massachusetts Infantry**—in July 1863. Overall, black servicemen established an admirable record, and twenty-one received the Congressional Medal of Honor. But the officers in black regiments were mostly white men. Only a handful of black soldiers were promoted to the rank of lieutenant or captain. Not until June 1864, was the pay of black and white soldiers equalized.

The Fifty-fourth Massachusetts Infantry was one of the first official black units in the United States during the Civil War. (Wikimedia Commons)

Throughout the war, blacks continued to face injustice and discrimination, despite their major contribution to the Union cause. From the beginning, their most influential spokesman, **Frederick Douglass**, looked on Lincoln as being much too conservative—and when the president delayed taking decisive steps toward freeing the slaves, Douglass was outspoken in his criticism.

Although Lincoln had his black supporters, including the beloved Harriet Tubman, he also gave offense by his continuing interest in some programs to move blacks out of the country to a colony in the tropics. In fact, there were some blacks who were so embittered that they welcomed the possibility of such separation. Martin R. Delany, who later joined with Douglass in working for black recruitment, favored the migration of American blacks to Haiti—a project that was tried unsuccessfully early in the war. After the rejection of black volunteers by the army, the subsequent mistreatment of black soldiers, and the attacks on both black soldiers and black civilians that had taken place in several Northern cities, there were blacks who agreed with white racists on one point: that the Civil War was indeed a white man's war in a white man's country, to which blacks owed no allegiance.

Nevertheless, there was progress. The Emancipation Proclamation was finally issued. The Thirteenth Amendment was adopted. The great slave population (which, as Douglass had repeatedly pointed out, had enabled the Confederacy to put so large a proportion of its whites into uniform) was finally freed. Many blacks, Union soldiers as well as former slaves, were also freed from the bonds of illiteracy by dedicated teachers—both black and white—and through their own efforts.

After the war, blacks were recognized as full citizens by the federal government, and campaigns against discrimination in the law courts, the polling places, the schools, and public conveyances won victories in several states. In 1864, black representatives from eighteen states formed the National Equal Rights League. The long, agonizingly slow march toward equality had begun.

14.3m Lincoln's Reelection and Assassination

In 1864, when the time came for a new presidential election, the Democrats nominated General McClellan to run against Lincoln. Some of the so-called Radical Republicans, who were dissatisfied with Lincoln's leniency, tried to block his renomination and put up the secretary of the treasury, Salmon P. Chase, in his stead. This effort failed, and Lincoln was renominated. In an effort to put the ticket on a broad, bipartisan basis, the party dropped the name Republican, called itself the Union Party, and nominated for the vice presidency a Southern Democrat who had stood firmly for the Union, Andrew Johnson of Tennessee.

In November 1864, Lincoln and Johnson were elected, carrying all but three Union states (New Jersey, Delaware, and Kentucky). In the following March, the new term began; and Lincoln delivered his second inaugural address, calling for "malice toward none and charity for all," in order "to bind up the nation's wounds." On April 9, Lee surrendered the Army of Northern Virginia. It was clear that the work of reconstruction must now begin in earnest.

On April 14, however—as celebrations still continued in the North in the wake of the Confederate surrender—Lincoln attended a performance at **Ford's Theater**, where he was assassinated by **John Wilkes Booth**. Booth broke into Lincoln's theater box and shot the president in the back of the head with a small pistol at point blank range, then jumped to the stage with a dagger in one hand—breaking an ankle in the process—and escaped through the back door of the theater. As he left the theater, Booth shouted the Virginia state motto, **"Sic semper tyrannis"** (thus always to tyrants). Lincoln died the next morning, without ever recovering consciousness. An attempted assassin also stabbed Secretary of State Seward in his bed—even as Lincoln was being shot across town—but he survived the attack with only a permanent scar on his cheek. An assassin also planned to kill Andrew Johnson, but lost his nerve; Johnson went on to become president of the United States.

Pictured is a depiction of the assassination of Abraham Lincoln at the hand of John Wilkes Booth, a Southern sympathizer. (Wikimedia Commons)

Unknown to Booth—a Southern sympathizer who had evidently killed Lincoln in the spirit of Southern revenge—he had probably just killed the South's best friend because it does not appear that Lincoln favored any sort of punitive reconstruction and was in favor of allowing the South to manage their own affairs as much as would be possible. With Lincoln out of the way, the path was much more open for those in the North who favored a more punitive peace.

Ford's Theater

Theater where John Wilkes Booth shot President Lincoln

John Wilkes Booth

President Lincoln's assassin

"Sic semper tyrannis"

The Virginia state motto uttered by John Wilkes Booth after shooting President Lincoln

Timeline

1809	Abraham Lincoln is born in a log cabin in Kentucky.
1816	Abraham Lincoln's mother, Nancy Lincoln, dies of "milk sickness."
1829	Sarah Bush Lincoln, Abe's stepmother, dies.
1832	Lincoln fights in the Blackhawk War.
1834	Abraham Lincoln is elected to the Illinois Legislature.
1835	Lincoln's girlfriend, Ann Rutledge, dies.
1842	Lincoln marries Mary Todd.
1846	Abraham Lincoln is elected to Congress.
1848	Treaty of Guadalupe Hidalgo ends the war with Mexico.
1854	Kansas-Nebraska Act stirs tensions over slavery.
1860	December 20, South Carolina is the first of eleven states to secede.
1861	April 19, Lincoln announces a blockade of the South.
	April 19, Baltimore erupts in riots.
	May 10–11, St. Louis erupts in riots.
	April 15, Lincoln calls for seventy-five thousand 90-day volunteers.
	July 21, First Battle of Bull Run (Manassas)
	August 1, Confederate Colonel John R. Baylor declares the "Confederate Territory of Arizona."
	September 20, Confederates capture a Union garrison at Lexington, Missouri.
1862	February 6–16, General Ulysses S. Grant takes Confederate Forts Donelson and Henry in Tennessee.
	February 21, Confederates under H. H. Sibley defeat a Union force at Valverde and take Albuquerque and Santa Fe for the Confederacy.
	February 25, Nashville, Tennessee, is the first Southern state capitol to surrender.
	March 8, sixteen thousand Confederates are defeated at Pea Ridge, Arkansas.
	March 9, a battle between the U.S.S. *Merrimac* (*Virginia*) and the *Monitor* ends in a draw.
	March 28, Confederate forces are defeated in New Mexico at Glorieta Pass and retreat back to Texas.
	April, the Confederacy institutes conscription.

Timeline

1862 Continued

April 6–7, 23,000 men die at Shiloh.

April 29, David Farragut takes New Orleans for the Union.

April–July, McClellan's campaigns to capture Richmond.

May 31–June 1, Confederate General Joseph E. Johnston is wounded at Seven Pines and is replaced by Robert E. Lee.

July 11, Lincoln replaces McClellan with General Henry Halleck.

September 17–18, McClellan forces Lee to retreat at Antietam.

October 8, Confederate offensive under General Braxton Bragg is pushed back at Perryville, Kentucky.

December 15, Union general Ambrose E. Burnside is defeated at Fredericksburg and is replaced by Joseph Hooker.

December 31, Confederates under Braxton Bragg are defeated at Murfreesboro and forced to abandon their offensive.

1863

January 1, Lincoln issues the Emancipation Proclamation.

March 3, Union general Joseph Hooker is defeated at Chancellorsville.

May, the Union institutes conscription.

July 1–3, the Confederate army under Robert E. Lee is defeated at Gettysburg and forced to withdraw.

July 4, General Ulysses S. Grant takes Vicksburg.

July 13–16, draft riots take place in New York City.

September 20, the Union is forced to retreat at Chickamauga Creek.

1864

May 5–7, the Battle of the Tangled Wilderness takes place in Virginia.

May 8–19, the Battle of Spotsylvania Courthouse takes place in Virginia.

June 15–18, the Battle of Cold Harbor takes place in Virginia.

September 2, Atlanta falls to General William T. Sherman.

November, Lincoln is reelected.

November 16 to December 21, Sherman's March to the Sea

1865

April 9, Robert E. Lee surrenders at Appomattox Court House, Virginia.

April 14, Lincoln is assassinated.

1869

May 10, a golden spike is driven at Promontory Summit, Utah, to commemorate the completion of the Transcontinental Railroad.

CHAPTER SUMMARY

$\mathcal{T}$he American Civil War was the bloodiest in American history, with 618,000 killed and over 20 percent of all white males participating—the highest participation rate of any American war. On both sides, men were fighting for what they deeply believed to be American values.

Southerners were convinced that their right to form a Confederacy was based on a principle of the Declaration of Independence—that governments derive their just powers from the consent of the governed. They were also fighting because they were being invaded by the North. The North was fighting to defend the flag and to prove that a democracy was not too weak to hold together. Abolition of slavery was not a motivation for most people at the outset of the war, but it eventually became one when Lincoln felt that the war needed a greater moral purpose.

Lincoln was born in a Kentucky log cabin in 1809 and suffered a life of tragedy that included the loss of his mother, stepmother, romantic love, and two of his children. Lincoln struggled to make a living all of his life until he rose from nowhere, politically, to seize the Republican nomination in 1860 and the White House that November. The next month, South Carolina seceded, followed eventually by ten other Southern states. Lincoln tried to resupply a Union fort in Southern territory (Fort Sumter), but Southerners fired on it; and the Civil War began on April 12, 1861. Originally, both sides viewed the war as a romantic test of courage, and Lincoln only called for seventy-five thousand ninety-day volunteers. The First Battle of Bull Run, where the Union troops were routed, proved that the war would not be swift; massive casualties in later battles, such as Shiloh, fairly well put to rest the notion that the war was, in any way, romantic.

The Confederates under Robert E. Lee hoped for a decisive victory in the North that would bring recognition or intervention from Europe, but Lee's Northern invasion was repelled at Antietam in 1862. The next year, Lee would suffer a defeat at Gettysburg on July 3 from which his army would never recover; and the next day, General Ulysses S. Grant would take Vicksburg. Nevertheless, the South fought on; and sentiments in the North turned against the war. Lincoln's approval rating in August 1864 was sufficiently low that he was expected to lose the election in November—but then Atlanta fell to the Union under General William T. Sherman on September 2, 1864. Lincoln's political fortunes reversed as Northerners suddenly believed they had won, and Southerners suddenly understood that they had lost. Sherman then reinforced that notion with a march across Georgia where he burned a sixty-mile wide swath across the state on his way to the sea.

Lee surrendered on April 9, 1865, at Appomattox Court House in Virginia after a bloody campaign to defend Richmond—where the outnumbered Southerners fought valiantly, but finally lost the war of attrition. Northern superiority in population, transportation, and manufacturing had eventually made the difference. Five days later, Lincoln—the man that might have been "the South's best friend" because he did not favor a punitive peace—was assassinated by John Wilkes Booth at Ford's Theater.

Meanwhile, the war had had a tremendous impact on life in America. The war boosted manufacturing and finance in the North, and the Transcontinental Railroad was finished four years after the war. African Americans were no longer enslaved, and some even served in the war itself—as did a number of women. Though Lincoln's Emancipation Proclamation had originally freed no one, since it applied only to the states in rebellion, it had given the Union a greater moral purpose and helped prevent English intervention into the American conflict.

KEY TERMS

BIBLIOGRAPHY

A

Ahlstrom, Sydney. *A Religious History of the American People*. New Haven, CT: Yale University Press, 2004.

B

Baker, Jean H., and Arthur M. Schlesinger. *The 15th President, 1857–1861*. New York: Times Books, 2004.

Baker, Jean H. *The Politics of Continuity: Maryland Political Parties from 1858 to 1870*. Baltimore, MD: Johns Hopkins University Press, 1973.

Brinkley, Alan. *American History: A Survey*. 11th ed. Boston, MA: McGraw-Hill, 2003.

C

Calvert, Robert A., Arnoldo De Leon and Gregg Cantrell. *The History of Texas*. 4th ed. Hoboken, NJ: Harlan Davidson, 2007.

Campbell, Randolph. *Gone to Texas*. New York: Oxford University Press, 2003.

Cash, W. J. *The Mind of the South*. New York: Knopf, 1941.

Catton, Bruce. *Bruce Catton's Civil War in Three Volumes: Mr. Lincoln's Army, Glory Road, and A Stillness at Appomattox*. New York: Random House, 1988.

Cooper, William J. and Thomas E. Terrill. *The American South: A History*. New York: McGraw-Hill, 1991.

Craven, Avery. *The Coming of the Civil War*. New York: Scribner, 1942.

Crook, David Paul. *The North, the South, and the Powers 1861–1865*. New York: John Wiley and Sons, 1974.

Cummings, Bruce. *Dominion from Sea to Sea. Pacific Ascendancy and American Power*. New Haven, CT: Yale University Press, 2011.

Curry, Richard Orr. *A House Divided: A Study of Statehood Politics and the Copperhead Movement in West Virginia*. Pittsburgh, PA: University of Pittsburgh Press, 1964.

D

Daniel, Larry J. *Soldiering in the Army of Tennessee: A Portrait of Life in the Confederate Army*. Chapel Hill, University of North Carolina Press, 2003.

Davis, William C. *Jefferson Davis: The Man and His Hour*. Baton Rouge, LA: Louisiana State University Press, 1996.

Donald, David Herbert. *Lincoln*. New York: Simon and Schuster, 1996.

Donald, David. *Lincoln Reconsidered*. New York: Vintage, 1961.

E

Engerman, Stanley L. and Robert E. Gallman. *The Cambridge Economic History of the United States, Vol. 2: The Long Nineteenth Century*. New York: Cambridge University Press, 2000.

F

Fehrenbach, T. R. *Lone Star: A History of Texas and the Texans*. Cambridge, MA: Da Capo Press, 2000.

Freeman, Douglas Southall. *Lee*. New York: Scribner, 1997.

G

Garraty, John A., and Robert McCaughey. *The American Nation: A History of the United States Since 1865*. 6th ed. New York: HarperCollins, 1987.

Gould, Lewis L. *Grand Old Party: A History of Republicans*. New York: Random House, 2003.

H

Harrison, Lowell Hayes. *The Civil War in Kentucky*. Lexington, KY: University of Kentucky Press, 2009.

Hughes, Jonathan, and Louis P. Cain. *American Economic History*. 8th ed. Englewood Cliffs, NJ: Pearson Prentice-Hall, 2010.

J

Jones, Howard. *Quest for Security: A History of U.S. Foreign Relations*. New York: McGraw-Hill, 1996.

K

Klein, Maury. *Days of Defiance: Sumter, Secession, and the Coming of the Civil War*. New York: Vintage, 1999.

Kolchin, Peter. *American Slavery: 1619–1877*. New York: Hill and Wang, 2003.

L

Lipset, Seymour M., and Earl Raab. *The Politics of Unreason: Right-Wing Extremism in America, 1790–1970*. New York: Harper and Row, 1970.

M

Massey, Mary E. *Bonnet Brigades*. New York: Knopf, 1966.

McFeely, William S. *Grant: A Biography*. New York: W. W. Norton & Company, 2002.

McPherson, James M. *Battle Cry of Freedom: The Civil War Era*. New York: Oxford University Press, 2003.

Muccigrosso, Robert. *Basic History of Conservatism*. Melbourne, FL: Krieger, 2001.

BIBLIOGRAPHY

N

Nichols, Roy F. *The Disruption of American Democracy.* New York: Collier, 1962.

Niebuhr, Reinhold. *The Irony of American History.* Chicago, IL: University of Chicago Press, 2008.

O

Olson, James S. *Encyclopedia of the Industrial Revolution in America.* Westport, CT: Greenwood Press, 2001.

Oren, Michael B. *Power, Faith, and Fantasy: America in the Middle East 1776 to the Present.* New York: W. W. Norton & Company, 2007.

P

Paludan, Philip S. *A People's Contest: The Union and the Civil War, 1861–1865.* Lawrence, KS: University of Kansas Press, 1996.

Parrish, William E. *Turbulent Partnership: Missouri and the Union 1861–1865.* Columbia, MO: University of Missouri Press, 1963.

Porter, Kirk H., and Donald B. Johnson eds. *National Party Platforms 1840–1968.* Urbana, IL: University of Illinois Press, 1972.

S

Symonds, Craig L. *The Civil War at Sea.* New York: Praeger, 2009.

T

Thomas, Emory. *The Confederate Nation: 1861–1865.* New York: Harper Perennials, 2011.

W

Wiley, Bell Irvin. *The Life of Johnny Reb: The Common Soldier of the Confederacy.* Baton Rouge, LA: Louisiana State University Press, 1989.

———. *The Life of Billy Yank: The Common Soldier of the Union.* Baton Rouge, LA: Louisiana State University Press, 2008.

Wooster, Ralph. *The Secessionist Conventions of the South.* Princeton, NJ: Princeton University Press, 1962.

POP QUIZ

1. Why did Abraham Lincoln eventually make emancipation part of the Union effort?
   a. He believed in the equality of white and black people.
   b. He believed that the North needed a greater moral cause for the war.
   c. He desired to incite slave rebellions in the South.
   d. He wanted the slaves to come work in Northern factories as laborers.

2. At the outset of the Civil War, for what reason(s) did Southerners believed that they would win?
   a. their "just cause," superior character, and because God was on their side
   b. their greater manufacturing capacity
   c. their greater rail capacity
   d. their greater naval capacity

3. Problems with Lincoln's blockade included which of the following?
   a. Blockades could only apply to sovereign nations.
   b. If the South was not an independent nation, then the blockade was not binding under international law.
   c. Both a and b
   d. None of the above

4. The area that seceded from the Confederacy during the Civil War and became a new state in the Union in 1863 was _____.
   a. Maryland
   b. Kansas
   c. Missouri
   d. West Virginia

5. Which of the following is true of the Seven Days' Battles (June 25–July 1, 1861)?
   a. Confederates under Robert E. Lee repelled the Union's Richmond campaign under George B. McClellan.
   b. George McClellan and the Union army took Richmond, causing Lee to retreat to North Carolina.
   c. The Union could have taken Richmond, but Lincoln ordered McClellan to withdraw.
   d. Southerner Thomas Jackson built a stone wall around Richmond in seven days, earning himself the name, "Stonewall Jackson."

6. Which of the following is true of Chancellorsville?
   a. It was a huge Union victory.
   b. It was a Confederate victory.
   c. Stonewall Jackson was accidentally shot by his own men.
   d. Both b and c

7. Which of the following is true about the Battle of Pea Ridge?
   a. It helped keep the Union supplied in vegetables.
   b. It secured Missouri for the Confederacy.
   c. It helped secure Missouri for the Union.
   d. It prevented Southerners from raiding Union pea fields.

8. The Union general who Lincoln replaced after Chickamauga, and who he described as "confused and stunned like a duck hit on the head," was _____.
   a. General George B. McClellan
   b. General William Rosecrans
   c. General William Tecumseh Sherman
   d. General Donald "Daffy" Duckard

9. The only Confederate executed by the Union after the war was _____.
   a. Jefferson Davis
   b. Robert E. Lee
   c. Henry Wirz
   d. Wilhelm Klink

10. The 54th Massachusetts Infantry was an _____.
    a. all-black infantry in the Union army
    b. all-female infantry in the Union army
    c. integrated infantry in the Union army
    d. all-Irish infantry in the Union army

11. The battle of Gettysburg is considered the turning point in the Civil War. T   F

12. In 1864, Lincoln ran as a Republican. T   F

13. Most of the money used to build the first transcontinental railroad came from private sources. T   F

14. The Union population was much _____ than that in the South.

15. The Emancipation Proclamation freed _____ in areas then at war with _____ _____.

Chapter 15

(CORBIS,© Stefano, Wikimedia Commons)

Emancipation and Reconstruction, 1865–1877

CHAPTER OUTLINE

15.1 Lincoln's Plan of Reconstruction

The process of readmission to the Union for Southern states had begun as early as 1862 when Union troops began reclaiming Southern territory. Lincoln then appointed provisional governors for those parts of the Confederacy controlled and occupied by federal troops. Although he had always opposed slavery on moral as well as political grounds, Lincoln was skeptical about the prospects for racial equality in the United States. The legacy of slavery and race prejudice, he believed, would prevent blacks from rising to the level of whites—or prevent whites from allowing blacks to rise to their level. This was why Lincoln had supported the deportation of freed slaves to a colony in Africa as a possible solution to the race problem.

By 1864, however, the president was convinced of the impracticality, if not the injustice, of this policy. The contribution of blacks to the Union war effort and the growing strength of Northern antislavery convictions also made him more hopeful about the chances for eventual black advancement and racial adjustment. On this question, though, Lincoln remained a moderate and a gradualist to the end of his life.

*Pictured is Lincoln's tomb in Springfield, Illinois.
(Wikimedia Commons, Robert Lawton)*

Wade-Davis Bill

Killed by Lincoln's pocket veto, the bill would have imposed stringent terms for the restoration of the former Confederates—including a requirement that Southerners could only establish state governments after the majority in a state had sworn a loyalty oath.

Ten-Percent Plan

Lincoln would have allowed Southerners to restore state governments after 10 percent had taken a loyalty oath to the U.S.

Andrew Johnson

Lincoln's vice president and seventeenth president of the United States

Johnson's plan for reconstruction

When the new Southern governments disavowed secession, accepted the abolition of slavery, and repudiated the Confederate debt, Johnson would accept them back into the Union; rights for blacks were left to the states.

Lincoln and the Northern moderates also believed that victory in war could not really restore the Union. It could only prevent secession. After that, the Union would be really restored only if the Southern people again accepted the Union and gave their loyalty to it. To bring them back, Lincoln wanted a conciliatory policy. So when, in 1864, Congress adopted a measure known as the **Wade-Davis Bill**, imposing stringent terms for the restoration of the former Confederates—including a requirement that Southerners could only establish state governments after the majority in a state had sworn to a loyalty oath—Lincoln quickly disposed of it with a pocket veto (the president did not sign the bill during the last ten days of a Congressional session, thus killing the bill through his inaction).

When people raised technical questions about the legal status of the Confederate states (Were they still states, or conquered territories? Had they committed "state suicide"?), Lincoln was impatient about such "pernicious abstractions." All that mattered was whether the states could be brought back into their proper relationship with the Union.

By 1864, the Union had regained enough control in Louisiana, Tennessee, and Arkansas to start the process of restoring these states to the Union; and Lincoln laid down generous terms on which this could be done. He would grant amnesty to former Confederates who took an oath of allegiance; and when as many as one tenth of the number who had been eligible voters in 1860 took the oath, he would permit them to form a new state government. Then, when this new state government accepted the abolition of slavery and repudiated the principle of secession, Lincoln would receive it back into the Union. States did not have to recognize the rights of blacks or give a single black person the vote.

Louisiana was the first state reorganized on this basis. Despite its denial of black suffrage, Lincoln accepted Louisiana—though he did ask the governor "whether some of the colored people may not be let in, as for instance the very intelligent, and especially those who have fought gallantly in our ranks." In Virginia, Tennessee, and Arkansas, also, Lincoln recognized state governments that did not enfranchise black Americans.

It was clear that Republicans in Congress were suspicious of these states—but it was more because of their leniency toward the former Confederates than because of their treatment of black people. In addition, the Radical Republicans favored a reconstruction policy that would punish the South, and they therefore opposed Lincoln's plan because it was not punitive. Radical Republicans in Congress also disliked Lincoln's conciliatory **Ten-Percent Plan** because it allowed the president to establish reconstruction policy rather than Congress. It was also clear that Congress might deny the reestablished states recognition by refusing to seat their newly elected senators and representatives.

15.2 Johnson's Policy of Reconstruction

Although a Southerner—in fact, the only Southern senator who had remained loyal to the Union—**Andrew Johnson** was expected to be more severe in his reconstruction policy than Lincoln had been. Johnson was the son of poor, illiterate parents in Raleigh, North Carolina, who could not afford to send their son to school. Instead, Johnson's mother apprenticed him to a tailor after his father died, and Johnson later worked as a tailor in Tennessee. The ambitious Johnson, who had been illiterate until his wife taught him to write, became not only a successful tailor but also accumulated a fortune in land—and at one time even owned five slaves. He was a man of strong emotions; and as a Southerner with the roots of a common man, he hated both aristocrats—whom he blamed for secession—and secessionists in general. But as **Johnson's plan for reconstruction** developed, it became clear that he disliked abolitionists and radicals even more. In the end, Johnson proved even more lenient toward former Confederates than Lincoln had been. Johnson was a strong states' rights advocate, who as a senator had voted against everything that smacked of increased federal power. He even once voted against a bill to pave the streets of Washington, D.C.

Johnson was also a defender of slavery and accepted emancipation only grudgingly. Johnson's eventual opposition to slavery developed more out of his dislike for the planter class than out of any moral outrage against slavery or sympathy for black Americans. Johnson believed black people to be intellectually inferior and naturally more suited to manual labor.

On May 29, 1865, he issued a broad amnesty to all who would take an oath of allegiance, including ex-Confederate government officials and military officers, though men with property valued at more than $20,000 (in other words, planters) were required to ask special pardon—which was freely given. In the six weeks after May 29, he appointed provisional governors in each of the Southern states to reorganize governments for these states. Only men who had been voters in 1860 and who had taken the oath of allegiance could participate in these reorganizations. This meant, of course, that blacks were excluded. When the new governments disavowed secession, accepted the abolition of slavery, and repudiated the Confederate debt, Johnson would accept them. As to what policy should be followed toward the freedmen—that was to be determined by the states themselves.

The Southern states moved swiftly under this easy formula. Before the end of the year, every state except Texas—which followed soon after—had set up a new government that met the president's terms. Two conspicuous features of these governments, however, were deeply disturbing to many Republicans.

First, these Southern states had adopted a series of laws known as **"Black Codes,"** which denied to blacks many of the rights of citizenship—including the right to vote and to serve on juries. Blacks could not testify against whites, and laws were passed against interracial marriage. Of course, blacks were also denied the right to bear arms. Other laws were passed that excluded them from certain types of property ownership and certain occupations. In some cases, black employment was limited to agriculture and domestic servitude. Unemployed Negroes might be arrested as vagrants and bound out to labor in a new form of involuntary servitude. Black workers truant from jobs were forced to do public service until they returned to their former employer to whom they were contractually bound.

Second, the former Confederates were in complete control. By December 1865, all but two former Confederate states had organized new governments, ratified the **Thirteenth Amendment** abolishing slavery, and elected Congressmen. Between them, the newly organized states elected to Congress no fewer than nine Confederate congressmen, seven Confederate state officials, four generals, four colonels, and the former Confederate vice president, Alexander Stephens.

An 1864 United States Republican presidential ticket shows a campaign banner for Republican presidential candidate Abraham Lincoln and running mate Andrew Johnson. (Wikimedia Commons)

"Black Codes"
State and municipal laws limiting black rights

Thirteenth Amendment
Abolished slavery

Pictured is a portrait of Confederate Vice President Alexander Stephens. (Wikimedia Commons)

BVT Lab

15.2a Congressional Radicals

When Congress met at the end of 1865, it was confronted by presidential reconstruction as a *fait accompli*. At this point, the Republicans were far from ready for the kind of all-out fight against Johnson that later developed—but neither were they ready to accept the reorganized states. They were especially resentful because these states could now claim a larger representation in Congress with the free black population (only three-fifths of the blacks had been counted when they were slaves), without actually allowing the blacks any voice in the government. It would be ironic, indeed, if the overthrow of slavery should increase the representation of the South in Congress, and if the rebels should come back into the Union stronger politically than when they left.

For some months, the Republicans in Congress moved slowly, unwilling to face a break with a president of their own party—and far from ready to make a vigorous stand for the rights of blacks. But they would not seat the Southern congressmen-elect, so they set up a joint committee of the Senate and the House to assert their claim to a voice in the formulation of reconstruction policy. They also passed a bill to extend the life and increase the activities of the **Freedmen's Bureau**—an agency created to aid blacks in their transition from slavery to freedom. One of the new duties Congress wanted to grant to the Freedmen's Bureau included federal protection of blacks against white oppression in the South.

Johnson vetoed this measure as an unnecessary and unconstitutional use of the military during peacetime, and also vetoed a civil rights bill that declared blacks to be U.S. citizens and denied Southern states the ability to withhold property rights on the basis of race. Tensions increased; and in April 1866, Congress re-passed the **Civil Rights Act of 1866** over Johnson's veto. This shifted the political upper hand to Congress, who would henceforth assume the lead in reconstruction policy.

In June 1866, Congress passed a proposed **Fourteenth Amendment**. This amendment clearly asserted the citizenship of blacks, stating, "All persons born or naturalized in the U.S. are citizens," thus effectively overturning the *Dred Scott* decision that held that blacks were not citizens and did not have standing to sue. It also asserted that they were entitled to the "privileges and immunities of citizens," to the "equal protection of the laws," and to protection against being deprived of "life, liberty, and property without due process of law." In effect, the amendment was designed to overturn the Black Codes.

Lawyers have been kept busy for more than a century determining exactly what these terms meant, but one thing was clear: The amendment did not specify the right of black suffrage. It did, however, provide that states that disfranchised a part of their adult male population would have their representation in Congress proportionately reduced. It almost seemed that Congress was offering the Southerners a choice. They might disenfranchise the blacks if they were willing to pay the price of reduced representation, or they might have increased representation if they were willing to pay the price of black suffrage. This might not help the blacks, but it was certain to help the Republicans. It would either reduce the strength of Southern white Democrats or give the Republicans black political allies in the South.

The Fourteenth Amendment also provisionally excluded from federal office any person who had held any important public office before the Civil War and had then gone over to the Confederacy. This sweeping move to disqualify almost the entire leadership of the South led the Southern states to make the serious mistake of following President Johnson's advice to reject the amendment. During the latter half of 1866 and the first months of 1867, ten Southern states voted not to ratify the Fourteenth Amendment. By March 1867, Tennessee was the only Southern state that had ratified the Fourteenth Amendment.

15.3 Radical Reconstruction

Southern rejection of the Fourteenth Amendment precipitated the bitter fight that had been brewing for almost two years. The congressional elections of 1866, however, gave Radical Republicans a two-thirds majority in Congress, thus solidifying their power to over-ride presidential vetoes and take the lead in the Reconstruction. Congress now moved to replace the Johnson governments in the South with new governments of its own creation. Between March 1867 and March 1868, it adopted a series of **Reconstruction Acts** that divided ten Southern states into five military districts under five military governors. The governors were vested with "all powers necessary" to protect the civil rights of all persons, maintain order, and supervise the administration of justice.

These governors were to hold elections for conventions to frame new state constitutions. In these elections adult males, including blacks, were to vote—but many whites, disqualified by their support of the Confederacy, were not to vote. The constitutions these conventions adopted must establish black suffrage, and the governments they established must ratify the Fourteenth Amendment. Then and only then might they be readmitted to the Union.

Congress followed with a second Reconstruction Act that required military authorities in the South to register voters and supervise the election of the delegates to state constitutional conventions. Furthermore, new constitutions had to be ratified by a majority of voters. Thus, two years after the war was over, when the South supposed that the postwar adjustment had been completed, the process of reconstruction actually began.

The period that followed has been the subject of more bitter feeling and more controversy than perhaps any other period in American history, and the intensity of the bitterness has made it hard to get at the realities. During 1867 the military governors conducted elections; and in late 1867 and early 1868, the new constitutional conventions met in the Southern states. They complied with the terms Congress had laid down, including the enfranchisement of black men. Still many Southerners resisted. Military authorities in many places found that they could not get together a majority of voters at the polls as Congress had required. In essence, the former Confederates protested their new constitutions—which they viewed as externally imposed—by staying home and not voting. In March 1868, Congress altered the rules to allow state constitutions to be ratified by the majority of those who voted in an election. Three months later, Arkansas fulfilled the requirements necessary for readmission to the Union; and within a year after the third Reconstruction Act (of July 1867), seven states had adopted new constitutions,

Map 15.1 Reconstruction

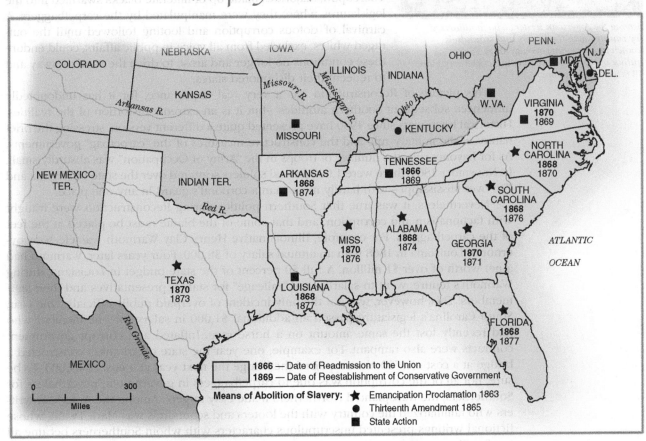

organized new governments, ratified the Fourteenth Amendment, and been readmitted to the Union. In Virginia, Mississippi, Georgia, and Texas, however, the process was for one reason or another not completed until 1870. In July 1870, Georgia became the last Southern state to be readmitted to the Union.

All of these new governments, except the one in Virginia, began under Republican control, with more or less black representation in the legislatures. In one state after another, however, the Democrats—supporting a policy of white supremacy—soon gained the ascendancy. Military and "Radical" rule lasted for three years in North Carolina; four years in Georgia and Tennessee (never under a military government); six years in Texas; seven years in Alabama and Arkansas; eight years in Mississippi; and ten years in Florida, Louisiana, and South Carolina.

The experience of this so-called "carpetbag" (so-named in reference to a popular nineteenth-century suitcase literally made from carpet and carried by many Northerners who moved south in search of economic opportunity) rule has been interpreted in completely different terms by historians of the past and those of the present. The earlier interpretation reflected the feelings of the Southern whites, who resented this regime bitterly, seeing it as one of "military despotism" and "Negro rule." According to this version, later elaborated by a pro-Southern school of historians, the South was, at the outset, the victim of military occupation in which a brutal soldiery maintained bayonet rule. Then came the **carpetbaggers**—unscrupulous Northern adventurers whose only purpose was to enrich themselves by plundering the prostrate South. The term *carpetbagger* was also used disparagingly by Southerners in reference to Northerners who moved south and became involved in Southern politics.

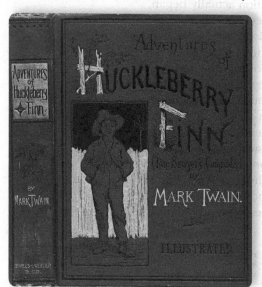

Among the American writers who familiarized the country with the looters and scoundrels known as carpetbaggers was Mark Twain, author of the American classic Huckleberry Finn. *(Wikimedia Commons)*

In the view of Southerners, in order to maintain their ascendancy, the carpetbaggers incited the blacks—who had been initially well disposed—to assert themselves in swaggering insolence. Thereupon, majorities made up of illiterate blacks swarmed into the legislatures where they were manipulated by the carpetbaggers. A carnival of riotous corruption and looting followed until the outraged whites, excluded from all voice in public affairs, could endure these conditions no longer and arose to drive the vandals away and to redeem their dishonored states.

This picture of Reconstruction has a very real importance, for it has undoubtedly influenced subsequent Southern attitudes—but it is an extreme distortion of the realities. Historical treatments since 1950 have presented quite a different version, stressing the brief nature of the military rule and the constructive measures of the "carpetbag" governments. As for bayonet rule, the number of troops in the "Army of Occupation" was absurdly small. In November 1869, there were 1,000 federal soldiers scattered over the state of Virginia and 716 over Mississippi—with hardly more than a corporal's guard in any one place.

Nevertheless, it was true that Southern politics during Reconstruction were fraught with factionalism and corruption, and that some of the blame must be placed at the feet of the carpetbaggers. For example, Illinois native Henry Clay Warmoth was elected governor of Louisiana in 1868 with an annual salary of $8,000. Four years later, Warmoth had a net worth of over $1 million. A full 50 percent of the state budget in Louisiana, during Warmoth's tenure, went to salaries and "mileage" for state representatives and their staff members. This, however, was not the only incident of overpaid public officials. One year, South Carolina's legislature passed an additional $1,000 in salary for one member who had recently lost the same amount on a horse race. Inflated and corrupt government contracts were also rampant. For example, one year the state of Arkansas constructed a bridge at a cost of $500, then repaired the bridge the next year at a cost of $9,000. To be sure, not all of the corruption was due to carpetbaggers in government; nevertheless for Southerners, the transplanted Northerners made easy targets. Among the American writers who familiarized the country with the looters and scoundrels was Mark Twain, whose fictional writings presented unscrupulous characters with whom Southerners became all too familiar.

Among the carpetbaggers, there were indeed looters and scoundrels; but there were also idealists who did all they could to improve conditions in the South. Many Northern women came to teach the freed slaves. Many men came to develop needed industry, which—though it enriched the Northern carpetbagger in the process—was good for the South as a whole. Many others worked with integrity and self-sacrifice to find a constructive solution for the problems of a society devastated by war and then left with a huge population of former slaves to absorb and provide for. Many native Southerners, who joined with the carpetbaggers in their programs and who were therefore denounced as "scalawags," were equally public-spirited and high-minded.

As for "Negro rule," the fact is that the blacks were in a majority only in the convention and the first three legislatures of South Carolina. Elsewhere they were a minority—even in Mississippi and Louisiana—where they constituted a majority of the population. In view of their illiteracy and their political inexperience, the blacks handled their new responsibilities well and tended to choose educated men for public office. Thus many of the black legislators, congressmen, and state officials they chose were well qualified. They were, on the whole, moderate and self-restrained in their demands; and they gave major support to certain policies of long-range value, including notably the establishment of public school systems, which the South had not had in any broad sense before the Civil War.

As for the "carnival of corruption," the post-Civil War era was marked by corruption throughout the country. All the Southern states combined did not manage to steal as much money from the public treasury as did the Tweed Ring in New York City, led by **William Marcy Tweed**, commonly known as "Boss Tweed." New York was also famous for fraudulent elections, and the corruption in government spearheaded by Tweed would become a major issue in national politics in the 1870s. It was true, however, that the impoverished South could ill afford dishonesty in government. Nevertheless, much that was charged to "corruption" really stemmed from increased costs necessary to provide new social services, such as public schools, and to rebuild the Southern economy laid waste by war.

Finally, it should be noted that the Southern whites were never reduced to abject helplessness, as is sometimes imagined. From the outset they were present in all of the Reconstruction conventions and legislatures—always vocal, frequently aggressive, and sometimes even dominating the proceedings.

15.3a The Fall of Radical Reconstruction

For an average of six years, then, the regimes of Radical Republican Reconstruction continued. After that they gave way to the "Democratic Redeemers"—those who wanted to "redeem" the South to white rule—delaying until the twentieth century further progress toward equal rights for blacks.

When one considers that the South had just been badly defeated in war, that radical Reconstruction was the policy of the dominant party in Washington, and that black and white Republicans constituted a majority of the voters in a half-dozen Southern states, it is difficult to understand why the radical regimes were so promptly—almost easily—overthrown. Several contributing factors must be recognized.

First, the former slaves lacked experience in political participation and leadership. Largely illiterate and conditioned for many decades to defer to white people, they grasped the new opportunities with uncertain hands. Very often they seemed to wish, quite realistically, for security of land tenure and for education more than for political rights. At the same time, however, a number of articulate and able blacks—some of them former slaves—came to the fore and might have provided effective leadership for their race if Reconstruction had not been abandoned so soon.

William Marcy Tweed

Also known as "Boss" Tweed, he was head of the New York City political machine in the late nineteenth century and notorious for fraud.

African Americans moved from the plantations to the state legislatures during the Reconstruction of the South. Of the conditions that the Southern states had to meet in order to be readmitted into the Union, the enfranchisement of black men was one of the most unpopular. (Library of Congress, Prints & Photographs Division, Popular Graphic Arts Collection, LC-USZC2-639)

The scare tactics of the Ku Klux Klan eventually escalated to extreme violence. (Wikimedia Commons)

Ku Klux Klan

Secret society that began in the 1870s as a social organization but quickly developed into a terror organization targeting blacks

First Ku Klux Klan Act

Imposed heavy penalties for violations of the Fourteenth and Fifteenth Amendments and gave the state governments the authority to take whatever action they deemed necessary against the Klan

Second, and more important, one must recognize the importance of the grim resistance offered by the Southern whites. With their deep belief in the superiority of their own race, these Southerners were convinced that civilization itself was at stake. They fought with proportionate desperation, not hesitating to resort to violence and terror.

15.36 The Ku Klux Klan

On Christmas Eve 1865, a half-whimsical secret society, known as the **Ku Klux Klan** (KKK), was formed in Tennessee by six Confederate army veterans who were bored and restless after the war and who sought something for their own amusement. The name *Ku Klux Klan* was derived from the Greek word *Kuklos*—the root of the English word *circle*. Since the six founding members were of Scotch-Irish ancestry, they added the word *Klan* and then added the made-up word *Klux* to add "mystery and baffle" as well as something "secret-sounding" and "nonsensically inscrutable." With nothing sinister in mind, Jon C. Lester reportedly said to the other five founding members, "Boys, let's start something to break the monotony and cheer up our mothers and girles. Let's start a club of some kind." The original purpose of the young men evidently was merely to play practical jokes and serenade women; initially, it had nothing to do with racism or terror.

In furtherance of their playful goals, the men dawned white regalia and rode through the Tennessee countryside in search of adventure. Inadvertently, the men discovered that their midnight marauding frightened the black refugees who were aimlessly wandering the Tennessee countryside in large numbers. This discovery then began to take on a more purposeful character, and the Klansmen began a campaign of scare tactics against the wandering black refugees. An unintended consequence was that blacks quickly began avoiding the roadways in the area where Klansmen were playing their games. Word of the KKK fun and games spread across the South. People in surrounding areas contacted the Klan wanting to know how they, too, could set up KKK dens of their own, for the express purpose of scaring vagrant blacks away from the roadways. Soon, every Southern state had its organization of masked and robed riders, either as part of the Klan or under some other name. Klan tactics quickly escalated from jokes and scare tactics to naked violence, contrary to the original intensions of the Klan's founders. By use of threat, horsewhip—and even rope, gun, and fire—they spread fear not only among blacks but perhaps even more among the Republican leaders. By 1868, the Klan claimed to have five hundred thousand members, and their expressed purpose had grown from playful mischief to overt resistance to the Congressional Reconstruction Act of 1867.

The Ku Klux Klan's expressed purpose had grown from playful mischief to overt resistance to the congressional Reconstruction Act of 1867. Klan members were sworn to secrecy and had to swear that they were opposed to Negro equality and in favor of a white man's government, including the "restoration of the civil rights to Southern white men." (CORBIS, © Stefano)

Klan members were sworn to secrecy and had to swear that they were opposed to Negro equality and in favor of a white man's government, including the "restoration of the civil rights to Southern White men." The Klan stated in its bylaws a reverence for the "majesty and supremacy of the Divine Being" and recognized the supremacy of the U.S. Constitution. The Klan claimed that it was an institution of chivalry, humanity, mercy, and patriotism that existed to protect the weak, defend the Constitution, and execute all constitutional laws.

In 1870, KKK violence had grown sufficient that it drew the attention of the Radical Republicans in Congress, who passed "An Act to Enforce the Provisions of the 14th Amendment to the Constitution of the United States, and for Other Purposes," more generally known as the **First Ku Klux Klan Act**. The act imposed heavy penalties for violations of the Fourteenth and Fifteenth Amendments and gave the state governments the authority to take whatever action they deemed necessary against the Klan. In furtherance of the execution of the act, Union troops and state militiamen arrested Klansmen and tried them for their crimes, sending many to prison. Under this pressure from the federal and state governments, the KKK was no longer a force by the end of 1872.

The dramatic quality of the Klan has given it a prominent place in the public's mental picture of Reconstruction. Though violence played a prominent role, the white South had other, less spectacular weapons that were no less powerful. Southern whites owned almost all of the land, controlled virtually all employment, dominated the small supply of money and credit that was to be found in the South, and dominated the legal system. In unspectacular ways, they could make life very hard for individuals who did not comply with the segregated system. These factors, perhaps more than the acts of night riders and violent men, made the pressure against radical rule almost irresistible.

Another important reason for the downfall of Radical Reconstruction was that it was not really very radical. It did not confiscate the land of plantation owners and redistribute it among the freed slaves like true radicals and abolitionists, such as Thaddeus Stevens and Wendell Phillips, had urged. It also did not reduce the former Confederate states to the status of territories for a probationary period, as many radicals also advocated. Furthermore, it did not permanently disfranchise the South's former ruling class, nor did it permanently disqualify more than a handful of ex-Confederate leaders from holding office. It did not enact Charles Sumner's bill to require universal public education in the South and to provide federal aid for schools there; hence, the former slaves were to remain largely uneducated. These would have been genuinely radical measures, but they went beyond what a majority of Northern voters were willing to support—and perhaps would have even risked the renewal of revolt in the South.

Indeed, even the limited radicalism of the Fourteenth Amendment and the Reconstruction Acts strained the convictions of most Northerners to the utmost. The North was not a racially equalitarian society. Black men did not have the right to vote in most Northern states at the time the Reconstruction Acts of 1867 enfranchised them in the South. The enactment of Negro suffrage in the South was accomplished by the Radical Republicans, not because of a widespread conviction that it was right in principle, but because it seemed to be the only alternative to Confederate rule.

Later, Republicans found that many Northern voters cared little about black suffrage in the South. They also found that the white South would not consent to a real reunion on this basis and that the restoration of former Confederates to political power did not threaten Northern or national interests. As a result, the Republicans let the existing forces in the South find their own resolution, which was one of white supremacy.

Yet Reconstruction was far from a total failure. It established public schools in the South that gradually brought literacy to the children of freed slaves. By 1900, illiteracy among blacks had dropped from 90 percent after the Civil War to an estimated 48 percent. It brought abolitionists and missionaries from the North to found such colleges as Howard, Fisk, Morehouse, Talladega, and many others. These colleges trained future generations of black leaders who, in turn, led the black protest movements of the twentieth century. Furthermore, though Reconstruction did not confiscate and redistribute land, many freed slaves became landowners through their own hard work and savings. In 1865 scarcely any black farmers owned their farms; by 1880, one fifth of them did.

Sharecroppers
Farmers who worked the land for landowners and paid a percentage of their harvest to the landowners

Sharecropping was a labor system where blacks worked the land for the white owners who paid them a percentage of the harvest. Sharecropping helped open the door for blacks to finally achieve economic freedom. (Wikimedia Commons)

15.3c Black Sharecroppers

A full 80 percent of black farmers were not land owners, even of small plots, but instead became **sharecroppers**—often working on the same plantation and for the same landowner who had once owned them. Sharecropping was a labor system where blacks worked the land for the white owners and paid the white owners a percentage of their harvest (normally 25 percent of the cotton crop and one-third of other crops) for the privilege of

BVT *Lab*

Visit www.BVTLab.com
to explore the student
resources available for
this chapter.

working on the owner's land. Planters generally divided their plantations into small twenty-five to thirty acre plots and signed contracts with individual black sharecroppers to work each plot. Land owners supplied the sharecroppers with the necessary mules, seed, plows, and tools, while blacks were responsible for their own food and necessities. A system of credit developed where local merchants would advance goods to black sharecroppers with payment due at the time of harvest.

Sharecropping allowed blacks the beginnings of economic freedom, but also the freedom to decide which family members would work the land, how long they would work each day, and how the labor would be divided. Blacks also typically moved out of the slave cottages and into their own dwellings. On some plantations, however, blacks worked for wages in gangs just as they had under slavery—complete with white overseers and even whippings in some instances.

Still, change did come with emancipation, in that a full third of the black women who had once worked in the fields abandoned that work either to tend to the home and child rearing, or for paid domestic servitude. Indoor work—even if it consisted of cleaning and laundry—was much preferable to working in the field in the hot Southern sun.

Pictured is an illustration from Harper's Weekly, 1868: *a bureau agent stands between armed groups of Southern whites and freedmen. The Freedmen's Bureau was created for the purpose of aiding the former slaves in their transition to freedom.* (Wikimedia Commons)

15.3b Freedmen's Bureau

Reconstruction also created the Freedmen's Bureau, which was perhaps charged with more responsibility than any federal agency in history. The Freedmen's Bureau was created for the purpose of aiding the former slaves in their transition to freedom. Though woefully undermanned and underfunded, the Freedmen's Bureau provided food, clothing, medical care, and shelter for former slaves. In the first two years after the war, the Freedmen's Bureau issued over $20 million to needy black Americans and treated 450,000 illnesses. The Bureau also constructed forty hospitals across the South to help meet the medical needs of the former slave population.

After the Civil War, the Southern roadways were literally clogged with free blacks who were released by Southern plantation owners who had no money with which to hire their labor. With nowhere to go, thousands of blacks wandered aimlessly across the South. Since they made easy targets without shelter on the roadways, many of these refugees would be among those terrorized by the night rides of the KKK. The Freedmen's Bureau helped transport the dislocated refugees to shelter, helped blacks find family members from whom they had become separated either before or after the war, and performed formal marriage ceremonies for many blacks who wanted legal sanction for the de facto marriages they had lived within under slavery. In the first two years after the war, the Freedmen's Bureau helped resettle thirty thousand displaced black Americans.

The Freedmen's Bureau also attempted to ensure fair trials for blacks in the South, provide for black education, and serve as an employment agency for the thousands of unemployed black refugees. In total, the Freedmen's Bureau constructed over 4,300 schools in the first two years following the Civil War.

Finally, Reconstruction also left as a permanent legacy the Fourteenth and Fifteenth Amendments, which formed the constitutional basis for the civil rights movements of the post–World War II generation.

15.3c Johnson Versus the Radicals

The Republicans did not abandon their program all at once. Rather, it faded out gradually—although the radicals remained militant while Johnson remained president. Johnson had used his administrative powers to evade or modify the enforcement of some Republican reconstruction measures. This convinced most Republicans that his removal was necessary if their policy was to be carried out in the South, and in 1868 they tried to remove him by impeachment. The immediate pretext for impeachment was Johnson's dismissal of Secretary of War Stanton in February 1868.

A year earlier Congress had passed a series of acts designed to strengthen the legislative branch at the expense of the executive. Among these laws was the **Tenure of Office Act**, which forbade removals of public officials who had been confirmed by the Senate without first obtaining Senate approval. The Tenure of Office Act was subsequently repealed by Congress in 1887. But at the time that Johnson had removed Stanton—who had been reporting to the radicals what went on within Johnson's administration—there had been no judicial ruling; and the House of Representatives voted to impeach Johnson, which meant that he must be tried by the Senate on the articles of impeachment.

Pictured is the impeachment trial of Andrew Johnson. (Wikimedia Commons)

The trial was conducted in a tense atmosphere and scarcely in a judicial way. Immense pressure was put on all Republican senators to vote for conviction. When a vote was finally taken on May 16, 1868, conviction failed by one vote of the two-thirds required. Seven Republicans had stood out against the party. Johnson was permitted to serve out his term; and the balance between executive and legislative power in the American political system, which had almost been destroyed, was preserved. Johnson, however, would fail to win the Democratic Party's nomination for president at their national convention two months later.

The determination of Republicans to achieve congressional domination of the reconstruction process also manifested itself in restrictions on the judiciary. When a Mississippi editor named McCardle appealed to the Supreme Court to rule on the constitutionality of one of the Reconstruction Acts, under which he had been arrested by the military, Congress passed, in March 1868, an act changing the appellate jurisdiction of the Court so that it could not pass judgment on McCardle's case.

Tenure of Office Act

Forbade the removal of public officials who had been confirmed by the Senate without first obtaining Senate approval for the removal of the official

15.4 **The Grant Administration**

In 1868 the country faced another election, and the Republicans turned to General Grant as their nominee. He was elected over the Democratic candidate, Governor Horatio Seymour of New York, by a popular majority of only 310,000—a surprisingly close vote. Without the votes of the newly enfranchised blacks in the seven reconstructed Southern states, Grant might have had no edge in popular votes at all. The Radical Republicans were alarmed at their narrow margin of victory and therefore sought to find ways to add more black voters to the ranks. Although the Fourteenth Amendment theoretically forced black suffrage on the South, the issue of suffrage for blacks had been generally ignored in a number of Northern states. Between 1865 and 1869, a number of Northern states had held referendums on black suffrage; and voters in Kansas, Ohio, Michigan, Missouri, Wisconsin, New York, and the District of Columbia all voted down black suffrage. The vote in the District of Columbia was an overwhelming 6,521 to 35 against black suffrage. Of the Northern states that held elections on the issue, only Iowa and Minnesota passed laws granting the franchise to blacks. To implant Negro suffrage

Pictured is President Ulysses S. Grant, delivering his inaugural address at the U.S. Capitol on March 4, 1873. (Library of Congress, cpb 3a19365)

permanently in the Constitution—for the North as well as the South—Congress in 1869 passed the **Fifteenth Amendment**, forbidding the states to deny any citizen his right to vote "on account of race, color, or previous condition of servitude." The amendment was ratified, in 1870, and had an almost immediate impact as black men—just five years removed from slavery—were elected to public office. Though blacks were still severely under-represented, in the 1870s seventeen black men served in Congress, one served in the U.S. Senate, and one black man served as chief justice of the South Carolina Supreme Court. For a brief interlude, blacks even held a majority of the seats in the South Carolina legislature.

President Grant supported the measures of the radicals and gave, in some ways, his backing to their policies. Like the good military man he was, he believed that where violence broke out, it should be put down uncompromisingly. Accordingly, he favored the adoption of Enforcement Acts for the use of federal troops to break up the activities of the Ku Klux Klan. When these laws were passed, he did not hesitate to invoke them; and troops were sent in on a number of occasions.

Fundamentally, however, Grant was not a radical. He wanted to see tranquility restored, and this meant reuniting North and South on any basis both would be willing to accept. Accordingly, he urged a broader extension of amnesty to all former Confederates, and he grew to resent the frequent appeals of Republican governments in the South for troops to uphold their authority. Though he realized that the tactics of the Redeemers were very bad—"bloodthirsty butchery," and "scarcely a credit to savages"—he became convinced that constant federal military intervention was worse in the long run.

In foreign affairs, Secretary of State Hamilton Fish was busy putting through an important settlement by which Great Britain and the United States adopted the principle of international arbitration as a means of settling American claims that had grown out of the raiding activities of the *Alabama* and other ships that British shipyards had built for the Confederacy. Though the U.S. did not get the $2 billion in "indirect" damages that it sought on the pretense that the British-built Confederate ships extended the war, it did get $15 million in damages from the British for their role in supplying the ships to the Confederacy.

15.4a The Collapse of Reconstruction

During the eight years of Grant's presidency, Republican governments were overthrown in eight of the Southern states. As Grant's second term neared its end, only three states—Louisiana, Florida, and South Carolina—remained in the Republican ranks. The program of Radical Reconstruction still remained official policy in the Republican Party, but it had lost its steam. The country was concerned about other things.

In financial circles, there was a controversy over what to do about the greenback dollars issued during the war. Since greenbacks were not backed by gold, people had saved the more valuable gold dollars and spent the less valuable greenback dollars, thus driving gold out of circulation. The government was willing to give gold for greenbacks even though such a policy would tend to increase the value of the dollar. Debtor interests (such as farmers), who wanted a cheap dollar, fought hard against the policy of redemption. Nevertheless, the policy was adopted in 1875. Not only did the policy limit the growth of the money supply and therefore hinder economic recovery in a cash-short economy, the decision also weakened the Republicans among farmers in the West.

15.4b Scandals Shake the Republican Party

In politics, public confidence in the Republican-led government was shaken by a series of disclosures concerning government corruption. In 1869, investors **Jay Gould** and **Jim Fisk** began purchasing gold futures for the purpose of driving up the price of gold, which skyrocketed from $4 per ounce to $25 per ounce. It was expected that, at a certain point, the U.S. Department of the Treasury would place U.S. gold reserves on the market in an effort to stabilize the gold market. Grant's brother-in-law in the Department of the Treasury, unknown to Grant, struck a deal with Gould to inform him in advance when the Department of the Treasury would release its gold reserves so that Gould could sell before the prices dropped. Grant's brother-in-law dutifully sent Gould a telegraph the morning that the Department of the Treasury released its gold to the open market, but Gould was out of the office and did not get the message. Prices quickly fell back to the pre-panic price of $4 per ounce, and Gould's losses were $16 million.

In 1872, it was revealed that several congressmen had accepted gifts of stock in a construction company, the **Crédit Mobilier**, which was found to be diverting the funds of the Union Pacific Railroad—including the funds the government had granted to it—with the knowledge of the officers of the road. In 1875 Grant's private secretary was implicated in the operations of the "Whiskey Ring"—which, by evading taxes, had systematically defrauded the government of millions of dollars. The following year, the secretary of war was caught selling appointments to American Indian posts. Meanwhile in the New York City government, the Tweed Ring, headed by Tammany boss William Marcy Tweed, was exposed as guilty of graft and thefts that have seldom been equaled in size—and have never been surpassed in effrontery.

The epidemic of corruption inspired a revolt by reform Republicans, who abandoned the party in 1872, organized the **Liberal Republican Party**, and nominated Horace Greeley, editor of the New York *Tribune,* for president. Although the Democrats also nominated Greeley and formed a coalition with the Liberal Republicans, Grant easily won reelection because most Northern voters were not yet prepared to trust the Democrats.

In the economic sphere, the country was trying to weather the financial depression that had begun with the panic of 1873. With the economic problems being experienced by whites in the North, the problems of Southern blacks seemed more and more distant, and less and less important, to the people of the North. Moreover, the economic recession weakened the Republican Party even further. In the 1874 mid-term elections, the Democrats won control of the House of Representatives for the first time since 1856. The next year, the Democrat-controlled House threatened to withdraw any appropriations for the Justice Department or the U.S. Army that were intended for use in the South.

In a number of Southern states, white Democrats created paramilitary organizations (the **White Leagues, Rifle Clubs, and Red Shirts**) who operated openly, unlike the Klan. In Louisiana, the Democratic paramilitary groups fought battles with Republican militias until President Grant sent the U.S. Army to restore order. Citizens on both sides of the Mason-Dixon line protested what they termed as Grant's "military rule" of Louisiana. Protests grew even louder after the U.S. Army ousted recently elected legislators in the Louisiana legislature due to electoral irregularities.

In Mississippi in 1875, Democratic Rifle Clubs broke up Republican Party rallies, shooting dozens of black Mississippi Republicans. The Republican Mississippi governor (a former Union soldier and native of Maine) called for sending federal troops to Mississippi to restore order. Grant considered sending troops, but refrained when Ohio Republicans warned him that such action could cost him the state of Ohio in the next election. In essence, the residents of Mississippi were left to fight out their problems amongst themselves. Governor Ames attempted to assemble a Republican militia to put down the unrest, but his efforts met with little success; and the Democrats won control of Mississippi in the state election of 1875.

15.4c The Courts and the End of Reconstruction

In the companion cases in 1876, *U.S. v. Reese* and *U.S. v. Cruickshank*, the Supreme Court struck down statutes that had provided for the enforcement of the Fourteenth and Fifteenth Amendments. With these rulings, federal officials could no longer prosecute individuals for violations of the equal rights of black people. Instead, the protection of individual rights was left to the states, and the rights of blacks in the South were left in the hands of the white Southerners who were now in control of Southern governments.

Crédit Mobilier
Construction company that was owned by the major stockholders of the Union Pacific Railroad and set up to make it appear that the Union Pacific Railroad was not profiting from the construction of the Transcontinental Railroad and that also bribed congressmen with shares in the company

Liberal Republican Party
Reform Republicans who abandoned the party in 1872 in reaction to scandals in the Grant administration, organized the Liberal Republican Party, and nominated Horace Greeley, editor of the New York *Tribune,* for president

White Leagues, Rifle Clubs, and Red Shirts
Paramilitary groups in the South that fought battles against the Republican state militias during Reconstruction

U.S. v. Reese and U.S. v. Cruickshank
The Supreme Court ruled that the Fifteenth Amendment did not confer voting rights on anyone; instead, if voting rights are denied, it cannot be on the basis of race.

Election of 1876

Disputed election in which Democrat Samuel Tilden won the popular vote, but Republican Rutherford B. Hayes won the electoral vote, when an Electoral Commission of eight Republicans and seven Democrats voted 8–7 to give all votes in dispute to Hayes

Rutherford B. Hayes

Republican elected president in the disputed election of 1876

Samuel J. Tilden

Democrat who won the popular vote but lost the electoral vote in the disputed election of 1876

15.5 The Hayes-Tilden Election of 1876

The **election of 1876** brought to an end the program of reconstruction, which probably would have ended soon in any case. In this election the Republicans, who were badly divided, turned to a Civil War veteran and governor of Ohio, **Rutherford B. Hayes**, as their nominee. Hayes was a conspicuously honest man, as was his Democratic opponent **Samuel J. Tilden** of New York, who owed his reputation to his part in breaking up the Tweed Ring.

Rutherford B. Hayes (Wikimedia Commons)

When the votes were counted, Tilden had a popular majority (obtained partly by the suppression of black votes in some Southern states) and was within one vote of an electoral majority. There were three states—Florida, Louisiana, and South Carolina—in which the result was contested, and two sets of returns were filed by rival officials—though Tilden had clearly won the popular vote in all three states. To count the votes in such a case, the Constitution calls for a joint session of the Congress; however, the House of Representatives—with a Democratic majority—was in a position to prevent an election by refusing to go into joint session with the Senate. Congress agreed to appoint an Electoral Commission to provide an impartial judgment, but the commission divided along party lines with eight Republicans and seven Democrats voting eight to seven to award all the electoral votes in dispute to Hayes. As late as two days before the inauguration, it was doubtful whether the Democrats in the House would accept the decision.

Map 15.2 Presidential Election of 1876

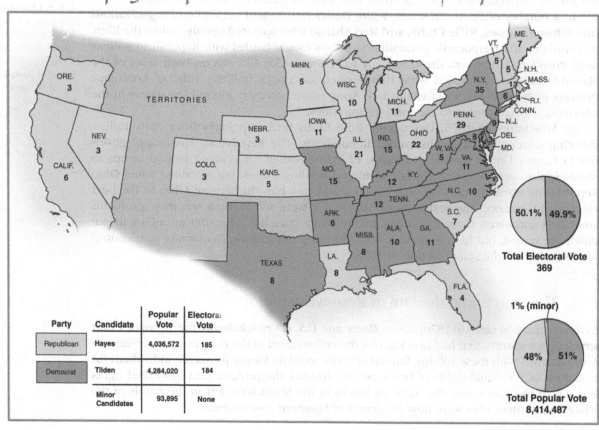

Party	Candidate	Popular Vote	Electoral Vote
Republican	Hayes	4,036,572	185
Democrat	Tilden	4,284,020	184
	Minor Candidates	93,895	None

50.1%   49.9%

Total Electoral Vote 369

1% (minor)

48%   51%

Total Popular Vote 8,414,487

Many Northern Democrats were prepared to fight to the finish against what they regarded as a stolen election, but the Southern Democrats had found that one civil war was enough. Moreover, various negotiations had been in progress behind the scenes. Important groups of Southern Democrats who had been left out when the government largesse of the Union Pacific-Central Pacific was distributed now hoped for a Texas and Pacific Railroad that would provide bountiful federal grants for Southern interests. They received assurances from friends of Governor Hayes that he would look with favor upon such programs of internal improvement. Moreover, they were assured that he would withdraw the last remaining federal troops from Louisiana and South Carolina, which meant that their Republican governments would collapse and the score of states would be: redeemed, eleven; reconstructed, none.

Pictured is the Electoral Commission of 1877. (Wikipedia)

With these understandings, Southern congressmen voted to let the count proceed so that Hayes would be elected. Later, when they were explaining their conduct to their constituents, they thought it best to say quite a great deal about how they had ransomed South Carolina and Louisiana and very little about their hopes for the Texas and Pacific Railroad and other such enterprises. Thus a legend grew up that there had been a "compromise" by which Reconstruction was ended.

What had really happened was that Southern Democrats and Northern Republicans had discovered that there were many features of economic policy on which they were in close harmony. The slaves were emancipated, the Union was restored, and bygones were bygones. The harmony of their views made reconciliation natural and reconstruction unnecessary. There was still the question of the blacks, but only a few whites had ever supported black suffrage or racial equality for its own sake. It had been an expedient; and now that the expedient was no longer needed, it could be laid aside. Such was the spirit of reconciliation.

Thus, the country ended a period of intense friction and entered upon a long era of sectional harmony and rapid economic growth—but this was done at the expense of leaving the question of racial relations still unattended to, even though slavery itself had, at immense cost, been removed.

Timeline

1862	Union troops begin reclaiming Southern territory; Lincoln appoints provisional governors for those areas controlled by federal troops.
1863	Lincoln outlines the Ten-Percent Reconstruction Plan.
1864	July, Lincoln disposes of Wade-Davis Bill with a pocket veto.
1865	January, Congress passes the Thirteenth Amendment abolishing slavery.
	May 29, Andrew Johnson offers broad amnesty to those who will take an oath of allegiance.
	December, all but two former Confederate states have organized new governments, ratified the Thirteenth Amendment, and elected congressmen.
	December 24, Ku Klux Klan forms in Tennessee.
1866	April, Congress passes the Civil Rights Act of 1866 over Johnson's veto.
	Congress votes on the Fourteenth Amendment, guaranteeing equal treatment under law and citizenship for the former slaves
	November, Radical Republicans gain a two-thirds majority in Congress.
1867	March, First Reconstruction Act is passed over Johnson's veto.
1868	January–May, House of Representatives votes to impeach President Andrew Johnson, but the Senate fails to convict by one vote.
	November, Ulysses S. Grant is elected president.
1869	Congress passes the Fifteenth Amendment prohibiting the denial of voting rights based on race.
	Jay Gould and Jim Fisk attempt to corner the gold market.
1870	July, Georgia becomes last Southern state to be re-admitted to the Union.
	First Ku Klux Klan Act prohibits violations of Fourteenth and Fifteenth Amendments.
1872	Crédit Mobilier scandal
	November, President Grant is reelected.
1873	Financial panic plunges the economy into depression.
1876	In *U.S. v. Reese* and *U.S. v. Cruickshank* the Supreme Court rules that the Fifteenth Amendment does not confer voting rights.
	Rutherford B. Hayes loses the popular vote to Samuel Tilden, but wins the electoral vote in a disputed election.
1877	Compromise of 1877 ends Reconstruction in the South and the South accepts Hayes as president.

CHAPTER SUMMARY

Reconstruction of the South actually began during the Civil War as the Union regained control in Southern states through military victory and began the process of restoring these states to the Union. Lincoln granted amnesty to former Confederates who took an oath of allegiance; and when as many as one-tenth of voters registered in 1860 took that oath, he would permit them to form a new state government. Then, when this new state government accepted the abolition of slavery and repudiated secession, Lincoln would receive it back into the Union, though new state governments did not have to recognize the rights of blacks.

Radical Republicans opposed Lincoln's plan as too lenient. After his tragic death they expected Andrew Johnson to be more punitive—but Johnson turned out to be perhaps even more conciliatory than Lincoln. Johnson issued a broad amnesty to all who would take an oath of allegiance, though men with property valued at more than $20,000 were required to ask for a special pardon. Johnson appointed provisional governors in each of the Southern states, and only men who had been voters in 1860 and had taken the oath of allegiance could participate. This meant, of course, that blacks were excluded. When the new governments disavowed secession, accepted the abolition of slavery, and repudiated the Confederate debt, Johnson would accept them.

In April 1866, Congress passed (over Johnson's veto) the Civil Rights Act of 1866, declaring all persons born in the U.S. to be citizens. In November, the radical Republicans won a veto-proof majority; in March 1867, Congress took over Reconstruction. In essence, Congress divided the South into five military districts, and required congressional approval for new state constitutions, that black men could vote, and that all Southern states ratify the Fourteenth Amendment.

Northern opportunists, labeled carpetbaggers by Southerners, moved South to exploit the political and economic situation. Some—such as Henry Clay Warmoth, who was elected governor of Louisiana—fleeced the taxpayers for millions. Southerners also objected to "negro rule" as blacks were elected to office on both the state and municipal level in the South. Most black men, however, became not elected officials but rather sharecroppers—paying landowners a percentage of the harvest for the privilege of working their land. The sharecroppers were among the poorest Americans in the late nineteenth century. The Freedmen's Bureau was established to assist blacks in their transition to freedom, but the bureau was understaffed and underfunded considering the scope of the problems faced by former slaves.

Whites reacted against black freedom with the formation of the Ku Klux Klan. Though the Klan began as a social organization for young men seeking fun and recreation, it quickly devolved into a terror organization that targeted blacks until it was squelched by federal authorities. Regardless, until the early 1870s the regimes of radical Republican reconstruction continued. After that, they gave way to the Democratic redeemers—those who wanted to "redeem" the South to white rule—delaying until the twentieth century further progress toward equal rights for blacks. Radical Republicans went as far as impeaching Andrew Johnson, but the Senate failed to convict the president by one vote.

General Ulysses S. Grant was elected in 1868; but his administration was fraught with scandals, including the Crédit Mobilier scandal in conjunction with the Transcontinental Railroad, and the efforts of Jay Gould and Jim Fisk to corner the gold market in 1869.

Reconstruction would finally come to an end with the Compromise of 1877, in which the Southern Democrats agreed to accept Rutherford B. Hayes, a Republican who lost the popular vote, as president in exchange for a federal withdrawal from the South. Real equality for black Americans would be an issue for future generations.

KEY TERMS

BIBLIOGRAPHY

A

Ahlstrom, Sydney. *A Religious History of the American People*. New Haven, CT: Yale University Press, 2004.

B

Baker, Jean H. *The Politics of Continuity: Maryland Political Parties from 1858 to 1870*. Baltimore, MD: Johns Hopkins University Press, 1973.

Brinkley, Alan. *American History: A Survey*. 11th ed. Boston, MA: McGraw-Hill, 2003.

Brock, William R. *An American Crisis: Congress and Reconstruction 1865–1867*. New York: Harper and Row, 1966.

C

Calvert, Robert A., Arnoldo De Leon and Gregg Cantrell. *The History of Texas*. 4th ed. Hoboken, NJ: Wiley, 2007.

Campbell, Randolph. *Gone to Texas*. New York: Oxford University Press, 2003.

Cash, W. J. *The Mind of the South*. New York: Knopf, 1941.

Cooper, William J. and Thomas E. Terrill. *The American South: A History*. New York: McGraw-Hill, 1991.

Croly, Herbert. *Progressive Democracy*. Somerset, NJ: Transaction Publishers, 1997.

Cummings, Bruce. *Dominion from Sea to Sea. Pacific Ascendancy and American Power*. New Haven, CT: Yale University Press, 2011.

Current, Richard Nelson. *Those Terrible Carpetbaggers: A Reinterpretation*. New York: Oxford University Press, 1989.

D

Donald, David Herbert. *Lincoln*. New York: Simon and Schuster, 1996.

———. *Lincoln Reconsidered*. New York: Vintage, 1961.

———. *The Politics of Reconstruction 1863–1867*. Bloomington, IN: iUniverse, 1999.

E

Engerman, Stanley L. and Robert E. Gallman. *The Cambridge Economic History of the United States, Vol. 2: The Long Nineteenth Century*. New York: Cambridge University Press, 2000.

F

Fehrenbach, T. R. *Lone Star: A History of Texas and the Texans*. Cambridge, MA: Da Capo Press, 2000.

Foner, Eric. *Reconstruction: America's Unfinished Revolution 1863–1877*. New York: Harper Perennial, 2002.

———. *Nothing but Freedom: Emancipation and Its Legacy*. Baton Rouge, LA: Louisiana State University Press, 2007.

G

Garraty, John A., and Robert McCaughey. *The American Nation: A History of the United States Since 1865*. 6th ed. New York: HarperCollins, 1987.

Gillette, William. *Retreat from Reconstruction 1869–1879*. Baton Rouge, LA: Louisiana State University Press, 1980.

Gould, Lewis L. *Grand Old Party: A History of Republicans*. New York: Random House, 2003.

H

Haas, Ben. *The Hooded Face of Vengeance*. Evanston, IL: Regency, 1963.

Hauss, Charles. *Comparative Politics: Domestic Responses to Global Challenges*. 2nd ed. St. Paul, MN: West Publishing, 1997.

Hughes, Jonathan, and Louis P. Cain. *American Economic History*. 8th ed. Englewood Cliffs, NJ: Pearson Prentice-Hall, 2010.

Hyman, Harold M. *A More Perfect Union: The Impact of the Civil War and Reconstruction on the Constitution*. Boston, MA: Houghton Mifflin, 1974.

J

Jacoby, Susan. *A History of American Secularism*. New York: Henry Holt, 2004.

Jones, Howard. *Quest for Security: A History of U.S. Foreign Relations*. New York: McGraw-Hill, 1996.

K

Keller, Morton. *Affairs of State: Public Life in Late Nineteenth Century America*. New York: Lawbook Exchange, 1977.

Kolchin, Peter. *American Slavery: 1619–1877*. New York: Hill and Wang, 2003.

L

Lipset, Seymour M., and Earl Raab. *The Politics of Unreason: Right-Wing Extremism in America, 1790–1970*. New York: Harper and Row, 1970.

Litwack, Leon F. *Been in the Storm So Long: The Aftermath of Slavery*. New York: Vintage, 1980.

M

McFeely, William S. *Grant: A Biography*. New York: W. W. Norton, 2002.

McKitrick, Eric L. *Andrew Johnson and Reconstruction*. New York: Oxford University Press, 1988.

McPherson, James M. *Battle Cry of Freedom: The Civil War Era*. New York: Oxford University Press, 2003.

Muccigrosso, Robert. *Basic History of Conservatism*. Melbourne, FL: Krieger, 2001.

BIBLIOGRAPHY

Nichols, Roy F. *The Disruption of American Democracy.* New York: Collier, 1962.

Niebuhr, Reinhold. *The Irony of American History.* Chicago, IL: University of Chicago Press, 2008.

Nieman, Donald G. *To Set the Law in Motion: The Freedmen's Bureau and the Legal Rights of Blacks 1865–1978.* Millwood, NY: KTO Press, 1979.

Olson, James S. *Encyclopedia of the Industrial Revolution in America.* Westport, CT: Greenwood Press, 2001.

Oren, Michael B. *Power, Faith, and Fantasy: America in the Middle East 1776 to the Present.* New York: W. W. Norton, 2007.

Paludan, Phillip Shaw. *A People's Contest: The Union and Civil War, 1861–1865.* Lawrence, KS: University of Kansas Press, 1996.

Perman, Michael. *Road to Redemption. Southern Politics 1868–1879.* Chapel Hill, NC: University of North Carolina Press, 1985.

Porter, Kirk H., and Donald Bruce Johnson eds. *National Party Platforms 1840–1968.* Urbana, IL: University of Illinois Press, 1972.

Rabinowitz, Howard N. *The First New South 1865–1920.* New York: Harlan Davidson, 1992.

Ransom, Roger L., and Richard Sutch. *One Kind of Freedom: The Economic Consequences of Emancipation.* New York: Cambridge University Press, 2001.

Seip, Terry Lee. *The South Returns to Congress: Men, Economic Measures, and Intersectional Relationships, 1868–1879.* Baton Rouge, LA: Louisiana State University Press, 1983.

Silbey, Joel H. *A Respectable Minority: The Democratic Party in the Civil War Era.* New York: W. W. Norton, 1977.

Summers, Mark Wahlgren. *The Era of Good Stealings.* New York: Oxford University Press, 1993.

Thomas, Benjamin Platt. *Abraham Lincoln: A Biography.* New York: Knopf, 1960.

Weisman, Steven R. *The Great Tax Wars.* New York: Simon and Schuster, 2002.

Woodward, Vann. *Reunion and Reaction: The Compromise of 1877 and the End of Reconstruction.* New York: Oxford University Press, 1991.

POP QUIZ

1. Which of the following is true of Lincoln's plan for Reconstruction?
   a. Blacks were granted equal rights.
   b. Blacks were granted voting rights.
   c. States did not have to recognize the rights of blacks or grant voting rights to blacks.
   d. Both a and b

2. Which of the following was included in the conspicuous features of the new Southern governments established under Johnson's reconstruction plan (that disturbed many Republicans)?
   a. Many Southern states had passed "Black Codes" that denied many citizenship rights to blacks.
   b. The former Confederates were completely shut out of control of politics in the Southern states.
   c. Many Southern states had reinstituted slavery.
   d. African Americans were now in control of politics in several Southern states.

3. Conspicuously absent in the Fourteenth Amendment was any mention of _____.
   a. black suffrage
   b. blacks' previous condition of servitude
   c. equal rights
   d. citizenship

4. Under congressional Reconstruction, blacks were the majority in the first three legislatures of _____.
   a. South Carolina
   b. Mississippi
   c. Alabama
   d. All of the above

5. What was one important factor that worked to limit black advancement in the South?
   a. Whites owned all of the land.
   b. Whites controlled most of the money and credit.
   c. Whites controlled all of the business and employment.
   d. All of the above

6. For what was the Freedmen's Bureau responsible?
   a. purchasing the freedom of slaves from their masters
   b. aiding the former slaves in their transition to freedom
   c. propaganda in support of black supremacy
   d. helping slaves escape to freedom via the underground railroad

7. What did the Fifteenth Amendment forbid?
   a. The denial of voting rights based on race, color, or previous condition of servitude.
   b. The denial of voting rights based on sex or gender.
   c. The denial of voting rights based on illiteracy.
   d. All of the above

8. The Hayes-Tilden Election was decided by _____.
   a. the popular vote
   b. the Electoral College
   c. the Supreme Court
   d. an Electoral Commission appointed by Congress.

9. How were Southern Democrats persuaded to accept the results of the election of 1876?
   a. They received assurances that Hayes would oppose any railroad in the South.
   b. They received assurances that Hayes would withdraw the remaining Union troops from the South.
   c. They received assurances that blacks would have equal rights in the South.
   d. They received assurances that all blacks would be removed to the North.

10. Lincoln favored the colonization abroad of freed slaves as a possible solution to the race problem. T F

11. Andrew Johnson was the only U.S. senator from a Southern state to remain loyal to the Union. T F

12. Reconstruction involved a very radical attempt to end racial discrimination in the South. T F

13. The Fourteenth Amendment asserted the citizenship of blacks and ensured black suffrage. T F

14. Andrew Johnson was charged with violating the _____ _____ but was not convicted.

15. The Reconstruction Acts abolished _____ _____ and created _____ military districts.

The Declaration of Independence

WHEN IN THE COURSE OF HUMAN EVENTS, it becomes necessary for one people to dissolve the political bands which have connected them with another, and to assume among the Powers of the earth, the separate and equal station to which the Laws of Nature and of Nature's God entitle them, a decent respect to the opinions of mankind requires that they should declare the causes which impel them to the separation.

We hold these truths to be self-evident, that all men are created equal, that they are endowed by their Creator with certain unalienable Rights, that among these are Life, Liberty and the pursuit of Happiness. That to secure these rights, Governments are instituted among Men, deriving their just Powers from the consent of the governed, That whenever any Form of Government becomes destructive of these ends, it is the Right of the People to alter or to abolish it, and to institute new Government, laying its foundation on such principles and organizing its Powers in such form, as to them shall seem most likely to effect their Safety and Happiness. Prudence, indeed, will dictate that Governments long established should not be changed for light and transient causes; and accordingly all experience hath shewn, that mankind are more disposed to suffer, while evils are sufferable, than to right themselves by abolishing the forms to which they are accustomed. But when a long train of abuses and usurpations, pursuing invariably the same object evinces a design to reduce them under absolute Despotism, it is their right, it is their duty, to throw off such Government, and to provide new Guards for their future security. Such has been the patient sufferance of these Colonies; and such is now the necessity which constrains them to alter their former Systems of Government. The history of the present King of Great Britain is a history of repeated injuries and usurpations, all having in direct object the Establishment of an absolute Tyranny over these States. To prove this, let Facts be submitted to a candid World:

He has refused his Assent to Laws, the most wholesome and necessary for the public good.

He has forbidden his Governors to pass Laws of immediate and pressing importance, unless suspended in their operation till his Assent should be obtained; and when so suspended, he has utterly neglected to attend to them.

He has refused to pass other Laws for the accommodation of large districts of people, unless those people would relinquish the right of Representation in the Legislature, a right inestimable to them and formidable to tyrants only.

He has called together legislative bodies at places unusual, uncomfortable, and distant from the depository of their Public Records, for the sole purpose of fatiguing them into compliance with his measures.

He has dissolved Representative Houses repeatedly, for opposing with manly firmness his invasions on the rights of the people.

He has refused for a long time, after such dissolutions, to cause others to be elected; whereby the Legislative Powers, incapable of the Annihilation, have returned to the People at large for their exercise; the State remaining in the mean time exposed to all the dangers of invasion from without, and the convulsions within.

He has endeavored to prevent the population of these States; for that purpose obstructing the Laws of Naturalization of Foreigners; refusing to pass others to encourage their migrations hither, and raising the conditions of new Appropriations of Lands.

He has obstructed the Administration of justice, by refusing his Assent to Laws for establishing Judiciary Powers.

He has made judges dependent on his Will alone, for the tenure of their offices, and the amount and payment of their salaries.

He has erected a multitude of New Offices, and sent hither swarms of Officers to harass our People, and eat out their substance.

He has kept among us, in times of peace, Standing Armies, without the consent of our legislature.

He has affected to render the Military independent of and superior to the Civil Power.

He has combined with others to subject us to a jurisdiction foreign to our constitution, and unacknowledged by our laws; giving his Assent to their acts of pretended legislation—For quartering large bodies of armed troops among us;

For protecting them, by a mock Trial, from Punishment for any Murders which they should commit on the Inhabitants of these States;

For cutting off our Trade with all parts of the world;

For imposing Taxes on us without our Consent;

For depriving us in many cases, of the benefits of Trial by Jury;

For transporting us beyond Seas to be tried for pretended offences;

For abolishing the free System of English Laws in a neighboring Province, establishing therein an Arbitrary government, and enlarging its Boundaries so as to render it at once an example and fit instrument for introducing the same absolute rule into these Colonies;

For taking away our Charters, abolishing our most valuable Laws, and altering fundamentally the Forms of our Governments;

For suspending our own Legislatures, and declaring themselves invested with Power to legislate for us in all cases whatsoever.

He has abdicated Government here, by declaring us out of his Protection and waging War against us.

He has plundered our seas, ravaged our Coasts, burnt our towns, and destroyed the lives of our people.

He is at this time transporting large armies of foreign mercenaries to compleat the works of death, desolation and tyranny, already begun with circumstances of Cruelty & perfidy, scarcely paralleled in the most barbarous ages, and totally unworthy the Head of a civilized nation.

He has constrained our fellow Citizens taken Captive on the high Seas to bear Arms against their Country, to become the executioners of their friends and Brethren, or to fall themselves by their Hands.

He has excited domestic insurrections amongst us, and has endeavoured to bring on the inhabitants of our frontiers, the merciless Indian Savages, whose known rule of warfare, is an undistinguished destruction of all ages, sexes and conditions.

In every stage of these Oppressions We have Petitioned for Redress in the most humble terms: Our repeated Petitions have been answered only by repeated injury. A Prince, whose character is thus marked by every act which may define a Tyrant, is unfit to be the ruler of a free People.

Nor have We been wanting in attentions to our British brethren. We have warned them from time to time of attempts by their legislature to extend an unwarrantable jurisdiction over us. We have reminded them of the circumstances of our emigration and settlement here. We have appealed to their native justice and magnanimity, and we have conjured them by the ties of our common kindred to disavow these usurpations, which, would inevitably interrupt our connections and correspondence. They too have been deaf to the voice of justice and of consanguinity. We must, therefore, acquiesce in the necessity, which denounces our Separation, and hold them, as we hold the rest of mankind, Enemies in War, in Peace Friends.

We, Therefore, the Representatives of the United States of America, in General Congress, Assembled, appealing to the Supreme judge of the world for the rectitude of our intentions, do, in the Name, and by Authority of the good People of these Colonies, solemnly publish and declare, That these United Colonies are, and of Right ought to be Free And Independent States; that they are Absolved from all Allegiance to the British Crown, and that all political connection between them and the State of Great Britain, is and ought to be totally dissolved; and that, as Free and Independent States, they have full Power to levy War, conclude Peace, contract Alliances, establish Commerce, and to do all other Acts and Things which independent States may of right do. And for the support of this Declaration, with a firm reliance on the Protection of Divine Providence, we mutually pledge to each other our Lives, our Fortunes and our sacred Honor.

The Constitution of the United States

WE THE PEOPLE OF THE UNITED STATES, in Order to form a more perfect Union, establish justice, insure domestic Tranquility, provide for the common defense, promote the general Welfare, and secure the Blessings of Liberty to ourselves and our Posterity, do ordain and establish this Constitution for the United States of America.

Article I

Section 1.   All legislative Powers herein granted shall be vested in a Congress of the United States, which shall consist of a Senate and House of Representatives.

Section 2.   1. The House of Representatives shall be composed of Members chosen every second Year by the People of the several States, and the Electors in each State shall have the Qualifications requisite for Electors of the most numerous Branch of the State Legislature.

2. No person shall be a Representative who shall not have attained to the Age of twenty-five Years, and been seven Years a Citizen of the United States, and who shall not, when elected, be an Inhabitant of that State in which he shall be chosen.

3. Representatives and direct Taxes[1] shall be apportioned among the several States which may be included within this Union, according to their respective Numbers, which shall be determined by adding to the whole Number of free Persons, including those bound to Service for a Term of Years, and excluding Indians not taxed, three fifths of all other Persons.[2] The actual Enumeration shall be made within three Years after the first Meeting of the Congress of the United States, and within every subsequent Term of ten Years, in such Manner as they shall by Law direct. The Number of Representatives shall not exceed one for every thirty Thousand, but each State shall have at Least one Representative; and until such enumeration shall be made, the State of New Hampshire shall be entitled to chuse three, Massachusetts eight, Rhode Island and Providence Plantations one, Connecticut five, New York six, New Jersey four, Pennsylvania eight, Delaware one, Maryland six, Virginia ten, North Carolina five, South Carolina five, and Georgia three.

4. When vacancies happen in the Representation from any State, the Executive Authority thereof shall issue Writs of Election to fill such Vacancies.

5. The House of Representatives shall chuse their Speaker and other officers; and shall have the sole Power of Impeachment.

Section 3.   1. The Senate of the United States shall be composed of two Senators from each State, chosen by the Legislature thereof,[3] for six Years; and each Senator shall have one Vote.

2. Immediately after they shall be assembled in Consequence of the first Election, they shall be divided as equally as may be into three Classes. The Seats of the Senators of the first Class shall be vacated at the Expiration of the second Year, of the second Class at the Expiration of the fourth Year, and of the third Class at the Expiration of the sixth Year, so that one third may be chosen every second Year; and if Vacancies happen by Resignation, or otherwise, during the Recess of the Legislature of any State, the Executive thereof may make temporary Appointments until the next Meeting of the Legislature, which shall then fill such Vacancies.[4]

3. No Person shall be a Senator who shall not have attained to the Age of thirty Years, and been nine Years a Citizen of the United States, and who shall not, when elected, be an Inhabitant of that State for which he shall be chosen.

4. The Vice President of the United States shall be President of the Senate, but shall have no vote, unless they be equally divided.

5. The Senate shall chuse their other Officers, and also a President pro tempore, in the absence of the Vice President, or when he shall exercise the Office of President of the United States.

6. The Senate shall have the sole Power to try all Impeachments. When sitting for that purpose, they shall be on Oath or Affirmation. When the President of the United States is tried, the Chief justice shall preside: And no person shall be convicted without the Concurrence of two thirds of the Members present.

7. Judgment in Cases of impeachment shall not extend further than to removal from Office, and disqualification to hold and enjoy any Office of honor, Trust, or Profit under the United States: but the Party convicted shall nevertheless be liable and subject to Indictment, Trial, judgment and Punishment, according to Law.

Section 4.   1. The Times, Places and Manner of holding Elections for Senators and Representatives, shall be prescribed in each state by the Legislature thereof; but the Congress may at any time by Law make or alter such Regulations, except as to the Places of Chusing Senators.

2. The Congress shall assemble at least once in every Year, and such Meeting shall be on the first Monday in December, unless they shall by Law appoint a different Day.

---

[1] *See the Sixteenth Amendment.*
[2] *See the Fourteenth Amendment.*

[3] *See the Seventeenth Amendment.*
[4] *See the Seventeenth Amendment.*

Section 5. 1. Each House shall be the judge of the Elections, Returns and Qualifications of its own Members, and a Majority of each shall constitute a Quorum to do Business; but a smaller number may adjourn from day to day, and may be authorized to compel the Attendance of absent Members, in such manner, and under such Penalties, as each House may provide.

2. Each House may determine the Rules of its Proceedings, punish its Members for disorderly Behavior, and, with the Concurrence of two thirds, expel a Member.

3. Each House shall keep a journal of its Proceedings, and from time to time publish the same, excepting such Parts as may in their judgment require Secrecy; and the Yeas and Nays of the Members of either House on any question shall, at the Desire of one fifth of those Present, be entered on the journal.

4. Neither House, during the Session of Congress, shall, without the Consent of the other, adjourn for more than three days, nor to any other Place than that in which the two Houses shall be sitting.

Section 6. 1. The Senators and Representatives shall receive a Compensation for their Services, to be ascertained by Law, and paid out of the Treasury of the United States. They shall in all Cases, except Treason, Felony, and Breach of the Peace, be privileged from arrest during their Attendance at the Session of their respective Houses, and in going to and returning from the same; and for any Speech or Debate in either House, they shall not be questioned in any other Place.

2. No Senator or Representative shall, during the Time for which he was elected, be appointed to any civil office under the Authority of the United States, which shall have been created, or the Emoluments whereof shall have been increased, during such time; and no Person holding any Office under the United States shall be a Member of either House during his continuance in Office.

Section 7. 1. All Bills for raising Revenue shall originate in the House of Representatives; but the Senate may propose or concur with Amendments as on other bills.

2. Every Bill which shall have passed the House of Representatives and the Senate, shall, before it become a Law, be presented to the President of the United States; If he approve he shall sign it, but if not he shall return it, with his Objections, to that House in which it shall have originated, who shall enter the Objections at large on their journal, and proceed to reconsider it. If after such Reconsideration two thirds of that House shall agree to pass the bill, it shall be sent, together with the objections, to the other House, by which it shall likewise be reconsidered, and if approved by two thirds of that House, it shall become a Law. But in all such Cases the Votes of both Houses shall be determined by Yeas and Nays, and the Names of the Persons voting for and against the Bill shall be entered on the journal of each House respectively. If any Bill shall not be returned by the President within ten Days (Sundays excepted) after it shall have been presented to him, the Same shall be a Law, in like Manner as if he had signed it, unless the Congress by their Adjournment prevent its Return, in which Case it shall not be a Law.

3. Every Order, Resolution, or Vote to which the Concurrence of the Senate and House of Representatives may be necessary (except on a question of Adjournment) shall be presented to the President of the United States; and before the Same shall take Effect, shall be approved by him, or being disapproved by him, shall be repassed by two thirds of the Senate and House of Representatives, according to the Rules and Limitations prescribed in the Case of a Bill.

Section 8. The Congress shall have Power

1. To lay and collect Taxes, Duties, Imposts and Excises, to pay the Debts and provide for the common Defense and general Welfare of the United States; but all Duties, Imposts and Excises shall be uniform throughout the United States;

2. To borrow money on the credit of the United States;

3. To regulate Commerce with foreign Nations, and among the several States, and with the Indian Tribes;

4. To establish an uniform Rule of Naturalization, and uniform Laws on the subject of Bankruptcies throughout the United States;

5. To coin Money, regulate the Value thereof, and of foreign Coin, and fix the Standard of Weights and Measures;

6. To provide for the Punishment of counterfeiting the Securities and current Coin of the United States;

7. To establish Post offices and post Roads;

8. To promote the Progress of Science and useful Arts, by securing for limited Times to Authors and inventors the exclusive Right to their respective Writings and Discoveries;

9. To constitute Tribunals inferior to the Supreme Court;

10. To define and punish Piracies and Felonies committed on the high Seas, and Offences against the Law of Nations;

11. To declare War, grant Letters of Marque and Reprisal, and make Rules concerning Captures on Land and Water;

12. To raise and support Armies, but no Appropriation of Money to that Use shall be for a longer Term than two Years;

13. To provide and maintain a Navy;

14. To make Rules for the Government and Regulation of the land and naval forces;

15. To provide for calling forth the Militia to execute the Laws of the Union, suppress Insurrections and repel invasions;

16. To provide for organizing, arming, and disciplining the Militia, and for governing such Part of them as may be employed in the Service of the United States, reserving to the States respectively, the Appointment of the Officers, and the Authority of training the Militia according to the discipline prescribed by Congress;

17. To exercise exclusive Legislation in all Cases whatsoever, over such District (not exceeding ten Miles

square) as may, by Cession of particular States, and the acceptance of Congress, become the Seat of Government of the United States, and to exercise like Authority over all Places purchased by the Consent of the Legislature of the State in which the Same shall be, for the Erection of Forts, Magazines, Arsenals, dock Yards, and other needful Buildings; And

18. To make all Laws which shall be necessary and proper for carrying into Execution the foregoing Powers, and all other Powers vested by this Constitution in the government of the United States, or in any Department or Officer thereof.

Section 9. 1. The Migration or Importation of such Persons as any of the States now existing shall think proper to admit, shall not be prohibited by the Congress prior to the Year one thousand eight hundred and eight, but a tax or duty may be imposed on such Importation, not exceeding ten dollars for each Person.

2. The Privilege of the Writ of Habeas Corpus shall not be suspended, unless when in Cases of Rebellion or Invasion the public Safety may require it.

3. No Bill of Attainder or ex post facto Law shall be passed.

4. No capitation, or other direct, Tax shall be laid unless in Proportion to the Census or Enumeration herein before directed to be taken.[5]

5. No Tax or Duty shall be laid on Articles exported from any State.

6. No Preference shall be given by any Regulation of commerce or Revenue to the Ports of one State over those of another: nor shall Vessels bound to, or from, one state, be obliged to enter, clear, or pay Duties in another.

7. No Money shall be drawn from the Treasury, but in Consequence of Appropriations made by Law; and a regular Statement and Account of the Receipts and Expenditures of all public Money shall be published from time to time.

8. No Title of Nobility shall be granted by the United States: And no Person holding any Office of Profit or Trust under them, shall, without the Consent of the Congress, accept of any present, Emolument, Office, or Title, of any kind whatever, from any King, Prince, or Foreign State.

Section 10. 1. No State shall enter into any Treaty, Alliance, or Confederation; grant Letters of Marque and Reprisal; coin Money; emit Bills of Credit; make any Thing but gold and silver Coin a Tender in Payment of Debts; pass any Bill of Attainder, ex post facto Law, or Law impairing the obligation of Contracts; or grant any Title of Nobility.

2. No State shall, without the Consent of the Congress, lay any Imposts or Duties on Imports or Exports, except what may be absolutely necessary for executing its inspection Laws: and the net Produce of all Duties and Imposts, laid by any State on Imports or Exports, shall be for the Use of the Treasury of the United States; and all such Laws shall be subject to the Revision and Control of the Congress.

3. No State shall, without the Consent of Congress, lay any duty of Tonnage, keep Troops, or Ships of War in time of peace, enter into any Agreement or Compact with another State, or with a foreign Power, or engage in War, unless actually invaded, or in such imminent Danger as will not admit of delay.

Article II

Section 1. 1. The executive Power shall be vested in a President of the United States of America. He shall hold his Office during the Term of four Years, and, together with the Vice President, chosen for the same Term, be elected, as follows:

2. Each State shall appoint, in such Manner as the Legislature thereof may direct, a Number of Electors, equal to the whole Number of Senators and Representatives to which the State may be entitled in the Congress; but no Senator or Representative, or Person holding an Office of Trust or Profit under the United States, shall be appointed an Elector.

The Electors shall meet in their respective States, and vote by Ballot for two persons, of whom one at least shall not be an Inhabitant of the same State with themselves. And they shall make a List of all the Persons voted for, and of the Number of Votes for each; which List they shall sign and certify, and transmit sealed to the Seat of the Government of the United States, directed to the President of the Senate. The President of the Senate shall, in the Presence of the Senate and House of Representatives, open all the Certificates, and the Votes shall then be counted. The Person having the greatest Number of Votes shall be the President, if such Number be a Majority of the whole Number of Electors appointed; and if there be more than one who have such Majority, and have an equal Number of Votes, then the House of Representatives shall immediately chuse by Ballot one of them for President; and if no Person have a Majority, then from the five highest on the List the said House shall in like Manner chuse the President. But in chusing the President, the votes shall be taken by States, the Representation from each State having one Vote; a quorum for this Purpose shall consist of a Member or Members from two thirds of the States, and a Majority of all the States shall be necessary to a Choice. In every Case, after the Choice of the President, the Person having the greatest Number of Votes of the Electors shall be the Vice President. But if there should remain two or more who have equal votes, the Senate shall chuse from them by Ballot the Vice President.[6]

3. The Congress may determine the time of chusing the Electors, and the Day on which they shall give their Votes; which Day shall be the same throughout the United States.

4. No person except a natural born Citizen, or a Citizen of the United States, at the time of the Adoption of

---

[5] *See the Sixteenth Amendment.*

[6] *Superseded by the Twelfth Amendment.*

this Constitution, shall be eligible to the Office of President; neither shall any Person be eligible to that office who shall not have attained to the Age of thirty-five Years, and been fourteen Years a Resident within the United States.

5. In Case of the Removal of the President from Office, or of his Death, Resignation, or Inability to discharge the Powers and Duties of the said Office, the same shall devolve on the Vice President, and the Congress may by Law provide for the Case of Removal, Death, Resignation, or Inability, both of the President and Vice President, declaring what Officer shall then act as President, and such Officer shall act accordingly, until the Disability be removed, or a President shall be elected.

6. The President shall, at stated Times, receive for his Services a Compensation, which shall neither be increased nor diminished during the Period for which he shall have been elected, and he shall not receive within that Period any other Emolument from the United States, or any of them.

7. Before he enter on the execution of his Office, he shall take the following Oath or Affirmation: "I do solemnly swear (or affirm) that I will faithfully execute the Office of President of the United States, and will, to the best of my Ability, preserve, protect, and defend the Constitution of the United States."

Section 2.   1. The President shall be Commander in Chief of the Army and Navy of the United States, and of the Militia of the several States, when called into the actual Service of the United States; he may require the Opinion, in writing, of the principal Officer in each of the executive Departments, upon any subject relating to the Duties of their respective Offices, and he shall have Power to Grant Reprieves and Pardons for Offences against the United States, except in Cases of Impeachment.

2. He shall have Power, by and with the Advice and Consent of the Senate, to make Treaties, provided two thirds of the Senators present concur; and he shall nominate, and by and with the Advice and Consent of the Senate, shall appoint Ambassadors, other public Ministers and Consuls, judges of the supreme Court, and all other Officers of the United States, whose Appointments are not herein otherwise provided for, and which shall be established by Law: but the Congress may by Law vest the Appointment of such inferior Officers, as they think proper, in the President alone, in the Courts of Law, or in the Heads of Departments.

3. The President shall have Power to fill up all Vacancies that may happen during the Recess of the Senate, by granting Commissions which shall expire at the End of their next Session.

Section 3.   He shall from time to time give to the Congress Information of the State of the Union, and recommend to their Consideration such Measures as he shall judge necessary and expedient; he may, on extraordinary occasions, convene both Houses, or either of them, and in Case of Disagreement between them, with respect to the Time of Adjournment, he may adjourn them to such Time

as he shall think proper; he shall receive Ambassadors and other public Ministers; he shall take Care that the Laws be faithfully executed, and shall Commission all the officers of the United States.

Section 4.   The President, Vice President and all civil Officers of the United States, shall be removed from Office on Impeachment for, and Conviction of, Treason, Bribery, or other high Crimes and Misdemeanors.

Article III

Section 1.   The judicial Power of the United States, shall be vested in one supreme Court, and in such inferior Courts as the Congress may from time to time ordain and establish. The judges, both of the supreme and inferior Courts, shall hold their Offices during good Behaviour, and shall, at stated Times, receive for their Services, a Compensation, which shall not be diminished during their Continuance in Office.

Section 2.   1. The judicial Power shall extend to all Cases, in Law and Equity, arising under this Constitution, the Laws of the United States, and treaties made, or which shall be made, under their Authority;—to all Cases affecting Ambassadors, other public ministers and consuls; to all cases of admiralty and maritime jurisdiction;—to Controversies to which the United States shall be a party;[7]—to Controversies between two or more States; between a State and citizens of another States;—between Citizens of different States;—between Citizens of the same State claiming Lands under Grants of different States, and between a State, or the Citizens thereof, and foreign States, Citizens or Subjects.

2. In all Cases affecting Ambassadors, other public Ministers and Consuls, and those in which a State shall be Party, the supreme Court shall have original Jurisdiction. In all the other Cases before mentioned, the supreme Court shall have appellate jurisdiction, both as to Law and Fact, with such Exceptions, and under such Regulations as the Congress shall make.

3. The trial of all Crimes, except in Cases of Impeachment, shall be by jury; and such Trial shall be held in the State where the said Crimes shall have been committed; but when not committed within any State, the trial shall be at such Place or Places as the Congress may by Law have directed.

Section 3.   1. Treason against the United States, shall consist only in levying War against them, or in adhering to their Enemies, giving them Aid and Comfort. No Person shall be convicted of Treason unless on the testimony of two Witnesses to the same overt Act, or on Confession in open Court.

2. The Congress shall have power to declare the Punishment of Treason, but no Attainder of Treason shall work Corruption of Blood, or Forfeiture except during the Life of the Person attainted.

---

[7] *See the Eleventh Amendment.*

Article IV

Section 1. Full Faith and Credit shall be given in each State to the public Acts, Records, and judicial Proceedings of every other State. And the Congress may by general Laws prescribe the Manner in which such Acts, Records and Proceedings shall be proved, and the Effect thereof.

Section 2. 1. The Citizens of each State shall be entitled to all Privileges and Immunities of Citizens in the several States.[8]

2. A Person charged in any State with Treason, Felony, or other Crime, who shall flee from justice, and be found in another State, shall on demand of the executive Authority of the State from which he fled, be delivered up, to be removed to the State having jurisdiction of the crime.

3. No Person held to Service or Labour in one State, under the Laws thereof, escaping into another, shall, in Consequence of any Law or Regulation therein, be discharged from such Service or Labour, but shall be delivered up on Claim of the Party to whom such Service or Labour may be due.[9]

Section 3. 1. New States may be admitted by the Congress into this Union; but no new State shall be formed or erected within the Jurisdiction of any other State, nor any State be formed by the junction of two or more States, or parts of States, without the Consent of the Legislatures of the States concerned as well as of the Congress.

2. The Congress shall have Power to dispose of and make all needful Rules and Regulations respecting the Territory or other Property belonging to the United States; and nothing in this Constitution shall be so construed as to Prejudice any Claims of the United States, or of any particular State.

Section 4. The United States shall guarantee to every State in this Union a Republican Form of Government, and shall protect each of them against Invasion; and on Application of the Legislature, or of the Executive (when the Legislature cannot be convened) against domestic Violence.

Article V

The Congress, whenever two-thirds of both Houses shall deem it necessary, shall propose Amendments to this Constitution, or, on the Application of the Legislatures of two-thirds of the several States, shall call a Convention for proposing Amendments, which, in either Case, shall be valid to all Intents and Purposes, as part of this Constitution, when ratified by the Legislatures of three-fourths of the several States, or by Conventions in three-fourths thereof, as the one or the other Mode of Ratification may be proposed by the Congress; Provided that no Amendment which may be made prior to the Year One thousand eight hundred and eight shall in any Manner affect the first and fourth Clauses in the Ninth Section of the first Article; and that no State, without its Consent, shall be deprived of its equal Suffrage in the Senate.

Article VI

1. All Debts contracted and Engagements entered into, before the Adoption of this Constitution, shall be as valid against the United States under this Constitution, as under the Confederation.[10]

2. This Constitution, and the Laws of the United States which shall be made in Pursuance thereof; and all Treaties made, or which shall be made, under the Authority of the United States, shall be the supreme Law of the Land; and the judges in every State shall be bound thereby, any Thing in the Constitution or Laws of any State to the Contrary notwithstanding.

3. The Senators and Representatives before mentioned, and the Members of the several State Legislatures and all executive and judicial Officers, both of the United States and of the several States, shall be bound by Oath or Affirmation, to support this Constitution; but no religious Test shall ever be required as a qualification to any Office or public Trust under the United States.

Article VII

The Ratification of the Conventions of nine States, shall be sufficient for the Establishment of this Constitution between the States so ratifying the same.

Done in Convention by the Unanimous Consent of the States present the Seventeenth Day of September in the Year of our Lord one thousand seven hundred and Eighty seven, and of the independence of the United States of America the Twelfth. In Witness whereof We have hereunto subscribed our Names.

[Names omitted]

---

[8] *See the Fourteenth Amendment, Section 1.*
[9] *See the Thirteenth Amendment.*

[10] *See the Fourteenth Amendment, Section 4.*

Amendments to the Constitution

ARTICLES IN ADDITION TO, and amendment of, the Constitution of the United States of America, proposed by Congress, and ratified by the legislatures of the several States, pursuant to the fifth article of the original Constitution.

Amendment I

[December 15, 1791]

Congress shall make no law respecting an establishment of religion, or prohibiting the free exercise thereof, or abridging the freedom of speech, or of the press; or the right of the people peaceably to assemble, and to petition the Government for a redress of grievances.

Amendment II

[December 15, 1791]

A well regulated Militia, being necessary to the security of a free State, the right of the people to keep and bear Arms shall not be infringed.

Amendment III

[December 15, 1791]

No Soldier shall, in time of peace, be quartered in any house, without the consent of the owner, nor in time of war, but in a manner to be prescribed by law.

Amendment IV

[December 15, 1791]

The right of the people to be secure in their persons, houses, papers, and effects, against unreasonable searches and seizures, shall not be violated, and no Warrants shall issue, but upon probable cause, supported by Oath or affirmation, and particularly describing the place to be searched, and the persons or things to be seized.

Amendment V

[December 15, 1791]

No person shall be held to answer for a capital or otherwise infamous crime, unless on a presentment or indictment of a Grand jury, except in cases arising in the land or naval forces, or in the Militia, when in actual service in time of War or public danger; nor shall any person be subject for the same offence to be twice put in jeopardy of life or limb; nor shall be compelled in any criminal case to be a witness against himself, nor be deprived of life, liberty, or property, without due process of law; nor shall private property be taken for public use, without just compensation.

Amendment VI

[December 15, 1791]

In all criminal prosecutions, the accused shall enjoy the right to a speedy and public trial, by an impartial jury of the State and district wherein the crime shall have been committed, which district shall have been previously ascertained by law, and to be informed of the nature and cause of the accusation; to be confronted with the witnesses against him; to have compulsory process for obtaining witnesses in his favor, and to have the Assistance of Counsel for his defense.

Amendment VII

[December 15, 1791]

In suits at common law, where the value in controversy shall exceed twenty dollars, the right of trial by jury shall be preserved, and no fact tried by a jury, shall be otherwise reexamined in any Court of the United States, than according to the rules of the common law.

Amendment VIII

[December 15, 1791]

Excessive bail shall not be required, nor excessive fines imposed, nor cruel and unusual punishments inflicted.

Amendment IX

[December 15, 1791]

The enumeration in the Constitution, of certain rights, shall not be construed to deny or disparage others retained by the people.

Amendment X

[December 15, 1791]

The powers not delegated to the United States by the Constitution, nor prohibited by it to the States, are reserved to the States respectively, or to the people.

Amendment XI

[January 8, 1798]

The judicial power of the United States shall not be construed to extend to any suit in law or equity, commenced or prosecuted against one of the United States by Citizens of another State, or by Citizens or Subjects of any Foreign State.

Amendment XII

[September 25, 1804]

The Electors shall meet in their respective States and vote by ballot for President and Vice-President, one of whom, at least, shall not be an inhabitant of the same State with themselves; they shall name in their ballots the person voted for as President, and in distinct ballots the person voted for as Vice-President, and they shall make distinct lists of all persons voted for as President, and of all persons voted for as Vice-President, and of the number of votes for each, which lists they shall sign and certify, and transmit sealed to the seat of the government of the United States, directed to the President of the Senate; The President of the Senate shall, in the presence of the Senate and House of Representatives, open all the certificates and the votes shall then be counted; The person having the greatest number of votes for President, shall be the President, if such number be a majority of the whole number of Electors appointed; and if no person have such majority, then from the persons having the highest numbers not exceeding three on the list of those voted for as President, the House of Representatives shall choose immediately, by ballot, the President. But in choosing the President, the votes shall be taken by states, the representation from each state having one vote; a quorum for this purpose shall consist of a member or members from two-thirds of the states, and a majority of all the states shall be necessary to a choice. And if the House of Representatives shall not choose a President whenever the right of choice shall devolve upon them, before the fourth day of March next following, then the Vice-President shall act as President, as in the case of the death or other constitutional disability of the President. The person having the greatest number of votes as Vice President, shall be the Vice-President, if such number be a majority of the whole number of Electors appointed, and if no person have a majority, then from the two highest numbers on the list, the Senate shall choose the Vice-President; a quorum for the purpose shall consist of two-thirds of the whole number of Senators, and a majority of the whole number shall be necessary to a choice. But no person constitutionally ineligible to the office of President shall be eligible to that of Vice-President of the United States.

Amendment XIII

[December 18, 1865]

Section 1. Neither slavery nor involuntary servitude, except as a punishment for crime whereof the party shall have been duly convicted, shall exist within the United States, or any place subject to their jurisdiction.

Section 2. Congress shall have power to enforce this article by appropriate legislation.

Amendment XIV

[July 28, 1868]

Section 1. All persons born or naturalized in the United States, and subject to the jurisdiction thereof, are citizens of the United States and of the State wherein they reside. No State shall make or enforce any law which shall abridge the privileges or immunities of citizens of the United States; nor shall any State deprive any person of life, liberty, or property, without due process of law; nor deny to any person within its jurisdiction the equal protection of the laws.

Section 2. Representatives shall be apportioned among the several States according to their respective numbers, counting the whole number of persons in each State, excluding Indians not taxed. But when the right to vote at any election for the choice of electors for President and Vice-President of the United States, Representatives in Congress, the Executive and Judicial officers of a State, or the members of the Legislature thereof, is denied to any of the male inhabitants of such State, being twenty-one years of age, and citizens of the United States, or in any way abridged, except for participation in rebellion, or other crime, the basis of representation therein shall be reduced in the proportion which the number of such male citizens shall bear to the whole number of male citizens twenty-one years of age in such State.

Section 3. No person shall be a Senator or Representative in Congress, or elector of President and Vice-President, or hold any office, civil or military, under the United States, or under any State, who, having previously taken an oath, as a member of Congress, or as an officer of the United States, or as a member of any State legislature, or as an executive or judicial officer of any State, to support the Constitution of the United States, shall have engaged in insurrection or rebellion against the same, or given aid or comfort to the enemies thereof. But Congress may by a vote of two-thirds of each House, remove such disability.

Section 4. The validity of the public debt of the United States, authorized by law, including debts incurred for payment of pensions and bounties for services in suppressing insurrection or rebellion, shall not be questioned. But neither the United States nor any State shall assume or pay any debt or obligation incurred in aid of insurrection or rebellion against the United States, or any claim for the loss or emancipation of any slave; but all such debts, obligations, and claims shall be held illegal and void.

Section 5. The Congress shall have the power to enforce, by appropriate legislation, the provisions of this article.

Amendment XV

[March 30, 1870]

Section 1. The right of citizens of the United States to vote shall not be denied or abridged by the United States or by any State on account of race, color, or previous condition of servitude

Section 2. The Congress shall have power to enforce this article by appropriate legislation.

Amendment XVI

[February 25, 1913]

The Congress shall have power to lay and collect taxes on incomes, from whatever source derived, without apportionment among the several States, and without regard to any census or enumeration.

Amendment XVII

[May 31, 1913]

The Senate of the United States shall be composed of two Senators from each State, elected by the people thereof, for six years; and each Senator shall have one vote. The electors in each State shall have the qualifications requisite for electors of the most numerous branch of the State legislatures.

When vacancies happen in the representation of any State in the Senate, the executive authority of such State shall issue writs of election to fill such vacancies: Provided, That the legislature of any State may empower the executive thereof to make temporary appointments until the people fill the vacancies by election as the legislature may direct.

This amendment shall not be so construed as to affect the election or term of any Senator chosen before it becomes valid as part of the Constitution.

Amendment XVIII

[January 29, 1919]

Section 1. After one year from the ratification of this article the manufacture, sale, or transportation of intoxicating liquors within, the importation thereof into, or the exportation thereof from the United States and all territory subject to the jurisdiction thereof for beverage purposes is hereby prohibited.

Section 2. The Congress and the several States shall have concurrent power to enforce this article by appropriate legislation.

Section 3. This article shall be inoperative unless it shall have been ratified as an amendment to the Constitution by the legislatures of the several States, as provided in the Constitution, within seven years from the date of the submission hereof to the States by the Congress.

Amendment XIX

[August 26, 1920]

The right of citizens of the United States to vote shall not be denied or abridged by the United States or by any State on account of sex.

Congress shall have power to enforce this article by appropriate legislation.

Amendment XX

[January 23, 1933]

Section 1. The terms of the President and Vice-President shall end at noon on the 20th day of January, and the terms of Senators and Representatives at noon on the 3d day of January, of the years in which such terms would have ended if this article had not been ratified; and the terms of their successors shall then begin.

Section 2. The Congress shall assemble at least once in every year, and such meeting shall begin at noon on the 3rd day of January, unless they shall by law appoint a different day.

Section 3. If, at the time fixed for the beginning of the term of the President, the President elect shall have died, the Vice-President elect shall become President. If a President shall not have been chosen before the time fixed for the beginning of his term, or if the President elect shall have failed to qualify, then the Vice-President elect shall act as President until a President shall have qualified; and the Congress may by law provide for the case wherein neither a President elect nor a Vice-President elect shall have qualified, declaring who shall then act as President, or the manner in which one who is to act shall be selected, and such person shall act accordingly until a President or Vice-President shall have qualified.

Section 4. The Congress may by law provide for the case of the death of any of the persons from whom the House of Representatives may choose a President whenever the right of choice shall have devolved upon them, and for the case of the death of any of the persons from whom the Senate may choose a Vice-President whenever the right of choice shall have devolved upon them.

Section 5. Sections 1 and 2 shall take effect on the 15th day of October following the ratification of this article.

Section 6. This article shall be inoperative unless it shall have been ratified as an amendment to the Constitution by the legislatures of three-fourths of the several States within seven years from the date of its submission.

Amendment XXI

[December 5, 1933]

Section 1. The eighteenth article of amendment to the Constitution of the United States is hereby repealed.

Section 2. The transportation or importation into any State, Territory, or possession of the United States for delivery or use therein of intoxicating liquors, in violation of the laws thereof, is hereby prohibited.

Section 3. This article shall be inoperative unless it shall have been ratified as an amendment to the Constitution by conventions in the several States, as provided in the Constitution, within seven years from the date of the submission hereof to the States by the Congress.

Amendment XXII

[March 1, 1951]

Section 1. No person shall be elected to the office of the President more than twice, and no person who has held the office of President, or acted as President, for more than two years of a term to which some other person was elected President shall be elected to the office of the President more than once.

But this Article shall not apply to any person holding the office of President when this Article was proposed by the Congress, and shall not prevent any person who may be holding the office of President or acting as President, during the term within which this Article becomes operative from holding the office of President or acting as President during the remainder of such term.

Section 2. This article shall be inoperative unless it shall have been ratified as an amendment to the Constitution by the legislatures of three-fourths of the several states within seven years from the date of its submission to the states by Congress.

Amendment XXIII

[March 29, 1961]

Section 1. The District constituting the seat of Government of the United States shall appoint in such manner as the Congress may direct:

A number of electors of President and Vice President equal to the whole number of Senators and Representatives in Congress to which the District would be entitled if it were a State, but in no event more than the least populous State; they shall be in addition to those appointed by the States, but they shall be considered, for the purposes of the election of President and Vice President, to be electors appointed by a State; and they shall meet in the District and perform such duties as provided by the twelfth article of amendment.

Section 2. The Congress shall have power to enforce this article by appropriate legislation.

Amendment XXIV

[January 23, 1964]

Section 1. The right of citizens of the United States to vote in any primary or other election for President or Vice President, for electors for President or Vice President, or for Senator or Representative in Congress, shall not be denied or abridged by the United States or any State by reason of failure to pay any poll tax or other tax.

Section 2. The Congress shall have the power to enforce this article by appropriate legislation.

Amendment XXV

[February 10, 1967]

Section 1. In case of the removal of the President from office or of his death or resignation, the Vice President shall become President.

Section 2. Whenever there is a vacancy in the office of the Vice President, the President shall nominate a Vice President who shall take office upon confirmation by a majority vote of both houses of Congress.

Section 3. Whenever the President transmits to the President pro tempore of the Senate and the Speaker of the House of Representatives his written declaration that he is unable to discharge the powers and duties of his office, and until he transmits to them a written declaration to the contrary, such powers and duties shall be discharged by the Vice President as Acting President.

Section 4. Whenever the Vice President and a majority of either the principal officers of the executive departments, or of such other body as Congress may by law provide, transmit to the President pro tempore of the Senate and the Speaker of the House of Representatives their written declaration that the President is unable to discharge the powers and duties of his office, the Vice President shall immediately assume the powers and duties of the office as Acting President.

Thereafter, when the President transmits to the President pro tempore of the Senate and the Speaker of the House of Representatives his written declaration that no inability exists, he shall resume the powers and duties of his office unless the Vice President and a majority of either the principal officers of the executive departments, or of such other body as Congress may by law provide, transmit within four days to the President pro tempore of the Senate and the Speaker of the House of Representatives their written declaration that the President is unable to discharge the powers and duties of his office. Thereupon Congress shall decide the issue, assembling within forty-eight hours for that purpose if not in session. If the Congress, within twenty-one days after receipt of the latter written declaration, or, if Congress is not in session, within twenty-one days after Congress is required to assemble, determines by two-thirds vote of both houses that the President is unable

Amendment XXVI

[June 30, 1971]

Section 1. The right of citizens of the United States, who are eighteen years of age or older, to vote shall not be denied or abridged by the United States or by any state on account of age.

Section 2. The Congress shall have power to enforce this article by appropriate legislation.

Amendment XXVII

[May 7, 1992]

No law varying the compensation for the services of the Senators and Representatives shall take effect, until an election of Representatives shall have intervened.

PRESIDENTIAL ELECTIONS

Year	# of States	Candidates	Party	Popular Vote	Electoral Vote**	Percentage of Popular Vote*
1789	11	**GEORGE WASHINGTON**	No party designations		69	
		John Adams			34	
		Other Candidates			35	
1792	15	**GEORGE WASHINGTON**	No party designations		132	
		John Adams			77	
		George Clinton			50	
		Other Candidates			5	
1796	16	**JOHN ADAMS**	Federalist		71	
		Thomas Jefferson	Democratic-Republican		68	
		Thomas Pinckney	Federalist		59	
		Aaron Burr	Democratic-Republican		30	
		Other Candidates			48	
1800	16	**THOMAS JEFFERSON**	Democratic-Republican		73	
		Aaron Burr	Democratic-Republican		73	
		John Adams	Federalist		65	
		Charles C. Pinckney	Federalist		64	
		John Jay	Federalist			
1804	17	**THOMAS JEFFERSON**	Democratic-Republican		162	
		Charles C. Pinckney	Federalist		14	
1808	17	**JAMES MADISON**	Democratic-Republican		122	
		Charles C. Pinckney	Federalist		47	
		George Clinton	Democratic-Republican		6	
1812	18	**JAMES MADISON**	Democratic-Republican		128	
		DeWitt Clinton	Federalist		89	
1816	19	**JAMES MONROE**	Democratic-Republican		183	
		Rufus King	Federalist		34	
1820	24	**JAMES MONROE**	Democratic-Republican		231	
		John Quincy Adams	Independent Republican		1	
1824	24	**JOHN QUINCY ADAMS**		108,740	84	30.5
		Andrew Jackson		153,544	99	43.1
		William H. Crawford		46,618	41	13.1
		Henry Clay		47,136	37	13.2
1828	24	**ANDREW JACKSON**	Democrat	647,286	178	56.0
		John Ouincy Adams	National Republican	508,064	83	44.0
1832	24	**ANDREW JACKSON**	Democrat	687,502	219	55.0
		Henry Clay	National Republican	530,189	49	42.4
		William Wirt	Anti-Masonic	33,108	7	2.6
		John Floyd	National Republican		11	
1836	26	**MARTIN VAN BUREN**	Democrat	765,483	170	50.9
		William H. Harrison	Whig		73	
		Hugh L. White	Whig	739,795	26	49.1
		Daniel Webster	Whig		14	
		W. P. Mangum	Whig		11	
1840	26	**WILLIAM H. HARRISON**	Whig	1,274,624	234	53.1
		Martin Van Buren	Democrat	1,127,781	60	46.9
1844	26	**JAMES K. POLK**	Democrat	1,338,464	170	49.6
		Henry Clay	Whig	1,300,097	105	48.1
		James G. Birney	Liberty	62,300		2.3
1848	30	**ZACHARY TAYLOR**	Whig	1,360,967	163	47.4
		Lewis Cass	Democrat	1,222,342	127	42.5
		Martin Van Buren	Free Soil	291,263		10.1
1852	31	**FRANKLIN PIERCE**	Democrat	1,601,117	254	50.9
		Winfield Scott	Whig	1,385,453	42	44.1
		John P. Hale	Free Soil	155,825		5.0

* Percentage of popular vote given for any election year may not total 100 percent because candidates receiving less than 1 percent of the popular vote have been omitted.

** Prior to the passage of the Twelfth Amendment in 1904, the electoral college voted for two presidential candidates; the runner-up became Vice President. Data from Historical Statistics of the United States, Colonial Times to 1957 (1961), pp. 682–883, and The World Almanac.

Year	# of States	Candidates	Party	Popular Vote	Electoral Vote**	Percentage of Popular Vote*
1856	31	**JAMES BUCHANAN**	Democrat	1,832,955	174	45.3
		John C. Frémont	Republican	1,339,932	114	33.1
		Millard Fillmore	American	871,731	8	21.6
1860	33	**ABRAHAM LINCOLN**	Republican	1,865,593	180	39.8
		Stephen A. Douglas	Democrat	1,382,713	12	29.5
		John C. Breckinridge	Democrat	848,356	72	18.1
		John Bell	Constitutional Union	592,906	39	12.6
1864	36	**ABRAHAM LINCOLN**	Republican	2,206,938	212	55.0
		George B. McClellan	Democrat	1,803,787	21	45.0
1868	37	**ULYSSES S. GRANT**	Republican	3,013,421	214	52.7
		Horatio Seymour	Democrat	2,706,829	80	47.3
1872	37	**ULYSSES S. GRANT**	Republican	3,596,745	286	55.6
		Horace Greeley	Democrat	2,843,446	***	43.9
1876	38	**RUTHERFORD B. HAYES**	Republican	4,036,572	185	48.0
		Samuel J. Tilden	Democrat	4,284,020	184	51.0
1880	38	**JAMES A. GARFIELD**	Republican	4,453,295	214	48.5
		Winfield S. Hancock	Democrat	4,414,082	155	48.1
		James B. Weaver	Greenback-Labor	308,578		3.4
1884	38	**GROVER CLEVELAND**	Democrat	4,879,507	219	48.5
		James G. Blaine	Republican	4,850,293	182	48.2
		Benjamin F. Butler	Greenback-Labor	175,370		1.8
		John P. St. John	Prohibition	150,369		1.5.
1888	38	**BENJAMIN HARRISON**	Republican	5,447,129	233	47.9
		Grover Cleveland	Democrat	5,537,857	168	48.6
		Clinton B. Fisk	Prohibition	249,506		2.2
		Anson J. Streeter	Union Labor	146,935		1.3
1892	44	**GROVER CLEVELAND**	Democrat	5,555,426	277	46.1
		Benjamin Harrison	Republican	5,182,690	145	43.0
		James B. Weaver	People's	1,029,846	22	8.5
		John Bidwell	Prohibition	264,133		2.2
1896	45	**WILLIAM MCKINLEY**	Republican	7,102,246	271	51.1
		William J. Bryan	Democrat	6,492,559	176	47.7
1900	45	**WILLIAM MCKINLEY**	Republican	7,218,491	292	51.7
		William J. Bryan	Democrat; Populist	6,356,734	155	45.5
		John C. Woolley	Prohibition	208,914		1.5
1904	45	**THEODORE ROOSEVELT**	Republican	7,628,461	336	57.4
		Alton B. Parker	Democrat	5,084,223	140	37.6
		Eugene V. Debs	Socialist	402,283		3.0
		Silas C. Swallow	Prohibition	258,536		1.9
1908	46	**WILLIAM H. TAFT**	Republican	7,675,320	321	51.6
		William J. Bryan	Democrat	6,412,294	162	43.1
		Eugene V. Debs	Socialist	420,793		2.8
		Eugene W. Chafin	Prohibition	253,840		1.7
1912	48	**WOODROW WILSON**	Democrat	6,296,547	435	41.9
		Theodore Roosevelt	Progressive	4,118,571	88	27.4
		William H. Taft	Republican	3,486,720	8	23.2
		Eugene V. Debs	Socialist	900,672		6.0
		Eugene W. Chafin	Prohibition	206,275		1.4
1916	48	**WOODROW WILSON**	Democrat	9,127,695	277	49.4
		Charles E. Hughes	Republican	8,533,507	254	46.2
		A. L. Benson	Socialist	585,113		3.2
		J. Frank Hanly	Prohibition	220,506		1.2

* Percentage of popular vote given for any election year may not total 100 percent because candidates receiving less than 1 percent of the popular vote have been omitted.

** Prior to the passage of the Twelfth Amendment in 1904, the electoral college voted for two presidential candidates; the runner-up became Vice President. Data from Historical Statistics of the United States, Colonial Times to 1957 (1961), pp. 682–883, and The World Almanac.

*** Because of the death of Greeley, Democratic electors scattered their votes.

PRESIDENTIAL ELECTIONS *(continued)*

Year	# of States	Candidates	Party	Popular Vote	Electoral Vote**	Percentage of Popular Vote*
1920	48	**WARREN G. HARDING**	Republican	16,143,407	404	60.4
		James M. Cox	Democrat	9,130,328	127	34.2
		Eugene V. Debs	Socialist	919,799		3.4
		P. P. Christensen	Farmer-Labor	265,411		1.0
1924	48	**CALVIN COOLIDGE**	Republican	15,718,211	382	54.0
		John W. Davis	Democrat	8,385,283	136	28.8
		Robert M. La Follette	Progressive	4,831,289	13	16.6
1928	48	**HERBERT C. HOOVER**	Republican	21,391,993	444	58.2
		Alfred E. Smith	Democrat	15,016,169	87	40.9
1932	48	**FRANKLIN D. ROOSEVELT**	Democrat	22,809,638	472	57.4
		Herbert C. Hoover	Republican	15,758,901	59	39.7
		Norman Thomas	Socialist	881,951		2.2
1936	48	**FRANKLIN D. ROOSEVELT**	Democrat	27,752,869	523	60.8
		Alfred M. Landon	Republican	16,674,665	8	36.5
		William Lemke	Union	882,479		1.9
1940	48	**FRANKLIN D. ROOSEVELT**	Democrat	27,307,819	449	54.8
		Wendell L. Wilkie	Republican	22,321,018	82	44.8
1944	48	**FRANKLIN D. ROOSEVELT**	Democrat	25,606,585	432	53.5
		Thomas E. Dewey	Republican	22,014,745	99	46.0
1948	48	**HARRY S. TRUMAN**	Democrat	24,105,812	303	49.5
		Thomas E. Dewey	Republican	21,970,065	189	45.1
		J. Strom Thurmond	States' Rights	1,169,063	39	2.4
		Henry A. Wallace	Progressive	1,157,172		2.4
1952	48	**DWIGHT D. EISENHOWER**	Republican	33,936,234	442	55.1
		Adlai E. Stevenson	Democrat	27,314,992	89	44.4
1956	48	**DWIGHT D. EISENHOWER**	Republican	35,590,472	457***	57.6
		Adlai E. Stevenson	Democrat	26,022,752	73	42.1
1960	50	**JOHN F. KENNEDY**	Democrat	34,227,096	303****	49.9
		Richard M. Nixon	Republican	34,108,546	219	49.6
1964	50	**LYNDON B. JOHNSON**	Democrat	42,676,220	486	61.3
		Barry M. Goldwater	Republican	26,860,314	52	38.5
1968	50	**RICHARD M. NIXON**	Republican	31,785,480	301	43.4
		Hubert H. Humphrey	Democrat	31,275,165	191	42.7
		George C. Wallace	American Independent	9,906,473	46	13.5
1972	50	**RICHARD M. NIXON*****	Republican	47,165,234	520	60.6
		George S. McGovern	Democrat	29,168,110	17	37.5
1976	50	**JIMMY CARTER**	Democrat	40,828,929	297	50.1
		Gerald R. Ford	Republican	39,148,940	240	47.9
		Eugene McCarthy	Independent	739,256		
1980	50	**RONALD REAGAN**	Republican	43,201,220	489	50.9
		Jimmy Carter	Democrat	34,913,332	49	41.2
		John B. Anderson	Independent	5,581,379		
1984	50	**RONALD REAGAN**	Republican	53,428,357	525	59.0
		Walter F. Mondale	Democrat	36,930,923	13	41.0
1988	50	**GEORGE BUSH**	Republican	48,901,046	426	53.4
		Michael Dukakis	Democrat	41,809,030	111	45.6
1992	50	**WILLIAM J. CLINTON**	Democrat	44,909,806	370	43.0
		George Bush	Republican	39,104,550	168	37.5
		H. Ross Perot	Independent	19,742,240		18.9
		Andre Marrau	Libertarian	291,631		0.3

* Percentage of popular vote given for any election year may not total 100 percent because candidates receiving less than 1 percent of the popular vote have been omitted.

** Prior to the passage of the Twelfth Amendment in 1904, the electoral college voted for two presidential candidates; the runner-up became Vice President. Data from Historical Statistics of the United States, Colonial Times to 1957 (1961), pp. 682–883, and The World Almanac.

*** Walter B. Jones received 1 electoral vote.   **** Harry F. Byrd received 15 electoral votes.   ***** Nixon resigned August 9, 1974; Vice President Gerald R. Ford became president.

Year	# of States	Candidates	Party	Popular Vote	Electoral Vote**	Percentage of Popular Vote*
1996	50	**WILLIAM J. CLINTON**	Democrat	47,402,357	379	49.2
		Robert Dole	Republican	39,198,755	159	40.7
		H. Ross Perot	Reform	8,085,402		8.4
		Ralph Nader	Green	685,128		0.7
		Harry Browne	Libertarian	485,798		0.5
2000	50	**GEORGE W. BUSH**	Republican	50,459,624	271	47.9
		Albert Gore, Jr.	Democrat	51,003,238	266	48.4
		Ralph Nader	Green	2,882,985		2.7
		Patrick Buchanan	Reform	449,120		0.4
		Harry Browne	Libertarian	384,440		0.4
2004	50	**GEORGE W. BUSH**	Republican	62,040,610	286	58.9
		John F. Kerry	Democrat	59,028,111	251	56.1
		Ralph Nader	Independent/Reform	463,653		0.0
2008	50	**BARACK OBAMA**	Democrat	69,456,898	365	52.9
		John McCain	Republican	59,934,814	173	45.6
		Ralph Nader	Independent	738,771		0.6
		Bob Barr	Libertarian	523,686		0.4
2012	50	**BARACK OBAMA**	Democrat	65,918,507	332	51.01
		Willard Mitt Romney	Republican	60,934,407	206	47.15
		Gary Johnson	Libertarian	1,275,923	0	0.99
		Jill Stein	Green	469,015	0	0.36
		Other	Other	637,706	0	0.49

* Percentage of popular vote given for any election year may not total 100 percent because candidates receiving less than 1 percent of the popular vote have been omitted.

** Prior to the passage of the Twelfth Amendment in 1904, the electoral college voted for two presidential candidates; the runner-up became Vice President. Data from Historical Statistics of the United States, Colonial Times to 1957 (1961), pp. 682–883, and The World Almanac.

GLOSSARY

Wade-Davis Bill 416
Killed by Lincoln's pocket veto, the bill would have imposed stringent terms to the restoration of the former Confederates including a requirement that Southerners could only establish state governments after the majority in a state had sworn a loyalty oath.

Wakeman, Sarah Rosetta 422
Woman who fought with General Nathaniel P. Banks in the famous loss at Mansfield and also at Pleasant Hill before dying of dysentery

War of 1812 217
War with England (1812–1815) essentially over American sovereignty rights and freedom of the seas

War on the Judiciary 207
Jefferson's conflict with the federalist Supreme Court of John Marshall

Washington, George 112
Commander of the Continental army

Webster-Ashburton Treaty 304
Set the border between Maine and New Brunswick and rounded the U.S. upper Minnesota

Webster–Hayne Debate 259
Famous 1830 Congressional debate over nationalism versus sectionalism and states' rights

West, Benjamin 134
Became court painter to England's King George III and successor to Sir Joshua Reynolds as president of the British Royal Academy, a painter in the so-called grand style, who specialized in huge canvases of such famous events as The Death of General Wolfe

Whigs 255
The political party supported by Daniel Webster and Henry Clay that opposed the policies of the Jacksonian Democrats and supported higher tariffs

Whiskey Rebellion 156
A revolt by Pennsylvania farmers in 1793–1794, against a federal excise tax on whiskey that was put down by George Washington and the federal troops.

Whitefield, George 99
A dramatic clergyman who toured the colonies from 1739 to 1740 and provided a spark for the Great

White Leagues, Rifle Clubs, and Red Shirts 447
Paramilitary groups in the South that fought bitter against the Republican state militias during Reconstruction

Whitney, Eli 179
Inventor of the cotton gin in 1793

William of Orange 90
England's Protestant King in 1689

Williams, Roger 18
Puritan who was banished from Massachusetts Bay for heresy and credited with founding the colony of Rhode Island

Wilmot Proviso 207
This Free Soil resolution was introduced in the House of Representatives by David Wilmot and proposed that slavery should be prohibited in any territory acquired from Mexico. The resolution passed the House where the North was stronger, but failed to pass in the Senate, where the South had equal strength.

Wilson, Harriet 343
Author of Our Nig in 1859 the first known novel by an African American woman

Winthrop, John 16
Puritan leader and author from whom we have a historical record of the Puritans in Massachusetts Bay

Wirz, Henry 420
Commander at Andersonville Prison, the only Confederate soldier executed by the Union after the war.

Wollstonecraft, Mary 168
Author of Vindication of the Rights of Women

Women's National Loyal League 425
Women's group for suffrage and the abolition of slavery founded by Susan B. Anthony and Elizabeth Cady Stanton

Wood, Jethro 7
Invented an iron plow in New York in the 1810s

Worcester v. Georgia 260
The U.S. Supreme Court recognized the Cherokee nation as a sovereign entity with its own territory in which the laws of Georgia had no force

Wright, Fanny 373
A woman who defied the taboo against women speaking in public and advocated reform for workers and marriage laws, along with "free love," in 1820

Writs of assistance 104
Empowered officers of the British customs service to break into and search homes and stores for smuggled goods

X

XYZ Affair 163
Incident in which three French diplomats demanded bribes from American diplomats prior to negotiations

Y

Yeoman 58
Land-owning farmer with little to smaller plots of land

Young, Brigham 282
Mormon leader who led the Mormons to Utah

INDEX